Midwest Studies in Philosophy
Volume XV

MIDWEST STUDIES IN PHILOSOPHY

EDITED BY PETER A. FRENCH, THEODORE E. UEHLING, JR., HOWARD K. WETTSTEIN

EDITORIAL ADVISORY BOARD
ROBERT AUDI (UNIVERSITY OF NEBRASKA)
JONATHAN BENNETT (SYRACUSE UNIVERSITY)
PANAYOT BUTCHVAROV (UNIVERSITY OF IOWA)
RODERICK CHISHOLM (BROWN UNIVERSITY)
DONALD DAVIDSON (UNIVERSITY OF CALIFORNIA, BERKELEY)
KEITH DONNELLAN (UNIVERSITY OF CALIFORNIA, LOS ANGELES)
FRED I. DRETSKE (UNIVERSITY OF WISCONSIN, MADISON)
GILBERT HARMAN (PRINCETON UNIVERSITY)
MICHAEL J. LOUX (UNIVERSITY OF NOTRE DAME)
ALASDAIR MACINTYRE (UNIVERSITY OF NOTRE DAME)
RUTH BARCAN MARCUS (YALE UNIVERSITY)
JOHN R. PERRY (STANFORD UNIVERSITY)
ALVIN PLANTINGA (UNIVERSITY OF NOTRE DAME)
DAVID ROSENTHAL (CITY UNIVERSITY OF NEW YORK GRADUATE CENTER)
STEPHEN SCHIFFER (UNIVERSITY OF ARIZONA)
MARGARET WILSON (PRINCETON UNIVERSITY)

Many papers in MIDWEST STUDIES IN PHILOSOPHY are invited and all are previously unpublished. The editors will consider unsolicited manuscripts that are received by January of the year preceeding the appearance of a volume. All manuscripts must be pertinent to the topic area of the volume for which they are submitted. Address manuscripts to MIDWEST STUDIES IN PHILOSOPHY, University of Notre Dame Press, Box L, Notre Dame, IN 46556.

The articles in MIDWEST STUDIES IN PHILOSOPHY are indexed in THE PHILOSOPHER'S INDEX.

Forthcoming Volumes.
Volume XVI 1991 Philosophy and Art
Volume XVII 1992 Wittgenstein's Legacy

Midwest Studies
in
Philosophy
Volume XV

The Philosophy of
the Human Sciences

Editors

Peter A. French
Trinity University

Theodore E. Uehling, Jr.
University of Minnesota, Morris

Howard K. Wettstein
University of California, Riverside

University of Notre Dame Press • Notre Dame, Indiana

Published by the University of Notre Dame Press
Notre Dame, IN 46556
Printed in the United States of America

Library of Congress Cataloging-in-Publication Data

The Philosophy of the human sciences / editors, Peter A. French,
    Theodore E. Uehling, Jr., Howard K. Wettstein.
        p.   cm. − (Midwest studies in philosophy : v. 15)
    Includes index.
    ISBN 0-268-01384-5   − ISBN 0-268-01385-3 (pbk.)
    1. Social sciences−Philosophy.   I. French, Peter A.
II. Uehling, Theodore E.   III. Wettstein, Howard K.   IV. Series.
B63.P48   1990
300′.1−dc20   90-12872
                                                            CIP

The University of Notre Dame
is an equal-opportunity
educator and employer

Midwest Studies in Philosophy
Volume XV
The Philosophy of the Human Sciences

Midwest Studies in Philosophy
Volume XV

Walking Together:
A Paradigmatic Social Phenomenon

MARGARET GILBERT

I f one were asked to characterize the standard concerns of contemporary philosophy of social science, two different problem areas would most likely come to mind. The first has to do with methodology broadly speaking. Key questions include: Are the methods of natural science appropriate to the study of social phenomena? Can there be a properly so-called social 'science' at all? The second problem area is a matter of ontology. Usually the question posed is a relational one. Roughly, what is the relationship between human social groups and the individual humans who are their members? Are groups simply aggregates of individuals, or what?

On the whole, those who have focused on the above questions have tended to work with a relatively inarticulate, intuitive understanding of the nature of social phenomena in general, and of social groups in particular. Though a more articulate understanding may not be required for certain purposes, one would think that it would benefit discussions of these questions. Thus it is plausible to suppose that an important task for the philosophy of social science is the detailed articulation of our central intuitive concepts of social phenomena.

In this essay I approach a concept crucial to this task, the concept of a social group or collectivity in general. I begin by focusing on something far less grand and general—the everyday concept of going for a walk together. The essay is intended to introduce some of the main ideas in my book *On Social Facts* (London, 1989) through a relatively self-contained discussion.[1]

I. A PROPOSAL ABOUT SOCIAL GROUPS

The sociologist Georg Simmel wrote:

> Sociation roughly, [the process of forming a social group] ranges all the
> way from the momentary getting together for a walk to founding a

1

family. . .from the temporary aggregation of hotel guests to the intimate bonds of a mediaeval guild.[2]

This suggests an idea that I endorse for my own reasons, as I shall explain.

The idea is that we can discover the nature of social groups in general by investigating such small-scale temporary phenomena as going for a walk together. This idea is attractive insofar as it should be relatively easy to understand what it is to go for a walk with another person. It may also seem somewhat farfetched.

When sociologists and others give examples of social groups they tend to mention only such enduring, complex phenomena as families, guilds, armies, even nations. And, clearly, important distinctions can be drawn between such phenomena as going for a walk together and families, armies, and so on. Be that as it may, such small-scale phenomena as two people going for a walk together, having a conversation, and the like, do occasionally find their place in sociologists' lists, witness the quotation from Simmel above. As I shall argue, there is good reason for this.

I shall propose, more precisely, that analysis of our concepts of 'shared action' discovers a structure that is constitutive of social groups as such. To this extent, then, going for a walk together may be considered a paradigm of social phenomena in general.

I start by arguing for a particular account of what it is to go for a walk together. This will be the major part of the discussion. I then argue that a plausible account of social groups in general can be given in similar terms. In an essay of this length, some sketchiness is inevitable.[3]

II. GOING FOR A WALK TOGETHER: PRELIMINARIES

What is it for two people to go for a walk together? Let us start with one person who is out on a walk alone and see what minimum addition allows us to say that this person and someone else are out on a walk together.

Imagine that Sue Jones is out for a walk along Horsebarn Road on her own. Suddenly she realizes that someone else—a man in a black cloak—has begun to walk alongside her, about a foot away. His physical proximity is clearly not enough to make it the case that they are going for a walk together. It may disturb Sue precisely because they are *not* going for a walk together.

It is possible, of course, that she is glad he is there. She has recognized him. He is Jack Smith, and she wants to get to know him. She waits for him to say something. He is in the same position. Thus they could be walking along next to each other, each wanting this to continue. Is each one's possession of the goal that they continue walking alongside each other logically sufficient for their going for a walk together? I would say not. Note that it is possible that each one's possession of the goal in question is not known by either one. Sue may look worried and Jack may suspect that she would rather be alone. Jack may be famous for his reclusiveness, leading Sue to conjecture that he is hoping she will stop and turn back. Once this possibility is made explicit it seems particularly clear that we must reject what I shall call the *weak shared personal goal analysis*. (Why I say 'weak' here will be clear shortly.)

What precisely is the problem here? One general, informal hypothesis is that giving both participants the personal goal that they walk alongside each other puts them no closer together *as far as they are concerned*.

Let us now consider the *strong shared personal goal analysis*. On this account, it is logically necessary and sufficient for a case of going for a walk together that it is *common knowledge* between Jack and Sue that each one has the goal in question. By this I mean, roughly, that each one's goal is completely out in the open as far as the two of them are concerned.[4] Such common knowledge could arise in various ways. In some contexts it may be enough for both parties to continue walking alongside each other for several minutes without any sign of discomfort. In any case, I shall now argue that even assuming that the conditions in question are fulfilled, a crucial feature of going for a walk together will be lacking. Let me first say something about the feature in question.

Let us assume that, at some point in time, Jack and Sue are indeed going for a walk together. That is, we assume that at this juncture the relevant logical conditions are fulfilled, whatever these are precisely. Now suppose that Jack starts drawing ahead. Failing some special circumstances, it would be odd if he were not to notice this. It would, moreover, be odd for him not to make any attempt to bring them closer together. So much is true, of course, if Jack genuinely desires that they walk side by side. For if this is what he wants, he will be acting against his interests if he fails to monitor the situation relatively carefully and to act accordingly. But there is more.

If Jack and Sue are indeed going for a walk together, and Jack has apparently drawn ahead without noticing what is happening, we can imagine Sue taking action in various ways. She might call out "Jack!" with a degree of impatience. She might catch up with him and then say, somewhat critically, "You are going to have to slow down! I can't keep up with you." In both of these cases she rebukes Jack, albeit mildly. She might not do this, of course, but it seems that, again failing special circumstances, her doing so would be *in order*. In other words, it seems that in the circumstances Sue is *entitled to rebuke* Jack. We would expect both Jack and Sue to understand that she has this entitlement.

The existence of this entitlement suggests that Jack has, in effect, an *obligation* to notice and to act (an obligation Sue has also). Particular acts Jack might perform in fulfilling his obligation to rectify matters include stopping and waiting for Sue to catch up, slowing his pace, smiling encouragement, asking if she is getting tired. These are the kinds of thing we expect to find if one party realizes he has drawn ahead of the other. Though he may not be obligated to do any one of these things, he is obligated to do something along these lines. The point can also be put in terms of *rights*: each has a right to the other's attention and corrective action. We would expect those out on a walk together to *realize* that they have the obligations, and the rights, just noted.

The foregoing suggests the following test for a putative analysis of the notion of going for a walk together. Are the proposed conditions such that the participants' failure to acknowledge the noted obligations and entitlements would necessarily throw doubt on the idea that the conditions are fulfilled?

I propose that the strong shared personal goal analysis fails the above test. In a word, those who are supposedly going for a walk in the sense defined by this analysis can deny that they have the obligations and entitlements at issue without necessarily bringing the supposition into doubt. Some clarification of this claim is in order.

Suppose Jack knows that he and Sue both have as a personal goal their continuing to walk alongside one another. (We can take this to follow from the common knowledge condition.) It is possible that Jack will judge that, all else being equal, both he and Sue have a *moral duty* to see that the goal is achieved. For this way overall happiness will be maximized. It seems equally possible, however, that Jack will not see things this way. In other words, he may fail to judge that either of them has a moral duty to promote the shared personal goal. Given that this is possible, it cannot be argued that his failure to draw the moral conclusion would necessarily throw doubt on the original supposition about what Jack knew. In order for this to happen we need some premise about Jack's moral views.

The reference to moral duties raises a more general question: Must those who lack the concept of a moral duty altogether be incapable of going for a walk together? This is not particularly plausible on the face of it. Nonetheless, if I am right, people out on a walk can *for that reason* be expected to recognize certain responsibilities and rights. This suggests that the rights and obligations in question are not moral rights and obligations. I take this to mean, roughly, that they do not have their basis in facts about objective value. This is something that a satisfactory analysis should illuminate further, for it should indicate what the grounds of obligation and entitlement are in the case of going for a walk together.[5]

Morality aside, if Jack's goal is to walk alongside Sue, *prudence* obviously requires him to monitor the situation carefully and to take what action he can to keep the two of them together. Common knowledge that Jack and Sue have the same personal goal seems to add to the prudential reasons available. Let us take it that, given common knowledge, Sue will know that Jack knows that both have the goal in question. She may well, in that case, deem Jack to be both irrational and inconsiderate of her if he fails to monitor the situation, and this could lead her to stop wanting to be with him. So it can be argued that the addition of common knowledge gives Jack an extra prudential reason to pay attention to and deal with the growing distance between them. In any case, one can say that, from a prudential point of view, that is what Jack is *obliged* to do. This does not help us save a shared personal goal analysis, however.

As is well known, H. L. A. Hart has stressed a conceptual distinction between 'being obliged' and 'having an obligation'.[6] It is clear that there is a significant distinction here. The distinction at its broadest is between a feature generated by prudential considerations, whatever we call it, and a feature differently derived. In the first case, we argue for the feature simply by noting what a person wants, and how he must act in order to get that thing. In the second case, such premises are insufficient. It seems clear that in the case of going for a walk we are dealing with an obligation of the latter kind. In this case, I have not only argued for the presence of an obligation—prior to that, I argued for an entitlement to rebuke. These features appear to be closely connected: *the obligation is such that Jack's failure to perform entitles Sue to rebuke him.* But in the case of the feature stemming from prudential considerations only, which Hart refers to as 'being obliged', there is no such tight connection between the feature and an entitlement to rebuke.

Supposing only the fulfillment of the conditions of the strong shared goal analysis, is there any basis for inferring that Sue is now entitled, all else being equal, to rebuke Jack for carelessly drawing ahead? On the contrary, fulfillment of these conditions does not seem to entitle her to interact with him in any way at all. By this I mean, roughly, that it does not by itself—without special ancillary premises—generate a right of some kind to interact with him. If this is so, one can infer, of course, that the right kind of obligation has not been generated either, by whatever means.

Someone in Sue's position may well feel herself to be in the following fix. She would like to call out to attract Jack's attention. Indeed, she would like to put the kind of pressure on him an appropriate rebuke would produce. But she does not feel entitled to behave in these ways. Quite generally, she does not feel entitled to *interfere* with his actions in any way. More precisely, she does not feel that the existence of such an entitlement has been *established* between them.[7]

In various places Charles Taylor has suggested that when there is common knowledge of some fact between two persons this does not yet make it what he calls 'entre nous' between them: according to Taylor it is not at this point 'in public space'. Meanwhile Taylor indicates that once the fact in question has been communicated, particularly by the use of language, it will be 'entre nous', 'in public space'. This suggests that it is worth seeing if there could be a difference for our purposes between the general common knowledge case and a case involving linguistic communication. What if, rather than simply positing common knowledge of the shared personal goal, from whatever source, we suppose it to be common knowledge that each has *told* the other that he or she has the goal in question?[8]

Here things are a little delicate, since more may be conveyed than is actually said, and more or less may be accomplished depending on the circumstances. But let us suppose in this instance that each is taking the other purely at face value, and this is common knowledge. (Perhaps it is common knowledge that they are members of the Literalists, or of the G. E. Moore Society.) Suppose, then, that Jack says, somewhat quaintly, "My goal right now is to go on walking in your company." Sue replies, "And my goal is to go on walking in your company!" In spite of this change in the situation, the crucial element needed to establish that the parties are out on a walk together seems to be missing. As before, each is safe in the knowledge that the other party will (if prudent) do what he or she can to ensure that the shared personal goal is reached. But, as before, neither one seems to have to conclude that any one has any obligations to the other to perform satisfactorily, or that anyone is entitled to rebuke the other for not doing what they can to reach the goal.

This is true even if each has averred: "I intend to do all I can to achieve my goal. For instance, if you draw ahead without noticing, I plan to call out to catch your attention. Given your own goal, this should help me attain mine." This does not seem crucially to change things. In the case now envisaged Jack will, if you like, be 'entitled to expect' that Sue will call after him if he unknowingly draws ahead, and Sue will be 'entitled to expect' that he will not be surprised at her doing so. This might make her less timid about doing these things. But here, saying that they are 'entitled to expect' these things is just another way of saying that their evidence is such that they can infer that performance will take place, all else being equal. No one yet seems to have the right type of *obligation to perform* or the corresponding *entitlements to rebuke* and so on. (Is a rebuke in order at all? This depends on whether one is entitled to complain about violations of *one's beliefs about what will be done*. Presumably Jack might in fact complain in such a way as this: "I believed you would alert me, so I was less concerned to monitor the situation!" Here I suggest the implicit appeal would be to moral considerations. Jack might add: "You *should have realized* that I might rely on you." Given a case of genuine walking together, however, he could afford to be much more peremptory, appealing to an *established understanding*: "Why didn't you alert me!?")

So far, then, three accounts of going for a walk together appear insufficient. I focused on the strong shared personal goal analysis, requiring common knowledge that it is each party's personal goal that the two of them walk along side by side. In such a situation reasons of morality generally, prudence, or, indeed, of 'care' could prompt each person to monitor the actions of the other and to do what they could to ensure that the goal each pursued was reached. I argued that, nonetheless, in this situation certain key obligations and entitlements fail to be generated. As long as people are out on a walk together, they will understand that each has an *obligation* to do what he or she can to achieve the relevant goal. Moreover, each one is *entitled* to rebuke the other for failure to fulfill this obligation. It is doubtful whether the core obligations and entitlements in question are moral obligations and entitlements. At the same time, they are not merely a matter of prudence or self-interest. Importantly, they seem to be a direct function of the fact of going for a walk together. Thus, though certain 'external' factors or considerations may lead to their being ignored, they are 'still there'. How might these various judgments about going for a walk together plausibly be accounted for?

III.   GOING FOR A WALK TOGETHER:
OUTLINE OF AN ACCOUNT

Suppose Jack Smith coughs to attract Sue's attention, and then asks if she is Sue Jones and would she mind if he joins her? "No," Sue says, "that would be nice. I should like some company." This is probably enough to produce a case of going for a walk together. Once the exchange has taken place, both parties will be entitled to assume that the attitudes and actions appropriate to their going for a walk together are in place.

What were the crucial elements in this transaction? I suggest, as an initial characterization, that each party has made it clear to the other that he is willing to *join forces* with the other in accepting the goal that they walk in one another's company. There are other ways of putting the point. I might have said that each has manifested his willingness to bring it about that the goal in question be accepted *by himself and the other, jointly.* For now, let me sum up by conjecturing that in order to go for a walk together each of the parties must express willingness to constitute with the other a *plural subject of the goal* that they walk along in one another's company. 'Plural subject' is a technical term of my own, whose meaning will be more carefully specified shortly.

I conjecture, further, that once this willingness to form the plural subject of the goal in question has been expressed on both sides, in conditions of common knowledge, the foundation has been laid for each person to pursue the goal *in his or her capacity as the constituent of a plural subject* of that goal. Thus we can consider that each one's expression of willingness to walk with the other, in conditions of common knowledge, is logically sufficient for them to be plural subjects of the relevant goal, and hence to go for a walk together.

If that is right, then once all this has happened, the relevant obligations and entitlements will be in place, and we can expect the parties to know this. Let me now argue that this will be so, provided that we construe the notion of plural subjecthood in a particular way. As it turns out, the way I (independently) want to put things bears a striking resemblance to the language of some classic political theorists.

Let me first say what I want to say about plural subjecthood. When a goal has a plural subject, each of a number of persons (two or more) has, in effect, offered his will to be part of a pool of wills which is dedicated, as one, to that goal. It is common knowledge that, when each has done this in conditions of common knowledge, the pool will have been set up. Thus what is achieved is a binding together of a set of individual wills so as to constitute a single, 'plural will' dedicated to a particular goal.

The precise mechanism by which this binding is understood to take place is rather special. The individual wills are bound *simultaneously and interdependently.* Thus we do not have, here, an 'exchange of promises' such that each person unilaterally binds himself to the goal in question, leaving himself beholden for release to someone else upon whom, through this particular transaction, he has no claim. Nor is it that one person in effect says: "You may regard me as committed once *you* have made a commitment" leaving it up to the other person to make an initial unilateral commitment. Rather, each person expresses a special form of *conditional commitment* such that (as is understood) only when *everyone* has done similarly is *anyone* committed. Thus all wills are bound simultaneously and interdependently. The character of each one's commitment is then as follows: no one can release himself from the commitment; each is obligated to all the others for performance; each is (thus) entitled to performance from the rest. This, I believe, is what is achieved in interchanges such as the one in my example, where Jack asks if he may join Sue, and Sue says that he may. Once this transaction has occurred, then all else being equal, the commitments in question are in place.

How can we best describe the content of the commitment? I have said very generally that the pool of wills is dedicated, as one, to the relevant goal. This, though vague perhaps, is the guiding idea. Other ways of putting it: each must act as would the parts of a single person or subject of action in pursuit of the goal. Or: they are to act as members of a single body, the body comprising the two of them. As we have already seen, in a concrete case one's sense of the range of responsibilities and rights becomes relatively precise.

The above account of what it is to become a participant in a plural subject can be used to throw light on, and is to that extent supported by, a semantic phenomenon involving the pronoun 'we'. (Since noticing this I have found that Wilfrid Sellars has remarked on it previously.[9])

It seems that premises of the form 'We seek goal G' license certain inferences about action. Thus, Sue's premise "We seek to walk along side by side" in conjunction with the premises "Jack is drawing ahead" and "The best way I can help achieve our goal is to tell Jack to slow up" seems sufficient to determine that (all else being equal) Sue should tell Jack to slow up. In other words we would expect Sue, if rational and accepting the premises, to act accordingly. Intuitively, I suggest, the conclusion follows from the premises without any kind of decomposition of the 'We' premise giving some 'I' premise about, say, Sue's personal goals.[10] Accepting this, how can we explain it? It turns out that the hypothesis that 'we' refers to a plural subject in the sense just elaborated gives us a satisfying account.

If 'we' refers to a plural subject of a goal, it refers to a pool of wills dedicated *as one* to that goal. In Sue's case, her use of 'we' refers to a pool of wills of which her own is a member. She understands her will to be bound in the service of the pool's established inclination. Hence she understands herself to be bound to perform what will best serve the goal in question. This gives her a (quite strong) reason to act accordingly. No reference to her own goals is necessary to effect the inference to this conclusion. For a premise about 'our goal' is as effective as one about 'my goal' in establishing a reason for action for a participating individual. In sum, then, the account of a plural subject in terms of a pool of wills dedicated as one to a given end, in conjunction with the assumption that 'we' refers to a plural subject of which the speaker is a part, plausibly explains the apparent inferences from an undecomposed 'we' premise.

Now, those out on a walk would quite appropriately refer to one another as 'we', at least in relation to their walk. They would quite appropriately say such things as "Shall we stop here?" "Shall we go through the woods?"[11] And inferences of the sort noted will seem appropriate at various junctures. This supports the idea that those out on a walk form a plural subject in the sense in question. For this assumption provides a satisfactory explanation of these uses of 'we'.

I have argued that going for a walk together with another person involves participating in an activity of a special kind, one whose goal is the goal of a plural subject, as opposed to the shared personal goal of the participants. Alternatively, going for a walk involves an 'our goal' as opposed to two or more 'my goals'. I take it that there are many activities of this kind, which may be referred to as 'shared', 'joint', or 'collective' action. Examples will include traveling together, eating together, dancing together, investigating the murder together, and so on.[12]

IV. SOCIAL GROUPS IN GENERAL

What has all this to do with social groups? To say it quickly, in my view, human social groups are plural subjects. That is, in order to form a social group, it is both logically necessary and logically sufficient that a set of human beings constitute a plural subject. Clearly this is a thesis about a concept, namely, our intuitive concept of a social group. The data includes, among other things, the open-ended lists of so-called social groups made by sociologists and others. These are not entirely unambiguous, but I believe the plural subject account gives them a plausible and compelling rationale.

Some immediate clarification of this thesis is in order. I have argued that those out on a walk together constitute the plural subject of a particular goal, roughly, the goal that they walk along side by side for a certain roughly specified period. Let us say that a given set of people have a 'joint', 'collective', or (in a strong sense) 'shared' goal when they are the plural subject of a goal. Now, some situations, which seem definitely to involve a social group, seem not to involve any joint goal in the appropriate sense. Witness, for instance, the committee imagined by John Updike in his story "Minutes of the Last Meeting" whose members are quite unclear about what general charge, if any, their committee has. Committees do standardly have some sort of goal, it is true. But what about families? We are not talking here about the useful effects family life may have, such as the satisfaction of individual needs for psychological intimacy. I do not find it obvious that, in constituting a family, a set of persons must have a *joint goal* or goals.

Suppose that we assume for the sake of argument that it is *not* the case that all social groups must have a joint goal. This does not, in any case, refute the claim that social groups are plural subjects. For the general, fundamental concept of a plural subject is not only embedded in our shared action concept, it can also be found, for instance, in our concept of a shared or collective belief and in the concept of a shared or collective principle.

There is no place here carefully to develop and defend detailed analyses of these particular concepts, but let us look at them briefly in action. Suppose that while they are out on their walk, Jack says: "What terrific weather!" and Sue concurs. If they subsequently run across Jill, a mutual friend, and she says "Whew! It's hot!" Sue could reply "Do you think so? *We* think it's great." It appears, in other words, that the previous interchanges between Jack and Sue will count as having established a view that they may properly refer to as 'ours'. My contention is that, more precisely, they are now members of the plural subject of a view. This carries with it a set of obligations similar to those involved with a shared goal. Roughly, they must endeavor to appear to be 'of one mind' – as we say – in relation to this view.

Similarly, Sue and Jack may constitute themselves the plural subject of a principle of action. Suppose that at each choice point, Jack tells Sue to choose where they will turn. After a while she chooses automatically, and Jack follows her lead. At a certain fork in the road, however, Jack seems to be 'taking the reins'. Sue says, with some amusement, "I thought I was supposed to make the decisions!" and Jack apologizes. Given some such scenario, we shall be able to say that Jack and Sue have come to constitute the plural subject of a principle of action. In this case the principle is a simple 'fiat', which means, I would say, that there is now a *social convention* in this particular population. (Sue's utterance might have been tendentious, but as long as Jack goes along with it, the right attitudes will have been expressed, and thus by these acts themselves a plural subject will have been constituted.[13])

Plural subjecthood, then, extends not only to goals but also, at least, to beliefs and principles of action. On my account of social groups, in order to constitute a social group people must constitute a plural subject *of some kind*. And *any* plural subject is a social group. This makes the account less restrictive. Updike's committee probably has many collective beliefs and principles, as do most families, whether or not they lack any clear collective goal.

My claim in this paper has been that if we are looking for the key to social groups we can find what we want in the phenomenon of going for a walk together. This claim can now be articulated as follows: it turns out that in order to go for a walk together two persons must constitute a plural subject. The key to social groups is the concept of a plural subject. For social groups are plural subjects. In the space that remains let me briefly attempt to back up this view of social groups.

Evidently, those who form a plural subject of whatever kind may properly refer to themselves as 'us' or 'we', to 'our goal' 'our belief', and so on. This supports the idea of a connection between plural subjecthood and social groups. 'We' is often used to emphasize or create a sense of group membership. Political rhetoric abounds with such phrases as 'We Americans' and 'We trade unionists'. And compare Tonto's reply to the Lone Ranger: '*We*, white man?'

Mention of politics may raise a doubt. Is the analysis too broad? In groups such as nations, clubs, and even families political questions are endemic. It may not be immediately clear that such issues can arise in such a small-scale enterprise as going for a walk. And so one might wonder if we can really have a social group here. Further thought resolves this doubt. Those out on a walk have many problems to solve. For instance, for how long should they walk and where will they go? Will they talk, and if so, what about? Both collective decisions and joint principles are likely to result. One may always question whether such decisions and principles have been arrived at in a fair way and whether their content is acceptable. Is Jack forcing conversation on Sue? Is Sue forcing her slow pace on Jack? Are Sue's interests likely to be ignored, the way things are currently arranged? Clearly, then, even going for a walk together has a political dimension.

It is, indeed, rather striking that the language I have felt it most appropriate to use in describing the constitution of plural subjects closely resembles some key passages in classic works of political theory.

Early in *The Social Contract,* discussing when we have an association as opposed to a mere aggregate of people, Rousseau writes:

> Since men cannot engender new forces, but merely unite and direct exist-ing ones, they have no other means of maintaining themselves but to form by aggregation a sum of forces. . .so that their forces are directed by means of a single moving power and made to act in concert.[14]

This is relatively obscure, and I do not claim, or need to claim, that I am certain what Rousseau had in mind. However, it and several other passages in the book clearly bear some resemblance to what I want to say about plural subjects.

So also does this, from Hobbes, who argues that in order to generate a commonwealth human beings must

> conferre all their power and strength upon one Man, or upon one Assembly of men, that may reduce all their Wills, by plurality of voices, unto one Will. . .this is a reall Unitie of them all, in one and the same Person. . . .[15]

Hobbes includes as a possibility that the 'one Person' in whom all are unified is an 'Assembly of Men'. In principle, this could presumably be the assembly of all the people. This does not seem such a far cry from the idea of people condition-ally committing their wills to common goals or views, the goals, it could be said, of a single person, that person they together constitute. Consider also what Hobbes says about the mechanism that generates the "reall Unitie": "A reall Unitie of them all, in one and the same Person, made by Covenant of every man with every man, in such manner, as if every man should say to every man, *I Authorise and give up my Right of Governing my selfe, to this Man, or to this Assembly of men, on this condition, that thou give up thy Right to him, and Authorise all his Actions in like manner."* [16]

These analogies with past accounts of association and commonwealth, though neither necessary nor conclusive for my argument, do lend a degree of support to the idea of linking social groups in general with plural subjects. Though Hobbes and Rousseau were concerned with whole nations, it can be argued that the essentials of the mechanism they envisaged is involved even in such phenomena as two people going for a walk together.

Georg Simmel himself regarded the two-person group or 'dyad' as impor-tantly different from larger groups. Something he stresses is that, in a dyad, each person knows that without him or her in particular the group will cease to exist. As long as there are at least three people, the group can survive the loss of any given person. People in a dyad, then, may feel less as if the group is something 'over and above' the individual members. One can accept this and related observations without having to reject the idea that a dyad can be counted as a fully fledged social group. It can simply be regarded as a social group with a special character.[17]

So much for the worry that, in embracing temporary dyads the plural subject account of special groups is too broad. One might also wonder if the account is too narrow. Let me briefly address two worries on that score.

First, it might be questioned whether there really is some jointly accepted principle, belief, or goal, in every social group. Consider the United States of America. Does every American constitute a plural subject with every other American? Let me answer this with another question: Is the United States of America a paradigmatic social group? By this I mean, does the population of the United States clearly satisfy the conditions for being a social group in a more than rough and ready way? Unless it does, a negative answer to the original question will not throw doubt on the plural subject account of groups. It is true that people often put nations in a list of social groups. And the United States of America is generally deemed to be a nation. But it is not obvious that all of the populations we are comfortable to think of as nations must be paradigmatic social groups.

The second worry I address concerns a type of population that has been the focus of much theorizing. Someone might ask, what of economic classes, such as the so-called blue-collar workers in a certain society? These are surely not always plural subjects. This I think is true, but I would not count that against the plural subject account. Usually the informal lists of social groups given by sociologists and others do not include economic classes as such. And the importance of such classes does not imply that they ought to be thought of as social groups. In sum, I do not think there is a problem in an account of social groups that may, in the event, not bring all actual economic classes within its scope. Of course, if a given class does constitute a plural subject then it will be counted a group according to this account. And recall that a plural subject may do no more than accept a certain credo.

In the end, I do not want to argue about a label. I have argued that those out on a walk together form a plural subject, and that there is some reason to suppose that our concept of a social group — that concept by virtue of which we list families, guilds, tribes, 'and so on' together — is the concept of a plural subject. In any case, I would argue that the concept of a plural subject is a key concept for the description of human social life. It informs and directs a great deal of that life, in nations, clubs, families, and even in the taking of walks.

POSTSCRIPT

There is no space here to enquire as to the implications of my argument for those methodological and ontological concerns mentioned in the preamble to this paper. It is clear, however, that once the centrality of plural subjects to the human social world is agreed upon, new and quite specific questions of methodology and ontology become salient.[18]

NOTES

1. Given this expository intention, I shall not attempt to survey the literature in this area or to compare or contrast my views with those of others. One who has for some while been discussing the nature of such phenomena as going for a walk together in a detailed way is Raimo Tuomela, whose work first came to my attention after my own analysis had been developed. See Tuomela, *A Theory of Social Action* (Dordrecht, 1984), and "Social Action," in *Social Action*, edited by G. Seebass and R. Tuomela (Dordrecht, 1985), 103–27, and elsewhere. I take Tuomela's conclusions to be significantly different from my own. In particular he does not ascribe to the phenomena the special type of intrinsic normativity I take to be central. There will not be space for any detailed comparison of our accounts here.

2. Georg Simmel, *On Individuality and Social Forms* (Chicago, 1971), 24. Original German publication, 1908. My attention was recently drawn to this particular passage by the quotation in Walter Wallace, "Towards a Disciplinary Matrix in Sociology," in *Handbook of Sociology*, edited by Neil J. Smelser (Berkeley, 1988), 33.

'Sociation' is a translation of the German *Vergesellschaftung*. "The process of forming a social group" is a more cumbersome but familiar-sounding rendering.

Simmel prefers to talk of 'sociation', a continuous process or event, as opposed to 'society' or 'social group', which have less dynamic connotations. See Simmel: ". . .society, as its life is constantly being realised. . .is something individuals do and suffer. To be true to this fundamental character of it, one should properly speak, not of society, but of sociation" (*Fundamental Problems of Sociology, in The Sociology of Georg Simmel*, translated and edited by K. H. Wolff (New York, 1969), 10. See also Wolff's note on his translation, p. lxiii.

3. For a more detailed discussion, see *On Social Facts*, especially chap. 4.

4. 'Common knowledge' is a technical term from David Lewis, *Convention* (Cambridge, Mass., 1969). See also Schiffer, *Meaning* (Oxford, 1972), on 'mutual knowledge'. Exactly how to define it is somewhat moot. See for instance David Lewis, "Languages and Language," in *Language, Mind, and Knowledge, Minnesota Studies in the Philosophy of Science*, vol. 7, edited by K. Gunderson (Minneapolis, 1975); Jan Heal, "Common Knowledge," *Philosophical Quarterly* 28 (1978). See also *On Social Facts*.

5. I am connecting these and related points to the problem of political obligation in my *Social Ontology and Political Obligation*, in progress.

6. See H. L. A. Hart, *The Concept of Law* (Oxford, 1961).

7. Even once an entitlement of the right kind has been established between parties, one may not feel able to make use of this. Sue may be loth to assert herself in certain ways even when she is, and recognizes that she is, entitled to do so. She might be reluctant to call Jack in a rebuking way if she knows that he has an aversion to criticism, of whatever kind, and is likely to flare up at her. Such circumstances may well provide enough motivation to inhibit action to which one knows one is entitled.

When it is understood that no entitlement of the relevant kind has been established, this will tend to act as a *break* on action. This does not, of course, rule out the possibility of impulsive action, or action one justifies in terms of beliefs about moral rights.

8. Possibly closest to Taylor's paradigm would be the case where Jack says "Obviously you and I have as a goal our walking along in one another's company!" and Sue endorses this. That is, the fact of the shared personal goal is communicated in a single statement. My conclusion on the case in the text seems to stand for this case also. I would agree with Taylor that in interactions of the sort at issue here an important type of change in the situation occurs. As I would put it, Jack and Sue can now be said *jointly to accept* the view that they both have as a goal their walking in one another's company. For what I take this to amount to,

see below and also Gilbert, "Modelling Collective Belief," *Synthese* 73 (1987): 185–201, and *On Social Facts,* chap 5.

9. See, for instance, Sellars, "Imperatives, Intentions, and the Logic of 'Ought'," in *Morality and the Language of Conduct,* edited by G. Nakhnikian and H.-N. Castaneda (Detroit, 1963).

10. For further defense of this idea, see *On Social Facts,* chap. 7. In particular, I argue against the fairly popular view that all reasoning rationally productive of action *must* include a reference to the agent's personal desires.

11. I have argued elsewhere that 'Shall we do *A*' is not *always* correctly said of a given speaker and hearer. See *On Social Facts,* pp. 175ff.

12. A caveat: the phrases used in this area can be somewhat ambiguous. 'Together' can mean little more than 'in close proximity' and such phrases as 'traveling together' may occasionally be intended accordingly. The head of a spy ring might say to a colleague "Kim and Don will be traveling together on Friday" meaning only that they will be on the same train and so on. He might add "Kim doesn't know Don will be there. I want Don to keep an eye on him." Standardly, though, traveling together is used of those who are engaged in the special kind of activity at issue in this section.

13. For more on social conventions in the sense at issue here, see *On Social Facts,* chap. 6, especially pp. 373ff. For some discussion of David Lewis's influential (and quite different) account, see my "Game Theory and Convention," *Synthese* 46 (1981):44–93; "Notes on the Concept of a Social Convention," *New Literary History* (1983):225–51; *On Social Facts,* chap. 6, and "Rationality, Coordination, and Convention," forthcoming in *Synthese.*

14. J. J. Rousseau, *The Social Contract* (Indianapolis, 1983), Bk. I, chap. 6, p. 23.

15. Thomas Hobbes, *Leviathan* (New York, 1982), Part II, chap. 17, p. 227.

16. Ibid., original emphasis.

17. Cf. Simmel, "Quantitative Aspects of the Group," in *The Sociology of Georg Simmel,* ". . .the simplest sociological formation. . .that which operates between two elements. . . itself is a sociation" (p. 122).

18. For a discussion of the debate between 'individualism' and 'holism' given that social groups are plural subjects, see *On Social Facts,* chap. 7.

An early version of this essay, entitled "Some Footnotes to Rousseau," was presented to the Department of Philosophy at the University of Connecticut, Storrs, in the spring of 1986. A later version, approximating the present essay, was presented to the Philosophy Department at the University of Michigan, Ann Arbor, April 5, 1989. I am grateful for all the comments I have received, and thank in particular Alan Gibbard, Peter Railton, and Crispin Wright for discussion of my work.

MIDWEST STUDIES IN PHILOSOPHY, XV (1990)

Rationality and Alien Cultures

LAWRENCE H. SIMON

S everal years ago, a controversy occurred in Kenya that threatened the fragile structure of Kenyan society. As reported in the American press, the controversy concerned the disposal of the corpse of the late S. M. Otieno, a prominent attorney in Nairobi. Mr. Otieno was a member of the Luo tribe, the second largest tribal group in Kenya. During his lifetime, however, Mr. Otieno had renounced tribal customs and in effect severed all connections with his family and tribe. His ultimate act of severance was to marry a woman of the Kikuyu tribe, the largest and by far the dominant tribe in Kenya. Not only are the Luo and Kikuyu rivals in modern-day Kenya, they are of different ethnic backgrounds, speak mutually incomprehensible languages, and practice different customs that in each case the other tribe finds morally and aesthetically repugnant. So alienated was Mr. Otieno from his tribal background that he agreed to have his children raised as Kikuyu.

The controversy concerned where Mr. Otieno's body was to be buried. Mr. Otieno's widow and children stated that the deceased had wished to be buried in Nairobi. Mr. Otieno's extended family and the Luo tribe went to court, however, to prevent this from happening. They argued that the burial had to be in western Kenya in the Luo homelands. Not to do so, they argued, would bring a host of calamities down upon the family and tribe.

Among the expert witnesses used in court to argue the Luo case were a philosopher and a witch doctor. As reported in the *Washington Post*

> Several Luo, including a philosophy professor at the University of Nairobi and a witch doctor, testified that members of the tribe live in mortal fear of improperly burying a tribal brother. The spirit of a dead Luo will haunt their families, they said, causing birth defects, car accidents and nightmarish sleep unless the body is buried back in Luo land in accordance with ancient rituals.[1]

The court ruled in favor of the Luo. In his decision, the judge made two comments worth mentioning here. The first is that he was dismayed by the lack of

15

respect for the Luo elders that the sons of the deceased had displayed in their testimony in court. The sons referred to the Luo, the judge wrote, as "being lazy, primitive and people who had a lifestyle of uncivilized people." Second, the judge argued that Kenyan law should honor tribal customs insofar as they do not conflict with the law and "unless they are repugnant to justice and morality. . . . The fear of supernatural consequences by those governed by them," he argued, "will not per se make the customs repugnant to justice and morality."[2]

I do not want to address the question of whether the tribal customs are repugnant to justice or morality, although I do think that a real question is involved here, especially for Western liberals who value individual autonomy and thus feel that a person's wishes concerning the disposition of his or her body after death should be honored. Rather my concern is with an additional question implicit in, but not directly raised by, the court proceedings. That question is: Should the tribal customs be considered repugnant to rationality? This question is indirectly raised by the fact that a philosopher and a witch doctor were treated as seemingly equal experts by the court. Here I am going to have to speculate on what happened and make claims that go beyond my limited knowledge of the case and its circumstances. By this I may be doing a disservice to the Kenyan judiciary, but it will best allow me to set up my problem.

The philosopher, let us assume, was trained in Anglo-American philosophy, perhaps in England. Let us assume, further, that a philosopher is considered from a Western point of view the model of the rational person. A witch doctor, on the other hand, would be considered by many people in our culture to be irrational, in a certain sense at least, in that he holds a set of beliefs that may be regarded as certainly false and potentially harmful to others. I do not know the specifics of the testimony each offered or what role it played in the proceedings, but let us assume that the philosopher took an "objective" stance towards the issue and described the tribal beliefs and customs somewhat as a Western anthropologist would. Let us also assume that the witch doctor, as a believer and practitioner, spoke as an insider and described the tribal beliefs as true and the rituals as efficacious. Let us assume, lastly, that the court took each testimony at face value, that is, in particular, took the witch doctor to be describing a set of phenomena in the world and how they behave. My question is, What do we want to make of this situation? Should the philosopher have denounced the witch doctor as an irrational fraud? Or should the philosopher, as a modern thinker who understands the precarious epistemological status of Western science and culture and who respects cultural diversity, have withheld judgment as to the rationality of the tribal beliefs and practices, feeling that to do otherwise would be to impose improperly his or her concept of rationality on others who do not share his views?[3] Was the court, in accepting the testimony of both at face value, as I am assuming it did, offending rationality? In general, when can we rightly judge that the beliefs and practices of alien cultures that we find puzzling and bizarre are irrational?

The problem of alien cultures is one of the oldest and abiding issues in the philosophy of the social sciences. The problem generally arises when we are confronted with beliefs and practices in an alien society that strike us as exotic and bizarre and that seem to defy our understanding as to why the people involved are acting as they are. The general problem involves a number of intertwined questions. The two most central ones are: How are we to understand the practices and beliefs of alien cultures? And can we criticize the practices and beliefs of alien cultures, and if so, from what standpoint? Can we claim that the beliefs and practices in certain traditional cultures concerning, for example, witchcraft and magic are deficient from the point of view of rationality, that they are irrational, or at least less rational than our beliefs and practices? I will survey a number of positions in the literature on these questions as a way of clarifying the issues. I will argue that we must avoid the opposing errors of ethnocentrism and relativism as well as the temptation to discount questions about the rationality of the agents we are attempting to understand, and that we can do so in a way that still allows us to criticize alien cultures. Since the type of criticism in question involves claims about the rationality or irrationality of beliefs and actions, I will begin with a general discussion of rationality in order to clarify the types of judgments involved and the various levels on which such judgments can be made.

I. THE NATURE OF RATIONALITY[4]

What is it to call something rational? There is a wide range of entities that are said to be rational – beliefs, preferences, choices, decisions, actions, behavioral patterns, persons, collectivities, institutions, and even emotions.[5] In all cases, questions of understanding and evaluation or assessment are closely connected. Rationality operates as both an explanatory term and a term of assessment. As an explanatory term, it helps explain why and how something came to be or how it proceeds. For example, to call an action rational helps explain why that action was done. To call a person rational helps us explain and predict that person's behavior. If we understand an action as rational, we have answered the two explanatory questions of what and why. So, for instance, we have explained the action of a person's waving his or her arm when we have understood the waving as a signal of warning and have seen that the agent has the intention of alerting us to a potential danger. For the most part, my concern will be with the rationality or irrationality of actions.

As a term of assessment, rationality conveys commendation, endorsement, or excellence that indicates the thing deemed rational meets certain specified standards of comprehensibility and procedural correctness. An action that we call rational is one that we understand in terms of what action it is and how it came about, and one that we certify as coming about in a suitably correct way. To call an action irrational is thus to indicate that there is some error or fault in how it came about and to criticize it in that regard, and also to indicate that in order to explain the action we have to make reference to factors beyond those normally involved in the explanation of rational action.[6]

When discussing the rationality of an action, there are three levels that must be taken into account. The first level concerns the relation of the action to the reasons for that action. The second level involves questions about the reasons themselves, and the third level introduces considerations about the overall culture in which the reasons may be embedded. I will say a little about each of these levels.

1. At the first level, the question is: Given a goal or desire and a set of beliefs about the world, what is the best action to achieve the goal? An action is rational if it is the action that best satisfies the desire. 'Best' here is understood in a subjective sense as relative to the beliefs of the agent.[7] Elster calls this level the thin theory of rationality, but it is often referred to as the model of instrumental rationality, *Zweckrationalitat*, to use Weber's term. Rationality here is basically a relation of efficiency of means to the achievement of specified ends.[8]

In discussions of this model, there are a number of different types of complications that must be taken into account. I am going to pass over most of these and, in particular, all the problems associated with situations in which there may be no best or optimal action or more than one optimal action and the related discussions in decision theory. For the sake of clarity, however, I must explicate the model a little further, following the lines suggested by Davidson's concept of the rationalization of action and Elster's discussions of rationality.[9]

Let us call the beliefs and goals or desires of the agent the agent's reasons. In a rational action, the reasons are connected to the action in a way that can be stated in three conditions. First, the reasons must be the reasons for that action; that is, we can understand the logic of choosing this action to satisfy that desire, given these beliefs. This is but another way of saying what I said above, that a rational action is the best action to satisfy a given goal, given the agent's beliefs.

The second condition holds that the reasons in fact cause the action for which they are the reasons. It may be that the agent has certain reasons that would lead to the selection of a certain action as the optimal one, and that, in fact, the agent so acts, but that due to some intervening factor the action is caused by something other than the agent's reasons. For example, I might want to signal to you and I might believe that raising my right arm is the best way to signal to you. And at the time I want to signal, I might in fact raise my right arm. But it might be the case that at that very time I want to signal, a third person comes into view, and distracted, I raise my arm in greeting to this third person. At least under the description, "signaling to you," my reasons for signaling do not cause the action and the action is not rationalized under that description. This condition is meant to rule out this sort of coincidence or other accidental or compulsive occurrences.

A third condition stipulates that the reasons cause the action in the right way, that is, that the reasons cause the action *qua* reasons. This condition is meant to rule out odd or non-standard causal chains. For example, I wish to surprise you and am hiding, waiting for you to come into the room. It may be that at the moment you enter, my desire to surprise you so unnerves me that it causes me to lurch forward and indeed surprise you. Still, while my desire can be said to be the cause of my surprising you, it was not the cause *qua* reason.

On this level of rationality, what is meant by criticizing an action as irrational? The central point is that to say that an action is irrational at this level is to point out an error in calculation that need not have been made and for which the agent could be held responsible. For instance, an action is irrational if the action was not the best means to achieve the goal, given the agent's beliefs, and the agent could have and should have realized this. He or she was remiss, somehow, in examining and understanding the implications of his or her available beliefs.

We might also want to introduce here considerations of the consistency of the agent's beliefs and desires. The idea is that an action can be considered irrational on this first level if the reasons for the action are in some relevant sense inconsistent. We might, for instance, want to regard the agent as having certain epistemic responsibilities that include being aware of inconsistencies among his or her standing beliefs. And we might also want to hold the agent responsible for being aware of desires that are either self-defeating or mutually defeating. Like most of the issues that I am mentioning, these considerations open up a large and difficult set of questions. It is difficult to get clear on the notion of epistemic responsibility and on the relation of rationality and inconsistent beliefs. And it is perhaps even harder to get clear on the notions of consistent desires, of how to formulate sufficiently focused goals to facilitate correct calculation, and of an agent's responsibilities in these regards. I will not attempt to explore these issues here.

2.   The second level of rationality introduces questions about the rationality of the agent's reasons, that is, the rationality of his or her beliefs and goals or desires. Rationality here involves more than considerations of more or less formal consistency. As Elster puts it, we need a theory of "the substantive nature of the desires and beliefs involved in action."[10] Following Elster, I will call this second level the broad theory of rationality to distinguish it from the first level, or thin theory.

The issues at this level are once again complicated and difficult. I will restrict myself to a brief discussion of the question of the rationality of beliefs, leaving aside the even more difficult question of the rationality of desires. Elster discusses the rationality of beliefs in terms of the notion of well-groundedness or as he sometimes puts it, how the beliefs are shaped.[11] He unpacks this notion in terms of three conditions, conditions that are similar to the three conditions specifying a rational action on the first level. A rational belief is a belief that: first, is the best belief, given the available evidence; second, is caused by the available evidence; and third, is such that the evidence causes the belief 'in the right way'.[12] In general, the idea is that a rational belief is formed "without distortion from belief-irrelevant causal processes," where such processes include distorting mechanisms such as wishful thinking, defensive avoidance, and processes of self-deception.[13]

There is a problem here, of course, concerning how to establish which cognitive processes are distorting and what exactly a non-distorting process looks like. There is also a problem concerning the notion of available evidence.

What is the scope of available evidence? What is the responsibility of the agent to gather additional evidence? How hard must he or she work at this? Can we judge an agent irrational for not gathering sufficient evidence? These are difficult problems and I just point them out to indicate that a full account would have to address them.

Leaving Elster's discussion aside, there is another way we might approach the broad theory of rationality, one that is not concerned *per se* with cognitive mechanisms and which brings us closer to the problem of alien cultures. At the first level of rationality, the thin theory, the concern is only with the relation of given reasons to an action. In that sense, one might say that it is a subjective or internal account of rationality. On the second level, we raise the issue of where the beliefs come from and whether the beliefs are those that a rational agent should, in some relevant sense, hold. Here a number of considerations could come into play.

Actions are meaningful in the context of some culture or other.[14] Likewise, beliefs are acquired by agents in a cultural context. That an agent acquires the beliefs that he or she does and thus acts in a certain way can largely be explained, at least on one level, in terms of the beliefs that predominate in the culture of which the agent is a member. We are all products of socialization processes that include socialization into ways of learning. In this sense, the rationality of a belief and the rationality of an action for which the belief functions as a reason are relative to the epistemic standards and belief structure of the agent's culture. In a culture in which the results of reading chicken entrails are taken as good evidence for certain types of beliefs, it is rational on this level for agents participating in that practice to acquire and hold those beliefs.

Elster talks as if the question of the well-groundedness of beliefs can be settled independently of considerations of context, or at least, questions of context are not brought into his discussions. I would argue that at least at this level of rationality, the issue of cultural context is of central importance. For we at least have to raise the question of whether different cultural standards might determine different beliefs as the best belief, given the available evidence, or even more strongly, whether different cultural standards might determine in different ways what the relevant evidence is.

If this is accepted, then it follows that we understand and appraise the rationality of an action in a fuller way at this level than at the first level. Our understanding of an action is fuller (or perhaps better, *richer*) because understanding the action requires not only seeing that the reasons cause the action in the right way, but in addition involves seeing that the reasons that cause the action are ones that make sense for the agent to hold, given his or her cultural context. Thus, we can judge that to believe in and act on the results of the reading of chicken entrails can be considered rational in a culture in which that practice is well established. Knowing the prevalence of the practice allows us to understand the beliefs and action. On the other hand, for someone in our culture to engage in the same practice can be considered irrational. Citing the fact that someone in our culture believes in the practice of entrails reading does not allow us to understand why that person acts as he or she does, for there is still a question of the rationality of such belief and action in our culture. We need to know why that person has the beliefs he or she does and why he or she acts on them before we fully understand the action. These beliefs are not normally held or rationally countenanced in our culture, and our suspicion would be that the person acquired the beliefs in a way that does not render their being held rational. This is the case even though in the narrower sense of rationality, the thin theory of the first level, the right sort of connection between the reasons and action might obtain.

The same sort of consideration that holds for understanding also holds for the assessment and criticism of the belief, action and agent. We can rightfully judge the belief and action of the entrails reader in our culture to be irrational and criticize him or her for so believing and acting, but we cannot in the same way criticize the agent in a culture where the practice is well established. The intuition here is that holding a belief is rational if, given the standards of evidence, belief acquisition, and the like in the believer's cultural context, the belief is the best one to hold in light of the available evidence. To judge a belief irrational on this level is to claim that it is not the best belief available and, also, to judge the believer responsible for not acquiring the better belief. We can, perhaps, hold a person responsible for not living up to the standards of his or her community, but it seems unreasonable to hold a person responsible for not living up to standards not available within his or her community.

I said that the first-level theory restricted itself to a subjective or internal point of view. The second level as discussed by Elster concerns cognitive processes and thus is focused on the individual. My expanded account of the second level, however, introduces a social or intersubjective perspective by making the notion of rational belief relative to cultural context. From this point of view, there are at least two ways one might understand what it is for a belief or an action to be rational appropriate to this level. The first is to hold that what it is rational to believe is what the average or normal member of the culture would believe, a sort of reasonable man theory. This is obviously a difficult notion to pin down, but one might talk of the normal process of socialization, the standard and widely held modes of learning, and the average degree of reflectiveness about epistemic matters that characterize the culture. One would also want to assume the prevalence of epistemically correct cognitive processes. Given this account, one could hold that a belief is irrational if it deviates too far from the accepted norms. An action informed by such a belief would be counted as irrational to the degree that the irrational belief serves as a central reason for the action. Likewise, one could hold an agent irrational to the degree that one could with justification hold the agent responsible for adjusting his or her beliefs to the norms of his or her culture.

The second way of making sense of the rationality of belief and action relative to a culture is by reference to the idea of an expert within that culture. We might want to say, for certain domains of belief at least, that some people in a culture are in a better position to endorse beliefs than is the average member.

The notion of rational belief, in this sense, is relative to the beliefs of the expert. The expert, that is, serves as the standard, or perhaps it would be better to say that the concept of the expert functions as an ideal of rational belief constructed within that culture. To be consistent with this level of analysis, we would have to hold that the expert is picked out by the standards of the culture in question and that being an expert is a status internally conferred.[15] From this point of view, a belief and related action could be held to be irrational if they deviated from the belief of the expert and the action the expert would perform in the relevant circumstances.[16]

3.   The third level introduces an additional, rather obvious consideration. It might be rational for a member of a culture to believe in certain magical practices and act on their results, given the beliefs and norms of that culture. But that in itself does not make such beliefs and actions *rational*. After all, the beliefs are false and it is not rational to hold false beliefs if true ones are available. Likewise, action informed by false beliefs, at least ones that are avoidable, cannot be rational in the fullest sense of that term. The move here is to invoke something like an objective standard of rationality, and from an objective point of view, false beliefs cannot be rational.

Of course, this move, at least as I have stated it, cannot be correct. Clearly truth cannot be a requirement of rationality. We are all fallibilists. If rational belief had to be true, and rational action informed only by true beliefs, then we would be much less rational than we rightfully hold ourselves to be.

The move to the third level needs to be restated then. The better question is: Are the epistemic standards and norms of action of an alien culture, for instance, Zande culture as presented in the anthropological literature, themselves rational? Surely, we want to say, magic, entrails reading, oracular practices, and the like are not rationally justifiable and therefore are not suitable processes for acquiring rational beliefs. While we might be able to understand how a member of a culture with those practices came to hold the beliefs that he or she did, we cannot countenance the beliefs and practices as rational. And we have a further problem, for we seem to need to understand how such manifestly irrational beliefs and practices came to be so widely held and to endure. After all, rain dances do not produce rain. Why don't the participants realize that and alter their beliefs and practices accordingly?

Is cultural criticism possible, and if so, how? When we raise the question of the rationality of the epistemic standards and the norms of action of a culture, by what standard do we make the judgment? The obvious answer is: by our standards, by the standards of our culture. What other standards could we use? But of course, our standards should not be confused with some objective, culturally independent set of standards. Our standards are the best we can come up with. That is why we hold them. But 'best' here is still relative to our epistemic structures.

If standards of rationality are in the end culturally relative, what sorts of judgments can we make on this third level of analysis? Can we judge the standards of another culture irrational? Can we judge an individual in another culture responsible for not recognizing the epistemic standards that we deem rational, and thus judge that person to be irrational? By what right do we dare impose our standards on another culture?

We have clearly arrived at the problem of alien cultures. And we seem to be confronted with two equally unacceptable options. Either we say (1) that our standards are correct (damn it), correct not just for us but objectively correct, correct for everyone; or we say (2) there are no judgments of rationality that can be made at this level, all such judgments are ultimately culture relative. According to the second option, if a belief and action is rational as judged at the second level, that is all we can say. The first option is a form of ethnocentrism (sometimes called cultural imperialism) that is often accused of involving cultural arrogance and insensitivity and seems to rest on somewhat shaky epistemological grounds. The second option is a form of relativism that prevents us from making certain judgments that we want to make.

I want to argue that in the end we cannot escape our epistemic structures and what we take to be our best standards of rationality. But at the same time, I want to argue that we can rightfully and with confidence make judgments about the rationality of beliefs and actions in alien cultures, in effect, third-level judgments. But there are better and worse ways of making these judgments and we have to be careful how we proceed.

II. THE DEBATE OVER ALIEN CULTURES

In the debate over the problem of alien cultures, a number of positions have been taken. I will discuss four of them that have been called the intellectualist, the functionalist, the symbolist, and the fideist. There are two intuitions at stake here. One is that many of the beliefs and practices in question do appear to be deficient from the point of view of rationality. The other is that we do not want, too easily at least, to judge that other people and cultures are irrational as if we were the arbiters and measure of all things rational. While the different positions balance these intuitions differently, all attempt to give accounts of the alien cultures that avoid charging such cultures with blatant irrationality. Part of my solution to the problem is to suggest that justice can be done to these intuitions by distinguishing the questions concerning rationality on the different levels that I have introduced.

There are three errors that need to be avoided and that one or another of these positions has been accused of falling into. Two have just been mentioned: ethnocentrism and relativism. We want to avoid imposing without justification our values and standards on others clearly different from us and we want to avoid paralyzing judgment by concluding that there is no standpoint from which one culture can with justification judge the rationality of another. The third error is what I call reducing away rationality. This occurs when, in an effort not to have people in another culture appear too ignorant or irrational, an explanation of beliefs and practices is given that in effect discounts their rationality by severing the links between reasons and actions.

In order to understand the debate, two questions need to be kept in mind. The first concerns how we understand alien belief systems and practices. Can we use our categories for dividing up cultural practices (e.g., science vs. religion vs. art) to understand another culture, or is it improper to impose our categories on the other culture? The second question has to do with assessment or criticism. When and from what standpoint can we judge the rationality of beliefs and actions in other cultures?

I will use three well-known cases from the anthropological literature as examples of alien practices in relation to which these questions are raised.[17] The first concerns the Zande belief in the inheritance of witchcraft. As reported by Evans-Pritchard, the Azande believe that witchcraft "is transmitted by unilinear descent from parent to child. The sons of a male witch are all witches but his daughters are not, while the daughters of a female witch are all witches but her sons are not."[18] There are a number of ways of detecting a witch, one of which is through post-mortem examination for witch-substance in the intestines. Evans-Pritchard draws the obvious conclusion that "to our minds it appears evident that if a man is proven a witch the whole of his clan are *ipso facto* witches, since the Zande clan is a group of persons related biologically to one another through the male line." Likewise, it should follow that "a post-mortem in which no witchcraft-substance is discovered in a man clears his paternal kin of suspicion." But, according to Evans-Pritchard, "Azande do not act as though they were of this opinion."[19] That is, "Azande generally regard witchcraft as an individual trait and it is treated as such in spite of its association with kinship."[20] Aside from the question of the belief in witchcraft *per se,* the issue here is a logical one. The Azande may treat someone as a witch in spite of a clear deduction to the contrary conclusion from facts that they accept. Yet the Azande do not seem to be aware of, much less concerned about, this apparent contradiction in their beliefs. Are they being irrational?

The second example is the well-known rain-making ceremonies among aboriginal tribes in Australia reported by Radcliffe-Brown.

> With reference to this purpose [producing rain] we have to say that from our point of view the natives are mistaken, that the rites do not actually do what they are believed to do. The rain-making ceremony does not, we think, actually bring rain. In so far as the rites are performed for a purpose they are futile, based on erroneous belief.[21]

Not only is the belief in the efficacy of the ceremony erroneous, it is an error that would be apparent to the participants through the application of elementary inductive logic. Are they being irrational by not drawing this inductive conclusion?

The third case concerns beliefs about physiological paternity among the Tully River Blacks in Australia. An early ethnographic study reported that the Tully River Blacks, when asked about how a woman becomes pregnant, gave four reasons. The two that I find most interesting are that the pregnant woman went hunting and caught a certain kind of bullfrog and that, alternatively, she may have dreamt of having a child put inside her. In any case, W. E. Roth, the ethnographer, concluded that the Tully River Blacks were ignorant of the connection between copulation and pregnancy. The question here is what to make of this reputed ignorance. The Tully River Blacks understood the connection between copulation and pregnancy in animals. Could they fail to understand such a basic biological fact about themselves? And if so, should we hold them irrational for failing to see what is so obvious to us?[22]

III. THE INTELLECTUALIST POSITION

The intellectualist position goes back to the fathers of British social anthropology, Frazer and Tylor. When they saw what they considered to be "primitive" people holding clearly false beliefs and doing strange things in light of them, they did not hesitate to judge the beliefs and actions by their own standards. They also held to a methodological principle of rational explanation of action. To quote Tylor, "It is, I think, a principle to be held fast in studying the early history of our race, that we ought always to look for practical and intelligible motives for the habits and opinions we find existing in the world."[23] That is, actions were to be explained in terms of the reasons, beliefs, and desires of the agent. The statements of beliefs and desires were to be interpreted literally.

For the intellectualist, then, practices such as magic, primitive religion, and witchcraft are to be explained in terms of their purpose as understood by the participants. What is their purpose? In general the intellectualist answer is that the purpose is to explain, predict, and control important events that impinge on human life. In effect, the belief systems that inform these practices are seen as primitive theories and the practices as sort of proto-science and technology which is to be understood on the model of our science. As primitive theories, the beliefs are taken to be oriented towards truth. The classical statement of this position is given by Frazer.

> From the earliest times man has been engaged in a search for general rules whereby to turn the order of natural phenomena to his own advantage, and in the long search he has scraped together a great hoard of such maxims, some of them golden and some of them mere dross. The truth or golden rules constitute the body of applied science which we call the arts; the false are magic. . . .magic is thus next of kin to science. . . .[24]

The emphasis here is on magical belief as a system of general lawlike statements, statements that function much the way scientific laws do.

In the most sophisticated modern statement of the intellectualist position, that of Robin Horton, a detailed comparison is made between modern scientific theories and traditional African religions. The focus is on the structure of theories and theoretical terms and not on lawlike statements *per se*. The aim of Horton's comparison is to show how traditional African religions, in a way no less impressive than Western science, "gave rise to theoretical systems whose basic *raison d'etre* was the extension of the magnificent but none the less limited causal vision of everyday commonsense thinking."[25] Part of this project involves showing that many of the seemingly paradoxical elements of what Levy-Bruhl had described as the mystical and prelogical thought of traditional cultures were mirrored by various theoretical moves and puzzles in our science.[26]

The intellectualist strategy is thus to stress the similarities between Western thought and magic and traditional religion. The latter, then, should seem no more irrational than the former. As Frazer puts the point,

> The flaw – and it is a fatal one – of the [traditional] system lies not in its reasoning, but in its premises; in its conception of the nature of life, not in any irrelevancy of the conclusions which it draws from that conception.[27]

But there is an obvious problem here, for surely we do not want to assimilate traditional religious and magical thought and modern science too closely. For one thing, many of the claims of magic or witchcraft are obviously false, and we feel that in many cases their falsity should be noticeable from within the system. It cannot be merely a matter of similar forms of reasoning operating on different initial premises as Frazer claimed. The intellectualist also needs to supply an account of the persistence of what we take to be false magical and religious beliefs.

The general move here is to claim that certain features of these systems of belief and the overall social contexts in which they exist operate as blocks to falsifiability. For instance, Evans-Pritchard, elaborating on comments by Frazer, offers twenty-two reasons why the Azande "do not perceive the futility of their magic."[28] And Horton argues that there is a basic difference between what he calls cognitive traditionalism and cognitive modernism, where the traditional mode of thought lacks the reflective and systematic monitoring of results and intertheoretic competition of modern thought and thus allows for the persistence of beliefs that we find obviously false. I might note in passing that I find this distinction, if it is drawn too sharply, suspect for reasons familiar to anyone aware of post-Kuhnian philosophy of science.[29]

How would the intellectualist position deal with the examples I gave above of apparently irrational belief and action? The first case concerned the fact that the Azande do not draw the contradictory implication of their beliefs about the inheritance of witchcraft. The intellectualist would have to take the charge of apparent irrationality seriously, for he or she holds to a literal interpretation of the beliefs and regards them as oriented towards truth. To help clarify the question, let me use the three levels of rationality I introduced above. At the first level, that on which actions are rationalized by reasons, I do not think there is a problem. Given the reasons, the actions can be perfectly rational. I did mention on this level a consideration of consistency of beliefs, but I would want to construe consistency here rather narrowly, so that it is a matter of the consistency of standing beliefs only and not a matter of consistency among the implications of standing beliefs.

The problem comes on the second level. Should we hold the Azande responsible for not drawing the implications of their beliefs and thus for not noticing the inconsistency in this expanded set? I introduced at the second level the consideration of the cultural context of the epistemic agent. The beliefs of the agent have to be judged in light of the governing standards of his or her community. If the governing standards are such that there is no general epistemic responsibility for drawing the implications of standing beliefs, then, on this level, we cannot convict someone who does not draw out such implications and notice the inconsistency that develops of irrationality. This is in effect what Evans-Pritchard argues. "Azande do not perceive the contradiction as we perceive it because they have no theoretical interest in the subject, and those situations in which they express their beliefs in witchcraft do not force the problem upon them."[30] And we might want to understand this disinterest in terms of the general context and nature of traditional thought and culture.

There is more that needs to be said, however. If, for instance, someone were to draw the attention of an Azande to the implications of his or her beliefs and the apparent contradiction that appeared as a result, then the intellectualist would have to expect the Azande to understand, acknowledge, and be concerned about the inconsistency. If the Zande system of witchcraft is in the first instance an explanatory system and oriented towards truth, then they cannot avoid basic logical requirements except at the cost of irrationality. A display of indifference to the inconsistency would thus be an indication of irrationality.

The same sort of consideration would operate for the intellectualist on the third level of rationality, the level on which the epistemic norms of the culture are judged. If traditional magico-religious thought is to be understood on the model of our science, then we can require that certain norms of logic and evidence be respected. If Zande culture does not respect these norms to the same degree that we do, then their belief system can be judged to be less rational than ours. The judgment is based on the fact that our science and technology, and the epistemic structures that support them, are more powerful and effective than the analogous system of the Azande, and we would account for our greater success as, at least in part, due to our greater critical scrutiny and the attention we give to logical implications. The intellectualist would have to make this judgment of inferior rationality regardless of how sympathetic and convincing a story he or she could tell about why Zande beliefs are as they are.

The second example requires a more complicated analysis. Here the problem is the failure to draw the inductive inference concerning the non-efficacy of the rain dance. Here, too, the charge of rationality may not be in order on the first and second levels of rationality. But if we point out to an Australian tribesman the obvious inductive inferences, should he acknowledge it? The answer is not straightforward. If probabilities, here, the probability of the rain ceremony to produce rain, are drawn against a body of evidence, and if the evidence includes beliefs about the causal structure of the world, then the tribesman might be able to avoid drawing our inference. He might be able to explain away what we take to be the failure of the ceremony in terms of a number of conditions and mitigating factors that are part of his general understanding of nature. This could be done without a violation of the canons of inductive logic. If this is so, then the intellectualist cannot accuse him of irrationality.

On the third level, however, the intellectualist can make a judgment about the comparable rationality of tribal standards. If the purpose of the rain ceremony is to produce rain, and it manifestly does not, then a system of beliefs and epistemic standards that does not allow this truth to be discovered upon sufficient evidence is less rational than one that does, even if there are no straightforward violations of standards of rationality in the application of the system.

The third example, unlike the first two, does not involve a straightforward question of logic. Here the problem is ignorance about a fact of nature that is apparent to us and we feel should be apparent to the Tully River Blacks. But if their belief system and epistemic standards are such as to support false beliefs about the causes of pregnancy, then the intellectualist cannot convict them of irrationality on either level one or two.

If we appealed to a Tully River Black's beliefs about pregnancy in other animals and pointed out to her the analogy between humans and animals, would she be irrational (in terms of the second level) if she did not agree with us? I do not think so, if her belief system and the communal epistemic norms support her belief about pregnancy. What about the judgment on the third level? If the intellectualist interprets beliefs about pregnancy in terms of an effort to explain and control a natural phenomenon, then here, as in the other two cases, I think that the intellectualist would have to say that the epistemic standards and norms of the Tully River Blacks were less rational than ours.

As I have analyzed the cases, then, the intellectualist position does allow judgments of irrationality to be made, but the judgments are aimed at the system of beliefs and epistemic standards, and not in the first instance at the actions or agents themselves.

IV.   THE FUNCTIONALIST AND SYMBOLIST POSITIONS

The second and third positions I will discuss, the functionalist and the symbolist, can be seen as direct reactions to the conclusions drawn by the intellectualist. These positions can be discussed together because they make the same basic move in relation to treatment of the beliefs of the people under study. In both cases they set aside the level of rational explanation in terms of the agent's beliefs and desires. Their focus is instead on analyzing the practices in question in terms of a level of meaning or function not immediately available to the participants in the practices.

The problem the functionalists and symbolists have with the intellectualist solution is that it in effect devalues the rationality of the people under study. The intellectualist ends up attributing to his or her subjects elementary logical flaws or ignorance of obvious and commonsense facts about the world in certain important areas of their lives. To the functionalist and symbolist, these attributions are inconsistent with the evidence indicating that in other aspects of their lives, the subjects seem to have an adequate understanding of their world and seem perfectly capable of manipulating the objects to satisfy their social and natural needs. No matter how elaborate an account of the basis and causes of these flaws and errors is given by the intellectualist, the position still offends the functionalist's and symbolist's sense that all people should be treated as equally rational agents.

The functionalist and symbolist are also struck by the apparent fact that the same or very similar practices occur in different societies and that the rational explanations of the practices given by participants differ greatly from society to society. This fact suggests that something deeper must be involved, some factor beneath the level of rationalization, that can be used to explain the apparent structural similarities across diverse cultures.

How, then, do the functionalist and symbolist deal with cases of apparent irrational belief and action? The first thing to note is that they focus on explaining actions and practices. Belief is of only secondary concern. Beliefs, interpreted in a literal manner, are necessary to identify practices, but they do not enter into the explanation of the practices. The second point to note is that functionalists and symbolists tend to divide actions and practices into two classes, those that can be understood instrumentally and those that cannot. Radcliffe-Brown, a typical functionalist, talks of the difference between technical activity and ritual activity.[31] Likewise, another anthropologist who is a leading symbolist, John Beattie, introduces the distinction between instrumental and expressive aspects of human activities. For our purposes, the distinction, in both cases, comes to the same thing, although Beattie does allow, in a way that Radcliffe-Brown does not seem to, that most human activities can be seen to have both instrumental and expressive aspects. In the words of Beattie,

> Instrumental activity is directed to bringing about some desired state of affairs; it is oriented towards an end. Expressive activity is a way of saying or expressing something; usually some idea or state of mind. The instrumental aspect of any activity is understood by seeing what it is aimed at; its expressive aspect by understanding what is being said.[32]

Explanation of action by rationalizing it in terms of the agent's beliefs and desires is appropriate to technical or primarily instrumental action. But a different form of explanation is appropriate to ritual or primarily expressive action. The cases of apparent irrational action or practices, ones that the intellectualist would judge to be irrational, are all seen as instances of ritual or primarily expressive activity.

Not to see the distinction between instrumental and expressive, the argument goes, and thus not to appreciate that different forms of explanation are appropriate in different cases, leads one to commit a basic error typical of the intellectualist view. Again to quote Beattie,

> Serious mistakes have arisen from attempts to interpret types of behaviour which are primarily symbolic in intention as though they were misguided attempts to be practical and scientific. I have already referred to Frazer's attempt to explain the symbolism involved in magic as though it were solely instrumental in intention; this led him to a mistaken view of magic

as a kind of inferior and erroneous science. There is an essential symbolic element in magic; it cannot be understood at all adequately if its expressive aspect is neglected.[33]

At this point the functionalist and the symbolist part company to some degree, although there is a lot of overlapping or shading of differences among the various proponents of the two positions. Again taking Radcliffe-Brown as our functionalist, he argues that a ritual activity should be explained by the effects it produces, "not the effects that it is supposed to produce by the people who practise it but the effects that it does actually produce."[34] The effects he has in mind are not the effects the agents intend the ritual to produce, nor are they the psychological effects the practicing of the ritual has on the participants. Rather, the effects that carry the explanatory burden for Radcliffe-Brown are the social effects of the practice, that is, the effects on the "network of social relations binding individuals together in an ordered life."[35] These effects can be seen as the social function of the ritual. So, for instance, with the aboriginal rain dance, the explanatory effect is the function of maintaining social solidarity or a sense of social identity.

The symbolist can be differentiated from the functionalist by the fact that the symbolist need not be concerned with the question of whether and what social function a ritual practice plays in a society. The symbolist's concern is with the level of symbolic meaning expressed in the practice, where symbolic meaning is to be distinguished from any literal meaning expressed by the participants either in or about the ritual. And it is important that the symbolic significance of statements uttered during the practice of a ritual be placed in the context of their role in the ritual. Rituals are to be understood as, in the first instance, saying something rather than doing something.

> The man who consults a rain-maker, and the rain-maker who carries out a rain-making ceremony, are stating something; they are asserting symbolically the importance they attach to rain and their earnest desire that it shall fall when it is required.[36]

So Beattie claims, in contrast with Frazer's view which understands magic instrumentally, that the correct view of magic is "the acting out of a situation, the expression of a desire in symbolic terms; it is not the application of empirically acquired knowledge about the properties of natural substances."[37]

Given the views of the functionalist and the symbolist, what would they say about our three examples of the inheritance of witchcraft, the rain dance, and the ignorance of physiological paternity? The answer is straightforward. In each case, they would agree that the problematic beliefs should be seen as part of ritual practices. To evaluate them in terms of logical mistakes or ignorance of instrumental connections is to ask the wrong questions. The standard questions of rationality, those raised on all three levels of my analysis, fall away. For the functionalist, the question of the rationality of a ritual practice becomes the question of how well the practice serves the assigned social function. For the symbolist, once the symbolic meaning is unpacked, the only further questions about rationality that seem appropriate are about the logic internal to the symbolic systems of meaning involved.

There are standard and well-known objections to both the functionalist and symbolist positions.[38] The basic problem for both is how to connect the level of meaning expressed in the reasons given by the participants for their actions, that is, in their beliefs and desires, to the level of symbolic meaning or functional significance in terms of which the ritual is explained. This problem becomes one of how to explain the persistence of what appears to be inadequately motivated behavior. The practices in question are actions done for reasons, and the reasons presumably serve as the intentions that motivate the agents to act as they do. But as we have seen, these reasons do not figure into the explanation of the existence or, importantly, the persistence of the practice. Typically in a functionalist account, the function served by a ritual practice is unknown to the practitioners. Nonetheless, this function is taken to be the cause of the practice and the successful satisfaction of the function is used as the explanation of the persistence of the practice. But there is a problem about how to make the production of an unintended consequence the cause of the behavior that will unintentionally produce it once again.

An analogous problem occurs for the symbolist. There is some disagreement among symbolists as to whether or to what degree and in what way the level of symbolic meaning is unconscious, hidden from the practitioners as it were. But for the symbolists' explanatory project to have force, it would seem that the meaning cannot be known to and understood as such by the people engaged in the ritual. If they knew that they were essentially uttering symbolic statements, then they would explain their beliefs and desires in these terms and the practice could be so rationalized. But if the symbolic meaning is hidden, and yet is central from an explanatory point of view, then we have once again the problem of the persistence of the ritual. How does the symbolic meaning get transformed into the agents' motivations to perform the ritual?

Furthermore, in both cases the questions about the rationality of the beliefs and practices have been discounted, but the problem does not go away. We still are left with the agents' accounts of what they are doing in terms of their reasons, and unless we want to say that their reasons have nothing to do causally with their actions, in which case it is not clear that they are genuinely acting, then we still are left with the puzzles about why they continue to engage in practices that involve the types of problems about rationality that we have been examining.

V. THE FIDEIST POSITION

The fourth position I wish to discuss is that of the fideist. This position is influenced by the late Wittgenstein and its best-known proponent is Peter Winch. Winch's position is complicated and I can only touch on one part of it here. Like the symbolist and the functionalist, Winch can be seen as reacting to the conclusions of the intellectualist program, in particular, to the judgments of irrationality or lesser rationality countenanced by that approach. He agrees with symbolists, for instance, that "Zande notions of witchcraft do not constitute a theoretical system in terms of which Azande try to gain a quasi-scientific understanding of the world."[39] In fact, he accuses the intellectualists of committing a category mistake by trying to impose our category of science on Zande magic and religious practices.

This might suggest that Winch is a symbolist who feels that we should view Zande practices as symbolic and evaluate them in terms of their symbolic richness and coherence. And there are places where Winch seems to suggest this sort of view. But I think that it is clear that he is not really a symbolist. For the symbolist, like the intellectualist, holds that alien beliefs have literal meanings that can be interpreted in a more or less straightforward way. The symbolist then adds to this literal meaning another level of symbolic meaning that is not accessible, in a straightforward way, to the person who holds the belief.

Winch, however, would say that to impose this additional and explanatorily important level of meaning is to distort the real meaning of, for example, Zande beliefs as much as by trying to force their beliefs into our scientific categories. Moreover, I mentioned that the notion of symbolic meaning was introduced by the symbolist in terms of a distinction between instrumental and expressive activities. But as Charles Taylor has pointed out, both terms in this dichotomy are our terms, are categories whose meanings are given by their role in our cultural set of beliefs and practices.[40] By viewing alien ritual practices as primarily expressive and symbolic, the symbolist is as guilty of ethnocentrism, of making, in Winch's terms, a category mistake, as is the intellectualist.

According to Winch, Zande beliefs and practices can only be understood by placing them in the context of the Zande belief system and general cultural context, within, to use the Wittgensteinian term, their form of life. Forms of life are understood by grasping the rules governing them. The point of beliefs and practices must be appreciated from the standpoint of the practitioners, how they understand and follow the rules, and we need to be careful not to read our rules or the purpose or meaning of our practices into their point of view.

In passing I might add that I do not think that Winch is guilty, as some critics have claimed, of requiring us to jump entirely out of their cultural skin and into another, of having to go native, in order to understand alien cultures. He appreciates that this task would be impossible. Rather, as he says,

> We are not seeking a state in which things will appear to us just as they do to members of [alien society] S, and perhaps such a state is unattainable anyway. But we *are* seeking a way of looking at things which goes beyond our previous way in that it has in some way taken account of and incorporated the other way that members of S have of looking at things. Seriously to study another way of life is necessarily to seek to extend our own.[41]

What, then, would Winch say about the examples of apparently irrational beliefs and practices among the Azande, the Australian aborigine tribes, and the

Tully River Blacks? Would he allow us to judge them irrational? It is clear that in relation to my first two levels of rationality Winch would only allow context relative judgments. And this context relativity is of a strong form. For Winch, not only are meanings relative to cultural contexts or forms of life, standards of rationality are as well.

> Something can appear rational to someone only in terms of *his* understanding of what is and is not rational. If *our* concept of rationality is a different one from his, then it makes no sense to say that anything either does or does not appear rational to *him* in *our* sense.[42]

If this is taken seriously, then it would seem that standards of deductive and inductive logic as well as canons of evidence and belief acquisition are culturally relative, and it would not be appropriate to judge a belief or action irrational except in relation to the standards of the society in which the belief or action occurred.

Winch seems to hold this even of such basic concepts as consistency. He allows that all languages and thus human cultures must have some basic notion of rationality and that this notion involves conformity to norms. But, he argues, "how precisely this notion [of conformity] is to be applied to them [members of society S] will depend on our reading of their conformity to norms—what counts for them as conformity and what does not."[43] Specifically in regard to the notion of consistency, he allows that all forms of rationality must include a formal requirement of consistency. Again, however, he argues that "these formal requirements tell us nothing about what in particular is to *count* as consistency. . . . We can only determine this by investigating the wider context of the life in which the activities in question are carried on."[44]

Thus Winch would say of the contradiction that Evans-Pritchard found in the Zande practice of witchcraft that it was a contradiction for us in their practice, but it was not a contradiction for them. To understand their practice, we need not and should not resort to our notion of contradiction. As for the assessment of rationality, Winch would have to say that there are no grounds for judging the Azande less rational than we. There are no standards, no point of view, from which this judgment could be made.

One still might feel that there is an additional question that can be raised on my third level of rationality. Accepting for a moment Winch's argument that we cannot rightly use our concept of rationality, even our standards of logic, to support a judgment that the beliefs and practices of an alien culture with a different concept of rationality are less rational than ours, can we not, nevertheless, judge their entire form of life, including their concept of rationality, from the view point of rationality?

Winch would reply, I think, that there is no judgment here that could be made. What standards of rationality could be applied? It would be inappropriate to use our standards, and it would be pointless to use the standards of the culture under question, since for all but perhaps a few internally very incoherent cultures, the answer would be that they are rational by their own standards.

Furthermore, for Winch, to raise this additional question is to miss the point of what is valuable in trying to understand an alien culture.

> What we may learn by studying other cultures are not merely possibilities of different ways of doing things, other techniques. More importantly we may learn different possibilities of making sense of human life, different ideas about the possible importance that the carrying out of certain activities may take on for a man, trying to contemplate the sense of his life as a whole.
>
> . . . My aim is not to engage in moralizing, but to suggest that the concept of *learning from* which is involved in the study of other cultures is closely linked with the concept of *wisdom*.[45]

The problem of alien cultures, for Winch, is thus really a problem of wisdom in the sense of the education of practical reason, and judgments of rationality seem out of place here.

I want to argue that Winch makes one point that is right in an important way and one point that is wrong in an important way. To take the latter point first, Winch is wrong to argue that we need not and should not invoke our standards of rationality in the effort to understand the beliefs and actions in an alien culture. This is for at least two reasons. First, I agree with Davidson that the correct theory of interpretation requires that we use our standards of rationality in interpreting the language, the beliefs, and hence the practices of alien cultures. We cannot interpret another culture by leaving our notions of rationality at home.[46] And we cannot understand an alien culture without interpreting it.

Second, the problems raised by, for instance, the three examples I am using can only be identified as problems by using our standards of rationality. The problem in the first example is that the Azande do not recognize a contradiction that we see in their belief structure and in the second example it is that the Australian tribesmen do not draw the obvious inductive inference that we do concerning the efficacy of the rain dance. These areas are problems for us because we cannot understand them in the same way that we understand more mundane beliefs and actions concerning, for instance, the normal everyday manipulation of objects and ordinary social relations. In the latter cases where there are no violations of the canons of logic or evidence there is no problem about understanding the beliefs and actions in terms of our model of rational action. It is in the problematic areas that this model breaks down in terms of either belief acquisition or of the relation of reasons to action.

But for Winch, this distinction between problematic and nonproblematic areas of understanding has no sense. All areas of life, all beliefs and practices, are to be treated on a par, and the strategy used to understand them is to grasp the rules used by the agents as understood by the agents. But this strategy, if it could be carried off, is an attempt to dissolve the problem rather than solving it. Since, presumably, the agents do not understand their own beliefs and practices to be irrational, the Winchian strategy would not allow us the possibility of understanding them as irrational either. Nevertheless, the problem resists dissolution, because we are still troubled by how people understand what they are doing, how they connect their reasons and actions, and why they agree to the rules governing certain practices as they do.

The point on which Winch is right is in his criticism of both the intellectualist and the symbolist. I think that we must be careful, when trying to understand alien cultures, not to impose our categories for distinguishing practices on them. Zande magic and witchcraft is not simply a proto-science oriented towards describing how the world really is, nor is it simply a symbolic activity expressing the culture's social structure and relation to nature. At the same time, it seems wrong to say that either or both of these ends or purposes is foreign to it. Rather, these purposes are combined in a way that is difficult to express in terms of our cultural categories.[47]

Charles Taylor uses the term "incommensurable activities" to capture this Winchian point. According to Taylor, incommensurable activities "are not just different but incompatible in principle."[48] They are activities or practices the constitutive rules of which are such that one cannot participate in both at the same time. One cannot, for instance, engage in the practices of a medieval samurai warrior and a contemporary Presbyterian minister at the same time. The demands the two roles and sets of practices make on one's beliefs, norms, and values are just too disparate to be held together and acted on by the same person. This is the relation Taylor sees between Zande witchcraft and magic and our cultural practices.

> Now the difficult thing about the relation of ritual magic in primitive societies to some of the practices of our society is that it is clearly not identical with any of our practices, nor is it simply different. . . . Rather they are incommensurable.[49]

If this is accepted, then it should be very difficult for us to understand alien practices such as Zande magic. We should be very careful when drawing analogies with any of our practices, whether it be science, religion, or aesthetics.

VI.   ON MAKING JUDGMENTS OF RATIONALITY

What implications do these conclusions have for whether we can make judgments concerning the rationality of alien practices? Here again I think that Winch is wrong in holding that all such judgments are inappropriate. The Azande do not recognize or seem concerned with the contradiction we see lurking in their belief system concerning witchcraft. The Australian tribesmen do not draw the inductive inference about the efficacy of the rain ceremony. The Tully River Blacks apparently do not make what is to us the obvious conceptual move of seeing that human procreation operates on the same principles as that of other animals. These are all cognitive mistakes that warrant the conclusion that the belief systems and epistemic structures that support these mistakes are rationally deficient compared to ours.

But if the practices are truly incommensurable, what is the basis for these judgments? To see why this is a problem, consider two literary genres that might be taken to be incommensurable (although I am not sure that they are), a scientific treatise and a poem. While we would not tolerate a contradiction in a scientific treatise, we surely allow contradictory claims to appear in a poem. In fact, some poems may gain their force and interest from the tension created by contradictions. It certainly does not seem right to judge that poetry is a less rational practice than science because it tolerates contradictions. If practices in alien cultures are truly incommensurable with our practices (science, religion, art), might not the proper relationship be like the one between scientific treatises and poetry?[50]

Thus, in order to make judgments of comparative rationality across incommensurable practices and the cultures and forms of life of which they are a constitutive part, it seems necessary to locate some common ground, presumably some interest or end that they share, however differently that interest may be organized or the end expressed. This common ground could then serve as the basis of a comparative judgment. Incommensurability, that is to say, cannot be the rule all the way down. Taylor appreciates this point, for he writes that although Zande magic and various of our practices are incommensurable, "yet they somehow occupy the same space."[51] Taylor is not very clear on what his metaphor of occupying the same space amounts to, but I take it that the point of common reference, what gives shape to the common space, is a set of interests or ends we share with the Azande and indeed with all human beings. In fact, in a different essay from the one quoted above, Taylor does talk of "human constants."[52] Winch, likewise, has a famous reference to what he calls three limiting notions that help define all human life.[53] And the original source for both of these ideas is the first three principles of Vico's *New Science*.[54]

Neither Taylor nor Winch is very helpful in explaining just what these shared interests are or how we are to determine just what is to be included on the list of them. It would seem, however, that the list would include basic concerns that grow out of the human predicament such as survival and death, the maintenance of health, sexual relations and child-rearing, hunger and material provisioning. It would, I think, be difficult to construct a definitive list of this sort that would be both inclusive and also applicable across all cultures. Nonetheless, it does seem uncontroversial that certain things such as the problem of health maintenance is a concern shared by all human beings.[55]

Let us take, then, the problem of the health maintenance as a common interest. What cultural practice in our society addresses this problem? Science and its application in the medical sciences and technology is the obvious answer. What about in Zande society? Here we have to be a little careful, but it would seem that their practices of witchcraft and magic are at least in part concerned with this problem.[56] If so, then we can ask, which practice is more successful in solving the problem? For most of us, the answer is fairly straightforward. Our medical sciences are clearly superior as a tool for maintaining our health. Not many of us, I presume, would go to a witch doctor instead of an

MD.[57] Why is our practice superior? Our sciences in general are superior from the point of view of manipulating and controlling nature, and in part, this is due to their respect for logical consistency, inductive inference, and the like. If Zande witchcraft is a less powerful tool for solving medical problems, then we can conclude that part, though not all, of the explanation of this inferiority is that the canons of logic are not respected as evidenced by the problem of the inherent contradiction. It follows that Zande magic, from this point of view, is rationally deficient.[58]

It is important to note that in the conclusion I just drew, I used the phrase "from this point of view," that is, from the point of view of the common interest in health maintenance. It may well be that Zande witchcraft also addresses other common interests, as would appear likely if it really is incommensurable with our practices. And it may be that in regard to these other common interests, Zande witchcraft may prove superior to the way our culture addresses them. This means that there is no easy judgment about the overall superiority or rationality of one practice compared to another and even less of a clear basis on which to judge one culture or way of life compared with another. And surely our culture exhibits its share of problems and failed practices. This last point may be a way of understanding Winch's claim that judgments of overall comparative rationality, those that would appear on my third level of rationality, are inappropriate, and that the problem of alien cultures is best seen as a problem of wisdom, of practical reason. While, as I have said, I do not agree with Winch that judgments on the third level are either inappropriate or avoidable, appreciating the limitations of such judgments should make us more open to the complexities of alien cultures and to the possibility of learning from them. We might well have as much, indeed perhaps more, to learn from how and why other cultures judge that our practices are irrational in various ways as they have to learn from our judgments of them.

One might object at this point that talking of incommensurable practices addressing the same interest or, to use Taylor's phrase, occupying the same space raises the question of who is to decide what the interest is that is being addressed, or how the common space is to be characterized. Who, in effect, is to decide on our theory of human constants, limiting notions, or universals? We certainly cannot assume that such a theory would be uncontroversial across distant cultures. If it is we who are to decide, if it is to be our theory, then are we imposing the theory on the alien culture and by so doing, recapitulating some of the errors of functionalism? If we claim that the alien practice is indeed addressing an interest in a way in which the members of that society are not aware and perhaps would not understand, or even, perhaps, an interest they would not accept as a common interest, are we not severing the connection between their reasons and actions?

There are two responses to this objection that I would like to suggest. First, we could require that in making comparative judgments of rationality, we and the members of the alien culture agree on there being a common interest and on the fact that both of our practices are addressing it in some way, whatever else each practice might be doing. In order to do this we would have to pay close attention to the point of the alien practice as described by the participants, and we would have to be open to adjusting our thinking on what a theory of common interests might look like in light of their comments.

Still, there might be cases where we would want to insist that two incommensurable practices are addressing the same common interest even where the participants in the alien practice refuse to accept our description of the practice or the interest. In such case, we might come to regard their refusal as an error and explain it in terms of a problem of rationality, perhaps with their epistemic structures or modes of learning. We should certainly be hesitant to do this and not do it until we were confident that the problem was not one of misinterpretation or misunderstanding. Taking this second option, however, does not put us in quite the same situation as the functionalist. For the sorts of errors we would be ascribing to the alien culture, errors concerning their understanding of a theory of human interests, would be much harder for the members of that society to detect than the errors with which the functionalist is typically concerned. If this is true, then the problem of the severing of the links between reasons and actions is less pressing here than in the other cases. We could still explain the actions in terms of the agents' reasons, although we would have to try to explain the persistence of the practice in terms of aspects of it other than how it addressed the interest in question.

One last point deserves mention. It might be thought that choosing a problem such as health maintenance as the example is easy, but that such easy cases will not take us very far. The judgments of rationality of the sort under discussion depend on practices sharing a basis in a common interest. But why should all cultural practices be related to a human interest? Can practices not exist that are truly incommensurable, in the sense that they are not ground in any basic human interest? In that case, they would not afford a basis on which to make judgments of comparative rationality.

I do not think that we can rule out such a possibility. Not everything in a culture need be grounded in a human universal or common interest. We can, of course, always ask about the point of a practice, and that might give us some basis for judging its rationality. But the answer to that question might not be very illuminating. We might be able to step back from the practice and regard it as part of a general culture and try to take a comparative measure of the culture overall. But that kind of judgment is notoriously difficult to make, and in any case it is no longer a judgment about rationality of the sort with which I have been concerned. In such cases, then, no judgment of rationality seems appropriate. We are, to adapt terms introduced by Bernard Williams, no longer in a real confrontation but rather in a notional confrontation. In such situations, the language of appraisal is suspended.[59]

Let me, finally, return to the story with which I began, the problem in Kenya concerning the burial of Mr. Otieno. Was the use of a philosopher and a witch doctor as expert witnesses of equal status an offense against rationality? I do not think that there is a straightforward answer to this question. Part of the difficulty is that Western philosophy and witchcraft are incommensurable practices, and it is not entirely clear how they interrelate and what the interest of the court was in securing testimony from the two experts. If the problem that the two witnesses were meant to address is the factual issue of the human soul or spirit, whether there is such a thing, whether it survives after death and whether it can cause the problems that the Luo believe it can, then I would have to say that the philosopher, presumably informed by knowledge of Western science, has the superior vantage point. In this regard, the court, in granting the witch doctor's testimony equal weight, was offending rationality.

But the point of the testimony may have been different. Western philosophy and Luo witchcraft may share another, different common interest, one that concerns something like the need to orient human beings in the world and supply perspectives on the large issue of human life and death. In relation to this problem, I am not sure that Western philosophy is superior to Luo witchcraft. In part my uncertainty comes from the fact that I am not clear as to what answers to this problem look like and how to judge whether one answer is better than another. This, of course is itself a philosophical problem. In any case, we should note in closing that the problem of how to relate philosophy and witchcraft is, in Kenya, not merely a theoretical issue about the nature of rationality. It is as well a concrete and practical problem that Kenyans are living out in their daily lives.[60]

NOTES

1. *Washington Post*, 14 February 1987, A28.
2. Ibid.
3. A third alternative exists, of course: that the philosopher, as a Luo, should have endorsed the beliefs and practices of his tribe. In that case, however, it is not clear why the philosopher's testimony would differ, materially or in significance, from that of the witch doctor's. Since I am taking the philosopher as a representative of a Western point of view, whether fairly or not, I will not consider this third alternative.
4. Talking about *the* nature of rationality seems to invite the question: Which rationality? Whose rationality? As the discussion proceeds, it will become clear that my answer is: *our* rationality. That is, I am presupposing a shared notion of rationality in our culture, one shared by my readers. This presupposition might be false in at least two ways. Our culture is composed of many subcultures and there may be no concept of rationality common to most or even many of these subcultures. Or it may be that some or many readers of this essay do not share the culture or the concept of rationality that I am discussing. Insofar as either of these circumstances is the case, it means that the problem of alien cultures may start closer to home than one might think. The problem is grasped most easily, I believe, when it is presented in terms of alien cultures whose cultural distance from us is matched by spatial and/or temporal distance as well. But the logic of the problem is essentially the same however close to home the line is drawn.

I should also add that by talking of *our* rationality I do not mean to imply that we (whomever that may refer to) are fully rational and beyond criticism by our own standards. I believe quite the contrary. There is undoubtedly a large gap between our theory of rationality and our practice, and turning our criteria of rational belief and action on ourselves and our practices will surely reveal many areas open to criticism. While this fact should keep us from becoming complacent or self-righteous, it should not, as I argue below, lead us to think that we cannot make judgments about others but only about ourselves.

5. See Jon Elster, *Sour Grapes: Studies in the Subversion of Rationality* (Cambridge, 1983), especially chap. 1.

6. It should be obvious but it nonetheless bears mentioning that either calling a belief or action irrational or criticizing a person for acting in an irrational way does not itself license any particular way of treating that agent. In particular, it does not follow that one is justified in interfering with the agent to try to correct the irrational belief or prevent further irrational action. It may be in certain cases that interference is called for, if the agent because of his or her irrationality is threatening harm to him or herself or others. But the kind of intervention that is labeled cultural imperialism is certainly not automatically condoned. All one needs to block such action is a robust principle of toleration.

7. See Jon Elster, "The Nature and Scope of Rational-Choice Explanation," in *Actions and Events: Perspectives on the Philosophy of Donald Davidson,* edited by Ernest LePore and Brian P. McLaughlin (New York,1985), 67.

8. The concept of efficiency as used here of course needs clarification. Among other things, a means should be proportional and appropriate to the ends sought.

9. See Donald Davidson, *Essays on Actions and Events* (Oxford, 1980), Elster, *Sour Grapes,* especially chap. 1 and Elster, "Nature and Scope of Rational-Choice Explanation," especially section 1.

10. Elster, *Sour Grapes,* 15.

11. See Elster, "Nature and Scope of Rational-Choice Explanation," p. 63, "Rationality," in *Contemporary Philosophy: A New Survey,* Volume 2, *Philosophy of Science,* edited by Guttorm Floistad (Hingham, Mass., 1982), 113, and *Sour Grapes,* 15.

12. "Nature and Scope of Rational-Choice Explanation," 63–64.

13. Elster, "Rationality," 113.

14. I am using the term "culture" somewhat loosely to refer to a shared set of beliefs, norms, practices, etc., that give shape to and help define a way of life common to a group of people. Of course, cultures are not homogeneous and within any larger culture there may be several subcultures. A person might live simultaneously within both a dominant culture and a subculture that are not mutually consistent. While these considerations clearly complicate matters, for the sake of my argument, I am going to put such complications aside. These considerations might if followed up lead us to conclude, as mentioned in an earlier note, that the problem of alien cultures starts closer to home than one might have thought.

15. Are there experts in picking out experts – second-order experts – or is being-an-expert a property that is determined according to the generally held standards and norms of the culture?

16. There are problems with both the reasonable man approach and the expert approach. According to both, a person can be no more rational than the epistemic norms of his or her culture, whether the norms are set by a notion of average or that of expert. But it might be that a person, an isolated genius, transcends the norms of his or her culture in a way that we would want to say, and the culture might also later want to say, was in the direction of greater rationality. An associated problem with the view as presented is that it seems to assume a picture of relatively static norms, while in fact epistemic norms in many cultures are often both controversial and undergoing modification. If one wanted to stay at the second level of analysis where rationality is relative to cultural context, one strategy to meet these problems might be to take the culture as a continuing tradition and make judgments of rationality relative to the latest stage of cultural development. One might also want to allow for regressive as well as progressive stages, but then a criterion of progress/regress is required. Alasdair MacIntyre's recent work attempts to make rationality relative to traditions in something like this fashion. See in particular his *Whose Justice? Which Rationality?* (Notre Dame, Ind., 1988).

My response to these problems is more to take them as indications that the analysis must proceed from the second to the third level.

17. Discussions of the problem of alien cultures generally draw on examples from the anthropological literature, but our predecessor cultures in the Western tradition are in many

ways equally alien to us and raise the same problems. The same sort of issues thus arise in a philosophically sensitive history of science.

18. E. E. Evans-Pritchard, *Witchcraft, Oracles, and Magic Among the Azande* (Oxford, 1976), 2.

19. Ibid., 3.

20. Ibid., 4.

21. A. R. Radcliffe-Brown, *Structure and Function in Primitive Society* (Glencoe, Ill., 1952), 144.

22. The original report by Roth can be found in W. E. Roth, "Superstition, Magic and Medicine," *North Queensland Ethnographical Bulletin* 5 (1903). For discussions of this case see Stephen P. Turner, *Sociological Explanation as Translation* (Cambridge, 1980), 48–52 and Steven Lukes, "Relativism in its Place," in *Rationality and Relativism*, edited by Martin Hollis and Steven Lukes (Cambridge, Mass., 1982), 282–92. The Lukes article has been of general use as a discussion of many of the points raised in this essay. Also see the debate between Edmund Leach and Melford Spiro: Edmund K. Leach, "Virgin Birth," in *Genesis as Myth and Other Essays* (London, 1969) and Melford E. Spiro, "Religion: Problems of Definition and Explanation," in *Anthropological Approaches to the Study of Religion*, edited by M. Banton (London, 1966).

23. E. B. Tylor, "The Religion of Savages," *Fortnightly Review* 6 (1886): 71–86 as quoted in John Skorupski, *Symbol and Theory* (Cambridge, 1976), 3.

24. Sir James George Frazer, *The Golden Bough*, one volume abridged edition (New York, 1922), 57.

25. Robin Horton, "Tradition and Modernity Revisited," in *Rationality and Relativism*, 201.

26. See Robin Horton, "African Traditional Thought and Western Science," *Africa* 38 (1967): 50–71 and 155–87 and "Paradox and Explanation: A Reply to Mr. Skorupski," *Philosophy of the Social Sciences* (1973): 231–56 and 289–314.

27. Frazer, *Golden Bough*, 306.

28. Evans-Pritchard, *Witchcraft, Oracles, and Magic Among the Azande*, 201–204. See Frazer, *Golden Bough*, 68.

29. Of course, some would make this point in a much stronger way. Feyerabend, for instance, argues that scientific thought is much more similar to traditional mythical thought than modern philosophy has been willing to admit. See his discussion of Horton in which he is sympathetic to Horton's description of African myth but not of Western science, thus, in effect, dismissing Horton's distinction between cognitive traditionalism and cognitive modernism, in Paul Feyerabend, *Against Method* (London, 1975), especially chap. 18.

30. Ibid., 4.

31. See Radcliffe-Brown, *Structure and Function in Primitive Society*, 143.

32. John Beattie, *Other Cultures* (New York, 1964), 71.

33. Ibid., 72.

34. Radcliffe-Brown, *Structure and Function in Primitive Society*, 143.

35. Ibid., 144.

36. Beattie, *Other Cultures*, 203.

37. Ibid., 206.

38. For a discussion of some of these objections, see Graham Macdonald and Philip Pettit, *Semantics and Social Science* (London, 1981), 38–44. The first chapter of this book is a generally interesting and helpful discussion of the problem of cross-cultural understanding from the point of view of a Davidsonian theory of interpretation.

39. Peter Winch, "Understanding a Primitive Society," in *Rationality*, edited by Bryan R. Wilson (New York, 1971), 93.

40. Charles Taylor, "Rationality," *Philosophy and the Human Sciences: Philosophical Papers, 2* (Cambridge, 1985), 140–41. This essay also appears in *Rationality and Relativism*.

41. Winch, "Understanding a Primitive Society," 99 (original emphasis).

42. Ibid., 97 (original emphasis).

43. Ibid., 100.

44. Ibid. (original emphasis).

45. Ibid., 106 (original emphasis).

46. See Donald Davidson, *Inquiries into Truth and Interpretation* (Oxford, 1984). For discussions of Davidson in relation to problems of understanding alien cultures, see Michael Root, "Davidson and Social Science," in *Truth and Interpretation: Perspectives on the Philosophy of Donald Davidson*, edited by Ernest LePore (New York, 1986), 272–304 and Graham Macdonald and Philip Pettit, *Semantics and Social Science,* chap. 1.

47. Alasdair MacIntyre makes a similar point about the difficulty of capturing alien practices in our classificatory scheme in "Rationality and the Explanation of Action," *Against the Self-Images of the Age: Essays on Ideology and Philosophy* (Notre Dame, Ind., 1978), section II.

48. Taylor, "Rationality," 144

49. Ibid., 145

50. This analogy is of only limited applicability. The contradictions that appear in a poem are most likely there intentionally to create a desired effect. It might be, however, that the poet is so intent on creating an effect through rhyme or color or some other aspects of the language that he or she loses sight of the fact that contradictory claims are made in the poem if the language is regarded literally the way a scientific treatise would be.

51. Taylor, "Rationality," 145.

52. Charles Taylor, "Understanding and Ethnocentricity," *Philosophy and the Human Sciences: Philosophical Papers 2*, 125 and 127.

53. Winch, "Understanding a Primitive Society," 107.

54. Thomas Goddard Bergin and Max Harold Fisch, eds., *The New Sciences of Giambattista Vico* (Ithaca, N.Y., 1968), para. 333. I discuss Vico's claim and its relation to Winch in my "Vico and the Problem of Other Cultures" (unpublished manuscript).

55. There are various ways one might go about constructing a theory of human universals. Obviously, our shared biological inheritance is basic. Beyond that, one would want to look at social and psychological factors that appear common across many cultures. Such a theory would not be empirical in a straightforward sense because a "universal" would not, strictly speaking, have to appear in every culture. A given culture might have no or only a very marginal way of addressing a particular human universal. The Ik as described by Colin Turnbull are sometimes taken as an example of this. Certain assumptions would have to be made about human beings and there might well be sharp disagreement about them. For some discussion of these issues, see Ruth Finnegan and Robin Horton, eds., *Modes of Thought: Essays on Thinking in Western and Non-Western Societies* (London, 1973) and B. Lloyd and J. Gay, eds., *Universals of Human Thought: Some African Evidence* (Cambridge, 1981).

56. This claim would have to be supported by looking at the ethnographic evidence about how the ill and dying are treated in Zande culture. Presumably this could be done without begging any questions about improperly using our classificatory scheme of practices.

57. Some would undoubtedly question the superiority of our medicine, even if most of *us* would choose an MD over a witch doctor. Recent results in the sociology of medicine indicate that medicine has perhaps taken more credit than it rightfully should for our improved physical health and longevity. If our medicine as a social practice is as narrow and exclusive as some claim, then it is open to much more criticism than my comment suggested. My claim, however, is not that our medical sciences are without problems or even that they are steadily improving. Nor would I claim that patients are psychologically better treated by medical doctors than by witch doctors. The claim rather is that our theories in chemistry, biology, physiology, infectious medicine, and the like provide a better basis for understanding and thus treating illness and curing the patient than do systems of traditional magic and witchcraft.

This last claim needs some qualification as well. Depending on the social context, the available resources, and, of course, the condition or illness of the patient, our medicine might not represent the best available option. It is possible that non-Western systems of healing might prove superior in certain ways. Acupuncture might be taken as such an instance. In these cases, judgments of comparative rationality would have to be refined and specified to give proper weight to the success of the non-Western practices. Nevertheless, we would still want in these cases to understand the non-Western practice and why it was successful in terms of our science and its theories.

It is possible, of course, that our medical practices might turn out to be inferior to those of some non-Western culture. Nothing in my argument requires the superiority of our practices of health maintenance. If our practices turned out to be inferior, however, we would want to decide whether the problem was epistemological, having to do with the nature of our science, or sociological, having to do with the nature and history of our institutions and practices, or, more likely, both.

58. In general, if we want to judge a practice of an alien culture to be rationally deficient, does that require explaining why it is so? For example, in the three cases I am using, is it necessary to explain the existence and persistence of the errors picked out? It would seem that a complete account would want to address this issue. My guess is that no generalizable answer could be found to explain various cases, but that in each case, specific historical contingencies would have to be addressed.

59. See Bernard Williams, *Ethics and the Limits of Philosophy* (Cambridge, Mass., 1985), 160–62 and Williams's essay, "The Truth in Relativism," *Moral Luck* (Cambridge, 1981), 137–40.

60. I would like to thank Tom Blackburn, Sara Dickey, Al Neiman and Howard Wettstein for their valuable comments on earlier drafts of this essay.

MIDWEST STUDIES IN PHILOSOPHY, XV (1990)

Ratifiability and the Logic
of Decision[1]

BRIAN SKYRMS

Happiness is achieved by prudence: prudence is found in right actions: a right action is one that, once performed, has a probable justification.

— Arcesilaus

1. INTRODUCTION

Richard Jeffrey introduced an equilibrium concept into the theory of individual rational decision in the second edition of *The Logic of Decision.* He called the concept *ratifiability.*[2] The system of the book originally was motivated by a desire to deal with cases in which states are not independent of acts and to do so without causally loaded concepts. Probabilities are defined on a large boolean algebra, whose elements are taken to be propositions and whose operations are to be taken as truth functions. Acts are construed as propositions in this space that can be directly "made true" by the decision-maker. The inclusion of acts in the boolean algebra over which probabilities are defined is an innovation which may provoke varying reactions.[3] However, one may argue that this feature makes the system attractive for dealing with sequential decision problems. In such problems, the choice of an option may change its status over time from consequence to act to part of the state of the world, and each change goes with an appropriate updating of subjective probability.

But examples like Newcomb's problem, where acts are evidentially relevant but not causally relevant to preexisting states of the world, convinced Jeffrey that choiceworthiness does not always go by the evidential conditional expected utility of his system. Savage's theory, with a suitable choice of states outside the causal influence of the acts, gives the right answers.[4]

Jeffrey introduced the concept of ratifiability to deal with these problematic cases within the framework of his system. Informally, a ratifiable act is one that is optimal if chosen. The erroneous choices were to be eliminated by the requirement that the act chosen be ratifiable. However, ratifiability was not given any precise definition within Jeffrey's system, and the discussion of its sensitivity to causal considerations has been inconclusive.

I will discuss here a precise definition of ratifiability within a Jeffrey-type framework supplemented with Savage-type distinctions. His definition is not new. It has, in fact, been discussed by both economists and philosophers. Given the definition, a certain version of the doctrine of ratificationism[5] is clearly correct. Pursuit of a ratifiable act cannot lead to an act which is not choice-worthy. However, another version of the doctrine of ratificationism — roughly the hypothesis that causal and evidential decision theory must agree at the moment of action — is much more problematic.

The plan of this essay is as follows: Section 2 sets up a framework in which Jeffrey-type and Savage-type expected desirabilities can be compared and gives a definition of ratifiability within this framework. Section 3 shows one sense in which the doctrine of ratificationism is clearly correct and section 4 discusses a different sense in which it is problematic. Section 5 notes the importance of ratifiability in the theory of games. Section 6 discusses the status of ratifiability as a principle of rationality. Section 7 comments on the significance of ratifiability for decision theory. Finally, section 8 serves as a brief guide to the literature.

2. DEFINITION OF RATIFIABILITY
IN A JEFFREY-SAVAGE FRAMEWORK

Before we can discuss the relationship between Savage and Jeffrey decision rules, we need a common framework in which they both can operate. In Jeffrey's framework, probability and value are defined on a common boolean algebra of propositions. Savage's framework distinguishes acts, states, and consequences with probabilities defined on the space of states, and acts being functions from states to consequences. In the application of Jeffrey's framework to a given decision problem, however, one needs to introduce one of the distinctions that is built into the Savage framework. One must identify a partition of *act*-propositions, each of which is "within the agent's power to make true if he pleases,"[6] that represents the relevant acts for the decision problem under consideration. Identification of the relevant act-propositions requires causal judgment. We will assume here a further exercise of causal judgment in identifying a partition of propositions which are surrogates for Savage states. The states are outside the influence of the decision-maker, and they, together with the acts, capture the causal conditions relevant to the payoffs.

Let us assume, for simplicity, a decision problem with a finite number of acts and states such that the acts do not causally influence the states, and the states together with the acts jointly determine the value of payoffs. Acts and states can now be thought of as partitions: $\{A_i\}$; $\{K_j\}$ respectively, on a Jeffrey space. We will assume that on the elements of the common refinement of these partitions, Jeffrey value and Savage utility coincide. This last assumption is made purely for convenience of exposition. Where it does not hold, a slightly more complicated form of causal decision theory is appropriate.[7]

Jeffrey expected value is defined for every proposition, P, and any partition, $\{Q_i\}$ as:

$$V(P) = \Sigma_i \, \text{pr}(Q_i|P) \, V(Q_i \, \& \, P).$$

Savage expected utility is defined here for acts as:

$$U(A) = \Sigma_j \, \text{pr} \, (K_j) \, V(A \, \& \, K_j).$$

For any proposition, P, we have Savage expected utility conditional on that proposition as:

$$U(A|P) = \Sigma_j \, \text{pr}(K_j|P) \, V(A \, \& \, K_j).$$

This is what the Savage expected utility would be if one conditioned on P to get new probabilities of the states. In this connection, it is worth noting that here the Jeffrey expected value of an act is just the Savage expected utility of that act conditional on itself:

$$(E) \quad V(A) = U(A|A).$$

There is only one formal definition of ratifiability that makes sense in this framework:

Def. (R): A_i is *ratifiable* iff $U(A_i|A_i) \geq U(A_j|A_i)$ for all j.

By (E), one can just as well say that A_i is ratifiable just in case its Jeffrey expected value is at least as great as the Savage expected utility conditional on it of each of its competitors:

$$(R') \quad A_i \text{ is } \textit{ratifiable} \text{ iff } V(A_i) \geq U(A_j|A_i) \text{ for all } i.$$

Jeffrey expected value is, in this sense, the figure of merit for the ratifiable act — but not for its contrast class.

Investigation of the concept of ratifiability requires use of elements from both the Jeffrey and the Savage frameworks. Ratifiability cannot be defined in a Savage framework because the relevant conditional probabilities, of states conditional on acts, do not exist. Ratifiability can be defined in the Jeffrey framework only when Savage's distinction between acts and states has been introduced.

3. RATIFIABILITY AND CHOICEWORTHINESS (YES)

Ratificationists[8] agree that an act which maximizes Savage expected utility is choiceworthy, while — in the tricky cases — one which maximizes Jeffrey expected value may not be. The injunction: "Choose a ratifiable act!" is supposed to guide decision-makers in operating within a Jeffrey framework to a choiceworthy act. Therefore, ratificationists cannot support any definition of ratifiability in substantive disagreement with that given in the previous section. On that definition, a ratifiable act is just one which maximizes Savage expected utility conditional on the hypothesis that it is carried out. In what sense can we show that pursuit of a ratifiable act cannot lead to a decision which is not choice-worthy?

We will consider three increasingly general models of deliberation. In the simplest model of deliberation the decision-maker chooses a ratifiable act, executes it, and conditions on the proposition that the act is done—and is then in a belief state in which Savage expected utility is maximized. In this sort of a model, prior ratifiability by definition coincides with posterior choiceworthiness, where posterior choiceworthiness is measured by Savage expected utility at the moment of truth.

In a slightly more sophisticated model of deliberation, decision-makers' beliefs change by probability kinematics on the acts (that is, the probabilities of the states conditional on the acts remain constant) until one act is done and gets probability 1. This model does not differ from the previous one in the relation of the starting to stopping points, but only on the description of the road in between. The posterior probabilities are gotten from the prior probabilities by conditioning on the act chosen. So again, by definition, choice of an act which is ratifiable *a priori* will lead to an act which *a posteriori* maximizes Savage expected utility.

But deliberation may be a much more complicated process than the simple model just described. Suppose deliberation is a process on the temporal interval [0,1], with the decision-maker being initially unsure at t_0 of which act to perform, and finally arriving at probability 1 for some act at t_1. Rather than assuming that the probabilities of the states conditional on the acts remain constant as in belief change by conditioning or probability kinematics on the acts, let us consider *any* deliberational process where the probabilities of the states conditional on the acts (where defined) change continuously with respect to time. In the large class of deliberational models satisfying this assumption many bizarre things can happen. Certainly it is possible that an initially ratifiable act may cease to be ratifiable during deliberation. But even in this model, there is still one precise sense in which we can easily show that pursuit of a ratifiable act cannot lead one astray. Conditioning and kinematics on the acts are special cases.

Theorem: If an act chosen, A^*, which gets probability 1 at time t_1, remains ratifiable for some stretch of time [x,1] with $0 \leq x < 1$ up to the moment of truth and if the deliberational process makes $\text{pr}(K_j|A_i)$ change continuously with time on [0,1], then A^* maximizes Savage expected utility at the moment of truth (t_i).

Proof: Suppose not. Then there is an act, A', such that at t_1 $EU(A') > EU(A^*)$. But at t_1, $EU(A_i) = EU(A_i|A^*)$ because $\text{pr}(A^*) = 1$. So at t_1 $EU(A'|A^*) > EU(A^*|A^*)$. By hypothesis for all j, $\text{pr}(K_j|A^*)$ changes continuously with time on [0,1]. For all i, $EU(A_i|A^*)$ is a continuous function of the probabilities: pr $(K_j|A^*)$. So $EU(A'|A^*)$ and $EU(A^*|A^*)$ vary continuously with time and so does their difference. By continuity throughout some neighborhood of $t = 1$, $EU(A'|A^*) > EU(A^*|A^*)$ contradicting the hypothesis that A^* is ratifiable throughout $[x,1)$.

4. RATIFIABILITY AND CHOICEWORTHINESS (NO)

Might it be the case that Jeffrey expected value and Savage expected utility coincide at the moment of truth? This is the leading idea of a number of discussions of the impact of causal counterexamples on Jeffrey's system. The question as it stands is ill-defined. The problem is not with the expected value of the act chosen—under the assumptions in force its Jeffrey expected value is indeed equal to its Savage expected utility[9]—but with the Jeffrey expected value of its competitors. This is not well defined because the relevant conditional probabilities are on conditions which at t_1 have probability 0.[10] (Thus an attempt to substitute V for U in definition R would produce nonsense.)

The next best thing is to compare the Savage expected utilities at the moment of truth with the limit of the Jeffrey expected values as the decision-maker approaches the moment of truth along an orbit of deliberation. The question is then meaningful only with respect to some model of deliberation. In certain special cases, a plausible model can indeed give the result that Jeffrey and Savage agree in the limit.[11] But can these special cases be extended for some reasonable model of deliberation to a general theorem?

Let us consider models of deliberation on the unit interval, as in the previous section, where the acts have probabilities unequal to 0 or 1 on t in [0,1], and one of the acts gets probability 1 at $t = 1$. The general case would require deliberation starting at any coherent prior probability in this class to end with Jeffrey and Savage in agreement in the limit. It seems reasonable to assume continuity of change of the probabilities of the states conditional on the acts throughout deliberation, as was also done in the previous section, in order to rule out imposition of agreement between Jeffrey and Savage by a kind of deliberational miracle. And it seems reasonable to require that deliberation be *coherent*. That is to say that it should not be the case that starting from a coherent prior the model of deliberation postulated leaves one open to a dutch book: a finite number of bets which one judges fair or favorable such that one suffers a net loss for every possible outcome. Under these conditions, we can show that no such deliberational model can exist.

Theorem: There is no coherent model of deliberation under which the probabilities of the states conditional on the acts change continuously with time, such that for any coherent prior Jeffrey and Savage coincide in the limit.

Proof: Consider the decision problem with the following payoffs and initial probabilities:

	Payoff		Probabilities	
	State 1	State 2	State 1	State 2
Act 1	1	0	.9	0
Act 2	0	2	0	.1

This can be thought of as a version of "The Nice Demon." A nice demon has predicted whether the decision-maker will chose 1 or 2 and has arranged the state so that the decision-maker will be rewarded if the nice demon's prediction is correct. According to the decision-maker's initial probabilities, there is .9 probability that the demon predicted Act 1 and arranged for State 1 to obtain; .1 probability that Act 2 was predicted and State 2 obtains. The decision-maker believes that the demon will be correct with probability 1. (To recast the example as a game, one may think of the decision-maker as playing a pure coordination game with the nice demon, and using "best response" reasoning.)

Coherence requires that the initial zero probabilities not be raised. Otherwise the decision-maker is open to a trivial dutch book. In our example, at time t_0 a cunning bettor buys from the decision-maker a bet which pays \$1 to the bettor if Act 1 and State 2 or Act 2 and State 1 obtains; nothing otherwise, for its fair price of exactly nothing. At time t_1 she sells back the bet for a price equal to the current probability of Act 1 and State 2 or Act 2 and State 1, making the dutch book.

So in a coherent model of deliberation, for all $t < 1$:
pr(State 1|Act 1) = pr(State 2|Act 2) = 1

because zeros are not raised and no act gets probability 1 until $t = 1$. At $t = 1$, one of these conditional probabilities goes undefined, but the other gets probability 1 by continuity. Jeffrey values of Acts 1 and 2 must be 1 and 2 respectively throughout deliberation so these must be the limiting values at $t = 1$. At $t = 1$, the decision-maker has decided which act to do, and that act gets probability one. If this act is Act 1 then at $t = 1$ pr(State 1 and Act 1) = 1, because at $t = 1$ pr (State 1|Act 1) = 1. By similar reasoning, the other alternative is that at $t = 1$ pr (State 2 and Act 2) = 1. In neither case does Savage expected utility coincide with Jeffrey expected value. If Act 1 is chosen, the Savage expected utility of Act 1 is 1 and of Act 2 is 0; if Act 2 is chosen, the Savage expected utility of Act 1 is 0 and of Act 2 is 2.[12]

5. RATIFIABILITY AND EQUILIBRIUM

Ratifiability is a kind of equilibrium concept for rational decision. As such, it takes on special significance in the context of strategic interaction among rational decision-makers — that is, in the sort of problem customarily treated by the theory of games. In fact, the concept of ratifiability plays a key role in

Aumann's (1987) argument that common knowledge of Bayesian rationality implies a correlated equilibrium, although he does not isolate the concept and is not in contact with the philosophical literature on the subject.

Let us begin in the context of individual decision making. Here we can show that more than self-knowledge of Bayesian rationality requires that the decision-maker be sure that she will choose a rationalizable act. Suppose that at the time t_0, a decision-maker is undecided about which act to do, and has determined to do an experiment before deciding. The possible experimental results form a finite partition of her belief space, each of whose elements has positive probability at t_0. Then she is informed which element of the partition is the true one, and conditions on this information. Finally, the decision-maker decides by t_1 on an act which maximizes expected utility with respect to this posterior probability. We assume that the decision-maker is equipped with an appropriate Jeffrey-Savage space, with finite act and state partitions. Now let us also assume that the decision-maker *knows* at t_0 that she will choose an act which maximizes expected utility at t_1 (and knows which act she will choose if there is a tie). Then we can show that the decision-maker knows at t_0 that one of the acts ratifiable at t_0 will be chosen at t_1.

Ratifiability Lemma: If the decision-maker about to perform an experiment with a finite number of outcomes knows at t_0 that she will receive an experimental result, condition on it, and then choose an act which maximizes expected utility, and knows which act she will choose for every possible experimental result, then she knows that she will choose an act that is ratifiable at t_0.

Proof: Conditional on each member of the information partition e, there is an act, A such that $pr(A|e) = 1$ and A maximizes expected utility conditional on e. Conditioning on an act, A, is equivalent to conditioning on the union of the members, e, of the information partition such that $pr(A|e) = 1$. It is an algebraic property of Savage expected utility that if an act, A, maximizes Savage expected utility conditional on one member, e, of a partition and on another member, e', of that partition, then it maximizes Savage expected utility conditional on their union. If an act A has any prior probability of being chosen, it must maximize expected utility conditional on some member of the partition. Then by the foregoing algebraic property of Savage expected utility it must maximize expected utility conditional on itself; it must be ratifiable. By contraposition, non-ratifiable acts get probability 0 at t_0. Since the act partition is finite, the decision-maker is sure at t_0 that she will choose one of the ratifiable acts.

Notice that there is nothing in the proof of the ratifiability lemma that requires the "experiment" to be a laboratory experiment in the ordinary sense. It might just consist of sitting and watching, or—if deliberation is conceived of as generating new information—of just sitting and thinking. The theorem applies in the degenerate case of vacuous information—where the information partition has only one member which is the whole space. In this case, we learn nothing so our probability at t_1 is the same as our probability at t_0. Then at t_0 the decision-maker must already have an act which she is sure that she will do, and which maximizes expected utility at t_0.

Let us now consider a finite non-cooperative game played by Bayesian decision-makers. Here each player's state of the world consists of the combination of acts of all the other players. We can then conveniently assume a common Jeffrey-Savage space whose points consist of combinations of acts of all the players, over which all players have their relevant beliefs. Aumann is interested in a model which gives each player the kind of decision setup we have just considered. At time t_0 players are undecided about what to do. At time t_1, each has gotten private information as to the true member of some information partition, has conditioned on that information, and decided on a pure act which then has probability 1 for the actor in question. Aumann wishes to prove that here common knowledge of Bayesian rationality at t_0 implies that the players are at a correlated equilibrium at t_0. Common knowledge of Bayesian rationality is construed as implying that at t_0, each player is sure that she will maximize expected utility at t_1. It is also assumed that each agent knows how she will break ties. Thus, each agent has at t_0 for every element of her information partition, an act which has probability 1 conditional on that element and which maximizes expected utility conditional on that element.

Then, by the ratifiability lemma, each player is sure at t_0 that she will do a ratifiable act. By the definition of ratifiability, if each player were told privately at t_0 what ratifiable act she would do at t_1, she would have had no incentive to deviate. This means that the players are at a *subjectively correlated equilibrium*[13] at t_0. If, in addition, they share the same probability at t_0, they are at an objectively correlated equilibrium. If, furthermore, they already know what they are going to do, they are at a Nash equilibrium.

Ratifiability is an equilibrium concept for individual decision making. Together with various degrees of common knowledge in game theoretic situations, it generates the main equilibrium concepts of the theory of games.

6. THE STRENGTH OF SELF-KNOWLEDGE

The assumptions of self-knowledge required by the ratifiability lemma may appear to be quite modest but they have dramatic consequences. As our first illustration, let us see how a decision-maker with such self-knowledge would probabilize a Newcomb problem. The following is stipulated:

| | *Payoff* | | *Probabilities* | |
	State 1	State 2	State 1	State 2
Act 1	1,000,000	0	x	0
Act 2	1,001,000	1,000	0	y

Now the sort of reasoning that Jeffrey had in mind when he introduced the concept of ratifiability goes through. By the ratifiability lemma, the decision-maker knows at t_0 that he will do a ratifiable act. But there is only one ratifiable act here. That is Act 2. So the decision-maker's initial probabilities at t_0 must already be $x = 0$ and $y = 1$. Self-knowledge of expected utility maximization in a curious way prohibits the existence of values for x and y such that Jeffrey expected value maximization is well defined and conflicts with Savage expected utility maximization. Under these conditions of self-knowledge, the problematic cases for Jeffrey *vs* Savage are ones like the Nice Demon rather than Newcomb's problem.

The power and scope of assumptions of self-knowledge should not be underestimated. Self-knowledge carries with it a kind of self-reference, and flirts with paradox. Consider the case of the Mean Demon. (As a game, take the decision-maker to be playing a zero-sum game with a mean demon. Mixed strategies are not available.[14])

The Mean Demon

	Payoff		Probabilities	
	State 1	State 2	State 1	State 2
Act 1	– 50	0	x	0
Act 2	0	–100	0	y

In Newcomb's problem, the assumptions of self-knowledge constrained the possible probabilities at t_0 so that only one initial probability was possible. Here these assumptions overconstrain the initial probabilities. There is no ratifiable act, so the assumptions of the ratifiability lemma cannot be met.

If we weaken the assumptions of self-knowledge slightly, by omitting the seemingly innocuous assumption that the decision-maker knows how she will break ties, then the remaining assumption of knowledge of expected utility maximization becomes barely consistent. Suppose that no matter what information comes in, at t_1 the values of x and y are $2/3$ and $1/3$ respectively. (Since coherence requires that prior probability be the expectation of posterior probability, the values of x and y at t_0 must be the same. We are in the degenerate case of an experiment, where no relevant information is produced.) Then at t_1 both acts maximize expected utility, and knowledge at t_0 that one will do something that maximizes expected utility at t_1 is just knowledge that one will do something. You can check that these are the *only* values for x and y at t_0 and t_1 which are consistent with the weakened assumption. In contrast, the bare assumption that the decision-maker will maximize expected utility (although she may not know it) is consistent with any probability values for x and y.

The question of the existence of ratifiable acts—and thus of the self-knowledge assumptions that guarantee existence—is a delicate one which calls for careful examination. Such an investigation would not be complete unless it paid attention to the possible deliberational processes which could take the decision-maker from a state of indecision to a state of decision. A myopic deliberator, who does not think about the moment of truth, may simply fail to converge to a decision in certain nasty cases.[15] A deliberator with foresight, who recognizes the problem as one which has no ratifiable decision, may as well forget about ratifiability and opt for the act with highest current expected utility,[16] notwithstanding the anticipated regrets.

7. CONCLUSION

The main significance of ratifiability does not lie in its use in handling causal pathology within the framework of *The Logic of Decision*. A proper implementation of ratifiability within that framework requires the identification of partitions which do the work of Savage's distinction between acts and states. Given those partitions, one can recover choiceworthiness most simply as maximum Savage expected utility. The real importance of Jeffrey's introduction of the concept of ratifiability into current philosophical discussion of individual rational decision is that it has opened up a rich array of topics for investigation: the status of equilibrium as a rationality concept, the nature of the deliberational process, the connections between individual decision theory and the theory of games, and the consequences of self-knowledge for rational decision-makers.

8. GUIDE TO THE LITERATURE

Jeffrey's system was introduced in Jeffrey (1965) as a more general framework than that of Savage (1954). Questions of interpretation arising from the inclusion of acts in the probability space in this system are discussed by Sneed (1966), Spohn (1977), Jeffrey (1977), and Shin (1989; forthcoming). The divergence between expected utility in the sense of Savage and expected value in the sense of Jeffrey is discussed in Gibbard and Harper (1981). The connection between maximization of Jeffrey expected value and the concept of Stackelberg equilibrium is pointed out in Walliser (1988). Gibbard and Harper (1981) advance an alternative "causal decision theory" formulated in terms of probabilities of subjunctive conditionals. For a survey of causal decision theories and a demonstration of their essential unity with each other and with Savage, see Skyrms (1980; 1984) and Lewis (1980). For a representation theorem for generalized causal decision theory, see Armendt (1986, 1988). For an explicit semantics for the relevant counterfactuals in normal form games, see Shin (1989).

In the second edition of *The Logic of Decision* (1983), Jeffrey gives an informal definition of ratifiability: "A ratifiable decision is a decision to perform an act of maximum estimated desirability relative to the probability matrix an agent thinks he would have if he finally decided to perform that act." The definition used in this essay is one way of realizing this basic idea. The definition of ratifiability proposed by Harper (1984; 1986; 1988) is equivalent to that given in section 2 of this essay, provided that the counterfactual in Harper's definition is given reasonable truth conditions in terms of the Savage states. This notion is called *stability* by Rabinowicz (1988). Walliser (1988) takes it as a natural interpretation of Jeffrey's informal definition. The same notion is independently introduced by Aumann (1987) to demonstrate the connection between *ex ante* optimality and his (1974) notion of correlated equilibrium. The significance of ratifiability is discussed by Eells (1988a; 1984b; 1985); Eells and Harper (forthcoming); Harper (1984; 1986; 1988); Rabinowicz (1988; forthcoming); Richter (1984; 1986); Shin (1989; forthcoming); Sobel (1986); and Weirich (1985; 1986).

For the relevant notions of dynamic coherence see Goldstein (1983), van Fraassen (1984), and Skyrms (1987a; 1987b; 1990). Some models of the deliberational process are to be found in Eells (1984b), Jeffrey (1988), and Skyrms (1988; 1990).

NOTES

1. This essay was delivered at a conference on probability and rational decision in honor of Richard Jeffrey at Dunwalke, New Jersey, in September 1989. Research was partially supported by the National Science Foundation.

2. Related ideas had been discussed by Ellery Eells (1982).

3. Spohn argues vigorously against this move.

4. As do a host of interrelated "causal decision theories." For simplicity and familiarity this essay will rely on Savage as a member of this group.

5. Jeffrey (1965, 19).

6. Ibid., 84. But also see the discussion of probabilistic acts on pp. 177–79 which I will not attempt to model here.

7. See the discussion in Skyrms (1985).

8. In particular, Jeffrey and Eells.

9. Since the probability of the act chosen, A, is here equal to 1, we have for each K_i, $\text{pr}(K_i) = \text{pr}(K_i|A)$, so:

Jeffrey Expected Value = $\Sigma_i \text{ pr } (K_i|A) \ U(K_i \ \& \ A) = \Sigma_i \text{ pr}(K_i) \ U \ (K_i \ \& \ A) =$ Savage Expected Utility.

10. If we were to model deliberation where the probability of the act selected fell short of 1 at t_1, there would be ample room for a Newcomb-type of spurious correlation to remain at the close of deliberation. In the second edition of *The Logic of Decision*, Jeffrey reports van Fraassen's dramatization of this kind of possibility in the case of Prisoners' dilemma with a clone.

11. See Jeffrey (1988).

12. This may not be a decisive argument against the program of showing that for certain special kinds of rational decision-makers, Jeffrey and Savage coincide in the limit. Perhaps the program can argue that such decision-makers should not be allowed to have the kind of prior given in the example.

13. For the definition of this equilibrium concept, see Aumann (1974; 1987). Limitations of space preclude a detailed discussion of game theoretic equilibrium concepts here.

14. Of course, if we expand the acts to include costless implementation of arbitrary random strategies, and preclude any correlation between the Savage states and *these* mixed acts, we get a ratifiable act. But perhaps implementation of a random strategy might carry with it a cost large enough to make any pure strategy preferable. Perhaps the mean demon might be

able to predict whether the decision-maker will randomize. Perhaps the mean demon could predict the outcome of the randomization. Solution of the existence problem is not something that we are entitled to take for granted.

15. Once the problem of convergence of deliberation is raised, it may be relevant even in cases where a ratifiable act does exist. For a problematic individual decision problem, see the shell game in Skyrms (1984). Similar examples have been discussed by Rabinowicz (1986) where mixed strategies are unavailable:

	C1	C2	C3
R1	1,3	2,0	3,1
R2	0,2	2,2	0,2
R3	3,1	2,0	1,3

The only Nash equilibrium is a (R2,C2). Therefore, under appropriately strong conditions of common knowledge, R2 and C2 are the only ratifiable options for Row and Column. But R2 is weakly dominated by both R1 and R3 and C2 is weakly dominated by both C1 and C3. For the application of dynamic deliberation models to this game, see Skyrms (1990).

16. As advocated by Rabinowicz (1988). See also the discussion in Skyrms.

REFERENCES

Armendt, B. 1986. "A Foundation for Causal Decision Theory." *Topoi* 5: 3–19.

Armendt, B. 1988. "Conditional Preference and Causal Expected Utility." In *Causation in Decision, Belief Change, and Statistics,* edited by W. Harper and B. Skyrms, 3–24. Dordrecht.

Aumann, R. J. 1974. "Subjectivity and Correlation in Randomized Strategies." *Journal of Mathematical Economics* 1: 67–96.

Aumann, R. J. 1976. "Agreeing to Disagree." *The Annals of Statistics* 4: 1236–39.

Aumann, R. J. 1987. "Correlated Equilibrium as an Expression of Bayesian Rationality." *Econometrica* 55: 1–18.

Eells, E. 1982. *Rational Decision and Causality.* Cambridge.

Eells, E. 1984a. "Causal Decision Theory." *PSA 1984*, vol. 2, edited by P. Asquith and P. Kitcher, 177–200. East Lansing, Mich.

Eells, E. 1984b. "Metatickles and the Dynamics of Deliberation." *Theory and Decision* 17: 71–95.

Eells, E. 1985. "Weirich on Decision Instability." *Australasian Journal of Philosophy* 63: 473–78.

Eells, E., and W. Harper. Forthcoming. "Ratifiability, Game Theory and the Principle of Independence of Irrelevant Alternatives." *Australasian Journal of Philosophy.*

Gibbard, A., and W. Harper. 1981. "Counterfactuals and Two Kinds of Expressed Utility." In *Ifs,* edited by Harper et al., 153–90. Dordrecht.

Goldstein, M. 1983. "The Prevision of a Prevision." *Journal of the American Statistical Association* 78: 817–19.

Harper, W. 1984. "Ratifiability and Causal Decision Theory: Comments on Eells and Seidenfeld." In *PSA 1984*, vol. 2, edited by P. Asquith and P. Kitcher. East Lansing, Mich.

Harper, W. 1986. "Mixed Strategies and Ratifiability in Causal Decision Theory." *Erkenntniss* 24: 25–36.

Harper, W. 1988. "Causal Decision Theory and Game Theory: A Classic Argument for Equilibrium Solutions, a Defense of Weak Equilibria, and a New Problem for the Normal Form Representation." In *Causation in Decision, Belief Change, and Statistics,* edited by W. Harper and B. Skyrms, 25–48. Dordrecht.

Jeffrey, R. 1965. *The Logic of Decision*. New York. 2d rev. ed. 1983. Chicago.
Jeffrey, R. 1977. "A Note on the Kinematics of Preference." *Erkentniss* 11: 135–41.
Jeffrey, R. 1981. "The Logic of Decision Defended." *Synthese* 48: 473–92.
Jeffrey, R. 1988. "How to Probabilize a Newcomb Problem." In *Probability and Causality,* edited by J. Fetzer, 241–51. Dordrecht.
Lewis, D. 1980. "Causal Decision Theory." *Australasian Journal of Philosophy* 59: 5–30.
Moulin, H. 1986. *Game Theory for the Social Sciences.* New York.
Rabinowicz, W. 1985. "Ratificationism without Ratification." *Theory and Decision* 19: 171–200.
Rabinowicz, W. 1988. "Ratifiability and Stability." In *Decision, Probability and Utility,* edited by R. Gardenfors and N. Sahlin, 406–25. Cambridge.
Rabinowicz, W. Forthcoming. "Stable and Retrievable Options." *Philosophy of Science.*
Richter, R. 1984. "Rationality Revisited." *Australasian Journal of Philosophy* 62: 392–403.
Richter, R. 1986. "Further Comments on Decision Instability." *Australasian Journal of Philosophy* 64: 345–49.
Savage, L. J. 1954. *The Foundations of Statistics.* New York.
Shin, H. S. 1989. "Counterfactuals and a theory of equilibrium in games." Read at the workshop on Knowledge, Belief and Strategic Rationality, Castglioncello, Italy.
Shin, H. S. Forthcoming. "Two Notions of Ratifiability and Equilibrium in Games." In *Essays in the Foundations of Decision Theory,* edited by M. Bacharach and S. Hurley.
Skyrms, B. 1980. *Causal Necessity.* New Haven, Conn.
Skyrms, B. 1984. *Pragmatics and Empiricism.* New Haven, Conn.
Skyrms, B. 1985. "Ultimate and Proximate Consequences in Causal Decision Theory." *Philosophy of Science* 52: 608–11.
Skyrms, B. 1987a. "Dynamic Coherence." In *Foundations of Statistical Inference,* edited by I. B. MacNeill and G. J. Umphrey, 233–43. Dordrecht.
Skyrms, B. 1987b. "Dynamic Coherence and Probability Kinematics." *Philosophy of Science* 54: 1–20.
Skyrms, B. 1988. "Deliberational Dynamics and the Foundations of Bayesian Game Theory." In *Epistemology* [Philosophical Perspectives v. 2], edited by J. E. Tomberlin, 345–67. Northridge.
Skyrms, B. 1990. *The Dynamics of Rational Deliberation.* Cambridge, Mass.
Sneed, J. D. 1966. "Strategy and the Logic of Decisions." *Synthese* 16: 270–83.
Sobel, J. H. 1986. "Defenses against and conservative reactions to Newcomb-like problems: Metatickles and Ratificationism." In *PSA 1986,* vol. 1, edited by A. Fine and P. Machamer, 342–51. East Lansing, Mich.
Sobel, J. H. Forthcoming. "Maximization, Stability of Decision and Actions in Accordance with Reason." *Philosophy of Science.*
Spohn, W. 1977. "Where Luce and Krantz Do Really Generalize Savage's Decision Model." *Erkentniss* 11: 113–34.
van Fraassen, B. 1984. "Belief and the Will." *Journal of Philosophy* 81: 235–56.
Walliser, B. 1988. "A simplified taxonomy of 2 X 2 Games." *Theory and Decision* 25: 163–91.
Weirich, P. 1985. "Decision Instability." *Australasian Journal of Philosophy* 64: 465–72.
Weirich, P. 1986. "Decisions in Dynamic Settings." In *PSA 1986,* edited by A. Fine and P. Machamer, 438–49. East Lansing, Mich.
Weirich, P. 1988. "Hierarchical Maximization of Two Kinds of Expected Utility." *Philosophy of Science* 55: 560–82.

The Idea of Science

HILARY PUTNAM

Poets like to issue statements about the nature of poetry, physicists to issue statements about the nature of physical science, economists to issue statements about the nature of economics—and, of course, philosophers love to talk about the nature of philosophy! Whether any of these activities is materially *advanced* by the issuing of these statements is another matter.

A by-product of this production of manifestos and ideologies is the endless debate about the exact status of the "social sciences." Are they "empirical sciences" at all? My contribution to this discussion will be modest indeed. I want to suggest that the notion "empirical science" is not one that can lend itself to clarifying, to "shedding light," on the problems of the special disciplines. The concept is, at bottom, too loose, its own structure too fragile, to support the weight that it is asked to bear in these discussions.

Perhaps this is not such a trivial claim at that! For, to hear people talk, it certainly seems as if "empirical science" is regarded as a firm notion. To ask whether history, or economics, or sociology, is (or, perhaps, could be) an "empirical science" is widely regarded as a perfectly meaningful (if controversial) question. But I do not think this question has a clear meaning at all.

The claim I shall defend is that the notion of an "empirical science" contains from the start a fundamental tension, and that this tension infects every attempt to use the notion to do serious philosophical work.

In saying this I am not saying that the notion has no use at all. Ludwig Wittgenstein taught us that not all concepts have "necessary and sufficient conditions." For many concepts, we have only paradigm cases, and more than one paradigm case at that. I believe that "empirical science" is a concept of this sort.

It is quite clear that the paradigm case *par excellence*, so to speak, is physics. But what makes *physics* so special? The possibility of divergent answers opens up, and it is these divergent answers that set up the tensions in the concept of an empirical science.

The two answers I am speaking of are answers that have appealed to scientifically minded philosophers from the beginning. Almost every empiricist has been attracted to both of them, and the greatest living empiricist philosopher has, in his own philosophical evolution, displayed the pull of first one and then the other of the two answers, the two purported distinguishing features, in a way that is especially perspicuous. I believe one can show the same tension in Carnap's writing, and especially in the seminar notes that were edited by Gardner and published under the title *Philosophy of Science*.

One of these "answers" to the question, "What makes physics so special," is that the distinguishing feature is *method*. Physics owes its success to a special method; an "empirical science" is, first of all, what uses this celebrated method. This is, perhaps, the root idea behind classical empiricism and classical positivism. In its purest form, it is represented by Comte's injunction to forget those musty questions about "why" and think only about "how." Freely interpreted, Comte was saying "Epistemology and not ontology is what matters."

But the rise of a school (or of several schools) of philosophy which "take the results of science seriously," as one says, has had consequences which might even have been foreseeable from the start. If we really take the results of science seriously, then why shouldn't we also take them *literally*? Classical empiricism took the methodology of science immensely seriously, but it felt free to reinterpret the *content* of science in the light of its current doctrines. Scientific talk about atoms and bacteria (and more recently, about black holes) or whatever the current theoretical entities happened to be, is really only "highly derived" talk about sense-impressions, or so empiricists used to be fond of claiming. But were these empiricists not taking their own philosophical theories – their theories of perception, for example – more seriously than science itself? Inevitably, philosophers were bound to ask themselves if a perfectly serious scientific philosopher should not believe science to be literally true (allowing for inevitable errors to be discovered in the future by science itself), or, anyway " as true as anything is." Shouldn't one be a *materialist* rather than some species of subjective idealist, if one really takes science seriously as the best knowledge we have?

In Quine's work one sees these two moments in philosophical reflection very clearly. In his early lecture, "On What There Is," material objects were described as "posits" and even as "myths," better than "Homer's gods" only in point of utility. But from "The Scope and Language of Science" and "Epistemology Naturalized" onward, Quine's claim has been that physics and physics alone gets to (or has the program of getting to) "the true and ultimate nature of reality." And nowadays we even find Quine describing his attitude to physics as "robust realism."

If the root idea of classical empiricism is the idea that method is what distinguishes physics, the idea that revealing the true and ultimate nature of the external world, the properties things have "in themselves," is the hallmark of physics, deserves to be called the root idea of classical materialism. What I am saying is that two philosophies, not one, claim and have always claimed to be "scientific philosophy," or "philosophy of science" in a proprietary as opposed to a merely topical sense. And since empiricism leads to a state of mind that finds materialism attractive, empiricism is unstable: the cycle, empiricism –

positivism — science worship — materialism — scientific method worship — empiricism. . . repeats itself over and over again.

Another way of putting the point, using terms corresponding to the two relevant subdisciplines of philosophy, is that one may think of physics as primarily distinguished *epistemologically* or as primarily distinguished *ontologically*. And the resulting images of science will be very different.

The difference in the images is partly accounted for by a certain vagueness in the notion of a "scientific method." Whether science even possesses a procedure clear enough and uniform enough to be called a "method" depends, always, on what alternative procedures are contemplated. In the age of Bacon the alternatives were the aprioristic and tradition-based methods of the late medieval/early Renaissance sciences. Then, it was clear enough to Bacon himself and to his contemporaries, that he was proposing something radically new in relation to these. Putting questions to Nature, relying on particulars and not on an intellectual intuition of substantial forms, and devising sequences of experiments so that Nature could be forced to answer the questions put to her were revolutionary ideas. Today, all the disciplines which engage in empirical research at all have eschewed *a priori* reasoning (or claim to have eschewed it) as anything more than a heuristic which aids in the construction of hypotheses. And the sort of appeal to authority and revelation that one found in the Middle Ages is a "thing of the past." The minimal Baconian standards for being an empirical science (being a part of Bacon's New Instauration) are met by a wide variety of enterprises, including, or so they claim, the "social sciences." So what is the problem?

The problem is that, while one can teach any graduate student in a few years what he or she must do to *make a case* for the acceptance of a scientific theory — he or she must make certain kinds of predictions or retrodictions, must observe and/or experiment, must rule out various kinds of error and statistical artifact — it is by no means the case that everything for which this kind of a case is made should be accepted. (What the graduate student learns is, so to speak, a "pre-method" rather than a "method"; a method for dealing with preliminaries, for bringing things to the point at which the question "should we accept this" can be seriously discussed.) Whitehead's theory of gravitation was not experimentally refuted (nor were a number of other special relativistic gravitation theories experimentally refuted) until the 1970s, for example, but Whitehead's theory (and other theories mentioned) was never accepted, and Einstein's General Relativity *was* accepted, simply because Einstein's theory was "plausible" and Whitehead's was judged "implausible." Questions of fit with "physical intuition" come into play in the decision to accept a scientific theory — as has often been remarked, the scientific method is not an algorithm. It is not a formalized method at all. And so, in an age in which everyone claims they are using it, the question who is "really" using "the" scientific method becomes a difficult one.

If one dimension of difficulty arises from the informality of the "scientific method," another arises from disputes over what constitutes observation. Purists in the Vienna Circle wanted to restrict observation to "protocols" in sense-datum language. Were we to agree with these epistemologists, we should have to deny that we observe tables and chairs; and then we might be led to wonder whether our commonsense belief in tables, chairs, ice cubes, etc., is not a folk theory, as Wilfrid Sellars believes, rather than a low-level empirical knowledge, as Karl Popper believes. As Peter Strawson has remarked, positivist epistemology tends to undercut everything that we ordinarily think of as the *evidence* for empirical science itself. For we ordinarily think of the perceptible evidence as the presence of certain continuous bodies, bodies which fill up certain regions of space and which bear colors on their surfaces and this is what sense-datum epistemology says we do *not* really observe.

The same problem arises in a more acute form when the alleged observations are in intentional language. Normally we think of lexicography, for example, as another sort of low-level empirical knowledge — as "descriptive" knowledge. The statement in the phrase book

'Parlez-vous francais' *means* Do you speak French

conveys inter-subjective knowledge; but of what sort if not empirical? But how was this knowledge obtained? The lexicographer (if he did not just rely on what he learned in school) might have asked bilingual "native informants." But how do they know?

Just this bizarre-seeming question was asked by Quine in *Word and Object*. Quine rejects the theory that there are such things as "meanings," and he also rejects belief-desire psychology. What we observe, Quine thinks, are forms of behavior. Quine does not say that "meanings" are behavior-dispositions; rather he thinks that meaning-talk belongs to a kind of folk theory which has heuristic value but no theoretical significance. The fact that no one has been able to suggest necessary and sufficient conditions for supposed intentional facts of the forms

"X" means that p
A desires that p
A believes that p,

that is to say, the fact that no one has been able to suggest necessary and sufficient conditions in physicalistic (or broadly behavioral) terms, confirms Quine in thinking that it is just a vestige of our (bad) mentalistic heritage to postulate such entities as meanings, beliefs, and desires.

How then does Quine describe whatever it is that the bilingual knows, if it is not the "meanings" of the words and sentences in his two languages? What he knows is how to find (where possible) a sentence or phrase in one language which he can use in the contexts in which he would use a sentence or phrase in the other, and expect much the same effect (much the same in the way of response) as if he had used the sentence or phrase in the other language. I say, "where possible" because sometimes this is impossible, or, at least, too difficult for most people to do: sentences and phrases in the context of an idiom or a proverb or a poem are notoriously difficult to translate, for example, not to mention the problem of "contexts" that are familiar to speakers of one language but not to speakers of the other.

Still, if Quine admits that this kind of knowledge is real, then what do his doubts about meanings come to?

Part of the answer is that the practice of correlating expressions with an eye to practical substitutability (when we move from one language group to another) does not really yield a theoretical account of what "sameness of meaning" is supposed to *be*. A famous sentence in Hopi has the morpheme-for-morpheme translation 'forked pattern produced in bush by hand action me'. The corresponding "idiomatic" translation would be 'I pull a branch of the bush aside'. Which translation has the same "meaning" as the original—the "literal translation" (the one I gave first) or the "idiomatic translation"? If we say the latter, we abandon a principle which has been held central to all meaning theory: that the meaning of a sentence is a function of the meaning of its parts and of the means of compositions (taxemes) in the language. If we say the former, we abandon the principle we used to characterize "what the bilingual knows": that a sentence and its translation are used in the "same" contexts and to the "same" effect. For we certainly will not get the desired effect if we say to the man on the street "Forked pattern produced in bush by hand action me"!

We might say that the Hopi sentence *means* "forked pattern produced in bush by hand action (agent-) me," and that this is understood in Hopi but not in English because this way of describing a certain state of affairs is familiar to Hopi speakers but not to English speakers. But then we have not said what *means* means. And this is Quine's point.

But there is another problem. To say that "contexts" are the "same" ignores the fact that the contexts themselves (as well as "responses") are frequently *linguistic*. If we say that a translation is successful if the translation of sentence S can be used in just the "contexts" in which sentence S can be used (and produce similar "responses"), and we intend this not just as a heuristic bit of information but as a theory of synonymy, then we have ignored the fact that the "contexts" and the "responses" are identified as "the same" by the very translation-scheme which is being tested for success.

Quine does not deny that this test is strong enough to disqualify many translation-schemes. What he claims—and this is the celebrated doctrine of Indeterminacy of Translation—is that this criterion, or any such criterion, is not strong enough to fix a unique translation for any sentence or a unique translation-scheme for any language. It is not even strong enough to determine translation up to truth-functional or extensional equivalence.

Before I sketch his argument, let me make one more point: "contexts" are identified, very frequently, by reference to beliefs and desires. But in all but the most primitive cases, beliefs and desires are the sort of thing to which we have access only through language. And if the language is not our own, we must, once again, depend on translation.

If we put all these points together, we see why Quine believes that there is "no fact of the matter" as to what a native speaker means by any given (non-observational) utterance. If we adopt a "bizarre" hypothesis as to what the speaker means, then we can still square this with the speaker's totality of dispositions to verbal and non-verbal behavior by making compensatory adjustments in our hypothesis as to what the speaker's beliefs and desires are. Any number of alternative descriptions of the whole "intentional" realm, of the subject's meanings, beliefs, desires, etc., can be rendered compatible with the totality of the subjects "speech dispositions." And these, the "speech dispositions," are all that is really *there*. Or so Quine claims.

If Quine were alone in going so far as to dispute the objectivity of discourse about the intentional, then we might record this as merely one more instance of the remarkable willingness of philosophers to hold views contrary to common sense. But he has recently been joined by an impressive community of "cognitive scientists." While some cognitive scientists, notably Jerry Fodor, continue to insist on the legitimacy and autonomy of international knowledge, many other workers (their philosophical spokespersons include Daniel Dennett, Paul Churchland, and Stephen Stich) have come to the conclusion that talk of "meanings," beliefs, and desires is just "folk psychology." Their reasons may not be as complex as Quine's, but they share a common scientific outlook with him — a common belief in physicalism, and a common distrust of whatever cannot be reduced to physical, or at least to computer-scientific, terms. If we have been unable to find any neat way of identifying beliefs, desires, and other ordinary language mental states with programs, computational features, etc. (let alone with neurological structures and activities), then, they suggest, we should not think that is because the problem is too hard, or because another thousand years of research is necessary: it is more likely that the cause is simply that these "crude" ordinary language notions were not really designed for scientific purposes in the first place. The ordinary language notion of colors as intrinsic properties of external things turned out to be wrong, the ordinary language notion of energy has little relation to the scientific notion, the ordinary language notion of work has little relation to the scientific notion, so why should we expect that ordinary language psychological notions would "cut nature at the joints"?

What I want to call your attention to is the uselessness of the question "Is lexicography an empirical science?" as a way of speaking to this dispute. Someone impressed by empiricist-epistemological criteria for deciding what is and what is not "science" might, indeed, point out that not all of Quine's alternative translation-manuals are equally simple. And he or she might say that accepting a translation manual on account of its greater simplicity, its fit with past background knowledge, and its instrumental efficacy is doing something very "similar" to what we do when we accept a scientific theory which is simpler, fits better with background knowledge, and is equal or superior to instrumental efficacy to its rivals. Indeed, this is exactly how Rudolf Carnap reasoned. Viewing science primarily through epistemological lenses as he did, he saw no reason not to consider translation (and mentalistic psychology) as "empirical."

But those who, with Quine, view science primarily through ontological rather than epistemological lenses will reply that the standard empiricist criteria of simplicity, minimum mutilation of background knowledge, and instrumental efficacy are not complete: the missing criterion is the (ontological) Unity of Science. Faraday, they will remind us, believed in the "reality" of *lines of force;* but today these are regarded as ideal objects, not as physical objects at all, in spite of the epistemological virtues of Farady's theory considered in isolation, because considering "lines of force" as real physical entities would not be conducive to the unification of our physicalistic worldview along lines that seem to be most promising. Saying that someone has "wonderful taste in painting" may pass as a good descriptive statement when we are in a culture in which there is reasonable agreement on aesthetic standards, but it would be foolish to accept "good taste in painting" as an objective fact. The integrity of the physicalistic world picture itself has to be the overriding standard to which specific theories must be asked to conform if they are to have the status of what Quine has called "first class science."

But if the question, "Is it an empirical science?" cannot even be answered in the case of knowledge which is (practically speaking) intersubjective (after all, everyone knows what 'parlez-vous francais' means in French), is it to be wondered at that the question cannot be answered in the case of really difficult intentional disciplines, such as history or sociology? The question cannot be answered, not because we do not know what history or sociology is, but because we are divided about what we want "empirical science" to be.

To this point I have played the role of an observer of the passing show, describing tensions and disputes but not attempting to adjudicate them. But many of you know my view: I believe that the project of deciding what is and what is not "science" or "reality" or "the external world in itself" on the basis of ontological criteria derived from seventeenth-century thought (which is what materialist criteria are) is now bankrupt. Quine, for example, rejects intentional notions as "second class" but admits "dispositions" as "first class"; but, as I have argued elsewhere, dispositional notions are no more "reducible" to the language of dynamical variables and space-time points (Quine's "furniture of the Universe") than are intentional ones. The ontology of the materialists has left them able to say almost nothing about warrant of justification—about the very topics which most concerned classical empiricism—and what little they have said has betrayed hesitation and extreme tension. Quine's "disquotational" theory of truth is a thinly disguised theory of the emptiness of the notion of truth—"is true" is just a linguistic device we use to "reaffirm" a sentence, and not a way of predicating a normative characteristic, on Quine's view. And all this is the case not because Quine is a bad philosopher, but because he is the best and deepest and most honest representative of his tendency. It is because Quine has pushed classical materialism so far that we can now see its bankruptcy, its inability to account for the cognitive status of the very science it esteems so highly, staring us in the face. As Wittgenstein and Husserl have seen, treating physical science as a description of reality "in itself" is a profound error. Physical science is a product of some of the same interests that underly our conceptual construction of our *Lebenswelt*; it is no more a description of reality "in itself" than is our everyday talk of colors or of meanings or of desires or of values or of anything else.

But if ontological approaches to "demarcation" are bankrupt and epistemological ones are hopelessly vague (or, in the case of the Popperian criteria, fantastic), what are we to do? The man on the street will not be troubled: he will go on saying that physics is a science, that chemistry is a science (it is close to the paradigm), that evolutionary biology is a science (it collects data meticulously, it has a theory which impresses him, and it has close links with subjects like molecular biology, which resemble the paradigm, even if it itself does not), and he will continue *not* calling history or sociology sciences (and being pretty skeptical about economics) — unless, that is, they have successes which impress him in the way physics (and more recently biology) have impressed him. In short, he will use science partly as an honorific notion, as he has been doing for several centuries. But what should we, we philosophers and "social scientists," do?

I suggest that we might do well to ignore the whole question. Collingwood deployed many of Quine's arguments to reach opposite conclusions. For Collingwood, the unavoidability of intentional notions in history, taken together with the fact that knowledge of a past belief or a past desire is never simply "observation" in the physicist's sense, showed that history is *sui generis*. It is "science" in one sense and not in another. Historians have learned that they must "put questions" to nature — they do not get answers if they do not approach data with questions. Historians learned in the nineteenth century to be meticulous with texts and carefully to evaluate evidence, which is why history had succeeded in becoming an ever more important discipline. But if history has gotten better, and will get better in the future, it is for the most part not by applying physics and certainly not by imitating physics. We learn to do better by doing history, not by doing anything else. I suspect the same is true of philosophy, of economics, of sociology.

What does it matter whether what we do is "empirical science"? The question was important as long as it seemed that physics had discovered the key to "objectivity." But there is no key to objectivity. Or rather, the idea of a kind of objectivity that does not spring from and is not corrected by a human practice is absurd. History, philosophy, sociology are human practices. Their standards of objectivity must be created, not found by some transcendental investigation (not even one that calls itself "epistemology naturalized"). But creating standards of objectivity is not, for all that, a matter of proceeding at hazard; whenever we stand within one of these practices, instead of looking for an Olympus from which to look down on them, we know perfectly well that there is a difference between competent and incompetent, informed and uninformed, fruitful and fruitless, reasonable and unreasonable, ways of proceeding. If there is any general advice to be given, it is simply not to abandon what we know perfectly well when we function as doers, practitioners, agents — that there is better and worse "social science" and better and worse philosophy, whether or not it all converges to final "laws" or final theories or whatever — for either the illusory certainties or the illusory skepticisms of the would-be Olympians. The standpoint of agents in an uncertain world and at an uncertain moment in history is not perhaps the one we would have chosen, but it is the one that has been given us to occupy; it is our part to occupy it with responsibility.

MIDWEST STUDIES IN PHILOSOPHY, XV (1990)

Paradoxes of Rationality

CRISTINA BICCHIERI

THREATS AND PROMISES

Game theorists have long known that a rationality assumption does not guarantee optimal results or, for that matter, results that agree with experience and intuition about how to play a game. Rational choice often yields paradoxical outcomes in finite, extensive form games of perfect information, as well as in finitely iterated noncooperative games involving simultaneous moves. In both cases, a backward induction argument recommends choices that seem counterintuitive, if not utterly unreasonable. The best-known example of this kind of result is the finitely repeated prisoner's dilemma, in which the only Nash equilibrium is to defect at every stage.

Attempts to reconcile rationality and common sense include changing the nature of the game by letting the players draw explicit contracts. Other kinds of incentive changes that involve threats, promises, and reputation effects can be attained in repeated games with discounting. Another group of solutions involve some kind of limited or bounded rationality. One way to depart from 'perfect' rationality is by introducing some uncertainty about the strategy played by an opponent; another way is by modeling players as automata that have a large but finite number of states.

The above solutions all involve the idea that rationality inevitably leads players to act in counterintuitive ways in some class of games, and hence the notion of rationality must be weakened. Alternatively, the nature of the game must be altered in order to provide the players with incentives to act in more reasonable ways. The epistemic conditions under which a game is played are not generally considered of particular relevance to the search for outcomes that are intuitively more appealing. Such conditions include players' mutual knowledge of rationality and of the structure of the game they are playing.

What I propose to show, on the contrary, is that even assuming perfect rationality, a very small breakdown in mutual knowledge of rationality is enough to bring about outcomes that are intuitively more reasonable. In repeated games of finite termination, an assumption of 'bounded knowledge' means that the players have iterated mutual knowledge of rationality up to any given order, but not enough to infer the classical, backward induction solution. Bounded knowledge is especially relevant in all those games that involve threats and promises. To be effective, threats and promises must be credible, but in a finite horizon game it takes some uncertainty about a player's rationality to generate expectations that punishments and rewards will in fact come forth.

Consider the following cases:

BARGAINING

A benefactor wants to test the hypothesis that poor people are more ready than more fortunate individuals to share what they have with others. He thus selects two individuals, let us call them A and B, whom he knows are needy and makes them the following proposition: I offer A $100 to divide with B. A can make an offer to B, and if that offer is rejected, I will lower the sum to $90 and ask B to make an offer. If B's offer is rejected, I withdraw the money, so neither A nor B gets anything. To the benefactor's surprise, A offers $89 to B and keeps $11 for himself, and the offer is accepted. He expected them to share the money, but could not fathom such generosity. But he is even more surprised when he repeats the experiment with two affluent individuals, A' and B', and gets the same result. Puzzled, he asks both A and A' why they made such an offer, keeping so little money for themselves. He gets the following answer from both:

Suppose I made an offer to B (B') and she rejects it. Then it is B's turn to make an offer. Now there is $90 to divide, and we both know that if I reject the offer, we both net $0. B knows that I am rational, so she knows I will prefer any amount of money greater than zero. Since the money you gave us came in one-dollar bills, the smallest number greater than zero B could offer me would have been $1, and I would have accepted. We both know that, and moreover I know that B knows that, since I know that B knows that I am rational. I also know that B is rational, so I expect that she will never accept any offer that nets her less than what she would get if she were to make me an offer. So I know that she will never accept less than $89, and this is precisely the amount I offered her, sure that she would accept it. I could not do better than that.

PROMISES

Anne and Bill can engage in a mutually profitable venture. To get the business started, however, Anne must lend $10 to Bill. Her problem is to decide whether or not to trust Bill. If she trusts him, he can either reward her trust or abuse it. If she trusts and he rewards, each nets $20. But if she trusts and he abuses, Ann loses $10 and Bill gains $30. In case she distrusts Bill, nobody gets anything. Bill promises Anne that if she trusts him he will reward her trust, but Anne cannot believe him. For if Anne chooses to trust Bill, he must choose between reward and abuse. Absent other considerations, Bill will choose to abuse, which nets him $30. Anne knows that Bill is rational, hence she is better off distrusting.

THREATS

Two countries, let us call them A and B, are involved in a territorial dispute over a group of islands that belong to country B but are geographically closer to A. Country B threatens to retaliate against a potential invasion by dispatching its fleet and engaging in military action. With this threat, B hopes to deter aggression in the first place. A conflict, however, will be very damaging to country B: besides the resources it will have to employ in retaliatory action, the government would risk its popularity in the event of a defeat. Moreover, after the invasion has taken place, it is futile to carry out the threat; the damage has been done and no punishment will restore the status quo. By punishing A, country B would only bear heavy costs, and since it is known that B's government acts rationally, the threat will not be credible. Therefore country A invades.

Note that in all three cases the parties are assumed to be motivated only by their payoffs, monetary or otherwise, and their interactions take place outside an institutional setup. Another feature common to all three examples is that at least one player has a dominant strategy and, since she is assumed to be rational, she is expected to choose it. A simple example will make this point clear. Imagine Anne and Bill are playing the game depicted in figure 1 just once.

B

	Reward	Abuse
Trust	20, 20	-10, 30
Distrust	0, 0	0, 0

A

Figure 1

Anne is the row player: she can either trust Bill or distrust him. In turn, Bill (the column player) can either reward trust or abuse it. The first payoff in each cell is Anne's, the second is Bill's. Note that Bill has a weakly dominant strategy (abuse), since if Anne trusts he is better off by abusing, and in case Anne distrusts him, he is indifferent between abusing and rewarding, since in this case he would not have to choose. So if Anne knows that Bill is rational, she predicts he will abuse her trust, hence she optimally chooses to distrust. The commitment problem faced by Bill is seen more clearly in the extensive form representation of the same game.

Figure 2

Here Anne moves first: if she chooses to distrust, the game ends and each nets $0. But if she trusts, then Bill has to make a choice between reward and abuse. Suppose Bill promised Anne that he would reward her trust. A promise is a declaration of a conditional choice for second move, but it is clear that when it is his turn to move, Bill has no incentive to keep the promise.

EXPLICIT CONTRACTS

Rationality seems to prevent individuals from coming up with efficient, cooperative outcomes, even in those cases in which both would be clearly better off by cooperating. This consideration grounds a well-known, traditional argument in favor of institutions as means to check and direct self-interested behavior. Indeed, the first proponents of a social contract as the legitimate foundation of government depicted individuals as involved in a permanent prisoner's dilemma, and unable to come up with a cooperative agreement unless forced to. In the Hobbesian model, individuals agree to surrender their powers of resistance to the Sovereign, a third party who will enforce cooperation. In the above examples, the institution that guarantees an optimal outcome need not be the state; it may be a legal system, an international treaty, an honor code, or even a set of shared moral principles. What matters is that one or both parties can credibly commit themselves to a given course of action, where credibility is afforded by the presence of an institution that punishes deviant behavior.

In the cases we are considering, one or both players would do better if they could credibly commit themselves to some course of action. In this way, a player can influence the opponent's expectations and deter or induce some action on his part.

Expectations are generally influenced by past behavior, but in the case of one-time interactions there is no past behavior to draw upon, so the players may try to affect each other's expectations by entering into some kind of enforceable contract.

In the bargaining case, the fact that B chooses second gives her an advantage. She can threaten to reject A's offer if she does not get $89, and since she is in the position of making the last offer, her threat is credible. The only way in which A could have done better is by committing himself not to offer less than, say $50. For example, he could have signed a contract that requires him to pay $60 to his lawyer if he gets less than $50. As long as the contract is enforceable it makes sense for A to sign it, provided that the costs involved in executing the contract are sufficiently small, say, smaller than $39. In the case of the incredible promise, both Anne and Bill would have been better off by choosing to trust and to reward, respectively. In this one-sided prisoner's dilemma, the only outcome is noncooperative and inefficient. Had both parties had the opportunity to enter into a binding agreement, it would have been in their interest to invest some resources in signing a contract that binds Bill to reward Anne's trust, as long the contract is enforceable. The same is true for country B's threat of retaliation. The threat would become credible if country B were to face punishment in the event it did not carry it out. For example, B may sign an international treaty with several other states that forces each party to respond to an invasion with military retaliation or face severe economic sanctions for failing to do so.

Contracts, however, are costly. There are costs involved in drafting and signing a contract, and costs involved with executing it, since in the absence of an enforcement mechanism, one or both parties will have an incentive to break the contract. Moreover, a contract will last only when it is possible for the parties to observe directly whether each of them complies with the terms of the agreement. Part of the monitoring problem is that it must be clearly understood what compliance means, and that circumstances do not change so quickly or are not so complex that it becomes ambiguous to define compliance in any of them. Truth telling among couples is an example. A truth-telling 'pact' is enforceable only if there is agreement as to what telling the truth means in different occasions, whether or not it is possible to attain reliable information, and under which circumstances it is permissible to lie. The fact that it is unlikely that two people can reach an agreement over such matters is one reason why such pacts are extremely rare. However, even in circumstances in which noncompliance is well defined and easily detectable, explicit contracts may be difficult if not impossible to draft. Some of the suggested solutions to the commitment problem are unlikely to be legally binding, but even if they were, if the 'transaction costs' involved in such contracts are sufficiently large, mutually beneficial transactions will be forgone.

IMPLICIT CONTRACTS

Entering into a binding, enforceable agreement solves the commitment problem by changing people's incentives, so that taking a dominated action becomes overall less costly than choosing the dominant strategy. Explicit contracts are not the only way to alter people's incentives, though. Strategic interactions are seldom one-time affairs, but are generally repeated over and over, if not with the same people, at least with somebody who knows how we have acted in the past. The repetition itself, with its possibilities for signalling, retaliation, and reputation formation, becomes an enforcement mechanism.

Suppose Anne and Bill are involved in the situation depicted in figure 1 not once, but repeatedly. Each time they play, there is a 20 percent chance that this is the last round, and an 80 percent chance that they will play again. Alternatively, we could imagine they play this game once a month forever, and that they apply a discount rate to their future payoffs. The total payoffs are the sum of what they win at each stage, and we suppose that each is interested in maximizing the expected sum of his or her payoffs.

Now the situation is quite different, since Anne can tell Bill that she will begin by trusting him, and will keep trusting until Bill abuses her trust. If Bill ever abuses her trust, she will distrust him forever. If Bill believes this statement, he will never abuse her trust. For suppose Bill were to abuse at some point. If Anne follows the announced strategy he will net $30 that round and $0 forever after. Since the game has a good chance of continuing, rewarding Anne's trust nets Bill $20 each round, so the expected value for the rest of the game far exceeds the $30 he could get by abusing once. Indeed, this combination of strategies is an equilibrium for the repeated game (if Anne plays her part of the strategy, Bill's best response is to reward trust), provided that the probability of continuation is sufficiently high. If there were a high discount rate, or a small probability of continuing for another round, or the payoff of abusing were very high, say $3000, then it would make sense for Bill to abuse Anne's trust.

What we have just described as an equilibrium for the repeated game is not the only one. For if Anne were to doubt that Bill believes that she will adopt the above strategy, and Bill in fact did not believe her, it would still be an equilibrium for Anne to distrust and for Bill to abuse if given the chance. Alternatively, Bill may tell Anne that he will reward her trust two-thirds of the time, provided she keeps trusting him all along. If either deviates from this pattern it will be distrust-abuse forever. If Anne believes Bill's statement, she is better off always trusting, and this is an equilibrium, too. The point is that whatever combination of strategies gives each player an expected payoff large enough to make 'cooperative' behavior more profitable than cheating and netting $0 afterwards is an equilibrium. This result is the subject of the folk theorem of game theory (Fudenberg and Maskin 1986), which states that, with low enough discounting of the future, any feasible vector of expected payoffs that are sufficiently above the worst that others can force upon a player is sustainable as an equilibrium.

The multiplicity of possible equilibria poses a serious problem for the theory, since there is no way to predict which one will emerge. In real life, the type of equilibrium reached will depend upon several factors such as the bargaining power of the parties, the possibility of monitoring the agreement, and the credibility of the threats. What is important to note is that repetition, combined with a small amount of uncertainty about future interactions, makes it possible endogenously to enforce agreements. Such agreements are like implicit contracts which are costlessly enforced by the threat of punishment, but in this case, as much as the explicit contracts, it is crucial that the parties are able unambiguously to define and monitor compliance.

REPUTATION

The folk theorem works only if the interaction is repeated with the same opponent, but what if one is engaged in repeated interactions with different opponents? Consider the case of the two countries involved in a territorial dispute. Their problem can be sketchily represented by the following game:

B

	Punish	Ignore
Invade	- 20, - 10	5, - 2
Not Invade	0, 0	0, 0

A

Figure 3

The payoffs represent ordinal utilities, and show that country B's retaliation in case of invasion is more damaging than acquiescence. Since B has a weakly dominant strategy (to ignore invasion) and B's government is known to act rationally, the obvious choice for country A is to invade. That the threat to punish is not credible is easily seen in the extensive form representation of the game, where country B would have to punish A after the fact, and since the lesser cost is to ignore, B can be expected to follow that course of action.

This game is close to what happened between Britain and Argentina over the Falkland Islands in 1982. The difference is that, when Argentina invaded the Falklands, Britain responded by dispatching the British fleet. It was quite obvious that the costs to Britain far outweighed the immediate benefits, since the Falklands do not have great economic or military value. So why did Britain respond aggressively? An obvious consideration is that, even if the conflict with Argentina can be viewed as a one-time event, Britain owns several foreign territories—such as Gibraltar—that might become the focus of future territorial disputes. What is irrational in the short run may well be rational in the long run

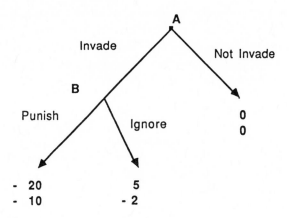

Figure 4

if it promises to affect the behavior of later opponents. In the case of Britain, the retaliation's aim was that of building a reputation for toughness that would deter future aggressions.

The possibility of repeated interactions with different opponents that can observe one's past behavior represents a means of changing the players' incentives to bring about more desirable outcomes. Suppose there is a sequence of players A', A'', A''',. . .who must choose whether or not to invade one of B's territories. Whatever B does with any of them will be known to all subsequent opponents, who will condition their behavior on B's choices. It is critical that players' expectations are influenced by past behavior, since in this way B's future opportunities are related to its past behavior and it retains an incentive to punish. There are many possible reputations that would work. For example, B might start out with a reputation for toughness that would be irreparably tarnished if it does not punish an aggression. If all the parties know this, it is rational for B to punish if invaded, and for every A not to try to invade. Alternatively, B might have the reputation of not retaliating with probability $1/3$ each time an invasion occurs. If an A who is planning to invade knows that there is a $2/3$ chance of being punished, it will still be deterred. Furthermore, B may *prefer* to only have a reputation for punishing with probability $1/3$, if some As will invade no matter what. In fact, any probability of punishment that makes the expected probability of invasion less than zero has a deterrent effect, provided it is believed that this is the true frequency with which B metes punishment.

Reputation, however, is something that takes time to build. Suppose that country B announces that it will punish with probability $2/3$ each round. What happens if B is observed to acquiesce twice in a row? Does it mean that B will not really punish with probability $2/3$, and can thus be harmlessly invaded? It can be shown that the "$2/3$" reputation can work with low enough discounting, but in general when the threat of punishment is expressed in probabilistic terms, ambiguity in detecting a pattern of play becomes an important problem, since the credibility of the threat crucially depends upon the possibility of monitoring its being carried out.

Another, no less important problem, is that reputation is a scarce good that people may compete for. Take the case of the bargaining game. Suppose there are several *A*s and *B*s that play sequentially. If there were only one *A* playing in turn with many *B*s, he may try to build a reputation for toughness by offering, say, $40 to *B* and, if *B* rejects the offer, by rejecting whatever offer *B* makes. If *A* is observed thus to behave, there is the presumption that he may do so again, and this limits the opportunities of future opponents. The situation would change quite radically if there were several *A*s competing with each other. Since now any *B* would prefer to deal with the *A* that has the reputation for making the most favorable offer. Unless the *A*s collude to 'share the pie', it is likely that competition among them will bring about the same outcome as the two-player game.

Up until now, we have considered several ways to change players' incentives in order to prevent them from getting stuck in inefficient outcomes. One way is to enter into an enforceable, explicit contract that binds one or both players to a given course of action. Another means to modify the incentives is by repeating the game, since repetition allows self-enforcing, binding agreements to emerge. Implicit contracts have the advantage of being costless, since their enforcing mechanism is by punishment, but unless there is a good chance of at least one more round of play, so that a breach of contract can be punished, such contracts have no chance of getting established.

FINITE REPETITION AND BACKWARD INDUCTION

Suppose the game depicted in figure 3 is repeated a finite number of times only. Both players know that there are *n* possible occasions for *A* to invade and for *B* to punish. The potential invader will thus reason: when the last occasion arrives, if I invade, it will be irrational for *B* to punish me, since punishment involves costs and will no longer serve as a deterrent. I know that *B* is rational, hence I will invade on the last round. Both players realize that this is so, hence in the next to last round *A* will invade and *B* will refrain from punishing, since retaliation would have no effect on the last round. But then there is no reason not to invade in the third to last round, and so on to the first round of play.

Backward induction leads to a unique result in which country *A* always invades and *B* acquiesces. In the case of the trust-reward game, the backward induction result is worse for both players: *A* will never trust because *B* will always abuse, if given a chance to make a choice. This problem has been first noticed by Selten in a famous example called the "chain-store paradox" (Selten 1978). Selten solved it by supposing that, at the outset, there is a small chance that *B* is the type of person who, for some reason, would never abuse trust. This small doubt in *A*'s mind is enough to restore the better outcome for most of the game. The idea is that of transforming the game into one of incomplete information (Harsanyi 1967–1968). In a game of incomplete information, there is an initial stage in which nature chooses a state (a combination of player types) according to some probability distribution, and gives each player a private signal about the state of nature. Each player knows his own type, which includes beliefs about other players' information, preferences, and beliefs, but does not know the other players' types. A strategy specifies an action to be taken by each player-type: if player i can get any of n signals and has m possible actions, then the player will have m^n possible strategies. Payoffs depend on the state of nature and the action that each player takes. An equilibrium for these games is defined as a combination of strategies in which the private strategy (i.e., the action specified by his actual type) of each player-type is a best response for that type to the strategies specified for the other players.

In our example, the argument runs as follows: suppose player B can be one of three types: type 1 always rewards trust, type 2 always abuses it, and type 3 is a strategic player. The probabilities that he is one of the three types are, respectively, p, q, and $1 - p - q$. Suppose that in the present round of play player B is supposed to play 'abuse' with probability 1 if he is type 3. So, if 'reward' is played instead, the conditional probability that B is of type 1 will be: $P(B$ is type $1|$ 'reward' is played) $= P(B$ is type 1 and 'reward' is played) $/P($'reward' is played) $= p/p = 1$. This induces A to choose trust for the rest of the game. Knowing this, player B can try to 'cheat' player A into believing that he is type 1, when he is in fact type 3, by playing 'reward' in any round but the last. Indeed, it would be irrational for B to abuse trust before the last round, since his choice would reveal he is not a type 1 player, and this would induce A to distrust forever after. Given these probabilities, it is an equilibrium strategy for player B to reward trust with probability 1 until the last round, since in this way A will never learn his true type and will keep trusting him.

The incomplete information framework allows the players to build a reputation even if the game has a known, finite termination (Kreps and Wilson 1982). For example, it can be shown that a slight change in the players' initial information yields cooperative outcomes even in the finitely repeated prisoner's dilemma game (Kreps, Milgrom, Roberts and Wilson 1982). If each player initially assigns a small probability to the other being, say, a tit-for-tat player, there are equilibria in which both cooperate with high probability until near the end of the game. In this case, each player finds it is beneficial to build a reputation as the cooperative type. The problem with this solution lies in the arbitrariness of the incomplete information assumption. Incomplete information is assumed exogenously, while one would like to see it emerge endogenously in the game.

BOUNDED KNOWLEDGE

The hypothesis underlying the backward induction solution is that how one behaves has no effect upon how one is expected to behave. At any point i, it is decided that whatever choice is made, it will have no effect upon an opponent's choice at $i+1$, since it is known that at $i+1$ what happened before has become strategically irrelevant. In other words, the expectation of what will happen at $i+1$ is unaffected by what happens at i. Under which circumstances are expectations unalterable?

Game theorists have customarily assumed that mutual rationality and the structure of the game are common knowledge among the players. By 'common knowledge of p' is meant that p is not just known by all the players in a game, but is also known to be known, known to be known to be known,. . .*ad infinitum*. In the games we are considering, however, common knowledge is neither necessary nor sufficient to infer the backward induction solution. Indeed, it can be proved that a finite number of levels of knowledge of rationality (and of the structure of the game) is necessary and sufficient for backward induction to work, their number depending on the length of the game (Bicchieri 1988; 1989). More specifically, at every stage of the game a player has to know what the following players (himself included) know: if she knows less than that, the result is indeterminate. But if she knows more than that (for example, she knows all that is known to the preceding players), then an inconsistency arises. In both cases, the number of possible solutions becomes very large.

A simple example will make this point clear. Imagine the following prisoner's dilemma game being played twice.

It is easy to verify that if player 1 had some doubt about player 2 being a tit-for-tat player, then it might be reasonable for him to cooperate in the first round and defect subsequently. But precisely under which conditions will some cooperation occur in both parts? In order to answer, we have to specify under which knowledge conditions the noncooperative equilibrium would occur. In our example, the game is played only twice, and in the last round each player, being rational, will choose that strategy that is a best response to the opponent's expected choice. Since both players have dominant strategies, it does not matter to them what the other player does: defecting guarantees each of them the highest payoff. In the first round, however, a slightly more complicated reasoning is required. Each player knows that he will defect in the last round, since defecting is a dominant choice. A strategy, however, is a complete contingent plan of action for the entire supergame, not just for a single round of play, so a player will have to decide at the beginning of the supergame which sequence of actions to choose. While in any round, if taken in isolation, a player's choice is independent of the expected choice of the other player (since to defect is a dominant strategy), a strategy choice for the supergame is no longer independent of what the other player is expected to do.

Consider the reasoning of player 1. If he knows that player 2 is rational, he expects 2 to choose D in the last round, therefore there is no point in trying to influence 2's choice with his behavior in the first round. Hence if it is first-order mutual knowledge that the players are rational, each player will defect throughout the game. Now suppose that each player is rational, but does not know that the other is. In this case, it is not evident that one should defect in the first round. For suppose there is some chance that player 2 is a tit-for-tat player. By definition, a tit-for-tat player will cooperate in the first round, and cooperate in any subsequent round $t + 1$ if the opponent cooperated in round t, while if the opponent defected in round t the tit-for-tat player will respond with defection in $t + 1$.

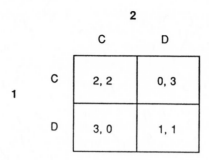

Figure 5

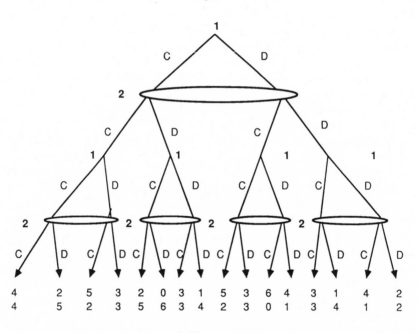

Figure 6

If player 1 were sure that player 2 is a tit-for-tat player, it would make sense for him to cooperate in the first stage, since by so doing he would induce 2 to cooperate in the second stage, too, thus netting $5 for himself (we assume that 1 is rational and defects in the last round). If 1 were to defect in the first round instead, his total payoff would only be $4, since player 2 would retaliate by defecting in the second round. We have assumed that player 1 does not know that 2 is rational, and does not know that 2 is tit-for-tat either. However, he may assign a positive probability to the event that player 2 is tit-for-tat. In our example, the probability of player 2 being tit-for-tat has to be greater than ½ to induce 1 to play the strategy CD. Note that we have been assuming that player 1 considers only two possibilities: either 2 is rational, or she is tit-for-tat. A more complicated case would be that in which player 1 considers the possibility that 2 is uncertain as to the type of player 1 is, and reasons along the same lines. If 1 takes into account this possibility, then he would have to assess the probability that player 2 assigns to his being a tit-for-tat player, since if he believes that player 2 believes with probability greater than $\frac{1}{2}$ that he is a tit-for-tat, then he would expect 2 to choose strategy CD, in which case it would be optimal for him to play strategy DD. It is interesting to notice that, were both players to know that the other player believes with probability greater than $\frac{1}{2}$ that he (or she) is tit-for-tat, each would have an incentive to defect throughout, so the equilibrium would still be noncooperative.

I have shown elsewhere that for the backward induction solution to obtain, at each stage of the game a player has to know what the successive player knows (Bicchieri 1988). In the two-stage game we are considering, in the first round it is sufficient that each player knows that the other player is rational for both to defect throughout. Given this state of information, if cooperation were to be observed in the first round, it could only be interpreted as evidence that the cooperating player (who is known to be rational) does not possess sufficient knowledge to predict what the other will do and indeed, since he is known to be rational, he must assign a high enough probability to the other player being irrational. Since each player knows that the other is rational, each knows that the other's response to a cooperative choice will be to defect. Under this state of information, therefore, no player has an incentive to try out an alternative strategy.

If, however, the players *did not know* their mutual rationality, they might end up doing better than if they knew. In this case it is not evident that one's deviation from the noncooperative equilibrium strategy will trigger a defection, since there is some uncertainty as to the other player's rationality in the first place. In fact, were both players to believe that the other is a tit-for-tat player with some small probability, both would have an incentive to play CD, and net $3 each, which is higher than the payoff they would obtain by defecting throughout.

Suppose that the same prisoner's dilemma is repeated three times. It is easy to verify that for the backward induction solution to obtain each player needs to know, at the start of the game, both that the other player is rational *and* that the other player knows that he is rational. Without this further level of knowledge, a player will have some doubt as to how the other player will react if he starts playing cooperatively. Player 1 may thus reason: I know that 2 is rational, so I expect her to choose D in the last round. However, I do not know whether 2 knows that I am rational. Suppose 2 has some doubts. Then, by playing cooperatively in the first round, I may induce 2 to believe that, say, I am a tit-for-tat player. If 2 so believes, it will be better for her to play C in the second round, since even if a tit-for-tat player will defect in the second round in response to her initial defection, he will reward her with cooperation in the last round, when she plans to defect again. So if player 2 can be induced to believe I am a tit-for-tat player, she will choose a DCD strategy, while I will play a CDD strategy that nets me $4.

Both players could do even better than that. For example, if player 2 reasons along the lines of player 1, she will cooperate in the first round, too. Even if each knows that the other is rational, the fact that each does not know that the other knows that he is rational is enough to induce both to cooperate twice, and defect only in the last round, thus netting $5 each. Each tries to 'cheat' the other into believing he is not rational, and even if nobody is cheated, everybody will act as if he were.

What happens if the players have *more* knowledge than is needed to infer the backward induction solution? In the three-stage prisoner's dilemma, this would mean that both players know the following things: (a) that the other player is rational; (b) that the other player knows that one is rational; (c) that the other player knows that one knows that (a) and (b). Suppose player 1 is considering playing cooperatively in the first round. How would player 2 interpret his move? By assumption, 1 knows that 2 knows the following things: 1 is rational, and 1 knows that 2 is rational. If 2 were to observe cooperation in the first round, she could not attribute it to player 1 being irrational, since by assumption she knows that he is rational. But she could not explain it by assuming that 1 has some doubts about her own rationality either, since by assumption she knows that he knows that she is rational. So it seems obvious that player 1 has no incentive to play cooperatively in the first round, as in so doing he can only lose. Observing cooperative behavior would leave player 2 without an explanation, and therefore without a prediction about player 1's next move. This consideration may motivate player 1 to play cooperatively, in the hope of convincing player 2 that he is, after all, completely irrational. Moreover, even if player 2 were convinced that 1 is pretending, she may well go along and pretend she believes he is indeed irrational, in order to encourage him to continue playing tit-for-tat.

So if insufficient knowledge can motivate the players to play cooperatively, too much knowledge, by potentially producing a discrepancy between what is observed and what is known about the other player, can be strategically exploited by the players to get mutually beneficial results. Note that in the previous examples we have implicitly made the strong assumption that it is common knowledge among the players that 'irrational' means 'playing tit-for-tat'. If this were not common knowledge, or if the players were to consider other alternatives to always defecting, we would get very different results.

The difficulty with determining the meaning of 'irrational' is best represented by the bargaining game in which two players have to divide $100. The 'right' amount of mutual knowledge of rationality leads to the (11, 89) outcome, since if A knows that B is rational and knows that he is rational, he can predict that, at the second stage, B will offer him only $1, sure that he will accept. Any starting offer different from $89 on the part of A may signal that he is irrational, or does not know that B is rational, or any other failure of mutual knowledge. So player B, when it is her turn to make an offer, has to assign probabilities to each possibility. In considering the possibility that A is irrational, B has to specify *which kind* of irrationality. For example, A may be the type that accepts any payoff greater than 1 or, conversely, he may be the kind of person that rejects any offer, thus getting both of them $0. Player B's uncertainty as to the type of irrationality of A can be represented by probabilities, where, in the absence of further information, every combination of payoffs has the same probability of being achieved. So the range of possible outcomes would go from (2, 88) to (90, 0), including the (0, 0) one. There are then 89 possible types of irrationality, each having an equal probability of being enacted by player A. Since $1/89$ is the probability of the disjunction of the various 'irrational' outcomes, the probability that A is rational must be $88/89$.

In games that involve threats and promises, it is not too farfetched to assume the number of irrational strategies to be quite small. Rational players will be likely to mimic irrational strategies that are best for them, so for example one would expect tit-for-tat or some variant thereof to be chosen in a repeated prisoner's dilemma, and a certain amount of retaliatory activity to be employed in the initial stages of a repeated game such as the one involving a sequence of territorial disputes. Whether something is a good reputation to have will of course depend on what the other player is believed to be like. In a finitely repeated prisoner's dilemma, when the number of repetitions is greater than two, each player knows that the other is rational, but a small breakdown in iterated mutual knowledge of rationality is enough to motivate the players to play cooperatively. Even if each player knows that the opponent is rational, each will try to deceive and pretend to be deceived.

It is important to realize that, contrary to common game-theoretic wisdom, there are other strategies that are rational, and may be even supported by a high degree of mutual knowledge of rationality, while at the same time being much more reasonable than those supported by backward induction.

REFERENCES

Bicchieri, C. 1988. "Backward Induction without Common Knowledge." *PSA* 1988, vol. 2: 329–43.

Bicchieri, C. 1989. "Self-refuting Theories of Strategic Interaction: A Paradox of Common Knowledge." *Erkenntnis* 30: 69–85.

Bicchieri, C. Forthcoming. "Norms of Cooperation." *Ethics.*

Fudenberg, D., and E. Maskin. 1986. "The Folk Theorem with Discounting and with Incomplete Information." *Econometrica* 54: 533–54.

Harsanyi, J. 1967–1968. "Games with Incomplete Information Played by 'Bayesian' Players." Parts I, II, III, *Management Science* 14: 159–82, 320–32, 468–502.

Kreps, D., and R. Wilson. 1982. "Reputation and Imperfect Information." *Journal of Economic Theory* 27: 253–79.

Kreps, D., P. Milgrom, J. Roberts, and R. Wilson. 1982. "Rational Cooperation in the Finitely Repeated Prisoner's Dilemma." *Journal of Economic Theory* 27: 245–52.

Selten, R. 1978. "The Chain-store Paradox." *Theory and Decision* 9: 127–59.

MIDWEST STUDIES IN PHILOSOPHY, XV (1990)

How Do I Presuppose Thee?
Let Me Count the Ways:
The Relation of Regularities to Rules
in Social Science

DAVID BRAYBROOKE

In these times of stress and tribulation, would we not do well to turn to the spirit of peace in Holy Scripture and take what comfort we can in what we find there? It is laid down in Deuteronomy 25:11-12, that

> When men fight with one another, and the wife of the one draws near to rescue her husband from the hand of him who is beating him, and puts out her hand and seizes him by the private parts, then you shall cut off her hand; your eye shall have no pity.[1]

That is a rule, indeed, perhaps more than one rule—to begin with, a rule about wifely conduct; but also a rule about enforcing the conduct. Even if we take just one rule from the passage, we have a choice of inferring directly a rule addressed to "you" the enforcers or inferring indirectly a rule about wifely conduct incorporating a provision for enforcement. I shall choose the indirect inference to one rule, because it leads to a prime case in respect to form of the sort of rule that I shall be concerned with—a rule in disjunctive form that says either do (forebear doing) this action or suffer this punishment. Is it a prime case with the substance of a settled social rule, that is to say, with the substance of the sort of rule that will occupy us? Can there have been, before the rule was brought in, so many instances in ancient Israel of the unseemly combat technique that it prohibits as to give the rule some point? After it was promulgated, were there a number of violations, and were measures of enforcement taken against them? If we are not to regard the rule as a gratuitous edict thought up in advance of any call for it by some prophet with an overactive heat-seeking imagination, we must have some combination of evidence about conformity, enforcement, and point; only then can we justify speaking of the rule as a settled social one.

For philosophers, asking, as is their wont, what is the content of rules that distinguishes them in significance from (say) universally quantified statements, it may seem too confining to consider only settled social rules for which such a combination of evidence exists. Social scientists, too, may well wish to have the concept of rules treated more broadly; social scientists are often interested, for example, in the discrepancies between the rules officially promulgated or cited and the rules actually followed—what I am calling "settled social rules." However, they can hardly make sense of such discrepancies unless they give due attention to settled social rules; and in fact they give them sustained attention in establishing the rules that characterize the kinship systems or the relations of production and so distinguish one culture from another. Moreover, for a program of argument (like the one I resume in this essay) which seeks to relate the inquiries of social science into rules to the inquiries of social science into regularities, the first order of business is with settled social rules. Moreover, it is with settled social rules that are prescriptions or prohibitions rather than with permissions, a more elusive and problematic category. I am going to ignore the claim of permissions to be counted among settled social rules.

Once we see what inquiries into these amount to, we can see that both sorts of inquiry have a legitimate place in social science and see as well that they are intimately related and mutually dependent. We do not need to take up all the interesting and important aspects of settled social rules to achieve these insights. Philosophers and social scientists are both deeply interested in how people internalize the rules that they follow; but internalization, though it is a common feature of settled social rules, is not an aspect that needs to be taken up at this stage of my program. It would be a distraction to try; I shall put internalization aside except for one brief mention in a late passage supplementary to my main argument.

No combination of evidence about conformity, enforcement, and point need be supplied for us to establish the existence of a regularity in social phenomena. Outward conformity alone will suffice; indeed, not to beg questions with the very term "conformity," which starts up implications of intending to act accordingly, all we need is to find that certain observable conditions are regularly followed by certain observable actions or forbearances. Men fight; their wives move in to grapple with their opponents, but either (in most cases) do not grasp the opponents' private parts or else (in a minority of cases) undergo an instance of what has been observed to be negative reinforcement. This, let us suppose, is a regularity of social phenomena. Moreover, if we take our license for using the term "causal" from men's fighting in the presence of their wives being what Mackie called "at least an INUS condition,"[2] that is to say, a condition that is at least an indispensable but necessary element in a combination of conditions that are unnecessary but sufficient for a certain effect, it is a causal regularity. When men fight in the presence of their wives and (another INUS condition) the wives attack their husbands' opponents, then either the wives refrain from grasping the opponents' private parts or they undergo negative reinforcement.

Causal regularities are a characteristic preoccupation of one side of social science; settled social rules, a characteristic preoccupation of another. Some philosophers of social science have cried up the first at the expense of the second; some have cried up the second at the expense of the first.[3] Social science has plenty of room for both. Indeed, to understand what social science is doing, one must understand that neither preoccupation can sever itself from the other and guide inquiry on its own. Inquiry into regularities is so intimately complementary to inquiry into rules that each line of inquiry depends on the other. So do the phenomena studied on either side, which (as we shall see) is what makes them both liable to radical variation. Social scientists looking for regularities affecting rates of employment must take into account the rules governing women's entering the labor force; indeed, they must take as given the rules surrounding the notion of having and holding a job. On the other side, social scientists interested in the rules for participating in the labor force must take into account the possibility that those rules may be modified if acute shortages of labor appear, for example, in wartime. Social scientists will not have full knowledge of those rules unless they know how variations in supply of labor and demand for it will modify them.

Suppose it is contended that the mutual dependence of the two lines of inquiry reaches so far that the existence of any settled social rule presupposes the existence of corresponding causal regularities in social phenomena, and vice versa—the existence of any causal regularity in social phenomena presupposes the existence of corresponding settled social rules. I am ready to contend this, though only with certain qualifications.[4] Is it too bold a contention? It may not seem bold enough. Even though rules originate in human intentions—sometimes in deliberate legislation—while regularities can in principle be observed without information about the intentions of the people involved, it may seem that the distinction between rules and regularities is an unstable one. Does mutual presupposition go far enough? Are rules and regularities not the same thing, viewed from different angles? Or, short of this, though going farther than mutual presupposition, are they things that in most cases have features characteristic of both regularities and rules?

Stephen Toulmin, in a suggestive article, argues that rules and regularities in human behavior belong in the same range of things; as we move from the polar extreme of a rule to the polar extreme of a regularity, rules change into regularities without any break.[5] Maybe there is a parallel here to Herbert Simon's demonstration that rational choice theories can be put on a continuum with behavioristic theories of adaptive responses, with the one passing smoothly into the other as we move, changing step by step from assuming fully informed agents to agents informed only very imperfectly, between the poles of the continuum.[6] There is no implication from our being able to arrange all cases on a continuum between polar cases of rules and polar cases of regularities that there is no difference between the polar cases. However, the existence of a continuum not only supports thinking that most cases between the poles will be things to different degrees both regularities and rules. It also suggests that the difference between the polar cases may be factitious, a suggestion that may carry greater weight when, in favor of limiting the issues in view to currently settled social rules, we set apart (as I am doing) rules just promulgated or dead letters on the statute books. On the other side, I also (as Toulmin does not) set apart, with an effect similarly favorable to the suggestion, biological regularities that human beings cannot overrule. Identity, or at least a continuum, would help to explain how a good deal of social science can be carried on without the investigators' pausing to distinguish between regularities and rules.[7]

There are grounds more specific than these that suggest identifying social rules and social regularities. On the one hand, the existence of a settled social rule implies the existence of a social regularity that not only corresponds to it, but is an exact counterpart. One of the most memorable accomplishments of the Trudeau governments (I used to say, the most memorable) was to cut out the delivery of mail on Saturdays. Thus, since Trudeau's time, the rule has been that postmen in Canada deliver mail on weekdays only. To this there corresponds a counterpart regularity: it may be observed that postmen deliver mail on weekdays only. On the other hand, moving from regularities to rules, it may be argued that regularities which do not begin by implying counterpart social rules will develop in that direction. People regularly seal envelopes before mailing them. One might hold that they do not do so under the compulsion of any rule; they simply act severally to make sure that the contents of their envelopes do not fall out. However, if they fail to seal the envelopes, will they not hear now and then from disappointed correspondents who have received only empty envelopes? Will they not try harder to make sure that the envelopes are sealed just to forestall the reproaches of friends, and creditors? Or consider how employers might insist on making sure that people in their employ seal envelopes sent out on their business. The regularities that seemed to operate unaccompanied by any counterpart rule may now seem to be just stages on one or another route to the settling-in of the rule. I do not say that the stages may not last indefinitely in some instances. However, when the regularity becomes fully established, after a history like the one that I have just imagined, will it not be more than just a regularity that people seal envelopes before mailing them? Will it not be also a settled social rule to which other people require them to conform?

In the end, except for philosophers who have a comprehensive ontological program with which identities here must harmonize, I expect that the issue of identity, and the issue about a continuum as well, will turn out to be a question of convenience; and I incline to think that it will be much less complicated, and hence much more convenient, to refrain from identifying rules with regularities, not just in some cases, but in any case whatever. I shall not try to settle the ontological issue. Before we get to the ontological issue, there is an issue about whether establishing the existence of a social regularity is the same thing as establishing the existence of a corresponding social rule.[8] I maintain that it never is. In respect to this issue, I maintain, only a qualified thesis of mutual presupposition can stand, and the most important qualification comes to light with an asymmetry in the arguments for presupposition when we begin with regularities and move to rules as against beginning with rules and moving to regularities.

In cases like the rule about wifely combat technique, the route from rules to counterpart regularities may have to go by way of a higher regularity involving all the rules in the book. Though we have no instances of the prohibited technique being used and hence no instances of the rule being enforced, we may know from what happens with other rules in the book that deviations from rules in the book regularly evoke measures of enforcement. In normal cases, however, we may expect to have clear evidence from enforcement and other matters particular to a given rule that it makes a difference to how people act, and in those cases, we can go from settled social rules to causal regularities, smoothly and easily: to every settled social rule there corresponds, among other regularities, a regularity with observed instances of actions that can be described as the actions required by the rule or as actions that fit the descriptions of the measures of enforcement, laid down by the same rule in its disjunctive form. We have a regularity that is an exact counterpart of the rule.

Things are not so easy on the other side. Much can be said for there being mutual presupposition going from causal regularities to settled social rules, but what can be said falls far short in this direction of maintaining exact counterparting in every instance. This discrepancy makes it impossible to reduce every regularity to a rule; there is, on occasion, no counterpart rule to reduce it to. It equally makes it impossible to hold that establishing the existence of a rule amounts to the same thing as establishing the existence of a regularity. In every case, more has to be done to establish the existence of a rule. When we do that more, we touch on the most important feature of social phenomena, the dependence, which rules found in those phenomena share with the regularities found there, upon human choices that might take a different course.

Much can be said for mutual presupposition going from causal regularities to settled social rules. In those cases where there is counterparting between rules and regularities we can move either way, and in every case reach from the regularity a rule expressed in the same terms. Canadian MP's are held to voting in Parliament with their parties; they regularly do so; whenever a vote is taken, they vote with their parties. In the case of some regularities, it is true, no rules at all can be said to be presupposed. Many of these, however, can be dismissed, without question-begging, as not belonging to social phenomena in a strict sense. Villagers who lose their lives to avalanches or to tidal waves regularly do less farming and less fishing in subsequent seasons. Social arrangements, whatever they can do to prevent or to mitigate such disasters, can do nothing to abolish the regularities mentioned. Given the persistence of these regularities, whatever human beings do individually or in the aggregate, they do not belong to social phenomena strictly so conceived, because a strict conception of such phenomena will set aside matters that are not subject to change following changes in behavior within the range of the current biological capacity of human beings. If we confine our view to social phenomena strictly conceived, on the other hand, regularities that lead us to counterpart rules will embrace a very large part of the phenomena.

They will not embrace the whole of the phenomena. Yet regularities that do not have counterpart rules commonly presuppose the operation of rules specially connected with them nonetheless. It is a regularity, I believe, that a larger proportion of the female population participates in the labor force when the proportion of the labor force employed rises above 95 percent. Whether this is so or not, however, there is no counterpart rule that calls upon employers to make sure of employing more women when the rate of employment rises above 95 percent. Yet rules come into the picture as soon as we ask what stops women from being employed in larger proportions at lower rates of employment? Or if we ask what does having a job or even being in the labor force amount to? To be in the labor force, the rule (a rule of practice on which the statistical convention is founded) is that a worker must be ready to take a suitable job if it is offered her; and accepting the job implies heeding rules about coming to work at appointed times and doing appointed tasks. So, though the regularity in question – and this is typical of innumerable social regularities – does not have a counterpart social rule, it presupposes, in the terms under which the statistics that it brings forward have been compiled, that the people in question are conforming to certain rules.

Unlike the regularity about female participation, which simply connects two macroeconomic variables, the regularity of people sealing envelopes before they put them in the mail might plausibly have a counterpart in a settled social rule. For now, however, it might be at most a stage in the development of a settled rule. Pending the actual development of the rule, the phenomenon presents us with a regularity to which no social rule corresponds. We have just parallel practices, by so many agents who rationally take precautions against having the contents of their letters fall out. Even here, however, without moving on to a further stage in the development of a rule, there is some purchase for the notion of social rules. Mailing a letter is something that falls under a social rule, indeed, under more than one; here as elsewhere what the agents are doing is something that is intelligible to them only as something to which familiar social rules apply.

There is purchase also for the notion of rules as exemplified by the rules that people make each for themselves.[9] N checks to see whether the envelope has been sealed before he mails the letter; having taken philosophical instruction in skepticism perhaps too often and too much to heart, he makes a point of doing this every time. This is still a rule, though not a social rule; and it is a rule that characteristically reflects the social rules that establish its notional context – indeed, inevitably does so, if we consider that the very notion of having a rule for oneself, of making a point of doing something, is learned in society. On top of this notion are piled, again, the concept of writing and sending a letter and the rules applying to exchanging letters in the mail.

The presence of personal rules of this kind enables us to connect yet another class of regularities with social rules, namely, regularities that are founded on behavior that is not parallel but disparate. Every available option comes to realization with the same frequency, though each individual case can be explained as arising from one or another personal rule. Suppose it is observed that as many people in a given group will shop for groceries on one day of the week as on any other. Some may go one day rather than the others for religious reasons; others choose a day because it is their pay day; yet others go when their babysitters do not have to go to school the next day.[10]

To this class of regularities founded on personal rules without any social rule intermediating we may add, stretching mutual presupposition further, yet still not breaking with it entirely, regularities founded on sporadic deviant behavior, where the individual cases are unprecedented in the individual's history and have no sequel for which a precedent has been created. Even here a person may be acting with an aim and with an understanding of her situation in which concepts of action — and with them traces of rules — learned from social life come to bear. She has become sick and tired of serving the menfolk first and eating her dinner later; just this once, she insists on serving herself first. From a number of different cases of this sort, let us suppose, there comes a regularity, that every year a cluster of cases of such defiance arise within a week or two at the end of the winter.

The connections that I have just been surveying combine in a hypothesis about the current state of social science. In its current state, social science contemplates only regularities that connect with rules in one or another of the ways that I have illustrated. Beyond this hypothesis, however, lies a modally more powerful thesis, which applies not only to the current state of social science but to anything that might obtain that title from us, even a social science that had broken utterly with ordinary language and bound itself to use exclusively specially created technical concepts, let us say the concepts of a social physics.[11]

The thesis is that regularities found in social phenomena would not have the foundation in personal choices and actions that they must have to be fully explained in our eyes as producers of social science or as consumers of it if they did not have a foundation in choices and actions guided by rules in one or another of the ways just surveyed. Instances of all those ways can be found for regularities from current social science as we move from one to another sort of case. We have already found instances; the illustrations given for the hypothesis can serve again as we bring current social science under the modally more powerful thesis. The illustrations given can serve once more when we turn with the modally more powerful thesis to a social physics, though here we shall have to set aside entirely the connections by way of counterparting.

I am not exactly sure what the regularities found by a social physics would look like, but perhaps this will serve as an example good enough to sustain analysis of the issue: it is found that, provided a certain minimum spacing between individual bodies is retained, aggregates of human bodies still locomoting from time to time attract other such bodies at rates that vary directly with the number of bodies in the aggregates initially. There is no settled social rule that is a counterpart of this regularity. People are not required by a rule to move their bodies about and for such clusters. Nor is there any use of terms that connect directly with the rules social or personal under which the people in those bodies choose and act. Nevertheless, we may ask, "What choices and actions did the people involved adopt that had the effect described in the regularity?" If they were attracted, as it were, against their will, sucked out of their present dwelling places and swept across hill and field until they came to rest in the largest of the aggregates within twenty kilometers, then we would be dealing with a regularity that does not belong to social phenomena strictly so conceived. We know, in fact, that this is not the way things happen. People choose to move; pack up their cars; drive to towns where there are jobs for them, or relatives who will put them up while they look for jobs. If we could not supply an explanation of this kind at the personal level, we could not supply what by present standards would be a full explanation of the regularity about social-physical attraction within social science. People make choices and engage in actions; if we leave these things, along with the rules that they reflect, aside without asking how the regularity connects with them, we are leaving aside connections that press for explanation.

Have I begged an important question by assuming methodological individualism? I am not assuming that all predicates of human groups reduce to predicates of the persons who belong to the group. That the population of one city is more numerous than the population of another does not imply that any person belonging to either population is numerous to any degree; and it does not suffice for every person in the larger population simply to be in proximity to every other; we have to count them to find how numerous the population is. Nor am I assuming that all explanations must be translated into explanations at the personal level before they count as explanations. The discipline of the parties in the Parliament of Canada can be explained at the group level by the presence in Canada of the British parliamentary system rather than the Congressional one. The regularity that I have attributed to a social physics could figure in various explanations of the growth of cities without our being able (for a time, even indefinitely) to find a corresponding explanation, involving choices and actions in a context established by rules, at the personal level. It would just remain mysterious – like, classically, gravitational attraction.

The much that can be said for a presupposition (or a set of presuppositions) connecting regularities to rules leaves some leakage in the presupposition, both in respect to the hypothesis and in respect to the modally more powerful thesis. In my earlier treatment of this topic, I said "a little leakage" – I wanted to emphasize how many regularities were captured for presupposition one way or another by the connections that I had surveyed. But here, wishing to emphasize the discrepancy between mutual presupposition when we try to go from regularities to rules as compared to going from rules (settled social rules) to regularities, perhaps I can say, without undue inconsistency, "quite a lot of leakage." If it is a social physics that we have in view, we must abandon counterparting. Even with current social science in view, counterparting takes us only part of the way. We may then find innumerable regularities that correspond nonetheless in other ways to settled social rules and to actions taken according to them. However, leakage sets in, one might say, as soon as we turn away from counterparting, even before we encounter parallel habits; increases when we move on from parallel habits to disparate behavior founded on personal rules that do not parallel one another; increases again when we consider deviant behavior founded on choices and actions that do not fall under personal rules at all.

The leak gushes more strongly still when we reach cases that I have not yet considered, but which must be allowed for: we have regularities, but the people involved in them are not acting or making choices; they are behaving impulsively. No rules in their social arrangements or in their personal histories gives us a basis for explanation. We may, if we encounter such regularities, have to treat them as utterly mysterious, like the regularity of social physics if, assuming that it belongs to social phenomena strictly so conceived, we have no explanation for it at the personal level. Or we may resort outside social phenomena to a biological explanation: suddenly casting a huge image of a vampire bat's muzzle and fangs, dripping with blood, upon the television screen terrifies people so much that they start from their chairs, rush out of the room, even out of the house and down the street. We could entertain a regularity based on instinctive reactions as a regularity putatively proper to social phenomena only while we remained uncertain that it was beyond the power of social arrangements – of social training in fortitude – to inhibit people from giving in to the terror.

The example derives some significance from the fact that we can easily think of reasons why people might wish (if they could) to control the impulses in question. It is less easy to assess the significance of many other regularities that persist (we may suspect) because not only has it never occurred to anyone to try doing something about them – it also seems hardly worthwhile trying. Negative formulations will give us infinitely many instances. It may be that in every known culture, without anyone's having noticed this before, there are no people who cut their toenails alternating from the little right toe to the little left one and then from the big right toe to the big left one and so on. People could upset the regularity by personal departures or by following some contrary rule. Does such a regularity presuppose anything like a settled social rule? We may, I think, hesitate to say "Yes" or "No" until we see whether the regularity has been given any significance.

Are there grounds in rules already identified in a given culture for thinking that people would wish to bring the regularity under those rules were they to discover it? If there were grounds for thinking that people would safeguard the regularity, those grounds might make a case for completing (for purposes of comparisons between cultures or otherwise) the system of rules ascribed to a given culture by adding a rule that prescribes forbearing to cut toenails on the pattern described. That would give us at least a marginal reason for inferring the existence of such a rule. Given the inference, we could take the regularity into account without augmenting the leakage in my argument.

Alternatively, we might ask whether an explanation of the regularity in question – here the regularity about cutting toenails – has been demanded. Without resorting to a category of permissive rules, we could say that there are no rules in any culture that require cutting toenails on the given pattern. That in turn implies something about the rules that do exist and their character. They correspond in a certain way—by leaving choices of other patterns of toenail-cutting open—to the regularity observed. It might be argued that by using this general form of explanation over and over again we could forestall leakage for any of these regularities, including the ones founded on impulsive behavior that has so far not been regulated. However, since it is not my present purpose to minimize the leakage, and most of the regularities in this case have not been taken up and will not be taken up by social science, we can perhaps leave it undecided how much leakage arises from the class.

We already have leakage enough in the thesis of mutual presupposition when we try to run it from regularities to rules to prevent us from thinking that establishing a causal regularity in social phenomena is the same thing as establishing a settled social rule. The leakage is something that should heighten our appreciation of the contingency of social science, a more radical contingency than we have to deal with in natural science. For how does the leakage come about? It comes from the freedom that people have to act independently of rules social or personal, even in defiance of them. It may be a freedom that it is hard for them to exercise individually. They may have internalized the rule so that they do not feel free to deviate from it regardless of the social penalties attached; it may not even occur to them that deviation is something that they might choose to do. Or they might be aware that they could so choose, and be tempted to, but feel deterred by the penalties. Even to exercise the freedom in concert may be costly; it might ruin arrangements for orderly government or for efficient production. Nonetheless the freedom is real: it is always open to human beings, acting individually or acting in concert, to make choices that undermine current regularities. This is the most important feature of social phenomena. Every one of the regularities proper to social phenomena is subject to vanishing—to vanishing very quickly, even within the span of a generation—when in sufficient numbers the people involved choose to act differently. It may help social scientists, reflecting on this fact, to preserve their equanimity if they consider that regularities about the behavior of birds can vanish when new regularities emerge in the train of mutations—some species have even become flightless; or consider that, even if regularities as enduring as those of classical mechanics may be beyond the reach of social science, it is still worthwhile knowing what regularities obtain even for the length of a generation, especially if it is our own generation. The regularities of social science are nevertheless—since choice goes much further in our species—much more liable to be transitory than regularities typical of natural science.

What I have expressed in terms of freedom and choice might be expressed, more obscurely, by using the term "intentional." We might say that the intentionality of settled social rules hovers behind social regularities, themselves discovered and expressed without any direct attention to intentionality. I shall not examine intentionality as such; but much of what is to be known under that head comes to light when we examine how some combination of evidence relating to conformity, enforcement, and point figures in establishing the existence of a settled social rule. I shall say a word or two about these matters.

If evidence as to conformity is to count in the absence (so far) of evidence as to enforcement or point, it must be more than evidence that the actions done or forborne are just in description the actions prescribed or prohibited by the hypothesized rule. So far we have observed no more than a regularity, which may (as we have been seeing several times over) not depend on any rule, and if it does, may not depend on a counterpart rule. We shall need testimony from the people concerned that they are deliberately trying to bring about what the rule prescribes or to refrain from what the rule prohibits. For example, they cite as a reason for sticking postage stamps onto envelopes that doing so meets a prescribed condition for having them carried in the mail.

We can dispense with this testimony when we have good evidence of deliberate enforcement – deliberate, hence itself a matter of choice falling under a rule with perhaps its own provisions for enforcement. The logical possibility of an infinite regress arises here; but in practice the possibility will not be troublesome; we may, for example, have testimony from the enforcers. It would be astonishing, even deeply perplexing, in such a case, if when we sought for such testimony from the people outwardly conforming (as we now might say) to the rule and subject to its enforcement, the testimony was not forthcoming; but beforehand we could reasonably assert the existence of a rule once given the combination of outward conformity and instances of enforcement.

Would it be equally reasonable to assert the existence of a rule given outward conformity, if in addition we had only some evidence of there having been a point to such a rule? There might be solid footing in at least some such cases. Had we evidence from ancient Israel that before the introduction of the rule about wifely combat assistance wives commonly did enter the fray and quickly moved to seize the private parts of their husbands' opponents, then we would be in a good position, given the abandonment of this technique after a given date, to hypothesize that a rule had been introduced prohibiting it. If we knew, further, that there had been a popular prophet at work just before the introduction of the rule who had instigated a wave of prudery in what had been hitherto a free-loving and free-fighting population, we would have a point not only in the sense of having something to stop; we would also be able to specify the grounds for stopping it.

Can we say anything as considerable to the point about (say) Canada in the present century? Quite possibly, as one aspect of the notoriously tame and boring character of social life in Canada, where we can still go to the grocery store without running into automatic rifle fire, there has been no instance whatever in the last several generations of Canadian wives using the combat technique in question, at least upon their husbands' opponents. So we have the semblance of perfect conformity, of what we could call perfect conformity were there a rule. Is there a rule? In Canada, the old-time religion has decayed so far even among its most fervent adherents that we cannot plausibly say that the conformity comes from wives bearing in mind Deuteronomy 25:11–12.

A bare possibility – a limiting case of intentionality – of finding some point for a rule in Canada against wives using the combat technique in question lies in the sort of marginal reason alluded to earlier, that to ascribe such a rule may complete the system of rules characterizing a given culture. Some historian or anthropologist might wish to distinguish Canadian society from others past and present in which the technique was freely used. I do not want to give this possibility too much weight; let us give it no more weight than suffices to make it clear that we do not want to prejudge how far someone concerned to give a comprehensive theoretical account of the system of rules in a given society may wish to stretch the application of the concept of rules. For systematic reasons, she might wish to ascribe rules in instances where, taking the instances by themselves, the ascription would have little motivation. Would the point of asserting the existence of such a rule then be point only for the systematist? It will not be easy to separate having a point for the systematist from having a point for the people that she is studying. Given their beliefs about female modesty and their other rules, could they not be expected to protest deviations from the rule, should they occur?

Let me attach a brief epilogue about free will. The freedom that I have emphasized, to have any given rule or not to have it, is freedom at a deeper level than political freedom – the freedom, in Hobbes's terms, to act without hindrance in whatever the Sovereign hath praetermitted, i.e., in connections not governed by rules that the Sovereign has laid down[12]; or the freedom from interference by others which Mill cherished, and specifically noted could be cherished and practiced regardless of how the issue of free will and determinism might be settled.[13] Freedom with respect to having any given rule is a deeper freedom because to abolish or abandon a rule can free people from the very regularities that on a naturalistic view of social science we depend to predict their behavior (unless we are directly predicting what they will do from a rule that we know them to adhere to). So, though those regularities are genuine ones, and genuine bases for scientific prediction, any determinism sustained by social science alone is not only consistent with human freedom; it is subject to upset by the exercise of that freedom. True, we do not in social science get to the bottom of the issue of free will. For whether people adopt a given rule or abolish it might be determined by underlying natural processes which work in ways beyond human control. However, do we have any comprehensively deterministic laws about these processes? And is not the great variety of human societies in the face of what often seem to be much the same natural circumstances – variety in the extent to which they are rulebound, variety as well in the character of their rules – some evidence that such comprehensively deterministic laws about underlying natural processes are not going to be found?[14]

NOTES

1. A reference to an article by Lyle M. Eslinger, "The Case of an Immodest Lady Wrestler in Deuteronomy 25:11–12," *Vesus Testamentum* 31, no. 3 (July 1981): 269–81, drew me

back to the Bible in search of this passage. I also looked up Eslinger's discussion of it; he has many interesting things to say.

2. J. L. Mackie, *The Cement of the Universe* (Oxford, 1974), 62.

3. Among the classical champions of regularities as the business of social science have been Karl Popper, for example, in *The Poverty of Historicism* (London, 1957), and Ernest Nagel, in *The Structure of Science* (New York, 1961), chaps. 13, 14. The most single-minded champion of rules has been Peter Winch, *The Idea of a Social Science* (London, 1958). Other advocates of interpretive social science (like Charles Taylor) can be brought into the rules camp with a little argument. Their concern with human intentions and choices gets some satisfaction from the study of rules that it would not get from the study of regularities.

4. I have so contended in *Philosophy of Social Science* (Englewood Cliffs, N.J., 1987), 110–23. What I say in that passage is, I think, correct enough, but I did not make the order of the argument quite so clear as I would have wished it. The present essay makes the order clearer; it also amplifies the argument in several respects and stresses the lessons to be learned from the discrepancy.

5. Stephen E. Toulmin, "Rules and Their Relevance for Understanding Human Behavior," in *Understanding Other Persons,* edited by Theodore Mischel (Oxford, 1974), 185–215.

6. Herbert A. Simon, "Mathematical Constructions in Social Science," in *Philosophical Problems of the Social Sciences*, edited by David Braybrooke (New York, 1965), 83–98 (a shortened and otherwise slightly revised version of "Some Strategic Considerations in the Construction of Social Science Models," in *Mathematical Thinking in the Social Sciences,* edited by Paul F. Lazarsfeld [Glencoe, Ill., 1954]).

7. For examples, we need look no further than the two prime specimens of social science that I continually refer to in *Philosophy of Social Sciences* — Epstein's account of party discipline in the Canadian Parliament as compared with the U.S. Congress, and Liebow's study of unemployed black men in Washington. Another example can be found in Jane Mansbridge's *Why We Lost the ERA* (Chicago, 1986); see especially chapter 1. Even in excellent works like these I suspect that insisting from point to point on the distinction between rules and regularities, though perhaps unnatural, would lead to further clarifications and discoveries. Suppose it did not; it would not follow that it was not correct and illuminating for philosophers to make the distinction and hold that one or the other was a leading feature of social phenomena. Furthermore, we have to explain how philosophers might fasten some upon the first, some upon the second, to the neglect (or even repudiation) of the other; and such an explanation, which can be gathered from the present essay, throws light upon the basic character of social science.

8. In general, to establish the $(\exists x)R_1(x)$ and to establish $(\exists y)R_2(y)$ leaves the question whether $x = y$ open, even when R_1 and R_2 are so closely connected that, empirically $R_1(x) \leftrightarrow R_2(x)$. Let $R_1(x) =$ "x is a settled social rule"; $R_2(y) =$ "y is a regularity." I am going to argue that $(\exists x)R_1(x)$ logically implies $(\exists y)R_2(y)$ — a y that moreover "corresponds" in one way or another to x; but that the implication the other way, from a regularity to a corresponding settled social rule, fails both for natural regularities and for regularities proper to social phenomena. Where it does not fail, furthermore, it is saved only by taking "corresponds" to cover a variety of ways of corresponding; whereas in the implication from a settled social rule to a regularity, "corresponding" can be taken narrowly to mean "counterparting."

9. Cf. Ronald Heiner, "The Origin of Predictable Behavior," in *American Economic Review* 73, no. 4 (September 1983): 560–95. Heiner argues that a person's behavior cannot be predicted unless it is founded on personal rules (which may be shared or idiosyncratic).

10. Not all regularities founded on disparate behavior need be the equal distribution sort. The demand curve may arise from disparate behavior. See Gary S. Becker, *The Economic Approach to Human Behavior* (Chicago, 1976), 158–59.

11. It was failing to distinguish as emphatically as I should have between the hypothesis about the current state of social science and the modally more powerful thesis that obscured the order of my argument in *Philosophy of Social Science*, 119–23.

12. Thomas Hobbes, *Leviathan,* chap. 21.

13. John Stuart Mill, *On Liberty*, chap. 1, at the beginning.

14. I have had the benefit of being able to deliver an earlier version of this essay to a colloquium held by the Department of Philosophy at Carleton University; and, making even more difference to my revisions, the benefit of a close reading of that version by Shelagh Crooks of St. Mary's University, followed by a stimulating conversation with her about it. It was she who brought up transitory regularities in bird behavior and the two senses in which rules have point. Something nearer to the present revision was read to the weekly colloquium of the Department of Philosophy at Dalhousie University, and the discussion there inspired me to make a number of further useful changes.

Causes of Variability:
Disentangling Nature and Nurture*
ARTHUR FINE

Was du ererbt von deinem Vätern hast, Erwirb es, um es zu besitzen.

(Goethe, *Faust*, Part I, Scene 1)[1]

1. OBJECTIVES

People differ. From the very beginning of life even the standard forms of behavior are plastic, varying not only in their quality but also in the schedule of their growth. For example, developmental studies (Bayley 1969) tell us that the age at which infants begin to make crawling movements can vary anywhere from three days to three months. Although infants usually respond to a voice by three weeks, that response may first occur in a range from one to eight weeks. When it comes to walking, taking the first few steps alone can happen anywhere from age nine months to seventeen months. Speech generally develops by fourteen months, at which time we may expect infants to say a couple of words, but this achievement can occur as early as ten or as late as twenty-three months. Thus even highly channeled behavior, like the development of motor skills or language acquisition, shows an enormous range and variability. The same is true for virtually all other items of human activity, including the many aspects of cognition and personality. Part of understanding human beings involves understanding the sources of individual differences that make up this variability.

Perennially, scientists and social thinkers have looked to two polar sources for this understanding; namely, to heredity and to the environment. The priority dispute that results from placing primary emphasis on one or another of these factors has come to be known as the nature-nurture controversy. There is no necessity, however, to regard these two sources as conflicting. For given the range of variability to be explained one could look for a compatibilist resolution and expect that both heredity and environment have contributions to make in

94

most cases. That is, one can expect that they each account for some portion of the total variability. (Indeed, one might anticipate that even when the contributions of nature and nurture are combined there will still be a significant amount of individual difference to be explained.) In the abstract, such a compatibilist strategy with regard to the nature-nurture controversy seems attractive and plausible. Whether it remains so in the field, however, depends on whether one can sort out the respective contributions of heredity and environment convincingly, and thereby effect a reconciliation.

When we describe heredity and the environment as sources of individual difference and when we propose to investigate the extent to which they can account for (or explain) behavior, we adopt a causal idiom and treat studies of human behavior as causal disciplines. This is certainly the idiom and attitude of dominant approaches to the human sciences, which makes these sciences an especially good testing ground for philosophical ideas concerning causality, its nature and implications.[2] The examination of the nature-nurture issue below uses this opportunity to examine the determinability of causes and the philosophical idea that causal analysis commits one to belief in the reality of the causal agents. Thus this essay has two objectives: to investigate the extent to which one can apportion individual differences to the effects of heredity or environment, and to investigate the extent to which the scientific techniques employed in this area support belief in a causal order and realism over the causes of behavior. These objectives are strongly connected.

2. NATURE AND NURTURE

In the 1970s public discussion of nature versus nurture centered on the IQ controversy that surrounded the writings of Jensen (1969), Herrnstein (1971) and Shockley (1972). Concern focused on the heritability of IQ and the implications for that of educational and social policy, and also for the conduct of scientific research (Tobach and Proshansky 1976). That controversy also generated reflections on the methodological problems involved in the nature-nurture issue; especially on the question posed above of whether for significant human behavioral traits we would ever be able to sort heredity from environment in a reasonably satisfactory way. One of the most thoughtful contributions to the public debate on this issue was made by David Layzer, who identified the conditions required for an adequate study.

> Nevertheless, heritability can still be defined as the purely genetic fraction of the phenotypic variation. The question now arises: Can this purely genetic contribution be estimated from the appropriate measurements of correlations between genetically related persons? The answer turns out to be yes—*provided that, in the sample population for which measurements are carried out, genotype and environment are statistically uncorrelated.* In experimental animal populations, this condition may be insured by placing newborn animals in random environments. In natural human

populations, on the other hand, it is probably impossible to eliminate genotype-environment correlation. Genotype-environment correlation is always present when children are reared by biologically related person. For adopted children, the effects are smaller but not entirely absent. Thus it would seem a hopeless task to determine the heritability of a phenotypically plastic trait in a natural human population. The data theoretically available in these circumstances are simply not adequate to the task. (Layzer 1976, 69)[3]

Almost as these words were being written, in 1974, at the Institute for Behavioral Genetics at the University of Colorado, Robert Plomin and John C. DeFries began plans for the Colorado Adoption Project (CAP), a landmark adoption study designed to answer questions about genetic versus environmental influences on human development. Indeed, the study was designed to address precisely the questions concerning which Layzer and others (e.g., Lewontin 1975) were so pessimistic. In work that is still going on, the project planned to study its subjects from infancy through adolescence. The report of the project published over ten years later (Plomin and DeFries 1985) covers only the first two years of life. It involves data from 182 infants adopted approximately within a month of birth and 165 matched control infants (nonadopted), all of whom were tested at 12 and at 24 months of age in lengthy home visits. The test data involve infant measures for cognitive development, communication, personality-temperament, behavioral problems, motor development, and health. The testers also made videotaped observations of mother-infant interactions. Data on the physical, social, and emotional aspects of the environment (everything from toys, verbal stimulation, and the family structure to noise levels, lighting, and the quality of the neighborhood) was extracted from lengthy interviews with the mothers, self-reports, and observation-interview instruments. The parents were also given a battery of tests covering cognition, personality, interests and talents, behavioral problems, drug use, and demographic background. The results involve a massive amount of information of all sorts, leading to virtually endless parent-child comparisons that can be processed and examined in many different ways. Although not perfect, the variety of techniques and tools used to collect information and the sensible way the information was handled is very impressive. A study on this scale, and executed with such care and good sense, is just the place to look if one wants to understand the possibilities of sorting nature from nurture.

The theory behind the study follows the random sorting paradigm alluded to by Layzer, above. Biological parents and their adopted-away infants share heredity but not environment. When the data from an adoption study is sorted for this combination the study approximates the ideal of randomizing family environment to reveal the effects of heredity on genetically related individuals. Adopter parents and their adopted infants share environment but not heredity. When the data is sorted *this* way the study approximates the ideal of randomizing heredity to reveal the effects of family environment on non-genetically related individuals. Thus adoption studies involve a powerful twofold design that seems, in principle, capable of disentangling the effects of heredity and environment, effects that covary in the nonadoptive family.[4] But they can do even more. For by adding a control group of nonadoptive families one can use this covariance to support further inferences by comparing the correlation of traits in the control, where the effects of heredity and environment are compounded, with the correlation of traits in the adoptive families where these effects, presumably, are not. Thus, for example, if one takes height to be a heritable trait then one would expect a greater correlation between parent height and child height among the control families than among the adoptive families. The same would be true for features of cognition, to the extent to which they are heritable. On the other hand if sociability, for example, were determined by environmental factors alone, then it seems that one would expect no difference in the correlation of parent sociability with infant sociability between the control and adoptive families, since heredity would not enter in.

3. CAUSAL ANALYSIS AND CAP

CAP uses path analysis and causal models to make the inferences sketched above quantitative and rigorous. The models employ directed arrows to indicate the path from cause to effect, and the techniques of partial regression (or "path coefficients") to quantify the causal influence and to compute expected correlations between the causal factors.[5] One can then check the model from the data in the normal hypothetical-deductive way. The makers of the study are quite clearheaded about the use of these models. There is, for example, no suggestion that one could extract causal conclusions from the correlational data alone. The causal conclusions that are drawn rely on the empirical goodness of fit of the causal models and on the network of causal hypotheses that go into their construction. There is, nevertheless, a special vulnerability in the modeling technique that shows up dramatically in this study (and in others in behavioral genetics); namely, the nonspecificity of the hypothetical causal factors. The study cannot identify exactly what genetic or environmental factors are at work nor describe how the putative causal effects are supposed to have been achieved. In short, there is no detailed causal story to tell. The crosschecks we normally expect for causal accounts, including independent information about the particulars of the supposed causes, are absent here. This is a failure of purely structural models in general, and one that makes it reasonable to hold off crediting their limited predictive success to the accuracy of their underspecified descriptive hypotheses, at least until some reliable, independent details are available. I take the critical point here to be very serious, but I shall not press it below for I want to look at other problems about the modeling in examining the causal conclusions of the study and how they are drawn.[6] Since the study is really too massive for any adequate survey here of its results, I will focus instead on just one of the conclusions, one that the authors themselves highlight, and concentrate the discussion there.

The conclusion I want to look at is one of the most intriguing results of the study; namely, that even where the environment clearly influences the development of a trait, that influence is also mediated by heredity. Thus, infant sociability seems to be influenced by the character of the home environment (i.e., open family styles make for more outgoing babies). But it would also appear that genotype controls the extent to which this environmental influence takes hold. The authors describe the evidence for this as the "most exciting" of several unexpected results of their analysis of environmental measures (Plomin and DeFries 1985, 340). The *New York Times* agrees and recently featured the finding in an article that began by referring to chromosomes as providing a "blueprint for personality" and then went on:

> The question today is no longer whether genetics influence personality, but rather how much and in what ways. The answers emerging in the last few years primarily from long-term studies of twins and adopted children, bring increasing clarity to the nature/nurture debate. While environmental forces *can* help shape temperament, it is apparently equally true that genes can dictate an individual's response to those environmental forces. (Franklin 1989, 36)

The CAP data showed a generally higher correlation between environment-infant characteristics among biological families than among adoptive families. In particular, the correlation between (roughly) family sociability and (roughly) infant sociability was more than twice as high (0.34) among the control families than it was among the adoptive ones (0.16) (Plomin and DeFries 1985, 219). Thus the authors infer that heredity mediates the effect of family environment on infant sociability. To support the inference the study makes use of causal models whose relevant features I reproduce below in a somewhat simplified form.

$$P \longleftarrow_e \quad E \quad \xrightarrow{\ \ } _e I$$

FIGURE 1a

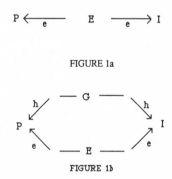

FIGURE 1b

Path models for parent (P)-infant (I) resemblance in (1a) adoptive families and (1b) biological families.

In these diagrams *E* represents shared family environmental influences and *G* (additive) genetic factors. The relevant parent and infant phenotypes are given by P and I, respectively, which we associate with the relevant CAP measures for parent and infant sociability.[7] The proportion of the phenotypic variation due to E is just the contribution that the path through E makes to the correlation Corr(P, I) between P and I. The simple rules of path analysis tell us to compute that contribution by multiplying the causal factors (path coefficients) associated with each causal arrow in the path. Thus both in figures (1a) and (1b) we find that E is responsible for the same fraction of the phenotypic variation; namely, e^2. The IQ controversy centered on the heritability of IQ; that is, on the proportion of the variance of IQ that results from genetic factors. For diagram (1b) above, heritability (in what is sometimes called the "narrow" sense) is just the contribution the path through G makes to the correlation Corr(P, I); namely, h^2. Finally, to find the correlation between factors in a path diagram just add up the contributions from all the paths connecting them. So in figure (1a)

$$\text{Corr}(P, I) = e^2 \tag{1A}$$

Whereas in figure (1b),

$$\text{Corr}(P, I) = h^2 + e^2 \tag{1B}$$

My pictures here oversimplify the causal analysis in several respects. I have ignored the fact that in the biological families only half the genes are shared between parents and offspring (which would reduce h^2 in (1B) by a factor of 2, assuming random mating). I have left out factors corresponding to non-shared environmental influences and, for the adopting parents, nonshared genetic influences too. These would add some arrows pointed at P and I, but no new paths connecting them. Hence these influences would not affect Corr(P, I). There are various other factors that could be introduced into the models to make them more realistic, but whatever their complications the basic logic would be the same as that represented above: the control parents contribute genes and environment to their children, the adoptive parents environment only.[8]

Equations (1A) and (1B) imply that, unless sociability is not heritable at all (i.e., unless $h = 0$), Corr(P, I) should be greater in the control group than in the adoptive group. Since the data does show greater correlation between family sociability and infant sociability among the control families, it seems to support the conclusion that heredity is a causal factor in the transmission of sociability. One could even do more and use the quantitative features of the model (or a suitable refinement), together with the correlational data, to estimate the heritability of sociability, i.e., the proportion of the variance in sociability that is due to genetic factors. It turns out, however, that the data on sociability used in these considerations is not so straightforward, and that the report in the *Times* is seriously misleading in this regard. The study used two different kinds of instruments to measure characteristics of the family and features of infant behavior. One kind we might call "interpersonal." It involved home visits, on-site observations, and independent evaluation by third parties of the family, the child, and the family-child interactions. When family and infant sociability is measured by these interpersonal means *no significant differences occur between the biological families and the adoptive ones.* There was, however, a different and "personal" measure as well. (See note 4.) It involved self-evaluation by the mothers of the family environment and of the child. It is only with respect to this personal measure that the correlations increase in the control group. What does this mean?

The higher sociability correlations in the control group are taken to support the conclusion that heredity is a causal factor. But it does not seem to be a causal factor in the genesis of infant sociability as such. If the conclusion is valid, then heredity is a causal factor in the genesis of the *mother's perception* of infant sociability. So it is not the case that insofar as open families make for more outgoing babies genes play a role. *The data do not support that inference at all.* Rather when the family environment is perceived as open and expressive, the child tends to be perceived as less shy. Genes (somehow) play a role in fostering that perception. So we are not talking about infant sociability here, but about parents' (more specifically, mothers') impressions of the temperament of their children. What the data suggest is that "heredity interfaces with the environment by altering perceptions of environment and experience" (Plomin and DeFries 1985, 239). If this is correct there ought to be features of the parents that are related genetically to their perceptions of family and child. The authors consider whether this genetic link to perceptions consists in personality traits of the parents, perhaps in combination with IQ. But the data rule this out (Plomin and DeFries 1985, 220–22). We are left with the finding that there is a genetically based tendency to see our children as sociable when we see the family as relatively open.

4. MODEL BUILDING

I have emphasized how that conclusion depends on using the correlational data in conjunction with a causal model. The inference to heredity as a causal factor in the mediation of family-infant perceptions is highly sensitive to this dependence. It only emerges when the causal arrows are placed just so. Consider, for example, the following models of the way heredity can mediate between parents' perception of the family (P) and their perception of the temperament of the infant (I).

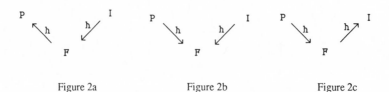

Figure 2a   Figure 2b   Figure 2c

In figure (2a) we might suppose that there is some genetic factor F such that *perception* of infant sociability (I) causally activates F (whose expected value changes with respect to I at rate h), and F in turn causally influences *perception* (*P*) of family sociability (at the same rate).[9] If this causal network were the operative one, from the point of view of heredity, then we could replace the *G*-path on top of figure (1b) by (2a). Equations (1) would still hold, and the CAP correlational data would support this revised model just as well as they do the original. But in the revised model that incorporates (2a) genetic factors are not a common cause of *P* and *I*, as in (1b), but rather a transmitting or intermediate cause. Indeed the supposition that (2a) incorporates is just this: that the way a mother perceives her biological child tends to trigger genetically based responses that influence the way she perceives the family unit. This is certainly a sensible suggestion, or at least not less sensible than the conjecture raised in the study that genes alter perceptions of both the family environment and the experience of the child. Figure (2c) represents a suggestion similar to that of (2a), but with the causal flow reversed. In (2c) the causal chain starts with the perception of the family, which influences the perception of one's biological child via some genetic intermediaries.

Figure (2b) represents something different. Here, presumably, there is some genetically related factor *F* that is the common causal *result* of the perception of infant sociability and of the perception of family sociability. What could *F* be? Perhaps one possibility relates to self-image. One tends to shape a self-image in terms of the way one experiences significant people. In the case of a biological child, perception of the child's temperament in conjunction with experience of the family might well influence how the mother conceives of herself. If the mechanism of this image formation were genetically tuned and sensitive to the biological connection between mother and child (so that the image of myself as mother is linked genetically to the fact that I actually gave birth to a child like *that*) then its development in the case of an adopted child would be negligible. The causal path represented by (2b) would then occur in the biological families but not the adoptive ones, and equations (1) could govern the correlations, in accord with the CAP data.[10]

The suggestion just raised is worth considering further. In building causal models there is a tendency to look for mediating factors that are "objective"; for example, factors like personality traits or IQ, which the study considered and rejected. But one should not overlook the possibility that causes and effects may well be mainly at the level of beliefs and ideas; that they are, as it were, in the head. Thus even in (2a) and (2b) we might look for causal intermediaries that are subjective and which would link children to their biological parents, but not to their adoptive ones. Here again the idea of self-image is suggestive. If there were a special kind of self-image that the mother forms from the experience of her own child *just because she knows that it is hers,* then that might in turn influence her perception of the family as in (2a). Since the causal path would be open only for biological families, equations (1) would obtain. Conversely, a self-image derived from perceptions of the family might selectively influence how a mother views her own child, again, *just because she knows that it is hers.* In that case the causal path represented by (2c) would only be operative for a biological family and equations (1) would once more result. One could even go back to the

CAP model with this idea of a subjective intermediary and note that the only requirement for the model is that the top G-path in the biological case of (1b) not be available in the adoptive case of (1a). A self-image selectively tuned to the idea that the child is one's own satisfies this requirement. Hence the common cause G in (1b) might itself be just such an image. That image, moreover, could be a cultural and social product. It might, for example, be constructed from the idea that there is an intimate connection between the sort of person I am and the sort of person my child is. The transmission could be entirely cultural. No genes and no heredity need be involved.

So far one might characterize the discussion as an exercise in underdetermination. The CAP project provides data in the form of correlations (or multiple regressions). To interpret the data we identify the range of factors we think might be involved in terms of culture or environment and in terms of heredity. We arrange these factors in a reasonable causal model, fit the data to the causal paths of the model and then examine the extent to which the data satisfy further constraints that the model requires (as in equations (1)). To the extent to which the satisfaction is good, we count that as confirmation of the causal hypotheses of the model, which we then hold to be the "findings" or "implications" of the study. The suggestion in offering the models in figures (2a, b, c) is that there are alternative ways of arranging the causal arrows that fit the correlational data equally well. Proliferation of this sort is a well-known feature of causal modeling, one that Woodward (1988) refers to as its "central methodological problem" (n. 6, p. 260). The usual tactic in general discussions is to suggest that we can cut down on the array of possible models in real applications because in real life not all possible rearrangements of causes make sense.[11]

The discussion above shows just the opposite. Precisely in the context of the CAP study and the personal measures of family and infant that give rise there to the question of the role of heredity in the transmission of perceptions, each of the possible causal paths does indeed make sense. In this instance, contrary to the general methodological maxim, in real life nothing is ruled out. Hence the conclusion that "heredity interfaces with the environment by altering perceptions of environment and experience" is just one of several equally well-supported causal interpretations of the data, ones that do not give hereditary factors a primary causal role at all. The inference to a causal role for genetic factors was based on stronger parent-child correlations among biological families than among adoptive ones. The existence of sensible alternative causal models consistent with these correlations shows that neither the data alone nor their combination with sound methodological maxims allow one to draw the conclusion about the influence of heredity. Moreover, the discussion suggests that where causal models involving genetic factors fit the data there are plausible competing interpretations of the models in terms of cultural mediation of beliefs that involve no factors related to heredity at all. Thus both the pattern of causal influences and the character of the causal factors are severely underdetermined by the CAP data. So, to make inferences from correlations to causes, even in the presence of well-fitting causal structures, is to put oneself on very shaky ground.[12]

The usual remedy for this prescribed by the causal theorists is to supplement the assumptions about what causal relations are sensible with even stronger assumptions about the completeness of the causal analysis. This is, for example, the sort of program that Cartwright (1989) develops, relying on the common cause principle (see section 5, below) and even more general causal considerations. The difficulty is that although strong causal assumptions can indeed imply causal conclusions, one needs to investigate the soundness of the assumptions before those conclusions are detachable. Insofar as this is an empirical question it is a matter of gathering further correlational data which, once again, will be liable to various causal interpretations. Further causal assumptions will be needed to sort the new data. So as we go down the line we will need to make more causal assumptions, not less. This is not a procedure for narrowing down the class of models, but rather for expanding it. The remedy appears to be worse than the disease.

Let me give just one illustration of the problem. One might try to sort out the differences in causal order between (1b) and (2) by making a strong causal assumption to the effect that heredity is the origin of social perceptions in general. Thus genotype would determine a selective framework that would affect how we experience the world socially. One might call such a view Social Kantianism. This would pick out the common cause arrangement of (1b) as the right connection between the mother's perception of the family as a social unit and of the child as a social being. But Social Kantianism has further consequences. For instance, if twins were raised apart in different family environments Social Kantianism would suggest that insofar as they share a selective genetic framework they would tend to see their different families as socially similar. To investigate this we could get older separated twins to do the same sort of family social ranking as was done by the CAP mothers and then look at the correlation between their assessments of family styles. In fact the study has been done (reported in Franklin 1989), and with the expected result; namely, that twins tend to rank their families similarly. Of course proponents of the different placement of arrows in figure (2) might also take to the road of high-level causal assumptions. They could suggest that heredity is not the causal origin of but only plays a role in transmitting social perceptions, in accord with (2a, c). In the family context this would imply a feedback mechanism: perceptions of the family would cause some genetically mediated responses in a child which would in turn influence further perceptions of the family, and so on. Even so, one would expect that since twins share the same genes, the repeated operation of the genetic feedback loop would tend to wash out differences in perception and to exaggerate similarities. Thus the study of separated twins and their family perceptions will not distinguish Social Kantianism from the feedback hypothesis. There are, moreover, other explanations for the similarity of separated twins' social perceptions that have little to do with either hypothesis, while adding further to the causal proliferation. For example, if genes influenced personality so that twins tended to be similar socially, then it would not be surprising to find that different families responded similarly to socially similar children, and that the children then perceived the families as similar. Since the assumption of genetic influence on personality runs counter to the CAP findings, however, maybe it is just that families tend to respond similarly to infants insofar as they look alike, as twins do, and the twins' perceptions of the families reflect that response. This raises an even further possibility. For maybe we tend to respond similarly to people who look alike because we *believe* that they *are* alike in terms of personality. (Probably we can all recall the experience of taking to new acquaintances right away just because they look like people we have known and cared for.) That tendency to respond to appearances may trade on beliefs about the relation of appearance to personality and to character, beliefs that may well be primarily social in origin and not genetic. What we see in all this is that checking on causal hypotheses simply generates more causal hypotheses. We are not eliminating the alternatives in figure (2) or the alternative social interpretations. We are not getting closer to the CAP conclusions, but moving farther away.

The situation, in fact, is even worse, as we can see by considering the model in figure (3) below.

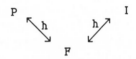

Figure 3

In accord with the conventions of path analysis, double-headed arrows signify correlations and not causal connections. Thus figure (3) represents a synthesis of figures (2) and the G-path of (1b), where all directed causal arrows, in whatever direction, are replaced by double arrows; that is, where all causal connections are replaced by correlations. Indeed it might be best to think of things the other way around. Since the CAP data are correlational to begin with, one might suppose that we start model building by arranging the data in a purely correlational representation as in figure (3). Notice that if we replace the G-path of (1b) with (3) then Corr(P,I) in the revised model will be exactly as in equation (1B). Thus when we represent the correlational data by correlational structures, we come out with a perfect fit. These structures, of course, do not permit causal inferences, but only inferences as to correlations.

Using the correlational structure of figure (3) one could not say that genetic mechanisms interface with the environment by *influencing* (or by *transmitting*) the perception of the family and the child. We could only say that genetic mechanisms interface with the environment in a way that shows a correlation with these perceptions. In stepping away from causal models in favor of correlational ones, however, we are still able to describe the central findings of the study and assess their implications for practice. For example, perhaps the most important finding about adoption was a negative one. The study found no important developmental differences between the CAP adopted and nonadopted children in infancy. This is a correlational finding, well represented by structures like figure (3), and not a causal one. We might gloss it causally by saying that, according to the study, adoption is not harmful to the adopted infants. Whether we choose to report it this way or not, the finding itself is still useful in making adoption decisions, and comforting to both the biological and adoptive mothers concerned with the welfare of their children. Similarly, those interested in gender might be surprised to learn that no significant gender differences show up in the analysis of environment-infant correlations for the 185 relations between environmental factors and infant development in the CAP and in a comparison of mother-infant correlations in the control and adoptive groups. The authors report this as showing that girls and boys are equally susceptible to environmental influences. Again, whether or not one likes that causal reading, the correlational structure that corresponds to the data (assuming, as the study does, that it is reliable for predictions) certainly gives no support to child-rearing practices that involve treating girls and boys differently because one supposes that, constitutionally, they require it.

Of course if one were to stick only with correlational structures to model the data there would be no point in looking to the CAP, or other such studies, to sort out the relative influences of heredity and environment on child development. From the point of view of purely correlational structures heredity and environment are not "influences," they are just intermediate nodes in the correlational paths. They mediate the statistical relationships between various determinable factors or traits. As illustrated above, this gives us a great deal of useful information, but not about causes. Nevertheless, it does enable one to divide the covariance in behavioral traits into the proportion mediated by heredity and the proportion mediated by the environment, and to see what is left over. Working with correlational structures also enables one to add further factors to a model, to experiment with different configurations and different interpretations. Indeed these structures offer the same advantages of model building that causal models do, and they have one less disadvantage. Whereas causal models for a given data set with fixed factors are numerous and highly undetermined by the data, the correlational structure is unique, being the unique substratum out of which causal models arise by imposing one-way paths on the two-way correlational traffic. Thus correlational structures escape one of the two sources of underdetermination described above. The other source, the possibility of reinterpreting the nodes in the structure, of course, remains. Still, reducing the range of possible models is an advantage to correlational structures that should not be overlooked. It is the dividend we can earn by foregoing talk of "influences" and the like.

Nevertheless I do not propose that we abandon causal talk and the causal analysis of behavior. Rather I highlight the utility of purely correlational structures in order to emphasize that there is a generically different and yet reasonable way to process information from a study like CAP and to report its findings. The point is not just to repeat that we only get causes out of the data if we put causes in (i.e., if we use causal models and auxiliary assumptions). It is especially to underscore that *with respect to each path* there is always a genuine choice of whether to treat it causally or not. The data do not determine which way to go. Real applications always present us with decisions about what to treat causally and what to treat as correlations only. Indeed, most working models do contain residual correlations: i.e., factors connected only by double arrows. Generally the choice of what connections to treat causally relates to the aims of the investigation (e.g., being set on determining the "influence" of heredity on IQ), the conception of the subject matter ("Surely," we say, "the way children are raised affects their character"), or other general causal convictions. Whatever the basis, there is a choice to be made. That means we have to recognize that one way of describing the relation of factors along a putative causal path is that they merely correlate with one another. This is always an option, and it might sometimes be a good one to take.[13]

5. CORRELATIONS AND CAUSES

There is a philosophical thesis, however, that runs counter to the liberal view advocated above; namely, Reichenbach's (1956) so-called principle of the common cause. That principle directs us to explain all correlations between factors as due either to direct causal connections between the factors or to common causes affecting both factors. It implies that in a *complete* causal model; that is, one in which all contributing (and inhibiting) causes are included, there will be no residual correlations; i.e., no double arrows. So we could rephrase the principle as requiring that a complete causal analysis leave no correlations unexplained. Why? Why must explanation be causal so that correlations are only explicable by means of causes? Why are correlations singled out in a completely context-free way so that they always need to be explained regardless of context or content? And why, finally, is explanation promoted as the primary mode in our approach to understanding nature?

The emphasis on explanation seems to me typical of an intellectualization of science that fails to appreciate the role played by experimental, practical, and policy considerations. The focus on explanations loses sight of how these practical concerns enter substantively into scientific inquiry. Like politics, science, too, is the art of the doable. Good scientific questions are the ones that we can get a handle on and investigate. The answers we get depend on the results of the investigation, which are a function of when we take the investigation to be over. Often enough that judgment depends critically on what resources and techniques are available, and whether we consider further effort likely to be relevant, from a practical or policy point of view. Thus experimental, practical, and policy considerations function crucially in determining what counts as a good question and what counts as an acceptable answer. Since scientific understanding accumulates with the accumulation of answers, explanation turns out to be just one element in understanding nature. This fact of scientific life suggests that sometimes the accumulation of reliable correlations that can be turned to a practical use may itself be counted as a suitable form of understanding. It is important to bear in mind that the unmasking impulse, which pushes one always to get "behind" the phenomena, may itself not always be appropriate or reasonable.

Thus the global character of the common cause principle, that correlations always require causal explanation, betrays its distance from scientific life. While in the social sciences especially, the maxim to look for causes is a useful heuristic principle it is not more than that. It is not a scientific Golden Rule representing the Ideal Form of investigation, one whose transgression consigns the investigator to a realm of inferior beings (e.g., empiricists or other philistines). Rather, in the search for causes, as in all areas of science, one has to judge in the context of a specific inquiry whether it is reasonable to go on. That means one will sometimes judge correctly that it is not. I believe there are no set rules or principles for the operation of such judgments. They are tempered mostly by the history of an investigation, the immersion in the details of the subject, and one's sense, given the subject and its history, of what seems fruitful to pursue and what not. Reasonable people may disagree on what constitutes a fruitful course of action, and further investigation may either vindicate a party or show them to have been wrong.

Finally it is a mistake, I think, to hold up causal explanation as the only suitable kind. For surely the form of understanding provided by a scientific discipline relates to the content of the covering stories (the theories or models or whatever) that the discipline provides in context. In the quantum theory, for example, one acquires considerable understanding from the capacity to make very accurate predictions of the outcomes of certain well-defined experiments, although the theory does not provide much by way of causal accounts of the details concerning the production of the experimental outcomes. This is not because the theory is probabilistic, but because the theory works in terms of certain general descriptions of the phenomena that are structural and not causal at all. Of course we all know that quantum theory is peculiar. But relativity, which respects causality, is not. Yet if we ask why light travels with a constant velocity or why no causal signal can be transmitted with a speed faster than light, there is no causal answer. The explanation is once again structural. The very structure of space-time requires (or perhaps even embodies) these features. A similar situation prevails in Freudian psychoanalytic theory, which is also strongly causal. Psychoanalytic method relies on a correspondence between certain chains of associations and causal relations that connect the associated items, or their surrogates, psychologically. If we ask why this correspondence obtains, why one tends to produce the psychological causal order by following the chain of associations, however, the theory has no causal answer.[14] The fundamental theoretical structure is defined by a group of permissible transformations, just as in space-time theories. Transformation by association is one of the permitted ones. So, if you like, the structure of the mind requires that associations of a certain kind correspond to the psychological causal order. The point is that where we have a good causal story to tell, we can sometimes tell it to explanatory advantage. But whether we have a causal story at all depends on the particular case at hand. Thus to demand causal explanation, as the common cause principle does, is to place a constraint on the form of a story independently of the subject matter. Since form and content are not dual, it is not the case that all correlations, or anything else, require causal explanation.[15]

6. CAUSAL CHOICE

Rejecting the common cause principle opens the door to incorporating some double arrows in causal models in a fundamental way; that is, without having to suppose that as knowledge develops in the future the double arrows will become single or become the terminus of some common causal arrows. It allows the possibility that even in a complete causal account, when all the causal arrows are in place, double-arrowed paths like figure (3) will still occur. As discussed in section 5, figure (3) signifies that heredity is not a causal factor in mediating perceptions of sociability of the family and the child. If data from the CAP do not discriminate between the G-path of (1b) and figure (3) then they do not determine whether to count heredity as a causal factor at all. Hence in rejecting the common cause principle we add to the query raised by figure (2), concerning what the causal connections are between heredity and perceptions of the family and infant, a further question as to whether those perceptions are connected to one another and to hereditary factors in a causal way at all.

If the argument concerning the possibilities raised by figure (2) is correct, then causes do not supervene on correlations, and the statistical data from investigations like the CAP underdetermine the causal order. Hence to place the various factors in a particular causal arrangement involves a judgment that goes beyond the information provided by the study. It represents a meta-empirical commitment to a particular causal flow. Although it may be reasonable to make such a commitment, it may also be reasonable to withhold it, or to place the causal order differently. I would say the same for the further question of whether, with regard to particular factors, one should be committed to connecting them causally. Since the findings of a study like CAP can be modeled in a number of different ways, it seems fair to urge caution over commitment to the details of any special representation, whether causal or not. Such caution, while not endorsing causal realism, does not amount to instrumentalism over causes either.

In general, instrumentalism cautions agnosticism with regard to the more theoretical elements (sometimes the "unobservables") of science. Instrumentalism correctly points out that we can use a theoretical structure, and take it seriously, without believing it to be literally true and so without believing in the reality of the entities that it employs (or to which it putatively refers). Agnosticism results when instrumentalism adds a recommendation that one tailor one's beliefs to accord with the following empiricist precept: do not believe what no empirical evidence can compel one to believe. Applied to the preceding discussion, instrumentalism would have us withhold belief in any particular causal order and in any particular causal connections. In short instrumentalism does not believe that causes are real.[16]

The position I have been trying to shape here is different. It does not begin with some entrenched scientific structure and recommend that we water down our beliefs about the structure to bring them in line with certain belief-warranting principles. That is bad belief management, requiring us to trade in scientific beliefs to pay for epistemological ones, regardless of context or content. Rather I have emphasized what all makers of causal models for data from a study like the CAP are well aware of; namely, that causal conclusions depend on a decision to employ models with particular causal arrangements, and that other models might equally well have been employed so far as the data go. I see no basis here for general agnosticism about causes. In particular, no special epistemological principles are imported to mold beliefs. Indeed, I recognize that there may be good reasons to impose models with certain causal connections and excellent reasons to accept such models, perhaps because of their fertility and the way they fit with other models or considerations that emerge from related investigations. I do not endorse any general epistemological strategy of restraint with regard to commitments or belief. Nothing of the sort follows from the fact that it is possible to believe less without suffering empirical loss. On the other hand, I point out that just because one *can* believe less the question of whether to do so may be an open one scientifically, and that withholding certain commitments, while not mandated, is possible and may be just as reasonable as the opposite, or maybe even more so. The situation in causal modeling presents us with the necessity to make judgments about how to proceed which are not forced on us by the data in the field. Such judgments, I would urge, are always to be found at the center of scientific life if we care to look with an open mind. The fact that we have considerable latitude in deciding whether to use causal models, and which factors to connect causally, does not support instrumentalism over causes. It does not support realism either.

The scientists involved in the CAP conclude that heredity is a significant causal factor in shaping our view of the social climate of the family and the temperament of our children. If we agree, then we accept genetic factors as causes. It is important to understand that we could do that instrumentally, merely accepting the genetic idiom as useful but without actually committing ourselves to believing that genetic factors are really there, acting as causes. For *acceptance* is a specification-hungry concept.[17] One accepts for a purpose, or with certain reservations, or under a certain description, and so on. We could also accept the conclusion realistically, admitting belief in some genetic causes whose exact specifications and mode of operation, as the authors suggest, are yet to be determined. But we may also just disagree with the conclusion drawn about heredity. The statistical inference to genetic causes that is based on higher correlations in the control group is not sound (section 4). Hence we might think it premature to put a causal gloss on the heritability factor at all. We might think that other causal models, ones that assign a different causal role to heredity, will stand the test of time better. We might raise the question of interpretation of the path diagrams. For example, we might believe that reinterpreting the *G*-nodes in terms of certain culturally transmitted factors, as suggested in section 4, will turn out to be a better construal than that of heredity when all the study data are taken into account, not just the material on perceptions of sociability. Each of these options (and certainly there are others as well) offers a reasonable basis for assessing the results of the study using desiderata that scientists in the field would certainly recognize as relevant. No specifically philosophical doctrines are required for that purpose, neither realism, nor instrumentalism, nor general skepticism.[18] The multitude of options plainly shows that the data do not interpret themselves and that the conclusions drawn by the study are not the only reasonable ones to draw.

We interpret and we choose. But not in a vacuum. Reflections about nature and nurture are part of a continuing cultural dialogue. It is a reasoned activity that engages social and educational policy, affecting what kind of creatures we take ourselves to be and, hence, what kind of people we become. The polar categories themselves reflect our social conditions and aspirations and draw their force from other polarities common in the culture. For example, they seem to relate to fundamental dualities connected with our bodies, the inner and the outer, which in turn relate to mobility and to what we can control and accomplish, and what not. Despite this entrenchment, I would argue (but not here!) that none of these dualities is necessary in the sense that we need to employ the posited categories in order to achieve an adequate understanding of ourselves or perhaps of life more generally. In particular, it may be better to think about ourselves without imposing the categories of nature or nurture with all their associations. Nevertheless, these alternatives constitute the categorial framework from which work like the CAP study draws its stock of causal factors. Because we have a choice about what to learn from such studies, the conclusions we accept are bound to involve our feelings about the background framework and the issues that relate to it for otherwise there would be no basis for choice at all. This entanglement with features of culture at large is always present in science, in physics no less than in sociology, for science always requires evidential and interpretive choice that must involve ordinary commonsense judgments; that is, judgments drawn from concepts common in our culture.

Given the data produced in studies like CAP, behavioral genetics will be inclined to credit heredity with considerable causal influence, if not on temperament itself, then on our perceptions of temperament. They have their reasons. That, after all, is what the factors drawn from the categories they employ put them on the lookout for. They frame their models for just that purpose. When the data are favorable, they are all set to go with their models. On the other hand, one may wonder about the framework of nature and nurture, or of environment and heredity, and therefore wonder whether it would not be better for social thinking and scientific talents to be engaged with different concepts. As explored above, there are also questions to be settled about the evidence for these particular models and the necessity for particular paths being causal at all. Then there are the problems of independence and underspecification that are serious for the credibility of any such structural undertaking. All in all, I am not inclined to credit heredity with causal influence. I have my reasons too.

NOTES

*I am grateful to the National Science Foundation for support of this research and to the Center for Advanced Study in the Behavioral Sciences for a fellowship year during which some of the thought reflected here first began. My thanks to Robert Plomin for introducing me to the Colorado Adoption Project and to Nancy Cartwright for useful discussions of causal modeling.

1. "What you have inherited from your fathers, acquire it to make it your own." Quoted by Freud (1949, 64) who holds the id to represent influences of heredity that we "make our own" through their interactions with family and cultural environment, represented by the development of the ego and superego.

2. I mean to include constructivist, hermeneutic, phenomenological, and ethnomethodological approaches in this characterization, for they use modalities such as "making," "constructing," "intending," "interpreting," "bracketing," "moving," "responding," and so forth, all of which are causal. The dichotomy that is sometimes drawn between these "interpretive" approaches and causal ones seems to me false. Both approaches are intermingled in all the sciences. To be sure, the formal techniques of causal analysis that are the focus of this essay may not be universal. The problems I develop about causal inference, however, are.

3. Note the callous attitude expressed here toward the separation of animal families for experimentation, an attitude more prevalent in the 1970s than it is now—or so I hope.

4. In adoption studies one has to worry about selective placement (i.e., matching adoptive to biological parents), whose effects amount to some covariance between gene and environment. However, the adoption agencies involved in CAP did not attempt to match adoptees to adopters, and other measurable sources of selectivity turn out to have been minimal. Still, the placement of adopted infants is far from random, and this is a possible weakness in the study to which critics, pursuing Layzer's line, could attend.

5. Kempthorne (1957) contains a standard introduction to causal path analysis. See note 9 for more on the path coefficients.

6. The problem about underspecification and the need for independent crosschecks in causal modeling is well illustrated by Horan (1989) and Lloyd (1989) in their discussion of biological models. Although they disagree about what can be pinned on or credited to the semantic view of theories, they do not disagree about the need for specificity and independence in taking predictive success to count in favor of the credibility of the model.

7. The study used a derived measure of family style called the FES (Family Environment Scales) personal growth factor, which we can take for P in the diagrams. This factor involves a self-rating by parents with regard to their being intellectual, active, permissive, and expressive. For I the study used the midparent CCTI (Colorado Childhood Temperament Inventory) measure for sociability. This measure is a rating by parents that relates to infant shyness, conceived of as a combination of emotionality-fearfulness and low sociability, rather than gregariousness. See Plomin and DeFries (1985), chap. 4.

8. For a detailed discussion of more complex causal models for the CAP data, see Fulker and DeFries (1983).

9. The path coefficient is derived from partial linear regression of the cause factor on the effect factor. It is best understood as an approximation to how much the average or expected value of the effect variable changes in the population as a result of a unit change in the variable representing the cause, other causes being held fixed.

10. I really have to emphasize the *could* here, for (2b) is different from the other path diagrams in that one cannot actually compute the correlation between P and I from it without additional assumptions. One could make such assumptions, however, or just put in the correlation "by hand" in a way that is compatible with the data.

11. E.g., see Blalock (1979).

12. Of course in some particular application it might happen that competing causal models and competing interpretations of the causal structures are ruled out by features of the context. The likelihood of such circumstances is pretty slim, but even so it would be

compatible with my conclusion here that inferences from correlations to causes, even in conjunction with causal models, are not reliable as such.

13. My (1989) argues that basic, residual correlations are a natural feature in an indeterminist worldview; for example, the worldview usually associated with the quantum theory.

14. Here may be one of the sources of Grünbaum's (1984) reservations about this aspect of psychoanalytic method. For a criticism of Grünbaum on this point, see Forbes and Fine (1986).

15. In this section I have concentrated on general considerations that lead one to reject the search for common causes as a sound requirement on theory construction. But there are more specific reasons, drawn from areas of biology and physics, where it appears that the common cause conditions simply cannot be met. For biology see Sober (1984), and for physics see van Fraassen (1985 and 1989), and my (1989). Cartwright (1989, chap. 6) makes an interesting suggestion for how to restore common causes in the physics' case, but acknowledges that her causal reconstruction has peculiarities of its own.

16. This is probably too broad. But it does come close to the point of view expressed by van Fraassen (1989, 109).

17. My (1990) develops this point about acceptance.

18. My (1986) explores the "no additives" theme touched on here and the nonskeptical reasons that lead one away from realism and instrumentalism more generally.

REFERENCES

Bayley, N. 1969. *Manual for the Bayley Scales of Infant Development.* New York.

Blalock, H. 1979. *Social Statistics.* New York.

Cartwright, N. 1989. *Nature's Capacities and Their Measurement.* Oxford.

Fine, A. 1986. "Unnatural Attitudes: Realist and Instrumentalist Attachments to Science." *Mind* 95: 149–79.

Fine, A. 1989. "Do Correlations Need to be Explained?" In *Philosophical Consequences of Quantum Theory,* edited by J. Cushing and E. McMullin. Notre Dame, Ind., 175–94.

Fine, A. 1990. "Piecemeal Realism." *Philosophical Studies* (forthcoming).

Forbes, M. and A. Fine. 1986. "Grünbaum on Freud: Three Grounds for Dissent." *The Behavioral and Brain Sciences* 9: 237–38.

Franklin, D. 1989. "What a Child is Given." *New York Times Magazine,* September 3: 36–49.

Freud, S. 1949. *An Outline of Psychoanalysis.* Translated by J. Strachey. New York.

Fulker, D. W., and J. C. DeFries. 1983. "Genetic and Environmental Transmission in the Colorado Adoption Project: Path Analysis." *British Journal of Mathematical and Statistical Psychology* 36: 175–88.

Grünbaum, A. 1984. *The Foundations of Psychoanalysis.* Berkeley, Calif.

Herrnstein, R. J. 1971. "IQ." *Atlantic Monthly* 228: 43–64.

Horan, B. 1989. "Theoretical Models, Biological Complexity and the Semantic View of Theories." In *PSA 1988,* vol. 2, edited by A. Fine and J. Leplin. East Lansing, Mich., 265–77.

Jensen, A. 1969. "How Much Can We Boost IQ and Scholastic Achievement?" *Harvard Educational Review* 39: 1–23.

Kempthorne, O. 1957. *An Introduction to Genetic Statistics.* New York.

Layzer, D. 1976. "Behavioral Science and Society: The Nature-Nurture Controversy as a Paradigm." In Tobach and Proshansky (1976), 59–79.

Lewontin, R. C. 1975. "Genetic Aspects of Intelligence." *Annual Review of Genetics* 9: 387–405.

Lloyd, E. A. 1989. "The Semantic Approach and its Application to Evolutionary Theory." In *PSA 1988,* vol. 2, edited by A. Fine and J. Leplin. East Lansing, Mich., 277–85.

Plomin, R., and J. C. DeFries. 1985. *Origins of Individual Differences in Infancy: The Colorado Adoption Project.* New York.

Reichenbach, H. 1956. *The Direction of Time*. Berkeley, Calif.

Shockley, W. 1972. "The Apple-of-God's-Eye Obsession." *The Humanist* (Jan.-Feb.): 16.

Sober, E. 1984. "Common Cause Explanation." *Philosophy of Science* 51: 212–41.

Tobach, E., and H. M. Proshansky (eds.). 1976. *Genetic Destiny*. New York.

van Fraassen, B. 1985. "EPR: When is a Correlation Not a Mystery?" In *Symposium on the Foundations of Modern Physics*, edited by P. Lahti and P. Mittelstaedt. Singapore, 113–28.

van Fraassen, B. 1989. "The Charybdis of Realism: Epistemological Implications of Bell's Theorem." In *Philosophical Consequences of Quantum Theory*, edited by J. Cushing and E. McMullin. Notre Dame, Ind., 97–113.

Woodward, J. 1988. "Understanding Regression." In *PSA 1988*, vol. 1, edited by A. Fine and J. Leplin. East Lansing, Mich., 255–69.

Probabilism

RICHARD FOLEY

According to probabilists, the central normative requirement governing an individual's degrees of belief is that they be coherent. Assume for the moment that a person's degrees of belief can be precisely measured on a scale from 0 to 1, with 1 representing maximum confidence in a proposition and 0 minimum confidence. Her degrees of belief are coherent, then, just if they can be construed as subjective probabilities. They must obey the axioms of at least the finitely additive probability calculus.[1] In effect, the probability calculus is used as a logic of opinion. So, to take some simple cases, it is irrational for her to believe a proposition with degree of confidence $x + n$ (where n is positive) and also to believe some proposition it implies with degree of confidence x: it is irrational for her to believe a proposition with degree of confidence x and also to believe some logically equivalent proposition with degree of confidence y where $x \neq y$; and it is irrational for her to believe a disjunction of mutually exclusive propositions with a degree of confidence x if she believes the first disjunct with degree of confidence y and the second with degree of confidence z and $x \neq y + z$.

An immediate difficulty for probabilism is that it seems to make being rational too easy. One sign of this is that an individual's degrees of belief might well be coherent even though he himself would be critical of them were he to be reflective. He himself would think that they need adjusting. Moreover, the worry that probabilism is not demanding enough will be all the more serious if, contrary to the above assumption, the individual does not have precise degrees of belief in a wide variety of propositions. For the less comprehensive and the less precise his degrees of belief, the less exacting is the requirement that they not be incoherent. So, it would be convenient for probabilists to be able to assume that he has some degree of belief or other in every proposition that he can understand, or at least in a wide variety of propositions, and that these degrees of belief are numerically precise.

Unfortunately, this does not seem to be the case. There are many propositions that a person can understand but that he has never explicitly considered. At least at first glance, he would not seem to have a precise degree of belief in each of them. But in addition, he would not seem to have precise degrees of belief even in all those propositions that he has explicitly considered. He may be significantly more sure than not that Sue will be on time for dinner, but his attitude might not be any more fine-grained than this.

It is important to resist the idea that this possibility can be safely ruled out from the start. It is perhaps true that an individual cannot help but have some degree of belief or another in those propositions that he understands and has explicitly considered, but it is something else again to say that these degrees of belief must be numerically precise.

Think of love, patience, jealousy, aesthetic pleasure, intellectual understanding, hope, and other such phenomena. They, too, come in varying degrees, but their strengths cannot be measured with numerical precision. The problem is not simply one of our presently lacking adequate techniques of measurement. The problem is with the phenomena themselves. They lack the requisite kind of richness. The distinctions among them with respect to strength simply are not fine enough.

Of course, we might force the issue by asking someone to make fine distinctions about how strongly she loves various people, for example. But if so, we are likely to encounter another problem, a problem with orderliness. The distinctions that she makes might not even be transitive, for instance.

Consider an analogy. A person's subjective perceptions of sweetness in a beverage cannot be calibrated in anything like the fine-grained way that the quantity of sugar in a beverage can be calibrated. Suppose we nonetheless force someone to make fine distinctions among her perceptions of sweetness. Then this can lead to problems with orderliness. If we put minutely increasing amounts of sugar in, say, twenty cups of a beverage, we can set up a sequence that in a blind tasting will tend to produce intransitive perceptions of sweetness. She may perceive cup 1 and 2 as equally sweet, cup 2 and 3 as equally sweet, and so on for each of the other adjacent cups but nonetheless perceive cup 20 as more sweet than cup 1.

Similarly, an individual is not inclined to make extremely fine distinctions about the strengths of her loves, jealousies, aesthetic pleasures, and the like, but on the other hand, if we forced her to do so, these too might turn out to lack the orderliness that they need to have if we are to be able to assign a numerical measure to them.

We must make allowances for this in whatever view we take of the nature of these phenomena. Suppose, for example, we think of love in phenomenological terms. It is essentially a feeling that is distinguished from other feelings not by its behavioral products but rather by its special phenomenological character. Maybe this is right, but if so, these feelings are diffuse in a way that precludes there being fine distinctions among them with respect to strength. On the other hand, suppose we think of love as a disposition of some complicated sort. If so, then this disposition is sufficiently embedded in a network of other like dispositions as to preclude once again fine distinctions with respect to strength.

It is undeniable that some loves, some jealousies, and some aesthetic pleasures are stronger than others. Nonetheless, it is a mistake to think they have numerically precise strengths. We can always devise tests—e.g., questionnaires, skin stimulation readings, etc.—that allow us to measure numerically the relative strength of an individual's reaction to a person or a situation or whatever. The problem is one of finding a rationale for thinking that it is the strength of her love or jealousy or aesthetic pleasure that we are measuring.

This is not to say that loves are not subtly different from one another, nor that jealousies and aesthetic pleasures are not. On the contrary, these phenomena admit of endlessly fine distinctions. It is just that the distinctions are not primarily ones of relative strength. Their subtlety is a more of a matter of the ways in which they can interact with comparable phenomena. Think, for example, of how love can be mixed with resentment or even hate of the very same person.

Something similar may be true of belief. Subtle distinctions can be made among them as well, but it may be that these distinctions are not primarily ones of strength. Indeed, this is just what first appearances would suggest. It would suggest, in particular, that the fine distinctions are ones of content, not strength. Neither casual introspection nor casual observation indicates that the strengths of our beliefs are finely distinct from one another. To be sure, someone may be more confident that Sue will be on time for dinner tonight than he is that she will remember the book he lent her, but at first glance there would not seem to be a numerically precise way to represent the relative strengths of these two beliefs. Indeed, if we were to request such numbers of him, he would probably be reluctant to supply them, and if we ourselves were to tell him what we think the numbers are, he would probably be skeptical. He would think that we are mistakenly assuming that his degrees of belief are more precise than they in fact are.

This does not settle the issue. The point is only that is it a mistake to assume from the start that an individual's degrees of belief cannot help but have precise strengths, the difficulty merely being one of finding out what they are. This may be right, but it is not obviously right. An argument is needed. Moreover, the best argument would be one that described how, contrary to first appearances, an individual's degrees of beliefs can be precisely measured.

Probabilists have tried to supply such arguments. Their basic assumption is that both casual introspection and casual observation are misdirected. Our feelings of conviction are the natural objects of the former, but the strength with which we believe something is not the same as the strength of these feelings. As Ramsey remarked, "The beliefs we hold most strongly are often accompanied by practically no feeling at all; no one feels strongly about things he takes for granted."[2] On the other hand, our everyday actions are the natural objects of the latter, but our everyday actions are enmeshed in contexts that make it impossible to see them as the produce of some particular degree of belief rather than another.

Nevertheless, according to probabilists, there is something right about this latter approach. Beliefs, they say, are dispositions that in combination with desires produce behavior. Thus, the right way to determine how strongly individuals believe something is to determine how strongly they are disposed to act on it, but this, they insist, is something best discovered in tests specifically designed to reveal strength of belief. The trick is to find test situations in which the individual's actions can only be interpreted, or at least are best interpreted, as the products of specific degrees of belief.

Various tests have been proposed, some of which are meant to determine simultaneously both strengths of belief and strengths of desire while others are meant to determine only strengths of belief, with minimal assumptions about value lurking in the background. For example, a simple test of the latter sort is one in which a person is asked to post odds on the truth of propositions, with his opponent then being free to determine all other details of the bets, including which side of the bet to take and its size. The odds that he would be willing to post are said to represent his degrees of confidence in these propositions. If the odds he would post on a proposition are $x:y$, his degree of confidence in it $= x/x+y$.[3]

The most obvious drawback about this suggestion is that if this person is like most other individuals, he would volunteer to post precise odds only on a very few propositions, perhaps only on those that concern games of chance and the like. On most others he would be unwilling to do so. Indeed, to post exact odds on a wide variety of propositions would be to commit the betting analogue of what informal logic text books call 'the fallacy of false precision'.

We can force him to set odds, of course, but then the question is whether he chose a particular set of odds rather than another simply because he was forced to choose something. Other odds might be equally agreeable to him. So, why think that the odds he would post reflect his preexisting degrees of confidence in these propositions? Why even think that they reflect his existing degrees of confidence – i.e., the degrees of confidence he has, given that he has been forced to post odds? Suppose I tell an bank teller that I do not care whether I am paid in tens or in twenties but that the teller nonetheless insists that I make a choice. I say: "Give me twenties then." Does this show that I was not telling the truth when I said that I was indifferent, that I really preferred the twenties all along? Does it even show that I now prefer the twenties?

Moreover, the odds a person would post will vary with what he takes to be the nature of the betting situation, including what he takes to be the knowledge and skill of his opponent. If he is convinced that his opponent is more knowledgeable than he himself is, this will typically cause him to adopt a more conservative betting strategy than otherwise, which in turn can affect the odds he is willing to post. For example, if he believes that his betting opponent is a perfect calculator of probabilities, he may be disposed to go to great lengths to avoid posting incoherent odds. On the other hand, if he believes that his opponent is a poor calculator, he may not be disposed to worry as much about avoiding incoherence.

Suppose we attempt to deal with this problem by specifying in detail what a person takes to be the nature of the betting situation, including his views about the knowledge and skill of his opponent. Then other problems arise. We have now used his beliefs about the betting situation to specify the relevant test, but this was supposed to be a test that we could use to measure his beliefs. Besides, which beliefs are the relevant ones? Should we assume that he believes with full confidence that his opponent is more knowledgeable than he himself is? Or should we assume instead that he believes with full confidence that his opponent is equally knowledgeable as he himself? Or should we perhaps assume that he has a significant degree of belief in each of these propositions? Or then again, should we assume something altogether different? Moreover, what would be the rationale for our choice? Why should a situation in which a person has one of these beliefs rather than the others be of special interest? Why is it privileged? Why should the odds that he would set in it be taken as a measure of his degrees of confidence?

There are yet other difficulties. If we say that his confidence in a proposition is to be measured by the odds he would set on it were he in a betting situation of a specified kind, we encounter a problem that plagues many counterfactual accounts — viz., how to handle propositions about the counterfactual situation itself. Consider the proposition that he is now in a betting situation of the specified kind. If he were in a situation in which this proposition is true, he might set very high odds on its truth. Yet this need not indicate that he is now highly confident of its truth.[4]

Problems analogous to these will face any other proposed test as well. There is, for example, no way to read off precise degrees of belief from an individual's expressed preferences. Consider a test in which a person is asked to pick a sum of money such that she would be indifferent between receiving this amount and receiving a ticket that pays her $100 if P is true and $0 if P is false. If she picks, say, $75 as the point of indifference, her strength of belief in P, it is said, must be 0.75.[5] The assumption is that her preferences between alternatives reflect her subjective estimated utilities. Thus, if her degree of belief were anything other than 0.75, she would not be indifferent between the above two alternatives.[6]

Suppose we ignore any worries about money not being a suitable unit of value. Even so, the same kind of problems as above arise once again. With most propositions a person would feel discomfort at having to state a precise point of indifference. She would not do so willingly. We can force her to do so, but then the sums she picks need not reflect her degrees of belief. She simply had to pick some sum.[7] In addition, whatever sum she chooses can be affected by the desirability of P itself as well as the desirability of the consequences she believes it to have.

We might try to deal with this last problem by imposing yet further conditions, but if so, these conditions cannot themselves make specific presuppositions about what a person believes, and the degree to which she believes it, since this is what we are trying to measure. On the other hand, if the conditions do not make presuppositions about what a person believes, they will not be able to get at the root of this problem. Consider, for example, Frank Ramsey's proposed method for measuring degrees of belief.

The first and most basic step in Ramsey's method is to determine an individual's degree of belief in an ethically neutral proposition. A proposition P is ethically neutral for the individual if two possible worlds differing only in regard to the truth of P are always of equal value for her. Suppose P is such a proposition, and suppose in addition that the individual is not indifferent between outcome A and outcome B; but that she is indifferent between the gambles $(A$ if P, B if $\neg P)$ and $(A$ if $\neg P$, B if $P.)$. Then, says Ramsey, her degree of belief in P must be 0.50.

But why? The definition of ethical neutrality guarantees that she does not intrinsically value P, but in certain situations she might nonetheless value it for the consequences she thinks it would produce. Ramsey attempts to rule this out by stipulating that A and B are something close to complete possible worlds. In particular, he stipulates that A and B must be maximally specific, subject to the constraint that each is compatible with either the truth or falsity of P. This stipulation is so strong that his test is no longer a feasible one for us to use, but it is not a theoretically sound one either, since what is relevant here is what the individual *believes* about A, B and P.

Suppose she believes with some degree of confidence that, say, $\neg P$ in conjunction with whatever is the less desirable of the two outcomes, A and B, would produce something else of value. Then she can be indifferent between the above two gambles even if her degree of belief in $P \neq 0.50$. Ramsey needs to rule out such possibilities, but he cannot do so simply by stipulating that she believes with full confidence that A and B are as specific as it is possible for them to be, since the point of his procedure is to determine her degrees of belief by her preferences.[8]

Consider, then, a different tack. We again ask the individual to pick a sum of money such that she would be indifferent between receiving this amount and receiving a ticket that pays her \$100 if P is true and \$0 if P is false, only now we ask her to make her choice as if she were indifferent between P and not P considered in themselves and as if, in addition, she were indifferent to whatever she believes its consequences would be. The advantages of this tack is that it does not make specific presuppositions about what she believes. On the other hand, she is now being asked to tell us what sum she *would* pick *were* certain conditions to be met. In effect, we are asking her to make a hypothesis about herself and her preferences. This is a step yet further away from a natural expression of her preferences, and hence there is even less reason to think that it invariably provides an accurate measure of her present degrees of belief.

Thus, none of these proposed tests succeed, and no other betting test can succeed either. They cannot succeed even if we grant the theoretical presuppositions of the tests. What these tests presuppose is that beliefs and desires are dispositions that combine to produce behavior and that the measure of beliefs and desires is not casual introspection or observation but rather the behavior or the preferences exhibited in these specifically designed tests. The problem, however, is that no piece of betting behavior and no expression of betting preferences is indicative of a specific degree of belief with a specific content. Rather, any number of combinations of degrees of beliefs and desires in any number of propositions might account for the behavior or the preferences and account for them not just in the sense that they might possibly be the product of any of these combinations. The point here is not one that requires some sort of verificationism. The point, rather, is that any number of vastly different combinations will be equally plausible given the theoretical presuppositions of the tests themselves.

What is true of betting tests is true of behavioral and preferential tests in general. And to make matters worse, it is not just that we cannot go from specific behavior or preferences to specific beliefs and desires. We cannot go in the other direction either. Even if we assume that an individual has a strong desire for_____ and a strong belief that X will produce_____, we cannot assume that he prefers X over the other alternatives. His other beliefs and desires can defeat this belief and desire, so that his strongest disposition may be to do or to prefer something other than X. This is just to say that the worst distorting factors of any proposed behavioral test for beliefs are the presence of phenomena of just the sort that we are trying to measure—other beliefs and desires.

So, even if we grant that beliefs and desires are best understood as dispositions that combine to produce behavior, there are special problems of measurement. The problem is not just the standard one of there possibly being distorting factors. The analogy is not one of measuring the weight of an object by putting it on a scale and then worrying about various factors that might possibly distort the result.[9] A better analogy is that of trying to determine the weights of the various parts of an object when our only tests are ones that involve placing the entire object on a scale.

This is a problem that cannot be made to go away by gathering more data. It might seem otherwise. If we found a way for an individual to express her preferences over a huge range of alternatives, we might seem to be in a better position to assign precise degrees of belief and desire to her. We could proceed in the usual way, assuming that the preferred alternative is always the one with the greater subjective estimated utility, only now we would have many more preferences with which to work. But in fact, gathering more information of the same kind does not help. The problem is still there smirking at us. Different combinations of beliefs and desires will still provide equally plausible interpretations of even these extended preferences.

The extra preferences do make a difference, however. They make the problems of measurement worse, since the more of an individual's preferences we have to work with, the less likely it is that they can be represented as following subjective estimated utilities. For them to be so represented, they must be transitive and trichotomous, and they must also satisfy what Savage calls 'the sure-thing principle'.[10] Unfortunately, the empirical evidence indicates that an individual's preferences concerning a wide and complex range of alternatives are unlikely to satisfy these conditions. Like the subjective perceptions of sweetness for beverages that differ minutely in sugar content, they are unlikely to have the requisite orderliness.[11]

This is not at all surprising. It is just what common sense would lead us to suspect. However, it does create a dilemma for anyone who thinks that precise degrees of belief and desire can be squeezed out from an individual's preferences with the help of the assumption that preference follows estimated utility. On the one hand, the method requires that we have access to a huge number of the person's preferences. Otherwise, we will not have enough data to be able even to begin making fine distinctions with respect to her strengths of belief. On the other hand, if we have access to a huge number of her preferences, they are unlikely to satisfy the ordering conditions that they must satisfy if they are to be represented as following subjective estimated utilities. Moreover, if we fiddle with them in order to get the required orderliness, or if we can ask her to do so, we lose whatever reason we had for thinking that they can be used to measure her current degrees of belief.[12]

We can always fall back on a normative claim. We can insist that if the individual's preferences are to be rational, they must meet these ordering conditions and, thus, they must be representable as following subjective estimated utility. This may be so, but it simply changes the subject. The argument in question requires assumptions about the individual's actual preferences. The hope was that we could use a theory about her actual preferences—namely, that they follow subjective estimated utility—to generate a plausible and precise measure of her degrees of belief.

The conclusion is inescapable. There are no tests for measuring precise degrees of belief. For any proposition P, it will be possible to devise a test that will allow us to extract a number that the individual be interpreted as assigning to P. The difficulty is one of finding a rationale for thinking that it is her current degree of belief in P that we are measuring. There is no solution to this difficulty.

Might not we nonetheless insist that the problem is merely one of measurement, that she does have precise degrees of belief but that we lack a way of determining what they are? This once again misconstrues the nature of the problem. It is not as if common sense or introspection or something else suggests that she really does have precise degrees of belief but that we run into troubles when we try to determine what they are. The difficulty, rather, is that finding an adequate reason for thinking that people typically do have precise degrees of belief in a wide variety of propositions. Casual introspection and casual observation suggest just the opposite. The strategy was to counter this initial appearance by finding an acceptable test for measuring degrees of belief, but all of the proposed tests are inadequate.

So, in the end we shall just have to admit that individuals typically do not have precise degrees of confidence.[13] This is especially obvious when the propositions are ones an individual has never explicitly considered, but it is also so for those propositions about which he does have an explicit opinion. Even these opinions are often irremediably vague. He is more confident that his keys are somewhere in his house than in his office, and likewise he is more confident that Sue will be on time for dinner tonight than that she will remember to bring the book he lent her, but there may be no precise way to rank his degree of belief in either of the first two propositions against his degree of belief in either the third or fourth proposition. Sometimes the most that can be said is that he is highly confident of a proposition's truth or that he is somewhat more confident of its truth than he is of the truth of its negation or that he is roughly as confident of it as of its negation.[14]

Probabilists have been increasingly willing to admit this. Consider Bas van Fraassen's views, for example. He concedes that we commonly have only vague degrees of belief, but he nonetheless insists that the probability calculus can be used as a logic of opinion. To illustrate how, van Fraassen introduces the notion of a representor. A person's representor is the class of all those probability functions that satisfy her vague degrees of belief. So, for example, suppose a person is more confident that the Yankees will win next year's World Series than she is that the Red Sox will win, and she is more confident of either than she is of the Cubs. Only those functions that make the probability of the Yankees' winning greater than that of the Red Sox's winning and that make the probability of the Red Sox's winning greater than that of the Cubs' winning can satisfy these degrees of belief. The total set of her degrees of belief is rational, then, only if there is some probability function capable of satisfying them. Of course, if there is one such function, there will be many, but this only shows that there are a variety of ways of making her degrees of belief more precise. On the other hand, if her representor is empty — if no possible assignments of probabilities can satisfy all of her degrees of belief — then there is no way compatible with the probability calculus to make her opinions more precise. On any interpretation, her opinions violate the probability calculus, and thus, says van Fraassen, they are irrational. This is irrationality by way of commission. There is also irrationality by way of omission. If every member of her representor class (i.e., if every assignment of probabilities that satisfies her overt judgments) entails that the probability of X is greater than Y but less than Z, then she is committed on pains of irrationality to believing X with greater confidence than Y but with less confidence than Z.[15]

This kind of view leaves intact the basic idea of probabilism — the idea that it is irrational for an individual's degrees of belief to violate the probability calculus — and it has the advantage of doing so without unrealistic psychological assumptions about the precision of her degrees of belief. The disadvantage of the view is that it leaves untouched the worry with which we began — *viz.*, that no such account is demanding enough. In recognition of this, it is not unusual for probabilists to admit that the avoidance of incoherence is only necessary for rationality. It is not sufficient. There are other requirements as well.[16]

This does not entirely do away with the problem, however. Probabilists want the requirement of coherence to have considerable bite, but the more vague a person's degrees of belief are, the less bite it will have. Indeed, the more vague his degrees of beliefs, the more the requirement of coherence will begin to resemble a mere requirement of consistency on his beliefs *simpliciter.* But then, just as no one would be tempted to say that mere consistency among his beliefs *simpliciter* is nearly enough to make them rational, so too no one should be tempted to say that mere coherency among his degrees of belief is nearly enough to make them rational. This, in turn, means that even if coherence is a necessary condition of rationality, most of the burden of an account of rational degrees of belief will have to be carried by something other than the requirement of coherence.

To make matters worse for the probabilist, there are even more devastating problems lurking in the other direction. To be sure, coherence is not nearly sufficient for rationality, but it is not absolutely necessary either. The probabilist's view, remember, is not just that it is rational for a person to try to avoid incoherence. It is not just that this is a goal that he must strive for. The idea, rather, is that if he is to be rational, he must actually succeed. A failure to do so is always and everywhere irrational. The idea, in other words, is that rationality requires him to be a perfect calculator of probabilistic relations and hence also a perfect calculator of logical relations.

But of course, he is not a perfect calculator. Nor can he be. Some logical and probabilistic relations are so complex that no one is capable of understanding them. This is so even if in principle all such relations could be broken down into simpler ones that the person can understand. Combinations of these simpler relations can still be so complex as to exceed his capacities. He does well enough in most circumstances, no doubt. It may even be a condition of his believing something at all that he recognizes many of its most obvious implications. Likewise, it may be a condition of his having beliefs at all that there is a limit to his incoherency. He must be an adequate enough calculator. His status as a believer and agent may depend upon it. On the other hand, it does not depend upon his being a perfect calculator.[17] Indeed, he lacks the cognitive powers to be such. Why, then, should we be interested in a theory of rationality that in effect presupposes the perspective of a perfect calculator to evaluate an individual's beliefs?

The lack of concern that probabilists have shown for this question might suggest that there is an easy answer to it, and in fact there does seem to be. The perfect calculator represents an ideal to which individuals aspire. As such it can be used to measure a person's irrationality, and this is so even if it is an idea that he is incapable of satisfying. It is enough that he can do better or worse jobs of approximating it. The more closely he approximates it, the more rational he is.

Compare this with idealizations in science. Scientists theorize about idealized entities in idealized circumstances, ones which model the real phenomena less than perfectly. The gas laws apply first and foremost to perfect gases. The laws of conservation and momentum apply first and foremost to closed and isolated systems. Nonetheless, such laws can help explain real phenomena. They can do so because the actual phenomena approximate the workings of the idealized model.

Why should something analogous not be true of theories of rationality? In particular, suppose we take it as a working assumption, a presupposition for our theorizing about rationality, that the best way to measure an individual's rationality is to compare what he does and believes and what an ideally rational being would do or believe in the same situation.[18] Doesn't this presupposition solve the difficulty? It would if it were both relevant and plausible, but it cannot be both. If construed in one way the presupposition is irrelevant to questions of human rationality, if construed in another it is implausible. If by an ideally rational agent we mean someone who is like the individual but who does and believes only what is rational, then the individual's rationality can be measured by comparing what he does and believes with what this ideally rational agent would do and believe in the same situation. However, this makes the above presupposition irrelevant to the question at hand, since such an agent is no more or less capable of determining logical and probabilistic relations than the individual is. So, insofar as the problem is one of showing that even those incoherencies that are beyond his ken can make an individual irrational, an appeal to what this kind of ideally rational agent would do or believe is useless. Indeed, it is worse than useless. For if there are incoherencies that not even this ideally rational agent would avoid, then these same incoherencies need not make the individual irrational either.

On the other hand, the above presupposition is implausible if by ideally rational agent we mean someone whose cognitive capacities exceeded the individual's. The problem now is that although it may always be rational for such an agent to avoid incoherencies, it is no longer clear what this has to do with the individual himself. What is the concrete action that it would be rational for Superman to take if he finds himself in the path of a speeding train? Perhaps to stick out his hand, since given his abilities this will stop the train. No one will suggest that this is the rational thing for an ordinary person to do in such a situation. It is no more plausible to suggest that it is always and everywhere rational for a person to believe only that which a logical Superman would believe in the same situation. It is one thing to measure a person's rationality by comparing what he does and believes with what he or someone with abilities recognizably similar to him would ideally do and believe. it is quite another to do so by comparing what he does and believes with what some ideally powerful being would do or believe.

Idealizations in philosophy have their limits. The limits are vague, just as they are in science, but if our theory is to be one of human rationality, the limits cannot be allowed to exceed that which is recognizably human. Theories of human rationality must be concerned with human points of view. The relevant point of view might be a person's point of view idealized. It might be a matter, for example, of what she would do or think were she to be ideally reflective and ideally careful. However, it cannot be a matter of what someone with ideal cognitive powers would do or think in her situation. The rough rule is that we are to limit ourselves to idealizations of the conditions under which she, as a normal human being, employs her various cognitive abilities and skills. Thus, we can legitimately idealize away various distorting conditions that interfere with her being able to employ these abilities and skills, but we are to avoid idealizations of the abilities and skills themselves. Ideal observer theories are no more plausible in epistemology than they are in ethics.[19]

The temptation to think otherwise can be discouraged by remembering that not every intellectual ideal is an ideal of rationality. An individual's degrees of belief are ideally accurate if she believes with full confidence all and only those propositions that are true, but no one thinks that the distance that she departs from this ideal is in general a measure of her irrationality.[20] Or less stringently, we might say that her degrees of belief are ideally accurate if they are perfectly calibrated with the objective probabilities.[21] But once again, no one should think that the distance she departs from this ideal is in general a measure of her irrationality. Being ideally rational is not the same as being ideally accurate. Indeed, any notion of rationality is in part a notion of understandable mistakes. The fact that a person made a mistake of belief does indicate that her belief system is less than ideally accurate, but it need not indicate that it is less than ideally rational.

Even so, it might be objected that the problem here is really just terminological. It can be resolved by distinguishing different senses of 'rational' and corresponding different senses of 'reason'. There is one sense of rational, an egocentric sense, that does not have coherency as a strict prerequisite. In this sense, being rational is roughly a matter of a person's not having an adequate internal reason for retracting her degrees of beliefs. So, incoherence that is beyond her ken need not make her irrational in this sense. On the other hand, there is also a more objective sense of rationality, and in this sense it is always and everywhere irrational for her to have incoherent degrees of belief. If the incoherence is beyond her ken, she will not have an internal reason for retraction, but there nonetheless will be objective reasons for retraction.

This much has to be admitted: there are different senses of rationality, some of which are more objective than others.[22] Nevertheless, distinguishing these different senses does not help with the problem here. For not only is coherence not a prerequisite of rationality in an egocentric sense, it is not a prerequisite of human rationality in any other interesting sense either. Any notion of rationality that makes coherence an utterly strict condition of rationality is in effect asking us to evaluate an individual's degrees of belief from the perspective of someone who is logically perfect but empirically imperfect. We are asked to imagine what someone with perfect knowledge of logical and probabilistic relations but limited empirical knowledge would do or believe in the same situation. Since such a being is always able to recognize incoherency, it is always irrational in the designated sense for an individual's degrees of belief to be incoherent. On the other hand, since such a being need not always be able to recognize merely contingent inaccuracy, it is not always irrational for the individual to have merely contingently inaccurate degrees of belief.

The question is why the perspective of these kinds of beings, with their strange combination of logical savvy and empirical ignorance, should be of interest to us when we are evaluating an individual's beliefs. Any such notion of rationality is asking us to think about questions of rational belief in a peculiar way. It is asking us to use the extent to which a person departs from logical omniscience as a measure of his irrationality but not to use the extent to which he departs from empirical omniscience as a comparable measure. But if a logically omniscient perspective, one in which we make no mistakes in calculating logical implications and probabilities, is an ideal perspective, one to which we aspire and one which we can do better or worse jobs of approximating, so too is an empirically omniscient perspective. So, if this were a reason to regard all departures from logical omniscience as departures from ideal rationality, it would be an equally good reason to regard all departures from empirical omniscience as departures from ideal rationality. But of course, no one wants to claim this.

Why, then, have epistemologists found it so tempting to regard all departures from logical omniscience as departures from some kind of ideal rationality? I have two conjectures, neither flattering. The first is that it is largely a matter of theoretical convenience. Epistemologists want rational belief-systems to have characteristic structure. Logic and probability conveniently provide them with such a structure. So, they are seduced into thinking that mistakes in calculating logical implications and probabilities are always symptomatic of irrationality while other mistakes are not, despite the fact that there is no obvious rationale for such an asymmetry and despite the fact that it forces us to conclude that, for example, Frege's beliefs about how to axiomatize set theory, as expressed in *The Basic Laws of Arithmetic,* were irrational, since they turned out to be inconsistent.[23]

The second conjecture is that the temptation arises out of a view of human reason that has been largely been discarded but whose influence nonetheless lingers. According to this view, reason is conceived as a special faculty that is tacked on, as it were, to our other cognitive faculties and whose operations are sharply distinct from them. These other faculties—those associated with perceiving, remembering, introspecting, and imagining, for example—are arational. They simply provide raw data for reason. Reason's job is to perform calculations upon this data, correcting inconsistencies as well as drawing out its implications. Without this special faculty we would be arational. With it we are capable of both rationality and irrationality. When reason performs its calculations well, we are rational. Otherwise we are not.[24]

Radical empiricist positions—phenomenalism, for example—constitute the purest expressions of such views. According to the phenomenalist, our various senses provide reason with arational data—sense data—and then reason performs its complicated computations on it. Of course, not many philosophers are prepared to defend phenomenalism anymore,[25] and likewise not many would be prepared to defend the view of rationality it presupposes. A more plausible view, we think, is that our cognitive faculties are reason-saturated. Judgment and hence reason pervades all our cognitive activities—perceiving, remembering, introspecting, etc.

Still, the outlines of the older picture can be discerned in views that make coherence a strict requirement of rationality. Beliefs have replaced sense data as the input. Perception, memory, imagining, and the like are belief-producing mechanisms. They produce a huge range of beliefs, from relatively simple perceptual ones to complex theoretical ones. However, reason's function is assumed to be essentially the same. It is to take this data which is given to it from other sources and to perform calculations upon it, checking it for inconsistency, incoherency, and the like. If these checks are not done accurately, if some inconsistencies and incoherencies remain, we are to that extent irrational. Thus, mistakes of logic and the like are invariably symptomatic of irrationality while other kinds of mistakes are not. The former are symptomatic of irrationality because they are due to the less than perfect workings of the special faculty of reason while our other mistakes are due to the less than perfect workings of essentially arational processes such as perceiving, introspecting, remembering, and so on.

Once we dismiss the idea that there is this special and distinct faculty of reason, we lose the rationale for thinking that mistakes in calculating probabilities are always and everywhere symptomatic of irrationality while other mistakes are not. Coherence is not an utterly strict prerequisite of egocentric rationality, and it is not an utterly strict prerequisite of human rationality in any other interesting sense either.

This is not to say that the probability calculus is epistemically irrelevant. It clearly is relevant. It has an especially important role to play in intellectual guidance, for example. The discovery of probabilistic incoherence, like the discovery of logical inconsistency, tells us as individuals that it it is not possible for all of our opinions to be accurate, and it thus puts us on guard about them. The mistake of the probabilists is one of oversimplifying this role. It is the mistake of making the avoidance of incoherence into an epistemic categorical imperative.

NOTES

1. In general, probabilists require not just finite additivity but also countable additivity. However, there are those (e.g., de Finetti) who resist this on the grounds that it might be rational to believe that the tickets in a denumerably infinite lottery are equally likely to win. For a defense of the stronger and mathematically more convenient form of additivity, see Brian Skyrms, *Pragmatics and Empiricism* (New Haven, Conn., 1984), especially pp. 21–23.

2. See F. P. Ramsey, "Truth and Probability," in *The Foundations of Mathematics and Other Logical Essays,* edited by R. B. Braithwaite (London, 1931), 156–98.

3. "One plausible measure of a man's partial belief is thus the odds he will determine to bet where his greedy but otherwise mysterious opponent subsequently decides both the stake size and the direction of the bet. From this situation the irrelevant effects are absent of a man's other beliefs, of his itch or distaste for gambling, or his preference for high or for low stakes, of his desires that some things should be true and others not and of the variable utility of money. The claim is that the only remaining factor disposing a man to settle on some odds in preference to others just is the strength of his partial belief, of which the odds are therefore a fair measure." D. H. Mellor, *The Matter of Chance* (Cambridge, 1970), 37. See also F. Jackson and R. Pargetter, "A Modified Dutch Book Argument," *Philosophical Studies* 29 (1976): 403–07.

4. Another complication is the phenomenon of anchoring. The odds a person would post on a series of propositions can be affected by the order in which he considers them. See Jon Elster, *Ulysses and the Sirens* (Cambridge, 1984), 128–33.

5. Compare, e.g., with H. Raiffa, *Decision Analysis* (Reading, Mass., 1968).

6. The assumption is not that a person consciously makes calculations of estimated utility but only that she ranks her preferences just "as though" she did. See Richard Jeffrey, "Ethics and the Logic of Decision," *Journal of Philosophy* 62 (1965): 528–39; and Ellery Eells, *Rational Decision and Causality* (Cambridge, 1982), 33–34.

7. Compare with Mark Kaplan, "Bayesianism Without the Black Box," *Philosophy of Science* 6 (1989): 49–69.

8. See Ramsey, "Truth and Probability."

9. See Eells, *Rational Decision and Causality,* 43.

10. See L. J. Savage, *The Foundations of Statistics,* 2d ed. (New York, 1972). Transitivity requires someone to prefer A to C if he prefers A to B and B to C. *Trichotomy requires that for*

any two outcomes A and *B* in the domain in question, either he prefers *A* to *B* or he prefers *B* to *C* or he is indifferent between them. The sure-thing principle requires that if acts *A* and *B* would have the same outcome given a possible state of nature, then which act he prefers is independent of that outcome; his preference of one over the other is instead wholly a matter of those states of nature in which the two acts would have different outcomes.

11. See, e.g., K. R. MacCrimmon, "Descriptive and Normative Implications of the Decision-theory Postulates" in *Risk and Uncertainty*, edited by K. Borch and J. Mossin (New York, 1968), 3–23; P. Slovic and A. Tversky, "Who Accepts Savage's Axiom?" *Behavioral Science* 19 (1974): 368–73; A. Tversky, "Intransitivity of Preferences," *Psychological Review* 76(1971): 105–10; *Judgement Under Uncertainty: Heuristics and Biases,* edited by D. Kaheman, P. Slovic, and A. Tversky, "Prospect Theory: An Analysis of Decision Under Risk," *Econometrica* 47 (1979): 263–91.

12. There are various ways of trying to explain away the empirical evidence that indicates our preferences do not always follow subjective estimated utility. We might try doing so, e.g., in terms of a special aversion to risk or in terms of second-order uncertainty about first-order desires and beliefs. These maneuvers might have some plausibility if we could presume that an individual typically has precise degrees of belief and desire. For then, the problem would merely be one of reconciling this presupposition with the recalcitrant empirical data. But in fact this is not our situation. What we are looking for is some argument for thinking that the individual really does have precise degrees of beliefs. But insofar as this is what we are looking for, all of these maneuvers seem *ad hoc.* Indeed, they all make the overall problem of measurement even more difficult. They thus make it more difficult to argue, as opposed to assume, that we typically have precise degrees of belief in a wide variety of propositions. Contrast with Eells, *Rational Decision and Causality,* esp. 33–41.

13. Suppose it is instead claimed that the individual has precise confidence-intervals for almost every proposition that he can understand, the idea being that although he may be of many minds about a proposition, there is nonetheless a unique upper bound to his confidence in a proposition as well as a unique lower bound. His overall attitude towards the proposition is defined by these upper and lower bounds. Proposals of this sort have been forwarded by Henry Kyburg, *Probability and the Logic of Rational Belief* (Middletown, Conn., 1961) and I. J. Good, *The Estimation of Probabilities* (Cambridge, Mass., 1965). For a related view, see Isaac Levi, *The Enterprise of Knowledge* (Cambridge, Mass., 1980). However, none of these proposals avoid the basic difficulty here either. Casual introspection and observation does not reveal that our confidence in various propositions typically has precise upper and lower bounds, and no behavioral test can plausibly be construed as revealing such bounds. We always can imagine a series of tests that would elicit precise bounds from an individual, but then the question is why this series of tests rather than a somewhat different one should be taken as a correct measure of an actual individual's confidence-intervals.

14. Might it be a condition of rationality that we strive to make our degrees of belief as fine as possible? Even if it were, we would be still left with the question of what degrees of belief are rational in the interim. But in fact, it is not always rational to try to make our degrees of belief more precise. For starters, there may not be much that we can do to make them more precise, but in addition, it would not always be rational for us to do so even if we could. We have better things to do. Doing so would sometimes even be positively harmful. The finer our degrees of belief, the more complicated our deliberations and inquiries become, and this in turn may increase the likelihood of our making mistakes. Indeed, having extremely fine degrees of belief might make deliberation on all but the simplest matters next to impossible. See Gilbert, Harman, *Change in View* (Cambridge, Mass., 1986).

15. See Bas van Fraassen, "Empiricism in the Philosophy of Science," in *Images of Science,* edited by P. Churchland and C. Hooker (Chigago, 1985). For similar views, see Brian Skyrms, *Pragmatics and Empiricism*, especially 26–29; Brian Ellis, *Rational Belief Systems* (Oxford, 1979); Richard Jeffrey, "Bayesianism with a Human Face," in *Testing Scientific Theories*, edited by J. Earman (Minneapolis, 1983), 133–156; Mark Kaplan, Bayesianism Without the Black Box."

16. "Indeed, the Bayesian framework is too roomy in that it permits belief functions that would be entertained only by a fool, and value assignments that would be entertained only by a monster. But I take it that the formulation and critique of particular probability and value assignments must be largely conducted in situ, with the aid of facts about the agent, his language, his community, and his special situation; and that although such activity should use the Bayesian framework, it belongs to other disciplines — say, to inductive logic, and to ethics". Richard C. Jeffrey, *The Logic of Decision*, 2d ed. (Chicago, 1983), 211. See also van Fraassen, "Empiricism in the Philosophy of Science" and Skyrms, *Pragmatics and Empiricism*.

17. Compare with Christopher Cherniak, *Minimal Rationality* (Cambridge, Mass., 1986).

18. See Brian Ellis, *Rational Belief Systems*. See also Robert Stalnaker, *Inquiry* (Cambridge, 1984), especially 84.

19. Contrast with Roderick Firth who in an uncharacteristically infelicitous phrase talks of an omniscient, disinterested, dispassionate but "in other respects normal observer." This cannot be read as anything other than an unintended joke. See Firth, "Ethical Absolutism and the Ideal Observer," in *Readings in Ethical Theory,* edited by W. Sellars and J. Hospers (New York, 1970), 200–221.

20. "In this ultimate meaning it seems to me that we can identify reasonable opinion with the opinion of an ideal person in similar circumstances. What, however, would this ideal person's opinion be? As has previously been remarked, the highest ideal would be always to have a true opinion and be certain of it; but this ideal is more suited to God than to man." F. P. Ramsey, "Truth and Probability."

21. See Bas van Fraassen, "Calibration: A Frequency Interpretation of Personal Probability," in *Physics, Philosophy, and Psychoanalysis*, edited by R. S. Cohen and L. Laudan (Dordrecht, 1983), 295–319.

22. See Richard Foley, *The Theory of Epistemic Rationality* (Cambridge, Mass., 1987).

23. In "Truth and Probability," Ramsey distinguished formal logic from human logic. The latter, according to Ramsey, tells us how to think. Ramsey went on to complain that "nearly all philosophical thought about human logic and especially about induction has tried to reduce it in some way to formal logic."

24. Theological concerns can also be seen at work here. The assumption is that we have higher and lower faculties, the lower ones (e.g, perception) we share with the animals and the higher one (reason) we share with God. This encourages the view of reason as an altogether discrete faculty, one whose operations are fundamentally different from those of other cognitive faculties. Compare with Edward Craig, *The Mind of God and the Works of Man* (Oxford, 1986).

25. There are exceptions. For the most subtle defense of phenomenalism that I know of, see Richard Fumerton's *Metaphysical and Epistemological Problems of Perception* (Lincoln, Neb., 1985).

Singular Explanation
and the Social Sciences

DAVID-HILLEL RUBEN

1. DIFFERENCE THEORY

Are explanations in the social sciences fundamentally (logically or structurally) different from explanations in the natural sciences? Many philosophers think that they are, and I call such philosophers 'difference theorists'. Many difference theorists locate that difference in the alleged fact that only in the natural sciences does explanation essentially include laws.

For these theorists, the difference theory is held as a consequence of two more fundamental beliefs: (1) At least some (full) explanations in the social sciences do not include laws; (2) All (full) explanations in the natural sciences do include laws. For example, Peter Winch criticizes and rejects Mill's view that "understanding a social institution consists in observing regularities in the behaviour of its participants and expressing these regularities in the form of a generalisation. . .[the] position of the sociological investigator (in a broad sense) can be regarded as comparable. . .with that of the natural scientist."[1] Daniel Taylor argues that "Scientific explanations involve universal propositions. . . . If you think of an historical event and try to imagine explaining it in a way which fulfills these criteria you will see the difficulties at once."[2] Michael Lesnoff claims that, quite unlike the explanations of physical science, ". . .at whatever level of detail a social phenomenon is investigated, the correct explanation may or may not conform to general laws."[3] Finally, A. R. Louch opposes "the univocal theory of explanation that all explanation consists in bringing a case under a law. This view has an initial plausibility when developed within the domain of the science of mechanics. . .but as applied to human performance it is totally irrelevant. . . ."[4] For these writers, and many more, full explanations of natural phenomena include laws; full explanations of social phenomena may not, or do not. Hence, explanations in the two types of science fundamentally differ.

These difference theorists are not really interested *per se* in there being a difference between explanations in the two types of science. Their basic belief is (1) that some full explanations in the social sciences do not include laws. Since they sometimes accept rather uncritically the covering law theory of explanation for the natural sciences, a view which does require the inclusion of laws in any full explanation, they are driven to being difference theorists. But if they could be convinced that full explanations in the natural sciences can also do without laws, that is, that (2) is false, they would not mind the defeat of difference theory. They would think that their most important view (1) had been further vindicated.

'Full explanations. . .can do without laws' might be ambiguous. Some of these difference theorists believe that there are full explanations in the social sciences which include no laws, because there are in principle no such laws to be had. On their view, no laws (at any level) governing these phenomena exist. That is, they believe that all or part of the subject matter of the social sciences is radically anomic. I am not concerned with their view here (although I think that it is of great interest). I assume, for the purposes of this essay, that everything that occurs, occurs nomically, is governed by some law or other (the law might be deterministic or stochastic). The question before us is not whether there *are* laws at some level governing everything, but whether every full scientific explanation must contain the statement of such a law.

I want to look at some old literature, which I think contains insights not yet fully appreciated. Michael Scriven rejects the difference theory on the grounds that (1) is true but (2) is false.[5] Moreover, Scriven never, as far as I am aware, supposes that anything occurs anomically. Rather, the question he sets himself is that of the place, if any, for those laws in full explanation. This essay argues against the difference theory when it is held as a consequence of (1) and (2). Like Scriven, I think that (1) is true and (2) is false, so no difference between the logic of explanation in the natural and social sciences has been demonstrated. Of course, it is consistent with my thesis that the difference theory may be true for some other reason.

However, there is a sting in my view that should cool the ardor of the proponent of (1) to some extent, and comfort his covering law opponent. Explanations in both natural and social science need laws in other ways, even when not as part of the explanation itself. Surprisingly perhaps, the covering law theorist, in his zeal to demonstrate that laws are a part of every full explanation, has tended to neglect the other ways in which laws are important for explanation. These other ways make explanations in both types of science somewhat more like the explanations required by the covering law theory than (1)'s truth and (2)'s falsity might have otherwise led one to suppose. The distance between my view and the covering law theory is not as great as it might at first appear to be.

2.   THE COVERING LAW THEORY

By 'the covering law theory', I refer to any theory of explanation which requires that every full explanation include essentially at least one law or lawlike generalization, whose role in the explanation is to "cover" the particular event being explained. Perhaps the best-known statement of such a theory is that by Carl Hempel. In a series of important writings, beginning with "The Function of General Laws in History" (1942), followed in turn by the jointly authored (with Paul Oppenheim) "Studies in the Logic of Explanation" (1948), "Aspects of Scientific Explanation" (1965), and *The Philosophy of the Natural Sciences* (1966), Hempel developed an account of singular explanation which has come to be widely known as the covering law theory. It is only singular explanation (e.g., the explanation of why some token event or particular phenomenon occurred or has some characteristic) which shall be the focus here; in particular, I will not discuss Hempel's account of the explanation of laws or regularities.[6]

Briefly, Hempel's covering law theory is that there are two distinct "models" of explanation: Deductive-Nomological and Inductive-Statistical.[7] What both models have in common is agreement about the logical form that all explanations have, and, as a consequence, the place of laws in explanations of both kinds. On Hempel's view, all full explanations (and hence all full singular explanations) are arguments. Let us call this view 'the argument thesis'. Some full explanations are deductively sound arguments; others are inductively good arguments. Hempel does not assume that there can be only one full explanation for an explanandum; there may be more than one sound or good explanatory argument for a single explanandum.[8]

Any plausible version of Hempel's argument thesis must have recourse to some distinction between partial and complete explanation since Hempel must recognize that actual explanations often fail to measure up to the requirements his models set for full explanation. On this view, sometimes the explanations which are actually offered are less than full: elliptical, partial, explanation-sketches, merely enthymemes, incomplete, and so on. There can be good pragmatic or epistemic grounds for giving partial or incomplete explanations, depending on context. On any theory of explanation, we sometimes do not say all that we should say if we were explaining in full. Laws may be omitted entirely from a partial explanation. Sometimes we assume that the audience is in possession of facts which do not stand in need of repetition. At other times, our ignorance does not allow us to fill all of the gaps in the explanation. In such cases, in which we omit information for pragmatic or epistemic reasons, we give partial explanations. But, on the argument thesis, all *full* explanations are sound or good arguments.

Different theories of explanation will disagree about what counts as a full explanation. Some will hold that explanations, as typically given in the ordinary way, are full explanations in their own right; I call the holder of such a view 'an explanatory actualist.' Others (like Hempel) are explanatory idealists, who will argue that full explanations are only those which meet some ideal, rarely if ever achieved in practice.[9] Most of those who have rejected the argument thesis have also been explanatory actualists, inclined to accept our ordinary explanations as full as explanations need ever be: "Now I have an alternative description of what Hempel calls explanation-sketches. . .I regard them as explanations as they stand, not incomplete in any sense in which they should be complete. . ." (Scriven, p. 446).

If Hempel's argument thesis is true, then all full explanations must essentially *include* at least one law or lawlike generalization among its premises. Let us call this 'the law thesis': "an explanatory statement of the form '*q* because *p*' [is] an assertion to this effect: *p* is. . .the case, and there are laws. . .such that. . .*q*. . .follows logically from those laws taken in conjunction with. . .*p* and perhaps other statements."[10] Roughly, if we restrict ourselves to full explanations in the natural and social sciences, the law thesis is equivalent to the denial of (1) and the assertion of (2).

True, there are valid arguments with singular conclusions, among whose premises there is no lawlike generalization. But, given some additional fairly uncontroversial assumptions about what explanations are like (e.g., that one cannot explain *p* on the basis of the conjunction, *p* & *q*), the argument thesis will imply the law thesis.[11] One will need a law to go, in a valid or good argument, from the singular explanans information to the singular explanandum.

It is important to see that the law thesis, as I have explained it, is not just a commitment to there *being* laws that in some sense or other lie behind or underpin the very possibility of explanation. Scriven and Hempel might have no disagreement about this. More specifically, the law thesis requires that a law or lawlike generalization be included in every full explanation.

What is a law? There are widely different responses to this question in the literature, and I do not want the argument of this essay to turn on the answer to that question. In what follows, I assume (like Hempel) that the 'orthodox' answer is correct: a necessary condition for a sentence's stating a deterministic law of nature is that it be a true, universally quantified generalization. There are unorthodox, 'stronger', conceptions of law in the literature, but I stress that nothing in my argument, as far as I can see, turns on the adoption of the orthodox view. If my argument works using the latter view, it would also work if the stronger view is adopted instead.

On the orthodox view, sentences which state deterministic laws of nature typically have or entail something with this form: $(x) (Fx \supset Gx)$.[12] Although the universally quantified conditional might be more complicated than this (e.g., the consequent might also be existentially quantified), it will make no difference to the argument if we only consider sentences with this simple conditional form. I recognize that there are stochastic natural laws; for the sake of simplicity, I restrict myself to the deterministic case.

Hempel expressly applied his models of explanation, and hence the argument and law theses, to the social as well as the natural sciences. Most notoriously, this occurred in his 1942 "The Function of General Laws in History" and the 1959 "The Logic of Functional Analysis." But the same eagerness for application of the models to social and behavioral science is apparent in "Aspects of Scientific Explanation": witness the section of the last mentioned, entitled "The Concept of Rationality and the Logic of Explanation by Reasons."

Why does Hempel subscribe to the argument and law theses? One reason is this. His theory of explanation is in essence a development of this idea: "The explanation. . .may be regarded as an argument to the effect that the phenomenon to be explained. . .was to be expected in virtue of certain explanatory facts."[13] An explanatory "argument shows that. . .the occurrence of the phenomenon was to be expected; and it is in this sense that the explanation enables us to understand why the phenomenon occurred."[14] This idea is summed up by Hempel in his symmetry thesis: every full explanation is a potential prediction, and every full prediction is a potential explanation.

Call the information used in making the prediction 'the predictans'; the event predicted, 'the predictandum'. There is no doubt that we need laws in order to make well-grounded predictions, because in making a prediction we do not have the predictandum event available prior to the prediction, as it were. We have to get to it from some singular event mentioned in the predictans, and the law is required to bridge the gap, to permit our moving from one singular event to another. If the symmetry thesis were true, the need for laws in predictions would transfer to explanation.[15]

Although I reject the symmetry thesis, I would not like to break entirely the connection between explanation and prediction. It is not true that every full prediction is a potential explanation, nor is it true that a full explanation (since, on the view I develop below, it can omit all laws) is itself a potential prediction. But I will argue that, if we have and *know* that we have a full explanation, then laws play a crucial role in that knowledge, and that therefore anyone with this knowledge will be in a position to make predictions.

3. OPPONENTS OF THE COVERING LAW THEORY

I believe that there are strong reasons to dispute the argument thesis; I do not believe that the idea of logical dependence of a conclusion on a set of premises can capture the idea of explanatory dependence, which is the essential contention of the argument thesis. I have argued elsewhere that explanations are typically not arguments, but singular sentences, or conjunctions thereof. I would not want to rest my case for this on the overtly non-argument grammatical form that explanations have as they occur in ordinary speech, but I cannot rehearse my arguments for the rejection of the argument thesis here.[16] A non-argument view of explanation has been developed by Achinstein, Ryle, and Salmon (the list is not meant to be exhaustive).

I argued above that the argument thesis, in conjunction with additional uncontroversial assumptions, leads to the law thesis. But the inverse is not true. Suppose that the argument thesis is false. It does not follow from the fact that not all full explanations are arguments that a law is not a part of every full explanation. It only follows that, if laws are a part of full explanations which are not arguments, the idea of their parthood in such cases is not to be cashed out as that of a premise in an argument. So the absence of laws from even some full explanations does not follow from the fact that some or all explanations are not arguments.

However, the idea that full explanations do not always include laws has been argued for by many of the same philosophers who reject the argument thesis. In numerous essays, Michael Scriven has said things similar to what I would wish to maintain about the role of laws or generalizations in explanation (although I do not need to agree with any of his specific examples). In "Truisms as the Grounds for Historical Explanations," he defended the view that the following was a perfectly *complete or full* explanation as it stood (what he actually said was that it was not incomplete; he was skeptical about the idea of a complete explanation): the full explanation of why William the Conqueror never invaded Scotland is that "he had no desire for the lands of the Scottish nobles, and he secured his northern borders by defeating Malcolm, King of Scotland, in battle and exacting homage."[17] The explanation is a conjunctive statement formed from two singular statements and contains no laws. Explanations which lack laws are "not incomplete in any sense in which they should be complete, but certainly not including the grounds which we should give if pressed to support them."[18]

Scriven's example above is an explanation of a human action. It is sometimes argued in the case of human actions that they are explicable but *anomic*. As I indicated at the beginning, the thought here is different. Human actions might be, perhaps must be, law-governed or nomic. The first of Scriven's claims is that although or even if human actions are always nomic, sometimes the laws or "truisms" which "cover" them form no part of their full explanation.[19] Similarly for explanations in the natural sciences. Natural occurrences, on his view, are covered by laws or truisms, but which may form no part of their explanation: "[A]bandoning the need for laws. . .such laws are not available even in the physical sciences, and, if they were, would not provide explanations of much interest. . . . When scientists were asked to explain the variations in apparent brightness of the orbiting second-stage rocket that launched the first of our artificial satellites, they replied that it was due to its axial rotation and its asymmetry. This explanation. . .contains no laws."[20]

What is a "truism"? Scriven's distinction between a genuine law and a truism is similar to Donald Davidson's distinction between homonomic and heteronomic generalizations.[21] Scriven's examples of truisms include these: "If you knock a table hard enough it will probably cause an ink-bottle that is not too securely or distantly or specially situated to spill over the edge (if it has enough ink in it)"; "Sufficient confidence and a great desire for wealth may well lead a man to undertake a hazardous and previously unsuccessful journey"; "Power corrupts"; "Strict Orthodox Jews fast on the Day of Atonement." Scriven says that truisms are *true:* "The truism tells us nothing new at all; but it says something and it says something true, even if vague and dull."[22]

How shall we represent a truism? Do they have the form: $(x) (Fx \supset Gx)$? If they did, they would be false, for, so construed, there are exceptions or counterexamples to each of them. Scriven says that the discovery of a devout Orthodox

Jew who is seriously ill and has received rabbinical permission to eat on the fast day does not disconfirm the truism. Truisms are, for him, a type of 'normic statement': "they have a selective immunity to apparent counterexample."[23]

> The normic statement says that everything falls into a certain category except those to which certain special conditions apply. And, although the normic statement itself does not explicitly list what count as exceptional conditions, it employs a vocabulary which reminds us of our knowledge of this, our trained judgment of exceptions. (p. 466)

"Other modifiers that indicate normic statements are 'ordinarily', 'typically', 'usually', 'properly', 'naturally', 'under standard conditions', 'probably'. But. . .no modifier is necessary. . . ."[24]

4.   ARE LAWS A PART OF ALL FULL EXPLANATIONS?

So, Hempel is an upholder of the law requirement for all singular explanations; Scriven a rejector for at least some singular explanations in both the natural and the social sciences. Neither is a difference theorist. But if Scriven is right, what many difference theorists really care about will have been vindicated.

Who is right, and why? Notice that the rejector certainly does not have to maintain that laws form no part of *any* singular explanation (see Scriven, pp. 461–62), only that laws do not necessarily form a part of *all* singular explanations in either type of science. It seems obvious that many full singular explanations do include laws, and this seems to be especially so in the natural sciences. Explanations in natural science frequently include relevant laws, although even when this is so, their inclusion in the explanation will not necessarily be as a major premise of an argument: '*o* is *G* because *o* is *F* and all *F* are *G*' is a (contingently true) explanatory *sentence* which includes a law, but is not an *argument*.

As we have already seen, even without the support of the argument thesis, the law thesis might still be true. Let us assume, for the remainder of the discussion, that the argument thesis (and the symmetry thesis) about explanation is false; this means that the upholder of the law thesis cannot argue in its favor on the grounds that without laws, there is no derivability of explanandum from explanans, and no potential prediction. In fact, I hope that the plausibility of my rejection of the law thesis will itself provide an independent reason to reject the argument thesis, thereby rendering that latter rejection somewhat less than a mere assumption. Is there anything convincing that can be said for or against the law thesis directly, independently of the argument and symmetry theses?

I think that there is something that can be said *against* it. It is this: in a singular explanation that is sufficiently full, there may simply be no work that remains for a law to do by its inclusion in the explanation. The inclusion of a law in a sufficiently full singular explanation may be otiose. Let me elaborate.

The non-extensionality of explanation is well known. Events or phenomena explain or are explained only as described or conceptualized. The point derives from Aristotle, who saw so much so clearly so long ago: what explains the statue is Polyclitus *qua* sculptor, but not Polyclitus *qua* the musical man or *qua* the pale man. A more modern terminology in which to make the same point is in terms of descriptions and the different properties they utilize. Any token event has an indefinitely large number of descriptions true of it. Suppose some token event is both the *F* and the *D*. Under some descriptions ('the *F*'), it may be explanatory, but under others ('the *D*') it may not be. If so, it is not the token event *tout court* that explains, but the event *qua* an event of type *F*. Hempel himself makes a point very similar to this; he says that we never explain concrete events, but only sentential events.[25]

To borrow and expand on an example from John Mackie: the disaster that befell poor Oedipus is explained by the event of his marrying his mother. Precisely the same event may have been his marrying the prettiest woman in Thebes, or his participating in the most sumptuous wedding in all Greece, but so described, the event does not explain the disaster that befell him. The event explains the disaster only as an event of the type, a marrying of one's mother. So properties matter to explanation and, in part, account for its non-extensionality. Two properties, like being renate and being cordate, can be coextensive, but an animal's being renate can explain things that its being cordate cannot explain, and vice versa.[26]

Suppose the law thesis rejector (I count myself among their number) claims that (A) *can* be a full explanation: (A) object *o* is *G* because *o* is *F* . The law thesis upholder will deny that this is possible, and say that the full explanation is (B); object *o* is *G* because *o* is *F* and $(x) (Fx \supset Gx)$. If so, then he has to motivate the thought that (A) could not really be a full explanation, by showing what of importance it is that (A) omits, which is not omitted by (B).

Can we pinpoint what it is that the law is meant to add to (A) as far as explanatory impact is concerned? What has (B) got that (A) lacks insofar as explanation is what is at issue? Of course, someone who held the argument thesis would say that there is no derivability of *o*'s being *G*, from *o*'s being *F* by itself, without the addition of a law. And he may no doubt wish to add something about the requirements for prediction. But the strategy here was to see what could be said for the law thesis, without assuming the argument thesis, or the symmetry of explanation and prediction, and so both the (purported) explanations with and without the law have been represented by sentences, not arguments.

Return to the thought, adumbrated above, that what matters to explanation are properties. When *o*'s being *F* does fully explain *o*'s being *G*, it is not (to put it crudely) that *o*'s being *F* explains *o*'s being *G*; there is nothing special about *o* in any of this. Rather, it is *o*'s being *F* that explains *o*'s being *G*. Explanatory weight is carried by properties, and properties are, by their very nature, general. If *o*'s being *F* fully explains *o*'s being *G* (and given our assumption that everything that happens, happens nomically), then for any other relevantly similar particular which is both *F* and *G*, its being *G* will also be explained by its being *F*. There is, to be sure, generality in singular explanation, but that generality is already insured by the properties ascribed to the particulars in (A) without the addition of laws.

Of course, there is one obvious sense in which an explanation of *o*'s being *G*, in terms of *o*'s being *F*, could be only partial. The explanation might fail to specify or cite all of the explanatorily relevant properties or characteristics of *o*. *But all of the explanatorily relevant properties of o can be cited without inclusion of any law or lawlike generalization.*

Suppose, for the sake of argument, two things: first, that it is an exceptionless law of nature that (x) $(Fx \supset Gx)$; second, that the *only* property of some particular *o*, relevant to explaining why *o* is *G*, is *o*'s *F*-ness. So, in the law or generalization in (B), the only information that could be relevant to the explanation of *o*'s being *G* is already given by the property linkage between *being F* and *being G* which is expressed by (A). The additional information in the generalization, which is about (actual or possible) *F*'s other than *o* which are also *G*, is simply irrelevant to the explanation of *o*'s being *G*. At most, what (B) does that is not done by (A) is merely to explicitly apply the connection between properties *F* and *G*, already expressed by (A), to cases other than *o*. And this cannot have any additional explanatory relevance to *o*'s case. The case of temporally and spatially distant *F*-objects which are *G* is surely not relevant to *o*. One might say about explanation what Hume said (but to which he believed he had a rejoinder) about causation: "It may be thought, that what we learn not from one object, we can never learn from a hundred, which are all of the same kind, and are perfectly resembling in every circumstance."[27]

The law thesis would make relevant to the explanation of *o*'s being *G*, the *F*-ness and *G*-ness of other actual or possible particulars, *a, e, i, u*, etc. To borrow and amend an example from Mill's discussion of deduction and real inference, it is hard to see, if the Duke of Wellington's humanity cannot fully explain his mortality on its own, how introducing the humanity and mortality of people other than the Duke (whether by a generalization or by the enumeration of other particular instances) could explain it. What is the explanatory relevance to the good Duke's mortality of the mortality of humans spatially and temporally far distant from him? It is only his being a human that explains his being mortal. If the world is nomic, then other humans will be mortal too, and it may be that the very possibility of explaining the Duke's mortality on the basis of his humanity presupposes this. But even if this were a presupposition of the explanation of the Duke's mortality by his humanity, that presupposition contributes nothing additional to the explanation of the Duke's mortality, and has no place in it.

5. LAWS GET THEIR REVENGE

But laws are still important, even to those cases of explanation which do not include them, in other ways. Indeed, the law requirement view, by insisting that laws are a *part* of every full explanation, has tended to neglect the other ways in which laws are essential to explanation. Let me add some remarks about how laws are still crucial for the explanation of the world about us, all consistent with my above claim; the remarks will also permit me to sharpen my view somewhat on the role of laws and generalizations in explanation.

Why did the match light? I struck it, and my striking of the match was, let us suppose, the penultimate thing that ever happened to the match. Or, my striking of the match was the event that caused the match to light. Why, then, can I explain the fact that the match lit by the fact that the match was struck, and not by the different facts that the penultimate thing that ever happened to the match occurred, or that the cause of its lighting occurred, even though these three singular facts (the fact that the match was struck, the fact that the cause of the match's lighting occurred, the fact that the penultimate thing that ever happened to the match occurred) are all facts about the same event, but differently described? We saw before that properties matter to explanation, and, because they do matter, it is redundant to include laws in all singular explanations. But in virtue of which of the features or properties of an event is that event fully explanatory of some other? How do we determine which properties of a thing matter for the purposes of explanation?

Aristotle's reply would have been that the explanatory features are the ones linked in a law (whether deterministic or stochastic).[28] In the case at hand, there is a law (or let us so pretend for the time being) that links the features, being a striking and being a lighting, of the two token events, but not other of their features, e.g., being a penultimate occurrence and being a lighting. Nor is there a *law* which links being a cause of lighting and being a lighting, even though it is a (contingent, if the scope is read correctly) general truth that causes of lightings cause lightings. On Aristotle's view, it is *not* that the laws are always part of the explanation (he does think that this is true of scientific explanation, but not of explanation generally); rather, the laws provide the properties for determining under which descriptions a particular fully explains another. Laws provide the appropriate vocabulary for full singular explanation.

The above allows me to make a closely related point about the role of theories in explanation. Scientists often cite theories in explaining a phenomenon. For example: the theory of gravity explains why the moon causes the earth's tides; the law of inertia explains why a projectile continues in motion for some time after being thrown; subatomic particle theory explains why specific paths appear in a Wilson cloud chamber. And theories consist (perhaps *inter alia*) of generalizations.

But (a) it does not follow that theories are explanatory in virtue of their generality, nor (b) does it follow that the way in which they are explanatory is in all cases by being part of the explanation. I have already argued for (b). But I now wish to argue for (a). Theories typically help to explain singular facts in virtue of supplying a vocabulary for identifying or redescribing the *particular* phenomena or mechanisms at work, which are what explain those singular facts.

The examples of "syllogistic explanation" that I have been using might have struck the reader as exceedingly artificial: whoever would have thought, the reply might go, that the Duke of Wellington's mortality could be explained by his humanity and the generalization that all humans are mortal? And, I have been working with this example form: '*o* is *G* because *o* is *F* and all *F* are *G*'.

These generalizations are "flat" in the sense that they are simple generalizations that use the same vocabulary as do the singular explanans and the explanandum descriptions. Flat generalizations do not contribute at all to singular explanation.

However, from the fact that flat generalizations are explanatorily useless, it hardly follows that all are. What is needed, so the reply might continue, are generalizations which employ a theoretical vocabulary with greater depth than 'human' and 'mortal'. Perhaps the vocabulary should be in *deeper* terms that refer to the fragility of hydrocarbon-based life forms. To explain why *o* is *G*, in terms of *o*'s being *F*, if a law is to be included, typically a scientific explanation will cite a law employing a theoretical vocabulary which is different from and deeper than the vocabulary of which *'F'* and *'G'* are part. Only as such could the generalizations be explanatory.

And such a reply is correct. But it confirms rather than disconfirms my view. If generalizations or laws were always *per se* explanatory, then flat ones ought to help explain (perhaps not as well as deep ones, but they should help to explain to some extent nonetheless). The fact that *only* ones that are deep, relative to the vocabulary of the explanans and explanandum singular sentences (in general, theories), will help explain *at all* is an indication that laws are explanatory only in virtue of offering a deeper vocabulary in which to identify or redescribe mechanisms, but not just in virtue of being generalizations. And even so, to return for a moment to (b), the generalizations that make up the wider or deeper theory may help to explain by offering that alternative vocabulary, but without being part of the explanation itself.

I have been arguing that full explanations do not always include laws, but that they sometimes may. Here perhaps is such an example (although it is not a singular explanation as it stands): "There are tides because it is a law that all bodies exert gravitational forces on all other bodies, and because of the fact that the moon exerts this force on the earth's seas." When laws are included within an explanation, as they sometimes are, the purpose of the inclusion is often to introduce a vocabulary different from the one used in the common or ordinary descriptions of the explanans and explanandum events and the particulars to which the events occur ('the tides', 'the earth', 'its seas', 'the moon').

On the one hand, if the common and less deep vocabulary used to describe the particular phenomena were wholly expendable, the theoretical vocabulary could be explicitly used to describe them, and any mention of the law in the explanation would be redundant. If on the other hand no deeper vocabulary were available, there would be no purpose for a law to serve in the explanation. Laws find their honest employment within singular explanations in situations between the two extremes: when the less deep vocabulary used to describe the singular explanans and explanandum is to be retained at the shallower level, but a deeper vocabulary is available and needs introduction.

One important role that theories play in science is to unify superficially diverse phenomena. In virtue of a unifying theory, what seemed like different phenomena can be brought under one set of deep structural laws:

By assuming that gases are composed of tiny molecules subject to the laws of Newtonian mechanics we can explain the Boyle-Charles law for a perfect gas. But this is only a small fraction of our total gain. First, we can explain numerous other laws governing the behavior of gases. . . . Second, and even more important, we can integrate the behavior of gases with the behavior of numerous other kinds of objects. . . . In the absence of the theoretical structure supplied by our molecular model, the behavior of gases simply has no connection at all with these other phenomena. Our picture of the world is much less unified.[29]

On my view, there is a difference between unification and explanation. Unification of a phenomenon with other superficially different phenomena, however worthwhile a goal that may be, is no part of the explanation of that phenomenon. It is true that a good theory unifies apparently disparate phenomena, and unification is a highly desirable goal for science. But that some particular mechanism is common to both what is being explained and other apparently disparate things is not relevant to the explanation of the first thing in terms of that mechanism. If other humans' mortality could not explain why the good Duke is mortal when his own humanity does not, then the fragility of other hydrocarbon-based life forms (which will 'unify' humans' mortality with that of other plants and animals) could not explain the Duke's fragility or mortality when his own hydrocarbon constitution does not. It does not matter, from the point of view of explanation, whether there are any other phenomena which get explained by the deeper vocabulary; the point is that the vocabulary gives a new and more profound insight into the phenomenon at hand and the mechanisms at work in its case, whether or not the vocabulary unifies it with other phenomena.

Consider a perhaps not perfect analogy. I want to explain both why Cicero was bald and why Tully was bald (thinking that they are two different men). I am informed that Cicero is Tully. There is a clear sense in which there has been unification, for there is now only one thing left to explain. Our view of the world is more unified. But has there been any explanatory gain? Only in the rather derivative sense that the identity explains why there are not two different things to be explained. If that is the substance of Friedman's claim, I accept it. But surely nothing else has been explained at all.

6. EXPLANATORY IDEALISM AND ACTUALISM

So far, it might seem that Scriven has won the toss against Hempel. On the specific question of the law thesis, I submit that he has won. But on the issue of explanatory actualism and idealism, I think he must be wrong, and some of the motivation behind Hempel's covering law account right after all. That is, I believe that few, if any, of the singular explanations commonly offered are full explanations. I, like Hempel, am an explanatory idealist.

There are two questions worth distinguishing: first, what is a full explanation; second, how can we justify a claim that some explanation is a full one? Let us look at the second question of how we might justify a claim that some singular explanation is full or complete, and at the role that truisms could play in such a justification.

Scriven addresses the second question in his remarks on laws as providing role-justifying grounds. Does some explanans really fully explain some explanandum? Perhaps it is not adequate to fully explain it; something may be missing. How can I justify my claim that the explanans fully does the job it is meant to do?

Suppose I claim that '*e* because *c*' is a full explanation. On Scriven's view (p. 446), if I am challenged about the adequacy or completeness of my explanation, I can justify my claim to completeness, and thereby rebuff the challenge, by citing a law (or truism), e.g., that all *C* are *E* (*c* being a *C*; *e* being an *E*). This is what Scriven calls the "role-justifying grounds" that laws and truisms provide in support of a claim that an explanation is not incomplete.

The law or truism plays an epistemic role in explanation. It can justify an assertion that *c* is the full and adequate explanation of *e*, without being any part of that explanation. On the basis of the law, I can justify my claim that no explanatorily relevant information about the particular explanans has been omitted. Although Scriven does not say so, there can be no objection to offering the full explanation and the justification for its fullness in a single assertion, but if this is done, we should be clear that what we have is a full explanation *and* something else, and not just a full explanation.

Scriven offers the following possible reply to his own views: "It may appear that we are quibbling over words here, that it is of little importance to decide exactly what is included in an explanation and what in its justification."[30] Like Scriven, I do not accept the sentiment expressed by such a reply. The distinction is important. There is quite generally a distinction between the correct analysis of an expression, and the grounds or evidence that one might have for believing that it is true. In particular, there is a difference between the roles that Hempel and Scriven assign to laws. On Hempel's view, the law is part of the full explanation itself; on Scriven's, the law provides the criterion for determining, concerning an explanation, when it is a full one.

Perhaps an analogy will help.[31] On Hempel's account, to know that an explanatory argument is a full one, one must know that the explanatory argument is valid. And the criterion for deciding validity is given by the rules of deductive and inductive logic. But neither the assertion that the explanatory argument is valid, nor the criteria for assessing validity is to be included as a further premise in the full explanation. *Pari passu*, on Scriven's account, to know that an explanation is a full one, one must know that no explanatorily relevant singular information has been omitted, and the criterion for assessing whether any such information has been omitted is given by the relevant covering laws or truisms. But neither the assertion that the explanation omits no such singular information nor the criterion for assessing whether this is so (the law) is to be included in the full explanation.

Suppose once again that *o* is *G* because *o* is *F* (Cortes sent out a third expedition to Baja, California, because of his considerable confidence in his own leadership and his prospect of gigantic booty). One can cite (1) grounds for thinking that o is F (or that o is G), (2) grounds for thinking that o's being F is *an* explanatory factor in o's being G, and (3) grounds for thinking that o's being F is the full explanation of o's being G. In the case of (1), one might cite various sorts of observational evidence; historical documents make o's being F highly likely or probable. In the case of (2), one might cite experimental evidence that showed that, in the absence of their being F, things otherwise relevantly similar to o failed to be G (Mill's Method of Difference).

It would be an error to include this historical or experimental evidence in the analysis of 'o is F' or 'o is G at least partly because o is F'. To do so would involve a kind of verificationism which conflates analysis and evidence. It seems to me a similar kind of mistake to include one's evidence for 'o is G because o is F' in its analysis.

But notice that even if this sentiment about the unimportance of the distinction between "what is included in an explanation and what in its justification" were accepted, it would cut more against the law thesis upholder than against its rejector. The law thesis upholder must think that it is an important insight that full explanations include laws; to hold that it is arbitrary whether one says that they do or do not include laws is contrary to the spirit of the thesis. At the very worst, the thesis of this essay would have to be that it is of little importance whether full explanations are said to include laws or not, and this is something the law thesis upholder should resist.

I agree with Scriven that a law can provide role-justifying grounds for full explanation, but I do not agree that a truism can do so. This raises the question of explanatory actualism, and on this question, I part from his company. A full explanation of o's being G is the fact that o is F, *only if* it is a law that all or a certain percentage of F's are G's, sans further exception. Suppose the law in question is a more complex law which says: (x) $(Fx \ \& \ Kx \ \& \ Hx \ \& \ Jx \supset Gx)$. A full explanation of why o is G would be the singular fact that o is $F \ \& \ K \ \& \ H \ \& \ J$. In this way, my view of full explanation is, in at least one way, closer to Hempel's than to Scriven's. Full explanations, on my view as on Hempel's, may well be close to ideal things; if almost no one ever gives one, that tells us a lot about the practical circumstances of explanation-giving, but provides no argument whatsoever against such an account of full explanation.

There may be perfectly good pragmatic reasons why we are entitled to give a partial explanation of o's G-ness; it may be that o's being $K \ \& \ H \ \& \ J$ is so obvious, that one never needs to say anything more than that o is F. But the law provides the criterion for what a complete or full explanation is. To turn to Scriven's second example, I am sure that the explanation of the variations in apparent brightness of the orbiting second-stage rocket that launched America's first artificial satellite in terms only of its axial rotation and asymmetry cannot be its full explanation. I agree that its full explanation, whatever it is, need not include a law, but since the explanation Scriven offers fails to contain any particular information about, for instance, the source of light that was present, it could not be a full explanation. Scriven's own remarks about the role-justifying grounds that laws provide help make this very point. The particular explanation Scriven offers as full can be seen to be merely incomplete, not because it does not include a law, but because the law provides the test for fullness which Scriven's explanation of the rocket's apparent variations in brightness fails.

On Hempel's (but not Lewis's) view of full explanation, which I have espoused, o's being F can explain o's being G, when it is a law of nature that (x) $(Fx \supset Gx)$. But suppose (as Elliott Sober reminds me) that this is a case of derivative or non-immediate explanation in the sense that there is some property H such that o's being F fully explains o's being H, and o's being H fully explains o's being G. The explanation with the greater information works in virtue of two laws: both (x) $(Fx \supset Hx)$ and (x) $(Hx \supset Gx)$. In this way, the explanation tells us more, since it tells us about the process or pathway *via* which being F explains being G.

We might capture this greater information in a single explanation in one of two ways: o is G because o is H and o is H because o is F; o is G because o is F and both (x) $(Fx \supset Hx)$ and (x) $(Hx \supset Gx)$ are laws of nature. I have no reason to resist this point if it is sound. First, I have allowed that some explanations do or may include laws, even though not necessarily as premises in an argument. Second, it seems a matter of pragmatic importance only in which of the two ways the information is captured. As Sober suggested to me, "Whenever adding a law would improve the explanation the same improvement can be effected by adding something that is not a law."

I certainly do not defend this Hempelian notion of full explanation on the grounds that this is the concept of full explanation that emerges from ordinary language or from common usage.[32] I have no interest in disputing about the ordinary sense of the term. If someone wishes to argue that there is a sense of 'full explanation' in ordinary language, on which Scriven-style explanations based on truisms can count as full, I will concede that this may be so.

The sense of 'full explanation' that I, following Hempel, urge is a technical one. I think that this technical sense is one that becomes plausible when we reflect upon the sort of understanding that science poses as a possibility. A full explanation is an ideal (as Hempel himself says). For such an ideal, a true law which 'backs' the full explanation of some token of a type must back the full explanation of any other token of that type. The amount of singular information in the explanans required in the full explanation of any token of a type is pulled upwards, as it were, to the level of the greatest amount of singular information required to fully explain any token of that type.

I do not offer this as a definition of 'full explanation' (if it were intended as such, it would be circular). Rather, it is a *constitutive* principle of what full explanation (in this technical sense) is. Such an ideal is constitutive, rather than regulative, to borrow a Kantianesque distinction. Ordinary or actual explainers are not required to try to offer, as nearly as possible, full explanations. Actual explanation-giving is governed by pragmatic considerations. The ideal is constitutive; it constitutes for us what, upon reflection, we intend by 'fully explaining why something happened.'[33]

But what this means is that one cannot justify the claim that one has produced a full singular explanation in the absence of knowledge of the appropriate deterministic or stochastic covering law. It may be that one has fully explained without knowing it; but knowledge that one has fully explained implies knowledge of the law. I am not supposing that one might explain without knowing that one had explained at all; whether or not that is possible, all that I am supposing is that one might know that one had explained at least in part, without knowing whether one had fully explained, even though one had, in fact, given a full explanation.

7. TRUISMS AND THE SOCIAL SCIENCES

This brings us back to the question of explanations making use of truisms, a question of special importance for the social sciences (the examples of Cortes and William the Conqueror employ such truisms). How could a truism be the backing for a complete or full explanation? It seems to me that when we use truisms, as of course we frequently do, we can at best claim partial or incomplete explanation. The completeness of the explanation can only be shown to be so when we see that all of the explanatorily relevant properties of William the Conqueror and Cortes have been included in their descriptions. For this, one must have available the relevant "strict" covering law.

It may be that these truistic, rough-and-ready generalizations are small fragments of fuller empirical generalizations. In the case of the social sciences, Ayer argues for this in "Man as a Subject for Science," and I do not think that his argument has ever been effectively answered.[34] If so, then we see what we must do to get full explanations: find the fuller and strictly true generalizations of which the truisms are only fragments.

But it is more fashionable to believe that Ayer's hypothesis is wrong, that the truisms will not reappear as fragments of fuller generalizations. Let us suppose that Scriven's truisms, like Davidson's heteronomic laws, are *incompleteable* within the terms of the vocabulary they use. As Davidson says,[35]

> The generalizations which embody such practical wisdom are assumed to be only roughly true, or they are explicitly stated in probabilistic terms, or they are insulated from counterexample by generous escape clauses. (p. 93)
>
> . . .[T]here are generalizations which when instantiated may give us reason to believe that there is a precise law at work, but one which can be stated only by shifting to a different vocabulary. We call such generalizations heteronomic. (p. 94)

On my view, singular explanations which rest on heteronomic (incompleteable within their own vocabulary) generalizations must fail to be complete explanations. Notice that 'incompleteable' for Davidson does not presuppose that a generalization is complete only when it is universally quantified. There are, or may be, stochastic laws which are less than universally quantified generalizations, and which may be as perfectly complete as any law need be. "Or perhaps the ultimate theory is probabilistic. . .in that case there will be no better to be had" (Davidson, p. 94). Heteronomic generalizations (and Scriven's truisms) do not just fail to be fragments of exceptionless laws; they fail, on their accounts, to be fragments of any kind of law at all, deterministic or stochastic.

I pretended earlier that it was a law that striking a match caused it to light. In truth, there is no law of nature that links strikings and lightings of matches. 'Striking a match will cause it to light' is also at best a truism, incompleteable within the terms of its own vocabulary.

I do not say, in the case of truisms such as this, that they cannot be explanatory *at all*. Clearly, it can be explanatory of a particular match's lighting to say that it was struck. Presumably, this is because 'striking' and 'lighting', although themselves no part of a law, are linked in some appropriate way with the vocabulary of the relevant underlying laws of physics or chemistry; Aristotle's criterion for determining when a description is one under which a particular is explanatory of another must therefore be amended to include this point. I only assert that such truisms, like the one about striking a match causing it to light, cannot provide a *complete* or *full* explanation of a singular occurrence, like the particular match's lighting.

If Ayer is wrong, and *if it is desirable to have complete explanations*, even of human action, then I think the drive towards homonomic laws, "correctible within [their] own conceptual domain" (Davidson, p. 94), even if it requires a switch to the vocabulary of brain neurophysiology, is irresistible. Many of these explanations would be similar to the ones I discussed above, in which the old terminology is retained at the level of the singular explanans and explanandum, but a law is included within the explanation, as a way of introducing a new, and deeper, vocabulary. To be satisfied with our practical lore as it stands for the explanation of human action, with its vocabulary that either is correctable in its own conceptual domain but stands in need of correction, or is uncorrectable in that domain, is to be satisfied with incomplete explanation.

It is no part of my view that it is always wrong to be satisfied with incomplete explanations, that it is always desirable that science look for complete explanations.[36] Perhaps these reflections pose the possibility of another angle from which to argue for a difference theory. Natural science, not strictly always but typically, with its emphasis on prediction and control, strives for completeness or fullness of its explanations. Recall what I mentioned in passing above. Explanations are not potential predictions, and predictions are not potential explanations (the symmetry thesis is false in both directions), but to know that we have fully explained requires knowing the relevant law, and the surest sort of prediction requires knowing the relevant law as well. If we know that our explanation is full, we have all we need in order to predict accurately. So predicting and knowing that our explanation is a full explanation have an overlapping requirement.

The social sciences lack this interest in control and prediction beyond the rough-and-ready, and as a consequence may not be as interested in pursuing complete or full explanations of things. Methodologically, partial explanations serve the needs and interests of social scientists tolerably well.

NOTES

I am grateful to Peter Lipton and Marcus Giaquinto, whose comments made this essay less bad than it would have otherwise been. An earlier version of this essay was read at the Royal Institute of Philosophy conference on explanation, held in Glasgow 8–11 September 1989. Discussion of the essay at the conference was helpful, and I am also grateful to all of those who contributed in this way.

1. Peter Winch, *The Idea of a Social Science* (London, 1967), 86.
2. Daniel Taylor, *Explanation & Meaning* (Cambridge, 1973), 75.
3. Michael Lesnoff, *The Structure of Social Science* (London, 1974), 106.
4. A. R. Louch, *Explanation and Human Action* (Oxford, 1966), 233.
5. Michael Scriven wrote extensively on explanation, but I will confine my remarks to his "Truisms as the Grounds for Historical Explanations," in *Theories of History*, edited by Patrick Gardiner (New York, 1959), 443–75.
6. I do not think that it is always easy to see when an explanation is an explanation of a singular event and when it is an explanation of a class of similar events, or a regularity. Grammatical form by itself may be a poor guide. Of course, there is a sense in which a token is *always* explained as a representative token of some specific kind. In a rough-and-ready way, though, I think we can see the intention behind the distinction between singular explanation and the explanation of a regularity.

Why did Vesuvius erupt in 79 C.E.? Why is there this unexpected reading in the light emission from such-and-such star? Why did Protestantism arise in northern Europe in the sixteenth century? These are requests for singular explanation. On the other hand, when a student explains the results of mixing two chemicals in a test tube in the laboratory, he is unlikely to be engaged in giving a singular explanation of the particular mixing at hand. He is in fact explaining why mixings of those types of chemicals have that sort of result. The claims of this essay are relevant only to genuinely singular explanations, not to ones which might have the grammatical form of a singular explanation but are in truth the explanation of a regularity.

7. He sometimes counts Deductive-Statistical as a third, but I ignore this here.
8. This assumption is made by David Lewis, since his conditions for something's being a full explanation are set so high: "Every question has a maximal true answer: the whole truth about the subject matter on which information is requested, to which nothing could be added without irrelevance or error. In some cases it is feasible to provide these maximal answers." David Lewis, *Philosophical Papers* II (Oxford, 1986), 229.
9. If, as Lewis asserts, a complete explanation is a maximally true answer, it is not easy to see how it could *ever* be feasible to provide one. Lewis's theory is bound to drive us into an extreme form of explanatory idealism. The causal history of each thing to be explained stretches into the indefinite past; surely I can *never* provide all of that. On my view, the whole truth about something will typically contain many full explanations for the same thing, so that we can proffer a full explanation about a thing without having to state the whole relevant truth about it. Lewis, *Philosophical Papers* II.
10. Carl Hempel, *Aspects of Scientific Explanations* (New York, 1965), 362.
11. Winch's criticisms of the covering law account of explanation were certainly not confined to the law and argument theses. He also argued against the view that having a reason is or can be the cause of the action it helps to rationalize. I consider the battle against this to be lost, principally due to the work of Donald Davidson. Once issues about causation, explanation, and law are disentangled, I can see no convincing argument against the claim that the having of reasons can be a type of cause.
12. No orthodox theorist would consider this condition by itself sufficient. Accidental

generalizations have this form, too. Further, universally quantified material conditionals are true when their antecedent terms are true of nothing. So, if this condition were by itself sufficient for lawlikeness, and if nothing in the universe was an F, then both of the following would be laws of nature: (x) $(Fx \supset Gx)$ and (x) $(Fx \supset \sim Gx)$.

There are various proposals for adding further conditions to the one above. Some are proposals for strengthening the generalization by adding a necessity-operator: laws of nature are nomically necessary universally quantified generalizations. See for example: William Kneale, "Natural Laws and Contrary-to-Fact Conditionals," *Analysis* 10 (1950): 121–25; Karl Popper, *The Logic of Scientific Discovery* (London, 1972), Appendix *10, pp. 420–41; Milton Fisk, "Are There Necessary Connections in Nature?" *Philosophy of Science* 37 (1970): 385–404. Others ascribe to the universally quantified generalization an additional special epistemic status, or a special place in science, or impose further syntactic requirements. See Richard Braithwaite, *Scientific Explanation* (Cambridge, 1964), chap. 9, pp. 293–318; Ernest Nagel, *The Structure of Science* (New York, 1961), chap. 4, pp. 47–78; D. H. Mellor, "Necessities and Universals in Natural Laws," in *Science, Belief, and Behaviour*, edited by Mellor (Cambridge, 1980), 105–19. Hempel himself is unclear about how to complete the list of sufficient conditions for something's being a law: "Though the preceding discussion has not led to a fully satisfactory general characterization of lawlike sentences and thus of laws. . ." (p. 343).

Suppose, though, that the orthodox view does not provide even a necessary condition, let alone a sufficient one, for a sentence's stating a law of nature. If so, my argument would have to proceed somewhat differently. I am sympathetic to some of these non-orthodox views, but I do not deal with any of them here, nor with how their acceptance would alter my argument. See Fred Dretske, "Laws of Nature," *Philosophy of Science* 44 (1977): 248–68; for a reply to Dretske, see Ilkka Niiniluoto, *Philosophy of Science* 45 (1978): 431–39; David Armstrong, *What Is a Law of Nature?* (Cambridge, 1987).

13. Hempel, *Aspects*, p. 336.

14. Ibid., 337.

15. In any event, Hempel himself, in *Aspects*, more or less abandons the view that every prediction is a potential explanation in his discussion of Koplik spots and measles. Another case worth considering is this: suppose c and d both occur. Both are potential causes of e, but, since c occurs and actually causes e, d is merely a potential but preempted cause of e. One can predict but not explain e's occurrence from the occurrence of d, its preempted cause; e's explanation must be in terms of c, its actual cause, and not in terms of its preempted cause.

16. I am convinced by the argument of Tim McCarthy, "On An Aristotelian Model of Scientific Explanation," *Philosophy of Science* 44 (1977): 159–66. See my *Explaining Explanation* (London, 1990), chap. 6, where I develop the point at considerable length.

17. Scriven, "Truisms as Grounds for Historical Explanation," 444.

18. Ibid., 446.

19. See Thomas Nickles, "Davidson on Explanation," *Philosophical Studies* 31 (1977): 141–45, where the idea that 'strict' covering laws may be 'non-explanatory' is developed.

20. Scriven, "Truisms as Grounds for Historical Explanation," 445.

21. See Davidson, "Mental Events," reprinted in his *Essays on Actions and Events* (Oxford, 1980), 207–27. Also in *Experience and Theory*, edited by Foster and Swanson (London, 1970), 79–101.

22. Scriven, "Truisms as Grounds for Historical Explanation," 458.

23. Ibid., 464.

24. Ibid., 465.

25. Hempel, *Aspects* 421–23.

26. I do not say that nothing but properties matter; names sometimes seem to matter to explanation, too. Naming in one way can be explanatory, naming in a different way can fail to be so. If I do not know that Cicero = Tully, I can explain why Cicero's speeches stopped in 43 B.C.E., by the fact that Cicero died in that year, but not by the fact that Tully died in that year. But in any case, properties matter to explanation, even if names do too.

27. David Hume, *A Treatise of Human Nature*, edited by L. A. Selby-Bigge (Oxford, 1965), 88. I think that much of the motivation for the inclusion of a generalization in every full explanation stems from the Humeian analysis of causation.

28. Aristotle gives us a definition of the incidental or accidental in *Metaphysics* V, 30, 20–5: 'Accident' means (1) that which attaches to something and can be truly asserted, but neither of necessity nor usually. . .for neither does the one come of necessity from the other or after the other, nor. . .usually. . . . And a musical man might be pale; but since this does not happen of necessity nor usually, we call it an accident. Therefore, since there are attributes and they attach to subjects, and some of them attach only in a particular place and at a particular time, whatever attaches to a subject, but not because it was this subject, or the time this time, or the place this place, will be an accident." For a defense of my interpretation of Aristotle, see my *Explaining Explanation*, cited in note 16.

29. Michael Friedman, "Theoretical Explanation," in *Reduction, Time, and Reality*, edited by Richard Healey (Cambridge, 1981), 7. See also his "Explanation and Scientific Understanding," *Journal of Philosophy* 71 (1974): 5–19, and the reply by Philip Kitcher, "Explanation, Conjunction, and Unification," *Journal of Philosophy* 73 (1976): 207–12.

30. Scriven, "Truisms as Grounds for Historical Explanations," 448.

31. The analogy was suggested to me by Peter Lipton.

32. This Hempelian notion of full explanation is to be contrasted with an even stronger sense of full explanation that one finds in the work of David Lewis. See notes 8 and 9.

33. To repeat again, this is the Hempelian ideal of full explanation. I described in notes 8 and 9 David Lewis's even more demanding ideal of full explanation.

34. A. J. Ayer, "Man as a Subject for Science," *Philosophy, Politics, and Society*, 3d s. (Oxford, 1967), 6–24.

35. Donald Davidson, "Mental Events," in *Experience & Theory*, edited by Foster and Swanson (London, 1970), 79–101.

36. I have discussed this briefly in "Marx, Necessity, and Science," in *Marx and Marxisms,* edited by G. H. R. Parkinson (Cambridge, 1982), 39–56. See pp. 54–56.

Moral Realism and Social Science*

ALEXANDER ROSENBERG

The traditional intersection between the philosophy of social science and moral philosophy has been the problem of value-freedom: whether theories in social science unavoidably reflect normative judgments, whether they can be or are free of them, and whether either of these alternatives is a good thing or not, given the aims and methods of empirical science in general. Despite its importance, this is a debate to which little both novel and reasonable has recently been added.

But the recent resurgence of interest in "moral realism" holds out the hope of a new approach to this issue, one likely to lend support to the opponents of moral neutrality, support from a direction in which they could not have expected it—the "scientistic" approach to theories about human behavior. For once moral realism is embraced, the attractiveness of deriving moral claims from descriptive social theories becomes very great.

1. REALISM AND NATURALISM

Moral realism is not just the thesis that at least some normative claims are definitely true or false. It also requires that at least some of them are in fact true. A moral realist who held that all ethical claims are just false could hardly be said to have offered a defense of ethical theories and claims.[1] But if at least some moral claims are true, it behooves the moral realist to show how we can know which ones they are, and what the evidence for them is. But providing the metaphysics and epistemology moral realism needs has long been a problem. As Sayre-McCord notes, "the common (mistaken) assumption is that the only realist positions available in ethics are those that embrace supernatural properties and special powers of moral intuition."[2] The assumption is said to be mistaken, because another "ism"—naturalism—has again become fashionable in metaethics. This is the brace of theses that (a) the conditions that make some moral claims true are facts about the world and its denizens, ontologically no different from the facts dealt with in physics or psychology, and (b) the way in which we can come to know such claims to be true is identical to the ways in which scientific claims in general are acquired – by the formulation and confirmation of theories that explain our observations.[3] To be plausible, moral realism needs to avoid any tincture of ethical intuitionism or metaphysical mystery mongering. Naturalism is the only option available to realism for avoiding the charge that its metaphysical and epistemological foundations are untenable.

This is where the social sciences and the philosophy of science come in. The relevant observations against which to test explanatory theories embodying moral claims must be observations of human behavior, individual and aggregate, and both the theories and the observations are the province of the social sciences.[4] If the case for social scientific theories embodying normative claims about the good, for example, can be made out, then not only will moral realism be vindicated in principle, but the normative bearing of social theory, independent of any further evaluative premises, will also be established. This would be a decisive refutation of the thesis that social science, like natural science, can be or should be value-neutral. No one currently writing on moral realism, and the social-scientific naturalism it requires, has noticed this special "dividend" of their theory. Nor have they noticed that a decisive argument for *vert-frei* social science will *ipso facto* be an argument against naturalism and moral realism.

Proponents of value-free social science and opponents of moral realism thus have common cause. Regrettably, they can only pursue their cause in a case-by-case piecemeal way. A general impossibility proof that no empirically adequate social theory that both explains the observations we make about human affairs and embodies moral claims is forever unavailable. For providing such a proof is equivalent to establishing a negative existential claim. This means that the only way to defend anti-realism in ethics and moral neutrality in social science is to attack the individual particular theories that are advanced as both empirically adequate and morally significant.

Surprisingly, though much has been written on the generic subject of moral realism and naturalism, few such theories have even been sketched. This is surprising since without such details, moral realism *cum* naturalism remains at best a pious hope, a bare logical possibility, instead of a robust foundation for ethics, a bulwark against ethical relativism, moral skepticism, and social nihilism.

2. RAILTON'S PROJECT

One recent attempt to fill out the details of the requisite social theory is that of Peter Railton. In "Moral Realism"[5] he offers an argument for moral realism that recognizes the obligation to say what the explanatory theory naturalism demands would look like. In the rest of this essay, I examine this theory and Railton's arguments for it. My doubts about it stem as much from reflection on the importance of value-neutrality in adequate social theory as they do from doubts about the notion that moral claims can be true or false. My strategy is mainly to focus on the substantive and the methodological defects of the social theory Railton adapts to ground his moral realism. But some of my arguments reflect traditional objections to moral realism and naturalism that go back to Moore and Hume. At a minimum, my objections will reflect strictures on subsequent theories in social science for which normative force is claimed. But perhaps some of the problems to be noted are unavoidable defects in any theory that aims to combine empirical adequacy and moral force. If so, these objections may help undermine the whole project of moral realism.

When we see what is wrong with Railton's theory and what is revealed by a wider view of social phenomena than Railton's, there remains little reason to endorse either his positive social theory or the integrally associated normative theory of moral goodness. And when repaired to avoid these defects, the result is either a positive theory without ethical ramifications, or one quite irreconcilable with strongly held moral convictions of the sort Railton seeks to justify and explain.

Railton is a naturalist. He sets himself the task of showing that "moral facts are constituted by natural facts"—that is, facts with an explanatory role in respect of human behavior. To do this, he writes, moral facts must exhibit two features: (1) existence independent from our own beliefs and a determinate character independent of these beliefs; and (2) it must be possible for these facts causally to influence our mentation and behavior (p. 172). These features, of course, do not make facts moral, they make them "real." That facts are moral consists in their instrumental rationality "from a social point of view, as opposed to the point of view of any individual" (pp. 190, 191). Thus, as Railton eventually notes, moral goodness will turn out to be consequentialist, interpersonally aggregative and maximizing (pp. 190–91, note 31). It will be what best serves the interests of all members of society somehow taken together. This approach to moral goodness already commits Railton to an empirical social theory that is both holistic and functional, as we shall see. It means that his moral theory will bear both the strengths and the weaknesses of such theories.[6] In this respect Railton's approach to moral realism is typical of attempts to combine ethical and empirical social theory (though his attempt is far more detailed than others[7].)

REALISM ABOUT NON-MORAL VALUE

Railton's strategy is to produce an account of what he calls non-moral value, and then to parlay this theory into an account of moral value, showing that the latter has all the reality of the former.

What is non-morally valuable to an agent is not what he actually values, but what he would value if he knew his "real" interests and employed this information rationally. Individuals are often notoriously wrong about their real interests, mainly as a result of epistemic and logical errors of omission and commission. Consider an agent with a certain set of preferences. Now deprive him of all of his false beliefs about himself, his situation, the consequences of acting on these preferences, and add all relevant knowledge about himself, his situation, and his preferences. The preferences that remain, and those that are added by this transformation of his doxastic states, are his "real" or "objective" interests. These interests obtain in fact and for all of us, whether we know it or not. Subjective preferences that conflict with them are not really in the interest of the agent, no matter how strongly he embraces them. Now, some state of affairs is "non-morally good" for an agent if it would satisfy an objective interest of the agent—"roughly, what he would want himself to seek if he knew what he was doing" (p. 176). The non-morally good thus turns out to "correlate well with what would permit the agent. . .to experience physical or psychological well-being. Surely our well- or ill-being are among the things that matter to us most, and most reliably, even on reflection" (p. 179). Thus, our well-being is intrinsically non-morally good, and whatever is instrumental in achieving this good is an "objective interest."

This account makes Railton's a thoroughly biological theory of the "non-morally good," perhaps more biological than he realizes. For interests are objective if they enhance well-being, and well-being is an intrinsic good for us because natural selection made us that way. It did so because well-being is causally connected to enhanced reproductive rates, and so secures evolutionary adaptation. This means that well-being is an intrinsic good to individuals because it is an instrumental good to the lines of descent in which they figure. Given environmental circumstances, certain of our ends are conducive to the demographic expansion (or at least the persistence) of each of our respective lineages. So, evolution has shaped us to treat them as objective interests. Railton's evolutionary explanation for our objective interests is consigned to a longish footnote (p. 179). But its importance is evident. Railton's naturalism requires that non-moral goods be grounded in biological facts; his instrumentalism about rationality precludes treating well-being as an intrinsic good, *tout court*.

Like any adaptation, an interest is objective only with respect to an environment. When an environment changes, an interest can go from objective to subjective, from adaptive to maladaptive. For example, in the time of the hunter-gatherer, eating as much protein as possible was adaptive, and in the objective interests of agents. Today in the West, it is highly maladaptive, and not in the objective interests of agents. Why? Because the environment has changed the amount of protein available to many people from barely sufficient to practically unlimited.

It is crucial to see that a theory of objective interests, of what conduces to well-being, must leave room for the environment as a variable: x is an objective interest for A in environment e. Railton does not omit mention of the environment in the exposition of non-moral goodness: he refers to the agent's circumstances. But he does omit it in his theory of moral goodness, with serious consequences.

Railton believes the notion of "objective interests" may yield counterintuitive results. In particular, he holds, it may turn out that quite aberrant and indeed repulsive preferences will figure among the objective interests of an individual, and thus be part of his "non-moral good." He writes, "some people. . .might be put together in a way that makes some not-very-appetizing things essential to their flourishing, and we do not want to be guilty of wishful thinking on this score" (p. 177). On the other hand Railton may wish to take some comfort in the "pluralism" about objective interests this possibility promotes. For few will want to adopt an account of the non-morally good that allows for little interpersonal variation in objective interests. But in fact, whether counterintuitive or not, this variability is not something Railton's theory really allows him. Because of its unavoidable biological character, Railton's conception of "objective interest" is more likely to homogenize agents than it is to reveal their divergent objective interests. To the extent that our interests – both objective and subjective – have what Railton calls a "reduction base" in our physiology and environment, acquiring complete knowledge about ourselves includes acquisition of information about this base as well. If, as seems reasonable, sadism, for example, turns out to be symptomatic of a physiological malfunction, then it will be in the objective interests of a sadist to treat the disorder. Similarly for more innocent pleasures. The insatiable craving for sweets, when viewed in the light of all its long-term effects, can be no part of an objective interest either.

This is true unless, of course, mental and physical malfunction can enhance "physical or psychological well-being." If so, a disorder or illness may figure in the objective interests of an agent. But it would be difficult for Railton to allow that there are some people whose objective interests are directly, intrinsically served by the exercise of cruelty or the onset of dental pain – unless our objective interests were somehow decoupled from evolutionary constraints, as indeed in modern life they sometimes seem to be. But in this case they would be decoupled from well-being and lose their standing as non-morally good. Such maladaptive objective interests might still be able to explain behavior, especially aberrant actions, as rational (in Railton's instrumental sense). But there would be no reason to identify such maladaptive interests as non-morally good. For a naturalistic approach would identify them as pathologies. Cut off from evolutionary adaptation, such interests no longer have the kind of naturalistic explanation in terms of adaptation that Railton's realism requires. Their naturalistic explanation is a matter of "break-down" or "malfunction." An interest which is the result of some malfunction, or deficiency, is indistinguishable from what Railton calls a subjective interest, one which may be the product of epistemic and logical errors of omission and commission, for, after all, these are malfunctions or deficiencies themselves. So aberrant objective interests are not really explained on Railton's theory as non-moral goods. And its prospects of accommodating the wide variation in human aims and objectives are not as great as Railton hopes.

In and by itself there is nothing philosophically very objectionable about Railton's theory of the non-morally good. It is, as noted, rather more biological than he indicates and may undercut conventional views about the degree to which individuals can differ in their real interests. But perhaps its gravest defect is not a philosophical one at all. Railton bills the account of "objective interest" as part of an explanatory theory of human behavior. But if there is such a theory, it is not a very interesting one. For consider, "objective interests" help explain agents' behaviors because the subjective desires that lead to action are supposed to evolve in the direction of these objective interests:

> [An individual's] desires evolve through experience to conform more closely to what is good for him, in the naturalistic sense intended here [his well-being]. The process [is] not one of an ideally rational response to the receipt of ideal information, but rather of largely unreflective experimenta-tion, accompanied by positive and negative associations and reinforce-ments. There is no guarantee that the desires "learned" through such feedback will accurately or completely reflect an individual's good. (p. 180)

Without the caveat of the last sentence this theory would be stigmatized as both Panglossian in its expectations about desires and patently false. On the other hand, the caveat deprives it of much explanatory power. For so qualified, the theory is consistent with the persistence of any kind of desires, no matter how non-morally bad, over any but the long run. In terms Railton employs later in his essay, the theory is guilty of a "complacent functionalism." Like another such theory, folk psychology, at best its explanations are highly generic or inevitably *ex post*. This fact bedevils the account of moral goodness which Railton wants to build on the model of non-moral goodness. It is to this account that I now turn.

3. MORAL GOODNESS

In line with the adequacy conditions set out at the beginning of "Moral Realism" (p. 172) Railton notes that to establish moral realism one must show that there are facts about what ought to be the case, and that these facts can be explanatory (p. 185). For facts about non-moral goodness, this should not be difficult. Hypo-thetical imperatives about what one ought to do in order to attain well-being may be said to have "derived" explanatory force for they rest on declarative state-ments about what in fact conduces to well-being, and on the presumption that agents seek well-being. Railton seems to adopt the view that 'A does x' can be explained by 'A ought to do x' because this latter can be unpacked into "Crea-tures like A have evolved in ways that make doing x conducive to their well-being, and they seek their well-being." (Railton's argument for the explanatory power of normative statements proceeds in a different way, exploiting examples to make the view plausible [pp. 185–87], but I think the sketch given above fairly represents the foundations of his reasoning.)

It is worth nothing that a categorial imperative will not have the sort of explanatory power a hypothetical one does. 'A does x' cannot be explained by 'A ought to do x, without qualification or condition." On the other hand, a catego-rial imperative is not vulnerable to the questions that a hypothetical imperative always leaves open: If A ought to do x because he seeks end e, then why does he seek end e, and why should he seek it? In the case of non-moral goods and individual agents, Railton's answers seem to be given in terms of the evolution-ary adaptiveness of individual well-being and the further end of the survival of the individual's lineage. What will the answer be in the case of moral goodness and social aggregates? Any answer to this question suggests that moral goodness is instrumental to some further end. Since moral goodness is part of an explanatory theory, all the imperatives it sustains will be hypothetical and will generate the question of why does the system which attains moral goodness do so and why should it do so? (I take up this point further in section 6 below).

Given his account of normativeness in terms of hypothetical imperatives with derived explanatory power, the steps Railton takes to an account of moral goodness and moral norms with explanatory power are pretty direct.

The non-morally good reflects what it is rational for an individual to want—his objective interests—in order to secure his individual well-being. The morally good reflects what it is rational to want, not from an individual point of view, but from "the social point of view" (p. 180). What is rational from the social point of view is "what would be rationally approved of were the [objective] interests of all potentially affected individuals counted equally. . . ." So, moral goodness is "what is rational from the social point of view with regard to the realization of intrinsic non-moral goodness." Moral goodness is thus supposed to involve increasing some aggregation of the non-moral goodness of individuals, the well-being of agents in society—not just any aggregation, such as average expected utility or well-being, but an aggregation that takes account of all affected individuals equally. Railton does not indicate which aggregation will do this, so, hereafter, I will refer to social rationality as requiring some aggregation, meaning a particular one, and leaving it open, along with Railton, which one.

Non-moral goodness pertains to individuals, moral goodness pertains to "social arrangements—a form of production, a social or political hierarchy, etc." When such arrangements depart "from social rationality by significantly discounting the interests of a particular group" there is "potential for dissatisfaction and unrest"—and therefore reduction in the viability of the "social arrangement," and of the whole society which it characterizes. Although he does not say it explicitly, a moral injunction will be a hypothetical imperative in which the end served by maximizing some aggregation of the well-being of the society's members is that society's well-being or survival. Thus there will have to be a social theory identifying the prerequisites for the viability of well-being of the society, and the conditions that increase and reduce it. Otherwise there is no end for social rationality to serve. But as Railton notes, rationality is always instrumental.

Railton is not shy about endorsing such a theory, for he needs it to establish moral realism as a claim about the causal and explanatory force of independently existing moral facts. The theory proceeds as follows: an optimally rational social arrangement minimizes social unrest and discontent. Departures from it lead to "alienation, loss of morale, decline in the effectiveness of authority. . .potential for unrest,. . .a tendency towards religious or ideological doctrines, or towards certain forms of repressive apparatus,. . ." etc. (p. 192). These conditions are not good for the society or for the social arrangements that lead to discontent. That is, as such departures from social rationality increase, the prospects for these arrangements' continued existence decline. Since those social institutions which have survived are ones which have been selected for survival-promoting features—i.e., social rationality—it follows that social rationality, like any adaptation, has an explanatory role to play in social theory. Or at least it does to the extent that the theory is a functional or teleological one, assigning either some stable equilibrium to social processes, or some end-state towards which societies evolve, given their environments. (As noted below, however, Railton seems to eschew the notion that a teleological account of social arrangements presupposes some kind of stable equilibrium. [Cf. p. 194.] This is simply incompatible with the adoption of a functionalist feed-back theory. A teleological process must track some variable over a range of conditions. So long as it keeps tracking, it is either at equilibrium or moving towards it and showing stability.)

Railton believes that recent work in social history and historical sociology tends to confirm such a theory. This work explains observed social change as movement in the direction of greater social rationality through a feedback between changes in the level of discontent and fuller recognition of the interests of social groups. Of course, Railton admits, actual short-term trends sometimes move away from social rationality, but the discontent this breeds tends to move society back in the "right" direction, one which tracks improvements in social rationality. Thus, social rationality constitutes a fact about moral goodness open to empirical study, and norms asserting the obligation to enhance social rationality can have some explanatory power. Besides endorsing particular works in social science that reflect this theory, Railton cites three gross trends, which he believes substantiate it: (1) "Generality"—the decline of tribalism, ethnic exclusivity, ethnocentrism, and xenophobia; (2) "Humanization"—the demystification of ethics and its separation from religious foundations; and (3) "Patterns of Variation"—greater approximations to social rationality in cases where such arrangements are more obviously in the subjective interests of all participants (p. 198).

I do not share Railton's confidence in the social science he cites, and I find at least two of his trends susceptible of interpretations which make them appear to be movements away from "social rationality." Thus, the first could equally well be described as the overwhelming of cultural differences in the interests of some covert or overt imperialist imperative; certainly the socially enforced abrogation of traditional ways of life has led to considerable discontent (cf. Iran under the Pahlavi dynasty), and could therefore be construed as a departure from social rationality. (Compare the biological irrationality of extinguishing species which provide a reservoir of variations we may need hereafter.) The "humanization," in Railton's terms, of moral prescriptions has certainly reduced their subjective force. When people thought that morality was God's command, they were more likely to embrace it. To the extent moral conduct is socially rational, this trend, too, seems in the opposite direction. Finally, in cases where "social rationality" can be explained in terms of individual rationality, it is in effect explained away, made superfluous as an explanatory concept. Naturally, there are possible counters to each of the objections briefly sketched here. But even if the gross historical trends are as Railton makes out, there is something crucial that is missing from his theory. Railton says that his theory is no mere "complacent functionalism or an overall endorsement of current moral practice or norms." He excuses himself from this charge by pointing out the account "emphasizes conflict rather than equilibrium and provides means for criticizing certain moral practices. . ." (p. 199). But conflict and equilibrium are by no means incompatible in a functionalist theory: indeed many such theories (including "complacent" ones, like "democratic pluralism") secure equilibrium through conflict. Consider game theoretical models of evolutionary interaction. And it is by no means clear that Railton's theory of social rationality provides the resources to mount serious criticism of any very long-standing social practice, present or past, as we shall see.

More seriously, Railton's theory is a complacent one, almost by default— because it fails to specify the environmental factors against which social institutions measure up for rationality or adaptiveness, it fails to indicate how they have changed over time and fails to indicate how these changes shift social arrangements from the adaptive to the maladaptive, the rational to the irrational, and back again. Instead he simply assumes that the background conditions always and uniformly favor increasing the aggregate well-being of all agents treated equally as socially rational.

To see how this assumption vitiates Railton's theory, we need to answer the question of for whose ends (and which ones) it is rational to optimize some aggregate of individual well-being. There are only two possibilities, optimizing aggregate well-being either serves the ends of individuals or of the society composed of them. Neither of these alternatives are satisfactory. Treating the ends of society as a whole, however, has the virtue of not making the theory empirically false.

Optimizing some aggregate of individual well-being is rational either for society as a whole, treated as an individual, or for the individual agents who compose it. There is no third possibility, since that is all there are: individuals and the aggregate of them. But clearly optimizing average, or median, or minimum, or maximum well-being or any such social welfare measure is not rational for the objective interests of every individual member of society. Some will be disadvantaged no matter what measure of aggregate well-being is optimized. In fact, under some circumstances of scarcity, for instance, that have been realized in the course of human history, the rational course may involve sacrificing the objective interests of a majority of the members of a society.

If social arrangements turn out to be morally good if and only if they are non-morally good, through some sort of disaggregation, for all the individual members of society, then of course there are almost no social arrangements that are morally good, and none that we could devise that would be. And if social arrangements are morally good because they are non-morally good for some subset, perhaps even a very large subset, of the individuals who compose a society, then we need a naturalistic explanation of what makes this subset the morally relevant one. For example, an evolutionary argument that the well-being of this subset is necessary or sufficient in most circumstances for the well-being of the society as a whole, or one that held its well-being was equally in the objective interest of every member of the society individually.

Railton does not give us such an argument. But his discussion of moral principles as "non-indexical" and "comprehensive," as reflecting "a social point of view" (pp. 189–90), suggests that social arrangements are rational to the degree they serve the ends of the whole society, as distinct from the individuals who compose it. This is not a view Railton will accept, for he holds that the only bearers of value are actual sentient beings, but it is the only way to reconcile his instrumental rationality with the maximization of aggregate well-being. So, in what follows let us explore the implications of this answer to the question of whose ends aggregate well-being is instrumentally rational for: it is instrumental for the ends of society as a whole.

Social rationality, like evolutionary adaptation, or individual rationality for that matter, is always relative to an environment. What is adaptive with respect to one environment is maladaptive with respect to another. Consider what happens to polar bears that move south. At a minimum, Railton needs to say that constant environmental factors make some aggregate maximizing of well-being an adaptation of all societies everywhere and always: he needs a convincing argument that environmental and demographic conditions have throughout history made movement in the direction of some aggregate maximizing of individual well-being a necessary condition of the continued existence of social arrangements and the societies that manifest them. Or at least he needs an argument that this has happened more often than not, or at the most crucial turns in human history. No such claim appears even vaguely plausible.

Indeed, the most convincing account of the evolution of human society that I know of proceeds on the well-supported hypothesis that this assumption is false. The evolutionary approach to anthropological theory developed in the work of Harris, Cohen, Harner, and others[8] is the most fully worked out functional theory of the sort Railton envisions, one quite explicit about explaining social change in terms of the interaction of individual objective interests with the changing biological environment. Harris, for example, traces an evolutionary sequence of social stages from the hunter-gatherer system, through neolithic agricultural organizations, to the pre-state village, chiefdoms, and eventually the state. Each evolutionary change represents, on his theory, an adaptation of social organization in order to meet the interests of individuals faced by environmental changes, in large part of their own making. The hunter-gatherer societies of prehistory include above 90 percent of all the human beings ever born. As Harris explains, not only was it chronologically the first social arrangement, it was the last to be characterized by what Railton would describe as optimal social rationality: "Political-economic egalitarianism is a. . .theoretically predictable structural consequence of the hunter-gatherer infrastructure," mainly because there is never any surplus to redistribute. "Egalitarianism is also firmly rooted in the openness of resources, the simplicity of the tools of production, the lack of nontransportable property, and the labile structure of the band. . .extremes of subordination and superordination are unknown. . . . Women would not be used as the rewards for male bravery [because warfare is unnecessary], sex-ratios would be in balance, and serial monogamy for both sexes would prevail." Indeed, Harris explains why "the slight degree of [human] sexual dimorphism would not impair the highly egalitarian bent of hunter-gatherer social life" (Harris, pp. 80–83).

But then environmental conditions changed in ways that would no longer support these social arrangements, so that survival of human societies required the abolition of these now maladaptive institutions that maximize well-being equally. The ice age, together with overhunting, extinguished the supply of game, and forced social groups to choose between extinction and agriculture. But agriculture increased reproductive levels and reduced mobility, thus fostering inter- and intra-group conflict. The appearance of storable and surplus food led to complex social organization, stratification, and inequities based on control of this surplus. Harris convincingly explains as adaptive for societies' survival—under these conditions—the appearance and persistence of female infanticide, obligatory marriage rules, male domination, warfare, despotic imperial state-systems, in fact, the whole panoply of past social practices we condemn as immoral, despite their enduring character. And Harris explains much of the underlying detail as well, in terms of a functional account methodologically indistinguishable from the functional theory Railton requires.

Harris's theory is not incompatible with the historical and sociological works that Railton cites. It is a much wider theory, that easily accommodates and provides a more general explanation of the sixteenth- through twentieth-century social processes which Railton's favored social scientists treat. Indeed, it may even underwrite Railton's claim that the moral goodness of social arrangements has increased over the very recent past, say, the period from the onset of the industrial revolution. For in this period, environmental and demographic forces may well have made some aggregation of well-being optimally adaptive for societies and social arrangements.

It is clear that Railton must reject this theory, for its reading of the role of social rationality in the evolution of social arrangements does not have the normative moral that Railton's does. If Harris is right, there is no reason to suppose that over the long term maximizing some aggregate individual well-being has been adaptive for society; in fact quite the opposite. But it is pretty clear that if Harris's theory is right for the whole of social history, Railton's claim, that moral goodness is whatever in general optimizes social rationality, must be false, when the latter is understood in its empirical guise as adaptation.

5. REINTERPRETING RAILTON'S MORAL THEORY

How should a defender of Railton's theory respond to this conclusion? He can either reject a theory like Harris's or revise his own account of moral goodness to accommodate it. There seems to be a way to do this latter: identify the morally good with every long-standing social institution for which an adaptational explanation is convincing; then attempt to find a way in which these institutions really did maximize some aggregate well-being of the members of their societies, no matter how repugnant these institutions may appear to us.

Rejecting Harris's view outright requires a specification of the environmental fact, which throughout human history has made aggregating well-being an evolutionary adaptation for all societies, and has made arrangements fostering inequities and disparities maladaptive. Without such a specification, Railton does not even have a challenge to Harris's theory, let alone a superior alternative. It is worth emphasizing that even if the details of Harris's reconstruction of the sequence of social institutions is wrong in detail, it is not this sequence that Railton must challenge. It is the environmental constraints, and changes in them that Harris identifies, which Railton must undercut and must find substitutes for.

Rejecting these environmental constraints is implausible. So, let us consider the ways Railton's theory might be revised or interpreted to accommodate them. Railton cannot simply say that many social institutions have persisted over long periods despite their tendency to decrease social rationality. For social rationality is supposed to be part of an explanatory theory about what has actually happened in the course of human history. A functional theory like Railton's cannot remain silent on the persistence of discontent-provoking institutions over the long term. It is not enough to say, as Railton does, that his mechanism, like those of evolution, "does not guarantee optimality or even a monotonic approach to equilibrium" (p. 194), especially in the face of theories (like Harris's) that explain departures from moral "optimality" on the basis of the same kind of evolutionary mechanism. Railton tells us, by way of excusing his theory from any commitment to monotonic improvement in the direction of social rationality, that "Human societies do not appear to have begun at or near equilibrium." Therefore, at best, "one could expect an uneven secular trend towards the inclusion of the interests of social groups." But a functional theory of the sort Railton envisions must postulate a mechanism for keeping a society within a stable equilibrium point, one determined by its environment, where this point is either itself an optimum or a sufficient condition for tracking an optimum, modulo the environment. To say that human societies do not appear to have begun near an equilibrium of any kind is incompatible with adopting a naturalistic evolutionary theory of how they change, as their environments change. The notion that starting far from any equilibrium point, an evolving system can survive and move towards it is worse than complacent functionalism. It is a species of immanent perfectionism.

If Railton had seen the need to specify environmental contingencies against which social changes could be measured for "rationality," i.e., adaptation, he might not have made this claim. He would have seen that any evolutionary theory of biological adaptation needs to have convincing explanations of departures from apparent optimality (e.g., random drift or changes in local conditions, etc.) just because it presupposes a long-term movement in the direction of optimization. To the extent such a theory lacks them, its explanatory power is minimal at best. The same must be said for Railton's theory. Thus, for example, we need to know why slavery, Railton's example of a "brutal exclusionary social arrangement" (p. 195), has persisted, not for hundreds of years, but through all of recorded history, in spite of the uneven secular trend towards social rationality.

On pain of fatally undermining the explanatory power of his theory Railton has to endorse as socially rational many of the social arrangements we hold morally repugnant today, but which typified long periods of past history, periods far longer than a millennium in some cases. Railton will have to allow that these arrangements reflected some aggregation of the objective interests of their subjects, and that therefore these apparently repugnant arrangements were, on aggregate, morally good. Now, every social system that succeeded the hunter-gatherer involved distributional inequalities, and most involved extreme social stratification, exploitation, gender discrimination, and violent preservation of the status quo. In all of these post-hunter-gatherer societies the subjective interests of the vast majority of the population certainly did not coincide with the actual arrangements, even though in most cases every one was better off—in regard to physical well-being—than had they remained hunter-gatherers (for in that case they would not have survived at all). Their objective interests thus justified the Railtonian judgment that societies characterized by slavery, warfare, and every conceivable violation of the person were morally better than they would have been had hunter-gatherer arrangements persisted. And what is more, to the extent each of these stages in the evolution of human societies was causally necessary for the ultimate appearance of still morally superior social arrangements, they were not just better than earlier states, but were morally good, *sans* phrase. Though it reconciles Railton's account with social evolution, this conclusion undermines Railton's defense against the charge of "complacent functionalism." At any rate it seriously compromises the application of the theory to criticize the most horrifying aspects of prior social practice, no matter what its power for criticizing present practice.

But in any case this tactic is not really available to Railton. He insists that in addition to having an explanatory function, a moral theory should also make sense of most of our moral intuitions: it should "insofar as possible capture the normative force of [our evaluative] terms by providing analyses that permit these terms to play their central evaluative roles. . . . they [should] express recognizable notions of goodness and rightness" (p. 205). This is something the tactic here envisioned surely cannot do.

Of course, Railton may want to jettison the requirement that an empirical theory of moral goodness should coincide with our relatively myopic moral judgments for they may be no better than our often mistaken views about our objective interests. Indeed, there is considerable impetus within his theory for doing exactly that. After all, as Railton claims, objective interests enhance biological well-being, and well-being is what broadly conduces to survival of the lineage of the individual. So, even though a vast majority of the members of a given society might be quite discontent with their lot, that lot might nevertheless foster the survival of each of their individual lines of inheritance, or at least the survival of some optimum number and distribution of agents, given the environment, population size, available technology, etc. The result is that at every stage of human history most of the prevailing institutions reflect the best of all possible worlds, though almost everything in them may be a necessary evil. Expressions of discontent, whether by organized or unorganized individuals would reflect mistakes about objective interest and would need to be suppressed in the interests of moral goodness.

This is true, unless, of course, at any or perhaps every stage of social evolution the objective interests of individuals are severed from their evolutionary bases. In such a case, it may turn out that the expressions of discontent will sometimes, perhaps even often, reflect unmet objective interests of individuals, even though they subvert social arrangements necessary for the survival of aggregates of them or their progeny. In these cases, meeting them will be morally good, even though it results in a heightened probability of extinction for the whole society. But one question this raises is whether moral goodness must take into account only agents alive at any given time and not also future generations? If the latter, we may not reconcile a theory like Railton's with discontent that threatens the survival of the society for satisfying such discontent can hardly be socially rational. But if we do not take the unborn into account in a theory about morality as social rationality, we not only deprive it of much explanatory power as an evolutionary explanation, but we also forgo any explanation for our intuitions that the interests of our and others' unborn offspring should count for something in our moral calculations. Surely no one supposes that moral goodness is whatever optimizes some aggregation of the objective interests of the present members of a society, regardless of its effects on future members of the same society. Indeed, Railton seems to include these future members, when he claims that socially rational institutions optimize some aggregation of the well-being of "all *potentially* affected individuals counted equally" (p. 180, emphasis added).

6. SOCIAL RATIONALITY-MORAL GOODNESS FOR WHAT?

Individuals ought to pursue their objective interests because this is instrumentally rational for achieving their well-being, their non-moral good. Why is well-being an intrinsic end of individuals and their objective interests instrumental ends? Because nature has fostered these ends for its own evolutionary ends. Societies, too, should pursue the objective interests of the individuals who compose them, for doing so is instrumental to the society's well-being, and so, to its chances of surviving and improving in its adaptation to the environment in which it is located. Optimizing some aggregation of individual well-being is "socially rational" because it is instrumental for attaining this end of the society. So far, there is nothing distinctively moral in this sketch of Railton's theory. Morality is introduced by the identification of the socially rational with the morally good.

But this identification of the socially rational with the aggregation of individual objective interests and the morally good will be mere fiat unless two other questions can be answered in a satisfactory way. First, why is it the case that optimizing some aggregation of individual well-being is necessary for the survival of the society? Second, and more important, why should, in the moral sense of should, societies survive?

Presumably Railton's answer to the first question is simply that the well-being of societies is a function of some aggregation of the well-being of their members, and its well-being is necessary for its survival. As we have seen, this is probably false for much of human history, though it might be true for some societies at some times under some environmental conditions. But how can Railton answer the second question. This is roughly the question, what is so valuable about societies? On Railton's instrumental notion of rationality, the question can always be posed "rational for what?" Identifying something as rational presupposes an end or objective whose attainment it fosters. Social rationality, *a.k.a.* moral goodness, has "reality" on this theory because a society's attaining or increasing it is an end instrumental to society's survival. But is the survival of society an instrumental end or an intrinsic one? If the former, then there is some other end, either of society or of some larger system within which it figures that must be identified. And if it is an intrinsic end, then all the problems that haunt traditional conceptions of moral realism return to unravel the whole of Railton's new argument for it.

To show that the survival of society is instrumentally rational for the biosphere, or ecosystem, or some other system that includes it, requires showing that its survival is necessary for the optimization of the well-being of the entire ecosystem. Even if, in the face of nuclear winter, overpopulation, the greenhouse effect, chemical pollution, destruction of species, etc., we could show this, the question of intrinsic *vs.* instrumental ends must recur at the level of the ecosystem as a whole. At some point, some end or other will have to be identified as morally good in itself. So, we might as well face, sooner rather than later in the regress, the question whether anything can be good in itself. This is the question arguments for moral realism must answer, for no one ever doubted that there are things that are good as means.

But Railton's argument for moral realism is anchored on showing the causal role of moral goodness in a functional network—one in which moral goodness is a means, and not an end. Even if the theory were empirically convincing, it would not succeed in showing that what he calls moral goodness is morally good.

In a way Railton recognizes this fact. He recognizes that whether social rationality is really morally good is, in Moore's phrase, an open question:

> Such "open questions" cannot by their nature be closed, since definitions are not subject to proof or disproof. But open questions can be more or less disturbing, for although definitional proposals cannot be demonstrated, they can fare better or worse at meeting various desiderata. (p. 204)

The desiderata Railton believes his definitional identification meets are actually adequacy conditions on the social theory in which the definition figures. But the theory does not, I think, meet them. First note that the issue of whether the identification is a definition or a central theoretical claim in a social theory with positive and normative ramifications is, of course, irrelevant to whether the theory meets adequacy criteria. To describe the identification of social rationality with moral goodness as a definition seems to ward off the question, "Is social rationality really everywhere and always morally good?" as silly, rather like the question "Is social rationality really social rationality?" But this ploy will not work among naturalists. For if there is one thing they agree on, it is then when it comes to scientific theories, the distinction between those sentences which are treated as definitions and those treated as axioms of the theory comes to very little. So the real test of whether this "definition" is a good one, or equivalently, whether this "axiom" is a well-justified one, is the explanatory and predictive power of the theory in which it figures. This is a point with which Railton, of course, agrees: "I have assumed throughout that the drawing up of definitions is part of theory-construction" (p. 204). So, in Railton's conclusion, whether definitional or not, his proposal is said to meet the following criteria on theory construction in this domain (the labels on these criteria are mine):

(1) Explanatory constraints: (a) Does the theory in which the definition figures systematize a large enough proportion of our actual judgments of moral goodness and rightness? (b) Do the moral notions defined in the theory actually do any explanatory work in systematizing the theory's subject matter?

(2) Evidential constraints: "[Are] the empirical theories constructed with the help of these definitions. . .reasonably good theories, that is theories for which we have substantial evidence and which provide plausible explanation" (p. 205).

If my account of the evidence is closer to correct than Railton's, then neither Railton's actual theory nor a reasonable revision of it can jointly meet these two sets of criteria. The best theory I know of consistent with the evidence identifies as instrumentally rational for the survival of societies many institutions we could never approve as morally good nor explain as persisting because of their moral goodness.

This leaves us with the question of whether the defects here alleged are restricted to Railton's particular attempt to yoke together empirical social theory and moral philosophy. Or do they reflect obstacles to any attempt to substantiate a naturalistic moral theory by means of social science. I venture to suggest that the moral to draw from this essay is not restricted to Railton's approach. The reasons are twofold. First, to be at all attractive to us, any moral theory will have to reflect our most basic moral beliefs. Secondly, the only tractable naturalistic theories in social science, and psychology for that matter, are all functional ones, of roughly the sort Railton appeals to. Since they are predicated on the assumption that their objects, individual people or whole societies, are either in a stable equilibrium that optimizes some quality or moving towards such an equilibrium, the moral realist has little choice but to link goodness with this optimized quality. To do otherwise deprives moral goodness of its explanatory role in the empirical theory, and so deprives it of its claim to reality. This means that every attempt to harness a theory of the good to an empirical social theory must face the charge of complacent functionalism.

NOTES

*The comments of Peter Railton and Russell Hardin on a previous draft of this essay are gratefully acknowledged.

1. This is a point well argued by G. Sayre-McCord, "Introduction: The Many Moral Realisms," in *Moral Realism,* edited by Sayre-McCord (Ithaca, N.Y., 1988), 1–23.

2. Ibid., 13.

3. This account of ethical naturalism is to be found, for example, in Nicholas Sturgeon, "Moral Explanations," in *Morality, Reason, and Truth,* edited by Copp and Zimmerman (Totowa, N.J., 1985), 49–78, and Richard Boyd, "How to be a Moral Realist," in *Moral Realism,* edited by Sayre-McCord.

4. Boyd's essay, "How to be a Moral Realist," provides an example both of this view about the relevance of social science and the one outlined in the previous paragraph about the importance of naturalism to realism: ". . .according to any naturalistic conception [of morals]. . .goodness is an ordinary natural property, and it would be odd indeed if observations didn't play the same role in the study of this property that they play in the study of all the others. . . . [G]oodness is a property quite similar to the other properties studied by psychologists, historians, and social scientists. . ." in *Moral Realism*, 206.

5. Peter Railton, "Moral Realism," *Philosophical Review* 95 (1986): 163–207. Page references in the text are to this essay, unless otherwise noted.

6. For a general discussion of the connections between alternative moral theories and alternative research programs in the social sciences, see Alexander Rosenberg, *Philosophy of Social Science* (Boulder, Colo., 1988), chap. 7.

7. Boyd is clearly committed to the same type of functional approach in his account both of individual and social goodness, although his "homeostatic" theory is not worked out in the sort of way that will reveal its connections to current social theories nor to the methodological problems that such theories face. See "How to be a Moral Realist."

8. M. Cohen, *Food Crisis in Prehistory* (New Haven, Conn., 1977); M. Harner, "Ecological Basis for Aztec Sacrifice," *American Ethologist* 4 (1977): 117–35; "Population Pressure and the Social Evolution of Agriculturalists," *Southwest Journal of Anthropology* 26 (1970): 67–86; Marvin Harris, *Cultural Materialism* (New York, 1979). Quotations from Harris in the text below come from this work.

The Methodological and Metaphysical Peculiarities of the Human Sciences

JOSEPH MARGOLIS

I t is very convenient, though hardly accurate, to date the decisive turning point in theorizing about the relationship between the natural and the human sciences from the publication of Thomas Kuhn's *The Structure of Scientific Revolutions*. [1] It is convenient, because, regardless of the endless quarrels about the precise form and tenability of Kuhn's thesis and its noticeably restricted purview, the major developments in the philosophy of science, particularly in the Anglo-American literature, has not been able or disposed to dispute the indissoluble connection—the theoretically critical connection—between the essential structures of the sciences as cognitive achievements and their history, the ongoing, actual living practice of the sciences themselves. The claim is not an accurate one, because: first of all, there have been many compelling anticipations in the Continental European literature of something like Kuhn's thesis featuring science as a historically changing practice;[2] second, giving the essential role of *Erlebnisse* in the classic formulations of the Vienna Circle's program, the ineliminability of such themes as those of experience, practice, and history were already (fatally as it proved) impregnably embedded in the Circle's fancies of precision;[3] and third, the naïveté of the anti-"metaphysical" bias of positivism and the early unity-of-science movement proved, quite apart from considerations of experience and history, to be utterly incapable of supporting the canonical vision or of segregating the phenomenological and theoretical standing of description, prediction, and the fate of scientific realism in general.[4]

The upshot of these remarkable changes in an interval of a little more than fifty years has, arguably, been to alter in a fundamental way the perceived relationship between the natural and the human sciences. The older canon of the unity of science, even when it had already pretty well shelved its positivist bent, still hewed very closely to the thesis that the physical sciences afforded the paradigm of what it was to be a science, *a fortiori* a human science. This is clearly the sense of Carl Hempel's well-known early discussion of history, for instance.[5] The two substantive philosophical theses (of those closely related programs) still actively debated at the present time—the various claims of extensionalism and physicalism—that link the 1920s and 1930s to our own time, have not fared very well in terms of actual achievement; although it is certainly true that, however attenuated, those two families of claims provide the pivot of a great many that acknowledge the need to rely on "folk" versions of the physical sciences on both scores, and that do not feel obliged either to support a strong reductive physicalism or a detailed and explicated extensionalism.[6]

The priority of the physical sciences, taken in a paradigmatic sense, rests, today, on a promissory note in just these two regards. On the argument that they are essentially flawed (extensionalism and physicalism), either it is the case that the methodology and epistemology of the physical sciences should be regarded as abstractions from whatever encompassing rigor may be assigned the human sciences, or else there is in principle no demarcation between the two. This dual conclusion is, in a fair sense, what is already adumbrated in an acceptance of Kuhn's argument (with whatever caveats may be needed). The human sciences are very much in the ascendent, then, without presuming any longer that it is possible to formulate an invariant overarching method that any bona fide science may be expected to instantiate, however approximately, or that such a canon can be drawn off from a review of the physical sciences themselves.[7]

I

We still cling, however, to our suspicions regarding the respectability of the human sciences. That is, we assess them disadvantageously in terms of a former canon that can no longer claim its former tribute. Part of the habit is undoubtedly due to the lag of a theorizing practice itself now largely discharged; part is due to the detachability of the objectives of extensionalism and physicalism from the special claims of positivism and the early unity-of-science program; and part is due to a reasonable puzzlement about how the world could possibly be other than one that conforms with those first two constraints.

What we may say is that, in a genuinely technical sense, it is still incumbent on those who mean to free the human sciences from the dependency in question to explain just how they intend to address those topics; but, beyond that, in a deeper sense, the very conceivability of a human world *not* so confined needs to be convincingly sketched. The opportunistic position that holds that the human or cultural *is* ultimately subject to just those constraints—but that we may nevertheless use whatever "folk" concepts we please, without bothering our heads to show, here and now, that they *are* so constrained—is always available, if it is available at all. Absolutely nothing is gained by that sort of stalemate.

There is only one sort of answer that genuinely affords the possibility of construing the human sciences as disciplines relatively distinct from the physical sciences. It is this: that the cognitive capacities of human investigators are antecedently structured (possibly in a hardwired sense biologically, as well as in culturally preformative ways), not infinitely plastic, horizontally skewed, reflexively intransparent to some extent; and, therefore, that there are tacit *endogenous* limitations on what humans can inquire into, understand, form concepts about, recognize, and analyze at conceptual levels thought to be more fundamental in the order of reality than that at which they first identify what they inquire into.

In a sense, the matter is an empirical one, at least to the extent that programs of analysis, reductive or not, that would replace what is specified at the usual level of familiar human functioning — what is fashionably now called "folk" science[8] — appear to be remarkably unsuccessful in their detailed projects. The thesis of endogenous limitations is a perfectly coherent, reasonable, empirically compelling, and resilient one. In fact, *whatever* gains can be made along the lines of extensionalist and physicalist regimentation can be easily accommodated within the folk position; but the contrary is either not successful or has not yet been successfully pursued. After all, such gains are the work of agents who belong in the folk world and are prepared to appraise them.

The largest, most important executive finding to be drawn from this relatively homely thesis is this: that there are at least two fundamentally different orientations to the human sciences (*a fortiori*, to the physical sciences), that are at one and the same time methodological and metaphysical (meaning, by 'metaphysical' to say that theories of how the world is structured are involved), that they are not asymmetrical merely because of their point of departure but are substantively different,[9] and that our preference for either need not be *a priori* but (generously construed) empirical, in the sense of 'empirical' in which, say, geometries are empirically validated within encompassing theories addressed to particular sectors of the world.[10]

The two programmatic orientations have pretty well come to be distinguished as *top-down* and *bottom-up*: meaning by that, in a formal sense, that the first is conducted in and controlled by "folk" concepts, even where bottom-up analyses are feasible for finitely demarcated, piecemeal subsectors of the folk-discriminated world; that folk categories are not themselves immutable; that bottom-up analyses are construed *factorially* as accounts of the *sub*functions or *sub*structures of what is discriminated at the folk (molar) level; and that the second is conducted in and controlled by the presumption that, in principle, there is some ultimate array of elements in accord with which all complex phenomena are *compositionally* formed, by processes ascribable to that fundamental array or, emergently, to higher-level combinations of whatever is so composed. Bottom-up theories are what is left of the reductive versions of the unity-of-science program (with respect to extensionalism and physicalism).

Top-down theories oppose physicalisms, both reductive and nonreductive, as failed programs; they also oppose unqualified extensionalisms for the same reason. But, as already remarked, they are resilient enough to accommodate *any* successful physicalist or extensionalist *sub*functional analysis.[11] And top-down theories open in principle to a variety of metaphysics (a Leibnizian or information-informed substrate) are usually formulated as *materialisms* but not as *physicalisms*. By this is meant that whatever is real is "material," in the sense that insofar as it is composed (though what is real may not be analyzable compositionally) it is composed of "matter"—of whatever the fundamental sciences determine to be the *materia* of the actual world. Physicalism maintains, by contrast, that whatever is actual possesses nothing but physical properties. Nonreductive materialism merely concedes that we need not refuse a "folk" language and that we need not supply a physicalist reduction of any serviceable language.[12]

II

The point of these distinctions is to draw attention to a series of questions that affect the inherent structure of the human sciences. The key question concerns the reasonableness of (i) an endogenous (cognitive) barrier. To grant (i) is to concede the initial eligibility of "folk"-level discourse: the apparent phenomena of the human world, the linguistic categories of analysis, the perceptual and conceptual capacities of the agents involved, and the conditions of validity on which their claims depend. To escape "altogether" the constraints of the folk sciences (physics as well as history) means, in effect, to be able to replace all categories of description, analysis, explanation, and validity that fail to behave extensionally and physicalistically)—all anthropomorphic categories. The admission of (i) is, therefore, the most fundamental admission we can make regarding the ineliminability of folk concepts and folk science. It is in this sense that the physical sciences are abstractions made *within* the human sciences or are inseparably linked to the human sciences.

It may be impossible to demonstrate the exclusive validity of either the top-down or bottom-up orientation. But the game goes on empirically, as we have said; and there, the inference to the best explanation distinctly favors the top-down orientation, *if (i) be granted.*. No one who denies the picture sketched will be willing to grant (i). Because, to admit (i) in the present philosophical context is to admit that *the cognizable world is constructed (not in a mere idealist sense) within the space of folk conceptions.* This is certainly part of the explicit heritage of Kuhn's and Kuhnian-like theories.[13]

Given (i), (ii) the viability of the folk or top-down conception of the sciences—if not its empirical superiority over the bottom-up—can hardly be denied. Top-down strategies are *not* a mere heuristic *for* some ulterior bottom-up strategy but a replacement for them.[14] Therefore, (ii) definitely obliges us to fit the *methodology* and *metaphysics* of the sciences to whatever prove to be the distinctive features of the world at the level of folk discourse. In particular, (ii) *prepares* us for, though it does not entail, the failure of both an unrestricted extensionalism and an unrestricted physicalism when applied specifically to the phenomena of the human or cultural world.

Here, a certain asymmetry between the human and the physical sciences may be conceded. The usual physical sciences have no use for *intentional*—or at least *intensionally complex intentional*—phenomena. Whether they require informational ("intentional") properties in biology or, in a "Leibnizianized" sense, in the physical world itself may be reasonably queried.[15] But the human sciences cannot characterize the world of human culture without the use of folk-level ascriptions. The top-down theorist maintains that such intentionally complex phenomena – natural language, linguistically informed thought, the action and production of linguistically apt agents, the artifacts of their form of life, institutions, traditions, histories, and the like – cannot be convincingly analyzed in terms that are exclusively extensionalist or physicalist in nature.

The methodological consequences are considerable. First of all, the human sciences will characterize their domain, consistently with (i)-(ii), in (a) intensionally complex ways. They will, nevertheless, insist that such phenomena are: (b) real or actual as such, (c) causally efficacious, (d) capable of rigorous explanation and of entering into the explanation of other phenomena, including physical phenomena (for instance, as in the explanation of someone's blushing as the effect of receiving an insult). As a result, they will form a conception of *objectivity* distinct from whatever may be supposed to obtain in the physical sciences, because the phenomena of human culture are, also, (e) not altogether separable from how they appear to the agents and observers of the society in question; they will also form a conception of rigor distinct from that of the physical sciences, because they admit properties that are (f) *intentional in intensionally complex ways (Intentional,* as we may now say).[16]

III

A number of misunderstandings are bound to arise. For one thing, the fact that the *real* properties of the human world depend in some ineluctable way on the consensual perception and participation of the agents of a given society (or, by reasonable proxy, the observers and agents of another society, in effect functioning now within the society in question) does not entail in any magical sense that the world simply changes with the intentional exertions of mere description and analysis.[17]

The illusion is due to the impossibility of escaping condition (i), the endogenous constraint, specifically in the vicinity of *reflexive* inquiry (ii) – the human sciences. The same is true, in a sense, in the physical sciences (since physics is now to be construed as a *human* science, *qua* science – and, as in the positivist idiom, as a discipline that depends on *Erlebnisse* or some suitable substitute that can only be reflexively posited; there, a realism regarding human culture entails (iii), the symbiosis of perceived and percipient, of real and known, of languaged world and worlded language, of the indissoluble realist and idealist aspects of human existence and cognition.

(iii) is a very complex thesis, one that, as it happens, has not actually had to wait for the late admission of (i) and (ii). On the contrary, there are hardly any philosophical positions of interest at the present time that deny (iii). It *may* be taken to be no more than a Kantian-like theme;[18] but radicalizing (iii) threatens to affect the methodology and metaphysics of the human sciences in ways that its more conservative adherents are hardly likely to favor.

In any case, (iii) forms part of a natural declension from (i) and (ii); and, because of the admission that the phenomena of the human world are Intentional, (iii) affects not only the meaning of objectivity in inquiry in general (the realist-idealist symbiosis) but also the meaning of objectivity in the narrower methodological sense suited to the human sciences. In the same sense, the admission of (iii) *and* the Intentionality of the human world—under (i) and (ii)—disallows *any* realist reading of nomic universals, of the covering-law model of explanation, for instance, of any weakened "nonargumentive" replacement.[19] The reason is that Intentional phenomena, if extensionally unreduced, are ineliminably *contextual,* subject to whatever contingencies affect intentional phenomena—*historicity,* for instance.

Roughly, then, if we construe the human world as formed of plural arrays of contexted practices mastered by "natural" acquisition (that is, merely by growing up among apt practitioners) and subject to historical change—what, broadly speaking, is a Wittgensteinian model *subject to a more profound sense of historical forces than Wittgenstein ever acknowledged*[20]—then: (1) causality *cannot* entail nomologicality, (2) causal explanation *must,* at least sometimes, fall under "covering institutions" that are merely general and subject to historical dissolution, and (3) causality sometimes obtains in irreducibly Intentional ways.[21]

(1)-(3) begin to afford a sense of the potentially radical difference between the physical and the human sciences. Put another way: the radicalizing of the physical sciences proceeds chiefly by way of radicalizing the work of *science (à la* Kuhn, say); whereas the radicalizing of the human sciences proceeds by way of radicalizing the nature of the *domain* addressed. There is a slippery slope here that threatens to lead from (i)-(iii) to the disruption of any sense of rational method.[22] At any rate, it is a simple enough misunderstanding that leads one to suppose that the affirmation of any or all of our claims (1)-(3) disqualifies any discipline from actually functioning as a science. The failure of the positivist and early unity canons, and the reasonableness of (i)-(iii), count heavily against any such verdict.

It also pays to take notice of the fact that many misunderstand the nature of Intentionality (intensionalized intentional phenomena). In a reasonable sense, *if* (iii) be conceded, then only a top-down conception of inquiry can account for *whatever* extensional procedures actually function (factorially) to regiment any given set of categories applied to the world. In addition, to admit that cultural phenomena are real—intrinsically *possess* Intentional properties—*and* to insist that those properties affect the individuation of the referents of pertinent discourse (for instance, that a chess move or an insult or an artwork must be identified *intentionally, not* merely by reference to its physical properties[23]) is to see at once the profound sense in which (i)-(iii) affect the methodology of the human sciences.

Nevertheless, in addition to this general complication, it is a further misunderstanding of the issue at stake to hold that "Intentionality is not a mark that divides phenomena from phenomena, but sentences from sentences. . . . Intentional objects are not any kind of objects at all. . . . What sort of things is a different thing under different descriptions? Not any object."[24]

Certainly it is true that no object changes merely by being described, changes merely because it is described by using whatever *sentences* are used. But the intentionalist does not hold that things do change as a result of description in that sense: he holds, rather, that *we* cannot always tell *whether* we have identified the same thing or another in moving from one (intentional) description to another. (That is just the problem of reference alluded to a moment ago.[25]) Extensional criteria will not help us here: we never possess unique descriptions that can be extensionally managed for everything we talk about; and we lack a means for regimenting extensionally the actual descriptions we do use in natural-language discourse. If we think of alternative descriptions of one and the same action, or if we think of contextual or story-relative descriptions of actions of a strongly intentional sort, we see that we lack any extensional rules for fixing identity in the first case, and we cannot fix the identity of actions in the second without attending to the complexities of context.[26]

Having said that, we must admit that another more radical form of intentional involvement *does* obtain — one that *does not* depend merely on the use of *sentences* but on the actual *acts* of human agents in which things *do* appear to change as a result of theorizing about them, describing them under shifting or alternative theories, or interpreting them. In fact, this is at least the point of Kuhn's famous puzzlement about the different "worlds" of Priestley and Lavoisier, of Aristotle and Galileo.[27] What is important here is that intentionality affects *all* discourse about the real world (*a fortiori,* the real world itself, *assuming the realist-idealist symbiosis*). In a more radical sense (a distinct sense), it affects *all* discourse about the human world because the human world is essentially Intentional.

For the moment, it may be enough to say that, in the generic realist-idealist sense, and in the sense in which description is theory-dependent, Intentionality infects discourse in a way that is not captured by the misrepresenting thesis cited above; and that, in the special sense appropriate to the human sciences, it is indeed possible that phenomena change there as a result not of mere *sentences* but as a result of actual activities of describing and interpreting. Consider, for instance, that the *properties* of Shakespeare's *Hamlet* may change as a result of our coming to understand the world in a Freudian-like way. There is no reason to deny that "things" like plays may change, under a distinctive kind of change that mere physical things cannot undergo, as a result of being "understood" historically. The changing history of persons includes their reflexive understanding of themselves and their cultural milieu.[28] The caterpillar that changes into a butterfly does not change in that profoundly different *way* — Intentionally — in which *Hamlet* changes under interpretation.

IV

We have begun to shift from methodological to metaphysical matters that affect methodology. We need to proceed as economically as before.

The distinctions that arise here presuppose the reasonable rigor of inquiries in accord with (i)-(iii), but they also have a metaphysical cast. Uncertainty about one pertinent distinction has probably fouled the tolerance of a great many who might otherwise be more hospitable to top-down strategies. Many feel that to concede condition (ii), the ability of cognitive functioning at the folk level, leads directly to metaphysical dualism. This is a mistake, a sheer *non sequitur*, that, admittedly, the literature tends to perpetuate. We had taken care, earlier on, to distinguish between materialists and physicalists, in the sense that materialists (but not physicalists) could admit *nonphysical* properties and ascribe them as the intrinsic properties of real things. In any case, the metaphysical counterpart of condition (ii) is (II), the denial or avoidance of metaphysical dualism. By "dualism," we mean here the positing of more than one ultimate *materia* for the real world—the Cartesian position, for instance, at least on the usual reading of Descartes's *res cogitans* and *res extensa* (which may well involve a textual mistake, or which may not be unequivocally prone to that interpretation).[29]

Part of the trouble rests with an unfortunate equivocation on the term 'nonphysical'. It could be used to mean what is utterly unlike, different from, the physical; or it could be used to mean what is not characterizable merely or exhaustively as physical, what exhibits features not expressible in terms restricted to the physical. Where the first reading is construed as designating some *materia*, or things composed of that *materia,* the distinction is taken to signify the advocacy of *metaphysical dualism*—on the grounds that what is different in the way of *materiae* cannot be really united as opposed to being joined in a merely verbal way. The second reading cannot be taken to identify a *materia*, but only either individuatable things or the properties of such things; and there, in either case, it cannot be construed dualistically. At worst, the second reading is insufficiently explicit about the issue of dualism; at best, it is consistent with the denial of dualism, but incomplete regarding the *nature* and *properties* of things. Nevertheless, when phenomena are said to be both "mental" and "physical," they are usually construed in a very strong dualistic way—hence, in a way thought to be scandalously untenable in the sciences.[30]

Schematically, the best sense in which individual things and their properties may be sorted metaphysically—corresponding to our condition (iii), the symbiosis of *realist* and idealist elements—is to admit (III), the ascribability of both physical and nonphysical properties to the same particular things. The best-known example of this way of putting matters appears in P. F. Strawson's *Individuals,* the important part of which, curiously, first appeared in *Minnesota Studies in the Philosophy of Science.*[31] But Strawson's solution was a merely formal one. He never explained the sense in which (III) *could* be satisfied; he merely showed that it was formally possible to make such ascriptions. In the process, he committed a mistake—not actually decisive against his specific solution—but a mistake that colored the reception of his entire view. On his own account, it was impossible for two distinct individuals to occupy the same place; but, in accord with his notion of "basic individuals," it proved impossible to deny that they could do so (a person and a body, for instance, that, otherwise, could be said to be that person's body).[32] Furthermore, the formality of Strawson's solution led his critics to affirm that he had done no more than refurbish a dualistic thesis.[33]

There is a viable solution, however—there may be many—that fits the entire range of what is needed for folk or top-down disciplines. It is this: merely construe the particulars or individuatable entities of human or cultural space as *indissolubly complex* within that space. They will then: (A) possess both Intentional and physical properties; (B) be real; (C) be active and effective; (D) be mutually intelligible within the shared practices of a natural society; and (E) be more or less as they appear to be, reflexively and consensually, at the level of folk discourse.

Of course, all this is still quite schematic. But it can be turned into an apt metaphysics by a number of small refinements. First of all, answering to the methodologically decisive constraint (i), the endogenous barrier, we must concede the real possibility (I) of (ontic) *emergence*. By 'emergence' is meant the existence, the coming into existence, of phenomena that are not describable or able to be explained in terms restricted to physicalist (or materialist) categories.[34]

The emergence of the human or cultural need not entail "nomological danglers" (in Herbert Feigl's sense), since: first of all, we need not (as we have seen) admit strict nomic universals; secondly, we need not insist that all lawlike regularities are expressible in physicalist terms; and (most important), thirdly, there are bound to be discontinuities of explanation (as well as of analysis), *if* condition (i) obtains—the endogenous barrier.

It is because of (I) that many (certainly Feigl) have supposed that top-down (folk) science is inexorably drawn to dualism. But that is a mistake. The discontinuities of emergent phenomena provide the basis for a dualism only *on* physicalist grounds. But here, it is merely the counterpart of an admitted limitation on what may be discriminated *at* the human level (at the "level," of course, at which *whatever* is discriminated *is* actually discerned). For example, there is no known analysis of natural-language behavior in physicalist terms. Does that mean that such behavior is not actually real; or that it could in principle, if real, be reductively analyzed; or that it could at least be replaced (again, in principle) by equivalent physical processes? Failure here counts *against* just those models of science in terms of which emergence *would* lead to dualism!

Certainly, we cannot deny the salience of natural-language behavior—or, therefore, its actual occurrence within our reflexively specified folk world. The same is true of whatever belongs to that emergent world subject to whatever correction we may concede. Michelangelo's *Pietà* is, as a sculpture, real enough (discernibly real "in the human world"). Is it real "in the physical world"? *It is. But it cannot* (on the argument being mounted) *be discerned in purely physicalist terms; its real properties cannot be confined to physicalist properties; it cannot be real unless its actual properties are suitably complex (unless they entail physical properties); and it cannot be identified except Intentionally.* These are the implications of condition (III), the (ontic) *complexity* of culturally emergent entities and properties. (III), of course, needs to be clarified.

V

We seem to have passed over the analogue of condition (ii), the viability of top-down or folk inquiry. The truth is that it holds the key to the entire puzzle. What is *emergent* at the human or cultural level must, in order to exhibit the *complex* "natures" and properties characteristic of what is salient at that level be such that it satisfies condition (II), the (ontic) *adequation* of "property" and "nature." By 'ontic adequation' is meant the conceptual congruity between what is specified as the "nature" of the individuated phenomena of the human world and what are ascribed as the intrinsic (*not* merely "external," relational) properties of such individuated things. Consider, for example, that John Searle straightforwardly maintains that "mental phenomena just are features of the brain" at the same time he denies mind-body identity and opposes reductive physicalism.[35] It would not be unfair to insist that, particularly in the light of the long history of the quarrel about the nature of mental phenomena, Searle should explain the sense in which such phenomena *could* be *ascribed to* brains. He does not do so.

The required answer is roughly this: that whatever is posited as the "nature" of an individuated thing – that in virtue of which it is individuated as the thing it is – permits us (trivially) to predicate intrinsically of it the properties of its imputed "nature"; and that whatever other properties may be said to be intrinsic to it must be able to be shown to be conceptually similar to and compatible with the trivially imputed properties of the first sort. For instance, being a horse is trivially adequated to possessing the properties intrinsic to having the "nature" of a horse; but having a spirited disposition could be an intrinsic property of a particular horse, in that there is a formulable conceptual congruity between (an ontic adequation between) its "nature" and its properties. The trick is to spell out its "nature" *and* to do so compatibly with the saliences of (I). Clearly, there will be a certain informality at the semantic level.[36]

Nevertheless, regardless of how difficult it may be to claim a criterion for "category mistakes," it is clear that there *can be no (ontic) adequation between a nature defined in physicalist terms and anything of that nature's intrinsically possessing Intentional properties* (that is, if those properties cannot be managed physicalistically). *If* brains had a "nature" defined in terms of intrinsic Intentional properties, then of course "mental phenomena" could be intrinsically predicated of them directly. But that is hardly the usual view. The obvious answer requires something like this: that there are *emergent* entities that intrinsically possess the Intentional properties salient at the level of reflexive folk behavior (I); that their possessing any of an entire range of Intentional properties discerned at that level must be *adequated* to their emergent "nature" (II); and that they cannot possess such properties, consistently with avoiding metaphysical dualism, without those "natures" and those properties being indissolubly *complex* (III).

This, then, supplies a very pretty parallel between the methodological and metaphysical features of the human sciences. The elements of each, within each set, implicate the others; and each set presupposes and supports the claims of the other. But, of course, we have yet to supply a full characterization of mental, cultural, historical, Intentional "things" or properties.

Let it be noted, however, that, in speaking of "natures," we are not subscribing to any form of essentialism. We are merely adhering to the grammatical constraints of ordinary discourse, to the ability to fix the numerical identity of the particular things we are talking about and to predicate of them whatever we wish to. It is entirely possible that the things of the world of human culture *have no natures*, in the strong sense of 'having a nature' in which natural kinds are subject to explanation under covering laws or nomic universals. Once we have come as far as we have, it is no longer unreasonable to hold that culturally emergent phenomena—persons, words and sentences, actions, institutions, histories, artworks—have no *natures* but only *histories*. To say that, of course, threatens the canonical picture of the sciences in the most radical way.[37] The full analysis, however, of that complication is obviously well beyond the scope of this essay.

Among our metaphysical conditions (I)-(III), (III) is the operative one. (I) simply says that phenomena of the (III)-sort emergently obtain in the reflexive world of human culture. (II) says that whatever of the (III)-sort obtains must (as everything must) meet adequational constraints, whatever they may be. The decisive unanswered question asks: What are cultural entities and properties like? Remember that the answer required must be such as to fit and facilitate the workings of the human sciences.

The answer—one viable answer—is this: that, insofar as they are emergent, adequationally sound, and complex, cultural phenomena are *embodied* (as entities) or *incarnate* (as properties). That is, *on* the argument that the human or cultural or folk or Intentional world is genuinely real, and *on* the argument that dualism is a conceptual scandal and physicalism (both reductive and nonreductive) a failed program, there appears to be no other metaphysical option than one that posits a distinctive kind of entity and property—one that has an Intentional "nature," one that is indissolubly complex at the "level" of emergence at which it is acknowledged to be real, one whose properties are monadic at that level.[38] Our own solution, consistent with these constraints (which do not depend on the particular solution we offer), is that cultural entities are *embodied* and cultural properties, *incarnate*. Now, what does that mean?

VI

We are not claiming that the "mental," the "psychological," the "human," the "cultural," the "social," the "historical," the "intentional," the "intensional," the "Intentional," the "linguistic," the "semiotic," the "subjective," the "functional," and a host of similar distinctions are identical or equivalent in sense or extension. They form a family of extremely subtle distinctions and need not be completely analyzed here. What we are saying, however, is that all entities and properties of these sorts are indissolubly complex, in that nothing so characterized can be so characterized without: (1) reference to physical or material properties; (2) reference to nonphysical properties (in the second of the two senses mentioned earlier on); (3) acknowledgment that the properties pertinent to (1) and (2) are such that those of (2) form indissolubly complex (emergent) properties (or cognate "natures") in which properties otherwise restricted to (1) are regarded as no more than abstracted features *of* the properties of (2); and (4) acknowledgment of the fact that the individuation and reidentification of embodied entities depend on the critical use of incarnate properties.[39] (4) clearly has profound methodological implications.

To say that physical properties are here *abstracted* is to say that properties that function as quite distinct properties at the *level* of analysis suited to the physical sciences also function in a logically distinct way at the *level* of the human sciences, at the level of reflexive folk life; and that, there, properties discernible as nonphysical (correspondingly, entities possessing such properties) do not and cannot obtain unless, for each instantiation, a coordinate instantiation (token-wise) of what would otherwise be a distinct physical property also obtains, and that such properties obtain only in instantiations that are indissolubly complex. (They thus appear within the space of our endogenous barrier.) In that sense, human or cultural properties are *incarnate* in physical properties: we may abstract their Intentional or functional *features* as we also can their physical features, but they themselves never obtain except as indissolubly embedded in some (not invariant — taken type-wise) physical properties.

The idea is that only embodied entities and their incarnate properties can satisfy (II), the constraint of (ontic) adequation: only entities or phenomena possessing "natures" specified in Intentional terms can be ascribed additional intrinsic Intentional properties. *No other metaphysical schema eschewing dualism and physicalism and admitting the reality of Intentional properties appears to be viable.* Persons, for instance, are *embodied* in the members of *Homo sapiens* (though, conceivably, there may be nonhuman, even nonliving, persons); artworks are embodied in physical media (the *Pietà,* in a block of marble: Dürer's *Melancholia I,* in a set of quite different token printings taken from the same engraved plate); actions are embodied in physical movements (the same chess move, type-wise, in a variety of token physical movements; the same physical movement, token-wise, being capable of embodying actions of different types); words and sentences are embodied in different sounds or other marks; and so on. Perceiving, thinking, desiring, feeling are *incarnate* in neurophysiological processes; the representational, expressive, denotative, significative, semiotic, purposive properties of artworks and actions are incarnate in their perceptible material properties; the historical, institutional, praxical, collective, habitual properties of social life are incarnate in the biology of aggregated persons; and so on.

There are many subordinate puzzles to be considered here — notably type-token distinctions. Also, the economies of discourse encourage our abstracting the Intentional features of incarnate properties — but the conceptual dangers are now sufficiently clear. What is critical is this: all and only cultural phenomena are embodied; embodiment is *sui generis* to cultural entities; the reality of Intentional properties can only be secured conceptually if they are incarnate;

incarnation is also *sui generis* to the world of human culture; and reference to embodied entities depends on the critical use of incarnate properties.

These are the bare bones of what must be supplied methodologically and metaphysically in order to afford a satisfactory account of the human sciences, given the present state of the philosophy of science itself. They entail departures that are radical enough. But there have been a great many recent changes in the general outlook of Western philosophy, hardly confined to the local questions of the philosophy of science, that have affected matters. We may mention them only in the most allusive way. What is important about them is that they cannot fail to radicalize even further our picture of both the physical and the human sciences. These may be construed as increasingly bold conjectures about joining the question of method and history in science—generalized now to the whole range of cognitive and active concerns. The least-debated development among them involves the rejection of every presumption of cognitive transparency—of foundationalism, correspondence, essentialism, universalism, and the like.[40] It is a development, in fact, entirely in accord with condition (iii).

In addition to intransparency, recent philosophical currents have urged such doctrines as: the cultural contingent, tacit, relatively impenetrable preformation of cognitive powers; the horizontal contingency of cognitive orientation due to changing plural histories within which such powers are first formed and function; a socially constructivist view of persons; a historicist interpretation of human existence, its rationality, conceptual resources, interests, conditions of understanding; the ineliminability of moderate (but not unintelligible) conceptual incommensurabilities; and the impossibility of conceptual closure under these conditions, of encompassing system, of trans-historical invariances of a philosophically decisive kind.[41] We are, therefore, really on the edge of a much more radical account of the structure of the human sciences than we have here sketched.

Central to these developments is bound to be the analysis of an increasingly radical sense of history: one in which human existence and cognition are intrinsically characterized in terms of a historical flux, and in which (accordingly) the conditions of objectivity, rationality, disciplinary rigor regarding the Intentional features of human life cannot fail to become increasingly problematic. Absolutely focal to this swarm of puzzles, for instance, is the resolution of questions regarding the conceptual relation between history as a true account of the practice of science (as it pursues what is true about the various sectors of the world it investigates) and history as the metaphysically changing space in which the practice of pursuing truth itself contingently changes.[42]

So seen, the foregoing constitutes no more than a provisional reorientation of the human sciences. It disallows a return to former canons, and it prepares the ground for bolder theories.

NOTES

1. Thomas S. Kuhn, *The Structure of Scientific Revolutions,* 2d ed. enl. (Chicago, 1970).

2. To mention a few representative texts, consider the following: Ludwik Fleck, *Genesis and Development of a Scientific Fact,* translated by Fred Bradley and Thaddeus J. Trenn,

edited by Thaddeus J. Trenn and Robert K. Merton (Chicago, 1979); Gaston Bachelard, *The New Scientific Spirit,* translated by Arthur Goldhammer (Boston, 1984).

3. Compare, for instance, Otto Neurath, *Empiricism and Sociology,* edited by Marie Neurath and Robert S. Cohen (Dordrecht, 1973), chap. 9, and Otto Neurath, "Protocol Sentences," translated by George Schick, in *Logical Positivism,* edited by A. J. Ayer (Glencoe, Ill., 1959).

4. For a sample of the recent exploration of the consequences of the failed vision of the early unity of science colored by the positivists' anti-metaphysical bias, see Nancy Cartwright, *How the Laws of Physics Lie* (Oxford, 1983); Ian Hacking, *Representing and Intervening; Introductory Topic in the Philosophy of Natural Science* (Cambridge, 1983); Arthur Fine, *The Shaky Game: Einstein Realism and the Quantum Theory* (Chicago, 1986); Richard N. Boyd, "On the Current Status of the Issue of Scientific Realism," *Erkenntnis* 19 (1983).

5. See Carl G. Hempel, "The Function of General Laws in History," *Aspects of Scientific Explanation and Other Essays in the Philosophy of Science* (New York, 1965); also, Paul Oppenheim and Hilary Putnam, "Unity of Science as a Working Hypothesis," in *Minnesota Studies in the Philosophy of Science,* vol. 2, edited by Herbert Feigl et al. (Minneapolis, 1958).

6. There is a recent convincing concession along these lines, in Richard N. Boyd, "What Realism Implies and What It Does Not," unpublished manuscript. See, also, at a greater remove from the literature of the philosophy of science, John F. Post, *The Faces of Existence: An Essay in Nonreductive Metaphysics* (Ithaca, N.Y., 1987); and Donald Davidson, *Essays on Actions and Events* (Oxford, 1980).

7. For an extended discussion of the issue in a wider context, see Joseph Margolis, *Science without Unity: Reconciling the Human and Natural Sciences (Oxford, 1987).* See, also, Bruno Latour, *Science in Action: How to Follow Scientists and Engineers through Society* (Cambridge, 1987); and Barry Barnes, *T. S. Kuhn and Social Science* (New York, 1982).

8. For a good sense of this sort of failure, not a principled failure of course, see Stephen P. Stich, *From Folk Psychology to Cognitive Science: The Case against Belief* (Cambridge, 1983); Paul M. Churchland, *Matter and Consciousness,* rev. ed. (Cambridge, 1988); and Daniel C. Dennett, *The Intentional Stance* (Cambridge, 1987). None of these three authors actually shows why the constraints of extensionalism or physicalism or both must be favored; but they increasingly accommodate *actual* "folk" discourse on the strength of the unearned promissory note that such discourse can eventually be abandoned.

9. Contrast, for instance, Daniel Dennett's unsupported claim to the contrary, in "Artificial Intelligence as Philosophy and as Psychology," in *Brainstorms* (Montgomery, Ala., 1978), 110–11.

10. See, for instance, John Stachel, "Comments on 'Some Logical Problems Suggested by Empirical Theories' by Professor Dalla Chiara," in *Language, Logic, and Method,* edited by Robert S. Cohen and Marx W. Wartofsky (Dordrecht, 1983); Abner Shimony, "Physical and Philosophical Issues in the Bohr-Einstein Debate" (as yet unpublished); and Richard Boyd, "The Logician's Dilemma," *Erkenntnis* 22 (1985).

11. For an overview of the top-down–bottom-up controversy, see *Science without Unity,* chap. 5.

12. For a thorough canvass of the physicalist issue, particularly with regard to the phenomena of the human world, see Joseph Margolis, *Texts without Reference: Reconciling Science and Narrative* (Oxford, 1989), chap. 6.

13. It is also, of course, ineliminable in such realist-oriented theories as those of Quine and Putnam and of all those philosophers of science who oppose the anti-metaphysical bias of the positivists – in light of the inseparability of theory and perception and the impossibility of fixing the nature of observable phenomena (in the context of the physical sciences) apart from the operative role of the unobservable entities posited by explanatory theories. See, for instance, Willard Van Orman Quine, *Word and Object* (Cambridge, 1960), chaps. 1–2; Hilary Putnam, *The Many Faces of Realism* (La Salle, 1987), Lectures 1–2.

14. There is an ironic suggestion of this sort in Robert M. Gordon, "Folk Psychology as Simulation," *Mind & Language* 1 (1986), but it does not supply more than a suggestion from the anti-"folk" camp.

15. See, for instance, Fred I. Dretske, *Knowledge and the Flow of Information* (Cambridge, 1981). An extremely suggestive empirical thesis regarding "intentional" properties in the physical world (*not* pressed in the direction of teleologism) appears in J. E. Lovelock, *Gaia: A New Look at Life on Earth* (Oxford, 1987).

16. See *Science without Unity*, chap. 9.

17. The point is correctly observed in both Quine, *Word and Object*, chap. 2 (particularly with regard to "analytical hypotheses") and in Peter Winch, *The Idea of a Social Science* (London, 1958), regardless of the paradoxes that must be resisted, for altogether different reasons, in either account.

18. As it is, for instance, in the "internal realism" Putnam favors. See, for instance, Hilary Putnam, *Meaning and the Moral Sciences* (London, 1978), particularly pp. 5–6. It is also essential, of course, to Kuhn's theory, which Putnam opposes.

19. At the very least, so seen, (iii) threatens the accounts of such strong covering-law theorists as Carl Hempel and Wilfrid Sellars. See Hempel, "Studies in the Logic of Explanation," *Aspects of Scientific Explanation*; and Wilfrid Sellars, "The Language of Theories," *Science, Perception and Reality* (London, 1963). The argument extends also to views like that of Wesley Salmon, despite Salmon's attempt to free the explanatory model from the inflexibilities of the Hempelian formulation; see Wesley C. Salmon, *Scientific Explanation and the Causal Structure of the World* (Princeton, 1984), for instance in the context of pp. 36–47.

20. See, for instance, Ludwig Wittgenstein, *Philosophical Investigations*, trans. G. E. M. Anscobe (New York, 1953).

21. (1)-(3) are irreconcilable, for instance, with the view expressed by Donald Davidson in "Mental Events," *Essays on Actions and Events.*

22. This, of course, is the point of the fatally inconclusive dispute between Imre Lakatos and Paul Feyerabend. See Imre Lakatos, *Philosophical Paper,* vol. 1, edited by John Worrall and Gregory Currie (Cambridge, 1978), particularly chaps. 1, 2; and Paul Feyerabend, *Against Method: Outlines of an Anarchistic Theory of Knowledge* (London, 1975).

23. This is the key to the perennial worry Herbert Feigl had dubbed the "many-many" problem, which he (rightly) feared might undermine all forms of the identity thesis. (I have been unable to locate the paper in which he develops the idea; but I recall his discussing it a number of times. It is, in any case, the subterranean theme of his *The "Mental" and the "Physical": the Essay and a Postscript* [Minneapolis, 1967].)

24. These remarks appear in Daniel C. Dennett, *Content and Consciousness* (London, 1969), 28–29. There is no reason to believe that Dennett has altered his view, for instance, in *The Intentional Stance.*

25. See *Texts without Referents*, chap. 7.

26. These considerations go entirely contrary to Davidson's use of Tarski and to his extensional account of action. See, Donald Davidson, "Actions, Reason, and Causes," *Essays on Actions and Events*; and Donald Davidson, "Semantics for Natural Languages" and "In Defense of Convention T," *Inquiries into Truth and Interpretation* (Oxford, 1984). See, also, *Science without Unity*, chap. 8. They also, of course, go contrary to Quine's program of extensional regimentation, *Word and Object*, chap. 4.

27. See Kuhn, *The Structure of Scientific Revolutions,* chap. 10.

28. It will be an alien theme to many analytic philosophers of science, but the notion here sketched is fairly close to the so-called hermeneutic ontology of the human condition developed in Hans-Georg Gadamer, *Truth and Method,* translated from 2d ed. by Garrett Barden and Robert Cumming (New York, 1975). This is not to endorse Gadamer's entire theory, but to suggest a dimension of the human sciences that has eluded the conceptual nets of analytic philosophy. For his part, Gadamer would reject the idea of a human *science.*

29. See, for instance, Lilli Alanen, *Studies in Cartesian Epistemology and Philosophy of Mind, Acta Philosophica Fennica,* vol. 33 (1982).

30. This is just the sense of Feigl's usage in *The "Mental" and the "Physical."* It is also, disastrously, the sense of the argument regarding the analysis of persons in Derek Parfit, *Reasons and Persons* (Oxford, 1984), part 3.

31. P. F. Strawson, *Individuals: An Essay in Descriptive Metaphysics* (London, 1959). See P. F. Strawson, "Persons," in *Minnesota Studies in the Philosophy of Science*, vol. 2 — the same volume in which the unity-of-science program is so centrally featured.

32. *Individuals,* chap. 1.

33. See Bernard Williams, "Are Persons Bodies?" *Problems of the Self* (Cambridge, 1973).

34. This *is* Feigl's straightforward usage, the one he associates with "nomological danglers," *The "Mental" and the "Physical,"* 139–40. See, also, Mario Bunge, "Emergence and the Mind," *Neuroscience* 2 (1977), for a notion of emergence relative to the physical world that does not accommodate Feigl's possibility; also, *Science without Unity,* chap. 10, for an overview of the emergence question.

35. John Searle, *Minds, Brains and Science* (Cambridge, 1984), 26–27. I have developed the notion of ontic adequation in *Texts without Referents,* chap. 6.

36. See Strawson's pertinent observations of regarding Gilbert Ryle: P. F. Strawson, "Categories," *Freedom and Resentment and Other Essays* (London, 1974).

37. See, further, *Texts without Referents,* chap. 8.

38. A ramified development of these distinctions may be found in Joseph Margolis, *Culture and Cultural Entities* (Dordrecht, 1984), chap 1; and *Texts without Referents,* chap. 6.

39. This accounts, incidentally, for the fatal functionalism of Putnam's early solution of the mind-body problem. See Hilary Putnam, *Representation and Reality* (Cambridge, 1988).

40. The most familiar Anglo-American exposé of these and related doctrines appears in Richard Rorty, *Philosophy and the Mirror of Nature* (Princeton, N.J., 1979). This is not to endorse more in Rorty's account than the validity of that exposé.

41. Recent developments along these lines are canvassed in *Texts without Referents.*

42. This is the paradox basic to Foucault's extraordinarily influential work, which has to a large extent baffled Anglo-American theorists. It is in a way, however, a provisionally radical development of the tradition from which Kuhn and the French philosophers of science (Bachelard, for example) proceed. This is the point, for instance, of Foucault's remark: "one 'fictions' history on the basis of a political reality that makes it true, one 'fictions' a politics not yet in existence on the basis of a historical truth." See Michel Foucault, "The History of Sexuality," *Power/Knowledge: Selected and Other Writings 1972–1977,* translated by Colin Gordon et al., edited by Colin Gordon (New York, 1980), 1193.

"Human Sciences" or "Humanities": The Case of Literature

FREDERICK A. OLAFSON

In the course of the last decade or so the term "human sciences" has been introduced into the academic vocabulary in this country. It appears to have been imported from France where it is in common use to designate the disciplines that are usually called "social sciences" here. On the surface, at least, this does not seem a very momentous difference. On the other hand, the reception here of this term has been marked by at least one curious feature. Unless I am very much mistaken, it is not so much people in the social sciences who have taken to referring to *their* disciplines in this new way. Instead, the currency of the term seems much more pronounced among people who are associated with the disciplines traditionally grouped together as "the humanities" and for whom the term "human sciences" apparently resonates in a way that is more congenial to their ideas about what they are or ought to be doing than does the former term. It is therefore fair to ask what this preference signifies and whether it has more to do with the "human" or the "sciences" part of the new locution.

If it were the former, it would be natural enough to suppose that such a preference might be motivated by a desire to underscore the specifically human character of the subject matter of the social sciences. The philosophical point associated with this terminological change might accordingly be that the logic of explanation in any discipline that has to do with human beings as active, purposive beings must be very different from anything one finds in the natural sciences. In the German discussions of these matters that took place at the end of the last century, the contrast between the so-called *Geisteswissenschaften* and the *Naturwissenschaften* loomed large; and there may still be those whose enthusiasm for the "human sciences" expresses a desire to reclaim, at least symbolically, some of the territory that was ceded quite some time ago to the newly emerging social sciences which at that time were understood in terms of the positivistic model of natural science. But if this is the hope that inspires at least some partisans of the human sciences at the present time, there cannot be many of them or at any rate this is what one would infer from the lack of interest in anything like a Diltheyan conception of the *Geisteswissenschaften* that is evinced in the current literature on this subject. Nor is it hard to divine the reason for this lack of interest. A great many of the people who find the idea of the "human sciences" attractive have been strongly influenced by another theme in recent French intellectual life: an emphatic anti-humanism. From such a standpoint, all the traditional terminology that was supposed to distinguish the *Geisteswissenschaften* from the sciences of nature—the language of "persons" and "purpose" and "value"—is automatically suspect. In these circumstances, it is hardly likely that the current interest in the "human sciences" expresses a disposition to reintroduce this language into the conduct of their business of such disciplines as economics or sociology. In that case, however, it must be the "science" part of "human sciences" instead of the "human" part that explains the appeal of this new term. But since the old term, "social sciences," already incorporated the "science" part within itself, the latter can hardly count as much of an innovation and so a mystery remains as to what the current excitement is all about.

It seems to me that a plausible explanation of the interest taken in the "human sciences" may be that it has more to do with the way the disciplines in which its principal sponsors work are to be conceptualized than it does with the social sciences as such. The conjecture I accordingly offer is that this new terminology is being welcomed because it is thought to offer a means of dropping the notion of "the humanities" altogether and of reconceiving the disciplines that make them up as human sciences. At least for the people who work within these disciplines and, as I hope to show, for the academic world as a whole, that *would* be a significant change. Although this is not the first time that a proposal of this kind has been made—one thinks, for example, of David Riesman's suggestion that classics departments be reborn as "Mediterranean Area Studies"—such proposals have, in the past, usually come from an external source. Now it appears to come from people in the humanities themselves and in good part from literature where enthusiasm for the conversion of the humanities into human sciences is surprisingly strong. I say "surprisingly" because literature has traditionally formed the central core of the humanities. This means that if literature were to reconstitute itself along the lines described above, the consequences for the humanities as a whole would be correspondingly more serious.

Certainly the idea that the study of literature should be conceived as a science is relatively new by comparison with similar developments that have taken place in history and philosophy, the other two principal humanistic disciplines. The aspiration of many historians to turn their subject into a sociology of the past is a familiar fact of intellectual life as is the project of associating philosophy with science by construing it as the logic of science. Both of these projects have made a good deal of headway and a point has been reached at which the continuing affiliation of these disciplines with the humanities is more than a little dubious, at least for any purposes that go beyond distribution requirements and administrative cartography. If literature goes in the same direction, the *Gleichschaltung* of the humanities will be complete; and so it is really the continuing viability within the university of any discipline that conceives itself in traditional humanistic terms that is at issue in the current debates about the human sciences.

In this connection it would be interesting to explore the intellectual background out of which this proposal has emerged; but for present purposes only a few points can be noted. One of these is that, for various reasons, the pieties to which humanists have traditionally subscribed find very few takers these days. It is, in fact, not too much to say that a fierce hostility toward humanism and all its works has established itself in many leading American universities and, paradoxically, in just those departments traditionally most closely identified with humanistic studies.[1]

The sources of this attitude appear to be in good part political and, at the deepest level, to stem from an intense animus against the whole ordering of life in advanced Western societies. Since the principal political and economic institutions of these societies have proved stubbornly resistant to the various attacks that have been mounted against them, it is as though that attack had been shifted to another front. For the last decade or two, the Western cultural and intellectual tradition has been the target of choice among dissident intellectuals, evidently in the belief that this tradition has offered ideological cover for the iniquities of bourgeois society. For purposes of dismantling and discrediting that tradition, almost any line of argument has seemed welcome that promised to shrink the prestige of some revered cultural object; and a political expectation of this kind very likely explains the excited (and often quite confused) response that has greeted "deconstructionism" in many departments of literature in this country. One can only assume that it is this same partisan zeal that accounts for the remarkable intensity with which convictions are held and expressed in these matters even when nothing political is directly involved.

Important as it is, this political motive is not the only one that is at work here. Even if the widespread disaffiliation from the older models and ideals of humanistic scholarship can be explained by reference to the influence exerted by a quasi-Marxist theory of culture along the lines just suggested, there is still the question of the new direction that scholarly work in literature should take. For some, the answer to this question is provided by this same Marxist orientation and, when that is the case, critical studies of the ideological function of literature are typically the result. This approach presupposes that the truth-claims of the texts being studied have been heavily discounted in advance; but there are other ways in which this can be done. For one thing, the motive guiding the operations a scholar performs on the texts with which he works may not be—at least overtly—political. Instead, it may have more to do with the level and style of conceptual prowess that is expected of a high-powered academic these days. By prevailing standards, which reflect the immense prestige of the explanation models that have been worked out in the natural sciences, the kind of commentary on texts that has typically been offered by old-fashioned humanists is held to be pretty unimpressive. It was couched, in large part, in the non-technical language of common sense and much of it was in a moralizing vein that is judged to be irreconcilable with the requirements of objectivity. The expectation now is that in order to be worthy of serious attention such commentary must be informed by something like a *theory*. It is theory that confers intellectual "clout" on what might otherwise be a set of rather inconsequential observations about this or that literary text and it is theory that qualifies the study of literature as a "human science" by giving it the essential attribute of a science: a technical vocabulary and with it the assurance that the insights being offered are not accessible to common sense.

The nature of theories about literature is a topic that deserves more consideration than it has received or than it can receive here.[2] One thing that is clear, though, is that there are great differences among the theories that command the most attention at the present time. Some of them come from an extra-literary source like psychoanalysis or Marxism and others have been inspired by models used in an associated discipline like linguistics. In some recent instances, the philosophy of language has been the source of theoretical approaches to literature. These differences among kinds of theory are so great that it may be that no single notion of theory is applicable to all the relevant cases. It is doubtful, for example, whether any theorists of literature seriously expect to discover, in literature, the kinds of regularities that could form the basis for prediction as they do in the natural sciences; and it is a real question whether the kinds of patterns they do claim to find would qualify as "laws." (Indeed, there are some cases in which the intention of the theorist appears to be to pull the discourse of the sciences into the orbit of literature rather than the other way around.)

Nevertheless, even these wide disparities do not cancel out certain common features that typically characterize the relationship between theory construction and what comes to be thought of as the object-domain of the theory in question. As this relationship is currently understood in the natural sciences and in philosophical accounts of their procedures, the role of theory in its relation to "facts" is very different from the one set forth in J. S. Mill's canons of induction. There is, of course, still room for inquiries that are heavily dependent on observation. After all, even high-level science must touch down every now and then on the common soil of observable fact. It does so, however, only on sites that have been carefully chosen and prepared by the theory that guides the inquiries in progress; and the idea that an adverse observation on such an occasion would straight away overturn the theory in question is widely treated as a piece of naïveté. One need not go to the point of claiming, as not a few are disposed to do these days, that "facts" are in some radical sense the creatures of theory to get a sense that under the present intellectual dispensation a humble empiricism does not command much respect. It is unmistakably "theory" that is running the store and any domain of pre-theoretical experience that we still recognize counts mainly as grist for a theory mill of one kind or other.

It is this relationship between theory and "data" that makes the assimilation of what we have thought of as the humanities to the status of sciences so profoundly problematic. There is, to begin with, the fact that the "objects" to which the humanist addresses himself and about which he has something to say are themselves typically texts of one kind or another. Not only that, but they are quite exceptional texts that have been preserved and studied over a considerable period of time in the belief that they have something of great importance to say to their readers. It is true that in its earlier stages modern natural science found itself dealing with texts like those of Aristotle and Galen and others; but these early scientists also had access to the same natural phenomena that their predecessors had tried to explain and it was these phenomena that were the focus of interest, not the texts as such. The interest of a humanist in an ancient text may also be mediated by an interest in something else—the date of an earthquake, say—for which that text offers independent evidence; but the more typical case is the one in which the text itself is held to justify the interest we take in it.

This somewhat reverential attitude of humanists toward their texts is often mocked at the present time by ironic descriptions of such texts as "sacred" and it is probably true that the attitude of humanists toward works in their canon has been influenced in some degree by the way the Bible was regarded. However that may be, it seems clear that a quite unceremonious demotion in status is implicit in the treatment of such texts as primarily occasions for the working out of some theory about them. At the very least, the point of view of the theorist is certain to be very different from that of any audience, either contemporaneous with the work in question or subsequent to it, to which the work in question may have been addressed; and it is questionable whether someone who stands in this new relation to it will be at all interested in hearing what *it* has to say. More specifically, because he is absorbed in the task of making good the truth-claims of his own theory, the theorist is unlikely to be interested in (or respectful of) any truth-claims that are implicit in the works that provide the raw material for his theorizing. And, of course, to the degree that the theorist also shares in or is influenced by the political orientation described above, he will feel justified in assuming that those claims are not, in any case, worthy of serious attention.

It is on just this point that the divergence from the humanistic tradition is most marked. The latter conceived the works it studied as vehicles of truth and it accordingly understood the responsibilities of the humanistic scholar primarily in terms of facilitating the apprehension of that truth. Since the texts in question were typically those of Greek and Latin antiquity, a primary task, once they had been discovered, was to make them available in an authentic version and this necessitated an immense labor of collating and editing that goes on to this day. There was also the task of learning the languages themselves in which these works were written and of preparing the dictionaries and encyclopedias and commentaries that enabled a modern reader to gain access to the historical and cultural circumstance in which a given work was composed.

A criticism that has often been voiced of the kind of teaching of the classics to which this regime of humanistic scholarship led is that it was almost exclusively philological and that it never reached the point at which the thought and vision of the works under study would have become the focus of attention although this was what was supposed to justify the expenditure of effort that was required. That *was* a failing of the older humanism and a grave one; and it may suggest a difficulty that in a variety of forms—some quite up-to-date—regularly besets the academic study of literature. Nevertheless, for all their crotchets, these scholars were serving the texts for which they made such great claims. The extraordinary availability of the literature of the classical world at the present time, when unhappily there is so little interest in it, is the achievement of generations of editors and translators who held that it was their function to enable these works to speak to new and different readers and who were sure that the resulting commerce of thought between past and present was an essential element in civilized life.

The heroic age of classical scholarship (and perhaps of historical scholarship as well) is now over. For many people it has become very difficult to share, even in imagination, the feelings of veneration for an author or a text or the expectations of a kind of secular revelation deriving from them that have motivated so much humanistic teaching and scholarship. Not only does the battle of the books appear to have been decisively won by the moderns, but the unproblematic availability of contemporary literature makes any thought of having to qualify oneself in some more or less elaborate way as a condition of gaining access to a text seem unattractive and archaic. Beyond that, the sheer proliferation of books of all kinds makes it very hard for any of them to maintain that aura of being exemplars of the Word that is surely what accounts for, say, St. Francis's insistence on rescuing a scrap of paper with writing on it from the mud. There is, finally, a widespread sense that there is nothing very exalted about the kind of under-laborer role that traditional humanism assigns to the scholar and the teacher and that the intellectual level of such work, by comparison with that of other kinds of work that is done in universities, is decidedly modest. It is clear, too, that "serving the text" is not exactly a recipe for achieving prestigious status in the contemporary intellectual world in which the professional student of literature often claims for himself and his "readings" a dignity that is at least equal to that of the work in question itself.

Even so, the expectation that there is something of great value that a poem or a novel can reveal to us remains the foundation of the humanistic tradition and something must be said, therefore, about the truth-claim that is implicit in this expectation. It is widely supposed that such claims make sense only against the background of some metaphysical postulation of an axiological reality for which no support can be found at the present time. It is all the more interesting, therefore, that the most considerable work that has been devoted to this topic in recent years—Hans-Georg Gadamer's *Truth and Method*—should have much that is deeply suggestive to say about "application" (*Anwendung*) as a pervasive element in the history of culture and especially in the interpretive appropriation of works of art and of thought that are in one way or another initially distant from (and even alien to) our own sense of what counts and of what is real. The root idea here is that of a dialectic of universal and particular such as is exemplified in the relationship between statutory law and judicial decisions, to cite just one illustration. Gadamer has also been deeply influenced by the Aristotelian view of moral reasoning as the interplay of some prior principle and new circumstances to which it is putatively applicable. Just as the import of such a principle is progressively amplified by being interpreted in the light of a wide range of cases to which it may or may not prove to be applicable, so a work of literary art, say, in being transmitted to successive generations takes on dimensions of meaning and of truth that an earlier audience could scarcely have found in it. Gadamer emphasizes repeatedly the fact that in this process there is and has to be at least as much learning from the work as there is adaptation of it to the life-situation of those who approach it (and he is certainly not offering a blanket justification for the modish and rather silly way in which plays and operas, especially, are now being kidnapped into the present by the people who direct them). What is central to Gadamer's argument, which is also a polemic against "method," is the idea that what we encounter in a work is a truth-claim that we ourselves must confront if we are to "understand" that work itself. In so doing, at least in favorable circumstances, we effect a rapprochement between the vision implicit in the work and our own prior beliefs and through our acknowledgment (or perhaps one should say "our negotiation") of the truth-claim it makes, it acquires a bearing on our lives. Examples of such application are not at all hard to find as any thoughtful reader of *Oedipus Rex* or *Don Quixote* will surely agree.

A work like Gadamer's suggests that the despair felt by many teachers and scholars in the humanities about the prospects for an intellectually defensible rationale for the kind of thought in which they engage is at the least premature. The humanities are certainly in trouble, but the reason may be as much that humanists are too ready to be impressed by what are supposed to be the devastating new insights that have been vouchsafed to one or another of the principal theorists of our day—insights that expose the self-diremptive character of the very utterances that have commanded so much respect and especially of the affirmations of value that are at the core of the works in the humanist canon. If this is indeed the case, it is surprising that these new arguments are as hard to come by as they prove to be even on diligent search. Instead of any such shattering insights, one finds plenty of evidence of a sudden recrudescence, among students of literature, of ideas remarkably like those of the positivism of the 1930s. It is almost as though minds that were previously immunized against such drastic theses by their lack of interest in philosophy and in theory generally, had, with the recent uptake of interest in theory, suddenly become astonishingly vulnerable to even the crudest among them. Certainly, there is now in these quarters an extraordinary prosecutorial zeal that sniffs out "metaphysics" everywhere and proclaims the underivability of any "ought" from any "is" in the best positivistic style. What is conspicuously absent is any sign of a disposition to subject any of these familiar exercises in iconoclasm to even the mildest kind of critical interrogation. It is not surprising that in these circumstances not just truth but reference and communication are discarded as though they represented nothing in which a disabused mind could think it had a stake.

This kind of effortless driving-through of even the most bizarre theses is a sure sign that an ideology, in the proper and pejorative sense of that term, is at work. The characteristic feature of an ideology is the apparent irresistibility with which it achieves its objectives as it deploys a system of definitions that is itself protected against critical scrutiny. When everything has been settled in advance in this way, the only residual question of interest concerns the exposure of the rhetorical strategy by which the patent fact of incoherence in the works of thought under study has been—imperfectly—concealed. It need hardly be added that under these auspices the sophisticated reader will not expect to learn something *from* the text before him. At best, such a text offers only the opportunity of watching it (or its author) struggling with its own internal contradictions.

This is not the place to enter into a discussion of the validity of such assumptions or of the strategies by which they are protected; and the case against them has, in any event, been effectively made elsewhere.[3] It may be worthwhile to point out, however, that the linkage between the political and the theoretical components in this alliance is an unstable one. The latter proceeds by convicting everyone and everything of "metaphysics" and in doing so it cuts the ground out from under every possibility of an alternative to the incoherence of the "discourses" it analyzes. While the political attitude may rejoice in this destruction of what it declares to be the cultural property of a class or an age and most certainly *not* that of humanity as a whole, it must at some point either give up the idea of any more attractive alternative of its own or make good the claim that the alternative does not disintegrate when the same criteria are applied to it as to its predecessors. There is, in other words, quite plainly a gross mismatch between the deconstructive program and any non-nihilistic form of politics, and that fact must eventually qualify the enthusiasm with which this project is pursued by most of its adherents. One can try to finesse this conflict by suggesting that the real target of deconstruction is some malicious form of thought-control that constrains thought and life by attributing stable meanings to words, but it is a strange sort of freedom that requires the sacrifice of even the concept of truth.

It is arguable that all of these antics should be understood as simply new instances of an all-too-common response on the part of academic disciplines to the discovery that they have no means of dealing with some aspect of their subject that is viewed—extra-murally—as centrally important to it. For example, although "meaning" had always been supposed to be the central fact of language, discussion of it was for many years placed under a strict interdict within linguistics. One might think that it ought to be possible for a discipline to make a candid admission that, in spite of their great value for other purposes, the modes of conceptualization and analysis currently available to it simply are not adequate to a serious treatment of the aspect of the subject that is being passed over in silence. In practice, however, such an admission is very unlikely to be made because it would acknowledge a fact that is deeply uncongenial to the owners and operators of theories. This is that, at least in those cases in which we ourselves are the "objects" with which the theory concerns itself, we have a certain pre-theoretical familiarity with the matters of which it treats and are not, therefore, wholly dependent upon the criteria that the theory itself uses to determine what is real and what is not. On the strength of this implicit and typically inarticulate understanding, we may on occasion even become bold enough to point out that the emperor has no clothes.

It is, of course, just this "pre-theoretical familiarity" with—at least—the human world that humanism has traditionally allied itself with. Interesting attempts have been made, in the phenomenological tradition and elsewhere, to develop the conception of a "life-world" that is both prior to and presupposed by the various theoretical reconstructions that supervene upon it. There is much to recommend such a conception and not least the fact that it suggests an alternative to a conception of themselves as human sciences that could be proposed to the humanities and especially literature, especially in the present conjuncture. It is, I think, a real question whether our universities will continue to make a place for any form of thought that does not at least try to conform to the theory-guided model of what a discipline should be. The issue this raises is whether a non-theoretical mode of thought of the kind that the humanities have cultivated, both in the works humanists study and in the commentary on them that they have offered, has any real value other than that of serving as the take-off point for some revisionary effort of theory construction.

To judge by our practice, both in the universities and elsewhere, one would have to conclude that almost no one takes the possibility of an affirmative answer to this question at all seriously. It may, of course, be the case that universities are just not a suitable venue for the kind of thought that goes into, say, the reading—much less the writing—of a poem and that the main result of trying to put our whole culture into the university is that people begin to write novels at the behest of a theory about novel writing. On the other hand, a university in which the interests that fall outside the purview of some theory or other are completely unrepresented is not an attractive prospect; and if those interests are to be a presence in the academic world at all, then it is surely the humanities and above all literature that should represent them. At any rate, if there is to be a "conversation of mankind" in which the things that matter most to us as human beings are sorted out in a language that we all speak, then it is especially important that people in the universities, for all their commitments to various special technical languages, be participants in it.[4]

One common objection to this line of thought points out how many people are and always have been effectively excluded from any such "conversation" and concludes that the very idea of a republic of letters must be a fraud. The factual element in this objection is sound enough but the inference is not. Here again, there is usually in the background of such an objection a strong political attitude; and so one assumes that there must also be some conception of what a juster society that does not exclude people in this way would be like. But in that case, one would like to know what kinds of communicative practices are envisaged for such a society by which its members might gain some understanding of one another's lives. If, as often happens in politically motivated projections of a new kind of future for mankind, no provision is made for anything of this kind, one suspects it is because all such matters are to be reassigned to an omnicompetent bureaucracy of some kind or — what is even more likely — because the political attitude in question is too primitive to acknowledge the need of human beings for this kind of expression. In any case, a society of whatever political complexion that does not even try to foster such a practice of thought within itself can hardly claim to honor in any meaningful way the idea of humanity.

A reply to this objection may therefore concede that the tradition of letters, like every tradition, undoubtedly bears the marks of the multiple distortions, occasioned by political and economic circumstances, to which the "conversation" that has gone on in it has been subject. To dismiss that tradition, however, on the grounds that women, for example, often had no part in it is to fail to perceive that it was within that same tradition that these distortions eventually came to be understood as such as, for example, in the writings of Mary Shelley and John Stuart Mill. That they did so testifies, moreover, to the sound elements that were already at work in this tradition even before their implications were understood in the relevant degree of generality. It should also be pointed out that this conversation has not always been harmonious or amicable as simple-minded polemics against the humanistic ideal regularly imply and that it has no logic that insures that it will issue in a happy resolution of all conflicts. Even so, it represents an investment of hope in the possibility that the ferocity that Erasmus so deplored in Luther can be made to yield, in some meaningful degree, to the civility proper to partners in a common pursuit.

What I am proposing can be misunderstood in any number of ways, but there is one that calls for special attention. I am not suggesting that departments of literature should become Ethical Culture Societies or that they should claim for themselves some privileged insight into "values." If the current interest in philosophy on the part of students of literature were to make them more skillful in their treatment of ethical questions and ethical concepts — a development that is thus far not detectable — that would be all to the good; but the purpose it could best serve would be that of giving a sharper sense of the ethical dimensions of "the field of selves" in which our lives are imbedded, and not that of "teaching values." This last is what a lot of people outside the universities think humanists should be doing; and the latter typically react very negatively to this suggestion because they are convinced that it would condemn them to a lifetime of platitudinous moralizing. In my view, both sides in this debate are on the wrong track — the outsiders because of the reified conception of values they presuppose and the insiders because they appear to think that this conception is the only one that could guide an ethical interest in literature.

If in place of this picture of ethics (and the antagonistic relationship to the whole subject that it tends to stimulate) something like a suitably adapted version of Hegel's conception of human beings as "universal particulars" were to inform our understanding of ethics, the idea that it has no interesting intellectual dimension would lose much of its plausibility. There is, of course, much that is of great importance to literary studies — various types of formal analysis come to mind — that is, at best, loosely linked to such a perspective on literature. I would suggest, however, that it would be far easier to accommodate these interests within a broadly ethical conception of literature than the other way around. On this point, our present situation, in which the bond between literature and life has been proudly severed in the favor of formal and theoretical interests, speaks loudly. My point here is simply that most of the preconceptions that surround this linkage are badly in need of reexamination and that there is good reason to think that it can be acknowledged by scholars of literature without detriment to their professional self-esteem. To be meaningful, of course, such an acknowledgment would have to be associated with an acceptance of the fact that literature, unlike endocrinology or plasma physics, addresses us in our capacity as human beings, and that this entails a different constituency and a different set of priorities for the *study* of literature from those that are appropriate for scientific disciplines. Unfortunately, the current vogue of the human sciences seems to me to reflect just the opposite disposition – an unwillingness to give any weight to these differences or to espouse the priorities that flow from them. Since these are the priorities that have been characteristic of the humanities, I think humanists should be more than a little cautious about the proposal that they become "human scientists."

NOTES

1. On this point a recent remark by Tzvetan Todorov should carry considerable weight. In discussing recent theoretical work in literature by American scholars, he states that "the dominant tendency of American criticism is its anti-humanism." *Times Literary Supplement* (1985), Nr.4305, p. 1094.

2. Two works on this subject with which I am familiar – *Literary Knowledge: Humanistic Inquiry and the Philosophy of Science* by Paisley Livingston and *Der logische Bau von Literaturtheorien* by Heide Gottner and Joachim Jacobs – both give a strong sense of the remoteness of their authors' concerns from any actual work of literature as well as of the immensely bureaucratized world of disciplines and theories that they actually inhabit.

3. I have in mind here the work of Wayne Booth, especially *Modern Dogma and the Rhetoric of Assent* (Chicago, 1974) and *Critical Understanding: The Power and Limits of Pluralism* (Chicago, 1979); and also Gerald Graff, *Literature Against Itself: Literary Ideas and Modern Society* (Chicago, 1979).

4. The practical difficulties this presents are suggested by an anecdote that is told about Andrei Sakharov. When he asked to be accepted as a student by the famous Russian physicist, Igor Tamm, the latter is said to have rejected his request on the grounds that Sakharov had too "humanistic" a way of thinking.

Social Science and the Mental

ALAN J. NELSON

The solutions of many outstanding general problems in philosophy of social science seem to await progress in philosophy of mind. This has a close parallel in the practice of social science. Important social scientists have thought that their theories should be developed in concert with psychology, or at least with attention to what psychology has to say. This essay argues that it is easy to exaggerate the significance of the undeniable connections between the social and the mental. I am particularly concerned to advocate caution in using our understanding of the mental to place methodological constraints on social scientific theorizing, but I shall also advance a formulation of a weak individualistic constraint.

We need to begin with a simple and selective history of how the philosophy of social science has become entwined with the philosophy of mind and psychology.[1] Let us confine the discussion to social sciences that use intentional concepts such as preference, expectation, perception, belief, knowledge, and the like to formulate laws that explain social facts, institutions, and actions as being partially caused by things possessing those concepts. This includes many of the most important theories in social science when they are interpreted in natural ways. "Economic *agents attempt* to *satisfy* their *preferences* by efficiently allocating their resources in light of their *information* about *perceived* conditions." This encapsulation of a large part of economic theory is chock full of intentional concepts.[2] Some notes on usage: I shall henceforth use 'social' and 'social science' for the sort of intentional theory just described. I shall assume that social science is "naturalistic": it seeks laws[3] and does not require Cartesian substance dualism. 'Mental' will refer to properties of what are commonly regarded as intentional states of individuals. Similarly, 'psychology' will refer to a science of lawlike explanations making use of intentional concepts.

One uncontestable bond between social science and individual behavior (and, hence, the intentional explanation of that behavior) is established by the fact that many interesting social phenomena consist in individual behavior in social contexts or in response to social constraints. "Why do people use drugs recreationally?" asks a question about what individuals do, and those asking it are usually expecting an answer in terms of social conditions. Another example is intrafamily behavior. In these cases, familiar from countless texts in social psychology and cultural anthropology, we are explicitly dealing with the actions of individuals even though we may hope for interesting regularities or averages taken over individuals.

Another, more complex, way the mental is clearly relevant to the social comes from some versions of the doctrine called Methodological Individualism (MI). MI has meant many different things, but one central meaning is that any acceptable scientific explanation of a social phenomenon must eventually be in terms of the individuals that make up the society.[4] MI is usually augmented with the requirement that individual actions, attitudes, dispositions, etc., themselves be explained in terms of individualistic concepts. There are some examples of social scientific explanations that appear to violate the explanation strictures of MI by making use of constructs describable only in macro-social terms.

But even for these cases there is a powerful argument concluding that the explanatory power of the macro-explanations rests upon mentalistic descriptions of the individuals. It might even be thought that such individualistic descriptions are a necessary *complement* of holistic explanations. I call this possible component of MI the Principle of the Individualistic Transmission of the Social (PITS).[5] Until near the end of this essay, PITS will remain implicitly defined by its application in the following example of an explanation that initially appears to violate MI.

A clear illustration is the casting into the PITS of some very influential metatheoretical theses of the famous holistic sociologist Emile Durkheim. Durkheim believed that there were social facts explanatorily autonomous (though not ontologically autonomous) with respect to the constitutive facts about individuals. Durkheim produced some philosophical considerations in favor of the concept of holistic social facts and made the disregard for facts about individuals into a methodological canon, but his best reasons for making use of social facts in sociological theory were empirical. A typical example is in his *Suicide* (1951)[1897] in which he argued that social facts concerning aggregate suicide rates could only be explained by the operation of social forces, and provided a theory of such forces. Individual psychology was inert in the explanation of suicide rates, he urged, because the data showed that suicide rates often varied dramatically among classes of people for whom the relevant individual motivations for suicide were similar.

The PITS are opened up before Durkheim by attending to the individual character of the act of suicide. Even granting that his account of social forces is correct, these forces must work on individual victims to cause them, at least partially, to commit suicide. The primary proximate cause of the particular suicide is the intention of the victim. Durkheim himself accepted that. So if he is right, it must be that these social forces are efficacious on individuals in virtue of effects on their states of motivation. But suicide rates are nothing more than aggregates of individual suicides, so it is natural to conclude that the complete explanation[6] of this social fact will involve mental states.[7] Generalizing from this example, we have PITS requiring that all causal connections at the social level operate through individualistic mechanisms.

PITS therefore also naturally creates a presumption that complete, lawlike explanations of the social are going to involve similarly *lawlike* explanations of whatever mental phenomena are involved. This is because interesting social regularities and generalizations will consist in aggregates of interesting regularities and generalizations concerning the actions of individuals and their chief causes, namely, the mental states serving as reasons for the actions. This presumption engages the notorious dispute in the philosophy of mind about the scientific status of the connections among reasons and actions. Since there are formidable philosophical arguments to the effect that explanations of individual acts in terms of their reasons cannot be scientific, and any unresolved difficulties for the scientific treatment of the mental will apparently infect social sciences as well, we are here obliged to make a foray into this part of the philosophy of mind and psychology.

The first group of arguments to consider are often called Wittgensteinian or, more circumspectly, neo-Wittgensteinian because they are either related to themes that were abroad because of Wittgenstein's later teachings or because they were propounded by those who had been associated with him.[8] The arguments all flow from considering the conceptual interplay among human actions, their causes, and their reasons. The conclusions of the arguments have the general form of denying that an explanation of an action in terms of the agent's reason for the action is a causal explanation. Since scientific explanations are presumably in the business of citing causes, it is a corollary that explanations in terms of reasons cannot be scientific. These conclusions are arrived at via one or more of the following observations: reasons are not the right kind of entities to serve as causes (e.g., they are dispositions instead of events); free will would be impossible if reasons were causes; reasons cannot be characterized as such independently of the acts that they actually give rise to, hence they are logically connected to them, and so cannot be causes; actions cannot be characterized as such without appeal to the rules they accord with or to the agents' conceptions of these rules (that is, part of the agents' reasons), hence they are logically connected with them, and so cannot be caused by them; when we ask for the explanation of an act we are not typically asking for a cause, instead we are asking for a justification or interpretation of the act. Especially relevant to this essay are the explicit extensions of some of these points to social science. For instance, Dray (1957) and Winch (1958) use some of these arguments to buttress Weberian concerns by saying that individual action in a social setting cannot be subsumed under causal laws, the hallmark of explanation in the physical sciences, because of the essential role of reasons in dealing with action. Donald Davidson is generally acknowledged as having exploded these arguments, but not in a way that ameliorates the problems for the social sciences that the neo-Wittgensteinians introduced.[9] We must now consider his position.

Davidson's brilliant attack on skepticism about causes for actions can be crystallized for present purposes as utilizing two principles. Anomalous Monism (this name runs the two principles together) concedes the neo-Wittgensteinian point that there are no causal generalizations to be had between physical and mental events or even among mental events for that matter (anomalism).[10] But, Davidson wrote, every physical event is lawfully connected with a physical cause and every particular mental event or "token" is identical to a particular physical event or "token" (monism). So the "logical connection" between reasons and actions is only an artifact of the logical connection between some of the linguistic descriptions of the events in question. The same events have other descriptions that make the contingency and causal nature of their connection clear. These principles enabled Davidson to say that although there cannot be psychological laws governing reasons (at least not "exact" ones like the ones found in natural sciences), there is no ground for rejecting what he took to be the intuitive view that reasons explain actions because they cause them. Since the causal relation requires lawlike connection, they cause them by courtesy of the physical laws subsuming the physical events they are token identical to.

It seems easy now to extend the conclusion of Davidson's analysis of individual action explanation into a convincing foreclosure of the possibility of scientific accounting for the causation of social phenomena. We need only consider the ways in which the social involve the mental. The case of social phenomena that consists in individual acts like the exchanging of gifts immediately requires laws governing individual actions — exactly what is ruled out by the Davidsonian system. With macro-social phenomena, on the other hand, it is first obvious that any strong reductionistic version of MI would have individual psychology being more basic than the social sciences so that laws in the latter would have to be derivable, in principle, from the non-existent former. And even if these strong versions of MI are rejected, it is hard to avoid the much more reasonable PITS. The complete explanations of macro-social phenomena like unemployment rates or degrees of social cohesion will directly incorporate mechanisms that connect these to individual actions. In both cases, therefore, the required explanation is committed to including information about the mental that is not amenable to scientific treatment. The apparently inexorable drift of all this is that there cannot be social laws because there are not mental laws.

I shall summarize. We have seen that MI and PITS suggest that social sciences can exist only if there is a science of individual action that can, at least in principle, be called upon to complement their explanations. Some neo-Wittgensteinians thought that since psychology is impossible (because reasons are not causes), it followed that (naturalistic) social sciences are impossible and the attempt to practice them needed to be abandoned in favor of interpretive social studies. Davidson reinstated causality in intentional explanations, but also left in anomalism. The contemporary approach to philosophy of mind that accounts for the trouble intentional psychology is in (if it is indeed in trouble) seems to lead directly to corresponding trouble for social sciences that deal in the intentional — almost all of social science. This has certainly attracted attention from those who are inclined to think that social science *is* in trouble and have been looking for an explanation of the predicament. Of course, a satisfying explanation would have to show not only what is wrong with social science, but also why the pursuit of social laws has seemed so reasonable. The approach outlined above seems to do these things. Social science by its very nature requires a firm foundation on a science of individual action, but this foundation is lacking. The apparent reasonableness of attempting to produce social science stems from the fact that our ordinary intentional folk psychology gives the false initial appearance of being the core of an improvable scientific theory.

This state of affairs seems to leave the fate of the social sciences in the balance while the real battle is waged in the philosophy of mind to determine whether successful scientific psychology is forthcoming. I propose to kick over the teetering balance by disengaging the social sciences from the mental cleanly enough to insure that the long-standing methodological and philosophical battle over the status of these disciplines can be settled on their own ground.

The greatest obstacle I face is that PITS all by itself seems to make the connection between the mental and the social quite tight. I find the prospect of denying the Principle repugnant, so I won't. I shall instead attempt to show how a satisfying version of PITS can be made compatible with anomalism. Despite PITS and the anomalism of the mental and the psychophysical, it is possible, I shall argue, that there be social sciences that give causes as well as reasons for aggregative social phenomena. Although I shall eventually grant it as an assumption that there can be no psychology of individual action, both the position and its application to social science have ramifications that should first be considered.

We should note to begin that even if Davidson is right about the multiple realizability and anomalousness of the mental, it seems that multiple realization by itself is compatible with nomologicity in other "special sciences" (J. Fodor's term for all sciences except "basic physics" [1975, 9–26]). The premise of the "holistic" and "hermaphroditic" character of intentional mental states is crucial for concluding that the mental is anomalous; a consideration of other examples shows this. For instance, even though 'river' and 'money' are multiply realized in physics, there may well be *nomological* relationships among such things in geology and economics. Or, in more Fodorian language, there may be natural kinds that are best described in the vocabulary of geology despite multiple realization, even if it turns out that there are no natural kinds best described in the vocabulary of intentional psychology-geology does not depend on psychology. Whether the special sciences of geology and economics will "finally" be vindicated or not is an empirical question, if the only potential problem is multiple realization. That should be uncontroversial — at least for geology.[11] We need, therefore, to consider the status of the anomalism of the mental doctrine.

Since the multiple physical realizability of the mental and the consequent extreme unlikelihood of psychophysical bridge laws are insufficient to distinguish psychology from other special sciences with respect to anomalism, great weight must be laid upon the main pillar of anomalism. This is what Davidson calls "the holistic character of the cognitive field" (1980, 231) and the "conceptually hermaphroditic character of its generalizations" (p. 240). I shall call it "Davidson's holism." Davidson's holism is brought to bear on the psychology-geology distinction as follows. Objects such as rivers are, *pace* Heraclitus, relatively sharp spatiotemporal particulars whose properties can be investigated by many means: they can be mapped, chemically analyzed, have their temperature gradients measured, and so on. On the other hand, the Davidsonian continues, mental states can only be imputed to agents on the basis of our interpretation of their actions in accordance with considerations of rationality, coherence, and the like. There is no independent empirical access to mental states to enable us to improve upon our folk psychological generalizations. In order to achieve a fully airtight, "exact" explanation[12] of an action one would, in the end, be forced to bring in an indefinitely long account of the interplay of factors in the agent's mental makeup. In the lawlike special sciences we can, however, always appeal "in principle" to other sciences for additional methods of observation and more exact means of measurement in order to improve and better confirm our generalizations.[13]

This reply to the appeal to an analogy between psychology and the other special sciences leads to a dilemma for the Davidsonian. I take the first horn of this dilemma directly from Fodor.[14] If the holistic and hermaphroditic character of the mental is supposed to be a consequence of the fact that folk psychological generalizations cannot be significantly improved and made more exact *within* psychology, then psychology has still not been distinguished from geology. Consider the geological generalization: Meandering rivers erode their outside banks. This is obviously grossly inexact; someone might build a concrete wall on the outside banks, the water might freeze, etc. Improving this generalization requires moving outside the taxonomy derived from the vocabulary of geology. "Concrete wall," for example, needs to be brought in. Making this geological generalization exact, even in principle, will require *ceteris paribus* clauses of complexity comparable to those required for action explanations because of the indefinite number of things that can go "wrong" with meandering rivers.

If, however, the Davidsonian relies on the fact that the mental cannot be measured and specified except by attending to actions and considerations of rationality, coherence, and the like, he must deal with the second horn of the dilemma. It is that Davidson's holism is not supported by the inexactness and *internal* unimprovability of psychological generalizations any more than an analogous and clearly false holism about geology is. Davidson's holism is an independent thesis, so the positive argument for anomalism only receives support from it that is proportional to the strength of the reasons for accepting it. And whether independent measurements, specifications, and individuations of the mental are available is partly a matter of how to interpret the *empirical* psychological evidence, and not a fully philosophical matter. (Compare debates about the epistemological status of Quine's Indeterminacy of Translation thesis.)

Let us recall that Davidson's rescue of causal individual action explanations from neo-Wittgensteinian difficulties can be regarded as employing two ideas—

token identity–multiple realizability and mental anomalism–holism. The first idea suffices to show how action explanations can make true, singular causal claims and to block heavy-handed materialism. That is the hard part. Davidson's anomalism–holism plays a relatively small role in the attack on the neo-Wittgensteinians. It has been thought to leave some room for free will that might not be available otherwise, and it makes plausible the inadequacies of psychological science in the 1950s and 1960s that the neo-Wittgensteinians had their eyes on. But problems about free will are tangential to our present concerns, and the present state of psychology puts anomalism in some danger of proving to be empirically unreasonable.[15] In this light, it seems safe to conclude that any threat to social science that depends on anomalism must appear shadowy.

A comprehensive evaluation of anomalism is not possible here and not fully germane to present purposes, so I propose to set aside the evaluation. In the rest of this essay, I shall write as though we can rely on it because my primary purpose is to examine anomalism's connection to the alleged anomalism of the social. In order better to enforce my main contention that philosophy of social science can be more separate from philosophy of mind I shall, in fact, consider the implications of an even stronger form of anomalism than Davidson's. While all of the philosophers being called neo-Wittgensteinian opposed taking reasons for actions also to be causes, they were not so monolithic, nor were they always so clear, about what reasons and the like *were*. They often wrote as though they were content to think of reasons as *mental states,* much as Davidson is. This is not to say that they thought that reasons were states of a mental substance, something that Davidson also repudiates; they were considered to be states of something else — a person perhaps. Insofar as the neo-Wittgensteinians were content with this way of thinking, they departed from the teachings of the Master. Wittgenstein himself, I believe, objected to characterizing reasons and the rest as *states* and especially as *mental states*. I cannot defend this view or its attribution to Wittgenstein here, but an example may serve to convey enough of the view to show how it results in a strengthened form of anomalism.

Recall Wittgenstein's (1958, 20) account of expectation, a typical "intentional mental state,"

> What happens if from 4 till 4.30 A expects B to come to his room? In one sense in which the phrase "to expect something from 4 to 4.30" is used it certainly does not refer to one process or state of mind going on throughout that interval, but to a great many different activities and states of mind. If for instance I expect B to come to tea, what happens *may* be this: At four o'clock I look at my diary and see the name "B" against to-day's date; I prepare tea for two; I think for a moment "does B smoke?" and put out cigarettes; towards 4.30 I begin to feel impatient; I imagine B as he will look when he comes into my room. All this is called "expecting B from 4 to 4.30." And there are endless variations to this process which we all describe by the same expression.

Wittgenstein goes on to characterize expecting as a family resemblance notion by which he meant, among other things, that there is no single thing that all instances of expectation have in common. The same points are made in the description of hope (1958 [1953], §584).

> Now suppose I sit in my room and hope that N.N. will come and bring me some money, and suppose one minute of this state could be isolated, cut out of its context; would what happened in it then not be hope? – Think, for example, of the words which you perhaps utter in this space of time. They are no longer part of this language. And in different surroundings the institution of money doesn't exist either.

He is saying, I think, that 'expects' and 'hopes' can be properly applied only when a complicated set of conditions is met, and these conditions are by no means exclusively mental. He is not making the highly implausible suggestion that mental occurrences are not involved, but instead that they are not the whole story. The same goes for believing, desiring, wanting, reading, understanding, and the rest. I am interested here in the ontological thesis that this suggests. When A purchases bonds expecting the interest rate to fall, his expectation is not, on this view, *spatiotemporally* confined to him or to his mind. It is only appropriate to attribute this expectation to him if a complex set of social institutions is in place and A is in this instance appropriately related to them. Moreover, the term 'expectation' will usually (but not always) be used inappropriately when it is confined to the mental.[16] If this is right, it might still be correct to say with Davidson that A's buying the bonds was partially *caused* by his expectation, but it is very clear on this view that psychology is in worse shape than he thinks and anomalism will rule. Psychology has had enough trouble with the purely mental. If it also has essentially to incorporate social and physical conditions that can be characterized only unsystematically by "family resemblance" relationships, the enterprise will indeed be hopeless.[17]

I do not, of course, allude to this iconoclastic and scientifically pessimistic position on the ontology of the intentional (which may or may not be Wittgenstein's) in order to convince the reader of its truth. My strategy is to argue that social science is not rendered impossible even on the assumption of an anomalism *stronger* than the one most neo-Wittgensteinians argued for.[18] We can reject the idea that individual actions performed for specific reasons such as desires, wishes, or fears, are explained primarily by some locally supervenient mental state while accepting the PITS injunction that social reasons need to be somehow analyzed into individual (though perhaps "non-mental") reasons. We can maintain sensible versions of MI and PITS, yet still give a non-miraculous account of how social science might work. In the rest of the essay, I shall mobilize two main kinds of arguments for a weakened social-mental connection and then provide the appropriate formulation of PITS.

The first consideration is based on a familiar type of phenomenon. Every action has consequences whose occurrence does not form part of the reason for the action, these consequences are unintended. Most of the time unintended consequences are so insignificant or so remote from the action and its intended consequences that they are of no interest to either the agent or someone trying to explain the agent's behavior. When one types on a keyboard, one also produces clacking or beeping noises, disturbs microscopic flora, and so on. The author of a philosophy paper is usually unaware of these relatively insignificant consequences of typing. Typing a philosophy paper might also lead through some weird and unforeseen causal chains to a truly momentous policy decision by the President (the First Dog may be disturbed by the clacking typewriter keys, start barking, interrupt the President's sleep, etc.; or, probably less likely, the President might actually read the paper). Psychology will be mostly powerless to explain unintended effects, and the explanations that we can sometimes give are rarely of any interest at the individual level. At the social level, however, the cumulative effect of the consequences of many unintended acts can be of great importance, and explanations of such effects will be interesting.[19]

A famous example of a significant aggregative social effect of individually unintended actions is the pollution of natural resources. An example of how unintended social regularities might arise is the Smithian emergence of an ordered economy from the selfish strivings of individual agents. In both of these cases it is easy to see why many have thought that interesting social scientific laws are awaiting discovery. Perhaps effects like pollution put nomological limits on the sizes or levels of development that societies can normally attain. Similarly, there are no strong *prima facie* reasons for thinking there are no scientific laws governing aggregate production and exchange in societies of certain kinds. The possibility of these laws need not rest in any way on psychology because the consequences of human actions that are important to these cases can be unintended and, therefore, outside its scope. Consequently, the question of anomalousness is irrelevant here because even if there were laws, they would in no way underlie the social laws in question—psychology might as well be anomalous for all the social scientists will care. I conclude that these examples provide a *prima facie* case against psychological anomalism entailing social anomalism. Let us postpone a consideration of objections to this until I bring out the second consideration.[20]

A second way of seeing how to break the connection between mental and social anomalism relies on another idea that is familiar in a different social scientific context. Suppose that anomalism rules at the individual level because the imprecision and extreme context dependence of family resemblance relations among reasons for action precludes interesting generalizations. It might still be possible to remove this impediment at the social level because the information that is lost in aggregating descriptions of individual reasons and actions into social ones might reveal lawlike regularities in what remains.

The following fantasy illustrates the idea. Lots of people may decide to buy bonds because (as we ordinarily say) they expect the interest rate to fall. At the same time, we may suppose that plenty of people who expect the interest rate to fall do not buy bonds and that plenty buy bonds for other reasons. Putting this together with Wittgenstein's reminder that "expecting the interest rate to fall" is realized in different instances in highly diverse ways, we suppose that a nomological connection between expectation and purchase is not forthcoming. Nevertheless, in a large economy it may well happen that there is a socially significant sale of bonds and that a good nomological explanation of this is that people (in general) expect the interest rate to fall. None of this depends on denying that it is *true* that lots of individuals, a majority say, expect interests rates to fall — Wittgenstein does not object to saying *A* expected *B*. Nor does it conflict with PITS. It is individuals that buy bonds and it is presumably their reactions to social conditions that usually lead them to individually expect that the interest rate will fall. Here is another example, this one loosely adapted from the theory of Durkheim's mentioned above. "Social cohesion" might turn out to be a quantifiable feature of societies and figure in significant social laws even though (a) it ontologically consists in degrees of cohesion among individuals, and (b) cohesion is inoperative or anomalous at the individual level. I am only relying on the assumption that the individual-transmission-of-the-social is, in this case, anomalous and that this case can be generalized.

A salient potential objection to this line of reasoning is that the envisioned aggregative explanation amounts to a winnowing that separates inessential complications from the kernels of law-supporting psychological natural kinds. If that is right, then the Wittgensteinian view is wrong and I am not, after all, entitled to assume anomalism. Some of the plausibility of this line of objection comes from what appears to be a close parallel between the imagined social law and the corresponding law for individuals. "When people generally expect the interest rate to fall, bonds sell faster" seems naturally related to "When an agent expects the interest rate to fall, he buys bonds." In other words, the objection continues, nomological relations at the social level that *result* from aggregation are the manifestations of psychological laws that are obscured by irrelevant complexity or "interference" at the individual level. Perhaps if it were possible to experimentally control for this interference, we could discover the psychological laws. Another thought is that such laws could emerge after numerous observations thanks to the "Law of Averages," if the interference is "random." Moreover, my examples from economics may be thought to work in just this way. A common (albeit not universally accepted) interpretation of how economic explanations work runs thus: first assume that individual agents act nomologically, attempting to maximize utility subject to income constraints. Next, use these (and some additional constraints) and mathematics to derive lawlike descriptions of some social entity, a market or an entire economy. Finally, insofar as the social descriptions are successful, it is supposed to be because the assumptions made about the nomological behavior of individuals are justified, either straightforwardly or by facts about averages. Even though few actual individuals might exhibit "average behavior," it is sometimes thought that the assumed law about individual behavior causally underlies the rather erratic behavior most actual agents exhibit.[21]

My reply to this objection comes in two parts. We should remember that economists' empirical descriptions of individual agents do not, as a matter of fact, work particularly well. It is undeniable, for example, that economists are more successful in empirically determining plausible supply and demand schedules for entire markets than they are for individuals. The thesis that individual economic behavior *directly* reflects utility maximization is no longer very popular. It can be concluded that the example of bond buying cannot be used to support the objection that social laws flow directly from analogous individual laws. So we should not be too quick to worry about the apparently easy reducibility of aggregate economic explanations to individualistic ones (compare Nelson 1984).

The point about averages is more subtle. With regard to economics in particular, it should be noted that derivations of successful macrolaws from postulated microlaws do not by themselves support the claim that success at the macro-level comes from successfully describing "average" individual behavior. Real macro-level regularities can exist even when behavior at the micro-level is highly diverse or random, so successful economics at what I am calling the social level does not clearly depend on individual or "average individual" nomologicity. It may be a law of some modest kind that the Dodgers team batting average is always near .270, but it can be true at the same time that no Dodger regularly hits near .270.[22]

We are now in a position to reexamine PITS. There are two main reasons for adopting it. One is ontological—we do not want social entities to be causally efficacious without all the real work being done by individuals. The second attraction of PITS depends on the intentional nature of social scientific explanations. It would seem mysterious if nomological concepts that social science borrows from intentional explanations of individual behavior were proven unscientific in psychology. For both of these reasons, it may still seem difficult to reconcile PITS with this essay's arguments for separating the fates of mental science and social science. I see two principal difficulties. The first step in resolving them is to dismantle unacceptably strong versions of PITS and state more precisely what should be required by the Principle.

It requires above all that there be a non-socially described mechanism through which social causes produce their effects. We now can see, however, that there is no good reason to require that the mechanism be psychological. Davidson said that reasons could be causes because reason/action pairs instantiated mechanisms covered by *physical* laws. Why should PITS require more? We need *some* mechanism covered by some laws to transmit social causes in an ontologically acceptable way, but a sociobiological, neurological, or even physical mechanism could do that job. It is a mistake to state PITS in terms of psychological transmission of the social. Why then is it called the Principle of the *Individualistic* Transmission of the Social if there are no descriptions of individual people in the approved mechanism?

PITS should indeed require that there be an analysis of social cause–effects pairs into individual behavior; it is the nomologicity that can be excluded. The problem is that when contemplating such analyses, there is a temptation to adopt two harmful Dogmas of Analysis. The First Dogma has it that the analysans and analysandum must be nomologically related to each other. For example, if pains are to be analyzed into C-fiber stimulations, it requires that it be true by law that pains are C-fiber stimulations. Davidson, Putnam, and Fodor have taught us that multiple realizability makes this First Dogma false. The Second Dogma says that the elements of the analysans must be covered by laws.[23] This Dogma seems better than the First. There are supposed to be laws governing C-fibers. Water is analyzed into bonded hydrogen and oxygen and these elements are covered by laws.

The Dogma is dangerous nevertheless. It is often possible to give a very enlightening scientific explanation of something by showing how it is instantiated at a more basic level of description. Pretend that we could show how consciousness could be instantiated in a machine. That would be enlightening even if the machine was very erratic and did not behave nomologically from the Maytag repairperson's point of view. Why-questions have to stop somewhere; optimistic mechanists like Boyle explained many phenomena in terms of colliding corpuscles, but they could not, and did not need to, produce a law explaining *why* solid corpuscles are inpenetrable. Successful explanatory analysis must, in principle, be able to strike laws of some kind at *some* level, that is partly why PITS requires a non-social mechanism, but not *every* level of analysis needs to be covered by laws. PITS is not violated by an analysis of the social into anomalous descriptions of individuals; it is only violated if there is no analysis into individuals.

I shall now state the suitably weakened and flexible version of PITS:

> Social scientific laws must in principle be (a) analyzable into individualistic instantiations, and (b) compatible with a nomological mechanism at some more basic level.

It is worth noting that nothing in this statement of PITS or the arguments leading up to it precludes the possibility of developing ways of using facts about individuals to measure and specify social properties. Surveys of individual expectations, for instance, may be a valuable source of information about "national confidence." Likewise, information derived from social observations might assist in the specification and measurement of individual properties. Nor does PITS require that these procedures be discoverable. Social science might or might not be improvable in Davidson's sense by reference to other sciences and vice versa. It also emerges that PITS is primarily an ontological restriction on theorizing and not an explanatory one. The individualistically inclined are suspicious of talk of social facts and even more suspicious of social forces so they are pleased to see more tangible mechanisms. It is not so much that social explanations are inherently unsatisfying, it is the worry that they essentially employ objectionable ontology that drives most individualists. PITS ensures that both social facts and social forces are ontologically acceptable and thus constitutes the true core of MI.

I shall consider one final apparent difficulty for my attempt to put some distance between the social and the mental. It is very natural to assume that the intentional concepts employed at the social and individual levels are *identical*. So when a social scientist asserts, "Americans believe that pork rinds are good" and a news reporter asserts, "Bush believes that pork rinds are good," it is often assumed that exactly the same thing is being asserted of Americans and of Bush. If that were right, then it really would be hard to accept an explanation of the social that did not build on an explanation of the individual. But the assumption of identity is unwarranted. If, as I have suggested, instances of intentional concepts are related only by family resemblance, then beliefs attributed to social entities obviously share no essence with individual beliefs. If they are in the same family as the individual beliefs, they will probably be distant relatives. Even those who reject the family resemblance story should be very wary of identifying the social and individual concepts. Much could be said here, but I confine myself to the following. "Bush wants pork rinds" on traditional accounts relates some pork rinds to the individual Bush, but "Americans want pork rinds" does not, on most traditional accounts, relate pork rinds to any individual. "Americans" do not even constitute a neat abstract individual like the University of California. Similarly (and more convincingly), on the traditional view, "Bush wants pork rinds" attributes a mental state to Bush, but "Americans want pork rinds" cannot sensibly be said to attribute a mental state at all. So why assume that the *relations* "*a* wants *x*" (individual) and "*B* wants *Y*" (social) are the same at both levels when there is this big difference in their behaviors?

I conclude that sensible guidelines for social science do not conflict with problems arising in attempts scientifically to explain the mental. I have tried to show that the natural seeming connections between the mental and the social are not strong enough to link their scientific fates.[24] Social scientists searching for laws incorporating intentional concepts are likely to benefit from examining advances in psychology, supposing that there are any. They might even be aided by studying the philosophy of mind. These benefits are not to be counted upon, however. Naturalistic social science should not be methodologically constrained by the results of our struggle to understand the mental.

NOTES

1. I shall not continue always to distinguish sharply between the philosophy of social science and the social sciences themselves. Philosophy and physics were fairly cleanly separated three hundred years ago, but the umbilical cord had not been cut at all in the social sciences until very recently and even now it has not been completely cut through.

A. Rosenberg has written a detailed genealogy of how the social sciences are enmeshed with the mental (1988). The organization of the present essay has been influenced by Rosenberg's work. Also useful in this regard are Macdonald and Pettit (1981) and Papineau (1978).

2. It is plain that some social scientific theories are not so clearly intentional. I do not know whether there are any interesting theories that have been completely purged of intentional concepts. It is also plain, however, that most theories presented as nonintentional are modeled after behavioristic psychology or are otherwise motivated by suspicions about the scientific tractability or, indeed, the very existence of the mental. Though I shall not discuss such theories, I note that they have been developed in accordance with methodological strictures against the mental. My conclusions are, therefore, also relevant to them.

3. I make this assumption to simplify the argument, but the essay's conclusions do not count against the possibility that interpretive social science is or will be more important than the "scientistic," naturalistic variety.

4. Discussions of MI that I have found especially useful are Miller (1978), Williams (1985), Kincaid (1986), Macdonald (1986a), and Sensat (1988). Taken together, these pieces reliably summarize the older literature.

5. The principle is very nicely developed for the following example in more detail in Rosenberg (1980, chapter 3). My summary is based on his treatment. Rosenberg also provides a thematic application of PITS to some structuralist anthropological theses. The PITS idea also appears in Macdonald and Pettit (1981, 127).

6. For a discussion of the relevant notion of "complete explanation," see Kincaid (1986).

7. It is this last consequence that Durkheim seems to have missed in formulating his radically anti-individualistic stance. It is sometimes suggested that he adopted this posture to facilitate the prizing of research monies from well-connected psychologists.

8. I shall roughly follow the exposition in Davidson (1980, 3–19). He gives a representative, though not complete, list of sources (p. 3). All references to Davidson's essays will be to page numbers in this edition.

9. The ideas appear throughout Davidson (1980), but they are most explicit in pp. 3–19, 207–24, and 245–59.

10. Unless otherwise indicated, I shall use 'anomalism' to refer to the thesis that there are no mental-mental laws.

11. Well, maybe not for geology. Geology (the example given in Fodor 1987, 4–6) in fact seems to be in the process of being devoured by geophysics whose vocabulary tends towards the basic: normal modes, wave propagation, forces, fields, etc. One is reminded of the way that "political economy" was mostly devoured by neoclassical economics in the 1950s and 1960s. Perhaps the only uncontroversially "physics-like" special sciences are chemistry and biochemistry. If that turns out to be true, it is not clear whether it would be good news or bad news for the special sciences. It could mean that they are all, natural and social, not "really scientific," or it could mean that they are all "scientific" but very different from physics and the few physics-like sciences. Time will tell; meanwhile let us pretend, if necessary, that geology has the same status as chemistry.

12. In this context, part of the meaning of "fully airtight explanation" is an explanation strong enough to convince us that it relied on a causal generalization, that is, it would conform to the deductive-nomological model that Davidson and his intended audience apply to scientific explanation.

13. For a clear, detailed, textual treatment of Davidson's view on this matter, see Rosenberg (1985).

Perhaps the starkest case of the difficulty Davidson has in mind is the revealed preference interpretation of economic utility theory. According to that doctrine, an economic agent's preferences (i.e., desires for commodities) are nothing more than a formal representation of some of the agent's intentional actions. For arguments concluding that economics so interpreted is patently unscientific, see Nelson (1986; 1990).

14. (1987, 4–6). Fodor is perhaps the greatest philosophical exponent of the view that fully intentional psychology is on equal methodological footing with other special sciences.

15. A very challenging critique of the doctrines, shared by Davidson and Fodor, about scientific properties and predicates that issue in this supposed difference between special sciences and physics can be found in Wilson (1985). Nelson (1985) is an unfortunately inadequate attempt to come to grips with Wilson's presentation. An interesting perspective on aspects of the Davidson-Fodor dispute is in Macdonald (1986b).

For a fresh defense of the optimistic view about psychology, see Cummins (1989). Two recent approaches to reconciling a fully intentional approach to mental states with developments in nonintentional (or at least less intentional) sciences can be found in Dretske (1988) and Cummins (1989, chaps. 10 and 11). I emphasize that optimism about cognitive science is consistent with the main conclusions drawn in this essay.

16. I find myself at odds here with the interesting reconstruction required by the interpretation of Wittgenstein in McGinn (1984, 95–110).

17. One might think that the considerations Wittgenstein draws our attention to can be accommodated by the distinction between broad and narrow contents of mental states. Tyler Burge has argued (1979, for example) that the contents of mental states, and therefore the states themselves, cannot be fully individuated by reference to what supervenes on a person's body, his environment needs to be considered as well. This might inspire someone to say that mental states have a narrow content that can be fully individuated by reference to what supervenes on the body and a broad content that is individuated by other facts as well (see Fodor 1987, chap. 2). One might continue to say (against Wittgenstein) that mental state terms refer to things that are entirely within the body, but (more or less with Wittgenstein) that these referents cannot be entirely understood without information about the context of use. So psychology might, after all, be able to proceed by attending only to the "purely mental." I acknowledge that psychology might be defended against the Wittgensteinian considerations adumbrated above by making use of the notion of broad (see Burge [1986] for a worked out example) or narrow (Fodor, 1987) content. But this is not the view that I am entertaining. I want the extreme case: if we insist on making *A*'s expectation an entity (and we probably should not), it is a spatiotemporally scattered object.

18. It should be mentioned that some have thought that even spatiotemporally scattered objects can be causally related (Thomson 1977, for example). A more moderate suggestion that has been applied to psychology (Horgan and Woodward 1985, 217–19) is that such objects can causally interact in virtue of some of their parts interacting in the ordinary way. A skeptical account of these theories is in Hornsby (1985). I shall not consider these ways of attacking anomalism.

19. This account could be enriched with a description of the different ways in which consequences of actions (and actions themselves) can be unintended, and the different kinds of remote effects of actions.

20. The complement of unintended consequences – unrecognized reasons – is also of interest here. The aforementioned social sciences of individual behavior often attempt to make use of unrecognized social reasons for individual actions. One may sometimes act for unrecognized or unacknowledged reasons of class membership, for instance.

21. A detailed description and critique of this interpretation is in Nelson (1986).

22. This point, along with a development of the conditions under which macrolaws *do* support claims about the average behavior of individuals, is worked out in Nelson (1989).

23. The term 'analysis' and the treatment of what I call the Second Dogma is fairly loosely adapted from the highly illuminating Cummins (1983, chap. 1).

24. I have argued that if psychology were a grand failure, that would not entail that the social sciences must fail. My primary purpose, however, is not to provide a philosophical defense of social science, it is instead to argue that the connection between the scientific explanation of the social and of the mental is not as secure as has often been thought. To reinforce this position, it should be pointed out that a kind of inverse thesis is reasonable. The lawlikeness of the mental would not entail the lawlikeness of the social. Some arguments for this are canvassed in Nelson (1990).

REFERENCES

Burge, T. 1979. "Individualism and the Mental." *Midwest Studies in Philosophy* 4:73–121.
Burge, T. 1986. "Individualism and Psychology." *Philosophical Review* 95: 3–45.
Cummins, R. 1983. *The Nature of Psychological Explanation*. Cambridge, Mass.
Cummins, R. 1989. *Meaning and Mental Representation*. Cambridge, Mass.
Davidson, D. 1980. *Essays on Actions and Events*. Oxford.
Dray, W. 1957. *Laws and Explanation in History*. London.
Dretske, F. 1988. *Explaining Behavior*. Cambridge, Mass.
Durkheim, E. 1951 [1897]. *Suicide*. Translated by J. Spaulding and G. Simpson. Glencoe, Ill.

Fodor, J. 1987. *Psychosemantics.* Cambridge, Mass.

Fodor, J. 1975. *The Language of Thought.* New York.

Horgan, T., and J. Woodward. 1985. "Folk Psychology is Here to Stay." *Philosophical Review* 94: 197–226.

Hornsby, J. 1985. "Physicalism, Events, and Part-Whole Relations." In *Actions and Events,* edited by E. LePore and B. McLaughlin. Oxford.

Kincaid, H. 1986. "Reduction, Explanation, and Individualism." *Philosophy of Science* 53: 492–513.

LePore, E., and B. McLaughlin, editors. 1985. *Actions and Events.* Oxford.

Macdonald, G. 1986a. "Modified Methodological Individualism." *Proceedings of the Aristotelian Society* 86: 199–211.

Macdonald, G. 1986b. "The Possibility of the Disunity of Science." In *Fact, Science and Morality,* edited by G. Macdonald and C. Wright. Oxford.

Macdonald, G., and P. Pettit. 1981. *Semantics and Social Science.* London.

McGinn, C. 1984. *Wittgenstein on Meaning.* Oxford.

Miller, R. 1978. "Methodological Individualism and Social Explanation." *Philosophy of Science* 45: 387–414.

Nelson, A. 1984. "Some Issues Surrounding the Reduction of Macroeconomics to Microeconomics." *Philosophy of Science* 51: 573–94.

Nelson, A. 1985. "Physical Properties." *Pacific Philosophical Quarterly* 66: 268–82.

Nelson, A. 1986. "New Individualistic Foundations for Economics." *Nous* 20: 469–90.

Nelson, A. 1989. "Average Explanations." *Erkenntnis* 30: 23–42.

Nelson, A. 1990. "Are Economic Kinds Natural?" *Scientific Theories: Minnesota Studies in the Philosophy of Science,* vol. 14. Minneapolis.

Papineau, D. 1978. *For Science in the Social Sciences.* London.

Rosenberg, A. 1980. *Sociobiology and the Preemption of Social Science.* Baltimore, Md.

Rosenberg, A. 1985. "Davidson's Unintended Attack on Psychology." In *Actions and Events,* edited by E. LePore and B. McLaughlin. Oxford.

Rosenberg, A. 1988. *Philosophy of Social Science.* Boulder, Colo.

Sensat, J. 1988. "Methodological Individualism and Marxism." *Economics and Philosophy* 4: 189–220.

Thomson, J. 1977. *Acts and Other Events.* Ithaca, N.Y.

Williams, B. 1985. "Formal and Substantial Individualism." *Proceedings of the Aristotelian Society* 85: 119–32.

Wilson, M. 1985. "What is this Thing Called "Pain"? – The Philosophy of Science Behind the Contemporary Debate." *Pacific Philosophical Quarterly* 66: 227–67.

Winch, P. 1958. *The Idea of a Social Science.* London.

Wittgenstein, L. 1958 [1953]. *Philosophical Investigations,* 3d ed., translated by G. Anscombe. New York.

Wittgenstein, L. 1958. *The Blue and Brown Books.* Oxford.

Narrative Time:
The Inherently Perspectival
Structure of the Human World

ROBERT PAUL WOLFF

This essay originated as a contribution to a symposium at Brandeis University chaired by Professor Egon Bittner on the topic "Whether scientific inquiry is, can be, or should be undertaken from positions of ethical and political neutrality." I chose to restrict my remarks to a consideration of the study of society, leaving to others the task of discussing the study of nature. I can say at the outset that my answer to all three of Professor Bittner's questions was *no.* The investigation of the human world cannot be, hence is not and ought not to be, undertaken from a position of ethical and political neutrality.[1] Such originality as I was able to bring to this much-discussed issue consisted in resting my case on ontological rather than moral considerations.

It may help to explain the origins of my argument if I report that when Professor Bittner's invitation arrived, I was reading Wilhelm Dilthey's observations on the construction of the historical world, in preparation for a graduate seminar on the philosophy of history. As will become obvious almost immediately, my reflections constitute an effort to extend into the realm of the human studies my understanding of Immanuel Kant's analysis of the transcendental ego's construction of objective time-consciousness as the foundation of the laws of phenomenal nature.

Let me begin, somewhat implausibly, by contrasting Kant's account of the status and structure of the natural world, as he gives it to us in the Transcendental Analytic of the *Critique of Pure Reason,* with the ontology of the worlds created, or constituted, by fictional narratives. Although I do not myself endorse the dramatically paradoxical doctrine promulgated by Kant in the Critical Philosophy, I do believe that it provides the essential clue to an understanding of the ontology of the human world, and thereby to an answer to Professor

Bittner's question. Here, as elsewhere, the extravagant metaphysical and epistemological doctrines put forth by Kant and his successors as analyses of the natural world turn out to be quite accurate guides to the structure of the social or human world.

I take as my text the extraordinary passage near the end of the Deduction of the Pure Concepts of Understanding in the first edition of the *Critique of Pure Reason*. Summarizing the argument which has been set forth, albeit erratically and somewhat inconsistently, over the previous fifteen pages, Kant writes:

> Thus the order and regularity in the appearances, which we entitle *nature*, we ourselves introduce. We could never find them in appearances, had we not ourselves, or the nature of our mind, originally set them there.[2]

And a page later:

> Thus the understanding is something more than a power of formulating rules through comparison of appearances [as David Hume had asserted]; it is itself the lawgiver of nature.[3]

In the Second Analogy of Experience, in the Analytic of Principles, Kant explains, with great precision and clarity, that the knowing mind constructs the objective world order essentially by establishing a necessary temporal succession of events that is in principle distinguishable from the subjective order in which the mind apprehends the diversity of its sense contents. To be an event, Kant argues, to be empirically real, *just is* to have objective time location. What is more, since, as Kant argues in agreement with Hume, causation is essentially necessary succession, it follows that to have objective time location precisely *is* to stand in necessary causal relation to everything that has preceded and will follow.

This doctrine is well known to students of the philosophy of Kant, but it is not an easy doctrine to understand, and since it will play a central role in my argument, let me devote a few words to explaining it. Consider the distinction between remembering an event and imagining it. The difference clearly does not lie in the *content* of the thoughts. So far as visual, auditory, or other images are concerned, there need be no difference at all between a scene recollected and the same scene imagined. What distinguishes memory from imagination is that memory involves the assertion of a proposition, and hence necessarily raises the issue of the truth or falsehood of what is being asserted. If I purport to *remember* that I dined last night at Maxim's in Paris, then I am implicitly asserting the proposition *that I dined last night at Maxim's*, a proposition which, alas, is false. But if I *imagine* having dined last night at Maxim's, since there is no assertion, there is no truth value. All experience, not merely memory, Kant tells us, is a structure of judgments, not a construction of sense contents.

If I ask, now, what is the most general and fundamental mark of objective experience, of the empirically real, Kant replies that it is not any particular sense *content* — not some special shade of blue that invariably signals the real, as it were — but rather a certain cognitive or judgmental feature in its *form*, namely necessary temporal succession. To say that something really happened, that it is part of the objective world order, is, at base, to say that it happened just *then*, that it came *after* this, that, and the other event which preceded it, and *before* these other events which followed it. Location in objective time succession is, Kant argues in the Second Analogy, *the* mark of the empirically real.

Fantasies can always be altered if I find them unsatisfactory. Daydreaming about a romantic affair, I imagine that I see a lovely woman on the street, speak to her, and strike up a romance. Then, dissatisfied with my imagining, I rewrite it, this time visualizing her as speaking first to me. Since nothing is being *asserted* in the daydream, no constraints limit the sequence in which I can conjure my images. But if I wish to *remember,* for example, what I did this morning, then I must represent my getting dressed as coming *earlier* than my having breakfast, for that is, in fact, the order in which those events occurred. (It is not at all necessary that I call up the image of my dressing before the image of my having breakfast in order to be true to the facts. I can perfectly well recall these events in reverse order, so long as, in doing so, I represent them *as* in reverse order. To repeat, experience is a structure of judgments, not a construction of sense contents.)

So to say of an event that it is *real,* that it really happened, is no more and no less than to assign it to an objective time location. But there is a problem here, as Kant notes in a passage added to the *Critique* in the second edition. "Since time. . .cannot itself be perceived, the determination of the existence of objects in time can take place only through their relation in time in general, and therefore only through concepts that connect them *a priori*."[4]

The problem is one which frequently confronts historians, especially those dealing with scanty data concerning ancient peoples. We are accustomed to saying that Julius Caesar was slain on the Ides of March in 44 B.C., as though it were possible to look at the time line stretching form infinity to infinity, and simply see that hanging up at the 44 B.C. mark, by a sort of cosmological clothespin, is the murder of Caesar. But in fact, as Kant notes, we cannot perceive time itself. Hence, to date a past event, we must trace a continuous regression of events from our present moment back to the event in question. There must, as it were, be an apostolic temporal succession connecting present time with that past event. Let there be merely one genuine break, and if we have no indirect evidence allowing us to ascertain how long the gap that cannot be filled, then we cannot date that past event. What is more, at the most basic epistemological level, we cannot then be sure of the reality of the event we are attempting to date.

How, for example, do we determine whether the stories of King Arthur are fact or fiction? Not by content, needless to say, for after the fabulous elements have been eliminated, there is nothing internal to the story to tell us whether in real time there were men and women corresponding to the Arthur, Lancelot, Guinevere, and Gawain of the old tales. We approach the question by attempting to set the persons and events of the story in some necessitated sequence with other persons and events whose provenance *can* be traced unbroken to the present. Thus it was that Schliemann sought to bring ancient Ilium into historical time, by setting it in the context of present-day physical remains that independent scientific knowledge permitted us to connect up with an already known historical sequence.

And now, perhaps, the reader may spy, distantly, the first glimmer of a connection between these remarks and the title of my essay, for the objective temporal sequence of which I have been speaking is, of course, a narrative. But there are other matters to be discussed before we can confront fully the significance of that fact.

Consider first a question which Kant neglects: the mind-constructed temporal sequence is, according to Kant, *objective* because necessitated. But is it *intersubjective*? Does each of us, Protagoras-like, live in a private time, or is there one time which is the single objective time for the experienced world? This question is in fact so deep that its full answer undermines the very foundations of Kant's ethical theory.[5] It suffices for our purposes to observe that Kant avoids the issue by assuming that the purely formal structure of the knowing mind is everywhere and always the same. Since the forms of sensible intuition—space and time—are the same for all minds, or for all human minds, at any rate, and since the pure forms of conception, or categories, which lie *a priori* in the mind, are likewise identical for all cognitive agents, it follows that there cannot be two or many objective times, but only one.

Put somewhat more formally, there is always a transformation that will allow us to translate the objective date of an event in any one system of time reckoning into the equivalent date in any other system. All peoples choose striking or memorable events as the zero-points of their calendars: the birth or death of a god, the creation of the world, the ascension to the throne of a ruler—it makes no difference. The defining mark of the real is intertranslatability from calendar to calendar. Thus, we might say that despite its brilliantly vivid verisimilitude, the Middle-Earth of Tolkein's *Lord of the Rings* is shown to be imaginary by the impossibility of establishing any temporal translation from *its* elaborate chronology, carried all the way back to the events of the first age of Middle-Earth, to the one chronology of the real world.

To summarize, then, the mark of the empirically real is objective time location, which is identical with inclusion within a sequence of causally connected events. And even if, as Kant claims, the structure of objective time is mind-created, nevertheless the formal identity of all knowing minds guarantees that objective time (and also objective space, though Kant does not say so) will have the characteristic intersubjective feature sometimes referred to as isotropy. To say of time that it is isotropic is simply to say that every moment of time or time-location is formally indistinguishable from every other. In isotropic time, there are no privileged times, no moments uniquely full of history, no hours in which eternity breathes. Hence, it is only their time relations, not their absolute time location, that is significant about a sequence of events.

It was the secular physics of the seventeenth century, and its antecedents in the teachings of the ancient agnostic atomists, that introduced the notion of isotropic time. Religious time is radically anisotropic. According to Christian eschatology, the flow of historical time is divided by a number of ontologically distinguished moments which segregate events in such a way that where one is located with regard to those moments determines entirely the existential status of one's being. I have in mind such moments as the Creation, the Fall, the Old Testament, or compact, made by God with Abraham, the Incarnation, Passion, and Resurrection of Jesus, when the Word is made flesh, fulfilling and superceding the Law, and the Last Trump, or end of time. Note—for this will become central to the development of my thesis—that the anisotropy of Christian time is intimately related to the narrative structure of the Christian story. Note also that here, as in the case of Kant's epistemology, intersubjectivity is preserved, for the story is God's story, and there is only one God, who is Lord and Creator of the universe.

Now let me turn to the apparently unrelated subject of fictional narrative, with particular attention to the ontological structure of the fictional worlds conjured, or, more precisely, created by those narratives. Think for a moment about the world brought to life in Edith Wharton's widely read novel, *Ethan Frome.*[6] The novel has a frame structure—it is a story within a story. The narrator undertakes to tell us about Ethan. His account of the events which constitute the story of the novel begins as he is stepping across the threshold of the Frome house. The entire inner story of the novel is told as he pauses, half in and half out of the door. When the tragic denouement has been revealed, he completes his step across the threshold, and the novel ends.

It is customary to assume that the 'location' of the novel is the western Berkshires in Massachusetts, roughly in the area between Springfield and Williamstown, and that the time is the early part of this century. But, of course, that is merely a manner of speaking, for this is a fictional narrative, and the events recounted stand in no causal or other relations to real places or events in the actual Berkshires of the early twentieth century. What is more (and this, if you will permit me a bit of crude finger-pointing, is the philosophically central idea of this entire discussion), the world of the novel, *Ethan Frome,* is ontologically, inherently perspectival. It is not simply *shown to us* from the narrator's point of view, so that, for example, the harshness of the winter or the timeless horror of the three souls trapped in that house are set center stage in the narrative. That world *exists* from the point of view of the narrator.

What do I mean when I say that the world *exists* from a point of view? I mean that the normal ontological relationship between representation and thing represented is reversed in a fictional world. In the real world, the object of our cognitive representations is ontologically prior to our representation of it. Truth is then conformity of representation to object, and perspective in representation is the consequence of the specificity of the spatio-temporal location from which the knowing mind apprehends what exists in isotropic space and time. Kant, as we have seen, inverts the ontological priority of representation and object of representations, but he restores the intersubjectivity and isotropy that are the two signal marks of the ontological priority of the object by his claim that the forms of intuition and conception are universal.

In a fictional world, however, the representations *bring the world into existence*. They are genuinely constitutive of that world. The narrator's account of Starkfield and those of its inhabitants whom he chooses to mention creates the world of *Ethan Frome*. Hence, the spatial, temporal, cultural, and linguistic perspectives of the narrator are constitutive of the structure of that fictional world. What the narrator tells us, and with what words, makes the world essentially what it is.

We are all familiar with these facts about fictional worlds, although we may not often bring them reflectively to mind. We understand that it is a confusion to wonder, for example, why Phineas Fogg never met Sherlock Holmes, or whether Raskolnikov would have struck up a friendship with Ivan Karamazov, had they met. It is equally confused, save as an independent literary and creative exercise, to ask how Pip looked to Miss Havisham, or what Nigger Jim's childhood was like. Such questions presuppose that the fictional world is ontologically prior to the narrative account of it, which account can then be called into question as incomplete, biased, (reprehensibly) perspectival. But although that supposition may be true for the real world (we shall consider that question presently), it is precisely *not* true for fictional worlds.

One more point about fictional worlds before I attempt to bring all this to bear on an analysis of the ontology of the human world. A fictional world is constituted by the words of the narrative. By intention in the fictions of a skillful novelist, and frequently unselfawares in such fictions as fairy tales, certain words, *as words*, take on a valence or power or significance in such a fashion that their appearance in the narrative objectively imbues certain places, times, events, objects, persons, or characteristics in that fictional world with special meaning. Dickens, for example, plays endlessly with the names of his characters as a way not of *revealing* but of *constituting* their nature. The Veneerings, Miss Murdstone, Ebenezer Scrooge, Lawyer Tulkinghorn, Herbert Pocket, and so forth.

Now, if a historian labels the economic, social, and technological changes of the seventeenth and eighteenth centuries an 'industrial revolution,' she is making a claim about their nature, asserting, we may suppose, that in the scope and depth of their effects they produced as great a change in Europe as the overthrow of the British or French monarchies. But when Dickens names a group of greedy poor relations the Pockets, he is thereby creating their distinctive trait by the act of naming.

The same thing is true, more subtly, with regard to the form of the narration. Where the author chooses to begin it, where he or she ends it, what is included and what omitted—all these are acts of creation and constitution, not acts of discovery or description. The fact that the world of *Tom Sawyer* has almost no significant positive adult male figures is an objective fact of that fictional world, *not*, as it would be if the book were a bit of social history, a fact about what aspects of that world the author has chosen to reveal to us.

Let me turn now to the nature of the human world, which, I shall suggest, has about it certain characteristics which ally it more closely with fictional worlds than with the spatio-temporally isotropic natural world.[7]

Let me begin with several passages by Dilthey from a draft for a critique of historical reason, published as part of his *Collected Works*. These words come from a subsection entitled simply "Awareness, reality: time."

[T]he parts of filled time are not only qualitatively different from each other but, quite apart from their content, have a different character according to whether we look from the present back to the past or forward to the future. Looking back we have a series of memory pictures graded according to their value for our consciousness and feelings. . . . When we look back at the past we are passive; it cannot be changed. . . . In our attitude to the future we are active and free. Here the category of reality which emerges from the present is joined by that of possibility. We feel that we have infinite possibilities. Thus the experience of time in all its dimensions determines the content of our lives. This is why the doctrine that time is merely ideal is meaningless in the human studies. We recollect past events because of time and temporality; we turn, demanding, active and free, towards the future. We despair of the inevitable, strive, work and plan for the future, mature and develop in the course of time.[8]

Although Dilthey's language is regrettably loose and imprecise, I think we can discern here a major philosophical break with the Kantian tradition, a break with extremely significant implications. The crux of the matter is the claim that moments in time "have a different character according to whether we look from the present back to the past or forward to the future." In short, human time, unlike the time of natural events, is anisotropic and perspectival. In the natural world, all moments in time have the same valence. It is only our arbitrary chronology that imposes a divided time line on the flow of events. What is more, the physical interactions of classical physics are all in principle reversible. But in the realm of human action, past and future are ontologically different. What is past can be recalled, savored, regretted, but not taken up as the object of intention, purpose, or action. What is future, by contrast, *can* be the object of a rational will. The distinction is not merely conventional, an artifact of the system of time measurement I am employing. It may be that I can, in imagination, situate myself in 44 B.C., but I do not thereby acquire the possibility of frustrating the attempt on Caesar's life.

Dilthey also calls attention to a second distinctive characteristic of human time, namely that it is organized by our affective and evaluative orientation toward the content of moments of time. The student of the natural world adopts an attitude of disinterested theoretical apprehension toward the events of the objective spatio-temporal order. She may be pleased or displeased by them — astronomers, we may suppose, have their favorites among the stars — but that affect plays no substantive role in the judgments she forms. Our experience of the human world, however, Dilthey clearly suggests, is in part constituted by our affective orientation.

This conclusion follows directly from his observation that it is as intentional, purposive, rational agents that we apprehend the human world. Since purpose presupposes ends, toward which we adopt an evaluative attitude, it is clear that the very structure of the human world—its asymmetry, its perspectival existence from the standpoint of the active mind—is affectively organized. In short, what is condemned by natural science as primitive animism and a pathetic fallacy is legitimate and necessary in the study of the human world.

As an illustration of this point from one of the classical texts of modern social theory, consider Karl Mannheim's well-known analysis of the affective constitution of human time in the section of *Ideology and Utopia* titled "The Utopian Mentality." Mannheim, with considerable flair, undertakes to distinguish the chiliastic, liberal-humanitarian, conservative, and socialist-communist political ideologies by their orientation to time itself. A few passages will indicate the direction of Mannheim's thought:

> The Chiliastic mentality has. . .no sense for the process of becoming; it was sensitive only to the abrupt moment, the present pregnant with meaning. . . . The Chiliastic absolute experience of the 'now', which precludes any possibility of experiencing development does. . .serve the sole function of providing us with a qualitative differentiation of time. There are, according to this view, times that are pregnant with meaning and times that are devoid of meaning.
>
> The time sense of [the conservative] mode of experience and thought is completely opposed to that of liberalism. Whereas for liberalism the future was everything and the past nothing, the conservative mode of experiencing time found the best corroboration of its sense of determinateness in discovering the significance of the past, in the discovery of time as the creator of value. Duration did not exist at all for the chiliastic mentality, and existed for liberalism only in so far as henceforth it gives birth to progress. But for conservatism everything that exists has a positive and nominal value merely because it has come into existence slowly and gradually.[9]

As for the socialist-communist mentality, Mannheim observes that "time is experienced here as a series of strategic points. . . . It is not alone through the virtual presentness of every past event that every present experience embodies a third dimension which points back to the past, but it is also because the future is being prepared in it. It is not only the past but the future as well which has virtual existence in the present."[10]

Which of these conceptions of historical time, we might wonder, is the *correct* conception? What is historical time *really* like? The familiar liberal-humanitarian bias of modern social science leads us to suppose that historical time is *really* isotropic, smoothly flowing like the time of the natural sciences. The chiliastic, conservative, and socialist-communist conceptions might then be understood as ideological or utopian distortions of the truth in the service of class or party interests. But this view, as Mannheim makes clear, is profoundly mistaken.

Let us recall Kant's observation that time itself cannot be perceived. This is as true for historical as for natural time. Historical time is the order of historical events. If historical events are *constituted* as anisotropic—if the history of a society has, in its very nature, distinguished moments, an asymmetrical structure, an orientation evaluatively determined—then the time of those events will *be* anisotropic, asymmetrical, affectively defined. It will not simply be that the members of that society *experience* their time in that way—much as schizophrenics subjectively *hear* voices. The time of the society's history will actually have that structure.

How can this be? The answer lies in the social character of human history. Max Weber introduced the notion of a 'social action' to capture the distinctive character and structure of the social, as opposed to either the natural or the individual. In *Economy and Society*, he explains that by a social action he means an intentional action which is oriented to the beliefs, expectations, intentions, and actions of others. As Weber says, "Not every type of contact of human beings has a social character. . . . For example, a mere collision of two cyclists may be compared to a natural event. On the other hand, their attempt to avoid hitting each other, or whatever insults, blows, or friendly discussion might follow the collision, would constitute 'social action.'"[11] In the full sense, social actions are acts of reciprocal orientations, in which the action *per se* is constituted by the shared expectations, evaluations—or, more generally, shared social meanings—by means of which the mutual orientation takes place. It goes without saying that social actions need in no sense be instances of harmony, cooperation, or rational agreement.

New let me introduce a bit of technical scholastic jargon—the Latin term *qua*. A hippopotamus is a mammal. But when I drop a hippopotamus from a helicopter, it does not fall *qua* mammal. That is to say, it does not fall in virtue of being a mammal. Its being a mammal is no part of the explanation for its falling. Rather, it falls in virtue of being, or insofar as it is, or *qua* heavier-than-air physical object. Were it a plaster cast hippopotamus, or a reptile masquerading as a hippopotamus, it would still fall. On the other hand, it *is qua* mammal that a hippopotamus bears its young live.

Consider a wedding ceremony, with minister, bride and groom, family and friends, all gathered for, and participating in, a social action essentially constituted by the reciprocal orientations that Weber calls 'social actions'. The flowers decorating the altar cannot be said, strictly speaking, to be present at the wedding *per se*, at the wedding *qua* wedding, for the flowers do not share a reciprocal orientation with the members of the wedding party. I wish to argue that it is also strictly correct to say that an uncomprehending anthropologist from a distant land or a visitor from another planet cannot be said to be present at the wedding *qua* wedding. To be sure, the wedding has a spatial location in physical space and also a temporal location in physical time. It would therefore be possible to construe the wedding purely as a natural event, noting, for example, the gravitational interactions between the bride's bouquet and the dust in the aisle or measuring the slight rise in temperature in the locality during the time of the event. But just as the hippopotamus does not obey the laws of motion of falling bodies *qua* hippopotamus, so these physical aspects of the wedding are not characteristics of it *qua* wedding.

The wedding as wedding exists in and through the shared meanings of the participants, and also of all the other members of the society through whose reciprocal orientation, directly or indirectly, weddings as social institutions and events have their being.

Social actions are grounded in normative mutual orientations which arise out of the purposiveness and affectivity of human life. A wedding has a normative structure which allows us, as participant observers, to judge that it has been conducted well or badly, successfully or unsuccessfully. What is more, a wedding is an objectively happy event, full of forward-looking promise and hope. Hence, an unhappy wedding—and, of course, there are such—is experienced objectively, not merely statistically, as an anomaly. That is to say, an unhappy wedding exhibits the same inner contradiction that we find in a man who sighs forlornly and announces that he is happy.

As many social theorists have observed, we naturally—I would maintain, inevitably—experience social roles, categories, and institutions as objective, existing independently of our choices or wishes in exactly the same way that trees, mountains, chemical reactions, or insects exist independently of our cognition and volition. Dilthey calls this phenomenon, rather quaintly, 'objectifications of spirit'.[12] Ask a little girl what she wants to be when she grows up, and she will invariably respond with the label of a social role (doctor, bus driver, president, saint) which she, and we, conceive to be the name of an objectively existing category.

Five facts about this universal phenomenon of objectification are relevant to my discussion here.

First, the objectification of social roles and categories *mis*represents the reality, which is that they are human products—for the most part originally intentional and deliberate products, but subsequently experienced as given, rather than as constructed.

Second, the process of construction and objectification is social or collective rather than individual. No one—not even the world-historical individual, if there ever was such a one—creates a social role himself or herself, and no one can, alone, carry through the process of objectification.[13]

Third, because social categories are collective *human* products, because they are the objectifications of purposive agents, they are intrinsically normative. Built into any social role or category are norms, purposes, intentions, and evaluations. Those who occupy the roles can embrace the evaluative structure of the role, resist it, play off against it, vary it, but they cannot avoid engaging with it in some way, because that structure is part of what the role *is*. In this way, social roles are entirely different from physical objects. A rock or stick has no purpose. It can be used for a variety of purposes, but it has no intrinsic purpose. Even an artifact which has been crafted for a human purpose does not bear that purpose within it. When I use a scalpel to open mail or a book to prop open a door, there is no objective contradiction between the *proper* purpose of the artifact and the *deviant* use to which I have put it. But when a doctor uses his skill to torture patients rather than to cure them, he violates the intrinsic normative structure of the role he is filling. To be a doctor in our society *is* to aim at relieving pain rather than at causing it. That is the element of truth in Plato's account or *technés* in the *Gorgias.*

Fourth, because the 'objectifications of spirit' are collective, they are inevitably historical. The objectification occurs as the structures of interaction are reproduced, day by day, and passed on from one generation to the next. The history of a social role or category is part of what it is—not simply of what has made it what it is. The way in which this carrying-along of collective memory takes place is by the process of personality development and enculturation through which infants become members of a society. To develop a coherently formed ego requires the internalization of a structure of social roles and categories which define who and what he is—and which, through the shaping of instinctual energies, determines even the *style* in which one desires, wills, reasons, or despairs.[14]

Finally, because who one is is a consequence, in large measure, of what normatively organized social roles one has internalized, because there is no coherently formed natural man or natural woman beneath a scrim of civilization who could stand back and achieve an objective cognitive or evaluative perspective on one's society, it follows that the perspectival, evaluative orientation to society and history in which each of us is embedded simply *is* social reality. Once one becomes reflectively aware of the nature of social reality, one can choose to alter one's social role, one's identifications, indeed even one's society. But every change is a change *within* a social context, not a step *out of* a social context. There have been many attempts in the history of philosophical analysis of the human world to find a way of achieving that evaluatively neutral, ahistorical extrication from the constraints of social reality. Among the most recent is John Rawls's "original position under the veil of ignorance," which is self-consciously a bracketing of precisely those perspectival aspects of our self-understanding. What Rawls neglects to notice is that by dint of this bracketing, he has accomplished also an abstraction from precisely the *social* in human experiencing, with the result that he has merely produced one more instance of what Marx, in a lovely turn of phrase, called "Robinsonades."

Let me now try to pull together the various strands of this discussion in some coherent form. What I wish to maintain is that the history of a society is a collective narrative, constituted by the members of the society as they construct their historical time through their projects, recollections, myths, and memories, and through 'objectifications of the spirit' in social, economic, and political institutions. The shared social meanings *are* the society, and the temporal organization of those meanings *is* their history.

Thus, to ask whether scientific inquiry—in the realm of the social—is, can be, or should be undertaken from positions of ethical and political neutrality is to ask whether there is a transcultural, transsocial privileged narrative standpoint from which one could retell the story of a society *objectively.* Alternatively, it is to ask whether there are translation rules enabling us to transform one historical account into another, from a different narrative perspective, without loss or distortion of information. My answer to this question is obviously, no. Every narration is, to use the term that the French so like, 'guilty'.

If objective social science is intrinsically impossible, what then are we to make of the normative debates that rage in the human sciences? Are they simply confusions? Dialectical efforts to advance what Charles Stevenson called 'persuasive definitions'? Crosscultural failures of communication?

I think it might be useful, at least up to a point, to construe such debates as struggles over control of the narrative voice in the story of a society. As Kant reminds us, it is the transcendental unity of apperception, the 'I think' that attaches to every proposition, that is the ground of the unity of the experienced world – a proposition incredible with regard to the natural world, but very close to the truth with regard to the human world. Very often, social and political struggles take the form of fights over which groups shall play a role in the telling of a society's story.

For example, the disputes between feminist and establishment historians in recent American historiography can be viewed not as disagreements over what actually happened in the past but rather as struggles over who shall tell the story of, and thereby constitute the nature of, the collective past of the American people. The same struggle has been waged for some time now by Black historians, just as, at an earlier time, it was waged by regionalists who struggled against the historiographic hegemony of the New England Puritan voice. The nodal moments in the time line of American history are reconstituted by the intrusion of new voices into the story-telling that is a collective culture.

Is there an 'original position', an 'ideal communicative situation', in which the historical truth can be voiced and rational principles of action enunciated? Is there a *correct* account, a suitable voice, one standpoint, perhaps encapsulating all the others, from which the story of the United States, or of any nation, can be told objectively? The answer is clearly no. For whose voice would that be? And where would he or she or they be standing?

There is a powerful tradition, going back at least to Plato, which seeks an objective, impartial standpoint from which to make political judgments or launch political actions. The attempts to derive a theory of the just state from cognition of eternal forms, to deduce it from an analysis of rational agency as such, to extract it from a model of a bargaining game among rational agents, or even to base it on a claim about the objective movement of history are all doomed to fail, for they all rest on the false supposition that there is a transhistorical, transcultural perspective from which we can grasp the nature of human nature, history, and society as they *really* are. Over and over, in some form or other, philosophers appeal to the image of the ideal observer, the impartial judge – in Lucretius' evocative image, the observer high on a hill, above the plain on which the battle is being fought.[15] But if the arguments of this discussion are sound, none of these attempts can possibly succeed.

What, then, are the implications for political action? If the stance of the judge, the impartial observer, is impossible to achieve, from what position should we launch into the struggle? Clearly, the answer is that we can only adopt, and hence must adopt, the stance of the *partisan*. A true story from my experiences at Columbia University during the student uprising of 1968 will help to explain. I was, at that time, deeply committed to the proposition that there are objective, universal principles of morality and society, a claim which I was struggling to explicate and justify both in my political writings, such as *In Defense of Anarchism,* and in my commentary on Kant's ethical theory, *The Autonomy of Reason.* One of my students was a serious, intense member of the Communist Party who divided such time as he could take from his studies between proselytizing on campus and organizing in a local factory. He challenged me to defend my belief in objective moral principles, and lacking good arguments, I tried to turn the question against him. If you don't believe that there are truths to be discovered in morals, I asked him, then on what do you base your own deep commitments in politics? He answered, somewhat like a parent explaining elementary matters to a child, that it all comes down to which side you are on. You have to make a choice, and after that, you will know who your friends and allies are, and whose interests you are prepared to fight for.

At the time, his reply struck me as hopelessly simple-minded – a refusal to face hard questions of justification and first principles. After almost two decades of reflection, I have concluded that in this, as in so much, my students have a great deal to teach me.

Political action grows out of felt needs, and out of identification with groups of men and women whose goals, needs, and demands one takes as one's own. By the time I begin to think about politics (or ethics, for that matter), I am already a historically and socially situated person whose self has been formed by identifications, internalizations, sympathies, and antipathies with other individuals and groups. Political deliberation consists partly in attempting to decide how (and whether) to advance the interests or projects of those with whom one identifies, and partly in reflective consideration of the soundness, the wisdom, the suitability of those identifications.

Depending on whom one is talking to, political debate is either a discussion with one's comrades about what is to be done, or an effort to find common ground with those whose overlapping commitments and identifications provide some possibility for persuasion, or else a form of non-physical combat in which the aim is to wound and defeat, not make common cause with or persuade, one's antagonist.

To this position, which can truly be described as banal in its manifest obviousness, it is frequently objected that if there is no firmer foundation for politics than shared identifications and sympathies, then there is nothing we can say to the committed Nazi or the historically and socially embedded Afrikaaner. If by this the objector means that we can find no arguments that will persuade the Nazi to give up Nazism and the Afrikaaner to give up Apartheid, that is certainly true, but scarcely relevant. Has anyone ever been so foolish as to imagine that she could legitimately act against Nazism only after she had found an argument that would persuade a Nazi (or even a 'rational' Nazi)?

But perhaps the objection means, How can I justify *to myself* acting against Apartheid if my opposition to it is 'merely' an expression of my identification with Black, Colored, and Indian South Africans (or, if I myself am Black, Colored, or Indian, an expression of my own interest in the defeat of Apartheid). If 'justification' consists in locating an objective, impartial standpoint from which any person, merely *qua* rational agent, would judge the opposing of Apartheid to be the right action, then justification is impossible since no such standpoint exists. If 'justification' means persuading my compatriots that this is the proper action, then justification will involve the usual sorts of strategic, tactical, factual, and purposive considerations which are the substance of real political discussion and with which anyone who has been at all active politically is familiar.

Nothing more can be obtained, nothing more is needed, and nothing more ought, therefore, to be sought.

NOTES

1. If 'one ought' implies 'one can', then 'one cannot' implies 'it is not the case that one ought', but that is not quite the same as 'one ought not', for this latter form of words carries with it the implication that one ought not even try. It is certainly possible to argue that one ought to try to investigate the human world from a position of ethical and political neutrality, even if one is doomed to fail, but I shall not undertake a refutation of *that* claim in this essay.

2. Immanuel Kant, *Critique of Pure Reason,* translated by N. Kemp Smith (New York, 1961), A 125.

3. Ibid., A 126.

4. Ibid., B 219.

5. For a demonstration of this claim, see R. P. Wolff, "Remarks on the Relation of the *Critique of Pure Reason* to Kant's Ethical Theory," in *New Essays on Kant,* edited by Bernard den Ouden and Marcia Moen (New York, 1987), 139–54.

6. Cf. Cynthia Griffin Wolff, *A Feast of Words* (New York, 1977), 159–84.

7. I have read a shorter version of this essay to a number of audiences, and almost invariably someone will observe, during the discussion afterward, that the study of the physical world does not in fact possess the objectivity which I attribute to it, and which I am contrasting with the perspectival character of the study of the human world. I must confess that I am, when it comes to the study of nature, an unreconstructed realist, but since that conviction is not part of my argument, the reader should feel free to substitute a different conception of our relationship to the physical world, particularly if that makes it easier to accept my thesis.

8. Wilhelm Dilthey, *Selected Writings,* edited, translated, and introduced by H. P. Rickman (Cambridge, 1976), 209–10.

9. Karl Mannheim, *Ideology and Utopia,* translated by Louis Wirth and Edward Shils (New York, 1936), 225–26, 235.

10. Ibid., 244, 246.

11. Max Weber, *Economy and Society,* translated by Ephraim Fischoff et al. (Berkeley, 1979), 23. I have read this brief passage a hundred times, and I still cannot tell whether Weber is deliberately satirizing the German mentality or intends the example seriously.

12. Dilthey, *Selected Writings,* 191–95, the section entitled "The Objectifications of Life [*Geist*]."

13. See, for example, the compressed but elegant development of this idea in Peter Berger and Thomas Luckmann, *The Social Construction of Reality* (Garden City, N.Y., 1966).

14. The deepest and most graceful exposition of this theme of which I am aware can be found in Michael Oakeshott's essay "Rational Conduct," in *Rationalism in Politics* (New York, 1962).

15. Cf. *De rerum natura,* Book II, opening lines.

Newcomblike Problems

JORDAN HOWARD SOBEL

R ichard Jeffrey's logic of decision is the best-known evidential decision theory. In it the desirability of an action is a weighted average of the desirabilities of its possible outcomes, in which average weights are conditional
probabilities of outcomes on the action. Conditional probabilities are assumed
to measure possible evidential bearings of propositions. Connectedly, the desirability of a proposition is said to measure its relative welcomeness as a possible
item of news.

> To say that A is ranked higher than B [i.e., *des* A > *des* B] means that the
> agent would welcome the news that A is true more than he would the news
> that B is true. (Jeffrey 1965b, 72)[1]

"The Bayesian principle [of this theory, which] is to *perform an act which has
maximum desirability"* (Jeffrey 1965b, 1) relates desirabilities to choiceworthiness. This principle can be given the aspect of an obvious truism.

> If the agent is deliberating about performing act A or act B. . ., there is no
> effective difference between asking whether he prefers A to B as a news
> item or as an act, for he makes the news.[2]

Since in choosing *A* over *B* the agent will make for himself the news that *A*, it
can seem obvious that he should do this only if he would *prefer* the news that *A*.
"What else?" Jeffrey tempts us to ask.
　　For present purposes the important feature of Jeffrey's theory is, put positively, its purely epistemic and unmetaphysical character. Put negatively this
feature is its acausal character, which feature has always been first among the
theory's Humean virtues in Jeffrey's view.

> The theory is *non-causal* in the sense that. . .[no] causal notion is taken as
> primitive. (Jeffrey 1965a, 292)

It [is] the principal virtue of the theory, that it makes no use. . .of any. . . causal notion. (Jeffrey 1965b, 409)

Newcomblike problems challenge this assessment of the evidential, acausal character of Jeffrey's theory. As Jeffrey himself reports,

[that] causal imputations play no explicit role [in his theory, is seen by Newcomb-critics and] partisans of causal decision theory as a defect.[3]

First, in part one, an analysis of Newcomblike problems is proposed, and their considerable variety is canvassed. Next, in part two, I defend Newcomblike problems from important objections, and maintain that they make coherent challenges to evidential decision theories, even refined ones. I am convinced that they make more than this, that they make refutations of evidential decision theories. But I am not concerned in the present essay to press this final substantive point.

I. ANALYSIS AND VARIETY

An Analysis of Newcomblike Problems

Newcomblike problems for Jeffrey's theory would have the following elements. (Problems cited by name are set out in Appendix One below.)

Element A. In a Newcomblike problem the agent would be sure that certain features relevant to the values of outcomes of his actions, for example, whether or not there is *$M* in the second box (Newcomb's Problem), or whether or not the other prisoner is going to confess (Prisoner's Dilemma), are *causally independent* of his possible actions and are things he can in no way influence.

Element B. These features would be for him *epistemically* or *evidentially dependent* on his actions, so that news of these actions would provide him with signs, with evidence for and against these features.

Element C. It is maintained, largely on the basis of Element A, that a certain action would be uniquely choiceworthy and rational.

Element D. It is maintained, largely on the basis of Element B, that the evidential desirability of this action is exceeded by that of some other action that is open to the agent. Given Element C, this entails that the choiceworthy action in the case is *not* the action news of which would be most welcome.

The Variety of Newcomblike Problems

Problems vary in the grounds provided in them for these elements. They vary in how they purport to secure the dependencies and independencies in Elements A and B, and in the character of explicit or implicit arguments for Elements C and D. Important differences among Newcomblike problems relate mainly to Elements B and C, but there is variety in the other elements as well.

Grounds for Causal Independence. In many cases the agent is sure that some feature is causally independent of his actions, because he is sure that this feature is already settled one way or the other. This may be because the feature relates to the past (for example, a past prediction) or because he views it as relating to the already determined future (for example, the development of a disease whose causes are already in place). But a belief that the feature is "already settled" is not a part of every problem. For example, it is not a part of every Prisoner's Dilemma. Whether or not the other prisoner will confess can be viewed as not yet decided and as not already settled. That a feature is already settled is only a particularly simple way of making reasonable an agent's belief that his actions can have no causal bearings on it.

Grounds for Epistemic Dependence. Most important differences between problems have to do with how, notwithstanding the absence of perceived causal bearings, *evidential* bearings of actions on certain features are made plausible.

Predictor cases. The agent may think that a feature depends on some good predictor's prediction, so that news of an action would provide a good sign that it had been predicted, and that the feature (for example $M in the second box) was as a consequence in place or not. The agent may be supposed to think that the predictor works with a theory, perhaps a causal theory. But predictor-cases need not be in any explicit way causal. For example, an agent may be supposed to think that the predictor is an intimate who understands him well and knows what he is going to do better and sooner than he does himself; *but* knows his coming actions only in something like the way in which he, the agent, often knows and can predict what he is going to do. Such a predictor will not be supposed, while reflecting from the agent's deliberating point of view, to think of the agent's actions as things that will be caused, anymore than the agent himself does from that point of view.

Causal cases. (1) The agent may think that there is a possible cause for the feature and a cause for his action and that these causes go together so that either both are present or both are absent (for example, he may think that it is possible that he has inherited a gene for a disease from a person who also carries a gene for tendencies to intellectualism [Nozick 1969, 125–26]). (2) He may think that there is a possible *common cause* for the feature and his action, for example, that there is a single gene that both inclines possessors to smoke and also makes them independently prone to cancer (*Sir Ronald Lights Up*). (3) He may think that the feature would cause his action; for example, that a signal on the screen that flashes when and only when there is popcorn to be had, would register subliminally and cause him to go for popcorn (*Popcorn Problem*).

Causal Newcomblike problems admit of further divisions. Suppose, for example, that the agent believes in a cause for his action. Then he may think that this cause will operate directly, or only indirectly and by way of causing his decision and choice for it. And, if indirectly by way of his decision, he may think that this will be caused by way of conscious factors (for example, his credences and preferences) of his decision making's being caused; or by way of unconscious factors being caused (for example, his implicit rule for translating credences and preferences into a decision—he might think that the common cause would cause him to be a desirability maximizer [cf., Nozick 1969, 127–29]); or by way of his being caused to be, in his choice, carried away or confused; or by a combination of these ways.

Similar-decision-processes cases. If the feature is an action, he may think that in whatever way he decides what to do, similar processes will lead to the other action. For example, he may believe that the other prisoner will think as he does, and he may believe this while being in considerable doubt concerning how he himself is going to think and decide (cf., Sobel 1985a, 271).

Signs of character cases. If the feature is a possible aspect of the agent's character or personality—for example, ruthlessness (see *Rising Young Executive*) or charisma (*Solomon's Problem*)—an agent's action could in yet another way be a good sign of something of which it was not considered to be a possible cause. He could think he was a person who learns things about himself by listening to what he says and seeing what he does. Most people are somewhat like that. "'How can I tell what I think till I see what I say?'—E. M. Forster" (Lewis 1981, 9–10). "How can I know, really know, what I am like, for example, what I am and am not capable of, until I see what I do when the chips are down?" These, for most persons, are sometimes apt rhetorical questions.

Arguments for the Choiceworthinesses of Bad News Actions. Choiceworthiness of bad news actions are made plausible in the best-known Newcomblike problems by dominance arguments, but this device is not a feature of every Newcomblike problem. Some use the more widely applicable common sense that an action is choiceworthy if it would probably have the best consequences. For example, not going for popcorn recommends itself in the *Popcorn Problem* even though the agent would prefer to go for popcorn if he thought there were some. Not going for popcorn is held to be his rational course, because he is nearly sure that there is not any popcorn and that he would be wasting his time going for some.

Arguments for the Desirability of Another Action. There is little variation in how relative desirabilities of actions are established. Most problems use assumptions concerning cardinalities of desirabilities of possible outcomes. One class of exceptions are probability-of-one problems. In these, ordinal relations of desirabilities for outcomes suffice. There are other exceptions, including a version of the *Popcorn Problem* (Sobel 1986b, 414–15).

Summing up, three bifurcations of Newcomblike problems divide these problems into predictor and non-predictor problems, into problems that involve causal hypotheses and problems that do not, and into problems that feature dominance arguments and those that do not. Crisscrossing these bifurcations produces an eightfold partition, each part of which contains either a problem that is already in the literature or a readily constructable one. It will be evident that very few objections to Newcomblike problems are, either as they stand or by easy extensions, objections to *all* Newcomblike problems.

II. OBJECTIONS

Objections to be opposed in this part are of several sorts. First come complaints that Newcomblike problems are too fantastic, too unrealistic, to be taken seriously and counted as refutations of otherwise satisfactory, ensconced theories.

Next come objections that these would-be problems are impossible in that they would have clearheaded deliberating agents view their possible actions as potential evidence for prior conditions. Then comes the objection that causal problems that would be test cases for theories of rational action are impossible in that they would have agents view their actions as, though caused, avoidable by choice. Following this are objections to cases in which agents believe their actions will be caused indirectly by way of their *choices* being caused. And last come objections that Newcomblike problems do not threaten properly qualified and formulated theories of rational choice that are addressed in the first place to choices of ideally rational and sophisticated agents, for such agents would be conscious of their credences and preferences and, by the time for making a decision, could not learn anything from news of what action they were about to do. For them, it has been argued, choiceworthiness must in the end go exactly by both evidential desirability *and* causal utility, so that the kinds of theories that Newcomblike problems would set at odds, when properly qualified and formulated, will in every case agree. (Whereas evidential desirabilities are computed using measures of evidential bearings of actions on likely outcomes, measures of probable causal bearings would be used in computations of causal utilities. The simplest causal decision theory uses unconditional probabilities of causal conditionals $P(a > o)$, instead of the conditional probabilities, $P(o/a)$, i.e., $P(a \& o)/P(a)$, used in Jeffrey's logic of decision.)

"That These Are Problems Only for Space Cadets"

Against predictors, it is sometimes suggested that their powers in problem cases need to be viewed as extraordinary, hardly human, and that cases based on them are always bizarre and farfetched. In fact, however, when the stakes are high, an agent can have a very low opinion of the predictor's power.

> Define *average estimated reliability* as the average of (A) the agent's conditional degree of belief that the predictive process will predict correctly, given that he takes his thousand, and (B) his conditional degree of belief that the process will predict correctly, given that he does not take his thousand. . . . Let r be the ratio of the value of the thousand to the value of the million: .001 if value is proportional to money. . . . We have a disagreement between two conceptions of rationality if and only if the expected value [i.e., the desirability] of taking the thousand is less than that of declining it, which is so if and only if the average estimated reliability exceeds $(1 + r)/2$. (That is .5005 if value is proportional to money.) This is not a very high standard of reliability. (Lewis 1979, 238–39)

For a proof, I employ certain simplifying numerical stipulations, and make one weak assumption. Simplifying stipulations: *des* \$0 = 0; *des* \$M = 1. Recall that $r = des$ \$T/*des* \$M. By the second stipulation it follows that $r = des$ \$T. Substantive assumption: *des* (\$M + \$T) = *des* \$M + *des* \$T. (This is weaker than the assumption that desirabilities are linear with money.) Letting 'C' abbreviate 'the predictive process will predict correctly', and 'T' abbreviate 'the agent takes his thousand', here is a desirability matrix for the agent's decision problem:

	C	¬C
T	r	1 + r
¬T	1	0

And here are the agent's desirabilities for ¬T and T:

$des \, \neg T = P(C/\neg T)$

$des \, T = P(C/T)r + P(\neg C/T)(1 + r)$

To prove:

$des \, \neg T > des \, T$ if and only if *average estimated reliability* $> (1 + r)/2$.

Here is a proof of the "only if"-part. Turned upside down it is a proof of the "if"-part.

$des \, \neg T > des \, T$
$P(C/-T) > P(C/T)r + P(\neg C/T)(1 + r)$
$P(C/-T) > P(C/T)r + [1 - P(C/T)](1 + r)$
$P(C/-T) > P(C/T)r + 1 + r - P(C/T) - P(C/T)r$
$P(C/-T) + P(C/T) > 1 + r$
$[P(C/-T) + P(C/T)]/2 > (1 + r)/2$
average estimated reliability $> (1 + r)/2$

Assuming that desirabilities are linear with money, as Lewis reports, $r = .001$, and $[(1 + r)/2] = .5005$. And, if .5005 is not already near enough to .5 to make no difference, by reducing the amount in B1 to $1, to 1¢, etc., it is possible to reduce the average estimated reliability required for the problem to a point where it is near enough to .5 to make no difference. It is not essential to a predictor-case that the agent believe in a predictor of preternatural powers. The agent can think that the predictor is barely better than a random one. Nor need the agent consider the stakes to be extraordinarily high. Stakes for the agent and his confidence in the predictor can both be moderate as far as the mathematics of predictor problems is concerned.

Newcomblike problems need not be farfetched, which is not to say that they are commonplace. But then decision theory, as practiced by philosophers, is not an empirical science, and as long as a kind of problem is possible it should not matter whether or not it arises often or even ever. Even if Newcomblike problems were never encountered in practice and were all problems only "for space cadets," they would, I think, *not* be problems "to which [in our theoretical exercises we could wisely]. . .apply the [practical wisdom] of Esther Marcovitz (1866–1944): 'If cows had wings, we'd carry big umbrellas'" (Jeffrey 1983, 25).

"That Deliberators Cannot View Their Choices
as Signs of Prior Conditions"

Some critics object to the idea that choices of deliberating agents in New-comblike problems would be, for these agents, evidence of causally independent states.

> Solomon, for example, when deliberating whether or not to send for the woman, should know "that he *is* deliberating" (Kyburg 1980, 162). He *"believes* that he has freedom of choice" (162). But then he must believe that "there is no connection between how he decides and whether or not he has charisma" (162). Since he "regards his choice as free, it cannot be taken [by him] as *evidence* of a prior state" (164).

However Solomon can, it seems, believe that his character is connected with his decisions, without thinking that it is causally connected. And, even if Solomon is a philosopher who thinks that connections between characters and actions can only be causal, still, as Ellery Eells has maintained, he need not think of his actions as inexorable consequences of his character:

> It seems perfectly consistent for Solomon to believe both that he has free-dom of choice and that. . .whether or not he has charisma is to some extent causally relevant to [and connected with] whether or not he sends for [the woman]. (Eells 1984a, 93)

These things are consistent at least according to ordinary understandings. (More is said about this in the next section.) And if Solomon believes his character is causally relevant to his actions, there is, I am sure Kyburg would agree, no reason why he cannot find in his actions evidence of that character. Others could learn of his character through his actions, and, assuming that he believes that it is causally relevant to these actions, so can he.

Furthermore, even if there is a problem with deliberating agents viewing their possible actions as evidence of their causes, because there is a problem with deliberating agents thinking their actions have causes, this difficulty does not extend to all Newcomblike problems. Shifting to an acausal problem, it is quite clear that I can consistently take my free choice to be evidence of what a wise friend and mentor has predicted I shall do of my own free will. That I think my predicting friend regards my choice as free could hardly be a reason for my thinking otherwise; nor would the fact that I regarded my choice as free, rule out my having confidence in my friend's predictive powers. Kyburg, if he means his objection to deliberating agents viewing their possible actions as evidence to apply against all Newcomblike problems, implicitly denies these things. Perhaps Kyburg thinks that in order for actions to be evidence for states, they must be viewed as connected with these states either as causes or effects. But this is not true, and it would not make Kyburg's point if it were.

Huw Price states in the abstract to an essay that he will show that "a free agent cannot take the contemplated action to be probabilistically relevant to its causes" (Price 1986, 195) in certain kinds of Newcomblike problems. In fact, however, freedom plays no role in his argument which, if successful, would show (only) that agents for whom conditional credences are relevant to choice, and whose relevant conditional credences for causes of actions on these actions would be formed by direct inferences from statistical correlations, made with attendance to all available evidence, cannot take contemplated actions as relevant to their causes. I will consider, and reject, his argument for this limited result, without considering here the usefulness for decision theory of this result, supposing it could be established. That larger issue is broached in note 11 below.

Suppose, for example, that Fred is an evidential desirability maximizer "or something like" one, and that in his conditional credences he abides by "the *principle of total evidence*" (Price 1986, 199). Assume that he is a smoker who believes that "the cancer gene occurs in 20% of smokers, and in 2% of nonsmokers" (196). Can he have conditional probabilities based by direct inference on these statistics (these conditional probabilities would be $P(G/S) = .2$ and $P(G/-S) = .02$)? Price says that he cannot, for conditional credences based on these statistics would not, once he had formed them, be based on *all* of the available evidence that needed then to be taken into account. These conditional probabilities would *themselves,* Price avers, be new evidence that *conflicted* with the old and made a difference to his view of the *pertinent* correlation between smoking and the gene among *Fred-alikes.* These conditional credences would, Price tells us, "be negatively correlated with smoking; they [would for Fred-alikes, evidential desirability maximizers that they are] increase the attractiveness of not smoking" (200).

Price contends (at least implicitly) that any conditional probabilities that would make Fred's smoking evidence for or against that gene can be shown to be for him untenable. His argument, however, is not sound even for the particular conditional probabilities he considers. For though the evidence provided by these conditional probabilities themselves *might* lead to revisions in the pertinent statistic, contrary to Price it is not true that it would need to do this. Let us grant that these conditional probabilities would be "negatively correlated with smoking" (200). Grant that Fred would expect there to be relatively fewer smokers within the class of Fred-alikes* (i.e., Fred-alikes all of whom, for one resemblance to Fred, have those conditional probabilities) than in the population at large, *or* in the larger class of Fred-like that includes some who (perhaps through inattention and lack of reflection) do not have those conditional probabilities. Suppose indeed that Fred would think that almost everyone in the class of Fred-alikes* would decide not to smoke, and that only a very few of this vast majority would then backslide, change their minds, and actually smoke. Even so he could think that in this now-refined sample space the cancer gene was *still* possessed by 20 percent of (the relatively few Fred-like*) smokers, and 2 percent of (the relatively many Fred-like*) nonsmokers.

Fred could consistently think that the evidence of those conditional probabilities was to the 20/2 percent correlations in the populations of smokers and nonsmokers at large and in the classes of Fred-alikes smokers and nonsmokers, as he might think that evidence that a fire in an empty building was started in a rubbish bin would be to correlations of fires in general in empty buildings with ones started by arsonists, and with ones started in other ways (cf., 198–99). He could think that the new evidence provided by those .2 and .02 conditional probabilities of his made no difference to pertinent correlations of the gene with smoking and not smoking by his alikes. Why not? And if he did think this, then the new evidence provided by those conditional probabilities would, according to Price, *not* need to be considered, for it would not "[conflict] with the old" (200). Alternatively, it can be allowed that even so it would need to be considered: for if the evidence provided by these conditional probabilities themselves makes no difference to them, they are not "self-defeating" (201) or "inherently unstable" (201). Contrary to Price, notwithstanding the relevance of the conditional probabilities to evidential desirability maximizer's actions, and notwithstanding his commitment to the principle of total evidence, these conditional probabilities *can* be supposed without contradiction to be his in the case. So, in this case, he *will* "take the contemplated action[s] to be probabilistically relevant" (195), and (*pace* 199) he will get what Price considers to be the *wrong* answer, he will not smoke.

Summing up, it seems that deliberating agents *can* take their well-reasoned choices and actions to be, though not causes, still evidence for prior conditions that would be relevant to the values of outcomes. And Price has not demonstrated (for what this result would be worth) that at least some agents for whom such evidence would be choice-relevant—for example, evidential desirability maximizers committed to the principle of total evidence—cannot, in what would be common cause Newcomblike problems, take their reasoned actions to be evidence for their causes. Other efforts, due mainly to Eells, to show that ideally rational and sophisticated agents, or at least ideally rational and sophisticated evidential desirability maximizers, cannot take their actions to be evidence for certain things, are considered below.

"Against Agents Who Believe in Causes for Their Actions"

Problem cases for Jeffrey's theory would be decision problems in which choiceworthiness and desirability seem to diverge. But for an agent to have a decision problem, it is necessary that he be sure that there is a decision he can make: it is necessary that he be sure that there are actions he can choose to do, each of which he would do were he to choose. However, it may be suggested, not against all Newcomblike decision problems, but against all of the causal ones, that an agent cannot consistently be sure that he has a *choice*, and that several actions are really open to him, if he thinks that he may be *caused* to do what he does.

Whether or not an agent can have a choice if what he will do will be caused is an old issue, one stand on which underlies the present objection to some Newcomblike problems. I do not take that stand. I think that an agent can have a choice even if he will be caused to do what he will do. I hold that a person can believe that under certain circumstances that he thinks may already obtain (for example, POPCORN!!! being flashed on the screen), he would be moved to do a certain thing; and, consistent with this thought, be sure that even if he is going to be so moved, though he will be caused to do the thing and not another, he will not *have* to do it, and he still has a choice. He can be sure, even when he is *sure* that causes for his action are already in place, that he can still choose to do otherwise than he will in fact do, otherwise than he will in fact be caused to do. All of that is, I think, consistent, given ordinary notions of agency and causation, and these, as distinct from various possible philosophic explications of them, are the notions of present relevance. The issue, I take it, is whether agents can, in their own terms, consistently think that they may be "caused" to do certain things, and be sure that even if they are being "caused" to do them, "moved" to do them, they have choices and are able not to do them.

There is no general difficulty here for ordinary thinking about causes and choices. Of course, *some* beliefs in causes for actions are not consistent with viewing these actions as avoidable by choice. If, for example, an agent believes that some predictor "hypnotically controls" his actions (Mackie 1977, 218), or that some predictor will "intervene [if necessary] via telekinesis. . .to *make* [him] choose the alternative she has 'predicted'" (Talbott 1987, 421), then he cannot think that he has a choice in the matter, or that what he does is up to him. (See Sobel 1988b, 9, for another example.) But not all ordinary beliefs in causes for actions are beliefs in such causes, or in causes that work in ways that quite remove control from the agent. Ordinary beliefs in subliminal stimuli and in character- and disposition-shaping genes can be of these stimuli and genes as causes that an agent can, even if he rarely or never does, override.

Some causes of actions are ordinarily viewed as contravenable. Furthermore, though not all philosophers approve of such views and provide explications for them, some do and thus can (as far as present objections go), consistently with their technical philosophies, be in causal Newcomblike decision problems. This can be so even for a philosophic determinist. Suppose, for example, that a philosopher believes that he will do A and that this is related to an already in place determining cause C by a law of nature L such that $(C \& L)$ entails A. Suppose furthermore that he believes that even if he were to choose to act otherwise, $Ch(A)$, that would make no difference to C, and that whatever he were to do would have a determining cause. He can, even so, think that he can choose to do otherwise, $Ch(A)$, and that if he were to choose he would *do* otherwise, A. For he can think (1) that up to the time of $Ch(A)$ there would be no change (C would thus remain in place), (2) that at that time there would be a small miracle (he could think that the "choice otherwise" would be this miracle, which, he might want to caution, though his and made by him, would not itself be an "action" of his or something he "did"), and (3) that from that time the world would unfold through A in accordance with the laws of the actual world modified minimally (presumably in ways peculiarly relevant to the agent's psychology and personal history) to allow for, and to make lawful, that small miracle (which while contrary to actual laws, given that the past to its time would remain fixed, would not be contrary to what, given it, would be the laws –

indeed, this small miracle might itself have a determining *cause* under the laws that would prevail were it to obtain) (cf., Gibbard and Harper 1985, 136 and 157–58, n.2; and Lewis 1981, 294).

But enough of metaphysical fancies. What is important to our subject is not whether beliefs in effective choices otherwise are consistent with various speculative technical opinions concerning causes and the past, and the semantics of standard "non-backtracking" act-consequence counterfactuals. What is important is the fact that persons, including most philosophers when they are not doing philosophy but simply getting on with life, can, in their own natural and everyday terms, think that sometimes, even when they are under the influence of causes to do things, they have choices and capacities *not* to do these things and to override those causes. What is important to the cogency of causal Newcomblike problems is that this is true of natural and everyday thought, and not whether or not, in the opinion of this or that metaphysician (opinions are, of course, divided) good philosophic sense can be made of the possibility of choosing to act otherwise, and then acting according to that choice.

Decision theories are not specific to the enlightened any more than they are specific to the humane.

> The logic of decision is concerned neither with the agent's belief function nor with his underlying value function. . . . The Bayesian framework. . . admits belief functions that would be entertained only by a fool, and value assignments that would be entertained only by a monster. (Jeffrey 1965b, 199)

Decision theories are *certainly* not specific to philosophic determinists. And so, though it is interesting that causal Newcomblike problems are possible even for some philosophic determinists, it is not important.[4]

An agent can have a decision problem even if he thinks that his action will be caused. However, though the belief that his action will be caused is consistent with his having a decision problem, the belief that it will be caused *quite regardless* of his decision and choice is not. An agent has a proper decision problem only if he is sure that what he does can depend on his choice or decision: an agent in a proper decision problem must be sure that he has choices which if made would be efficacious.[5]

Consider now these words of Jeffrey's:

> Fisher's problem belongs to the Newcomb species only if it is the *choice* of smoking that the agent takes the bad gene to promote directly. . . . If he takes the performance itself to be directly promoted by presence of the bad gene, there is no question of preferential choice: the performance is compulsive. (Jeffrey 1983, 25)

Jeffrey's words suggest, and it can seem true, that an agent in a proper decision problem cannot think that his action will be caused *directly* by some already in place condition, and not merely indirectly and only by way of this condition causing his choice or decision. I think, however, that what are excluded are not beliefs in direct causation, but only, as has already been said, beliefs in *quite regardless* and *uncontrovertible* causation. And, I maintain, to say that an action is caused, caused this way or that, directly or whatever, is *not* to say that it will take place quite regardless, and that the agent has no choice in its connection. Consider that even if an action will be caused directly by some already in place condition, e.g., a subliminal stimulus, it is possible that it will also be chosen, and possible for both the in place direct cause and the choice to be necessary causes, as well as sufficient in each other's presence. It is possible for an action to be counterfactually dependent on a directly operating cause, and *also* counterfactually dependent on a choice: it is possible that if that cause were absent, then so would be the action, notwithstanding the continued presence when its time comes of this choice, and *also* that if this *choice* were not merely absent, but replaced by an alternative choice otherwise, then the action would be absent, and indeed replaced by that chosen action otherwise, the action's absence taking place this time notwithstanding the continued presence of that already in place direct *cause.*

But is it possible for an action caused directly, and not by way of its choice being caused, to be rational? Yes it is, just as it is possible for such an action to be irrational, and for things the agent could have done by choice instead to be rational. Whatever way rational actions must be related to credences and preferences, this caused action can be related in this way to credences and preferences, or not so related. And this is true, whether the required relation is purely structural (e.g., having maximum evidential desirability, or maximum causal utility), or not purely structural but, as William Talbott would have it (Talbott 1987, 423) somehow causal. For a proper causal condition for rational actions must tolerate the causal pattern described in the previous paragraph.

"Against Agents Who Believe in Causes for Their Choices"

Causal Newcomblike problems do not need to be indirect causation problems, for direct causation of actions is not necessarily causation quite regardless. Still, cases in which agents believe only in indirect, and by way of their choices, causation of their actions are important, and it can be felt that there are objections to *such* cases being *Newcomblike.*

There are no special difficulties with an agent's believing that his action will be caused by way of his choices being caused, where these in turn will be caused by way of his credences and preferences. For he can still think that his choice will be up to him, and that he will not have to make the one that he will make. He can think that he does not have to choose as he will, and that were he to choose otherwise he would act otherwise, and think that these things are so whether or not his act will be rational relative to his credences and preferences, and even though his choice will be caused by way of his credences and preferences being caused.

But it can seem that an agent who believes that his actions will be caused only indirectly by way of his credences and preferences and thence his choice being caused cannot be in a Newcomblike decision problem. For it can seem that, *if* an agent believes just before the time for choice that just before the time for his choice his credences and preferences, and thence his choice, will, depending on certain crucial circumstances (for example, whether or not the popcorn message is flashing), be caused to take on a particular character; *then* he will at least at this last minute have views about those circumstances, views that will bring into alignment the choiceworthiness and desirabilities of his possible actions. The objection is not that an agent in a decision problem cannot have the beliefs in question, but that, if he does have them, then at least in the *end* his case cannot constitute a Newcomblike decision problem, and be a case in which, for Newcomblike reasons, choiceworthiness and desirability diverge.

This objection supposes that an agent will, at least just before the time for his choice, be aware of the character of his beliefs and preferences, and that he will not then be able to learn from news of his impending action anything regarding its causes that he has not already learned. But a competent agent need not be supposed to have perfect and complete self-awareness, he need not be supposed to be at the time of choice fully and accurately aware of his perhaps just then attained beliefs and preferences. And, for another difficulty with the objection, even if we concentrate on agents who are always aware of their credences and preferences, we need not suppose that they always know what time it is. Agents can, in important ways, sometimes not know what time it is. In particular, an agent can fail to know, just before the last time for a choice, that the time then *is* just before the last time for that choice. All this is true of actual agents, including very competent ones. Verging towards science fiction, I note that a self-styled super-agent could think that there never were times just before the times of *his* last times for choice. He could think that until an action was actually done there was always time left for *him* to reconsider and to change his mind.

Finally, in addition to these *difficulties* with the objection now under discussion, we should note its *limitations.* This objection is only to problems in which it is to be believed that choices may be caused by various features of situations affecting the credences and preferences on which these choices will be based. But circumstances can affect choices in other ways that need not involve intermediate conditions in place before the decision, and discoverable then by introspection. Circumstances can be supposed to determine an agent's choices by affecting the very way he will translate his ultimate credences and preferences into action: circumstances can be supposed to affect choices by affecting how, when making them, the agent will take into account his credences and preferences, and that is something which, even just before the decision is made, may still remain to be seen. The present form of objection admits of no easy extension to cases in which the agent believes that his choice may, depending on circumstances, be caused in *this* way.

The fact seems undeniable that a competent and clearheaded agent need not think that he knows what he is going to do, not even just before the time for choice, and not even if he thinks that his decision will be caused by his final credences and preferences. And so he can learn from news of his impending action things he has not already learned. He can learn not only what he is going to do, but learn things of which that news would be evidence. A competent and clearheaded agent can be in causal Newcomblike problems, both direct ones and indirect ones.

Perhaps, however, while such problems are possible for ordinary agents, they are not possible for appropriately *ideal* agents. Reasons due mainly to Eells for this view will be taken up at some length in the next section. I conclude the present section by noting, without discussion or response here, a reason that has affinities to ideas of Talbott's (cf., Talbott 1987, especially sections 6 and 9). It can be argued with some plausibility that though competent and clearheaded agents can be in indirectly causal Newcomblike problems, *ideally* competent, clearheaded, and self-confident agents cannot be. It can be contended that agents in these cases have views concerning possible causes of aspects of their credences, preferences, ways of thinking, and actions that imply that they, the agents, are possibly *not,* in the circumstances of the case, ideally competent and clearheaded, and responsive only to objective evidence and good reasons.

For a related Talbott-like point, I note that it can be argued that (1) it is a condition of every *properly qualified* theory of rational action, that an action is rational in the subjective circumstances of a case only if a *belief* on the agent's part that it is would not be undermined by ideal reflection on these circumstances; that (2) in any indirectly causal Newcomblike problem, ideal reflection conducted by a competent, clearheaded, and self-confident deliberator *would* undermine his confidence in his competence in a way that would undermine any conclusion he had tentatively reached concerning what it was rational to do; and therefore that (3) even though indirectly causal Newcomblike problems in which causal utilities and evidential desirabilities differ are possible for competent, clearheaded, and self-confident agents, no indirectly causal Newcomblike problems are possible for them for which *properly qualified* causal and evidential theories of rational action *diverge.* The suggestion is that properly qualified theories, when applied to such cases, will all say that *nothing,* that *no* action, would be rational, since no belief in the rationality of any action would be maintainable on ideal reflection.[6] A response of sorts is made to these Talbott-like objections in note 11 below.

"That Newcomblike Problems Are Not Possible for Ideally Rational Agents"

Eells has two arguments that would show that Newcomblike problems are not possible for ideally rational agents. He tells us that a difficulty with the first one makes welcome the second. And if he is right, if in particular the theories of causal utility and of evidential desirability maximizing agree for ideally rational and sophisticated agents in the manner maintained in his second argument, then a fully general evidential theory that, without in any way "going causal," prescribes correctly for all agents can seem in the offing.

After considering Eells's original defense of evidential decision theory and attending to objections to it, I take up his second one and give reasons why, as a defense of evidential decision theory, it can be only a partial success. One reason to be stressed is that ideally rational and sophisticated evidential and causal maximizers would *not* agree in their actions in *all* Newcomblike problems in which ordinary agents can find themselves. These paragons would, I claim, end up deciding for different actions in some *non-dominance* problems. In these problems the decisions that would be made by ideally rational and sophisticated evidential maximizers would be wrong, if not for themselves, at least for the ordinary agents in these problems that would be their clients. Another reason for considering Eells's second defense as, at best, only a partial success is that all-of-a-piece maximizers of these two sorts would end up *hoping* for different acts in some third-person Newcombesque problems and for different *states* in some non-action Newcombesque problems, which is relevant if, as I think, decision theory, or the theory of the *choiceworthiness of acts,* should fit smoothly into a theory of the *desirabilities of all possible facts,* as distinct from the desirabilities of possible items of news.

Eells's first static argument, his "original defense" (Eells 1984a, 73–76). In paraphrase: In a common cause problem[7] an ideally rational agent would be sure that the feared cause (*C*) could cause his act (*S*) only by affecting the credences and preferences on which his decision will be based (*R*). And such an agent, in his sophistication, would be fully conversant with these credences and preferences. That information would "screen off" possible further information concerning that common cause, and make that cause probabilistically irrelevant to his act. But then, by symmetry of irrelevance, his act would be made probabilistically irrelevant to that cause. There could not be, for an ideally rational agent, the kind of evidential bearings of acts on causes that is essential to a common cause Newcomblike problem. For such an agent, there would be probabilistic independence *as well as* causal independence of circumstances from acts. The two paradigms, causal utility maximization and evidential desirability maximization, would thus *agree* in their prescriptions for any ideally rational agent, and they would both be right.[8]

I think that, while arguable, the thing is not true of, for example, Prisoner's Dilemma Newcomblike problems. For an agent can reasonably think that his, and another's, acts are correlated without thinking that either are caused. But I will not press this point. My concern is to show that Eells's metatickle defenses are not good even against the common cause Newcomblike problems to which they are explicitly addressed.

Horwich's Objection. This argument is, as Eells has come to realize, at least incomplete: to say that an agent is sure that certain of his credences and preferences convey all of some possible common cause's *causal* relevance to his act is *not* to say that his knowledge of them encompasses all relevant information that could be provided by knowledge of that common cause, or that these credences and preferences already have for him all of the *evidential* relevance to his decision and eventual act that news of that common cause could provide. This is so because, though an ideal agent is to know for sure what his credences and preferences are, Eells takes care *not* to assume for this argument that his ideal agent knows what rule he will use to translate his credences and preferences into a decision.

> It is worth noting that the argument does not assume that DM actually will apply PMCEU, or even that DM knows what decision rule he will use. The argument is intended to show that PMCEU would, *if applied,* give the right answer. (Eells 1985a, 212 n.19).[9]

Indeed, Eells does not *insist* that his rational agent, the decision maker of his argument, has a fixed decision rule. Eells supposes that "the assumption that an agent is rational should be enough to ensure that the presence or absence of a common cause will not affect which decision rule is used," but he writes that this latter condition "is not essential to [his] argument" (Eells 1985a, 203, I have transposed his text). It is thus clear that information concerning the presence or absence of that common cause could help this agent to see what he will probably make of them his preferences and beliefs [cf., Eells 1984a, 78], and so could *be* further evidence for what he was going to do, which conversely would then be evidence for it.

Eells calls this objection to his original static defense "Horwich's Objection" [Eells 1984b, 76ff]. He thinks that it may be possible to meet it by insisting on very strong conditions of rationality, but rather than developing such a response he undertakes, "in the interest of defending evidential decision theory as applicable to agents who do not satisfy such strong conditions of rationality," a second dynamic answer to Horwich's Objection: he tries "to show that the required independence. . .should in fact, *eventually*. . .hold of the agent's probabilities" (Eells 1984a, 78–79, emphasis added). Eells leaves open the exact relationship between his original defense and this new one:

> By taking a closer look at the "dynamics" of the process of deliberation, I shall try to put. . .objections to rest, not trying to decide here whether the ideas involved. . .constitute a revision, rather than an elaboration of the original defenses. (Eells 1984b, 72)

Eells's second dynamic argument—his theory of "Continual CEU-Maximization" (Eells 1984b, 83–92). Here is a paraphrase, made with license, but I trust without prejudice, of this second defense: Let a problem be *ripe for decision* if and only if the agent in it is sure that he will receive "no new [possibly practically relevant] information 'from outside' [and that] all he will learn [of possible practical relevance] during the course of his deliberation is information about how his deliberation is going" (Eells 1984b, 87). According to Eells's second argument, an ideally rational desirability maximizer can *begin* deliberation with credences and preferences that make a Newcomblike problem that is ripe for decision. Strong idealizing conditions are being avoided that would bar him from, and thus compromise his relevance to the problems of ordinary variously limited agents (including, perhaps, even "the dithery and the self-deceptive" ones [Lewis 1981, 10]).

However, though this ideal desirability maximizer can *begin* deliberations in such a problem, he will proceed, very quickly if need be, to size up his credences and preferences according to his way of thinking, and he will not, Eells assures us, ever *end up* in such a problem. His initial credences and preferences in such a problem will, to his way of thinking, favor the good news act (e.g., not smoking). Reflecting on this, of which he has introspective knowledge, provides him with evidence that he will *do* that favored act, and that a decision for it is what he would make of those initial credences and preferences, were they his final credences and preferences. After conditionalizing on this evidence, he thinks again—indeed, ideally rational agent that he is, time permitting and as required in order to reach stable credences, preferences, and inclinations, he conditionalizes anew and rethinks, *again and again*. As "the agent [deliberating continuously in this way] carries out sufficiently many calculations. . .before the time of action, accommodating [before recalculations] the information learned from previous calculations" (Eells 1984b, 91–92), he becomes more and more confident both of what his final credences and preferences will be, *and* of what he will make of them. Eventually, at *some* point before the moment of decision and from that point on, he "knows" (that is, he is, at least for all practical purposes of the case, as near to certain as makes no difference) what his final credences and preferences will be, and knows what decision he will make of them, perhaps what decision he is *just about* to make of them (cf., Eells and Sober 1986, 228 n.5, and 235). "That is," as an *ideally rational and sophisticated* desirability maximizer deliberates, he gets "*precisely* the kind of information whose earlier absence was *precisely* the reason for the non-independence between [common causes] and acts" that the "original defense" failed clearly to exclude (Eells 1984b, 88).

"Horwich's objection [is thus] answered by supposing that the agent continually. . .calculates [desirabilities] with appropriate alterations in his subjective probabilities in the light of the results of previous calculations" (Eells 1984a, 92). Though an ideally rational evidential desirability maximizer can find himself initially undecided in a ripe-for-decision Newcomblike problem in which feared common causes are probabilistically *dependent* on his acts; *in the end,* when he makes his decision, his knowledge of his credences and preferences *and* of what he is about to make of them screens off those causes from his acts, and makes them probabilistically *independent* of one another (either completely, or nearly enough for all practical proposes).

And so "the principle of [desirability] maximizing will, in the end, even if only after a false start, prescribe the correct act," and the same act that is then prescribed by the principle of maximizing causal utility maximizing (ibid., 91–92). And it seems that this result opens up the possibility of a completely general evidential decision theory, that addresses itself to the problems of all agents, and not just to those of ideally rational evidential desirability maximizers. Ignoring ties in order to simplify, it can seem (here comes a suggestion made in Sobel 1988, 128 n.5) that this result provides a basis for the general rule that an act in a decision problem that is ripe for its agent is rational if and only if this act is the one an ideally rational evidential desirability maximizer would decide to do were he in precisely the same ripe-for-decision problem.

Some parts of this second argument of Eells's are very plausible. In particular, it is very plausible that always in the end, for an *ideally rational* evidential desirability maximizer, there will be probabilistic or *evidential* independence from acts, of conditions that are seen to be *causally* independent of these acts. It is plausible that even if such an agent begins deliberation in a Newcomblike problem, he will end up in a problem that is *not* Newcomblike. It may be, as Eells maintains, that, given plausible assumptions concerning the dynamics of ideally rational deliberation, no terminal Newcomblike problems are possible for suitably characterized ideally rational agents, and this even while allowing these agents *entry* into all kinds of decision problems. These would be marvelous results. But they would not be sufficient to a defense of desirability maximizing as a fully general theory of rational action. *One* problem is that, in order that the general theory envisioned should give right answers to all decision problems, it is necessary that ideally rational evidential maximizers would reach decisions in their ripe-for-decision problems that were always right not only for themselves, but right for all ordinary agents in identical ripe-for-decision problems. It is necessary, one might say, that what would be the decisions of these paragons of evidential reasoning would always be right for their clients. It will be argued that this condition is not met and that, even giving metatickles every possible due, there remain decisions that ideally rational desirability maximizers would get *wrong* for their clients. A *second* problem is that, *even if* this second defense of Eells's yielded a satisfactory fully general theory of rational *decisions,* it could not be made into a defense of the larger evidential theory of rational *desires*, of which an evidential theory of rational decisions would be only a proper part. To get the larger umbrella theory right, there seems to be no recourse but "to go causal" in at least parts, and, to keep it simple, it seems best to go causal throughout.

Eells's argument does not work as a fully general evidential desirability maximizing theory of rational action. For even if, as is plausible, continual desirability maximizing, by converting crucial probabilistic dependencies into independencies, gives correct answers for all *dominance* Newcomblike problems; it gives wrong answers for some *non-dominance* problems staffed by ordinary agents who are not ideally rational evidential desirability maximizers. I have used the Popcorn Problem to make this point (Sobel 1988); here, for a change, I consider *Brian Skyrms's Uncle Albert*.

Uncle Albert is not feeling well. He realizes that for him going to the doctor would be a further symptom that he is genuinely ill. But he knows that it would have no tendency to make him ill, and that staying home would certainly not help him to get well, if he really is ill. And so he goes to the doctor, notwithstanding the inferior subjective prospects of his doing so. "He's no fool" (Skyrms 1982, 700).[10]

Nor is Uncle Albert an ideally rational desirability maximizer. But suppose that he were. Consider, that is, a ripe-for-decision case exactly like his in which, however, the agent, IDesM, is an ideally rational continual-desirability-maximizer deliberator (thus his name). IDesM will calculate, discover that his calculation favors staying home, and take this good news as evidence that he is going to stay home, and that he is not sick after all! Recalculations by this ideally rational desirability maximizer will in this case only *confirm* first comparative results, and first tentative dispositions to action. And so, even if, as is plausible, they will lead to probabilistic independence of his health from his acts, and to a *non*-Newcomblike problem, they will *not* lead to the *same* non-Newcomblike problem to which the deliberations of an ideally rational *causal utility* maximizing agent would lead. Desirability and utility maximizers (whether or not they are *ideally* rational) would both decide to *stay home* in an ideally rational *evidential desirability* maximizer's final problem. Whereas they would both decide to *go to the doctor* in an ideally rational *causal utility* maximizer's final problem.

An ideally rational evidential desirability maximizer in a ripe-for-decision problem exactly like Uncle Albert's would decide to stay home. And that seems the *right* decision *for him,* since he would acquire while deliberating what would be for him good evidence that he was not sick after all. Ideally rational evidential desirability maximizer that IDesM is to be, "[he believes] that, for him, the way in which [it could happen that his being ill would cause his going would be] by causing. . .beliefs and desires [on which] evidential decision theory [would]. . . prescribe going. . . . [We have seen that IDesM eventually] finds [*not* going] maximal [and prescribed by evidential decision theory]. This is evidence against [his illness]" (Eells 1989).[11]

But though IDesM would acquire good evidence that *he* was not ill, he need learn nothing of necessary relevance to *Uncle Albert's* condition. Indeed, if he knew, as we do, that Uncle Albert is not an evidential desirability maximizer, let alone an ideally rational one, IDesM would realize that he had learned nothing of relevance to Uncle Albert's condition, which IDesM would still, just as Uncle Albert does, fear was grave. But then IDesM's decision to stay home, while right for him, would be wrong for Uncle Albert (though IDesM, applying evidential decision theory to Uncle Albert's case, would deny this). The probability that Uncle Albert is really ill (both IDesM's probability for this, and Uncle Albert's own) is high enough for *us* to agree (notwithstanding the benighted official positions of hypothetical evidential theorist kibitzers) that Uncle Albert is right, he better go to the doctor.

The two paradigms diverge in Uncle Albert's ripe-for-decision problem, and would take ideally rational and sophisticated maximizers in different directions, the causal ones to and the evidential ones away from the doctor. And the way in which these theories can diverge in non-dominance problems, strongly suggests that even if an evidential decision theory can, by metatickle elaborations, be made to give right answers in all dominance Newcomblike problems it will not, in them, or in *any* problems, in *anyone's* problems, give "right reason" (Lewis 1981, 10).

Eells's dynamic defense does not work. It is not true that the two paradigms converge at least for suitably characterized ideal agents, and that a theory of evidential desirability maximizing can be made to deliver correct answers in *all* problems including non-dominance ones, for *all* agents including most prominently agents who are *not* ideally rational evidential desirability maximizers (as few if any real agents are), and deliver these answers "on the cheap" and without more or less explicit recourse to causal primitives. And even if it *could,* the gain in conceptual economy would be disappointingly local and of only limited Humean comfort. This is my second major response to Eells's dynamic defense of evidential decision theory.

A theory of rational *decisions* should fit smoothly into a general theory of rational *hope* (cf., Sobel 1985, 199 n.7). For it should be rational to choose to *do* what it is rational to *hope* that one will do. I note that Jeffrey situates his own evidential logic of decision, which would have the choiceworthiness of acts go by their desirabilities, in a theory of desirabilities that extends beyond given agent's action propositions to propositions in general (Jeffrey 1965b; 1983). However, even if, as may be so, the true choiceworthiness of acts of ideally rational and sophisticated evidential desirabilities in every case go by their eventual evidential desirabilities, the true hopeworthiness of facts in general, and not just facts concerning one's possible acts, need not for *any* person invariably go by this person's final evidential desirabilities.

Consider a case in which I know that my friend is in Newcomb's Problem, so that I am in what we can term a *third-person Newcombesque Problem* in which my question is, what, for his sake, I should *hope* that he will do. Every consideration that makes it seem that he should for his sake *take* both boxes makes it seem that I, as his friend, should *hope* that he will take both boxes. For I know that whatever he thinks, and whatever he has tentatively, or finally even, decided to do, he will, if he takes both boxes, get more money than he will if he takes just the second box. I should, it seems, find his taking both boxes more hopeworthy, more desirable, more welcome as a *fact.* Of course, if we suppose that I do not know what the predictor has predicted, am ignorant of what is in the second box, and have great confidence in that predictor's powers; then "news" (by which I mean, a new subjective certainty which, I caution, may be false, thus the scare quotes) that my friend is going to take just the second box, or that he already has, might be for me most welcome *news.* It might be, for me, far more welcome than would be news that he was going to take both boxes, and this even though I do hope that he will take both boxes. Regarding the *complex* issue, what I should hope to *learn* is *a fact* concerning his act, I can be of two minds, and this without being in any way confused (cf., Sobel 1985, 199 n.7). The divergence between what it would be rational for me to hope is *a fact* in this case, and what might be for me best *news* and most welcome as a new subjective certainty, could survive any amount of reflection on my part about the case, including any amount of reflection on my part about the probable course of my friend's deliberations and efforts to decide what to do, *and* including any amount of reflection on my part about the course of my *own* efforts to make up my mind what to hope he will in fact do, and on my efforts, if any, to make up my mind what news to hope for concerning his act.

I should, in this case, *not* hope for the fact that would be hoped for by an ideally rational person. IDesH, whose hopes in every case go by his final desirabilities for propositions in the case. For I should hope for the best fact, which we have seen is that my friend take both boxes, and IDesH would hope for the fact news of which would be for him, and for me, best news, which fact is that my friend takes just the second box.[12]

It thus seems that even if a metatickle-enhanced evidential theory could be made to give right answers for all decision problems what to make true, it cannot be made to fit smoothly into an evidential theory that gives right answers to all attitude problems what to hope is true. But wait. My proposal, that the theory of rational acts should be a part of a general theory of rational desires for facts, is formally similar to the proposal on which Frank Jackson and Robert Pargetter build a response to "tickle defenses." They hold that the first-person theory of rational decisions should be imbedded in theory that yields not only *agent* assessments, but also *spectator* assessments, of the rightness of acts (see Jackson and Pargetter 1983). And so it may seem that Eells's reply to their argument (Eells 1985b) can be revamped and addressed to mine. This has been tried. Regarding the case of my friend, Eells has said:

> I should take *my* subjective probabilities and *his* desirabilities [with which, friend that he is, I presumably agree]. . .and then *hypothetically* deliberate (evidentially), as if my beliefs and his desires are all my own. Then I should hope that he does the act that has maximal (evidential) expectation from my hypothetical perspective. . .doing this, with the evidential theory, will, with metatickles, give the appropriate prescription. (Eells 1989)

This approach can be extended beyond friends to foes, whom I wish ill, and in general to all others, by having me deliberate from the hypothetical perspective of others with not only my own probabilities but also my own desirabilities.

But there is a problem with this recycling of Eells's reply to Jackson and Pargetter, for my proposal is only somewhat similar to theirs. It differs most notably in being more *general*. They would imbed a theory for personal decisions in a general theory for prescriptions to all persons. I hold that a theory for what to do, should be, as Jeffrey's theory is, imbedded in a general theory for what to hope. And so, *even if,* a metatickle enhanced evidential theory could be made to the right answers not only to all decision-problems-what-to-do, but also to all attitude-problems-what-to-hope-*others*-will-do, *more* is required for a *complete* theory for what to hope. Even supposing that an evidential theory could be made to yield right decisions and hopes for all *acts,* a purely evidential theory cannot be made to yield right hopes, not only for all possible acts, but for absolutely all possible facts. Evidential theories are quite stymied I think by some *non*-action Newcombesque problems. Here are two.

How Do You Spell Relief? Consider a young person who believes that there is a gene that, in adults, causes cancer and tends to *prevent* heartburn. What should he in his youth hope for when he grows up? Should he hope for heartburn? Given assumptions summarized in matrices in Appendix Two below, heartburn should be for him most welcome as an item of news (or new subjective certainty) in view of its evidential potency. News that when he grows up he will be *free* from heartburn would be bad news. And (on these assumptions) heartburn (i.e., the proposition that he will get heartburn when he grows up) will excel in evidential desirability, and could continue to excel throughout any course of ideal reflection on the matter that included reflection on the credences and hopes being firmed up. But even so, that he will be free from heartburn when he grows up should be most welcome as a *fact* in view of its probable causal potency, and the differences it might make. For who wants heartburn, whether along with or without cancer?!

Three things may be stressed: First, while there is certain causal *in*dependence of value-relevant circumstances from possible facts, there is evidential *de*pendence: that is, the case is Newcomblike. Second, this dependence could survive any amount of reflection on the youth's part to determine which proposition, -H or H, to hope for as a fact or truth, or which to hope for as an item of news, and this no matter what maximizing principles operated for him in these reflections. And third, there is no point of view to which his credences and preferences might be transported, from which point of view ideal reflection to maximize, addressed to either of these issues, would, by metatickle mechanisms, need in the end to resolve this dependence.

Pennies for Heaven? For a theological case to the same point, consider someone who believes "that a rich man shall hardly enter into the kingdom of heaven" (Matthew 19:23), that "it is easier for a camel to go through the eye of a needle, than for a rich man to enter into the kingdom of God" (Matthew 19:24), and that "many that are first shall be last" (Matthew 19:30); but who thinks that these things are so *not* because riches make it difficult for a person to be good and deserving, but because God, for His own reasons, rarely bestows both saving grace and worldly riches on the same person. Consider, that is, someone who believes that riches, while in no way causal obstacles to eternal bliss which is already settled yea or nay before one is born, are reliabile signs that it is not forthcoming. And wonder whether or not such a person should want to be rich.

Non-dominance Newcomblike problems, such as Uncle Albert's, establish that not even a correct limited theory specifically for rational acts of highly sophisticated evidential desirability maximizers can be purely evidential. Third-person Newcombesque problems argue, and non-action Newcombesque problems argue more forcefully, that even if a purely evidential theory of rational acts could be developed that got right answers for all agents in all decision problems, no purely evidential theory for desires for facts will give right answers even regarding the desires of the ideally rational evidential desirers, and that for right answers a general theory needs to be causal at least in part, and for simplicity is best made causal throughout. Third-person and non-action problems provide further grounds for thinking that though evidential theories can be made to give right answers to a range of questions what acts to do, and for what facts to hope, they never give right reasons.

Summary: While Eells's dynamic metatickle defense of evidential theories is promising against dominance Newcomblike action problems, it fails against non-dominance ones. And all metatickle defenses have difficulty with third-person Newcombesque problems including dominance ones, and cannot even get started against non-action Newcombesque problems. Probably he would have given up on tickles or never started with them, if he had not concentrated exclusively on problems that are like Newcomb's Problem itself, not only in that they are problems in which simple evidential and causal decision theories diverge, but like it also in that the action selected by *causal* theories is a *dominant* action; or if he had seen his task as that of defending a general evidential theory of the hopeworthiness of facts, rather than a special theory confined to the choiceworthiness of acts.

CONCLUSIONS

Problem cases for Jeffrey's 1965 logic of decision come in many varieties, and, depending on their details, occasion objections of several sorts. The best cases for displaying the putative error of identifying an action's choiceworthiness with its desirability are predictor-cases in which the predictor is a friend of whose predictions the agent is reasonably respectful. Such cases avoid the science-fiction-like aspects of Newcomb's Problem, and need not include the idea that the agent thinks of his actions and/or choices as things that will be determined by causes. Prisoner's Dilemma cases are less good for the purpose stated, because of the relative difficulty of making plausible within them that a reasonable agent might still, even just before the time for action, view his actions (both the one he then presumably considers reasonable, *and the other one*) as sufficient evidence for like actions on the part of the other agent (see Sobel 1985a). But while I think that certain predictor cases have dialectical advantages, in my view most Newcomblike cases that have been brought against Jeffrey's logic of decision are, when generously interpreted, coherent challenges even against properly qualified evidential decision theories, challenges that need to be taken seriously.

Critics of that theory hold that at least some Newcomblike problems are good challenges that dramatize the point that when news of an act would provide evidence of states that the agent is sure it would not affect, though, in his act, "the agent indeed makes. . .news, he does not make all the news his act bespeaks" (Gibbard and Harper 1985, 146). Critics hold that for such an agent, as Jeffrey a sometimes critic himself puts it, preferring "A1 over A2 *as a news item*. . .is compatible with [a] preference for A2 over A1 *as a course of action*" (Jeffrey 1981a, 381).

Partisans of causal decision theories think that Newcomblike problems should convince one that in order to get things right a theory needs to take more or less explicitly into account opinions about causes and objective chances. I note that Jeffrey himself at times agrees with this:

Purists like de Finetti hold that the concept of objective chance is meta-physical hocus-pocus. . . . But I am persuaded that the notion of objective chance often plays a useful rôle in our practical deliberations – maybe, an essential rôle. Perhaps the clearest example is a. . .Prisoner's Dilemma. . .[in which the prisoners] are pretty sure they'll decide alike *but don't know how.* . . .[and in which I, a prisoner] see my decision as a rather good indicator of his. . . . Confession, the wiser choice, is ruled out by judgemental c.e.u. maximization if you see your choice as a strong but ineffectual symptom of his. (Jeffrey 1986, 10–11)

Jeffrey 1986 includes "a version of 'causal' decision theory" (16, n.6).

I suspect, however, partly because of subtleties in the essay form which I have quoted, that Jeffrey is still inclined to think that the logic of decision (1965), unadorned and unrevised, may yet retake the high ground. He seems at times to think that one might gracefully withdraw from the fray and maintain the equation of rational preferences with desirability maximization, not as a rule for making decisions, but as a fundamental principle of decision theory that connects consistent and rational decision, credences, and preferences. He writes that in a Prisoner's Dilemma in which the agents

[are] pretty sure [they will] confess. . . . [the] description, "They are pretty sure they'll decide alike *but don't know how*", is inaccurate. I do not know, not by c.e.u. maximization [that is, not by judgmental conditional expected utility, or desirability, maximization] but by a dominance argument that refers to causal considerations. That's all right, or, anyway, not all bad. As Sandy Zabell urges, [the principle of] c.e.u. [maximization] enters decision theory as a way of connecting preference, probability, and utility: A is preferred to B if $P(u/A) > P(u/B)$. It is a mistake to view this biconditional as showing that preference is determined by P and u, not vice versa. (Jeffrey 1986, 12).[13]

I have, by implication, urged that though the biconditional according to which final preferences for actions go extensionally by desirabilities may be right for ideally sophisticated rational agents; third-person and non-action problems suggest that it is wrong when extended from 'first-person' action propositions to all propositions. While rational preferences for news may for the most part go by desirabilities, rational preferences for facts sometimes do not. Reflection on Newcomblike problems, especially non-dominance ones, and on third-person and non-action ones, challenges the idea that desirabilities enter decision theory, or the theory of rational preferences for action facts, in any important way at all.

APPENDIX ONE: SOME NEWCOMBLIKE PROBLEMS

Newcomb's Problem. "Suppose a being in whose power to predict your choices you have enormous confidence. . . . There are two boxes, (B1) and (B2). (B1) contains $1000. (B2) contains either $1,000,000 ($M), or nothing. . . . You have a choice between two actions: (1) taking what is in both boxes, (2) taking only what is in the second box. Furthermore, and you know this. . .: (I) If the being predicts you will take what is in both boxes, he does not put the $M in the second box. (II) If the being predicts you will take only what is in the second box, he does put the $M in the second box. . . . First, the being makes its prediction. Then it puts $M in the second box, or does not. . . . Then you make your choice" (Nozick 1969, 114–15).

For a mechanically simpler version of Newcomb's Problem we have the following: "A preternaturally good predictor of human choices does or does not deposit a million dollars in your bank account, depending on whether he predicts you will reject or accept the extra thousand he will offer you just before the bank reopens after the weekend. Would it be wise on Monday morning to decline the bonus?" (Jeffrey 1983, 15. See Sobel 1985b, 198–99 n.6).

It seems the reasonable thing would be to take both boxes, or accept the offer of the thousand, and end a thousand ahead no matter what. Yet news that you were going to take just the second box, or reject the offer, would be good news. Given it you would be confident that you were going to be rich.

The Prisoner's Dilemma: "Two men are arrested for bank robbery. Convinced that both are guilty, but lacking enough evidence to convict either, the police put the following proposition to the men and then separate them. If one confesses but the other does not, the first will go free (amply protected from reprisal) while the other receives the maximum sentence of ten years; if both confess, both will receive lighter sentences of four years; and if neither confesses, both will be imprisoned for one year on trumped-up charges. . .the police are convinced that both will confess, even though both would be better off if neither confessed" (Jeffrey 1983, 15).

Reflection on the matrix,

	He confesses.	He does not confess.
I confess.	−4	0
I do not confess.	−10	−1

can explain why the police are convinced that each prisoner will confess. "But the Bayesian principle [of *The Logic of Decision,* 1965] advises each prisoner *not* to confess, if each sensibly sees his own choice as a strong clue to the other's and therefore assigns high subjective probabilities. . .to the other prisoner's doing whatever it is. . .that he himself chooses" (p. 16).

Sir Ronald Lights Up. "In 1959, R. A. Fisher argued that the undoubted correlation which had been demonstrated between cigarette smoking and lung cancer admitted of three explanations, among which [was]. . . . (iii) Smoking and lung cancer are effects of a common cause, viz., a certain genetic makeup. Fisher urged that the evidence then available made (iii) a lively alternative. . . .

Coupled with his reference to 'the mild and soothing weed,' this leads me to guess that Fisher was a smoker who thought that while abstinence might be of prognostic interest, it was probably useless either as prophylaxis or as therapy" (Jeffrey 1981b, 476). Fisher's smoking, notwithstanding its predicting cancer, seems reasonable, if he would think that it had no chance of causing the disease.

The Popcorn Problem. ". . .I want very much to have some popcorn," but "I am nearly sure that the popcorn vendor has sold out. . . . And so. . .I have decided not to go for popcorn. . . . Still, I am also nearly sure that in *this* theatre, when and only when there *is* popcorn. . .the signal—POPCORN!!!—is flashed on the screen, though at a speed that permits only subliminal, unconscious awareness. . . . [And, since] I consider myself to be a highly *suggestible* person. . .I am nearly sure that I will change my mind and *go* for popcorn if and only if I am influenced by this subliminal signal to do so. . . . [And so] while I think it is very unlikely that I will go for popcorn. . .I think it is *much more* unlikely that I will go for popcorn though there is none. . .to be bought. . . . In short. . .my going for popcorn would provide me with a near certain sign of. . . there being popcorn. . . . And my *not* going would provide me with a near certain sign that there is *not* popcorn. . ." (Sobel 1986). News that I was going for popcorn, would be good news, but, since I am nearly sure that there is no popcorn, it would seem a mistake to go for some.

Evidential potencies "are. . .founded on beliefs concerning possible causes of my actions, but they could be provided with very different kinds of bases. For example, I could be supposed to think that the manager was a very reliable predictor who acted on his predictions in order to sell as much popcorn as possible, and waste as little as possible" (Sobel 1988a).

Uncle Albert's Problem. "Uncle Albert believes that, for him, going to the doctor is a symptom of being genuinely ill. Indeed, he believes that, whatever his other symptoms, if he finds himself in the doctor's office in addition, he is more likely to be ill than if not. This need not be an irrational belief. Now, in certain cases, conditional expected utility will recommend staying home because of diminished prospects associated with going in to be examined. But Uncle Albert goes anyway. He's no fool. He knows that staying home won't help him if he's really ill" (Skyrms 1982, 700).

The Problem of the Rising Young Executive. "Robert Jones, rising young executive of International Energy Conglomerate Incorporated. . .and several other young executives have been competing for a very lucrative promotion. . . . Jones learns. . .that all the candidates have scored equally well on all factors except ruthlessness. . . . Jones [before the promotion decision is announced]. . .must decide whether or not to fire poor old John Smith. . . . Jones knows that [his] ruthlessness factor. . .accurately predicts his behavior in just the sort of decision he now faces" (Gibbard and Harper 1985, 142–48). If Jones wants not to fire old John, it seems he shouldn't even though it would make him confident of the promotion he covets.

Solomon's Problem. "Solomon faces a situation like" the one David faced. He covets a married woman and fears possible civic consequences of public adultery, ". . .but he, unlike David, has studied works on psychology and political science which teach him" that "a king's degree of charisma. . .cannot be changed in adulthood," that "charismatic kings tend to act justly," that "successful revolts against charismatic kings are rare," and that it would not be the unjust act of public adultery that caused civic unrest and revolution, but the lack of charisma that it signalled, and the sneakiness and ignoble bearing that go with lack of charisma (Gibbard and Harper 1985, 141).

Problems for Some Pregnant Women. "Many physiological states produce quite specific symptomatic effects on choice behavior. Pregnancy, for example, often affects what a woman chooses to eat. Any such physiological effect is a potential source of a medical Newcomb problem. All else that is needed is that the attitudes of the person concerned about the possession of the underlying physiological state and the performance of the symptomatic act should conflict. . . . If the agent is someone who knows that pregnancy tends to make her decline garlic, then the problem will arise if either she likes garlic (*ceteris paribus*) but wants to be (now) pregnant; or doesn't like garlic (*ceteris paribus*) and doesn't want to be pregnant. Clearly she shouldn't refuse the delectable garlic in order to be already pregnant, in the former case; or eat the distasteful garlic in order not to be, in the latter" (Price 1986, 196).

APPENDIX TWO:
FURTHER STRUCTURE FOR TWO PROBLEMS

1. Brian Skyrms' Uncle Albert

A Possible Consequence Matrix for Uncle Albert's Problem

	He is really ill.	He is not really ill.
Go to the doctor.	genuine illness, bother, and medical assistance	bother
Do not go.	genuine illness	—

Desirabilities and *Utilities of Acts in Circumstances*

	Ill	¬Ill
Go	−90	−10
¬Go	−100	0

Conditional Probabilities of Circumstances on Acts				Probabilities of Act-Circumstance Practical Conditionals		
	Ill	¬Ill			Ill	¬Ill
Go	14/15	1/15		Go	9/15	6/15
¬Go	4/15	11/15		¬Go	9/15	6/15

These probability matrices reflect the assumptions that Uncle Albert's probability for his being genuinely ill is 9/15, and that acts Go and -Go would be equally good further evidence, respectively, for his being genuinely ill, and his not being genuinely ill—news of either would make a 5/15 difference to the probability of the condition for which it would be evidence.

Given assumptions summarized in these matrices, while ¬Go would be best news, Go would be the best act:

$$Des(Go) = -84\ 2/3 < Des(\neg Go) = -31\ 2/3.$$

and

$$Util(Go) = -58 > Util(\neg Go) = -60.$$

2. How Do You Spell Relief?

A Possible Consequence Matrix for This Problem

	I have the gene.	I do not have the gene.
No heartburn.	cancer	—
Heartburn.	cancer, and heartburn	heartburn

Evidential Desirabilities and *Factual Desirabilities* for Possible Facts in Circumstances

	Gene	¬Gene
¬H	− 1000	0
H	− 1001	−1

Conditional Probabilities of Circumstances on Facts		
	Gene	¬Gene
¬H	20/100	80/100
H	2/100	98/100

Probabilities of Fact/ Circumstance Practical Conditionals		
	Gene	¬Gene
¬H	11/100	89/100
H	11/100	89/100

Given the assumptions summarized in these matrices, while possible fact or proposition H would be best news, -H would be the best fact:

$$EvidDes(H) = 2/100(-1001) + 98/100(-1) = -21 >$$
$$EvidDes(\neg H = 20/100(-1000) + 80/100(0) = -200;$$

but

$$FacDes(\neg H) = 11/100(-1000) + 89/100(0) = -100 >$$
$$FacDes(H) = 11/100(-1001) + 89/100(-1) = -111.$$

That $FacDes(\neg H)$ exceeds $FacDes(H)$, of course follows without calculation, given that (1) ¬H dominates H in the factual desirabilities in circumstances matrix, and (2) circumstances, Gene and ¬Gene, are independent of facts, ¬H and H, in the matrix relevant to factual desirabilities.

NOTES

1. For reservations concerning this interpretation of desirabilities, see Sobel (1986b, 410), and Eells (1987).

2. Jeffrey (1965b, 73–74), corrected as in Jeffrey (1983, 84).

3. Added in December 1981 to Jeffrey (1981b, 492).

4. On the subjectivity of rationality: Whether or not an agent has a decision problem depends on whether or not he thinks he has a choice, but not also on whether or not he really does have a choice. Similarly whether or not a choice would be rational depends on what choices the agent thinks he can make, but not at all on what choices he really can make. "But what if an agent is mistaken about what choices he can make?" There are no real problems with this case, though it is perhaps worth remarking that in it there may be no choice that the agent can make that would be rational. Suppose (1) that an agent is sure he can choose to continue smoking Camels, to switch to a low tar cigarette, or to stop smoking altogether; (2) that his beliefs and preferences recommend his stopping altogether, and, as between what he takes to be his other two options, recommend his choosing to switch from Camels to low tar; (3) that he chooses to switch to low tar; and (4) that of the options that he is sure are open to him, while the first two really are open, the third is not. The agent has made an irrational choice even though he has made the choice that, of those he can make, is recommended by his beliefs and preferences. For his choice is not, of those he *thinks* he can make, recommended. He thinks he can stop smoking, and he may have impeccable reasons for this confidence, as good as anyone ever has for such confidences. But, we assume, he cannot do this. And so, *possibly through no fault of his of any kind, intellectual or practical*, no choice he can make would be a rational choice.

5. I have maintained elsewhere that an agent's options in a proper decision problem *are* choices, i.e., "organizations of will" in which actions are made certain or given specific

objective chances. In the theory I endorse the requirement that choices be viewed as efficacious for chosen options in a proper decision problem is satisfied by trivializing identification. See Sobel 1983, 159.

6. I endorse a principle that makes it a condition of a rational action that a *decision* for it would be ideally stable (Sobel 1983; 1985c; 1990). The condition presently before us is that a certain *belief,* specifically the belief that the action would be rational, would be ideally maintainable. While these conditions are different (the maintainable belief condition, in contrast with the stable decision condition, builds into practical rationality a modicum of theoretical rationality), they are formally similar.

7. Regarding the apparently limited character of his defenses, Eells writes:

> Notice that this defense relies essentially on the agent's believing that there *is* a common cause. . . . In some of the decision problems that are taken to be *prima facie* counterexamples to the traditional theory, no common cause is explicitly mentioned. . . . It is arguable, however, that if the agent believes that there is a correlation between an act and some outcome, where he believes that the act doesn't cause the outcome and the outcome doesn't cause the act, then he should postulate a common cause of the two things—even if he cannot say what that causative factor is. (Eells 1984b, 75)

8. Cf. ". . .I do not assume that the agent knows what rule he will use," Eells 1981, 324.

9. See Appendix Two, in which numbers are stipulated for a case of the problem.

10. I have made Eells's own references to Uncle Albert into references to our IDesM. For Uncle Albert himself is no kind of evidential desirability maximizer. If he notices that not going maximizes evidential desirability, he quite sensibly makes nothing of this and is not at all disinclined on that account to go.

11. On the relevance of this case to the ideas of Price and Talbott: Reflections of mine *qua* agent on my efforts to make up my mind would not threaten to unsettle the credences on which initial tentative sentiments would be based in ways Eells could lead one to fear. Neither would they need to threaten conditional credences in ways in which Price might have us fear. For I could realize that my credences had nothing to do with what the agent was to do, as distinct from what I was to hope he would do. Nor would reflections on my efforts to make up my mind and to settle my desires need to threaten my confidence in my competence in the ways Talbott might have us fear. For in third-person problems (causal or acausal), the first person need have no unsettling views concerning the causes of *his* credences, preferences, or ways of thinking and making up his mind. And so as has been said, regarding the complex issue of what I should hope to learn is true concerning what someone other than myself will do in a Newcomblike problem, I can be of two minds all along, and in the end after giving the issue every thought that could make a difference to my attitudes. I can be of two minds all along without being at any time confused, inductively irresponsible, or in doubt concerning my competence, or the causal credentials of my credences, preferences, or ways of thinking.

12. $P(u/-)$ is "c.e.u. . . .computed via judgmental prevision" or judgmental conditional probabilities (p. 11): $P(u/A)$, for example, is des A.

REFERENCES

Campbell, R., and L. Sowden, ed. 1985. *Reality, Cooperation and Paradox: The Prisoner's Dilemma and Newcomb's Problem.* Vancouver.

Eells, Ellery. 1981. "Causality, Utility, and Decision." *Synthése* 48:285–329.

Eells, Ellery. 1984a. "Newcomb's Many Solutions." *Theory and Decision* 16:59–105.

Eells, Ellery. 1984b. "Metatickles and the Dynamics of Deliberation." *Theory and Decision* 17:71–95.

Eells, Ellery. 1985a. "Causality, Decision, and Newcomb's Paradox." In Campbell and Sowden, 1985. (From Ellery Eells, *Rational Decision and Causality,* 1982, chaps. 3–6, abridged and revised, and from Eells 1984a.)

Eells, Ellery. 1985b. "Reply to Jackson and Pargetter." In Campbell and Sowden, 1985.

Eells, Ellery. 1987. "Learning with Detachment: Reply to Maher." *Theory and Decision* 22: 173–80.

Eells, Ellery. 1989. "Comments on Jordan Howard Sobel's 'Non-Dominance and Third-Person Newcomblike Problems'." Paper delivered in April at APA meeting in Chicago.

Eells, Ellery, and Elliott Sober. 1986. "Common Causes and Decision Theory." *Philosophy of Science.*

Gärdenfors, Peter, and Nils-Eric Sahlin, eds. 1988. *Decision, Probability, and Utility: Selected Readings.* Cambridge.

Gibbard, Allan, and William L. Harper. 1985. "Counterfactuals and Two Kinds of Expected Utility." In Campbell and Sowden, 1985. (Abridged from *Foundations and Applications of Decision Theory,* vol. 1, edited by Hooker et al. [Dordrecht, 1978]. The original essay is reprinted with corrections in Gärdenfors and Sahlin, 1988: "Czesław Porebski pointed out to us a number of errors in previously published versions.")

Howich, Paul. 1985. "Decision Theory in Light of Newcomb's Problem." *Philosophy of Science* 52: 431–50.

Jackson, Frank, and Robert Pargetter. 1983. "Where the Tickle Defense Goes Wrong." *Australasian Journal of Philosophy* 61: 295–99. (Reprinted with a postscript on 'meta-tickles' in Campbell and Sowden, 1985.)

Jeffrey, Richard C. 1965a. "New Foundations for Bayesian Decision Theory." In *Logic, Methodology, and Philosophy of Science: Proceedings of the 1964 International Congress,* edited by Y. Bar-Hillel. Amsterdam.

Jeffrey, Richard C. 1965b. *The Logic of Decision.* New York.

Jeffrey, Richard C. 1981a. "Choice, Chance, and Credence." *Contemporary Philosophy: A New Survey,* vol. 1. The Hague.

Jeffrey, Richard C. 1981b. "The Logic of Decision Defended." *Synthése* 48: 473–92.

Jeffrey, Richard C. 1983. *The Logic of Decision: Second Edition.* Chicago.

Jeffrey, Richard C. 1986. "Judgmental Probability and Objective Chance." *Erkenntnis* 24: 5–16.

Kyburg, Henry E. 1980. "Acts and Conditional Probabilities." *Theory and Decision* 12: 149–71.

Lewis, David. 1979. "Prisoners' Dilemma Is a Newcomb Problem." *Philosophy and Public Affairs* 8: 251–55. (Reprinted in Campbell and Sowden, 1985.)

Lewis, David. 1981a. "Causal Decision Theory." *Australasian Journal of Philosophy* 59: 5–30. (Reprinted in Gärdenfors and Sahlin, 1988.)

Lewis, David. 1981b. "Are We Free to Break the Laws?" *Theoria* 3: 113–21.

Mackie, J. L. 1977. "Newcomb's Paradox and the Direction of Causation." *Canadian Journal of Philosophy* 7: 213–25.

Nozick, Robert. 1969. "Newcomb's Problem and Two Principles of Choice." In *Essays in Honor of Carl G. Hempel,* edited by N. Rescher et al. Dordrecht. (Reprinted in Campbell and Sowden, 1985.)

Price, Huw. 1986. "Against Causal Decision Theory." *Synthése* 67: 195–212.

Skyrms, Brian. 1982. "Causal Decision Theory." *Journal of Philosophy* 79: 695–711.

Sobel, Jordan Howard. 1983. "Expected Utilities and Rational Actions and Choices." *Theoria* 49: 159–83.

Sobel, Jordan Howard. 1985a. "Not Every Prisoner's Dilemma Is a Newcomb Problem." In Campbell and Sowden, 1985.

Sobel, Jordan Howard. 1985b. "Circumstances and Dominance in a Causal Decision Theory." *Synthése* 63: 167–202.

Sobel, Jordan Howard. 1985c. "Predicted Choices." *Dalhousie Review.*

Sobel, Jordan Howard. 1986a. "Metatickles and Ratificationism." *PSA 1986,* vol. 1, edited by A. Fine and P. Machamer.

Sobel, Jordan Howard. 1986b. "Notes on Decision Theory: Old Wine in New Bottles." *Australasian Journal of Philosophy* 64: 407–37.

Sobel, Jordan Howard. 1988a. "Defenses and Conservative Revision of Evidential Decision Theories: Metatickles and Ratificationism." *Synthése* 75: 107–31.

Sobel, Jordan Howard. 1988b. "Infallible Predictors." *Philosophical Review* 97: 3–14.

Sobel, Jordan Howard. 1990. "Maximization, Stability of Decision, and Rational Actions." *Philosophy of Science* (March).

Talbott, W.J. 1987. "Standard and Non-standard Newcomb Problems." *Synthése* 70: 415–58.

Soft Laws

TERENCE HORGAN AND JOHN TIENSON

1. LAWS AND THE HUMAN SCIENCES

There is a long-standing controversy about the nature of knowledge and under-standing in the so-called "human sciences." This has often taken the form of questioning whether these disciplines can be genuinely scientific, or scientific in the sense or way in which the physical sciences are scientific. There has been controversy about the kind of understanding these disciplines can offer—about, for example, whether they contain lawful generalizations, whether they involve causal explanations, or whether they propound scientific theories. And there has been controversy about the kind of understanding they require—about, for example, whether their methodology fundamentally involves empathic or intui-tive understanding (*verstehen*) or "interpretation," as opposed to the experimen-tation and intersubjectively observable data of the physical sciences. Obviously, these two kinds of questions are not unrelated.

In our view, the disputing parties have frequently shared mistaken presup-positions about the nature of science, and in particular about the nature of scien-tific laws, and hence about what would be necessary for there to be genuine laws in the human sciences. This, in turn, has created misconceptions about the explanation of human behavior and institutions, and correlatively, about expla-nation in the human sciences.

We do not suppose that clearing away misconceptions will resolve any disputes. But it might help the disputants to find more stable positions in the logical landscape and to aim their attacks more accurately at their opponents.

In this essay we will focus on the notion of law. On the standard conception of scientific law, proper laws permit no exceptions. For the special sciences, including the human sciences, this must be qualified to say that they have no exceptions within their domain. This conception of laws as exceptionless is virtually unchallenged in the philosophy of psychology and philosophy of the social sciences, as well as in the philosophy of science in general, and it plays a significant role in much scientific research.

We will argue, to the contrary, that *proper* laws in intentional psychology always have exceptions. Laws *should have exceptions.* We do not mean to be saying anything paradoxical. The kind of laws that should be sought in psychology and the other human sciences are laws to which exceptions are *to be expected.*

These are not merely terminological issues about what deserves the honorific labels "law" and "scientific," for they have implications for how inquiry, both empirical and conceptual, should proceed in psychology and the human sciences in general, for what the goals of these disciplines should be, and for what should count as success. Theories, for example, are sometimes criticized on broadly methodological, rather than empirical, grounds because there are obvious and ineliminable counterexamples to their proposed "laws" or generalizations. Some such theories, we hold, are perfectly correct and empirically well-supported scientific theories, certainly not to be criticized on this ground alone.

Our discussion will concentrate on intentional psychology, that is, on psychology that posits contentful mental states and cites such states in its explanations.[1] For the most part the discussion will apply, *mutatis mutandis,* to the other human sciences, in part because they presuppose intentional psychology and thereby inherit some of its basic characteristics.

We will first, in section 2, describe the standard conception of law, to which it is generally, if sometimes only implicitly, held that all genuine scientific laws must conform. In section 3, we argue that classical cognitive science, which embodies the standard conception of law, involves a fundamentally mistaken conception of human cognition, a theme we have developed extensively elsewhere. We will then, in section 4, suggest a different conception of cognition, and describe a notion of law that we think is appropriate for this conception. In section 5 we will argue that this notion of law provides correctly for psychological explanation. We conclude in section 6 with the suggestion that, given the proper understanding of law, explanation requires laws.

2. THE STANDARD CONCEPTION:
QUASI-EXCEPTIONLESS, GENERAL LAWS

Taking what is accepted to be the case in the physical sciences as paradigmatic, scientific laws are standardly supposed to have three important features. They are exceptionless (at least in a way that is appropriate to their domain). They are general, over and above merely being exceptionless. They are precise, again in whatever way is appropriate to their domain. Obviously the first is the most important for our present purposes, but all three will figure in the subsequent discussion. We will discuss each in turn.

2a. Quasi-Exceptionlessness

Fundamental laws of the physical sciences are thought to be *exceptionless*: they purport to hold without qualification, rather than holding *ceteris paribus*, "all else equal." A law can be thought of as a universally quantified conditional. Circumstances under which the antecedent is satisfied and the consequent is not constitute an exception to the law. If there are such exceptions, then the (putative) law has not yet been properly stated. Those exceptional circumstances must be explicitly excluded in the antecedent of a correct, fully explicit law.[2]

In psychology, it seems excessive to demand that the laws be strictly exceptionless. Typical laws concern psychological processes, and hence relate earlier and later events. If the subject has a stroke or is hit by a bus before the later event can occur, then strictly speaking, this is an exception to the law. But, intuitively, it is a kind of exception that should not count. It is commonly held that all permissible exceptions to the laws of the special sciences are of this kind. Fodor, for instance, remarks, "I assume that the laws of the basic sciences are strictly exceptionless, and I assume that it is common knowledge that the laws of the special sciences are not."[3] But,

> Exceptions to the generalizations of a special science are typically *inexplicable* from the point of view of (that is, in the vocabulary of) that science. . . . But of course, it may nevertheless be perfectly possible to explain the exceptions *in the vocabulary of some other science*. In the most familiar case, you go 'down' one or more levels and use the vocabulary of a more 'basic' science. . . .[T]he same pattern that holds for the special sciences seems to hold for common-sense psychology as well.[4]

Thus the only kinds of exceptions there would be to proper psychological laws would come from outside of psychology, and hence would be stateable only in some other vocabulary—hit-by-a-bus or had-a-stroke exceptions. We will call laws of a (special) science which have no exceptions stateable in the vocabulary of that science *quasi-exceptionless* laws.

Each special science concerns a domain organized or structured in a certain way. The laws of the science presuppose for their applicability the integrity of that structure. This integrity can be disrupted by events pertaining to the structured entities, and explicable only in "lower-level" terms—had a stroke. Or it can be disrupted strictly from without—hit by a bus. For convenience, we will call exceptions stateable in the vocabulary of the science under discussion *same-level exceptions*.

Quasi-exceptionless laws are exceptionless in their domain. Insofar as one takes the fundamental laws of physics as providing the model for scientific laws in general, it is quite natural to regard the laws of nonbasic sciences as quasi-exceptionless.

It is commonly acknowledged that there are same-level exceptions to the fairly simple and uncluttered generalizations we appeal to in ordinary explanations of behavior. But typically, these are viewed as "rough and ready" generalizations and hence as only first approximations to genuine, respectable, psychological laws. For instance, Paul Churchland says of some examples he gives (cf. section 2b, below), "As baldly stated above, no doubt they want qualification in certain respects, but those details are of no particular concern to us here."[5] The picture seems to be this: (1) commonsense intentional psychology explanation requires a set of psychological laws; hence, (2) these must be formulable in a way that eliminates any same-level exceptions. Moreover, (3) stating these exceptionless laws is essentially just a matter of filling in the "details" in our commonsense generalizations.

The putative implication from (1) to (2) is widely accepted, and quite naturally so. We do sometimes back up our explanations with generalizations, if only *ceteris paribus* generalizations, and we often would be able to do so if called upon. But if there are exceptions to a generalization, then—so the intuition goes—citing (an instance of) its antecedent cannot explain why (an instance of) its consequent occurred. For the present case might have been one of the exceptions. Thus, the true explanation must involve a (quasi-) exceptionless law to which we only gesture with our rough and ready generalization.

Controversy centers on (3). Those who believe in an intentional psychological science in roughly commonsense terms believe that the details can be filled in to render our ordinary generalizations exceptionless (though few, probably, would think it as easy as Churchland's remark suggests). Many who deny the possibility of a science of psychology, or who think of the human sciences as fundamentally different from other sciences, do so because they believe that the details cannot, in principle, be filled in. Generalizations in these terms cannot be rendered exceptionless. Hence there cannot be a science like any other in these terms.[6] There are, indeed, a remarkable variety of different positions that accept the inference from (1) to (2) and reject (3). Some deny (1), that explanation, or at least understanding, requires laws. Others deny the possibility of a genuine science of (intentional) psychology.

Our point here is that it is assumed by virtually everyone in this controversy that laws must be quasi-exceptionless. Insofar as one takes fundamental physical laws as providing a model for laws in general, this attitude seems quite natural. We will argue, however, that this attitude is incorrect.

2b. Generality

The generality of the fundamental laws of the natural sciences does not consist merely in their having the logical form, All A's are B's. It consists, rather, in the fact that they are systematic in scope and structure, so that a wide range of phenomena are subsumable under relatively few laws. One major source of their systematicity is that (1) the laws cite *parameterized* properties—viz., quantitative magnitudes, where the parameters are numerical values that these magnitudes can take on when instantiated; and that (2) the laws contain universal quantifiers ranging over the values of these parameters (in addition to the universal quantifiers ranging over the non-numerical entities in its domain).

Newtonian velocity, for example, is not a single property but an infinite array of determinate properties, one for each real value of V. The resultant generality of a physical law consists largely in the existence of a whole (typically infinite) set of specific nomically true principles, each of which is a specific instantiation of the law with specific numeric values "plugged in" for the quantitative parameters.[7]

Intentional psychology might or might not turn out to employ *quantitative* parameters. But its concepts will certainly have propositional (or *intentional*) parameters—the kinds typically specified by 'that'-clauses. Belief, desire, and the other so-called propositional attitudes are state-types involving propositional parameters. Intentional psychology will contain either these concepts or some refinement or replacement of them. Thus, suitably general psychological laws will quantify over such propositional parameters, as, for instance, in the following list of candidate laws of commonsense intentional psychology, due to Paul Churchland.[8]

$(x)(p)[(\text{Wants}(p)x$ & Discovers $(p)x) \supset$ Pleased $(p)x]$
$(x)(p)[\text{Fears}(p)x \supset \text{Wants}(\sim p)x]$
$(x)(p)(q)[(\text{Believes } (p)x$ & Believes(if p, then $q)x) \supset$
    $(\text{Believes}(q)x \lor \text{Reconsiders } (p)x \lor \text{Reconsiders}(\text{if } p, \text{ then } q)x)]$
$(x)(p)(q)[\text{Wants}(p)x$ & Believes(if p, then $q)x) \supset$
    $(\text{Wants}(q)x \lor (\exists s)(\text{Wants}(s)x$ & Believes(if q, then $\sim s)x))]$

Thus, wanting, believing, etc., are seen in these laws as vast (possibly infinite) highly structured arrays of properties, a different specific property for each value of p.[9] Correlatively, each of these candidate laws implies numerous more specific (putative) nomic principles that are instances of the (putative) law.

The kind of generality represented by quantitative parameters in the physical sciences and by intentional parameters in psychology is essential to science. Imagine, for example, that dynamics consisted of nothing more than a huge set of principles, each relating *specific* sizes, velocities, or whatever to later specific sizes and velocities. Suppose that together these principles allowed us to predict the motion of middle-size objects of interest to us, but that there was no way to systematize or reduce the list, so all one could do was look up specific principles as needed or memorize portions of the list. This, we take it, would not constitute scientific understanding.

Likewise, imagine that the only true psychological generalizations mentioned *specific* propositional attitudes, perhaps in a form like: when a cognizer is in $S1$, he goes into $S2''$, where $S1$ and $S2$ are lengthy specifications of the specific beliefs, desires, and so forth in total psychological states. And suppose there were no interesting structure or systematicity to the set of such transition principles, so that, for example, they could not be specified recursively.

Such a hodgepodge would not capture generalizations in a way that would give point to seeking out laws at the psychological level in the first place. They would not constitute a theory and would not give us any understanding of what they permitted us (piecemeal) to predict.

So the frequent emphasis in philosophy of psychology on capturing generalizations is most naturally construed as presupposing that if the generalizations are to count as genuine *laws,* then they should involve universal quantification over the parameters embodied in the state-types that figure in those generalizations – in particular, they should involve universal quantification over propositional/intentional parameters.

2c. Precision

The fundamental laws of physics are precise, in that they apply to precisely specified quantitative magnitudes. This virtually follows directly from the quantitative parameterization discussed in the previous section. It also follows from this that they are precise in the sense of not being vague. As we usually think of these laws, the conditions under which their predicates apply are precisely determined. If there are problems about application, they are epistemological or practical problems.

Both of these features are thought to be important virtues for theories in general. Vagueness is thought to be a serious defect in a proposed law, and much effort is expended in efforts to expel vagueness from predicates of theories in psychology and the social sciences.

In both psychological theorizing and philosophy of psychology, quantitative precision is often treated as something that is at least highly desirable, if not absolutely necessary, for genuine laws. For instance, the folk-psychological notions of belief and desire get transformed in decision theory and game theory into the corresponding quantitative notions of subjective probability and subjective utility. And such quantized notions are sometimes appealed to in psychology and other human sciences, e.g., economics. Psychological concepts would thereby be doubly parameterized, with numerical as well as propositional/intentional parameters.

Some who are attracted to quantitative precision in psychology see in this a way of overcoming the *ceteris paribus* nature of our non-quantitative psychological generalizations. The belief that p, for example, corresponds to a large number of different possible cognitive states, depending, for example, on how firmly p is believed. Especially when there are many different cognitive states instantiated in a creature, this vagueness has the effect that no single outcome can be determined from a characterization of the creature in terms of beliefs, desires, and so forth. If, however, these psychological concepts get replaced by their quantized analogs (subjective probability, subjective utility, etc.), then – it is hoped – it will be possible to formulate laws that are precise and exceptionless. No matter how complex a creature's total psychological state might be, the relevant psychological laws still should determine the subsequent effect of this state. Given the precise numerical magnitudes of the various component states, the relevant instantiation of the relevant law will specify the "weighted sum" of these states and will determine the outcome as the effect of this weighted sum – much as decision theory's rule of expected utility maximization determines which action has highest expected utility given a set of contemplated actions, envisioned possible outcomes, and associated subjective probabilities and utilities.

To summarize this section: It is widely, though partly implicitly, held by both philosophers and psychologists that in order for a bona fide science of psychology to be possible, there must exist psychological laws that are quasi-exceptionless and general. *Ceteris paribus* generalizations with same-level exceptions are regarded as no more than approximations. They must be replaceable by, or refinable into, laws with these two features. This assumption is typically held in common both by those who think that a scientific psychology is possible and those who question this. The former believe that there are such laws, the latter believe there are not.

Furthermore, it is widely considered at least highly desirable for psychological laws to be quantitatively precise as well; and the ideal of quantitative precision comports very naturally with those of generality and quasi-exceptionlessness.

3. THE KUHNIAN CRISIS IN COGNITIVE SCIENCE

The theoretical orientation that has dominated the interdisciplinary field of cognitive science since its inception is often called the "rules and representations paradigm" (for short, the RR paradigm). This view is a species of the standard conception of scientific laws. It is, in effect, a hi-tech version of that conception. But there is at present a Kuhnian crisis in classical cognitive science, brought on by a series of recurrent and recalcitrant problems.[10] An analysis of these problems shows, we believe, that the RR paradigm embodies a fundamentally mistaken view of cognition,[11] and reveals furthermore that cognitive systems do not conform to (cognitive-level) quasi-exceptionless laws.

The fundamental idea of classical cognitive science is that cognition is what the classical computer does, rule-governed symbol manipulation. This view of cognition posits structurally complex mental representations, many of which encode propositional information syntactically via language-like sentential structure. Mental activity is construed as processing of mental representations in conformity with programmable, representation-level rules (for short, PRL rules)—*programmable* in the sense that they could constitute a computer program, and *representation level* in the sense that they are stateable over the representations themselves. (Although processing may also conform with programmable rules stateable at one or more lower levels, e.g., at the level of machine language in a computer, such lower-level rules are not the kind that count.)

The RR paradigm is thus committed to the standard conception of psychological laws. Programmable rules must be *hard*—that is, precise and exceptionless. Computers are stupid; they do all and only what we tell them to do—that is, put into the program—as long as the device is working properly. A program, in other words, constitutes a set of quasi-exceptionless laws or rules. These must be general, because for a task of any complexity, a mere list of transition principles would quickly produce an explosion of rules. Thus, the rules and representations view entails that cognitive processing conforms to a set of precise, general rules.

3a. The Relevance of Anything to Anything

There is a crisis situation in classical cognitive science because it has proven impossible to find the kinds of PRL rules that the RR paradigm requires. The difficulties can be seen as turning upon two clusters of problems. One involves multiple soft constraints. The other involves the fact that any bit of common-sense knowledge might turn out to be relevant to any task or other knowledge. We will concentrate upon the latter cluster, which contains, as perhaps two ends of a spectrum, the so-called "frame" problem, and what we call the "folding" problem.

Any single bit of information we acquire will change our total system of beliefs. Some of our earlier beliefs must be deleted, and we must make some obvious inferences from other beliefs. But the new bit of information will be irrelevant to most of our beliefs, and those will remain unchanged. The frame problem can be seen as the problem of determining, in an effective and general way, what to change and what to leave the same when any new bit of information is added.

One instance of the frame problem arises from the fact that, given other factors, any item of information one has might be needed to solve a current task. The problem is to determine which old beliefs are in any way relevant to the current stage of the current task. Humans do this naturally; it has proven very difficult for the classical computer.

For a system of any size, of course, it is utterly inefficient to search through each bit of old information to see whether and how it is relevant. Thus, the problem is sometimes seen as the problem of representing commonsense information (in a way that makes for efficient relevance determination). And it is sometimes seen as the problem of content addressable memory – that is, of organizing memory in such a way that it can be accessed by content and not simply by computer location (address).

But we suspect that these labels tend to obscure the extent of the difficulty. First we must see that a bit of information is relevant. Then we retrieve it. But how can we see that it is relevant until we find it? Apparently we must find it and see that it is relevant all at once. As Hume said, "One would think that the whole intellectual world of ideas was at once subjected to our view, and that we did nothing but pick out such as were most proper for our purposes" (*Treatise* I,I,vii). Problems of this sort have resisted progress long enough to produce a crisis.

But the depth of the problem of the relevance of anything to anything has not been sufficiently appreciated. Consider the problem of programming a computer to perform some complex task that humans perform routinely. This means giving it explicit directions for how to perform under all circumstances, i.e., stating the (supposed) quasi-exceptionless laws that characterize how we perform that task.

A widely discussed example of a program that is supposed to do this is Shank's program that is able to "understand" simple stories about restaurants.[12] It has what is called a "script" about restaurants, which generates inferences that allow the system to answer questions not explicitly answered in the story, like, "Did the man eat the hamburger?"

But now, just about anything we might think of could come up in a restaurant or in a restaurant story. The man ate with his son. Who paid the bill? We do not know. The man ate with his small child. Now we know. The waitress ate with the customer. Who paid her bill? No one. The policeman did not pay for his meal. Why not? The waitress ate the customer. Was that what he expected?

The program may be able to answer some of these questions. To the ones it cannot answer, there is a tendency to respond, "You ask too much. This is only a beginning. We haven't gotten to that yet. We'll put it in version 5.7."

But that misses the point. It is an *in principle* objection. No matter what finite amount of information about restaurants a script has, there will be questions that people can easily answer about restaurant happenings that it cannot answer. If the script is large enough, it might be hard to trip up the machine. But one strategy would be to make up bizarre stories. Another would be to let one of the questions be, "Were the customers surprised?" and simply describe possible situations as they occur to us. Eventually, the program will be stuck where a human being would not be stuck.

Given *any* finite list of things we can understand about the goings on in a restaurant, there are more things we can understand (over and above the deductive consequences of the items on the list). There is always something else. That is, there are always exceptions to any finite list of quasi-exceptionless laws supposedly governing human restaurant story understanding.

The reason for this involves two facts. What we can represent is essentially open-ended. For any finite list of possible situations, a human being could think of another. And just about anything one could think of might make a difference in a restaurant story, given the rest of the story. The same goes, of course, for innumerable other kinds of things we do. Human cognition is open-ended. Computer programs — and quasi-exceptionless laws — are essentially closed.

So, since the RR paradigm's commitment to PRL rules precludes the kind of relevance-sensitive open-endedness that human cognition displays so abundantly, the moral is that the problem of the relevance of anything to anything is unsolvable within that paradigm. Although the problem itself has been recognized within the RR paradigm, this moral has been less well appreciated.

Furthermore, focusing on isolated chunks of information, single scripts, has had the effect of obscuring a further difficulty, and a ubiquitous feature of human cognition. Information may come in chunks, but real human understanding does not come in *isolated* chunks. A small child can form reasonable prior expectations about, for example, the first birthday party she attends at a restaurant from her knowledge of parties and restaurants. Likewise, we can imagine a faculty meeting at a restaurant (or at a birthday party). We easily "fold" together "scripts" that have never before been combined in our thinking. Yet cognitive science in the RR paradigm has contributed essentially no insight into this kind of cognitive folding, and as far as we know, no one has the slightest idea how one might program a computer to do it.

It is very difficult to see how this cognitive ability *could be* programmable. For there is little reason to suppose that there are general purpose, domain independent, PRL rules that govern the folding together of knowledge about any two (or more) arbitrarily chosen domains. Yet the alternative suggestion, that there are domain specific PRL rules for folding together knowledge, faces a severe loss of generality, and with it an exponential explosion of rules.

3b. Multiple Soft Constraints

The problem of multiple soft constraints has to do with the fact that many tasks involve many, possibly conflicting, considerations. In general, adding conditions or constraints makes a task easier for a human being. But adding constraints makes it more difficult for a computer because the number of computations required expands exponentially with the number of factors involved, leading to an unmanageable computation explosion.

Furthermore, where there are multiple constraints, they are frequently soft. That is, they can be violated while the system is operating properly. Although dogs are four-legged, we readily recognize certain three-legged animals as dogs. To deal with this phenomenon in a computer context requires adding still further conditions, compounding the explosion of computations and rules.

The upshot of our discussion so far in this section is that human intelligence is fundamentally different in kind from computer "intelligence." But the RR paradigm, which sees cognition on the model of the modern digital computer, is just the view one gets from the idea that cognition is describable by quasi-exceptionless laws. Furthermore, the problems that have precipitated the Kuhnian crisis call this underlying conception directly into question. We conclude that human cognition is not so describable.

3c. Going Quantitative Will Not Help

Fans of decision and game theory might hope to avoid this conclusion by invoking the "weighted sum" conception of psychological laws mentioned at the end of section 2. This conception envisions psychological laws that include *quantitative* parameters that would govern the interaction of any combination of distinct psychological states, irrespective of their specific contents.

We think it unlikely that there is any aspect of cognition that is governed by such laws. But surely the weighted sum conception cannot be correct for cognition in general. For any given cognitive domain, this view presupposes that when processing starts, each item of relevant knowledge (desire, etc.) is already actively represented, i.e., is an *occurrent* mental state alongside the other occurrent mental states. But this assumes that each relevant item has already been retrieved from memory. And relevance driven memory retrieval is one kind of cognitive process probably not describable by quasi-exceptionless laws. That is, this conception of processing *assumes* an independent solution to the frame problem, rather than offering a solution.

This view also implies that cognitive folding can be described by domain independent, quasi-exceptionless, "cognitive summation" laws of some kind, laws that supposedly would characterize folding as the net result of some sort of "parallelogram of forces." But in the domain of intentional phenomena, assigning a numerical parameter merely specifies a *potential* "force." The proper "direction" of that "force" depends upon contentful relations with other intentional states, because folding is a content dependent process. Assigning numbers to intentional states will not alter this fact, and will not help in determining the relationships of content on which folding depends. Thus a "cognitive summation" process that works purely as a function of numerical parameters would be a content independent process, and thereby would be incapable of subserving effective cognitive folding. So it is highly unlikely, to say the least, that adding a content independent quantitative aspect to psychological laws will solve problems concerning content dependent processing.

Furthermore, even if effective folding could be accomplished in a particular case by means of some non-content-specific weighted summation process, still, the specific numerical values that would subserve effective folding in the given case would surely have to be dependent upon the specific domains being folded together. The same values would not effect folding with any two distinct domains. Hence prior cognitive processing would be required to "set" the contextually proper numerical values. This prior activity, being a necessary preparatory step for the application of the "cognitive summation" laws, would constitute the real work of cognitive folding.

To summarize this section: The human ability flexibly and efficiently to accommodate the relevance of anything to anything (and to deal smoothly with multiple soft constraints) is not subserved by PRL rules, and is not describable by quasi-exceptionless psychological laws of any kind. On the contrary, any cognitive system whose mental processing is describable by such laws is likely to perform quite badly on the (vastly many) kinds of cognitive tasks on which the relevance of anything to anything (and multiple soft constraints) figure prominently.

4. HUMAN COGNITION AND SOFT PSYCHOLOGICAL LAWS

There are no quasi-exceptionless general laws of intentional psychology. This does not mean that human cognition is anarchy and chaos nor that a scientific psychology is impossible. There are causal/explanatory laws of cognition, and it is the business of psychology to discover those laws. They are just not quasi-exceptionless laws. In this section we will briefly describe the picture of cognition to which our reflections on cognitive science lead, and the notion of scientific law that is appropriate to that picture of cognition.

4a. Soft Cognition

Suppose Jane wants a beer and believes there is beer in the refrigerator. She walks over to the refrigerator, reaches in, and pulls out a beer. The following generalization of commonsense psychology evidently figures in explaining her action.

(G) $(S)(D)(A)$(If S wants D and S believes that doing A will bring about D, then *ceteris paribus*, S will do A).

But suppose Jane did not want to offend the person speaking or did not want to miss this particular bit of conversation. Then she might have sat a while longer before getting her beer. Or suppose she thought that drinking a beer now would conflict with her diet. Perhaps her will power would win out. Suppose she smelled smoke. She would, perhaps, have gone to see if the house was on fire instead of going for a beer. And if she heard her phone ringing, she probably would have gone to answer it first.

Clearly, (G) is not quasi-exceptionless. There is a virtually limitless range of possible same-level exceptions excluded by the *ceteris paribus* clause. Equally clearly, she went to the refrigerator *because* she wanted a beer and thought that was a way to get one. None of the possible exceptions came up. So her belief and desire did result in that action.[13]

What (G) expresses, then, is a *defeasible causal tendency*. More exactly, each instance of (G) expresses a defeasible causal tendency. (G) gives us a potentially infinite array of such causal tendencies, all based in the same way upon structural relationships among contentful states.

The *ceteris paribus* clause in (G) adverts to the fact that in each instance, other psychological states might interact with S's belief and desire in a way that would bring it about that she does not do A. Each of these possible defeaters is itself an instance of (G) or a similar law expressing a different array of content-determined defeasible causal relations.[14] Thus, what can defeat a defeasible causal tendency is another defeasible causal tendency — a tendency to an incompatible state or act.

The fact that a cognitive system is subject to certain defeasible causal tendencies is a basic or fundamental fact about that system. A psychological law such as (G) is a generalization about such defeasible causal tendencies, where the generality comes from quantifying over intentional/propositional parameters. As such, it is no part of the laws' role to delimit all the possible ways that this tendency might get defeated when interacting with other causal tendencies.

It is a mistake to think that psychology should seek to "refine" generalizations like (G) into more complicated generalizations that lack same-level exceptions. Laws like (G) already express fundamental facts about the cognitive system. Such a refinement would be *less* revealing about the nature of the system. The point here is not, as it was in section 3, that the goal of exceptionless laws is unattainable. The point is.that this goal is wrongheaded: the laws themselves should not be expected to catalog all of the ways the tendencies they express might get defeated.

We will call laws that express defeasible causal tendencies *soft*, in analogy with the distinction between hard and soft constraints. Hard constraints are inviolable. Soft constraints are constraints that can be overridden, and hence violated when the cognitive system is working properly. Likewise, soft laws are laws that might get overridden. Quasi-exceptionless laws might, in contrast, be called hard.

4b. Competition and Conspiracy

Mental activity, on this view, typically involves a variety of intentional mental states, all present in the cognitive hopper at once, simultaneously exerting causal influence on one another and simultaneously clamoring for attention. These states, either individually or in certain combinations, have various tendencies to cause certain new psychological states and/or behavior, tendencies determined by their intentional structure and content and expressed in soft laws.

The simultaneous causal tendencies will sometimes compete with, and sometimes conspire with one another. Some of the tendencies will end up being *defeated* – i.e., completely overridden by other, competing tendencies. Some will end up *deflected* – i.e., exerting an influence on the outcome of processing, although the outcome is not what it would have been had other competing factors not been present, but a "compromise." And some will end up being neither deflected nor defeated. For them, *ceteris* is *paribus*.

The separate causal tendencies that are involved in this competitive/conspiratorial processing will be separately describable by the appropriate instances of (G) or of other soft psychological laws. There will be no comparably fundamental, comparably general psychological laws that specify, for complex combinations of occurrent mental states, what the outcome of their mutual interaction will be. Even if there happen to be psychological generalizations that apply to such complex combinations (and there very well may not be, as shall be explained presently), such generalizations would be a consequence of, and would be far less general than, the fundamental laws describing defeasible causal tendencies. They would thus be theoretically secondary and nonfundamental, and would collectively constitute an unsystematic, exponentially explosive hodgepodge.

These remarks apply, not only to the propositional attitudes of commonsense psychology, which we have used for illustration, but to *any* laws of intentional psychology. Perhaps it will be helpful to note the similarity between this conception of psychological laws and a familiar position in philosophy. W. D. Ross held that certain principles of normative ethics express *prima facie* duties. That is, they specify conditions under which something is a duty, provided it is not overridden or mitigated by other *prima facie* duties. A feature of Ross's view is that there are no systematic general principles of normative ethics for determining the right action where there is a conflict of *prima facie* duties. (We take no stand on the normative issue, but) this, on our view, is the right story to tell about *descriptive* ethics, that is, about moral reasoning and moral judgment formation. There is no systematic general way to determine what moral decision a person will settle upon when two or more of that person's moral principles come into conflict. A person's operative moral principles are soft laws of moral judgment formation for that person. (Similar points, we believe, can be made about both normative and descriptive principles of belief formation – inductive logic and the like.)

There are two further features which, while not essential to this conception of cognition, are very likely to go along with it. First, the cognitive system's memories and prior knowledge are not stored away, in the same form in which they are used, in a mental file cabinet called "memory." The contents of such a memory would have to be fetched and updated as appropriate. This is the source of the frame problem in classical cognitive science. Rather, known and remembered information takes the form of cognitive *dispositions* – dispositions to produce new occurrent mental states from present occurrent mental states in an appropriate manner. Memories are literally *recreated* as needed. As with all cognition, these dispositions to recreate information as needed are soft, i.e., defeasible.

Second, mental processing will frequently exhibit *psychological indeterminacy*. That is, there will be no fact of the matter – on the basis of a total psychology level description of a cognitive system plus all of the relevant soft laws – about what will be the psychological or behavioral outcome of the interaction among various competing psychological factors. There will be no psychological determination of which defeasible causal tendencies will win out.

One reason for this is that psychological states are multiply realizable. That is, there are many different subpsychological states that can constitute a particular psychological state like believing there is beer in the refrigerator. This goes for each particular component of a total psychological state. Often, then, the particular psychology level outcome of processing will depend on details of realization that are left open by any psychological level description. [15]

4c. Soft Laws

The defining characteristic of soft laws is that they contain an essential *ceteris paribus* clause, either implicitly or explicitly. The *ceteris paribus* clause involves universal quantification over properties at the same level as the law – *all* else equal, if *nothing* defeats or deflects. [16] This clause is ineliminable because there are essentially limitless same level properties that could constitute exceptions (defeaters or deflectors). But even without this it would be essential, because laws expressing defeasible causal tendencies are the fundamental laws in the domains for which soft laws are appropriate.

But of course, a serious science of intentional psychology requires the kind of generality represented by intentional parameters. Hence, the soft laws of psychology will include quantifiers ranging over intentional/propositional parameters.

In addition to these three essential features – intentional parameters, *ceteris paribus* clauses, and essentially limitless same-level exceptions – the soft laws of psychology are likely to exhibit three additional attributes. First, it is likely that systems conforming to them will be diachronically indeterminate in the manner described above. Hence, the psychological *laws* are likely to be indeterminate in that they will not predict a determinate outcome for every situation to which they apply.

Second, the concepts that figure in soft laws, and in particular, the concepts of intentional psychology, are likely to be vague. That is, typically for such a concept there will be certain situations, actual or possible, for which there is no definite fact of the matter about whether or not the concept applies. The reason for this is that the conditions for applying those concepts are likely to include soft laws.

Third, the concepts employed in soft laws are likely to be non-quantitative, i.e., lacking in quantitative parameters. One reason for this is that their vagueness is apt to preclude the kind of precise, non-arbitrary, measurability that quantitative magnitudes normally require. Being non-quantitative does not mean, however, that there could not be (possibly vague) comparative concepts such as wanting *a* more than *b*, or believing *p* more firmly than *q*.

In addition, for psychology (and by extension, for other human sciences whose concepts include intentional parameters), there is not likely to be sufficient theoretical motivation for positing quantitative parameters anyway. For the laws already possess generality by virtue of containing quantifiers that range over intentional/propositional parameters. And as we argued above, the prospects are dim for quantitative psychological laws that achieve additional generality.

It should be stressed, however, that lack of quantitative parameters does not mean that quantitative *methods* have no proper place in psychology or the other human sciences. On the contrary, such methods can play a crucial role in experimental design and in hypothesis testing. For instance, empirical investigation in psychology can quite appropriately seek quantitative measurable data (about e.g., reaction times, error rates, and the like), and such data can be subjected to sophisticated statistical analyses.

It should also be stressed that softness does not render putative laws immune from empirical verification or falsification. Soft laws describe defeasible causal tendencies. Standard statistical techniques for data analysis can be very effective in uncovering such causal tendencies, even, or especially, when the data involve multiple causal factors operating at once, and even when the theoretical hypothesis being tested does not itself employ quantitative concepts. Given such techniques, it is implausible and naive to claim that if a putative psychological law has a *ceteris paribus* clause, then the proposed law is thereby rendered immune from empirical falsification (because, for example, one can stubbornly insist, in the face of any conceivable recalcitrant evidence, that *ceteris* was *paribus*). Suppose a law is proposed of the form, if *A*, then *ceteris paribus B*, and *A* occurs but *B* does not. Then if nothing can be found that would make this an exceptional case, then we have evidence against the proposed law. And defeasible causal tendencies are, in general, only defeated by other defeasible causal tendencies. Thus, finding something that makes this an exceptional case requires finding something that can figure in a competing soft law.

5. SOFT LAWS AND THEORETICAL EXPLANATION

It is widely believed that genuine scientific explanations require exceptionless nomic principles. This is one major reason why it is so commonly believed that full-fledged scientific *laws* must lack same-level exceptions. In this section we will argue, to the contrary, that soft laws can undergird perfectly respectable scientific explanations.

5a. Deductive Nomological Explanation

Jane went to the refrigerator and fetched herself a beer. She wanted a beer, she believed there was beer in the refrigerator, and had no overriding reason not to do it. These facts about her, together with the generalization (G) cited earlier, provide a perfectly fine explanation of her behavior.

Would it be a better explanation if we added that she did not have to answer her phone first? Would the explanation get better still if we said she did not think that getting up just then would offend the person speaking? And that she did not fear that the house was afire? And on and on indefinitely? When we explain in this manner, we *presuppose* that these and all other possible exceptions are excluded. That is, the explanation presupposes that *ceteris* was *paribus*. (Sometimes, of course, it is appropriate to mention some *particular* possible exception that might have been thought to be operative in the present case.)

Causal explanations that rest upon soft laws presuppose that the law's *ceteris paribus* clause was satisfied in the given situation. That *ceteris* is *paribus* is an implicit premise in the explanation. Thus, the explanation of Jane's behavior, when reconstructed in fully explicit form is: (G), Jane wanted a beer and believed she could get one in the refrigerator, and *ceteris* was *paribus*. So she went to the refrigerator for a beer.

Deductive explanations of this kind are faithful to an intuitive idea that largely motivates the *D-N* model in the first place, viz., "like causes–like effects." Jane's belief and desire led to her action. In any other case *exactly like that one, ceteris* would again have been *paribus,* and a like action would have occurred. Indeed, in any case *relevantly* like this one, *ceteris* would have been *paribus.* We cannot—in practice, and probably in principle—spell out all of the ways that things could fail to be relevantly like the present case. But that does not alter the fact that where a soft law applies, same causes do lead to the same effects.

A soft law does not delineate its own exceptions. Perhaps it is worth pointing out that quasi-exceptionless laws, if there are any, do not delineate their own exceptions either. Explanation on the basis of a quasi-exceptionless law presupposes that the domain of the law is not disrupted from below or from outside. Thus, advocates of the standard conception of psychological laws are committed to claiming that a *D-N* explanation can properly contain an assertion that *ceteris* was *paribus* among its premises.

5b. Some Consequences

When a law has a *ceteris paribus* clause, an asymmetry can arise between explanation and prediction. Often one knows after the fact that a certain combination of mental states were *operative* in the circumstances, even if one could not know beforehand that those mental states would win out.

Often, of course, one can predict with reasonable confidence on the basis of soft laws. One has good grounds in advance both for attributing certain mental states to someone and for believing that *ceteris* will be *paribus* with respect to those states. Reliable expectations about others are the norm.[17] Think of appointments and meetings, or of forming expectations about what drivers on the freeway will and will not do. There are "crazy drivers," but they really are the exception.

Sometimes, however, one cannot predict reliably even when one largely knows what all of the relevant psychological states are, because one cannot know in advance which combination of states will win out. The most familiar case is where one knows that someone has competing motives for performing each of several incompatible actions. After the person performs an action from among these alternatives, one will be able to explain this action by citing a relevant belief-desire combination that one knew about beforehand. But before the fact, one did not know which motive would prevail, and so could not predict the person's action.

Often this unpredictability is not simply epistemic. Rather, there is no determinate fact of the matter, given (only) a total psychology-level specification of the person prior to the decision about which action he will settle upon. (It will depend upon the details of the global, subcognitive state that realizes this total psychological description.) Even so, after the fact one will be able to explain the outcome psychologically by adverting to those motives that ended up being neither defeated nor deflected.[18]

Thus, explanation and prediction come apart. There are events, like the action in question, which can be explained, but which could not be predicted. There is a further consequence of this discussion: Some psychological phenomena are not psychologically explainable. In the kind of case just mentioned, we can explain why the person acted as he did. He acted from a certain motive. But we cannot give a psychological explanation for why that motive prevailed.[19]

Not only is there before the fact psychological indeterminacy about which motive will prevail, but there is no after the fact psychological explanation for why it did, for there is no (soft or hard) psychological law that explains why the given motive prevailed over the others. From the point of view of intentional psychology, it simply did.[20]

There is nothing metaphysically mysterious going on here. There is, of course, *an* explanation, even though there is no *psychological* explanation. The explanation will require "dropping levels," i.e., adverting to the subpsychological states of the person (as well as to certain subpsychological laws which determine the evolution of subpsychological states in this person, and to laws concerning the realization of psychological states by subpsychological states).

So if psychological theories employ soft laws, then these theories are likely to be explanatorily incomplete within their own domain. But even if *some* psychological phenomena lack psychological explanations, it hardly follows that they all do. On the contrary, many psychological and behavioral phenomena will still be explainable on the basis of soft psychological laws. Explanatory incompleteness in psychology is not objectionable; it is just a fact.

5c. Functional Explanation

Some philosophers hold that functional analysis is a species of scientific explanation that is importantly different from deductive nomological explanation, and that this species figures importantly in psychology. Robert Cummins gives a careful exposition of functional explanation:

> Functional analysis consists in analyzing a disposition into a number of less problematic dispositions such that programmed manifestation of these analyzing dispositions amounts to a manifestation of the analyzed disposition. By "programmed" here, I simply mean organized in such a way that could be specified in a program or flow chart. . . . [T]he explanatory force of the analysis derives largely from a specification of how the analyzing functions [i.e., dispositions] interact, a manifestation of one precipitating manifestation of another in the characteristically systematic way that is naturally specified in a flow-chart or program.[21]

This kind of explanation, he claims, is ubiquitous in cognitive science: sophisticated cognitive capacities are subjected to proposed functional analyses into simpler capacities; these, in turn, are subjected to further proposed functional analyses into still simpler capacities; and so on. (The process is supposed to end when one reaches fairly simple capacities, directly instantiable by the physical components of the system.)

It does seem quite natural to construe many of the cognitive models produced within the RR paradigm as proposed functional analyses of cognitive capacities. These models, of course, quite literally describe "programmed" interactions among intentional states. But several points should be made, in light of our discussion in earlier sections.

First, even if functional analysis (as described by Cummins) is indeed a form of explanation distinct from *D-N* explanation, nevertheless it still makes central use of *generalizations*. For, on Cummins's account, the analysis is supposed to be expressible in a *program,* and a program is a set of general rules of a certain kind.

Second, Cummins's account also commits him to the position that functional explanation requires generalizations that are *quasi-exceptionless*. For, in order to constitute a proper program, a set of generalizations or rules must be free of same-level exceptions.

But third, this latter commitment seems inessential to the conception of functional analysis he seeks to characterize. As far as we can tell, it would be quite consonant with the spirit of his approach to allow the principles governing interactions among analyzing dispositions, in a functional analysis, to be *soft*, rather than being formulable as quasi-exceptionless rules. The analysis could not then be formulated as a program, but it still could be formulated as a "flow chart," although arrows on the chart would now reflect defeasible causal tendencies.

Fourth, this liberalization of the account actually looks quite plausible on independent grounds. One reason, already stressed above, is that the Kuhnian crisis in the RR paradigm indicates that the search for PRL cognitive rules is hopeless; hence, functional explanations adverting to such rules will not be forthcoming. But as Cummins remarks, the analyzing properties in a functional analysis are *dispositional* properties. Why suppose that the full range of interactions among such properties can be expressed by quasi-exceptionless principles? On the contrary, aren't dispositions themselves better viewed as defeasible causal tendencies?

So the upshot is that functional explanation in psychology, although sometimes characterized in a way that presupposes the existence of quasi-exceptionless psychological generalizations, can perfectly well employ soft psychological generalizations instead. This position is fully consistent with the spirit of functional explanation, and indeed is more plausible than a position which requires a functional analysis to be literally formulable as a set of programmable (and hence quasi-exceptionless) generalizations.

5d. Rationalizing Explanation

Much has been written in philosophy of psychology about so-called "rationalizing explanations." These explain an action, or perhaps a specific mental state like a belief or desire, in a way that provides a *rationale* for the action or mental state. *Reasons* are cited for the action or state. These reasons reveal what can be said in favor of it from the agent's point of view; and if the explanation is correct, then the agent acted (or believed, etc.) as he did *because of* these reasons. The most commonly discussed form is the explanation of actions in terms of beliefs and desires, in accordance with a principle like (G) above.

At least four broad and interrelated issues are at the center of philosophical debates about rationalizing explanations. (1) Are reasons a species of cause? (2) Are rationalizing explanations a species of causal explanation? (3) Are generalizations like (G) genuine laws, rather than having some status that is incompatible with their being laws? (4) Do generalizations figure in rationalizing explanations at all?

In our view, the answer to each of these questions is "Yes." But our discussion in this essay has an important moral even for those who think otherwise. As long as one's position includes an affirmative answer to question (4), then the following further question arises: Are the generalizations that figure in proper rationalizing explanations *soft* generalizations, rather than being quasi-exceptionless? The broad moral of our discussion is this: If "Yes" is the correct answer to question (4), then it is also the correct answer to this further question, regardless of the proper answers to questions (1)–(3).

Another general moral is that many who answer "No" to question (4) may be motivated largely by two beliefs: (a) the mistaken belief that an affirmative answer carries a commitment to generalizations of the quasi-exceptionless kind; and (b) the correct belief that there are few if any such generalizations in the human sciences. If so, then they should repudiate the mistaken belief and should reconsider their answer to (4). Insofar as this mistaken belief has played a role in determining answers to the other questions, these, too, should be reconsidered.

6. EMPATHETIC UNDERSTANDING, COGNITIVE SIMULATION, AND EXPLANATORY FORCE

We shall conclude with some remarks about the view that the methodology of the human sciences fundamentally involves empathetic or intuitive understanding, rather than a kind of explanation that rests upon generalizations.

To begin with, the human sciences seek to provide *explanatory* understanding, as opposed to something that falls short of explanation. The goal is to understand *why* individuals or groups act as they do, believe as they do, and so forth. An informative answer to a why-question is an explanation. Thus, the real issue is not whether the human sciences provide a kind of understanding distinct from the explanatory kind. Rather, it is whether they provide a kind of explanation that does not rest upon generalizations.

In our view, those who take an affirmative stand on this question have failed to describe a form of explanation in the human sciences which does not ultimately rest upon generalizations. Their discussions typically exhibit two defects: (1) the sample explanations they cite turn out to rest upon generalizations after all; and (2) their attempts to provide a positive account of the putative alternative form of explanation are either uninformative or plainly deficient. Avoiding these problems becomes especially difficult once one realizes that explanatory generalizations in the human sciences typically are soft, not quasi-exceptionless.

As an example of the first problem, consider an explanation which Arthur Ripstein makes the centerpiece of a recent article defending *verstehenism*. In "Looking Back on the Spanish War," George Orwell recalls passing up one of his few chances to shoot at an enemy soldier. Here is the key passage from Orwell, quoted by Ripstein:

> At this moment, a man, presumably carrying a message to an officer, jumped out of the trench and ran along the top of the parapet in full view. He was half dressed and was holding up his trousers with both hands as he

ran. I refrained from shooting at him. It is true that I am a poor shot and unlikely to hit a running man at a hundred yards, and also that I was thinking chiefly about getting back to our trench while the Fascists still had their attention fixed on the aeroplanes. Still, I did not shoot partly because of that detail about the trousers. I had come here to shoot at 'Fascists'; but a man who is holding up his trousers isn't a 'Fascist', he is visibly a fellow creature, similar to yourself, and you don't feel like shooting at him.[22]

Ripstein maintains that although Orwell has indeed provided an explanation of his refusal to shoot, it does not rest upon any discernible psychological generalizations. But the trouble is, it does. Although Orwell does not make this fully explicit (he is writing in journalistic rather than philosophical style), he is clearly presupposing some such generalizations as these:

> *Ceteris paribus,* if one sees a person running and holding up his trousers with both hands, then one perceives that person as a fellow creature.
> *Ceteris paribus,* if one perceives a person as a fellow creature, then one does not feel like harming that person.

An example of the second above-mentioned problem is also provided by Ripstein's own positive account of the putative structure of explanations like Orwell's. Ripstein maintains that the facts cited in an explanation have explanatory force provided one has assurance that they "make a difference" to the phenomenon being explained. Concerning the explanatory force of Orwell's description, he writes:

> Your own capacity to find Orwell's description gripping. . .can take the place of articulate (general) principles. . .because it does exactly the same job: it allows you to tell that what Orwell saw made a difference to what he was willing to do.[23]

But the trouble is that one can know that certain facts "made a difference"—i.e., that if those facts had not obtained, then the phenomenon being explained would not have occurred—even if one has no inkling about *why* the facts made a difference. That is, one can know *what* caused the phenomenon (say, by learning this from a reliable source, in this case Orwell himself) without understanding *why* the actual cause had the effect it did. Explanatory understanding requires the latter kind of knowledge, not just the former. It requires *seeing the connection* between cause and effect. Yet Ripstein tells us nothing about what it might be to see the connection between cause and effect, other than to be aware of a (soft) generalization linking the two. Thus, he provides no genuine alternative to the claim that explanatory force rests upon generalizations that link the cited facts to the phenomenon being explained.

We do not deny that the psychological process whereby one acquires explanatory understanding of another person often involves putting oneself imaginatively "in that person's shoes," and then (as it has become fashionable to say) "running a cognitive simulation" of what someone in that person's environmental and psychological situation would or might do (or believe, or desire, etc.).[24] Nor do we deny that explanatory understanding often is experienced, phenomenologically, as the intuition that the person's actual action (or belief, etc.) "makes sense." Nor do we deny that it is possible to achieve such explanatory understanding without being able to articulate it explicitly. However, as far as we can see, cognitive simulation *requires* (soft) laws. Such laws must govern both our own cognitive processes when we simulate, and also the cognitive processes of the person or culture we are simulating.

First, in order for us to be able to simulate someone else at all, there must be (soft) laws that connect our own representations of the subject's prior mental states to our own representations the subject's later behavior (or mental states). We must have processes that produce appropriate expectations about what that person would do (or believe) in the envisioned environmental and psychological situation. And this means having our own mental states governed by appropriate soft laws. (We might not always be able to predict what the subject would do [or believe], even when we can understand it after the fact. But this is a feature of soft-law explanation in any case. And surely we must *sometimes* be able to predict correctly.)

Second, in order for our processes of cognitive simulation to constitute a *correct* simulation of what happens in the mind(s) of the person or group we are simulating, their mental states and behavior must conform with (soft) laws that are suitably mirrored by the laws governing our own simulation processes. And those are precisely the laws that would figure in an explicit, articulated, explanation of the phenomenon whose etiology is being cognitively simulated.

In the earlier sections of this essay we argued that if there are laws in intentional psychology at all, then they are soft laws. In this final section we have argued that psychological explanation evidently requires such laws. Analogous conclusions hold, we think, for the human sciences generally. Numerous issues in the philosophy of psychology and in the philosophy of the human sciences deserve to be reconsidered in light of these conclusions. Important new issues also arise in the philosophy of science generally — for instance, how best to understand the intertheoretic connections between soft theories in the human sciences and hard theories in the natural sciences. It is time for philosophers to take a hard look at soft laws.

NOTES

This essay is thoroughly collaborative; order of authorship is alphabetical. These matters are discussed at greater length in our forthcoming book, *Connectionism and the Philosophy of Psychology* (Cambridge).

1. Thus, what we say will apply to commonsense psychological explanations and to the generalization of so-called "folk psychology," whether or not it is properly regarded as a theory or as "protoscience."

2. The Newtonian model still gives most philosophers their ideal of a scientific theory. Perhaps, then, exceptionlessness is most often thought of in terms of deterministic theories. However, the notion applies equally to probabilistic theories. The laws will involve precise and specific probabilities and will not contain any *ceteris paribus* clauses.

3. Jerry A. Fodor, "Special Sciences," in *Representations* (Cambridge, Mass., 1981), 141.

4. Jerry A. Fodor, *Psychosemantics* (Cambridge, 1987), 6.

5. Paul M. Churchland, *Scientific Realism and the Plasticity of Mind* (Cambridge, 1979), 104.

6. Churchland, notoriously, rejects the possibility of an intentional psychology, but not on these grounds.

7. The kind of generality that results from universal quantification over parameters has been underemphasized in much of philosophy of science, e.g., in classical formulations of the deductive-nomological model of explanation.

8. Churchland, *Scientific Realism*, 104.

9. We take no stand here on the ontological significance of this quantification.

10. The notion of a Kuhnian crisis is, as we understand it, in large measure sociological. There is a crisis because sufficiently many practitioners perceive certain problems as sufficiently vexing to justify looking outside the paradigm. But of course, the problems they perceive are genuine problems.

Evidence of the crisis includes the rapid rise of connectionism in the 1980s, and the defection of several central figures of classical cognitive science, for example, David Rumelhart, co-editor of the "bible of connectionism" (*Parallel Distributed Processing,* edited by David E. Rumelhart, James L. McClelland, and the PDP Research Group, 2 volumes [Cambridge, 1986]); Terry Winograd, author of the well-known SHURDLU program (see Terry Winograd and Fernando Flores, *Understanding Computers and Cognition* [Norwood, N.J. 1986]); and Michael Dyer, a prominent student of Roger Shank, whose story understanding program is discussed below.

11. This is a theme we have developed at length elsewhere. See T. Horgan and J. Tienson, "Settling into a New Paradigm," in *Connectionism and the Philosophy of Mind: Proceedings of the 1987 Spindel Conference, Southern Journal of Philosophy* 26, Supplement; "Representations without Rules," *Philosophical Topics* 17 (1987): 147–174; *Connectionism and the Philosophy of Psychology* (Cambridge, Mass., forthcoming).

12. Roger C. Shank with Peter Childers, *The Cognitive Computer* (Reading, Mass., 1984).

13. It might be thought that a "refinement" of (G) such as the following would be a good candidate for a quasi-exceptionless law.

(G′)   (S)(D)(A)(If S wants D, and S believes that doing A will bring about D, and S has no other desire that outweighs S's desire for D, then S will do A).

But the key clause in (G'), asserting that S has no desire that "outweighs" the desire for D, is just another way of saying the D is neither defeated nor deflected by other desires. Thus, this phrase is itself a *ceteris paribus* clause.

14. For expository purposes, we are writing in a way that presupposes the truth of (G) and of commonsense psychological explanation in general. But this is for convenience only. We do not suppose such laws and explanations must be true. Whether they are or not is an empirical question. Our concern at present is with the *form* of laws that govern psychological phenomena.

15. This kind of indeterminacy is possible in connectionist networks, but not in classical computers. Cf. Horgan and Tienson, "Settling into a New Paradigm," for discussion.

16. We leave open the question of what the proper form of the *ceteris paribus* clause should be. Perhaps it should depend on the science. In any event, our purpose in this essay is to draw attention to soft laws and advertise their importance. It would detract from this purpose to commit ourselves prematurely to a specific view on this question.

17. Cf. Fodor's discussion in the first chapter of *Psychosemantics*.

18. In such a case, although one might say after the fact that the given motive was the "stronger" one, this will be quite *literally* an after the fact description, which does not correspond to any pre-outcome psychological relation.

19. There are *other* kinds of cases where the question of why the given motive prevailed might have an answer, say in terms of a second order belief the person had concerning the relative importance of the competing motives, plus applicable soft psychological laws concerning this second order belief.

20. Another interesting sort of case where there may be no psychological explanation is creative compromise. There may be several competing factors and the final outcome is one in which the defeasible causal tendencies of each of them are at least deflected. It seems plausible that there will be no psychology-level explanation of how the final outcome was thought of. (It may be that once the potential solution was generated it was subject to cogency testing that is governed by soft laws.) In general, generate and test cognitive processing may frequently be amenable to psychology-level explanation only at the testing end.

21. Robert Cummins, *The Nature of Psychological Explanation* (Cambridge, 1983), 29–31.

22. Quoted in Arthur Ripstein, "Explanation and Empathy," *Review of Metaphysics* 40 (1987): 470f.

23. Ibid., 472.

24. See Robert Gordon, "Folk Psychology as Simulation," *Mind and Language* 1 (1986): 158–74; and Alvin Goldman, "Interpretation Psychologized," *Mind and Language*, forthcoming.

Do Social Structures
Govern Action?

THEODORE R. SCHATZKI

Questions concerning the relations between individuals and society are as old as social thought itself. Two prominent such issues are: Are social formations nothing but or something more than the individuals found in them? and Are social formations the products of individuals or *vice versa*—or both? In modern times from Hegel and Mill onward, philosophical attention to these issues has ebbed and flowed, the most recent sustained treatment occurring in analytic philosophy during the 1950s and 1960s. Since then, some of the most creative work in social theory has focused upon the relations between agency and structure.

Contrary to what the instigators of this shift suppose,[1] theoretical questions about agency and structure do not merely update traditional issues concerning individuals and society. Individuals and agency are roughly coextensive phenomena, since that aspect of individuals of typical interest to social theory is their agency. Social formations and social structures, however, are entities of different sorts. Social phenomena are the phenomena comprising human coexistence, e.g., corporations, clubs, economies, political systems, and racial prejudice. Social structures are orders that either characterize or organize social formations. Until recently, structures were standardly modeled after the anatomy of an organism: as patterns formed by the activities that constitute social formations. As such, they were purely descriptive features of these formations, having no explanatory power. The structures discussed by recent theorists, on the other hand, are not patterns. Modeled after Saussure's *la langue* or the corpus of grammatical rules (allegedly) governing speech acts, they are abstract entities that govern, organize, and hence explain the patterns exhibited by social formations.

Far from simply updating traditional issues, therefore, the theorists of agency and structure have opened a new area of investigation: Are there structures of the type they envision? If so, what are they, and how do they relate to action? A second innovation characterizing this recent movement lies in the generic answer it proposes to the latter issue: structures are both the medium and outcome of action. Structures, that is, govern actions while at the same time being their product. According to the new structuralists, this way of thinking overcomes both the voluntarist illusion that individuals willfully create social phenomena and the determinist illusion that individuals are the playthings of all-powerful forces. For these thinkers, structures do indeed govern actions, but actions, in reproducing structures, can at the same time transform them. Human activity, however, does not willfully create structures—it can at best merely modify the already existing structures that constrain or determine it.

This essay examines the new structuralist school of thought. With an eye to the central thesis that differentiates its viewpoint from the traditional one, I will organize my discussion around the question: Do social structures govern action? The bulk of my remarks will critically analyze this school's answer to this question. In my conclusion, however, I will suggest that, although many structures in social reality instantiate the traditional conception, some social structures do indeed govern action. They are of a different nature, however, than the new structuralists imagine.

I. THE NEW STRUCTURALIST SCHOOL

The three central theorists of this school are Pierre Bourdieu, Anthony Giddens, and Roy Bhaskar, by training an anthropologist, sociologist, and philosopher respectively. What unites them is an allegiance to the formula that structures both govern and result from action. What divides them are divergent accounts of action, of structure, and of the relations between them. In this essay, I discuss Giddens and Bhaskar alone. My reason for setting Bourdieu aside is that his theoretical ideas about action and structure, despite their great interest, remain relatively unknown to English-speaking social theorists and philosophers fifteen years after their development.[2] Giddens, on the other hand, stands at the forefront of Anglo-American sociology. Together with Bhaskar, moreover, his work is the central impulse underlying the current theoretical renaissance in geography. Hence, it is of greater practical significance to examine and to deflate their notions of structure-in-action.

According to Bhaskar, social reality exhibits "ontological depth" or "stratification": a division into an experienceable component, comprising actions and the material products of action, and an unexperienceable component, society, comprising social relations and the mechanisms that operate within these. With this analysis, Bhaskar contests empiricist construals of social reality that treat it as either the contents of experience (the empirical) or the totality of events (the actual). In Bhaskar's eyes, the empirical and actual must be complemented by the nonempirical, nonactual real, which is a layer of relations and mechanisms causally generative of what happens on the first two levels.

The real is composed of two sorts of entities. There are, first, social relations, which hold not between particular individuals, but between "the *positions* (places, functions, rules, tasks, duties, rights, etc.) occupied (filled, assumed, enacted, etc.) by individuals, and. . .the *practices* (activities, etc.) in which, in virtue of their occupancy of these positions (and vice-versa), they engage" (*PN* 51). Examples of such relations are those between capitalist and worker, between MP and constituent, between worker and machine, and between husband and wife (*PN* 36). Unfortunately, Bhaskar neglects to analyze further the constitution of social relations. Is, e.g., the relation between husband and wife an irreducible *ens realissum*? Or does it consist of items such as the rules, tasks, duties, and rights mentioned in the above quotation? I will later return to this question.

The second component of the real is generative mechanisms that operate "within. . .structured sets of social relations."[3] What I think Bhaskar has in mind is twofold: that social relations form systems and that these systems are such that relations of necessity govern actual social affairs through them. Such relations of necessity, moreover, are described by laws paralleling those that describe the mechanisms at work in physical reality. To understand Bhaskar here, we must briefly consider his general analysis of causality and laws.

In an earlier work,[4] Bhaskar, following Harré and Madden, argues that it is an error to analyze laws as or even to base them on empirical covariances. Among the reasons he marshalls against empiricist doctrine is the fact that empirical covariances rarely occur since, in the open systems characteristic of physical (and social) reality, events are the products of multiple causes, each of which partly determines what happens. Even if events of one sort would regularly, in the absence of other causes, be followed by events of another sort, the omnipresent co-action of other causes prevents this regularity from manifesting itself in actuality. For Bhaskar, furthermore, the plurality of causes that co-produce an event is a plurality of mechanisms, not a manifold of events. These mechanisms are real relations which govern events and which, because they arise from the natures of things, cannot be reduced to regular sequences of events. They are described by laws of the form: the properties of Z are such that in conditions C event X will occur (or state of affairs Y will be the case). For example, water will freeze at 32°F by virtue of its molecular structure. This statement formulates a real relation of necessity. However, when conditions C occur, i.e., when it is 32°F, we need not expect X to occur, i.e., water to freeze. For any number of other mechanisms (e.g., those arising from the molecular structure of antifreeze) might co-determine what occurs and frustrate the actual expression of the first mechanism. Laws, consequently, describe tendencies, not regularities. And even if conditions and other mechanisms are such that a particular mechanism is never realized in actuality, it still exists in reality. The conclusions follow (1) that in open systems such as nature and social life where multiplicities of mechanisms co-determine events, the laws describing particular mechanisms are useless for predictive purposes; and (2) that the existence of mechanisms cannot be determined on the basis of what occurs in these systems. Putative mechanisms can be confirmed only in the laboratory where the potential interfering effects of other mechanisms can be eliminated or held constant.

Bhaskar believes that mechanisms of this sort govern social life and that they arise from the properties of systems of social relations. An example of such a mechanism, discussed by a follower of Bhaskar, is: "the competitive structure of capitalist production forces each firm to increase output per unit of labour costs as a condition of its survival."[5] A firm is a system of relations among manager, worker, capital, and means of production. Similarly, the capitalist economy is a totality of relations among, among other things, the sets of social relations comprising firms. The putative law claims that this totality is such that the systems of relations comprising individual firms must, in order to survive, be transformed in ways having a particular type of statistical effect. This statement formulates a "real" relation of necessity that supposedly governs what occurs in social life. Exactly what changes in firm organization result from its operation, however, will depend on what other mechanisms, reflecting, e.g., the degree of organization of labor and the range of available technologies, also operate. Thus:

> In the transport industry, the effects may take the form of a change towards fewer but larger mobile units. . .or more frequent faster units. . . . For other firms, this lowering of transport costs can either enable them to centralize production towards existing agglomerations or, conversely, decentralize their production.[6]

Finally, even though social relations do not hold among individuals, they are continually reproduced through the actions of individuals. The worker-manager relation, for instance, is maintained and possibly also transformed, in small or large measure, by the actions of particular workers and managers. Actions also carry out the mechanisms that operate within social relations. It is, again, the actions of particular managers and workers that, in transforming and conforming to the new organization of the firm, bring about increased productivity and thereby realize the law. At the same time, social relations and mechanisms preexist and govern human activity. I will postpone until part II my examination of how structures allegedly accomplish this. In any case, society, the ensemble of relations and mechanisms, is "both the ever-present *condition*. . .and the continually reproduced *outcome* of human agency" (*PN* 43).

Bhaskar characterizes his position as "transcendental realism." Society is a necessarily unexperienceable stratum of being distinct from, though not independent of, the experienceable realm of actions and their material products. For Giddens, on the other hand, actions and structures do not constitute distinct strata of existence. Social reality is nothing but systems of actual social interactions. Structures are simply abstract features of these systems visible from a particular perspective.

Giddens writes that people "draw on" rules and resources when acting. This means that they follow rules and utilize resources in their interactions with one another. Since actors repeatedly draw on the same rules and resources, rules and resources also organize people's interactions into systems of continuous and patterned practices. When rules and resources are viewed not as items that actors draw on but as that which organizes practices over space and time, they are viewed as elements of the *structures* of practices. Structures thus pertain to the continuity and patterning of interactions over time and space (the "stretching" of social practices over space-time). Unlike structures of the traditional type, however, Giddens's structures are not patterns. They are that which organizes and is responsible for patterns. Social structures are abstractions (*CS* 189) "recursively implicated" in the stretching of practices as that which, in governing interactions, gives them systematic form over space and time.

Giddens's conception of rules is relatively straightforward. Rules are (1) codes of signification and modes of typification with which actors grasp and communicate meaning, and (2) norms (rights and obligations) with which actors carry out, legitimate, and criticize actions and states of affairs.[7] His notion of resources, on the other hand, is more problematic. The role that resources play in social interaction is clear: they are the media through which power is exercised,[8] where power is understood, generally, as the capacity to bring about changes and, in a narrower sense pertinent to social theory, as the capacity to bring about changes where the realization of these changes depends on the agency of others (*CP* 93). Functionally, therefore, resources are that which, through the utilization of or reliance upon, actors can bring others to perform actions by which specific outcomes are secured. At key moments when defining resources nonfunctionally, however, Giddens writes that resources are "capacities that generate commands" over objects or persons (*CP* 100; *CS* 33). This formulation is backwards. An example of a resource is land (property). Neither land nor its possession is a capacity. It is ill-conceived, therefore, to analyze the possession of land as a capacity that generates commands. Rather, possession of land is *itself* a command over material entities. And what this command yields is capacities, capacities to perform certain actions, to induce others to perform certain actions, and thus to secure certain states of affairs. Resources, consequently, are commands over persons and objects that yield capabilities (as Giddens sometimes seems to realize, cf. *CS* xxxi, 283).

Now, the specific structuring function that rules and resources play *vis-à-vis* action is to open up particular actions as possibilities, thereby excluding other actions as not possible. (Giddens claims, as a result, that structure is both enabling and constraining.) Similarly, the function that structures play *vis-à-vis* practices is to "bind space and time" (to regulate "time-space distanciation"); that is, to open up certain ways of stretching over time and space as possible, thereby closing off other ways as not possible (*CS* 17, cf. 181). It is important to keep in mind that it is the opening up of possible actions by the rules and resources that actors continually draw on that opens up the ways in which practices can stretch. These structuring functions also explain the sense in which structures are both the medium and outcome of activity. Structures are the medium of activity since activity is tied down to what rules and resources make possible. Structures are equally the outcome of activity since human activity, in realizing that to which it is tied down, reaffirms what determines this.

Rules and resources, however, are only the building blocks of structures. Structure, at one level of abstraction, consists of "convertability sets," each of which is composed of rules and resources that can be converted into one another. For instance, since private property can be converted into money, thence into capital, thence into labor contracts, and thence into profits, private property, money, capital, labor contracts, and profits form a set. Convertability sets conglomerate, moreover, under higher-level structural principles. These principles describe the organization of the sets of rules and resources that organize those practices having the greatest spatial-temporal extension. They are *post hoc* descriptions of the patterns formed by that which governs action. They are not at all akin to Bhaskar's laws which specify what will happen under such and such conditions.

Finally, it is important to emphasize that structures are not concrete phenomena. Their space-time being consists solely in: (1) instantiations in practices, i.e., the continuity and patterning of interactions; and (2) practical knowledge (memory traces) about how things are to be done which "orients the conduct of knowledgeable human agents" (*CP* 64, cf. *CS* 17). Sets of rules and resources form a "virtual order," an "order of differences," absent from but implicated in the space-time manifold of interactions. The components of structure, on the other hand, are embodied in this manifold. Rules are embodied in interactions because the tacit knowledge (practical consciousness) that orients interactions is a knowledge of rules (*CP* 68, *CS* 21). One assumes, though Giddens is not very clear on this point, that resources, too, are embodied in practices primarily because actors' practical knowledge about how to act, together with their discursive knowledge about things such as rights, obligations, and material objects, *is* (in part) a knowledge of who has a command over what.[9] In short, for Giddens the constituents of structure exist as contained within knowledge: "structure has no existence independent of the knowledge that agents have about what they do in their day to day activity" (*CS* 26).

Bhaskar and Giddens disagree on two important issues: the identity of structure and its mode of being. While Bhaskar construes structures as social relations and generative mechanisms, Giddens views them as sets of rules and resources. However, their positions on this first issue might have more in common than initially meets the eye. Bhaskar occasionally hints that he would analyze social relations in terms of rules and resources; and at one point Giddens writes, footnoting Bhaskar, that some structural properties of social systems are best understood as position-practice relations (*CS* 83). Regardless of how much overlap exists between social relations and rules and resources, however, Giddens has no equivalent for Bhaskar's generative mechanisms. For necessity appears nowhere in his account. Sets of rules and resources are "hierarchically organized in terms of the time-space extension of the practices they recursively organize" (*CS* 17). Structural principles are simply the "most deeply embedded structural properties implicated in the reproduction of societal totalities" (ibid.). They are descriptions of the organization of that which gives systematic form to practices (*CS* 181): both the rules and resources embodied in these systems and the causal action loops and processes of reflexive self-regulation that also hold these systems together (cf. *CS* 27–28; these loops and regulations are mixes of

intended and unintended consequences of action). But there is not anything necessary about the organization of either the rules and resources or the mixes of
intended and unintended consequences that bestow systematic form upon practices. Structural principles are simply higher-order descriptions of these system-
determining phenomena, not relations of necessity that operate through them.
The difference here between Giddens and Bhaskar reflects a fundamental philosophical divide in social theory: principles can be viewed either as laws determining how things are in concrete reality or as *ex post facto* descriptions
summarizing general features of that which organizes reality.

A second philosophical schism dividing Bhaskar and Giddens concerns the
mode of being of social structure. Bhaskar argues that reality is stratified: in
addition to experiences and events, there also are structures and mechanisms.
What is more, experiences and events are the products of the transfactual activities of mechanisms, where 'transfactual activity' means the operation of a mechanism irrespective of its expression or lack thereof in actuality. Of course,
structures are not things (*SRHE* 152); they are not objects akin to unexperienceable physical objects such as protons. But relations and mechanisms do form a
realm of "entities" or "phenomena" distinct from that comprised by actions and
material objects. Bhaskar remarks that structures are "aspects" of the concrete
flux of social life (*SRHE* 152, 124). I am not sure how the implication of this
remark, that the real is an aspect of the actual (assuming that a "concrete flux" is
an actuality), coheres with the thesis of ontological stratification, the thesis of a
categorical distinction between the real and the actual. Even if it does, however,
the meaning of this remark remains unclear so long as Bhaskar fails to analyze
social relations more precisely. The uncertainty of Bhaskar's conception of the
ontological status of structures is revealed by his statement (*SRHE* 132) that
social structures are more like elements of a system than like the powers of a
particular (these being the two paradigms for the nonactual real). For in *PN*,
Bhaskar repeatedly describes society as, e.g., "an articulated ensemble of tendencies and powers" (49). Perhaps this statement points toward a distinction
between the ontological statuses of social relations and social mechanisms (cf.
his Giddensesque remarks at *SRHE* 124), but Bhaskar does not say this.

In Giddens, on the other hand, there is no ontological stratification. Social
reality is the concrete world of social interaction. Rules and resources are not a
distinct order of phenomena but something embedded in this world, which,
when reconstructed and viewed as that which organizes this world is treated as
its structure. Rules and resources are thus "aspects" of practices in being the
reconstructable contents of the practical knowledge underlying patterned interactions. The structures they comprise, accordingly, are "aspects" of practices in
being sets of reconstructable contents of knowledge. Notice that social structures are not themselves contents of knowledge. Only the rules and resources of
which they are composed have this status. Structures are abstractions visible to
the investigatory gaze of social scientists. And this is ultimately why Giddens
writes that social structures are 'virtual orders' absent from concrete reality.[10] In
any case, Bhaskar's social relations and mechanisms, however they connect with

actions, practices, rules, and resources, are neither contents of actors' knowledge/consciousness nor sets of such contents. So Giddens's structures are more straightforwardly aspects of the concrete flux of social life than are Bhaskar's. In fact, since rules and resources are at one and the same time contents of tacit knowledge and elements of practice-organizing structures, agents and structures are not two distinct realms of reality:

> The constitution of agents and structures are not two independently given sets of phenomena. . . . Structure is not 'external' to individuals; as memory traces, and as instantiated in social practices, it is in a sense more 'internal' than exterior to their activities in a Durkheimian sense. (*CS* 25)

Similarly, Giddens's structural principles are aspects of actuality *qua* higher-order descriptions of the contents of tacit knowledge. So their ontological status sharply contrasts with that of necessities which hold of social life on the basis of systems of social relations that govern actuality.

II. CRITIQUE

Bhaskar's account of social science parallels his analysis of natural science. In both realms, scientific work consists in moving from manifest phenomena, physical events or actions, to the entities that generate them, physical or social structures/mechanisms. In his discussions of social being, accordingly, Bhaskar constantly refers to generative mechanisms, powers, the nomic or tendency statements describing these, and, e.g., "shifting deep structures. . .[that] produc[e], in myriad forms, the turbulences and routines of our historical experience, the manifest phenomenology of everyday social life" (*SRHE* 207). Such language makes it sound like social structures govern actions in the way that physical structures govern physical events: by causing them (bringing them about). Likewise, the occasional appearance in *PN* of the image of a magnetic field (e.g., his description of society as "totalities of internally related fields of force" [*PN* 194]) suggests that, just as a magnetic field causes iron filings to line up in certain patterns, so, too, does, e.g., economic structure cause people to act in certain ways. However, if this is what Bhaskar has in mind, he needs to explain the parallel. For it is not at all obvious how the first component of structure, systems of relations, can bring about actions. Exactly how does the capitalist-worker relation bring about the actions of particular workers and capitalists? What immediately governs action are the states of affairs to which people respond, those that mold the intelligibility governing what they do, and this intelligibility itself. If social relations cause actions, they can do so only by linking up with these phenomena in some way. Bhaskar, however, nowhere provides an account of this connection. As we will shortly see, this is because he does not really believe, *pace* his typical mode of expression, that social relations bring about actions.

Similar comments apply to his notion of social mechanisms. Like the laws describing the physical mechanisms that generate physical events, those describing social mechanisms specify real necessities: what, under certain conditions, will happen or be the case given the natures of certain entities. The structure of capitalism, for instance, forces firms to increase output per unit labor costs as a condition of their survival. Just how, however, do social mechanisms such as this govern human activity?

How does the necessity, that enduring firms in a capitalist economy sustain increasing output per unit labor costs, relate to the actual actions of particular managers and workers? Bhaskar certainly does not believe that people become aware of this necessity and act accordingly. Nor does he suggest that the necessity operates by compelling, in a manner unmediated by individuals and thus akin to Althusser's structural causality, the self-reorganization of the relations comprising the firm and the competitive economy. Rather, social mechanisms, as noted, are "exercised by the intentional activity of men" (*PN* 49). What Bhaskar means, I think, is that necessities are *carried out* by people who, finding themselves in particular situations occupying positions charged with the execution of specific ends and projects, act in ways which result in certain changes. Thus, managers who aim to maintain healthy levels of profit, who exert control over specific material objects and organizations of people, and who compete against other managers with similar ends and controls, reorganize these material objects and organizations in ways which increase their firms' output per unit labor costs.

However, if this is what there is to the operation of social mechanisms, it is not clear why such increases are the *products* of transfactually active real mechanisms. In the state of affairs as I have described it, the causal forces at work are people's actions, the intelligibility governing their behavior, and the states of affairs that induce actions and mold intelligibility. Whatever statistical changes occur are products of these forces. If, then, real mechanisms are what govern, cause, or generate what happens, they must be responsible for the operation of these (as opposed to other possible) forces. For this, in turn, to be the case, there must be some connection between the mechanisms and the actual causal forces at work. Bhaskar, however, fails to specify this connection. Until he does, there is no justification for the claim that the real *governs* the actual. Notice that this problem does not arise for Giddens. Since structural principles are *post hoc* descriptions of the organization of that which governs action, they possess no governing power of their own.

I indicated earlier that Bhaskar might analyze social relations in terms of rules and resources. This possibility is suggested by a number of facts, for instance: (1) that Bhaskar refers parenthetically to "rules, tasks, duties, rights, etc." immediately after first mentioning positions (*PN* 51); and (2) that in a number of places in *SRHE* while discussing structure, he speaks of rules and resources (e.g., 123, 127, 149; cf. *PN* 52). I explained earlier that, for Giddens, rules and resources govern action by making actions possible. Accordingly, if Bhaskar does mean to analyze social relations in terms of rules and resources (though there are passages opposing this supposition), he can claim that social relations govern actions by making them possible. This interpretation appears confirmed by his statement that structures are the material causes of action while beliefs are their efficient causes (e.g., *PN* 43; *SRHE* 119, cf. 122). What he means is that structures provide the materials necessary for acting, the rules, resources, media, and "functions" without which acting and speaking could not proceed. In providing these materials, structures make a range of actions possible. Bhaskar's position does not collapse into Giddens's, however, because, in clearly separating the competences and skills of agents from the facilities or possibilities offered to agents by social structures (*SRHE* 175; cf. *PN* 66), Bhaskar refrains from embedding structures or their elements in knowledge as the latter's implicit content.

If this is Bhaskar's position, then the parallel between physical structures and social structures, at least social relations, is weaker than he admits. Whereas physical structures are generative causes, social relations are preconditions. Moreover, his notion of social relations now seems to contravene his claim about ontological depth. Social relations no longer form a layer of reality distinct from the concrete actuality of activity. They are merely logical constructions built from or contained within entities (rules and resources) which one assumes are aspects of actuality. (Bhaskar says nothing about the ontological status of rules and resources.) Although this analysis both elucidates how social relations can be "aspects" of actuality and brings Bhaskar's account of social relations closer to Giddens's analysis of structures, its undermining of ontological depth further weakens the parallel between social being and nature. Insofar as social relations do consist in rules and resources, my later criticism of Giddens simultaneously assails Bhaskar's position.

The idea that structures govern actions by making them possible also offers a way of interpreting the connection between action and social mechanisms. Necessity can now be understood as social relations being such that, in certain circumstances, there is but one possible way for actors to proceed. Thus the claim, that in a capitalist economy firms must increase output per unit labor costs in order to survive, can be understood as follows: the relations constituting a capitalist economy are such that a manager, in order to preserve her firm, has no choice but so to alter the firm's organization and operations that a particular statistical measure of its activity increases. It does not, of course, undermine the validity of this law that in the actual world this claim is never true.

But one can still question whether the mechanism, interpreted in this way, *governs* action. Consider a particular manager. The rules and resources relevant to her behavior open up to her a realm of possible actions. The economic, political, and legal environments in which she acts similarly open up and limit what she can do in order to preserve her enterprise. Within these limits she pursues a particular course of action which may or may not result in increased output per unit labor costs. Which course she pursues will depend on a host of factors in addition to the ones mentioned, e.g., her moods, the counsel and information she receives, and the other ends she pursues in her life. So much for actuality. What, however, does the theoretical state of affairs, that the only course of action open in certain circumstances is such and such, have to do with her actions? As far as I can see, nothing (assuming knowledge of this theoretical construction does not guide her actions). She does what she does as determined by particular factors and within the confines of what rules and resources set up as possible. (Remember that in the actual world the narrowing of possibilities to one does not occur.) The theoretical state of affairs, on the other hand, is that so and so will happen when such and such alone is the case. But since such and such is not alone the case, and since the actual circumstances resemble these to an unspecified degree, what would happen if they were alone the case has no imperativeness in actuality. Hence, the "real" necessity has no particular bearing on what actually happens. It still holds true in the constructed theoretical world. And theoretical constructions of this sort can be useful in social science, for instance, in modeling. But there is no sense in which this theoretical necessity governs what actually occurs.[11] What governs actions are the rules, resources, and other action-governing factors that give possibilities to and otherwise determine specifically what people do.

We must now focus on the (Giddens's) claim that rules and resources govern action. Structure, according to Giddens, has three dimensions: signification, legitimation, and domination. For our purposes, this means that rules and resources are found in these three dimensions. More specifically, rules are found in the first two dimensions, as codes and typifications and as norms (rights and obligations) respectively, while resources are found in the realm of domination. There are, moreover, two categories of resources: allocative resources, which are capacity-engendering commands over objects (e.g., coins, raw materials, instruments of production), and authoritative resources, which are capacity-engendering commands over persons, more specifically, over the organization of activities, the placement of individuals within those activities, and people's opportunities for acquiring aptitudes and competences (see *CS* 258–63).

Giddens fails, however, to acknowledge a crucial difference between rules and resources. While the governing power of rules is, so to speak, a primitive, irreducible phenomenon, the governing power of resources depends on that of rules and other entities. For a resource, most crucially, the possession of command over objects or persons, depends intrinsically on other phenomena, for instance, behavioral norms, the threat of physical violence, and emotional ties between people. It is not merely the case, as Giddens writes, that resources are *mobilized* only in conjunction with codes and norms (*CP* 104, cf. 107) or that the constraining aspects of asymmetrical distributions of resources (power relations) are *experienced* as sanctions (*CS* 175). Rather, a resource is nothing apart from codes, norms, and sanctions among other phenomena (cf., interestingly, *CS* xxxii, 33). It is simply a label for a particular open-ended bundle of other action-governing phenomena. So the governing power that Giddens ascribes to resources actually arises from such bundles. That is, the possibilities opened up to a person by her having control over these coins, these production apparatuses, these organizations of activities, and the like are in fact opened up by the norms, sanctions, emotional ties, threats, etc., that pertain to these entities or to the persons connected with them. Giddens seems to realize something analogous to my point when he writes that structural constraints do not operate independently of actors' motives and reasons (*CS* 181). I assume he means that what possibilities rules and resources open up is not independent of motives and reasons (cf. *CS* 309). He fails, however, to transform this realization into a general insight concerning the governing power of resources.

This is a crucial oversight because resources can be elements of structures of the governing sort promoted by the new structuralists only if they govern action. Since their governing power is nothing but that of other phenomena, however, they do not perform this function. So they cannot be components of structure. Moreover, since their governing power is that of rules, among other phenomena, Giddens's claim, that structures govern action, resolves into the claim that rules govern action. So our examination of his notion of structure must focus squarely on his concept of rules.

Giddens claims (1) that the practical knowledge generally underlying action is knowledge of how to go on, and (2) that the latter knowledge can be analyzed as knowing a rule (*CP* 67; *CS* 21; knowing a rule does not entail being able to formulate it). All actions, consequently, are rule-governed. By 'rules', however, Giddens does not mean formulated codes and norms. Rules are essentially unformulated; a formulation is an *interpretation* of a rule (*CS* 23). When, accordingly, he writes that actors "draw on" rules, he does not mean that they consciously or nonconsciously observe already formulated rules. Rather, he means that their actions are governed by a "tacit" (*CS* xxiii, 22) grasp of unformulated codes and norms. Since this tacit grasp of rules determines how people act, it also gives rise to the continuities and patterning of their interactions over space and time. Rules, as a result, are "recursively implicated" in and extractable from practices.

Giddens highlights the important fact that people continually rely on their knowledge of how to go on. As I will now explain, however, he errs in equating knowing how to go on with knowing a rule. He is mistaken, consequently, in claiming that rules underlie the continuity and patterning of practices. The succeeding criticism applies *mutatis mutandis* to any conception of social structure as rules to the extent that the rules in question are unformulated.

Wittgenstein developed strong reasons for thinking that understanding a concept is not equivalent to understanding a rule. No set of rules (in Giddens's language, of "interpretations" of rules), formulated either by an actor or by an observer on the basis of a finite number of uses of a concept, will be able *pre facto* to cover all possible acceptable uses. Moreover, there are indefinitely many rules (interpretations) that adequately capture any finite number of uses.[12] It follows that the uses are no more in accordance with any one than another of these rules;[13] on Giddens's way of thinking, no one of these interpretations is truer or more accurate than the others. Hence, if there are any rules underlying the use of a concept, it is impossible to *state* (accurately interpret) them. Why, then, should he believe that people, in using a concept, follow an unformulated rule? Wittgenstein did not believe that such rules exist. For him, understanding a concept is simply being able to go on speaking and acting in ways intelligible to others. If he is right, then the continuity of and patterns formed by the use of concepts must not be explained as the application of rules (except, of course, where explicitly formulated rules are at work). Even if he is wrong, this sort of explanation remains worthless because, since it is not possible to state the relevant rules, it is not possible to formulate specific (true) explanations of this form.

I believe that similar remarks apply to actions *überhaupt*. The ability to go on that underlies behavior should not be treated as knowledge of rules. For there are no specifiable rules (interpretations of rules) capable of covering all the things people do on the basis of their know-how that are continuations of ongoing activities, consistent with past practices, and intelligible to others. Moreover, an indefinite number of rules can adequately capture the continuity and patterning displayed by any finite collection of such actions. Giddens errs, consequently, in assuming that it is possible to state the rules he claims underlie practices. In the face of this impossibility, moreover, he needs but fails to provide evidence that actions nonetheless are governed by a tacit grasp of unformulated rules. In any case, we have seen that it is futile to want to explain behavior in this way.

Social science is impossible to the extent, which for Giddens is great, that it rests upon the identification of the unformulated rules governing human behavior. It would be overhasty, however, to call for the cessation of social investigation. We should abandon instead the ideas that knowledge of unformulated rules governs action, that unformulated rules organize the patterning and continuity of practices, and that social structures consist consequently of rules of this sort. Notice that if we accept this chain of conclusions, it also follows that the possibilities opened up by resources cannot arise, even in part, from rules.

Hence, social structures, as Giddens and Bhaskar analyze them, do not govern action. Bhaskar's social mechanisms have no governing connection with actual activity; since the resources with which Giddens analyzes structure and Bhaskar social relations lack their own governing power, they fail to qualify as elements of structures of the governing sort; and the rules which form the ultimate basis of Giddens's structures and Bhaskar's systems of social relations do not exist. If, consequently, there are social structures that govern by making actions possible, they consist of phenomena other than rules and resources.

The possibilities open to a person are what it is possible for him to do given (a) the range of actions he might perform, (b) the range of actions that others might perform, and (c) a collection of other factors: the physical and communications connections that exist between settings, people's practical skills, the properties and possible uses of physical, man-made or natural objects/processes, biological facts, and space-time packing constraints.[14] Furthermore, since what a person does on any occasion is determined by a set of factors of various types (moods, emotions, known states of affairs, ends, projects, ideas, explicitly formulated rules, paradigms, and customs), the range of actions that a person might perform is delimited by the range of sets of factors that can determine his behavior. This latter collection is in turn circumscribed by the breadth of action-governing factors with which he is familiar. Consequently, a person's possibilities are delimited by the range of factors with which he and others are familiar together with the items listed under (c).

Notice that the range of possibilities open to someone is wider than the gamut of possibilities that Giddens and Bhaskar believe social structures open to people. Only if one assumes, e.g., on the presumption of rationality, that specific ends, ideas, states of affairs, and so on are sure to determine what people in certain circumstances do, does then totality of possibilities open to someone approximate the dimensions the new structuralists envision. Notice, too, that what centrally opens up people's possibilities are the totalities of action-governing factors with which they are familiar. So, to draw one last implication, because the variety of social phenomena determines the range of factors with which people can be familiar, it is ultimately the variety of social phenomena that centrally opens up possibilities to people.

III. CONCLUSION

Social life does contain structures of the governing type advocated by the new structuralists. They are composed, however, of phenomena other than rules and resources. Of course, social reality also contains structures that instantiate the traditional conception of structure. A comprehensive account of social structure must analyze structures of both sorts. Now, there is hardly space in this essay to develop my own account of social structure. To conclude, I will simply list the key features of my position:

(1) In addition to the structured totalities of action-governing factors that determine individual actions, a second type of action-governing structure is intensional orders composed of the related, coordinated, and mutually implicating contents of the factors governing different people's actions. This order is a network of interrelated permissions, restrictions, instructions, schemes of identification, procedures, and the like which inform how people comprehend and act toward entities in the world. Kinship structure is an example. To the great extent that people have knowledge of individual factors, the elements of structure, as Giddens contents, are embodied in knowledge. As Giddens also maintains, however, intensional orders (sets of rules and resources on his account) are not themselves embodied in knowledge. Being sets of knowledge-embodied items, they live a "virtual" abstract existence.

(2) The only other structures in social reality are those constructed by social scientists through the application of logical, typological, and mathematical operations to concrete social reality. There are many subtypes of constructed structures, including patterns of logical constructions, patterns of types, and statistical distributions. Examples are, respectively, the role structures of institutions, many of Levi-Strauss's matrix descriptions of social phenomena, and employment rates. Since these structures are scientific constructions, they are rarely present in actors' knowledge.

(3) While totalities of factors govern action by determining what people do, the larger systems of factors with which people are familiar govern action by

helping to open up possibilities. The latter is also true of intensional orders formed by the contents of action-governing factors. Here, consequently, lies the truth in the claim that structures govern action. *Vis-à-vis* intensional orders, moreover, the new structuralists are further correct that actions and practices reproduce structures. The same cannot be said, however, about action-governing totalities since such totalities do not usually predate the actions they govern.

(4) Constructed structures often are patterns and in all cases are based on patterns. They are, moreover, merely the upshot of action and of what determines it. They do not, as a result, govern action in either the determining or making possible sense of governing. Herein, consequently, lies the truth of the traditional conception of structure.

(5) Finally, structures of all the above types can govern action in at least one way neglected by the new structuralists. When a person possesses knowledge of structures (typically through the work of social science, though action-governing totalities and intensional orders are often at least partly known to people in everyday life), structures can govern her behavior either as items to which she reacts or as items in the knowledge of which a particular action makes sense to her to perform. For example, Levi-Strauss's matrix descriptions of kinship structure might govern someone's actions by inducing her to nod in agreement or being that in the knowledge of which it makes sense to her to visit the library and check out Saussure.

NOTES

1. E.g., Anthony Giddens, *The Constitution of Society* (Berkeley, Calif., 1984), 62. References to this book are henceforth given as *CS*. See also Roy Bhaskar, *The Possibility of Naturalism* (Atlantic Highlands, N.J., 1979), 39–47. References to this book are hereafter given as *PN*.

2. For a detailed critical analysis of his ideas, see Theodore R. Schatzki, "Overdue Analysis of Bourdieu's Theory of Practice," *Inquiry* 30 (1987): 113–35.

3. Roy Bhaskar, *Scientific Realism and Human Emancipation* (London, 1986), 176. References to this book are henceforth indicated by *SRHE*.

4. Roy Bhaskar, *A Realist Theory of Science* (Atlantic Highlands, N.J., 1977). See especially the postscript to the second edition.

5. Andrew Sayer, "Explanation in Economic Geography," *Progress in Human Geography* 6, no. 1 (1982): 71. If it is believed that the "in order to survive" clause disqualifies this statement as a law of the above described sort, the statement can be rewritten as: "the competitive structure of capitalist production is such that enduring firms maintain steadily increasing output per unit of labour costs." So rewritten, the law is of the same form as Bhaskar's example of a social law: in a capitalist economy, rates of profit on enterprises [i.e., surviving enterprises] tend to equalize (*PN* 68). For an analysis of the latter law along the lines here discussed, see Andrew Sayer, *Method in Social Science: A Realist Approach* (London, 1984), 100.

6. Sayer, "Explanation in Economic Geography," 71–72.

7. In *CS,* Giddens describes rules as techniques or generalized procedures about what to do (e.g., 21). I am unsure whether this formulation analyzes codes, modes, and norms or identifies a further type of rule.

8. Anthony Giddens, *Central Problems in Social Theory* (Berkeley, Calif., 1979), 91. References to this work are henceforth indicated in the text by *CP*.

9. It is thus a little misleading for Giddens to claim that the space-time being of structures consists equally of memory traces and of instantiations in practices. For structures are "instantiated," i.e., implicated, in practices only because the rules and resources constituting them are embodied in the knowledge (memory traces) that underlies practices.

10. This interpretation of Giddens tallies with that of Derek Gregory (cf. Derek Gregory, "Solid geometry: notes on the recovery of spatial structure," in *A Search for Common Ground*, edited by Peter Gould and Gunnar Olsson [London, 1982], 208).

11. Giddens writes that the "inevitability" of social forces consists in rational actors having few options (*CS* 178). This claim differs from Bhaskar's since Giddens is talking about options available in the *actual* world, and 'social forces' refers to forces in the actual world, not to real necessities.

12. For discussion, see Michael Rosen, "Critical Theory: Between Ideology and Philosophy," in *The Need for Interpretation,* edited by Sollace Mitchell and Michael Rosen (London, 1983), 90–117.

13. Ludwig Wittgenstein, *The Blue and Brown Books* (Oxford, 1969), 13.

14. On the last, see Törsten Hagerstrand, e.g., "Space, Time, and Human Conditions," in *The Dynamic Allocation of Urban Space,* edited by A. Karlqvist, L. Lundqvist, and F. Snickars (Lexington, Mass., 1975), 3–14.

Group Action and
Act Consequentialism

RICHARD FUMERTON

In this essay I want to explore once again certain familiar objections to act consequentialist analyses of moral and rational action. Specifically, I want to examine the charge that the act consequentialist cannot account for the rightness and/or rationality of certain actions when the consequences of the action are insignificant but where the action can be seen as falling under a rule such that the consequences of people generally following the rule are momentous. The bulk of my discussion will focus on the well-known voter's paradox for I think that it crystallizes the issues in a way that is very useful. But my concern is much broader than any particular objection. More specifically, I want to examine critically the methodological assumptions underlying certain sorts of objections by counterexample to act consequentialism. Although my primary aim is not to argue for any particular act consequentialist analysis of the rightness or rationality of actions, I shall begin by at least sketching the kind of theory I am interested in defending. I do so to call attention to some interesting and overlooked distinctions that an act consequentialist can make; some of which might be used in defending the view against counterexamples.

I

From the above introduction, one might immediately wonder why I am intent on treating questions of morality and rationality together. It is surely difficult enough to discuss either without trying to discuss both simultaneously. As might be expected, however, my reason for discussing questions of morality and rationality together is simply that I think the two are conceptually linked. As others have also argued, it seems to me that one divorces the question of what one morally ought to do from the question of what one has the most reason to do only at the cost of replacing questions of morality with questions of rationality as the most fundamental questions that rational people must answer in deciding what to do.[1] In short, as I have argued elsewhere, I think that at least our first person questions about what we ought to do are univocal.[2] In any event, if one argues successfully that one might not have the most reason to do what one morally ought to do, so much the worse for morality. It is an *analytic* truth that rational people do what they rationally believe they have the most reason to do. And that makes questions about what they have the most reason to do the most fundamental questions involved in making decisions. We shall focus, then, on the question of how to understand the concept of reasons for acting.

An act consequentialist thinks that reasons for acting are ultimately to be understood in terms of some fact about the consequences of particular actions, or at least in terms of some fact about rational *belief* about the consequences of particular actions. One way of distinguishing different versions of act consequentialism is by reference to whether it is *actual, probable,* or *possible* consequences that define what one has reason to do. Another is by reference to what makes a consequence of an action *relevant.* With respect to this latter question, fundamental rifts develop among philosophers. If we understand by "objective" property, a property whose presence or absence is not defined in terms of some subjective (i.e., intentional) state of a subject, it has always seemed obvious to me that it is not some objective property of the consequence of some action that makes it relevant. On the relativistic view I defend, the fact that some action X might lead to Y gives *me* a reason to pursue X only if I take an interest in Y, only if I value Y. The fact that X might lead to Y can give me a reason to pursue X even though if another person were placed in a similar situation she might have no reason to do X. We can say that something Y is a goal or end for someone S if S values Y for itself. The fact that one intrinsically values Y is neither rational nor irrational (intrinsically). It is one's goals or ends that give one reasons to act. The court of goals is the ultimate appeal on all questions of rationality. One can, of course, raise the question of whether it might be rational to alter one's goals or rid oneself of certain goals, but even this question must be taken to that court on which *all* goals preside, including the goal in danger of being impeached. This is no doubt an extreme, albeit familiar view. It has been attacked both by philosophers sympathetic to the general framework which I defend and by objectivists in value theory who would claim that it is only the objective goodness of something that can make something I value something that is rational for me to value.[3] I have argued against those views elsewhere and I will not try to repeat those arguments here.[4]

How precisely do my goals or ends relate to the concept of what I have a reason to do and ultimately to the concept of what I have the most reason to do? One can understand the relationship between goals or ends and reasons for acting in a number of ways. Perhaps the most straightforward suggestion is the following:

(D1) S has a reason to do X when X has as either a logical or nomological consequence some Y which is an end for S (where we can treat X as a logical consequence of itself and thus allow that X itself being an end for S can give S a reason to do it).

I believe this concept of reason does exist and occasionally finds expression in ordinary discourse. I am also convinced that one needs to recognize more sophisticated concepts of reasons for acting in order to capture a plausible conception of justificatory reasons. In the sense of reason captured by (D1) one can have reasons to do X even when one has no reason to believe that those reasons exist. If the medical researchers have miscalculated once again, for example, and it turns out that high salt intake *prevents* high blood pressure then according to (D1) (and obvious assumptions about my goals) I have a reason to maintain high consumption of salt. But there is surely a sense in which as long as I have every reason to believe that high salt intake is bad for my health I have a reason to avoid high salt intake. Indeed, if we want reasons for acting to be action guiding we must surely tie the concept of reasons for acting to an epistemic perspective. We might then modify (D1) as follows:

(D2) S has a reason to do X when it is *probable* relative to S's evidence that X will have as either a logical or nomological consequence some Y which is an end for S.

Once we decide to make the concept of reasons for acting sensitive to epistemic perspective, it is obvious that (D2) is too restrictive. It seems clear that I can have a reason for doing X even if I justifiably believe that X will frustrate all of my goals or ends. To use a familiar example, if I have the opportunity of entering a lottery for \$1 when the odds against winning are only ten to one and the prize is \$1,000,000, it is surely true that I have a rather powerful reason to enter the lottery (again making obvious assumptions about my goals). And this is true despite the fact that it is quite likely relative to my evidence that nothing I value will come from my action. In fact it is likely that I will be out the dollar (something we may presume I disvalue). The obvious conclusion to infer is that the mere *possibility* of satisfying some goal or end by acting in a certain way gives one at least some reason to act in that way:

(D3) S has a reason to do X when relative to S's evidence it might be the case that S has as either a logical or causal consequence some Y which is an end for S.

The *strength* of this reason is clearly a function of how likely this possible consequence is. The less likely the possible consequence, the weaker the reason. In the case of extremely unlikely possible consequences the reason will become vanishingly small unless the value attached to the possible consequence is enormous.

There are still other concepts of reasons for acting that can be defined in terms of an agent's mere *beliefs* (justified or not) about the consequences of acting. Thus we could say that S has a reason to do X when S believes that X will satisfy some end. This "subjective" conception of reasons, however, seems to be irrelevant to understanding the justificatory concept of rational action. The epistemic irrationality of a belief, the epistemic *defect* of a belief, seems clearly to affect the rationality of an action based on that belief. In the sense of rational action relevant to agents interested in guiding their lives by their conclusions about what is rational to do, it seems clear that one cannot discover what one has reason to do merely through introspection. We want to understand justificatory reasons for acting in such a way that we can understand how one can easily be confused about what one has a reason to do, how one can easily make mistakes about what one has a reason to do. But if reasons for acting are defined in terms of mere beliefs (justified or not) about consequences it seems that discovering what one has a reason to do would be no more difficult than introspecting.

These three concepts of having *a* reason to act can be used to define corresponding concepts of rational action. What is rational to do, all things being considered, is a function of what one has the *most* reason to do. Corresponding to (D1), we will have a concept of rational action defined in terms of the sum of the value of the consequences that would actually be produced by each alternative compared to the others. Corresponding to (D2), we will have a concept of rational action defined in terms of the sum of the value of the consequences that would probably be produced by each alternative compared to the others. While there is a concept of rational action defined in terms of actual consequences that finds expression in ordinary discourse, I have argued elsewhere that it is not primary and that it is the concept of rational action corresponding to the concept of reasons defined by (D3) that is fundamental.[5] For that reason I focus on it. The *initial* account of rational action suggested is a version of the view that rational action is action that maximizes expected utility. In other places I have also referred to it as value-adjusted possible consequence consequentialism to mark off the specific version of the view I defend, a version which, as I noted earlier, stresses the importance of viewing the concept of practical rationality as parasitic upon the concept of epistemic rationality. The account presupposes that I can intrinsically value one thing more than another and that this allows me to rank on an open-ended scale the value and disvalue attached to possible consequences. We can then define rational action as follows:

(R)   *S*'s action is rational when *S* has more reason to choose *X* over any of its alternatives; *S* has more reason to choose *X* over its alternatives when the collective weight of *S*'s ends that might (relative to *S*'s evidence) be satisfied by *X*, when the value of each end is adjusted for the probability (relative to *S*'s evidence) of its occurring, is greater than the collective weight of the ends calculated in a similar fashion that might (relative to *S*'s evidence) be satisfied by any of the alternatives to *X*.

The above account is intended to be an account only of what it is for there to be more reason for *S* to do *X* than anything else. It is not intended to be an account of acting rationally where that is understood as acting *with* or *for* reasons. As I use this term, an agent may have more reason to choose *X* than anything else but do *X* for completely irrational reasons. Perhaps he does *X because* his astrologer informs him that this is the right time of the year to do X-like things. In such a situation we can reasonably conclude that the agent is acting irrationally even if that agent does what he has the most reason to do in the sense defined by (R). We could say that an agent acts rationally only when the action results from the agent's awareness that his action is rational but, as we shall see, this will need to be modified slightly.

I have argued elsewhere that (R) captures a fundamental concept of rational action, a concept that identifies the intentional object of a rational agent's deliberations in calculating what he ought to do. I have also argued, however, that there are a number of important and overlooked derivative concepts of rational action. Suppose, for example, that it is false that X is rational for S in the sense defined by (R) but that S has an epistemically justified belief that X is rational in the sense defined by (R). Has S more reason to do X than anything else or not? It seems to me that there is a clear sense in which we might allow that for such an agent X is the rational thing to do. Notice that if we take this to be a defect of (R), it will almost certainly be a defect of *any* analysis of rational action. No matter how we define rational action, we must allow the possibility that an agent can have epistemic reasons to believe that his action is rational in that sense even though it is not. The solution, it seems to me is to allow a derivative "second-level" concept of rational action:

(Rd1a) S has more reason to choose X over any of its alternatives   =Df S is justified in believing that in the sense defined by (R), he has more reason to do X than anything else.

Of course our reasons for allowing this derivative concept of rational action would presumably also suggest that there is a sense (Rd1b) in which it is rational for a person to do X if that person has a justified but false belief that his action is rational in the sense defined by (Rd1a)! And there is nothing to prevent us from allowing infinitely many derivative concepts of rational action defined in terms of justified beliefs about one's action satisfying lower-level conditions of rationality. But this is only one (non-vicious) regress of derivative concepts of rational action.

It is entirely possible to find oneself in a situation where one is faced with alternatives, say X, Y, and Z, and one's evidence indicates that X has the *best chance* of being rational in the sense defined by (R) even though it is not likely relative to one's evidence that it is rational in that sense. It may be that one is able to consider only relatively few consequences of the alternatives but that relative to such consideration X has developed an "early lead" in terms of valued-adjusted possible consequences. Nevertheless one realizes that the evidence is so slight that it is still more likely that either Y or Z will eventually win out. In such a situation, if one is forced to choose among the three alternatives, there is surely a sense in which one is acting rationally by choosing X. We can, then, recognize the following derivative concept of rational action:

(Rd2a) S has more reason to $=$Df S is justified in believing that
choose X over its alterna-   of the alternatives X has the
tives   best chance of being rational
                                      in the sense defined by (R).

And as was the case with the (Rd1) series of derivative concepts of rational
action, we can again recognize indefinitely many levels of concepts of rational
action in a (Rd2) series. Thus there is a sense in which we might say that X is the
rational thing for S to do by virtue of the fact that X has the best chance of being
rational in the sense defined by (Rd2a), and so on. Furthermore, we can easily
see that it is possible to "mix and match" concepts of rational action employing
both the (Rd1) and (Rd2) series of derivative concepts of rational action. We can
recognize, for example, a sense in which X is rational for S by virtue of its
having the best chance of being rational in the sense defined by (Rd1b) or by
virtue of S justifiably believing that X is rational in the sense defined by (Rd2a).

Earlier I distinguished X's being rational for S and S's acting rationally.
When we had developed only our primary concept of rational action (R), I
suggested that we might say that S acts rationally when his action is caused by
his awareness of his action's being rational in the sense defined by (R). We can
now see that we might equally well have said that S is acting rationally when his
action is caused by his having reason to do X in the sense defined by (Rd1a). But
having recognized a byzantine structure of derivative concepts of rational
action, we can now allow as many different concepts of acting rationally as we
have concepts of rational action. Whenever we recognize a sense in which S has
reasons for acting we can recognize a corresponding sense in which S acts for
those reasons by acting out of an awareness of his having those reasons. Reflection should indicate that this will always be equivalent to S's action being produced by the fact that he has reasons for acting in one of the derivative senses
recognized above.

I have spent so much time developing a specific act consequentialist
approach to understanding rational action because I think it is important to recognize the complexities and subtleties introduced by the availability of derivative concepts in responding to objections to act consequentialism. Let us turn
now to some of these objections.

II

By far the most common objections to act consequentialist accounts of morality
and rationality are arguments by counterexample. Although the kind of objection we are about to consider is still most familiar in a discussion of morality, it
must be taken to have equal force against act consequentialist accounts of
rational action if we recognize that the significance of morality rests on our
ability conceptually to tie moral action to rational action. The class of counterexamples I am most interested in here involves hypothetical situations in
which an individual action is rational by act consequentialist standards even

though if everyone acts "rationally" the results will be disastrous (everyone's goals will be frustrated). In such a situation, the critic says, it is obvious that act consequentialism has implausible and unacceptable consequences.

Not all counterexamples to act consequentialism explicitly involve behavior which if practiced by groups would be destructive. Harman, for example, argues that an act consequentialist cannot explain why a doctor should not carve up one relatively healthy patient to save the lives of several important people in need of assorted vital organs.[6] But even here one can certainly argue that it is our concern about a general *practice* rather than an isolated incident that is the source of our intuition.

Standard objections to act consequentialism that explicitly trade on situations in which general practice of a certain sort of behavior has bad consequences include the claims that an act consequentialist cannot account for the obvious immorality and/or irrationality of littering, breaking promises, cheating on taxes, cutting across the grass rather than staying on the sidewalk, or ignoring various civil responsibilities. Perhaps the most striking example that illustrates the alleged difficulty for act consequentialism is the example of voting. We all *know* that we ought to vote, particularly in important national elections. Voting is both moral and rational. But it is notoriously difficult for an act consequentialist to accommodate this conviction. It seems obvious that my single vote's consequences get "lost" in a sea of votes cast by conscientious voters. Assuming that it takes some unpleasant effort to vote, it is difficult to see why rational people will engage in the ritual knowing that there is virtually no realistic chance of their votes making a difference to either the outcome or the "health" of the election.[7]

Before examining the objection in more detail, let us make some general observations about its structure and the kinds of replies available to argument by counterexample.

It is not implausible to maintain that from Plato to the present, argument by counterexample or *reductio ad absurdum* is one of the cornerstones of Western analytic philosophy. It is one of the few genuinely effective ways of getting philosophers to abandon even well-entrenched philosophical positions. Almost all of us have had the unpleasant experience of having another philosopher exhibit for us some unforeseen and unacceptable consequence of a position we are maintaining.

Argument by counterexample, of course, takes the form of *modus tollens*. The critic first asserts of the view being attacked that if it is true a certain consequence follows. The second premise asserts that the consequent of the conditional is false. *Modus tollens* becomes argument by counterexample when the falsity of the consequent is something that is supposed to be "obvious," i.e., part of the prephilosophical "data" which any plausible philosophical view must accommodate.

Given the structure of the argument, it seems obvious that there are at least two kinds of responses available to philosophers under attack by counterexamples. The first is to deny that their view has the alleged consequence. The second is to deny that the consequence is false. For example, many philosophers today will reject a philosophical account of perception and its relation to the physical world if it follows from that account that we cannot know or even justifiably believe that physical objects exist. Representative realism leads to skepticism, some would argue, and skepticism is absurd. Representative realism, therefore, is absurd. Most representative realists try to defend their view by denying that it leads to radical skepticism (the first kind of response to *a reductio*), but a few philosophers will grimly embrace both representative realism and skepticism, rejecting the charge that skepticism is an absurd and obviously false position.

Of the two standard responses to argument by counterexample, the first is relatively unproblematic in structure. The second raises a number of methodological questions. On the one hand it hardly seems worthwhile doing philosophy if one must enslave one's philosophical views to the dictates of *prephilosophical* beliefs about what is and is not absurd. On the other hand, if one is trying to illuminate *our* conceptual framework, it seems that we must allow that there is a process of discovery that involves *testing* proposed philosophical analyses by appeal to something like relatively stable dispositions to regard situations as correctly described in certain ways, dispositions that one can find without reference to one's philosophical view and through which one can test one's philosophical view. I have tried to describe these dispositions and the way in which they are relevant to the adequacy of philosophical analyses elsewhere.[8] For our present purposes, I want only to stress that one ignores argument by counterexample at the risk of casting adrift philosophical analyses from the only moorings they have. I do think that once one agrees that one's conceptual analysis has a consequence most people take to be absurd one has a responsibility minimally to explain why people might find this consequence of the view absurd even when the view is supposed to accurately reflect their conceptual framework. But enough abstract discussion. Let us return to the use of argument by counterexample against act consequentialism.

III

When faced with the counterexamples discussed earlier, proponents of act consequentialism have used both kinds of response distinguished above. At least some act consequentialists deny that their views do sanction the morality/rationality of such intuitively immoral/irrational actions as killing one innocent to save three, of breaking promises for relatively minor gain, of ignoring one's civil responsibilities come election day. Others admit that their views have these surprising consequences but regard them as truths to which the majority of people are simply blind—they refuse to be cowed by the fact that their act consequentialism might outrage conventional morality/rationality. Let us examine each response in more detail and let us begin by examining attempts to reconcile act consequentialism with the dictates of conventional views about morality and rationality.

Is it true that act consequentialism does sanction the rationality of violating certain dictates of conventional morality, particularly of allowing an individual to act in a kind of way which would result in disaster were everyone to behave in a similar fashion? Certainly, if one embraces the relativistic conception of act consequentialism I sketched earlier, where the relevant consequences of an action are those that the agent intrinsically values, one would be hard pressed to identify *any* prephilosophical "intuitions" that the act consequentialist cannot in principle accommodate.

If one is a Humean about what one can intrinsically value or disvalue, then there is nothing to preclude the possibility of intrinsically valuing *anything*. One can, for example, intrinsically value telling the truth, refusing to kill innocents even when inaction results in many more deaths, or even participating in an electoral process. Moreover there are no *a priori* restrictions on the amount one can value or disvalue such things. In short, it seems that an act consequentialist can "juggle" the numbers representing the values of possible outcomes in any way he pleases so that the view together with these facts of human nature entails the rationality of actions prephilosophically regarded as rational. You don't like sacrificing freedom for material well-being? Jack up the value you attach to freedom. You want to keep your promise to Aunt Mary even though it means losing half the world's population? Just make sure you value keeping a promise strongly enough. In trying to accommodate our prephilosophical conviction that it is rational to join groups acting in certain ways even when one's contribution to the group's accomplishment is insignificant, we can even speculate that at least some of the relevant values we will need to posit are there as a result of evolutionary programming. Perhaps we just like being part of a group when the group's actions have certain consequences that we like.

Now while formally possible, this approach to reconciling act consequentialist views and "commonsense" intuitions can easily become strained if it is not combined with a realistic and plausible view of human nature. Let us focus on the question of voting. Is it true that we intrinsically value participating in the electoral process? Speaking for myself the suggestion strikes me as almost bizarre. And I would say the same thing about telling the truth and keeping promises. It is, however, far more plausible to suggest that people either get pleasure from participating in the electoral process (telling the truth, keeping promises, etc.) or feel pain in the form of guilt when they do not, and for well over two thousand years pleasure and pain have been leading contenders for states that people value and disvalue intrinsically. The explanation for the occurrence of feelings of guilt is, of course, relatively straightforward. Most of us have been raised on conventional morality and have been effectively conditioned to flinch at least when we violate its dictates. Come election time we are inundated with praise for voters and disdain for those who refuse to participate in the electoral process, and it is not particularly surprising given human nature that we would rather be the subject of praise than disdain. In short, the fact that we have been conditioned to respond to our violation of conventional morality the way we do gives us act consequentialist reasons to abide by those conventions.

There are, however, two difficulties with this attempt to disarm arguments by counterexample by reconciling act consequentialism with the dictates of conventional morality concerning social responsibility. The most obvious is that it still leaves unexplained the *origin* of conventional morality and its widespread acceptance. Theoretically, one can easily account for the existence of propaganda concerning civil responsibilities if one adopts a Thrasymachian conspiracy theory concerning those in power. It has been observed by many that consistency does not require that act consequentialists preach act consequentialism. Parents may well have very good act consequentialist reasons to condition their children to believe in some false view about what makes acts right. Children are notoriously poor at evaluating consequences and may well be better off acting as implicit rule utilitarians. We do not tell young children that it is *usually* wrong to lie. We tell them instead that they should always tell the truth. Particularly in their dealings with us, we do not want them to think as act consequentialists. Similarly, if I were a politician running for office, I do not think I would spend a lot of time emphasizing the extreme improbability of a single vote affecting the outcome of an election. I would probably do everything I could to condition people to feel very guilty if they did not support me with their votes, and *I* would have good act consequentialist reasons for engaging in this conditioning process, a conditioning process that might very well affect the outcome of an election.

Having said this, however, one cannot help but feel that there is something a little too Machiavellian about the explanation. People in power are almost certainly *not* act consequentialists surreptitiously trying to foist false theories of morality and rationality on the populace. Most people in power are already committed to, and in some sense genuinely accept, the conventions of morality that they also recommend to others. Of course, one could assume that they were themselves conditioned to accept conventional morality just as we were, but that simply pushes back again the question of how all this conditioning got started and one will still need to posit some act consequentialist in power who recognized that the good of society required that people be convinced of certain falsehoods.

The second obvious problem with the above attempt to reconcile act consequentialism and conventional wisdom about the morality and rationality of accepting one's social obligations is the obvious fact that people do not *cite* pleasure and guilt as relevant considerations in their calculations about what they ought to do. People who are convinced that they ought to vote have not the slightest inclination to identify the enjoyment they get from voting or the guilt they would feel from not voting as their reasons for voting. Indeed, they would probably feel that someone who acted for those reasons was acting for ignoble reasons, i.e., had not fully realized the importance of voting for the moral/ rational person. An act consequentialist who wants to accommodate conventional wisdom concerning voting has to show not only that there can be act consequentialist reasons for voting but that those reasons have nothing to do with such trivial considerations as pleasure and guilt that voters might get from participating in the electoral process.

We discussed earlier the existence of widespread efforts to condition people to accept the dictates of conventional morality/rationality concerning such social activities as voting and admitted that by itself this would seem to leave the act consequentialist without any obvious explanation for the origin of efforts at such conditioning. This admission, however, should not overshadow the extent to which such facts are grist for the act consequentialist's mill. Recall that in developing a sketch of an act consequentialist view I emphasized the importance of recognizing derivative concepts of rational action. Specifically, I suggested that we should allow a sense in which an action can be rational for a person by virtue of the fact that the person has a justified belief that the action is rational. Now one might certainly argue that the dictates of authority figures on social responsibilities give ordinary non-philosophical people epistemic reason to believe that these actions *are* moral/rational. To be sure appeal to authority is usually included in a list of the informal fallacies, but we must surely admit that a good many of our commonplace beliefs about the world are based on nothing other than the word of people we trust. If we can legitimately defer to authorities in other fields, it is not clear why we should not be able to do so in matters concerning the morality or rationality of certain sorts of actions. And it is further not implausible to suggest that the existence of widespread "propaganda" concerning the morality or wisdom of living up to the dictates of conventional morality gives ordinary people a good epistemic reason to suppose that these actions really are moral/rational. But if this is so then those actions *are* moral/rational for those people in the derivative sense we recognized.

Again we must emphasize that this hardly gets the act consequentialist off the hook for we are still in need of an explanation of why there exists the widespread support on the part of authority figures for the dictates of conventional morality (even when conventional morality *seems* to run afoul of act consequentialist criteria for moral/rational action). And we have yet to find any more plausible explanation for this than the Machiavellian conception of act consequentialist rulers out to deceive (for good act consequentialist reasons) the unwitting public.

There are, of course, more straightforward attempts to reconcile act consequentialism with conventional wisdom concerning the morality or rationality of living up to social and political responsibilities. I have basically left unchallenged the claim that in various sorts of situations an act consequentialist cannot find plausible act consequentialist reasons for refraining from littering, for keeping promises, and particularly for voting. In chapter 3 of *Reasons and Persons*, Derek Parfit warns against certain mistakes of "moral mathematics" that people can easily make. I think a careful reading will indicate that some of these alleged "mistakes" essentially involve making decisions as act consequentialists. This kind of mistake is usually illustrated through counterexample and it is just this sort of argument that we are here examining.

In other places, however, Parfit warns against making mistakes even within a purely act consequentialist conception of moral/rational action. One such mistake is ignoring very small probabilities. Parfit points out that in the case of voting the "experts" put the odds of affecting the outcome of a national election at only(!) a hundred million to one *if* the voter lives in a populous state with a great many electoral votes and *if* the election is close. Now as value-adjusted *possible* consequence consequentialists, we would not only admit but insist that in calculating the rational course of action one must take into account even very remote possibilities. And *if* you care very much who wins the election, particularly, if you think the fate of the world hinges on the outcome, I suppose you might think that the possible effect of your vote remains significant even after taking only one one-millionth of its value. Of course this presupposition is rarely satisfied. Speaking for myself it is rarely clear to me that one candidate rather than the other in a presidential election will make things significantly better for many Americans. That is not to say I do not have views as to who would improve matters the most, but I am not foolish enough to suppose that there is any great likelihood of my views being correct. As one factors in *these* probabilities, the adjusted value assigned to the possible consequence of winning the election for a chosen candidate starts dipping back down towards zero. Meanwhile, of course, one must take into account other equally remote possible outcomes of voting. If one must drive a fair distance through traffic to the polls, I suspect there is at least an equal chance of killing oneself or some other very nice person on the way to vote. Furthermore, this solution of Parfit's to the voter's paradox is hardly going to make the residents of Wyoming happy. I am sure they wanted to think that they had just as much reason to vote as the Californian and that that reason was a *powerful* reason—not the kind of reason that might just barely survive the diminishing value of the extremely unlikely consequence of affecting the outcome of the election.

Before leaving this suggestion, I might point out that the attempt to identify relatively unlikely but possible and important relevant consequences of actions that might help act consequentialists reconcile their view with conventional morality fares much better with at least some other examples. Certainly in the case of littering, for instance, it simply is not true that a tiny bit of litter is extremely unlikely to produce any relevant consequences. Anyone with an ounce of aesthetic sensibility can say how truly ugly human handiwork can be intruding on the beauty of nature. And if one has any altruistic values or one is an empathetic egoist, one will have a reason not to create in others this kind of aesthetic suffering. Still other counterexamples to act consequentialism posit hypothetical situations in which the agent "knows" that his violation of law or conventions will remain undiscovered. But healthy skepticism requires us to recognize that we are virtually never in a position to rule out the possibility of discovery. As long as there are possible (if unlikely) punishments we need to fear (punishments that others may have good act consequentialist reason to inflict) we might well have enough act consequentialist reason to refrain from acting in ways that might otherwise be perfectly rational.

So far we have been considering attempts by the act consequentialist to deny that act consequentialism is at odds with commonsense, conventional views about what is rational or moral, particularly in situations where an individual action seems to have few if any relevant consequences but where a group acting in the same way can make a huge difference. But let us finally turn to the act consequentialist who tires of attempts at reconciling act consequentialism with conventional views about the morality or rationality of certain actions but who wants to argue that the act consequentialist has correctly identified our concept of right/rational action despite these genuine conflicts. Again, let us focus on the case of voting, for it is certainly as difficult a case as any for the act consequentialist.

I am myself convinced that act consequentialism is correct and I am also convinced that unless one takes pleasure form voting (the way, for example, one might take pleasure from throwing darts at a picture of a hated politician), or is the victim of conditioning and feels guilt from not voting, or is concerned about the dispraise of others who might discover one's political inaction and revile it, one probably does not have any good reason to vote. Furthermore, despite what I said earlier, I am inclined to think that ordinary people are not simply relying on the wisdom of authority figures in reaching the false conclusion that they have reason to vote. How, then, can I reconcile the conviction people have that they ought to vote with my claim that they implicitly accept act consequentialist conceptions of rational action? The answer I will suggest is one that on the face of it is wildly implausible. My proposal is simply that people do believe, falsely and irrationally, that their single vote makes a difference. If I can make good the claim that people have this belief then that is all I need to do in absolving act consequentialism of any conflict with the ordinary person's firm prephilosophical intuitions. If people vote because they believe their single vote makes a difference or is likely to make a difference, or has a reasonable chance of making a difference, then there is no reason to suppose that they are not making their decision to vote as act consequentialists.

But why should anyone think that people are so misguided as to think that their single vote has a significant chance of affecting the outcome of an election? I call attention to two relatively uncontroversial empirical facts. First, people are more likely to vote in close elections. The most obvious explanation for this fact is that they think their vote is *more* important, i.e., *more* likely to affect the outcome of the election. And of course, it *is* more likely to affect the outcome of the election. But if this is a significant factor in the common person's calculations, that strongly suggests that the common person is making decisions precisely as a value-adjusted possible consequence consequentialist trying to affect the outcome of an election.

The second familiar empirical fact is even more suggestive and concerns the consequences of early projections of national elections on voter turnout. As the networks become more and more adept at projecting the final vote from tiny samples of exit polling it becomes possible for them to predict accurately the final outcome long before the polls close. And this seems to give many people a great deal of concern. The reason cited most often for this concern is that early projections will cause those who have not yet voted to stay at home. Why, the argument goes, should people bother to vote when they already know that their vote will not affect the outcome of the election? Notice that once again the presupposition of all this concern is that people really are approaching the question of whether or not to vote as act consequentialists. The presupposition of the concern is that they are, through their vote, trying to affect the outcome of the election. Now for the life of me *I* cannot understand why it would make any difference to someone if the networks project at nine o'clock in the morning the outcome of the election. It is true I can conclude after such projections that my vote is extremely unlikely to affect the outcome of the election, but, of course, I could have concluded *that* in the absence of any projections. Anyone who votes in a national election anticipating that there is some realistic chance of their vote affecting the outcome of the election is wildly and hopelessly unrealistic. My point, however, is that as long as people are influenced by such factors as early projections, we can reasonably infer that they are making decisions as irrational act consequentialists. And if they are making decisions as act consequentialists we have no reason to abandon an act consequentialist *conception* of rational/ right action.

Since the suggestion that people actually do think of their votes as having a realistic chance of affecting the outcome of an election might strike the reader as so highly implausible, let me conclude by adding some qualifications concerning the nature of the alleged belief that I am attributing to people.

The human mind is extraordinarily complex, particularly when it comes to the nature of belief. Without examining too closely the metaphysics underlying belief, it seems safe to say that there are various levels at which people believe things. There are all kinds of people who seem quite sincerely to believe, or at least sincerely to assert that they believe, that there is an afterlife – indeed, an afterlife far more pleasant than any life here on earth. I suspect, however, that there is at least some sense in which, or some level at which, people do not really believe this. One must certainly wonder why people who really believe in pleasant afterlives cling so desperately to this life.

Consider a more trivial example. It is striking to me that people can become so emotionally involved in a fictional book, play, or film. When a person is moved to tears at the tragic demise of the heroine of a dramatic film there is surely a sense in which, at that time, it is as if the person believed that the tragedy was really taking place. Indeed, I would go so far as to suggest that at the moment the person moved by the film at some level really believes that the scene depicts reality. Of course we must surely recognize that at a deeper level the person realizes that none of these things that so moved him are really happening, that it is all make-believe.

One more example might be particularly useful in trying to understand the phenomenon of voting. Most of us who watch games like football and basketball on television have engaged in the curious practice of shouting encouragement at those images on the screen. When our side attempts the field goal that looks as if it might just make it inside the upright we almost involuntarily apply "body english" in an "effort" to affect the flight of the ball. Do we really believe that our shouts of encouragement or that "body english" will have any effect whatsoever on the performance of the athletes or the flight of the ball? Obviously, at some level the answer is no. Indeed, if we reflect on our behavior we might even be puzzled or embarrassed. But that does not stop us from continuing to behave in these ways. Something similar, I would suggest, may very well be at work when individuals join groups whose behavior brings about certain valued outcomes. The voter, I suspect, is not all that different from the spectator swaying with the flight of the ball. At some level the voter probably does realize, or at least can easily be brought to realize, that a single vote is quite literally insignificant. At a more superficial level, however, I suspect that that voter really does go to the polls hoping with that vote to make a difference. And as long as this is a fact of human psychology we have all we need to diffuse the voter's paradox and related counterexamples to act consequentialism.

Notes

1. Brandt argues convincingly for the need to tie useful concepts of right action to rational action in the first chapter of his book, *A Theory of the Good and the Right* (Oxford, 1979).

2. For a detailed discussion of this issue see chapter 3 of my *Reason and Morality* (Ithaca, N.Y., forthcoming).

3. The former include Brandt in *A Theory of the Good and the Right* and Darwall in *Impartial Reason* (Ithaca, N.Y., 1983). The latter include Butchvarov in *Skepticism in Ethics* (Bloomington, Ind., 1988) and, I would argue, Parfit in *Reasons and Persons* (Oxford, 1984).

4. See again my forthcoming *Reason and Morality*.

5. Again, in *Reason and Morality*.

6. See Harman, *The Nature of Morality* (New York, 1977), 3–4.

7. I am here assuming that the notion of a contributory cause is of no use to a consistent act consequentialist. We can say that my vote contributes to the health of an election meaning that it, along with all the other votes, makes for a healthy election. But as an act consequentialist I must surely concern myself with the *difference* my vote makes taking other things as they are. See Regan's discussion of this issue in *Utilitarianism and Co-operation* (Oxford, 1980), 13.

8. See my "Paradox of Analysis," *Philosophy and Phenomenological Research* (1983): 477–97.

Some Social Benefits
of Uncertainty

GREGORY S. KAVKA

U ncertainty, we normally think, is a bad thing.[1] A small amount may add spice to our lives—we would not want everything to be perfectly predictable. But when important consequences are involved, we want to know the results of various courses of action, so that rational choice is both easier and effective in attaining our ends. This is especially true when we shift our focus from the private sphere to the public. There the consequences of action are typically greater in magnitude and wider in scope. And those who make public policy are generally accountable to those who suffer (or enjoy) the consequences. Hence, decision-makers in the public sphere, as well as the private, are likely to consider uncertainty an implacable foe whose very existence is to be regretted. But this, I shall argue, is a mistake.

Uncertainty, despite its interference within the effective pursuit of our ends, is in important respects a blessing. In a world of individuals, social groups, and sovereign nations, with conflicting aims and interests, it promotes certain vital social benefits—solidarity and stability within nations (especially democratic nations),[2] and relatively peaceful relations among sovereign nations. This does not mean we should cut back efforts to expand our practical knowledge, for these efforts are unlikely to ever reduce uncertainty to the extent necessary to erase its main social benefits. But it suggests a different understanding of the role of uncertainty in the social world, one in which uncertainty is no longer viewed as an unmitigated evil.

1. UNCERTAINTY AND SOCIAL SOLIDARITY

Knowledge of the consequences of the actions available to one allows one to select that action which best promotes one's ends. But different individuals seldom, if ever, have ends which are fully mutually compatible. And in large groups, there are sure to be many significant conflicts of aims and interests among their members. Hence, in many important areas of public policy, any policy selected will, in the end, benefit some while harming others.[3] Suppose the harms were substantial and *were known with certainty ahead of time.* Then the individuals who would suffer them would not, if they had any choice, peacefully accept the policy, unless provided with compensating benefits. And if the harms were non-compensable (such as death, serious disability, or loss of loved ones), these individuals would be strongly inclined to join together forcibly to resist implementation of the policy, even if it were arrived at by fair democratic procedures.

But in the real world, the consequences of policy alternatives within a large group are never known with certainty. Hence policies which will probably provide substantially more overall benefit than harm can be accepted by most all citizens as policies that promote the general welfare. Even those who expect they are more likely than average (or more likely than not) to suffer from the policy will oppose the policy less vehemently than if they were sure they would suffer. And since losses are, at most, probable, potential losers may regard themselves as sufficiently compensated by the benefits provided by other policies.

Uncertainty thus promotes social solidarity in two closely related ways by preventing the most severely affected victims of any social policy from being preidentified. First, it discourages these victims from violently resisting the policy. And, second, it allows citizens to share a sense that "we are all in this together," and a belief that the policies are chosen to promote the general welfare. This would not be possible if policies were forced upon preidentified certain "victims" by preidentified certain "beneficiaries."

These sources of social solidarity are especially important in any political system, such as a democracy, that depends for its sustenance largely on continued public consent rather than physical coercion. Such systems cannot function effectively if enough citizens perceive themselves as victims who do not receive compensating benefits for the risks that public policies expose them to, or if the general public loses the sense that—as a whole—policy is aimed at helping all citizens. For it is the belief that all can expect to benefit that sustains the high levels of voluntary compliance necessary for the effective functioning of political systems that are not sustained by excessive coercion.[4]

The role here attributed to uncertainty is like that played by stipulative information constraints (such as Rawls's veil of ignorance) in hypothetical contract theories of justice or morality.[5] The common idea is that individuals may be able to reach agreement on principles and policies to live under if they lack certain information (e.g., about how their particular interests would be affected), while they would be unable to agree if they possessed this information. Since real world uncertainty is a less severe information constraint than most such devices in hypothetical contract theories, it may be less able to promote agreement on social policies. But, if I am correct, it has *some* such effect, and—unlike the hypothetical constraints of moral theory—has it in the real world.

Our general point can perhaps be made clearer by use of a pair of simple examples. Consider first the so-called Trickle-Down hypothesis, which says that certain tax benefits to the wealthy in a democratic free enterprise system will, in the long run, stimulate the economy so that members of all social classes benefit. We do not know whether, to what extent, and under what conditions, the hypothesis is true. Given this, those who predictably benefit in the short run from designing public policy in light of the hypothesis, i.e., the wealthy, are more inclined to accept the hypothesis than those who might expect to suffer heavier taxes or reduced public services in the short run. But there are arguments and evidence on both sides of the issue. And if tax cuts are made based on this hypothesis, no one really knows what the long-run effects will be, or knows for sure what groups and individuals will benefit and by how much. (If the theory is grossly wrong, even most wealthy individuals may suffer in the long run from indirect economic or political effects. And either way, some members of both groups will likely end up as beneficiaries and victims of the policy.) So while there may be considerable political struggle in a democracy over a tax cut of this kind, this struggle can take the form of a genuine debate about the public interest. And the losers of the struggle need not feel that all is lost, since many of them may actually end up benefiting from the policy they have opposed. If the results of the proposed tax cut were fully known, however, the political process could only take the form of an open power struggle among beneficiaries and victims. This could well undermine commitment on both sides to the society and its democratic procedures.

A proposal to spend less money on highway safety is an example of a rather different kind. Here no preidentified *group* can be singled out as even probable victims. But the individuals who would be killed or disabled in auto accidents if and only if the policy were enacted would suffer noncompensable harm from this enactment. But if, purely hypothetically, there were a complete absence of uncertainty,[6] these individuals would know who they were, and would fiercely, even violently, resist the cut in expenditures.[7]

The differences between these two examples reveal that, so far, we have not been precise enough in speaking about "uncertainty." We have used the term to refer to an absence of knowledge of the consequences of available policies. But we can distinguish at least five different types of uncertainty concerning public policies. Let us call uncertainty about the kinds of significant effects a policy would have *general* uncertainty. An example of a policy that might involve substantial general uncertainty would be a policy to subsidize genetic research, for the very nature of the effects on human society of future developments in this area are highly unpredictable. Sometimes we know the kinds of effect a public policy would have, but do not know the direction of these effects. Our tax cut example involves *directional* uncertainty of this kind, for while we can be reasonably sure that the tax cut will have some aggregate effect on economic growth, we cannot tell whether it will accelerate or retard such growth.

A third sort of uncertainty, *distributional* uncertainty, concerns how many individuals will experience the various consequences of a policy and to what extent. Such uncertainty can exist even when we know the aggregate results of policy with considerable accuracy. If, for example, we sell a fixed number of lottery tickets, at fixed prices, with fixed prizes and relatively high probabilities of winning, we can know exactly what the aggregate net loss of the ticket-buying public will be. But since we do not know how many people will buy multiple tickets or win multiple prizes, we do not know how many people will win or lose how much. *Group* uncertainty will be said to exist when we do not know how major social groups (defined in economic, racial, religious, sexual, ethnic, or occupational terms) would fare, in aggregate, as a result of a given policy. Group and distributional uncertainty will often go together, but are, in principle, separate. We would have distributional, but not group, uncertainty in our lottery, for example, if we sold a preset percentage of tickets (including a preset percentage of winners) to members of various specific social groups. We would have group, but not distributional uncertainty, if we effectively prohibited multiple ticket purchases, but could not predict how many people from various social groups would buy tickets or winning tickets.

Our last type of uncertainty, *individual* uncertainty, can exist even when none of the others does. We have individual uncertainty when we cannot predict what consequences particular individuals would experience as the result of the adoption of a given public policy. Since public policies are usually general, and may have a variety of direct and indirect effects on individuals (often via their effects on other individuals), a large degree of individual uncertainty exists for most all individuals with respect to most all public policies.

We may look back at our two initial examples in the light of these distinctions among types of uncertainty. The primary sorts of uncertainty present in the tax cut example are group and directional. The key unanswered question is how this sort of tax cut would economically affect the "non-wealthy" economic group in the long run. But the directional question is also open; if the Trickle-Down hypothesis is wrong about the cuts spurring growth, even the aggregate economic effects will be negative. In the highway safety case, the main type of uncertainty is individual. We may be able fairly accurately to predict specific savings in tax dollars and a specific increase in highway casualties resulting from the measure which cuts safety expenditures, but we have no way of knowing *which individuals* would suffer.

Of course, in these cases, as in nearly all others, there is some degree of uncertainty of each type. For virtually any public policy, there may be some effects of totally unforeseen kinds, and the direction of predicted effects may not turn out as anticipated. Further, the distribution of effects cannot be predicted with great accuracy, and the effects on particular groups can only be estimated with wide degrees of error. Finally, the effects on particular individuals can only be guessed by looking at the average effects on members of various relevant groups to which they belong (including perhaps the population as a whole). The type of uncertainty which is most significant will vary from case to case.

My argument for social solidarity benefits depends mainly on uncertainty at the *group* and *individual* levels. This is because groups are the main effective actors in the domestic political process. To the extent they are convinced that their interests will be harmed by a policy, without adequate compensation, they will resist that policy and undermine solidarity. Individual uncertainty is even more important, because individuals are more likely than groups to suffer *noncompensable* injuries as the result of public policies.[8] Hence, the victims of these harms would have reasons to resist these policies by practically any means, at practically any cost. Individual uncertainty ameliorates this problem, by preventing the individual victims from identifying themselves and fellow victims until it is too late to band together to veto the policy.

The three other sorts of uncertainty, while nearly always present to a considerable degree in public policy making, are not crucial to producing the solidarity benefits of uncertainty. Reductions in general and directional uncertainty are for the most part unmitigated goods; in fact too much uncertainty of either kind renders rational policy making virtually impossible. Reductions in distributional uncertainty are also unmixed blessings, insofar as concern for social justice requires us to take account of distributional as well as aggregate effects of policies. Reduction in group uncertainty, however, is a mixed blessing. Sometimes it will enable specific groups and their sympathizers to identify and combat systematic neglect of the group members' interests. But it threatens solidarity among groups and the ability to enact public policies that are at least acceptable to all major groups. Reduction in individual uncertainty may, up to a point, be beneficial. But too great a reduction – in the limit, its total elimination – would be an unmitigated disaster for a democratic state. By producing maximally motivated resisters to every significant policy proposal, it could eliminate peaceful democratic policy making.

Having clarified the meaning of uncertainty, for our purposes,[9] it remains to consider some major objections to my claim that some types of uncertainty contribute to social solidarity, and therefore should be prized. Before turning to this task, however, it may be useful briefly to note two analogies between benefits of uncertainty in the social and personal spheres. These analogies are not intended as arguments for the existence of social benefits or uncertainty. They serve instead to clarify the claim that there are such benefits.

Uncertainty about the effects of personal choices can benefit some individuals by allowing them to avoid making unbearably painful tradeoffs between conflicting values or aspects of the self. Thus, an addicted smoker can avoid choosing between what she loves and a shortened life by noting that smoking may not kill *her.* For those who cannot give up smoking no matter what, or cannot do so without falling apart, the uncertainties of the effects of smoking in their own case allow them to avoid a self-destroying choice. Of course, there are costs of this uncertainty. First, some smokers, who would give it up if they knew for certain that it would cause their early demise, will keep smoking and die sooner. And second, some smokers will give up what they love unnecessarily, believing falsely that this is necessary to prolong their lives. It is likely that the net effect of this uncertainty, over all smokers, is negative. But a society is most analogous to the fragile smokers, those who cannot handle the tradeoff among values. For, in society, the conflicting values represent the interests of distinct groups who generally cannot be compensated for their losses by the gains of others. Under complete certainty, neither set of conflicting values can give way, and the society – like the self of the unreformable smoker – would come apart. It is better to be held together by the thought derived from uncertainty that "It may not happen to me (or us)," than to disintegrate as a society, or a self.

A second analogy concerns personal knowledge of the time of one's death. Such knowledge would provide some benefit, in allowing one more rationally to plan one's activities over one's lifetime. On the other hand, it would in most cases have damaging effects on one's morale and attitude toward life. The net effect of uncertainty here seems positive. On balance, I suggest few of us would want to know this information about ourselves. Social uncertainty carries analogous benefits and burdens. Elimination of group and individual uncertainty would allow more effective public policy making and more rational political action by individuals and groups. But, it would likely destroy social morale by turning public policy making into an exercise in which beneficiaries openly force rules upon desperately resistant victims. Here too, on balance, we should be glad of the existence of uncertainty.

2. IS THE SOLIDARITY EFFECT REAL?

My claim that there are social benefits due to uncertainty is subject to two main objections. One says that there are no solidarity-increasing effects of uncertainty. The other says that if there are such effects, they are not social *benefits*. Let us consider these objections in turn.

According to the former objection, group and individual uncertainty does not promote social solidarity in the ways suggested in the last section. For individuals and groups will resist expected harms based on probabilities just as fiercely as they would resist known harms. Three replies disarm this objection in its present form. First, it is irrational to invest as much effort in resisting a probable harm as in resisting a certain harm of the same magnitude. Thus, if we expect rational behavior, on average, in the political sphere, we would expect less resistance to public policies under uncertainty, on average. Second, cognitive psychologists have discovered that decision-makers tend to give disproportionate weight (according to the canons of expected value maximization) to outcomes that are certain compared to those that are merely probable.[10] So, to the extent that there *are* departures from rationality in average political behavior, they are likely to be in the direction suggested in section 1: probable harms will produce *proportionally less resistance* than certain harms (i.e., merely probable harms will be overdiscounted relative to certain harms). Third, under uncertainty, individuals will very rarely know – at the time of policy choice – that they would suffer a noncompensable harm as a result of the policy. Suppose, for example, that the issue is abolishment of capital punishment for future crimes. Few – if any – would know that they would become executed murderers if the death penalty were retained, or victims of undeterred murder if it were not. Taken together, these three factors prevent a maximally motivated group of self-defending opponents from forming to oppose significant public policy proposals. As a result, peaceful democratic policy making by consensus, compromise, and tradeoffs across issues is possible.

At this point the objector may back off a bit, and modify the objection to apply only to groups. Groups, it will be said, will fight harms as strongly when they are probable as when they are certain. Their experienced political leadership will be less likely than most people to be subject to overvaluing outcomes that are predictable with certainty. Also, policy effects on groups will generally be more predictable than those on individuals. Finally, groups are not subject to noncompensable losses, as are individuals, since even the worst losses of individual members can be balanced off by gains to other members. So, with or without certainty, groups will proportion their resistance to *expected* net gains and losses, and will peacefully accept losses – and the system that produces them – if and only if there are compensating gains.

The specific points the revised objection makes are valid ones, and they do imply that individual uncertainty is a proportionately greater contributor to social solidarity than is group uncertainty. Nonetheless, group uncertainty will still make a significant contribution to social solidarity, over and above the contribution of individual uncertainty. There are at least two reasons for this. First, group uncertainty will increase the power of subgroups within the group who may favor a policy the group opposes. Without uncertainty, this subgroup would have to admit the policy was harmful to the group as a whole and would not have much leverage. To the extent that uncertainty allows them plausibly to claim (and believe) that the policy will not, or may not, harm the group, these subgroups can effectively moderate the degree of the overall group's opposition to the policy and the group's alienation from the system producing it.

The second reason is that even some groups' losses may, *in practice,* be noncompensable because relevant norms of the society prevent compensation from being acknowledged as appropriate. For example, suppose a specific military recruitment policy makes it likely that a particular social group will suffer heavy casualties in a war. It may be impossible to compensate the group for this because of social norms that say military service is a patriotic duty, not a harm that is to be traded off for compensating benefits. Thus, overall, group uncertainty should reduce resistance to public policies and promote social solidarity (at least in a democratic political system) in a manner that reinforces and extends the effects of individual uncertainty.

3. IS INCREASED SOLIDARITY A BENEFIT?

Suppose that the previous section is correct, and that both individual and group uncertainty promote social solidarity. The other main objection we must consider is that this kind of increase in solidarity is not a social benefit at all, but a social harm. On this view, social harmony purchased at the price of victims of social policy being ignorant of their victimization is not desirable. By reducing victims' levels of protest, uncertainty is a tool of oppression. It is hardly a good thing if a society, even a democratic one, is kept stable and harmonious by the victims of its injustices falsely believing policy is made for the good of all. If this is how uncertainty promotes social solidarity, so much the worse for uncertainty.

The error underlying this objection is the assumption that a policy is unjust or oppressive if it harms specific groups or individuals. Unfortunately, almost every significant public policy has the effect of harming *some* individuals and groups (relative to the status quo and/or available alternative policies). What constitutes social injustice or oppression is a situation in which identifiable groups or individuals are systematically harmed by most all social policies, so that society can be divided into general beneficiaries and general victims. But this sort of systematic oppression is generally clear, at least to the victims, even with uncertainty. No doubt uncertainty can have some negative effect on the propensity of those oppressed in this sense actively to oppose and transform the social system from which they suffer. But other factors, such as lack of power, organization, and leadership, are likely to be much more important.

The point is that uncertainty does not prevent group politics. It does not even prevent violent social upheavals. But it does limit the number of situations in which political conflict is likely to become violent and destabilizing. Uncertainty makes it possible to keep group politics within certain civil bounds, especially in societies that have achieved a reasonable level of social justice. Since constrained, though vigorous, political competition within a stable society is nearly always preferable to an unconstrained war of group against group, uncertainty provides social benefits.

In fact, one specific benefit it provides directly promotes social justice. This benefit is the promotion of package-deals.[11] As noted above, without individual uncertainty, many individuals would refuse to accept package-deals involving some policies harming and some policies benefiting them, because the harms are noncompensable. Without group uncertainty, it would also be harder for *groups* to make package-deals. For subgroups expecting to suffer net harm from the package would often be able to prevent group support for the package by stressing the harm certain to accrue to the group as a result of one part of the package.[12] The shroud of uncertainty can thus make package-deals acceptable to various domestic groups in somewhat the same way that deliberately ambiguous language can make an international agreement possible among nations. Each side can expect the uncertainty or ambiguity eventually to work out to its advantage, and can use this expectation to dampen domestic critics who might otherwise scuttle the deal.

In the end then, the social solidarity effects of uncertainty are genuine social benefits. Uncertainty does not much support oppression, but it does promote peaceful and civil politics by facilitating package-deals among groups and by inhibiting highly motivated opposition to particular public policies.

4. COMPARISONS

My argument for the domestic solidarity benefits of uncertainty is essentially complete. However, before turning to other potential benefits of uncertainty, I wish to clarify the solidarity argument further by comparing it to related arguments in the recent social science literature. We may begin with Calabresi and Bobbitt's influential book *Tragic Choices*.[13] Calabresi and Bobbitt are concerned with how American society deals with decisions in which there is a "tragic" choice between some particular individuals suffering a high risk of death (or similarly grave consequences) and other particular individuals suffering such risks. They claim that our society benefits from upholding the myth that every life is infinitely valuable. We therefore do—and *should*—employ various shifting procedural devices to make choices about who shall live and die without admitting that we are making, and have to make, such choices.

There are some affinities between Calabresi and Bobbitt's theses and the argument presented here. Both start from the premise that many policies in a large society will inevitably inflict severe harm on some individuals. And both claim that, despite this fact, social solidarity can be upheld by a certain belief among the populace (including victims of public policies and their close associates). For Calabresi and Bobbitt, it is the belief that society values individual lives infinitely. For me, it is the belief that public policies are enacted for the common good or general welfare.

Still, there are two fundamental differences between the claims made here and those of Calabresi and Bobbitt. First, I have emphasized, as Calabresi and Bobbitt do not, that practically any significant public policy is going to have tragic consequences for someone, hence that virtually all policy making has a "tragic choices" aspect to it. Second, and more important, the argument of this essay does not endorse myth making (or myth continuation) as Calabresi and Bobbitt do.[14] The claim that society accords each individual life infinite value is simply false (perhaps even nonsensical), unless interpreted in some purely symbolic way. But the belief that public policies (or "packages" of them) serve the common good, in the sense of yielding *expected* benefits (or at least a tolerable balance of benefits and burdens) for all is not always false, given the uncertainties we face in the real world. In fact, a key point of my argument is that in the *absence* of uncertainty, we could derive social solidarity via belief in the common good only by myth making. But since uncertainty is not a myth, but a reality, belief in the common benefits of public policy need not be mythical—if the society in question is reasonably just and non-oppressive. This is why uncertainty can be a blessing, though surely a mixed one.

Robert Goodin makes a point similar to Calabresi and Bobbitt's when he observes that we are less uncomfortable about making allocative decisions that have inequitable results, when uncertainty shrouds who the losers will be.[15] He attributes this to the fact that the norm of impartial treatment, which we prize, is fully consistent with unequal outcomes when we do not know who will receive the less-than-equal benefits. This thesis of Goodin's resembles my earlier claim that uncertainty can reconcile the fact that public policies harm some people with the belief that these policies are designed to promote, and do promote, the public good. But the main theme of this essay extends beyond this bit of intellectual common ground. It says that peoples' concern for the victims of public policy, whether motivated by moral norms like equality and impartiality, or by self-interest and self-preservation, is normally consistent with effective policy making only because of the effects of uncertainty in hiding the identities of those victims. Partial or impartial, we would find it much more difficult to make policy in the absence of uncertainty.

Over the last two decades, a number of economists have also noticed that uncertainty can have beneficial effects in a variety of special contexts. It has been suggested, for example, that uncertainty can increase the efficiency of certain securities markets, and that uncertainty about tax rates can spur productivity.[16] However, the closest analogues to the argument in this essay can be found in some of the literature on the valuation of life. Economists ask whether public policies should be evaluated *ex ante* (in terms of people's preferences regarding their *expected* effects), or *ex post* (in terms of people's preferences regarding their *actual* outcomes). They note that individuals may assign virtually infinite negative value to the loss of their own lives, but much less than proportionate negative value to *risks* of losing their lives. Hence, there is a problem about which is the appropriate valuation to put on loss of life for purposes of public policy making.

More to the present point is an objection that has been raised against *ex post* evaluation. If people assign virtually infinite negative values to the certain loss of their own lives, it will turn out that virtually no public policies could pass *ex post* evaluation by the popular Wicksellian criterion.[17] This criterion says, in effect, that a policy is acceptable if and only if unanimous approval could be obtained for the policy together with a suitable arrangement for winners to compensate losers. The problem, of course, is that no scheme of compensation (or certainly none the winners would find it worthwhile to pay for) could capture the consent of those who would lose their lives (or suffer other noncompensable losses).

My own main point is closely related to this objection, but goes beyond it in a number of ways. First, whatever the appropriate normative standpoint for evaluating public policies (*ex post* or *ex ante*), I am emphasizing that it is only the fact of uncertainty that makes it possible to avoid this objection as a devastating *practical* political problem. For, without uncertainty, the noncompensable victims of particular public policies would make their own *ex post* (i.e., actual-outcome based) evaluations and would fiercely resist the adoption of such policies. In addition, given the now well-known propensity of people to value identifiable lives over statistical lives,[18] many would strongly oppose public policies with preidentified victims on altruistic grounds, even if they were not themselves among the victims. With uncertainty, however, our policies may be chosen with particular winners and losers unknown until it is, for practical and political reasons, too late for the losers and their altruistic sympathizers to act.

Further, economists' discussions of these issues seem to assume that rationally chosen public policies can be adopted and implemented without unreasonably high transaction and enforcement costs, or other negative social side effects. This may, in general, be the case. But if so, it is only because of the omnipresence of uncertainty. My discussion emphasizes that the costs of agreeing on, and enforcing, social policies (given the rational resistance of known victims and their sympathizers) would be prohibitive, save for the beneficial effect of uncertainty in shielding the identity of victims.

These considerations suggest two additional points about uncertainty. It is well known that precommitting oneself to a future course of action can have various advantages in situations of self-management or strategic interaction. Uncertainty may be viewed as allowing society to precommit itself to actions that will uncompensably harm some individuals while benefiting the group, without paying unbearably high bargaining or compensation costs.[19] Who will pay the uncompensable costs is shrouded in uncertainty until after the (more or less) irrevocable precommitment of adopting a policy is made. As a result, society may minimize the social costs of bargaining, keep compensation payments within affordable bounds, and minimize social disruption (provided that the burdens of policy do not always fall on the same groups).

In addition, it can now be seen how society may benefit from deliberately introducing uncertainty in special contexts. In particular, where some must suffer noncompensable harms, and society can (partly) determine who in particular will, there may be reasons of social solidarity for employing a lottery procedure. Thus, if we collectively precommit ourselves to a lottery to decide who goes to fight in foreign wars, or who receives scarce body-parts for transplant,[20] we might lower both decision costs and resistance to implementation of the decisions made. These are benefits over and above the inherent moral advantages of employing a fair procedure to determine such vital matters.

5. UNCERTAINTY AND DEMOCRATIC GOVERNMENT

There is another *potential* domestic benefit of uncertainty in societies whose government takes the form of a democracy. In such a system, government officials must pursue policies that please the electorate or risk being voted out of office. Thus, if there is genuine electoral competition among parties, or candidates, there will be a long-run tendency for governments to promote the interests of the citizens they govern. (If they do not, enterprising competitors will offer voters a more attractive alternative and take over power.) More metaphorically, via the mechanism of free elections, the citizens of a democracy hold their governors on a leash.

The potential uncertainty benefit in question shows itself once we inquire how long and flexible this leash of citizen control ideally ought to be. There are at least three reasons why the leash should not be too short. Officials may concern themselves with the interests of those beyond their constituents – people in other legislative districts, people in other countries, or future generations. Officials will typically have more information and expertise about how to achieve given social ends than do their average constituents. And, more controversially, it is possible that officials tend to be more enlightened about appropriate social goals than most citizens. To the extent that officials possess these characteristics of broader concern, greater technical expertise, and greater moral expertise, it is desirable that they be given some leeway to deviate from the most popular alternatives in their choice of social policies.

But, in the absence of uncertainty about the effects of policies, democratic politicians would not receive such leeway. For if any of their policies promised outcomes that were less favored by their constituents, they could be defeated by a rival who duplicated their stand on other issues and favored the more popular position on the matter in question.[21] In the presence of uncertainty about effects, on the other hand, democratic politicians can, to a certain extent, exercise their moral and technical expertise and express their broader concerns, without dooming themselves to electoral defeat. With policy outcomes shrouded in the mists of uncertainty, democratic politicians can act with some discretion to promote public (and human) welfare and still get reelected.

I refer to this politician-protecting effect of uncertainty as only a *potential* benefit because there is a downside to it. Uncertainty can also shield the democratic politician whose scope of concern is too narrow (e.g., himself, his friends, or a special interest group), or whose technical or moral expertise is below that of the average voter. To the extent it does this, uncertainty has a harmful social impact on policy-choice in democracies.

Whether the protection of politicians by uncertainty is a net social benefit or loss will depend upon the characteristics of particular democratic societies and their politicians. If politicians are more expert and more broadly concerned, on average, than are voters, the net effect will tend to be beneficial. Cynics may scoff at this idea, but I see no reason why politicians in some democracies might not possess more than average amounts of these desirable characteristics. In the area of technical expertise, for example, one would strongly expect specialization alone to produce higher average levels of competence among politicians than among voters. And I would not be shocked to learn that in some democracies, elected officials possess a breadth of concern and level of moral expertise at least equal to that of the average citizen. If this is so, uncertainty may benefit certain democratic societies by allowing their officials to operate on a somewhat longer leash than would otherwise be possible.

6. UNCERTAINTY AND WAR

Uncertainty constrains conflict and maintains peace at the international as well as domestic level. At first glance this may seem wrong. For uncertainty sometimes leads to wars in which both sides believe they will win. Without uncertainty, on the other hand, it would seem that all wars would be avoided, since no nation will enter a war it knows it is going to lose.

To see what is wrong with this "certainty would benefit us by preventing war" reasoning, let us proceed in three stages. First, suppose it were true that there was certainty about the outcome of any potential war and that no nation would fight a war it would lose. Then any predictably winning nation could simply dictate terms of surrender to a predictably losing opponent by simply threatening to attack if its terms were not accepted. In a world such as this, the bloodshed of actual war would be avoided, but at the tremendous cost of the surrender of the independence of most all nations. For stronger nations could, and probably would, conquer weaker nations at will and without material loss. In fact, the predictable long-range result would be a series of conquests by mere threat of war, leading to larger and larger competing empires facing off until only one remained and dominated the world.[22]

Proceeding to our second stage, we should note that contrary to the above assertion, nations may fight wars they know they will lose. This is because there are degrees of losing a war, and because it can be costly to fight (or continue fighting) a winning war. Thus a nation may rationally prefer to fight and lose a war if it can achieve substantially better armistice terms than the terms demanded by its opponent as the price of avoiding war. And achieving such terms will sometimes be possible, because it would be more costly for a winning nation to continue fighting a war than to accept a less than total victory. As a result, even an obviously losing side may have considerable bargaining power during, or prior to, a war. Indeed, in view of the finding of cognitive psychologists that people are inclined to take great risks to avoid losses, but are much more conservative in pursuing gains,[23] the weaker side may well have substantial bargaining success.

Noting that a potential war situation has certain features of a bargaining game opens the way for a third stage of our rebuttal of the "certainty would benefit us by preventing war" view. There are at least two distinct sorts of uncertainty that may face a nation contemplating (or fighting) a war. *Military* uncertainty concerns the forces, strategy, and tactics the other side would use and the military outcomes of the various possible engagements that might take place. *Motivational* uncertainty concerns the values and will of the opponent—how much he is willing to endure to obtain what ends.[24] Though conceptually distinct, these two sorts of uncertainty are linked, since will and values can influence strategy, and military tactics or outcomes may affect will and values. (For example, civilian casualties may strengthen resistance by increasing the perceived importance of defeating a foe who callously inflicts them.)

The key point to be made is that uncertainty of either sort can serve to deter war even in the complete absence of uncertainty of the other sort. Even if military outcomes were completely predictable, the expected winner may not know that the losses it can inflict will be sufficient to achieve its political ends, because it does not know enough about the opponent's values to determine if the opponent's anticipated losses would be worse—in the opponent's eyes—than conceding the winner's political aims. Similarly, knowing the limits of the other side's endurance of wartime losses will not allow one confidently to predict achievement of one's aims in war, if one is uncertain whether losses can be inflicted beyond those limits.

We may now summarize our general observations about war and uncertainty. Complete certainty on military and motivational matters implies the absence of war only on the false assumption that a nation will never fight a war it knows it will lose. Further, even if this assumption held, certainty would avoid war only at the price of inviting world domination by a single empire. Since it is sometimes rational for nations to fight a losing war, even predictably losing nations may have considerable bargaining power to deter wars or conclude wars on terms acceptable to them. Uncertainty about military outcomes and national motivations adds to the bargaining power of weaker nations, since stronger nations cannot generally be confident they can fight and win wars at an acceptable cost. Uncertainty thus helps both to deter war and to preserve the independence of sovereign nations, at least to the extent that national leaders tend to be rational and risk averse when it comes to starting wars. In particular cases (e.g., when an aggressive nation starts a costly losing war that it expects to win), uncertainty may produce a war. But the overall deterrent and nation-protecting effects of uncertainty seem well worth the cost of the wars produced in this way. International peace among nations, to the extent it exists, is like domestic peace within nations, in being an offspring of uncertainty.

What about nuclear war and nuclear deterrence? Does my claim about the benefits of uncertainty apply in this special case? Interestingly, the strategic literature contains different informed analyses attributing the effectiveness of nuclear deterrence to uncertainty and to certainty. McGeorge Bundy uses the term 'existential deterrence' to refer to nuclear decision-makers being deterred from nuclear weapons use by the grave *uncertainties* about the nature and consequences of nuclear war, this uncertainty deriving largely from our fortunate lack of experience with nuclear wars.[25] The Harvard Study Group, on the other hand, attributes the success of nuclear deterrence to the crystal ball or *certainty* effect: decision-makers know—because of nuclear weapons' characteristics and the size of nuclear arsenals—that a nuclear war would have disastrous consequences for both sides.[26]

Though, on the surface, these views seem directly contradictory, they actually are compatible, and each is largely correct. It is a particular *mixture* of certainty and uncertainty that makes nuclear deterrence effective, and hopefully will continue to do so as long as these horribly destructive weapons exist. The main operative uncertainties concern whether any use of nuclear weapons in war could be kept under control so as not to escalate into a large-scale nuclear war. The main operative certainty is that such a large-scale nuclear war would be an unprecedented catastrophe for both sides and for humanity. Together these imply that any nuclear use could well result in unprecedented catastrophe for the users (as well as others), and they thereby produce powerful inhibitions against such use.

Turning back from the special case of nuclear deterrence, we may conclude by pointing out the common theme in arguments presented here about the domestic and international benefits of uncertainty. Uncertainty implies that agents (individuals, groups, and nations) cannot be sure they will suffer from policies determined by peaceful bargaining, politics, and diplomacy. In particular, they cannot be fully confident that they could do better by forcibly resisting such policies. Thus, at both the domestic and international levels, uncertainty makes possible controlled competition where we might otherwise have all-out war or brutally direct coercion. The practical lesson to be learned is simple. We should strive to increase social knowledge; but we should at the same time be thankful for the remaining residue of uncertainty that makes social peace possible.[27]

NOTES

1. Daniel Dennett writes, "We would like to. . .face the world with as much elbow room (as large a margin for error and as little relevant uncertainty) as we can get." (*Elbow Room* [Cambridge, Mass., 1984], 72–73)

2. On this point, see also my *Hobbesian Moral and Political Theory* (Princeton, N.J., 1986), sec. 6–4, where it is observed how uncertainty renders many potential revolutions irrational.

3. That is, relative to an appropriate baseline (e.g., the status quo), few policies in such a group would be what economists call "Pareto-improvements."

4. Of course, no large political system can sustain itself without some coercive apparatus. But there are important differences of degree here. See my "Rule by Fear," *Nous* 17 (1983): 601–20, sec. VII.

5. John Rawls, *A Theory of Justice* (Cambridge, Mass., 1971), sec. 24.

6. When we carry the absence of uncertainty to these limits, we encounter certain conceptual puzzles—e.g., couldn't a preidentified victim avoid victimization by avoiding auto travel? Would not a world without uncertainty have to obey simpler natural laws than the actual world? Would beings like us have ever come into existence in such a world? These puzzles, which I leave aside, reveal how much our ordinary conceptual scheme and understanding of the world presupposes a context of uncertainty.

7. Imagine, for example, how powerful and dedicated groups like Mothers Against Drunk Driving would be if many potential members knew (ahead of time) that they could save their own children by, and only by, politically effective action through such groups.

8. A group can be compensated for noncompensable injuries to some members by benefits to other members.

9. These distinctions among types of uncertainty cut across the familiar distinction between choices under risk, where probabilities of outcomes are known, and choices under uncertainty, where the decision-maker lacks such information. "Risk" and "uncertainty," in this familiar sense, actually name the end points of a continuous scale from full probability information to none.

I use the term "uncertainty" in its generic sense to cover all situations in which the consequences of alternatives are not known with certainty. This usage encompasses the "risk-uncertainty" continuum inclusively from end-point to end-point. My examples range over a large portion of this continuum, with some lottery examples falling near the "risk" endpoint, and other examples, like the tax cut, falling nearer the "uncertainty" end-point.

When I speak of *reductions* in uncertainty, I mean either (1) movement toward the risk end of this continuum, or (2) changes in probability estimates toward the extremes of the zero to one probability scale. For example, if I want to draw a red marble from an urn, there is less uncertainty in the first sense if I know the percentage of red marbles in the urn than if I know nothing of the color of the marbles; while there is less uncertainty in the second sense if I know there are 95 percent red marbles as opposed to knowing there are 50 percent.

10. See Daniel Kahneman and Amos Tversky, "Prospect Theory," *Econometrica* 47 (1979): 263–91.

11. By "package deals," I mean A accepting policy P which benefits B (and harms A) on condition that B accept policy P' which benefits A. This is a familiar generalization of the notion of log-rolling or vote-trading within legislatures.

12. Of course, proponents could stress the certain benefits of the other elements of the package. But, especially if individuals fear losses more than they value gains, as Kahneman

and Tversky observe in "Prospect Theory," the remaining individual uncertainties may cause the package to lose out in intragroup politics.

13. Guido Calabresi and Philip Bobbitt, *Tragic Choices* (New York, 1978).

14. For cogent criticisms of Calabresi and Bobbitt's endorsement of maintaining the "infinite value of life" myth, see Brian Barry, "Tragic Choices," *Ethics* 94 (1984): 303–18.

15. Robert Goodin, *Reasons for Welfare* (Princeton, N.J., 1988), chap. 3, sec. 2.

16. See Lawrence Glosten and Paul Milgrom, "Bid, Ask and Transaction Prices in a Specialist Market with Heterogeneously Informed Traders," *Journal of Financial Economics* 14 (1985): 71–100; and Joseph Stiglitz, "Utilitarianism and Horizontal Equity," *Journal of Public Economics* 18 (1982): 1–33.

17. John Broome, "Uncertainty in Welfare Economics, and the Value of Life," in *The Value of Life and Safety*, edited by M. W. Jones-Lee (Amsterdam, 1982), 212–13; and Dan Usher, "The Value of Life for Decision Making in the Public Sector," in *Ethics and Economics*, edited by Ellen Paul et al. (Oxford, 1985), 174–75. It should be noted that while there are problems with the idea of individuals assigning literally infinite value to their own lives, this notion is considerably less problematic than the mythical notion of *society* infinitely valuing each member's life. In particular, the latter notion borders on incoherence when tradeoffs have to be made among the lives of different members.

18. Thomas Schelling, "The Life You Save May be Your Own," in *Problems in Public Expenditure,* edited by Samuel Chase (Washington, D.C., 1968).

19. Richard Thaler, "The Value of a Life," in *Value of Life and Safety,* 171–83.

20. On lottery allocation of tragic burdens, see Calabresi and Bobbitt, *Tragic Choices,* 41–44. They observe, as do writers going back at least to Hobbes (*Leviathan*, chap. 15), that "first come, first serve" is a kind of natural lottery.

21. Anthony Downs, *An Economic Theory of Democracy* (New York, 1957).

22. Even purely defense-minded nations might be forced into a maximal-conquest-by-threat-of-war strategy to protect themselves. There are parallels here to the part of Hobbes's classic argument against anarchy which is discussed in chapters 3 and 4 of my *Hobbesian Moral and Political Theory.*

23. See Kahnemann and Tversky, "Prospect Theory."

24. Actually, a nation may face military and motivational uncertainty about itself (i.e., about its own tactics, will, and values in the event of war). I will ignore this complication.

25. McGeorge Bundy, "Existential Deterrence and Its Consequences," in *The Security Gamble*, edited by Douglas MacLean (Totowa, N.J., 1984).

26. The Harvard Nuclear Study Group, *Living With Nuclear Weapons* (New York, 1983), 43–44.

27. The University of Texas Medical Center Library supplied the quiet needed for writing the first draft of this essay in June 1985. At a University of California, Irvine philosophy colloquium in November 1987, Tyler Cowen and several of my philosopher-colleagues provided helpful suggestions. An ACLS/Ford Fellowship supported production of the penultimate draft in 1988. I thank them all.

Foucault's Genealogical Method[1]

GARY GUTTING

M ichel Foucault was famous not only for the strikingly original content of his intellectual histories but also for the innovative methodologies he deployed in writing them. Both the "archaeological" method that he developed throughout the 1960s and the "genealogical" method to which he turned in the 1970s have attracted considerable attention and controversy. An understanding of Foucault's intellectual enterprise requires careful reflection on the nature of the two methods and on their relationship. I have recently offered a detailed analysis of Foucault's archaeological method.[2] Here I want to make a start on the question of how to understand his later turn to the genealogical method. My focus will be on Foucault's explicit methodological reflections on genealogy, particularly his 1971 essay, "Nietzsche, Genealogy, History," his 1970 inaugural address at the Collège de France, "L'ordre du discours," and his methodological comments at the beginning of *Discipline and Punish*. To place these reflections in context, I will begin with a general characterization of Foucault's intellectual enterprise, drawn primarily from his comments in the essays and interviews of the 1970s collected in *Knowledge/Power*.

I. FOUCAULT'S HISTORICAL PROJECT

Foucault was both a historian and a philosopher, but he did not derive his approach to history from *a priori* philosophical commitments. His historical methodology depended more on a sensitivity to the particularities of historical events and structures than on fundamental views about knowledge and reality. On the other hand, Foucault was not a "pure" historian, simply displaying neutral truths about the past. His histories originate from specific experiences and concerns about contemporary society: a concrete awareness that something is wrong with our treatment of mental patients or prisoners, with our sexual attitudes and practices. He says, for example, that he undertook a historical study of psychiatry (in *Folie et déraison*) "because I had had a certain amount of practical experience in psychiatric hospitals and was aware of the combats, the lines of force, tensions and points of collision which existed there. My historical work was undertaken only as a function of those conflicts" (*PK* 64).

It is this origin in contemporary experience that led Foucault to characterize his work as "history of the present" (*DP* 30–31). But this origin does not mean that Foucault thought his histories provided expert solutions to our social and political problems. His history of madness, although taken up by Laing and others in the anti-psychiatry movement, was not intended as a call for abolishing asylums or for any other specific reforms in our treatment of the mad. In Foucault's view, decisions about how to deal with political and social problems are the province of those immediately involved in and familiar with them. Disengaged intellectual analysis is important but only as a background suggesting possibilities, not as a normative summons to action. "The project, tactics and goals to be adopted are a matter for those who do the fighting. What the intellectual can do is to provide instruments of analysis, and at present this is the historian's essential role. . . . [He provides] a topological and geological survey of the battlefield. . . . But as for saying, 'Here is what you must do!', certainly not" (*PK* 62).

On the other hand, Foucault does think there is a sort of intellectual who does have the right to recommend particular policies and tactics. This is the "specific intellectual," who "has at his disposal, whether in the service of the State or against it, powers which can benefit or irrevocably destroy life" (*PK* 129). Included under this rubric are all those experts (teachers, engineers, doctors, consultants) who develop and deploy domains of knowledge within the power structures of society. Foucault distinguishes the specific intellectual from the "universal intellectual," a free spirit, "the spokesman of the universal," "speaking in the capacity of master of truth and justice" (126). He suggests that such autonomous intellectuals – Voltaire is no doubt a premier example – once played an important role. But today the relation between theory and practice has changed, and we can no longer expect universal systems of morality to provide effective responses to social and political domination. We need, rather, specific responses formulated by those concretely involved in the problems. Foucault's "specific intellectuals" are, of course, not the only ones so involved; there are also the direct objects of society's power structures (e.g., prisoners, asylum inmates, students), their families, as well as a network of nonintellectual functionaries (e.g., prison guards, office workers). But specific intellectuals' specialized knowledge and reflective capacities make their efforts particularly important.

The intellectual role Foucault sees for himself does not seem to be that of either the specific or the universal intellectual. His work is grounded neither in the latter's general moral principles nor in the former's specific responsibilities within society's power structures. We might (though Foucault does not use the term) call him rather a "critical intellectual." A critical intellectual does not speak with the authority of universal principles or of specific social or political responsibilities but simply on the basis of his historical erudition and analytic skills. He is neither "the rhapsodist of the eternal" nor "the strategist of life and death" (*PK* 129); and his analyses provide the intellectual tools—awarenesses of strategic and tactical possibilities—needed to combat arbitrary constraints on human freedom.

Although the critical intellectual's social and political concerns explain his choices of particular historical phenomena for analysis, they do not account for the historical methods he employs or for the results these methods yield. Foucault, for example, chose to study the historical origins of certain disciplines and institutions because he regarded them as particularly dangerous contemporary threats to freedom. But his studies themselves were intended to help generate reliable strategies for combatting these threats. Consequently, they had to be designed to yield accurate historical accounts, not ideological caricatures. Foucault was committed to struggles for freedom in the manner of an intelligence analyst, not a propagandist. Consequently, he always aimed at a reliable understanding of the historical phenomena he was investigating. He sought, as he said, "a discourse which would be both true and strategically effective,. . .a truth which could have a political effect" (*PK* 64).[3]

This construal of Foucault's work may seem at variance with his often-cited characterizations of his writings as fictions. In a 1977 interview, for example, he said: "I am well aware that I have never written anything but fictions" (*PK* 193). However, a look at the context of this remark shows it to have quite a different meaning than we might think. Immediately after saying that all his writings are fictions, Foucault continues, "I do not mean to say, however, that truth is therefore absent" and goes on to explain that there are cases in which "a true discourse engenders or 'manufactures' something that does not as yet exist"; for example, one can help create "a politics not yet in existence on the basis of a historical truth." In such a case, one can be said to "fiction" a politics by means of the historical truth (*PK* 193). This fits nicely with my claim that Foucault aimed at accurate history as a basis for effective social and political action.

There is also a passage in a 1967 interview with Raymond Bellour that has been taken (e.g., by Megill) as saying that *The Order of Things* is novelistic fiction. In the course of a discussion of *The Order of Things,* Bellour asks about Foucault's relation as author to this text. Foucault replies with some general comments suggesting that books are more expressions of the system of discourse characteristic of a given cultural epoch than of the intentions of an author. He goes on to say: "My book is a pure and simple 'fiction'; it's a novel, but it's not I who invented it; it is the relationship between our period and its epistemological configuration and this mass of statements."[4] I see no reason to take this as a specific reference to *The Order of Things.* It is much more plausible to read Foucault as saying, quite generally, that, even if I (or anyone else) have written a novel (which we tend to regard as a paradigm of individual creativity), it is still the case that what I have written is more the product of my culture's system of discourse than of my own invention. Certainly, the passage in question is not a response to a question about *The Order of Things'* historical accuracy, and nothing else Foucault says in the interview suggests that he regards it as unconstrained by historical fact.

None of this is to say that Foucault approached the past with no methodological presuppositions. Like any good historian, he began from a standpoint suggested and warranted by what seemed to him the best current work in his and related fields. For Foucault, this was that of recent French historians of science (particularly Gaston Bachelard and Georges Canguilhem) and that of Braudel and his *Annales* school.

Two key aspects of Foucault's approach to history derive from the historians of science: skepticism about progress and distrust of global accounts. Regarding the former, he says, "I owe to the historians of science. . .the methodological precaution and radical but unaggressive skepticism which makes it a principle not to regard the point in time where we are now standing as the outcome of a teleological progression" (*PK* 49). He does not, however, deny the possibility of progress; like Bachelard and Canguilhem, he agrees that science has produced successively better accounts of the natural world. But he wants to question our ready assumption—particularly regarding social knowledge and practices—that "what happens now is. . .better, more advanced, or better understood, than what happened in the past" (*PK* 50). Foucault also follows Bachelard and Canguilhem in directing his historical concerns toward carefully limited, regional domains of inquiry. Bachelard denied that there was any helpful notion of scientific rationality in general and limited his studies to various specific "regions of rationality." Similarly, regarding our efforts to understand social and political embodiments of rationality, Foucault emphasizes "the inhibiting effect of global, *totalitarian* theories" such as Marxism and psychoanalysis. He agrees that such general viewpoints have "provided. . .useful tools for local research" but insists that this has happened only when "the theoretical unity of these discourses was in some sense put in abeyance. . . . In each case, the attempt to think in terms of totality has in fact proved a hindrance to research" (*PK* 81).[5]

In Braudel and other members of the *Annales* school, Foucault found the very fruitful idea that historical discoveries could result not only from "magnifying something whose presence is already known (e.g., studying a particular institution or practice in great detail)" but also from "a change of level, addressing oneself to a layer of material which had hitherto had no pertinence for history. . ." (*PK* 50). Braudel's history of the Mediterranean, for example, lengthened the temporal scale of historical analysis in a way that made considerations of climate, mining technologies, and agriculture more important than the political, military, and individual biographical events that have traditionally concerned historians. Much of Foucault's work was an effort to do for the history of thought what Braudel had done for political and social science.

Specifically, Foucault's goal was to develop a history of thought that operated at a level more fundamental than that of the conscious life of thinking and experiencing subjects. This, of course, did not mean the simple elimination of a role for individual thinkers in the history of thought. Foucault did not think there were thoughts without consciousness or that thought was ultimately the function of some transhuman absolute consciousness. Thinking for him remained the exclusive domain of individual human subjects. But he saw thinking as itself pervaded and constrained by factors not discoverable by investigations of consciousness. Although Foucault does not eliminate the conscious subject from the history of thought, he does decenter it, regarding its activities as derived and delimited by deeper structures.

This decentering of the subject was not only an expression of Foucault's Braudelian historical methodology, it was motivated by his philosophical views and by his practical goals as a critical intellectual. Foucault's original philosophical stance was most strongly influenced by existential phenomenology (especially Heidegger's), which gave a fundamental role to the phenomenological subject. His original project in writing his book on madness (*Folie et déraison*, 1961) was, as he later said, to understand the phenomenological subject in historical terms.[6] But he eventually concluded that "the problem [could not] be solved by historicising the subject as postulated by phenomenologists." Instead, "one has to. . .get rid of the subject itself, that's to say, arrive at an analysis which can account for the constitution of the subject within a historical framework" (*PK* 117). This dissatisfaction with existential phenomenology (and, in general, any philosophy of the subject) was partly due to the sorts of purely philosophical difficulties he discussed in *The Order of Things* under the heading, "The Analytic of Finitude." But these difficulties converged with his historical sympathy with the Braudelian approach.

They also converged with his desire to contribute as a "critical intellectual" to the cause of human liberation. This was because Foucault's historical studies, from *Folie et déraison* on, convinced him that the sources of constraints on human freedom operate beneath the level of conscious thoughts and decisions. Even the apparently most "enlightened" policies of letting agents make their own choices and encouraging the free play of their thoughts (in, for example, matters of education or sexuality), might well be subtle instruments of control. As a result, the project of liberation required a move beyond the standpoint of the subject.

Foucault characterized his non-subject-centered approach to the history of thought as one developed in spatial rather than temporal terms (*PK* 70-71). The idea of a nontemporal history seems contradictory on the face of it, but Foucault was here using time as an image of continuity and progress, contrasted with space as an image of differentiation and incommensurable differences. So construed, a temporal view of history reduces to one that is centered in the subject as a continuously enduring focus: "Metaphorising the transformation of discourse in a vocabulary of time necessarily leads to the utilisation of the model of individual consciousness with its intrinsic temporality" (*PK* 70). By contrast, Foucault used space as a metaphor for "the forms of implantation, delimitation and demarcation of objects, the modes of tabulation, the organisation of domains" that reveal the nature of the "processes—historical ones, needless to say" in which he is interested (*PK* 70). This shows that what critics have seen as Foucault's rejection of temporality—and hence of history—*per se* is in fact just his non-subject-centered reconstrual of historical time.

The point is borne out by Foucault's attitude toward the notion of an event. Although Braudelian history has often been characterized as rejecting *l'histoire événementielle,* Foucault saw it as rather a move to a new level and type of events (cf. *AK* 3–4). Rather than reject the event as an essential historical category, he emphasized the need of "realising that there [is] actually a whole order of levels of different types of events differing in amplitude, chronological breadth, and capacity to produce effects" (*PK* 114). He regarded his focus on events as a major difference between his work and that of the structuralists. "One can agree that structuralism formed the most systematic effort to evacuate the concept of the event, not only from ethnology but from a whole series of other sciences and in the extreme case of history. In that sense, I don't see who could be more of an anti-structuralist than myself" (*PK* 114). We can succinctly summarize Foucault's much discussed relation to structuralism by saying that he tried to develop an account of thought in terms of non-subject-centered structures without eliminating the essential historical reference to events.

In sum, Foucault's historical methodology was rooted in both his practical goals as a critical intellectual and in his appreciation of the power and relevance of Bachelardian and Braudelian approaches to history. These two factors led him to develop a history of thought that decentered the subject and opened up new levels of the historical analysis of thinking. This approach to the history of thought converged with but by no means derived entirely from his philosophical critique of phenomenology. His method incorporated an emphasis on structures and "spatiality" while reconstruing but not eliminating the events that make history history.

II. FROM ARCHAEOLOGY TO GENEALOGY

Foucault called the methodology of his first three historical studies (*Folie et déraison, The Birth of the Clinic,* and *The Order of Things*) "archaeological," and devoted a methodological treatise (*The Archaeology of Knowledge*) to its codification and elucidation. Its most fully developed practice was in *The Order of Things.* There it was essentially a technique for analyzing the linguistic systems ("epistemes" or, in the terminology of *The Archaeology of Knowledge,* "discursive formations") that, in Foucault's view, determined the range of objects, concepts, methodological resources, and theoretical formulations available to thinkers in a given domain at a given time. Thus, Foucault delineated the linguistic systems underlying the classical (seventeenth- and eighteenth-century) disciplines of general grammar, natural history, and analysis of wealth as well as those of the modern (nineteenth- and twentieth-century) disciplines of philosophy, biology, and economics that replaced them. He argued that, at the archaeological level of his analysis, there were strong structural similarities among the three classical disciplines and among the three modern disciplines; but that there was a sharp break between classical and modern modes of thought taken as wholes. On this basis he rejected, for example, the common view that the work of nineteenth-century biologists such as Darwin could be treated as continuous developments of the work of eighteenth-century natural historians such as Lamarck. Specifically, he maintained that there is no hint of the Darwinian concept of evolution in Lamarck or any other classical thinker. He took such results as illustrative of the superiority of his archaeological approach to the methods of standard history of ideas, which focused on the specific concepts and theories of particular thinkers and not on the linguistic structures underlying them.

Although Foucault most fully developed his archaeology as a method of analyzing systems of discourses, he clearly intended it also to apply to the study of nondiscursive practices and institutions. This is apparent from his practice in *Folie et déraison* and the beginning of *The Birth of the Clinic,* where such things as houses of confinement, clinics, and social systems for controlling the poor are a major concern. Foucault is particularly interested in showing the structures common to discursive practices (e.g., modern psychiatry) and their nondiscursive counterparts (e.g., the asylums founded by Tuke and Pinel). Also, the methodological reflections of *The Archaeology of Knowledge* explicitly allow for both discursive and nondiscursive applications of archaeological analyses.[7]

Archaeology's goal of revealing the deep structures of discourse and knowledge lying beneath the consciousness and intentions of individuals fits well with his historical project of decentering the subject and moving the history of thought to new levels of analysis. Further, archaeology's revelation of the "unconscious"[8] of thought made it a prime means toward Foucault's ultimate goal of discovering and dissolving constraints on thought.

Foucault's archaeological analyses typically revealed sharp discontinuities ("epistemological breaks," in Bachelard's terminology) between chronologically successive discursive formations. Critics quickly noted that these analyses seemed essentially incomplete since they delineated structures on either side of such breaks but gave no account at all of how the move from one structure to another was accomplished. Instead, for example, of explaining *how* modern biology came to replace classical natural history, Foucault merely described each discipline in its own terms. Some critics concluded that Foucault was so enamored of discontinuity that he rejected the possibility of any account of how thought had gotten from one point to another. In fact, however, Foucault regarded archaeological analysis as only an initial (though essential) descriptive stage that required complementing by a causal account. In his own terms, archaeology could not be the exclusive method of a history of thought precisely because it ignored the event as such; that is, it treated events only as fixed givens for analyses, not in their full dynamic reality.

In both *Folie et déraison* and *Birth of the Clinic,* Foucault occasionally alluded to standard social and economic causal factors, connecting, for example, the classical age's internment of idle citizens (including the mad) to the collapse of the Spanish economy. By the time he wrote *The Order of Things,* however, he was disillusioned with the standard approach. "The traditional explanations— spirit of the time, technological or social influences of various kinds—struck me for the most part as being more magical than effective." However, Foucault had at this point no alternative sort of explanation to offer and so thought "it would not be prudent. . .to force a solution I felt incapable, I admit, of offering. . . ." Consequently, he says, "I left the problem of causes to one side; I chose instead to confine myself to describing the transformations themselves, thinking that this would be an indispensable step if, one day, a theory of scientific change and epistemological causality was to be constructed" (*OT*, Foreword to the English edition, xiii).

The only further suggestion Foucault makes in *The Order of Things* about causal accounts is that they will require reference to factors outside the realm of thought. "Discontinuity — the fact that within the space of a few years a culture sometimes ceases to think as it had. . .and begins to think other things in a new way — probably begins with an erosion from outside, from that space which is, for thought, on the other side, but in which it has never ceased to think from the very beginning" (*OT* 50). But he immediately adds that it is probably too early to pose this question of causal explanation and that "we should wait until archaeology of thought has been established more firmly. . .before attempting to encompass thought and to investigate how it contrives to escape itself" (*OT* 50–51).

III. NIETZSCHE AND GENEALOGY

Foucault's first extended discussion of the causal question is his essay "Nietzsche, Genealogy, and History," originally published in 1971 in a memorial volume for Jean Hyppolite. Perhaps as an elegantly modest reference to Foucault's debt as Hyppolite's student, this discussion takes the form of a meticulous *explication de texte*, with Foucault scrupulously summarizing Nietzsche's view of genealogy but never commenting in his own voice about the validity of the view. For this reason, we cannot simply assume — as critics such as Habermas have — that Foucault himself endorses every formulation of this essay. In some respects, it is clear that the position Foucault presents is not his own. He would not, for example, agree with Nietzsche's frequent references to the feelings and intentions of subjects (the rivalries of scholars, the inventions of the ruling class, NGH 142) as primary engines of the history of thought; nor with Nietzsche's claim that the degeneracy of the nineteenth century is due to racial mixing (NGH 159). In attempting to move from this exposition of Nietzsche to Foucault's own views, it is well to keep in mind a comment Foucault made five years later: "I am tired of people studying [Nietzsche] only to produce the same kind of commentaries that are written on Hegel or Mallarmé. For myself, I prefer to utilise the writers I like. The only valid tribute to a thought such as Nietzsche's is precisely to use it, to deform it, to make it groan and protest. And if commentators then say that I am being faithful or unfaithful to Nietzsche, that is of absolutely no importance" (*PK* 53–54).

Nonetheless, there can be no doubt about Foucault's acceptance of the core of Nietzsche's view: "If I wanted to be pretentious, I would use 'the genealogy of morals' as the general title of what I am doing" (*PK* 53). Although we should not take "Nietzsche, Genealogy, and History" as Foucault's own explicit and unqualified methodological statement, we may assume that what he later calls his "genealogical" approach to the history of thought at least belongs to the same genus as Nietzsche's genealogy. The essay therefore provides a good preliminary statement of some of the general features of Foucault's approach to the explanation of change in the history of thought.

Of particular value are Foucault's discussions of the senses in which genealogy does (and does not) reveal the "origins" of things and of how it differs from the methods of traditional historical analysis. Regarding the former, Foucault notes that Nietzsche challenges the idea that we can understand present realities by discovering their origin (*Ursprung*) in the sense of a privileged initial state in which their essential truth and perfection are contained and from which they have only deviated in the course of their subsequent history. He sees claims of such glorious origins as lies hiding a much less savory story: "Historical beginnings are lowly: not in the sense of modest or discreet like the steps of a dove, but derisive and ironic, capable of undoing every infatuation" (NGH 143). Properly understood, however, these beginnings are of the greatest significance for our understanding of things.

In this regard, Foucault notes that Nietzsche employs two further terms referring to origins that have a positive connotation for him: *Hernunft* (stock or descent) and *Entstehung* (emergence). Tracing the descent of an idea (or institution or practice) does not reveal an implicit essence that has unfolded over time. To tell the story of a descent is rather "to identify the accidents, the minute deviations—or, conversely, the complete reversals—the errors, the false appraisals, and the faulty calculations that give birth to those things that continue to exist and have value for us." What such a story reveals is not "truth or being. . . but the exteriority of accidents" (NGH 146). Foucault particularly notes the connection of Nietzsche's *Hernunft* (with its suggestions of blood and race) with causal processes that operate on the human body: "Genealogy, as an analysis of descent, is thus situated with the articulation of the body and history: Its task is to expose a body totally imprinted by history and the process of history's destruction of the body" (NGH 148). This aspect of genealogy becomes of central importance in Foucault's own development of a genealogical method in *Discipline and Punish* and the first volume of *The History of Sexuality*.

The "emergence" denoted by *Entstehung* is not "the final term of an historical development" but an interim stage in the unending struggle of forces that Nietzsche sees as the essence of history. We may agree that our "truths," along with the institutions and practices they justify, have an unseemly past of struggles for domination but still maintain that we have eventually replaced the violent coercion of power with the rational constraints of rules. According to Nietzsche, however, humanity never "arrives at universal reciprocity, where the rule of law replaces warfare." Rather, it "installs each of its violences in a system of rules and thus proceeds from domination to domination" (NGH 151). A society may pretend that the rules underlying its practices and institution express the authentic meaning of human existence, that its interpretation of man is simply an expression of his essential truth. But according to Nietzsche, such rules and the interpretation they express are always vehicles for the powers that dominate a society; and their alleged objectivity is nothing more than a neutrality that allows them to be "bent to the purposes of whoever seizes them." It is always possible to "invert their meaning and redirect them against those who had initially imposed them" (NGH 151). Rather than revealing a privileged interpretation expressing the historically emergent true meaning of human reality, genealogy presents every effort at interpretation as "the violent or surreptitious appropriation of a system of rules, which in itself has no essential meaning. . ." (NGH 151).

Traditional history attempts to ground human reality in fixed meanings expressed through "apocalyptic judgments" that in fact introduce "a suprahistorical perspective" (NGH 152). By contrast, Nietzsche sees his genealogy as a real or effective history (*wirkliche historie*) that "deprives the self of the reassuring stability of life and nature, and. . .will not permit itself to be transported by a voiceless obstinacy toward a millennial ending" (154). As a result, it reverses traditional history on three key counts. It gives primacy to the singular contingent event rather than to ideal continuities of necessary development. It focuses on those ignoble things that are near at hand (e.g., the body and its processes) rather than on the distantly noble. Finally, disdaining the cloak of absolute objectivity, it acknowledges the limited and perspectival character of its own viewpoint.

The contrast between traditional history and Nietzsche's genealogy is particularly well expressed in the opposition between the former's Platonic reliance on reassuring identities and the latter's persistent subversion of them. For example, traditional history offers "the confused and anonymous European. . .the possibility of alternative identities, more individualized and substantial than his own" (NGH 161). Thus, the French Revolution could be read through parallels with Roman history and Romanticism through parallels with medieval chivalry. The genealogist effects a destructive parody of this effort to give historical substance to the present by overwhelming us with the dizzying multitude of possible identifications. Once we realize the immense range of radically different ways of construing ourselves out of our past, we may be forced out of the consolations of pregiven identities and "can discover a realm where originality is again possible" (cited, NGH 161). Similarly, where traditional history moves beyond historical parallels to attempt a grounding of our identity in causal origins ("tracing our roots"), the genealogist shows the irreducibly multiple ways of characterizing these origins. The purpose of genealogical history "is not to discover the roots of our identity but to commit itself to its dissipation" (NGH 162).

For Nietzsche—and here Foucault is surely in strong agreement with him—the fundamental identity traditional history provides modern man is that of a conscious subject, capable of achieving an objective knowledge (of itself and its world) that will constitute it as a free, morally autonomous agent. Traditional history (like the post-Kantian philosophical project Foucault examined in *The Order of Things*) sees itself as a primary source of this liberating knowledge. "Presenting itself as neutral, devoid of passions, and committed solely to truth," it claims to provide the self-knowledge that grounds the authentic identity of men as free subjects. Genealogy, by contrast, undermines even this identity by showing how the allegedly liberating ideal of objective self-knowledge is in fact a subtle instrument of domination. Man's identity as a free subject is revealed as merely a mask for multifarious techniques of control. The will to knowledge is just an instance of the will to power, to which it sacrifices the subject of that knowledge.

Nietzsche saw his genealogies as revealing our most revered institutions and practices as "human, all-too-human." Foucault clearly accepts the negative side of this conception of genealogy; he too sees it as deconstructing the official meanings and evaluations that constitute a society's or culture's self-understanding. Genealogy in this sense well complements his fundamental historical project of dissolving constraints on thought and his earlier archaeological efforts to carry out this project. However, Foucault does not follow Nietzsche in his tendency to construe the "human, all-too-human" factors revealed by genealogy in psychological terms. The decentering of the subject means that for Foucault there are no parallels to Nietzsche's deployment of Socratic weakness and Pauline rancor as key genealogical determinants. Nor is Foucault's insistence on the irreducibly regional character of historical analysis and his distrust of "totalitarian" theories consistent with Nietzsche's (sometime) attraction for global reduction of history to a monolithic will-to-power. Similarly, there is no reason to think (as Habermas and others have suggested) that Foucault accepts the strong epistemological relativism that can be read into some of Nietzsche's formulations.[9]

IV. "THE DISCOURSE ON LANGUAGE"

To get a more specific idea of Foucault's own conception of genealogy, we must turn to his *"L'ordre du discours"* (translated as "The Discourse on Language"), the inaugural address given for his installation as a professor at the Collège de France. Here he provides an analysis of the variety of specific constraints on our discourse, constraints that determine the nature of the historical method that would seek to reveal and dissolve them. Foucault begins with the idea, illustrated, he says, both by his own reluctance to give an inaugural address and the highly structured, ritualistic institutional setting provided for it, that discourse is inherently dangerous. Because of this, he says, "in every society the production of discourse is. . .controlled, selected, organized, and distributed according to. . .procedures whose role is to avert its powers and dangers. . ." (DL 215). Some of the mechanisms of this control are entirely familiar, e.g., the exclusion via taboo of certain forms and topics of speech; others, e.g., the sharp distinction between the rational discourse worthy of our attention and the "meaningless" rantings of the mad, were the subject of Foucault's early historical studies. To these Foucault adds, as another means of controlling discourse, the distinction between truth and falsity.

He realizes the oddity of treating this distinction as just another way a society has of excluding forms of speech it happens not to want. Surely, we instinctively urge, this distinction is no contingent or arbitrary mode of exclusion! Foucault in fact agrees that, if discourse is considered simply on its own terms (on what he calls "the level of the proposition"), "the division between true and false is neither arbitrary, nor modifiable, nor institutional, nor violent" (DL 218). He maintains, however, that we must distinguish truth simply in its own terms (e.g., as a property of propositions in a linguistic system) from truth as the product of social structures and forces. This latter he calls, in a Nietzschean phrase, "the will to truth" (or alternatively, "the will to knowledge").

Foucault suggests that, within Western culture, the separation of truth from the will to truth corresponds to Plato's separation of philosophy from poetry. Prior to this—in, e.g., Hesiod and Homer—true discourse inspired "respect and terror, to which all were obliged to submit, because it held sway over all and was pronounced by men who spoke as of right. . ." (DL 218). From Plato on, however, the truth of a discourse depends not on the source or manner of its pronouncement but merely on its logical and semantical content. In this sense, truth is separated from social mechanisms of constraint and control. Without denying the reality and importance of truth in this objective (even absolute) sense, Foucault makes two further crucial points: (1) that, at every stage of its post-Platonic development, Western society has generated specific projects for attaining objective truth (specific forms of the will to truth); (2) that these projects have, in addition to producing objective knowledge, expressed and served society's goal of constraining discourse. As a result, even though objective knowledge no doubt exists (and increases daily) within our society, the means for attaining this knowledge are essentially tied to social power structures.

Just how does the will to truth lead to constraints on discourse? First of all by stigmatizing particular statements and, more importantly, entire modes of discourse as false. This is the fate of what have been revealed as pseudo-sciences (astrology, phrenology), religious superstitions, old-wives-tales, etc. Excluding such areas of discourse as false not only eliminates objectively incorrect statements; it also alters the power structure of society by undermining the authority of the sources of such discourse (e.g., astrologers, priests, women). There is, of course, also the possibility that what is judged to be simply true and simply false is not actually so; frequently, what we take as an exclusion of the false in favor of the truth is really the installation of one domain of partial truths in place of another. But even an entirely accurate exclusion of falsehood may be undesirable because of its consequences for power relations. Foucault neither disparages the social value of objective truth nor assumes that it should be the sole criterion for the worth of discourse. His point is simply that judgments of truth and falsity have ramifications in the realm of power that require careful scrutiny and assessment.

According to Foucault constraints on discourse via the true-false distinction, like those via taboo or the reason-madness division, constitutes a system of exclusion that simply cuts off certain modes of discourse as outside the realm of legitimacy. In addition, there are various principles of constraint that operate within domains of socially and culturally legitimate discourse. These internal principles are further ways in which our projects for generating true discourses (our will to truth) introduce constraints on discourse.

Foucault notes three different internal principles for the limitation (or "rarefaction") of discourse: commentary, the author, and disciplines. On one level, of course, all of these categories are creative sources of, rather than constraints on, discourse. Commentary, based on the distinction between fundamental discourse (e.g., religious, judicial, literary, or scientific) and its interpretation, certainly sustains the unending production of new discourses, since, in Montaigne's phrase, there is no end to books about books. But the project of commentary also limits discourse since its goal is always only to re-express what has already been said in the fundamental discourse. The infinite proliferation of commentary is essentially limited to a framework defined by the fundamental text.

Similarly, the author, considered simply as "the individual who delivered the speech or wrote the text in question" is undoubtedly a creative source of discourse. But once we think of an author as "the unifying principle in a particular group of writings or statements, lying at the origins of their significance, as the seat of their coherence" (DL 221), we introduce a principle of limitation. For the significance of any particular statement or group of statements depends on the way it fits in with the unified authorial project. Consider, for example, the extensive system of interpretive constraints that apply to a famous set of letters once they are definitely assigned to Plato.

Disciplines (roughly, organized efforts to attain knowledge, with the sciences as the premier but not sole examples) are, of course, explicitly intended to formulate new truths. But the very principles by which they are creative sources of truth also limit the range of truths that they can express. This is so first because any discipline is, at any given stage of its historical development, in fact based on errors, as further historical development will reveal. At a minimum, a discipline denies us access to the truths that are the denials of these errors. But even apart from this, a discipline allows the formulation of only truths that can be expressed in terms of its categories (i.e., in terms of its ontology, concepts, and range of theoretical frameworks). It will always exclude a range of "monstrous" truths ("a whole teratology of learning," DL 223) that cannot be formulated in its terms. Foucault gives Mendel's results on heredity as an example of truths that could not be accommodated by the biological disciplines of his time.

To the external and internal constraints that operate on systems of discourse themselves, Foucault adds a third group of constraints that operate on the speakers or writers who express themselves within a system of discourse. For example, religious rituals and doctrines (and parallel elements in other social and political structures) impose rules specifying just who may speak and with what authority in various situations.

Given this account of the nature of the constraints on our discourse, Foucault is in a position to give a sharper characterization of the historical methods by which he hopes to show their contingent and arbitrary character and thus pave the way for modes of talking and thinking that go beyond them. The first of these methods, which he here calls "critical," takes a system of discourse (e.g., the classical discourse on madness) as given and studies the forms of exclusion associated with that system. Critical analyses distinguish the various forms of constraint that exist within a system of discourse, show how the system generated and modified them, and describe the precise effect they have had on the history of thought. It seems clear that what Foucault here calls "criticism" corresponds to the method he earlier characterized as "archaeological," since both are essentially analyses of discursive structures independent of causal questions about their origins. In switching to the term "criticism," Foucault may want to emphasize what he (here at least) sees as the primarily negative thrust of archaeological analysis; or he may be responding to the fact that some of his earlier "archaeological" studies (especially *Folie et déraison*) in fact illustrate both the critical and the genealogical approaches. In any case, Foucault's subsequent discussions return to "archaeology" as the characterization of his non-causal mode of historical analysis.

The second mode of analysis he calls "genealogical." This does not begin with systems of discourse as givens; it rather deals with the processes whereby systems of discourse are formed. Critical analysis focuses on the negative, exclusory functions of discourses; consequently, Foucault presents it as defined by a methodological principle of reversal whereby "in all those factors which seem to play a positive role, such as the author, discipline, will to truth, we must rather recognise the negative activity of the cutting-out and rarefaction of discourse" (DL 229). By contrast, genealogy, precisely because it examines discourses at their points of origin, sees them as positive, creative factors, generating new modes of language and knowledge. He sees genealogy's causal analyses as governed by three methodological principles: that of discontinuity, that of specificity, and that of exteriority. The principles of discontinuity and specificity introduce, in the genealogical context, Foucault's familiar view that systems of discourse must be regarded as unique and irreducible units, not derived through the continuous transformation of other systems or understandable via the categories of these systems. The principle of exteriority embodies the Nietzschean injunction to eschew the alleged "deep meanings" in terms of which a culture understands its modes of discourse and instead "look for its external conditions of existence, for that which gives rise to the chance series of these events and fixes its limits" (DL 229).

"The Discourse on Language" advances Foucault's conception of genealogy by explicating the sorts of constraints it must be able to reveal. Particularly important, in the light of Foucault's subsequent case-studies, is the idea that the true-false dichotomy is a constraint on discourses. Beyond this, however, "The Discourse on Language" is far from a completely satisfactory explication of genealogy. This is primarily because it fails to formulate in a concrete, specific way, the differences between genealogy and archaeology. The extremely general characterization of the latter as dealing with negative aspects of discourse and the former with positive aspects is misleading. As Foucault admits (DL 233), this distinction of negative and positive is not sharp, since negative procedures of control may be at work in the production of a system of discourse and, conversely, control mechanisms may come to have a creative role within discourse. Further, two of the methodological principles said to be distinctive of genealogy (those of discontinuity and specificity) in fact correspond to major concerns of Foucault's earlier archaeological works. Similarly, the principle of reversal, said to be distinctive of archaeology (criticism) is surely implicit in the genealogical search for hidden constraints on discourse.

V. GENEALOGY AND THE BODY

The unsatisfactory character of "The Discourse on Language" derives primarily from the fact that Foucault has still not found very much to say about the nature of the causes that create new systems of discourse. We are told little more than that they are like those of Nietzsche's genealogy in being multiple and "ignoble" and unlike them in being nonpsychological. This defect is remedied with Foucault's first application of genealogy in *Discipline and Punish,* where both his practice and his methodological comments reveal genealogical causes as essentially concerned with control of the human body.

Discipline and Punish is a study of how nineteenth-century changes in the punishment of criminals introduced the ways of thinking and talking that are characteristic of modern social sciences. It is, accordingly, a paradigm case of a genealogical analysis, as Foucault makes clear at the outset, when he says "this book is intended. . .as a genealogy of the present scientific-legal complex" *(DP* 23). Obviously, a complete understanding of the genealogical method would require a close analysis of Foucault's practice in *Discipline and Punish.* We can, however, get a good preliminary idea of the book's distinctive contribution to the genealogical method by attending to the explicit methodological reflections with which it begins.

These reflections take the form of four rules that Foucault sees as guiding his study of punishment. (1) Treat punishment not merely as a means of repressing undesired forms of behavior but as "a complex social function" that produces a series of positive effects. (2) Do not regard methods of punishment as simply "consequences of legislation" (as traditional legal history does) or "indicators of social structure" (like Durkheimian analysis); rather treat them as autonomous causal factors, operating independently of the political and social causes recognized by standard histories. (3) Do not treat the history of penal reform and the history of the human sciences as separate (even if interacting) developments; rather, "see whether there is not some common matrix or whether they do not both derive from a single process of 'epistemological-juridical' formation" *(DP* 23). (4) Try to seek the appearance of the "soul" (Foucault's term for the conception of man involved in both the modern age's penal system and its human sciences) as the result of a transformation of the way power operates on the body.

The first three of these methodological rules restate major themes of Foucault's earlier adumbrations of the genealogical method. The first corresponds to the basic idea of "The Discourse on Language" that genealogy should regard the causes it analyzes as positive sources of new modes of discourse. The second reflects the fundamental resolve, prominent in "Nietzsche, Genealogy, History," to seek alternatives to the progressivist, teleological accounts of standard history. The third expresses Foucault's basic genealogical hypothesis that systems of discourse (and the bodies of knowledge they formulate) are produced by nondiscursive causes. The fourth rule, however, provides the distinctive, specific feature of genealogical causes that was lacking in Foucault's previous discussions and that is the key to his analysis in *Discipline and Punish*. This is the crucial idea that the productive causes of new systems of discourse and knowledge are new techniques for the control of human bodies.

As we have seen, Foucault previously noted the connection of Nietzsche's genealogy with control of bodies in the notion of *Hernunft*. Now, in placing this connection at the center of his own work, he also develops the Nietzschean theme that genealogy sees effects following from a wide variety of diverse "petty causes." Ironically citing Jean-Baptiste de La Salle, he says genealogy reveals the "little things" on which everything depends. There is never a question of some single major stroke of invention but rather of very many minor, disparate, uncoordinated developments eventually converging to produce a major new development. In *Discipline and Punish,* for example, Foucault shows how, among many other things, the invention of more effective rifles, more efficient ways of organizing the space of hospitals, and changes in the methods of teaching children penmanship all contributed to the formation of a radically new system of social control. Thus, genealogy continues Foucault's Bachelardian project of avoiding the grand teleological schemes of much traditional history of thought.

The full specification and deployment of the genealogical method in *Discipline and Punish* is particularly important for clarifying the relation between genealogy and archaeology. For one thing, it makes clear that genealogy is by no means a replacement for archaeology. The latter plays an essential role in the description (as opposed to causal explanation) of forms of punishment. For example, Foucault presents the distinctively modern technique of punishment by imprisonment in terms of the four main categories of archaeological analysis that he distinguished in *The Archaeology of Knowledge*. Imprisonment constitutes delinquents as a new class of *objects,* characterized by the *concepts* distinctive of the criminal character; moreover, it distinguishes various *modes of authority* (that of the judge, of the parole board, of the criminologist) and alternative *lines of strategic action* (for example, different ways of using solitude and work in the treatment of prisoners). In this case, the four key archaeological categories are applied to nondiscursive practices, rather than to the discursive practices that are more typically associated with the archaeological method. *Discipline and Punish* also employs the standard archaeological analysis of discursive structures when, for example, it presents the ideas of eighteenth-century humanitarian reformers who proposed to eliminate crime by manipulating the representations offered to the mind. Archaeology remains needed to describe the fields of practices (both discursive and nondiscursive) in which genealogical causes operate.

Foucault's continuing employment of archaeological methods in his genealogical studies corresponds to the key theme of those studies: the inextricable tie between knowledge and power. A genealogical study of the origins of the means whereby a society physically controls its members must eventually call on archaeology to analyze the bodies of knowledge invented and deployed by the project of control. An archaeological study of historically successive bodies of knowledge inevitably raises causal questions that can be answered only by a genealogical account of the involvement of knowledge in systems of control. Further, just as Foucault's archaeological method is designed to analyze knowledge without giving a privileged role to the epistemological subject (whether individual or collective) so too genealogy, with its marshaling of an immense complexity of petty factors into a "micro-physics of power," decenters notions such as sovereign, state, and class as controlling subjects of power. Thus, archaeology and genealogy are complementary instruments towards Foucault's goal of uncovering the controlling structures that operate below the level of human subjectivity. As such, they are both essential methods in his fundamental project of a history of thought in service of human liberation.

NOTES

1. The following abbreviations will be used in references to Foucault's writings:
AK: *The Archaeology of Knowledge,* translated by A. Sheridan (New York, 1972).
DL: "The Discourse on Language," included as an appendix to *AK*.
DP: *Discipline and Punish,* translated by A. Sheridan (New York, 1972).
NGH: "Nietzsche, Genealogy, History," in *Language, Counter-memory, Practice,* edited by D. Bouchard (Ithaca, N.Y., 1979).
OT: *The Order of Things,* translated by A. Sheridan (New York, 1970).
PK: *Power/Knowledge,* edited by C. Gordon (New York, 1980).

2. Gary Gutting, *Foucault's Archaeology of Scientific Reason* (Cambridge, 1989).

3. Here I disagree with Alan Megill. Cf., for example, his "Foucault, Structuralism, and the Ends of History," *Journal of Modern History* 51 (1979): 499.

4. "The Discourse on History," translated by J. Johnston, in *Foucault Live,* edited by S. Lotringer (New York, 1989), 20.

5. Nevertheless, we do find in Foucault's histories some speculation of a global character. In this regard, cf. my comments on *The Order of Things* in *Foucault's Archaeology of Scientific Reason.*

6. Cf. "Postscript: An Interview with Michel Foucault," in Michel Foucault, *Death and the Labyrinth: The World of Raymond Roussel,* translated by Charles Ruas (Garden City, N.Y., 1986), 174.

7. Thus Foucault says, "Archaeology also reveals relations between discursive formations and non-discursive domains (institutions, political events, economic practices and processes)" (*AK* 162).

8. Foucault characterizes archaeology in terms of an analysis of an unconscious in, for example, an interview with J.-P. El Kabbach, "Foucault repond à Sartre," *Quinzaine littéraire* 1–15 March (1968): 21.

9. See my discussion of this issue in *Foucault's Archaeology of Scientific Reason,* chap. 7.

The Contractarian Explanation
of the State

JEAN HAMPTON

How do governments originate? How are they maintained? These are two causal questions about how states originate and persist through time that have always been of interest to anthropologists and historians. To answer them, however, one also needs to know the answer to a conceptual question "What is a state?" This essay attempts to answer all three questions by using ideas drawn from the social contract tradition. Together the answers constitute what I will call an explanation of the state.

It may seem fantastic to some that the social contract argument could provide plausible answers to the two causal questions. Doesn't the contract argument make the state's creation and maintenance the result of each subject's contractual consent to it? And isn't this a wildly inaccurate explanation of virtually every state's origin and continued existence? As Hume wryly observes:

> [W]ere you to ask the far greatest part of the nation, whether they had ever consented to the authority of their rulers, or promis'd to obey them, they wou'd be inclin'd to think very strangely of you, and wou'd certainly reply, that the affair depended not on their consent but that they were born to such obedience. (*Treatise,* III, ii, viii; 1978 548)

In response to such ridicule, supporters of the contractarian methodology have tended to back away from claiming that their contract talk has any explanatory import. The contracts in the argument are generally represented as "hypothetical" occurrences and not historical events: the theorist is, on this view, using the contract talk not to give any dubious history lessons but merely to justify the state in terms of what people *could agree to* in an equal and impartial setting.

However, I do not want to give up on the idea that the contract methodology has explanatory power. In this essay, I will construct an explanatory theory which I will argue is implicit in the traditional social contract argument but which does not make use of the literal notion of contract. I will conclude by considering, first, in what sense this is a *contractarian* model given that it incorporates only an attenuated notion of agreement, and second, whether or not the explanation is true, and thus usable by an historian or anthropologist exploring the origins and histories of particular states, or by a political or legal theorist attempting to understand the nature of the institution itself.

It is important to stress that as I attempt to answer these questions, at no point will I be discussing the justificatory force which contractarians have believed their argument has. Whether or not one can construct a social contract argument justifying the state's authority (and in this essay I take no position on that issue), I am arguing that this form of argument can at least offer a partial explanation of what kind of institution the state is. I leave for another day a discussion of how much justificational force the social contract might have in political contexts.[1]

I. SOLVING THE LEADERSHIP SELECTION PROBLEM

There are a variety of social contract arguments concerned with the justification of the state: my claim that we can distill from all of them a single explanatory theory of the state means that I believe they share, despite their differences, a common causal account of the state's creation and maintenance, and a common conceptual analysis of the state. It is one of the difficulties of my project that I must isolate these two common threads even while acknowledging the differences that divide members of this tradition.

We can find the end of that common thread by reflecting on the fact that those who present an argument in which people in a state of nature create a government are assuming that political subordination is not a natural feature of our social world. In contrast, those who believe that political subordination is natural will insist that one has no more reason to explain the subjugation of a human population to their ruler than one has to explain the subjugation of a group of mares to a stallion. Such subjugation is understood as inevitable, either because the natural masters are born with the power to dominate the natural slaves, or because the natural slaves are, for psychological or intellectual reasons, incapable of assuming the leadership role.

However, someone can believe that there is a hierarchy of talents and abilities which *ought* to be—but frequently is not—respected in the structuring of existing political societies. Or, more radically, he can deny that any such hierarchy exists and insist, as the traditional contractarians did, that human beings are similar enough in talent and abilities to make them equal, such that any of them could be leader. Either view is consistent with the contractarian methodology insofar as each accepts the fundamental tenet of that methodology, namely, that the state is an "artificial" institution (to use Hume's term) created (albeit perhaps not intentionally) by the actions of the human beings who would be rulers or subjects in it. (However, note that the second view would make not only political power but also the *reasons* entitling anyone to hold that power a human creation.) Most members of the contract tradition also believe that the state is not only created but also *maintained* by human action. The model I will present aims to clarify the nature of this maintenance activity.

If states are not only created but also maintained by the people, then this suggests that the people want them. In order to persuade his readers of the desirability of political society, the contractarian paints life without government in a "state of nature" as conflict-ridden, and presents people concluding that the state is a remedy (either the best or the only remedy) for that conflict. In the process of telling that story, the contractarian constructs a psychology which explains both why people tend to engage in conflict in a natural state, and why they would prefer to leave this state of conflict and enter political society. The psychologies of the traditional social contract theorists and the reasons they give for state-creation have varied considerably over the years. But if one looks closely one sees that although their arguments differ on the questions of why the state is desirable and what kind of state people have reason to generate, all of them contain roughly the same account of how the state is created and maintained.

I want to propose that the reason why contractarians share a common explanation of the state is that, despite the use of different psychologies and ethical theories which justify the institution of different kinds of political regimes, each believes that the generation of the state involves solving the same game-theoretic problem. In order to make this claim plausible without going into taxing detail describing every contract argument in the tradition, I will sketch how it is true for the two most important members of that tradition, Hobbes and Locke. If this common element exists in their importantly different arguments, then we have at least the basis for a claim that it is definitive of the contractarian explanatory strategy.

Let us start with Hobbes's theory. People in his state of nature are largely, but not exclusively, self-interested, and pursue above all else their self-preservation. Their desire for this latter goal, along with their desire for glory, generate violent competition for objects that leads to a climate of distrust precipitating more violence. Hobbes presents the institution of a sovereign as not only a sufficient but also a necessary condition for peace. The people in his state of nature believe this, and hence desire to institute a sovereign. But they still face considerable disagreement on the question of *who* should be sovereign. What precisely is the nature of their disagreement?

To specify it exactly, suppose there are three people in Hobbes's state of nature who are unable to resolve prisoner's dilemma problems and who are therefore inclined to aggress against one another. Suppose further that these individuals accept the Hobbesian argument that the warfare in this state can only be remedied by the institution of a sovereign. To simplify the problem for the time being, let us also suppose that they agree with Hobbes that the state will operate best if sovereignty is invested in one person, so that they aim to create an absolute monarch. Their preferences over the various possible outcomes in this situation are as follows. First, each party will rate lowest the situation in which he is not a member of the state while the other two are, because here he is a lone individual in a partial state of war facing a unified group of two who can likely beat him in any conflict. Each of them will rate the partial state of war in which he is a subject in a two-person state higher than this, because here he would enjoy the increase in security which association with another person brings. He would prefer even more being subject in a state in which all three of them are members because in this situation peace finally prevails. Hobbes also tells us that individuals would rather be rulers than subjects in any state;[2] hence, each would prefer being ruler of a two-person state rather than a subject in it, and each would prefer even more being ruler in a three-person state. But the importance of avoiding war and imminent death or injury is such that (assuming these people are not badly vainglorious) each individual would prefer being a subject in a three-person state to being the ruler in a partial state of war. So the question to be settled is, "Who shall reign?"

This situation is actually a kind of conflict-ridden coordination game much discussed in the game-theoretic literature called "the Battle of the Sexes" after Luce and Raiffa's unfortunately sexist example of a husband and wife who each prefer different evening activities (he prefers a prize fight, she prefers a ballet) but who would also rather go with the other to his or her preferred evening activity than to go to his or her own favorite alone.[3] A two-player version of this game is given in figure 1.

Figure 1 (with ordinal numbers):

	B:	
	Choose A as ruler.	Choose B as ruler.
A: Choose A as ruler.	3,2	1,1
Choose B as ruler.	1,1	2,3

It is important to note that this type of interaction is a *coordination* rather than a conflict problem because it has coordination equilibria. Coordination Equilibria are defined as those situations where the combination of the players' actions is such that no one would be better off if any one player, either himself or another, acted differently.[4] In the matrix in figure 1 there are two coordination equilibria (AA and BB), which come about when A and B choose the same person as ruler. Each prefers either of these outcomes to the outcomes that result when they choose different leaders, because their disagreement prevents them from installing a government. For a population of n people in the state of nature, the matrix representing their deliberations will be n-dimensional, with n coordination equilibria, but that game will be closely analogous to this two-dimensional game.

So the major problem people with these preferences face in their efforts to create a commonwealth is a coordination problem with considerable conflict of interest on the issue: "How shall we be governed?" I call this the "leadership selection problem." And it really has two components. In the example above, the players agreed that only one of them would rule — amounting to an agreement to create a state with an absolute monarch. But of course there can be a dispute over whether to invest sovereignty in one person or a group of persons, which is, in effect, a dispute over what form of government to institute. Resolving this dispute involves determining how many leaders will rule them, and what power he/she/they will have, and it, too, would likely have a battle-of-the-sexes structure.[5]

After resolving these matters, the people must decide (as in the example above) *which* person or persons to choose as leader to fill whatever offices in the government they have defined. If there is no disagreement on these questions, the people's dilemma is an easily solvable coordination problem with only one coordination equilibrium. Disagreement makes the coordination problem conflict-ridden, but unless it is so severe that people would rather remain in the state of nature than accept someone other than their favorite candidate as ruler (a preference driven by the desire for glory which Hobbes would condemn as irrational), it will not destroy the coordination character of the game.[6] As long as irrationality is not widespread, there should be sufficient support for achieving some resolution to generate an institution powerful enough to coerce any recalcitrant glory-seekers into submission. Later I will discuss procedures, e.g., voting, that help to create a salient solution to this kind of coordination problem, which could be used to generate the state.[7]

Does Locke's argument for the state also assume that a conflict-ridden coordination game describes the problem of creating government? It does. Consider that unlike Hobbes's people, Locke's people can be motivated not only by self-interest but also by God's "Fundamental Law of Nature" which directs them to preserve the life, health, and possessions of others as long as their own preservation will not be compromised by doing so.[8] Were people to act strictly in accordance with God's law, the state of nature would be a state of peace. But warfare is precipitated by irrational members of society, who either harm others for their own gain ("In transgressing the Law of Nature, the Offender declares himself to live by another Rule, than that of Reason and Common Equity"[9]) or fail (because of personal bias) to interpret the Fundamental Law of Nature correctly, especially when they use it to justify the punishment of offenders.[10] In virtue of the violent or uncooperative actions precipitated by this irrationality and self-bias, "nothing but Confusion and Disorder follow."[11] Reason directs men to pursue peace, but like Hobbes, Locke believes they can only do so by instituting a government:

> I easily grant, that *Civil Government* is the proper remedy for the inconveniences of the State of Nature, which must certainly be Great, where Men may be Judges in their own Case. . . .the State of Nature is therefore not to be endured.[12]

Hence, for self-interested, religious, and moral reasons, men "are quickly driven to [political] Society."[13]

Locke argues that political society remedies the disorder by providing impartial bodies which can fairly interpret the Fundamental Law of Nature and impartially adjudicate disputes using that law, and also by providing agencies that enforce the law effectively through punishment:

> Mankind in general, may restrain, or where necessary, destroy things noxious to them, and so may bring such evil on any one, who hath transgressed that Law, as may make him repent the doing of it, *and thereby deter him,* and by his Example others, from doing the like mischief.[14]

In other words, Locke believes that the use of fear can control the actions of those who refuse to live by the law of reason; on his view only the state can effectively and fairly generate that fear.

Given that this is the solution to their problems, what difficulties do Locke's people face creating that solution? Let us again consider our three-person state of nature, this time described in Lockean terms, and assume once again that they each prefer that only one of them rule. Consider that because Locke's people want the state in order to promote greater respect for a divine law that defines their obligations to one another, they desire political power not only for self-interested but also for moral and religious reasons. For all three reasons, each person would prefer least being a lone individual facing a unified group of two, because outside the state a person does not enjoy the enforcement of his rights according to this law. Locke would represent being a subject in a two-person state as better than this insofar as it would allow a person to enjoy some enforcement of rights and an increase in security (both of which are, at least in part, moral goods). Better still would be membership in a three-person state; here the person would enjoy a cessation of violence (or at least, depending upon the effectiveness of the ruler's enforcement, a lower threshold of violence). What about preferences for being ruler rather than subject in a two- or three-person state? Locke is not as committed as Hobbes is to the idea that each person would rather be ruler than subject, so it is theoretically possible that everyone would have the same favorite candidate, making the selection of a ruler easy. But if there were disagreements, Locke is clear that because it is highly desirable to institute government for moral as well as self-interested reasons, each would prefer being subject in a three-person state to being ruler in a two-person state.

So, once again, we have battle-of-the-sexes preferences, although these preferences are a function of both the moral, religious, and self-regarding interests of the people. The game-theoretic situation underlying the creation of the Lockean state is therefore the same as that which underlies the creation of the Hobbesian state.[15] Locke also believes that there can be reasonable disagreements over the form that government should take, as well as over who should be ruler in it (although he himself argues for a government with divided powers and legislative dominance). But again, note that as long as each party does not prefer a continuation of war to compromise on a non-favorite form of government, their disagreement will have a battle-of-the-sexes structure, and thus present them only with a conflict-ridden coordination game.

So we have actually discovered the two common threads running through the Lockean and Hobbesian arguments. First, both assume that the preferences of people regarding the creation of government in the state of nature give rise to a series of coordination games (most likely conflict-ridden) which must be solved and maintained to generate and sustain that institution. So in answer to the causal question, "How is a state created and maintained?" both say, "Through the generation and maintenance of conventions." Second, both see the state's role as primarily that of resolving, preventing, or punishing conflict among the people (although they disagree about exactly what reasons people have for desiring to create an institution that plays this role). And it is this role which they would regard as fundamental to understanding what a state is.

Granted that coordination games underlie the state's creation, and not prisoner's dilemmas, how are games of this kind solved and a desirable coordination equilibrium reached? Are contracts necessary to do so?

II. CREATING LEADERSHIP CONVENTIONS

Although the word 'contract' is sometimes used loosely to mean any sort of agreement, it is generally understood to be a certain kind of agreement, one in which one or more promises figure. The American Law Institute defines a contract as "a promise or set of promises for the breach of which the law gives a remedy, or the performance of which the law in some way recognizes a duty."[16] The species of contract which the traditional contractarian invokes is known as a bilateral contract, in which a promise or set of promises by one side is exchanged for a promise or set of promises by the other side.[17] Contracts are made when parties to an agreement believe that the performance of the actions to be agreed upon is only collectively and not individually rational for each of them, such that an exchange of promises among them (i.e., a contract) to perform the actions seems necessary to secure performance. The prisoner's dilemma nicely represents the game-theoretic structure of this situation, and is depicted in figure 2.

Figure 2 (with ordinal numbers):

		B: action x	action y
A:	action x	2,2	1,4
	action y	4,1	3,3

In circumstances such as the state of nature, in which no law exists to enforce the contract, performance would only occur if the parties to it were able and willing to keep their contractual promises.

So if people in a state of nature needed a contract to institute the state, this would be because there were one or more prisoner's dilemmas associated with its institution, and that institution would only occur if people had the ability to keep a contractual promise to perform collectively rational but individually irrational actions. But we have seen that prisoner's dilemmas do not underlie the institution of the state in Hobbes's or Locke's theory. Although they are the sort of problem *precipitating* conflict for which the state is supposed to be a solution, they are not the problem which must be solved to create that solution. Another and more easily solved problem underlies the state's creation—i.e., the conflict-ridden coordination game. Might contracts, nonetheless, be necessary to solve these games?[18]

The idea that a promissorial agreement is necessary for the state's creation is puzzling, because promises are not usually taken to be either necessary or desirable for the solution of any coordination dilemma—even those with conflict. Consider that the task of the participants of such a dilemma is to realize only one coordination equilibrium. An effective way of doing so, if circumstances permit, is to communicate with one another so as to *reach an agreement* to pursue only one of the equilibria (e.g., players in a traffic coordination dilemma might specifically agree with one another to drive on the right rather than the left). Such agreements work as solutions to these problems because they give each party the "common knowledge that each prefers to conform to [the equilibrium chosen] conditionally upon conformity by others involved with him in [the game]."[19] How does that common knowledge help to effect a solution to this dilemma? I propose the following answer.[20] The fact that the agreement is commonly known causes each player to make a high assessment of the likelihood that the other player(s) will choose the agreed-upon equilibrium, such that an expected utility calculation performed by each of the players will dictate the action realizing that equilibrium by each player. Henceforth I will call such agreements "self-interested" or SI agreements, because self-interested rational calculation, rather than the sense of "duty" arising out of a promise or fear of a coercive power, is the motive for each person's performance of the act agreed upon.

But as David Lewis explores,[21] SI agreements might not be necessary for the resolution of a coordination problem. What is needed for its resolution is the generation of a *convention* governing which equilibrium to realize, and that convention can be generated even without agreement if there is an obviously salient equilibrium, one that stands out from the rest by its uniqueness in some conspicuous respect. If it is common knowledge that this equilibrium stands out in an obvious way, each will estimate the probability that they will perform the action leading to that equilibrium as higher than the probability that they will perform any other action, so that an expected utility calculation will dictate the pursuit of that equilibrium. In such situations it is "as if" there were an agreement on the pursuit of that salient outcome; hence it is common to hear people speak of there being a "tacit agreement" in these situations. Literally, of course, no one explicitly agreed with anyone on anything, but each did act by making reference to the beliefs and preferences of the others in the pursuit of this particular outcome, just as she would have done if there had been an explicit agreement among them to pursue it. If this coordination problem persists and is repeatedly solved in this way, the participants have developed (without explicit agreement) a *convention* to solve their coordination problem.

So in order to solve their leadership problem, people who want to create a state must generate a leadership convention. As we shall discuss, either of the strategies involved, or some combination of the two, could be used to do so. Moreover, *something like* a contractual process *could* produce it. If each member had explicitly agreed with the others on who should rule and how, where that agreement involved a compromise by members of the group whose favorite outcome was not selected, then the conflict in the situation would be resolved and coordination achieved. However, notice that this compromise agreement *would not literally be a contract* because promises would not be necessary to keep it. Once the agreement was made it would already be in each party's interest to realize the coordination equilibrium agreed upon. This agreement would only be more difficult to make, requiring capitulation or compromise by some or all of the parties.

Another more historically plausible scenario used by Hobbes to explain the institution of a sovereign involves voting,[22] a method that is actually used by democratically organized states to select their rulers (although they use it in a situation where there is already a convention on how these leaders will rule, what powers they will have, and how long their term of office will be). Consider the problem facing any political party of selecting a viable candidate to represent the party in a general election. All members of the party realize that it is overwhelmingly in their interest to select someone from among their ranks to represent them, but there is often considerable disagreement as to who shall do so. Political parties such as the Democratic Party in the United States or the Labour Party in Britain resolve this controversy by holding successive elections (either in different geographical areas at different times, or successively at one national party convention), with those who get the majority of the votes staying in contention, and those who get small percentages of support dropping out. As the process continues, there is a gradual "snowball" or "bandwagon" effect, with one person usually emerging as the clear-cut favorite. The snowball effect in these elections is a clear indication that they are tactics for effecting a solution to a conflict-ridden coordination problem. The results of each successive election give people a way to determine the probability that their favorite leader will be able to receive support from the rest of the electorate, and thus allow them to calculate whether or not it is rational for them to hold out for that leader's selection. Those people who find themselves supporting candidates with little or no support from the rest of the electorate will find it rational to switch to a more popular candidate they prefer less in the interest of getting a resolution to this coordination problem.

If this election technique ever fails to effect a solution to a leadership selection problem, it is because a significant number of those whose favorite candidates lose refuse to accept that their candidates are effectively out of contention for selection, in just the same way that the loser of a coin-flip might repudiate that coin-flip as a strategy for solving this sort of problem. Such a refusal in a political context can produce stalemate and even civil war, but Hobbes would insist that this refusal is generally irrational. Holding out for a better deal means risking no solution to the problem, and thus a return to the state of war; it is a risk that an expected utility calculation in the state of nature would likely tell one not to take (unless, of course, the winning candidate posed a threat to one's life).

Historically, people have not been so rational or so moral, and have frequently resorted to warfare to choose their leaders and their governmental structures. But warfare is another device for achieving a resolution to a battle-of-the-sexes problem relying on natural saliency rather than SI agreements. To see this, imagine a pre-political situation in which war has gone on for some time and consider the plight of a very unsuccessful inhabitant. Unless he is badly vainglorious, such a person knows that he will never score a complete win over all the others in this state. Such a person is ripe for the following offer by a more successful inhabitant whom I will call a "sovereign-entrepreneur." This entrepreneur says, "Look, you are getting nowhere on your own. But if you join forces with me and *do my bidding* (so that I am your ruler), then you will have more security than you now have." If this person does not accept this rather attractive-looking positive incentive by the sovereign-entrepreneur, he might be "offered" the following negative incentive: "Do my bidding or else I will harm you!" And this threat will be real since, as we said, the sovereign-entrepreneur is a better warrior.

In general, both of these incentives are important tools for successful warriors to use in attracting subjects. The advantage of submission to this sovereign-entrepreneur are substantial: the subject will receive greater protection from other members of the confederacy, he will have a greater chance of warding off attacks from outsiders if he is allied with this leader than he would have on his own, and he might receive a share of the spoils of any victory achieved over the forces of these outsiders. However, negative incentives are useful as a method of encouraging some reluctant members of the state of nature to "give in" and accept the sovereign-entrepreneur as leader. Hence, the threats help to resolve the battle-of-the-sexes problem over who should be declared ruler.

As entrepreneurs attract subjects in these ways, a certain number of powerful confederacies may emerge. But with their emergence comes a real market choice for the people in this state, as Robert Nozick actually noticed in his own attempt to construct a scenario of the creation of government.[23] In Nozick's scenario the forces of the two competing "protection agencies" do battle. One of these agencies will emerge as the usual or continual winner of these battles. And since the clients of the losing agency are ill-protected in conflicts with clients of the winning agency, they leave their losing agency to "do business" with the winner. Eventually one confederacy emerges as winner over all others and is thus the "best buy" in protection for everyone in this state. So the inhabitants of the state of nature looking for a protection agency are in a market. Heads of different confederacies essentially say to them: "Buy me if you want protection." And the confederacy that wins more often than any other will be the best buy for the people in that state.

There are two important points to notice about this scenario. First, coordination on who should be leader is being achieved *not* via explicit agreement among the inhabitants of the state of nature, but via a series of independent choices of a salient sovereign candidate by each inhabitant. Second, the negative incentives in this scenario are particularly useful in solving the *sort* of coordination problem which leadership selection presents: in particular, it breaks the conflict over who should rule (and how). Nor does the sovereign-entrepreneur have to threaten *everyone* in the state of nature. He need only threaten enough people to get a cadre of support enabling his confederacy to dominate in the state of war. Thereafter his confederacy will be the "best buy" in the state of nature and, as such, the salient choice for subjugation by everyone else.

The fact that warfare is not generally regarded as a *legitimate* way to solve this type of conflict-ridden coordination problem does not alter the fact that it can succeed in effecting a solution to it. Nonetheless, most social contract theorists have not used this warfare scenario in their argument because it does not serve their justificatory interests. Any theorist interested in showing what kind of state we *should* create and maintain does not want to use stories of state creation such as the warfare scenario in which the mightiest, but not necessarily the most just leadership faction would prevail. It is natural to present a just government, which takes account of the rights of each individual subject, as the product of an agreement process in which those rights are respected. But Nozick's scenario has other advantages. In my restatement of his scenario I attributed to people the intention to leave the state of nature and create a government. But I needed to attribute to them at each moment only the intention to subjugate themselves to the best confederacy leader at that moment, and given the structure of the situation, this intention on the part of each of them would more than likely lead to the creation of a confederacy leader with a monopoly of power. Insofar as this "invisible hand" explanation need only make use of this limited intention, it not only has certain desirable explanatory features,[24] but may also be closer to what actually occurred in the generation of existing political conventions than explicit-agreement scenarios.

The fact that traditional contractarians all resorted to the notion of an explicit agreement to construct a scenario of the state's creation has obscured the two causal explanations of the state that their arguments are making, namely, that states are created via the generation of a leadership convention, and second, that states persist through time for as long as this convention is maintained. As we noted above, this convention can be generated without the people having the explicit intention to create a state. So despite what Nozick himself says, he is not any less of a "contractarian" because he uses in his argument a story in which the leadership convention is not generated by explicit agreement; instead, his successful use of a non-agreement story simply points up the fact that creating and maintaining a government involves the generation and maintenance of a conventional solution to a (probably conflict-ridden) coordination problem.

III. EMPOWERMENT

Thus far, this model makes the creation and maintenance of government a result of people's participation in a convention empowering rulers in a certain form of government. But we still do not know what participation in a leadership convention involves, such that the state is created and maintained. What actions must people take such that someone becomes their ruler?

Consider that a person is only a ruler—i.e., only has *power*—when his subjects do what he says, so people presumably make someone a ruler when they (or at least most of them) obey his commands. According to the contractarians, each subject gives the ruler the power of command over him: in Locke's words, "the first *Power, viz. of doing whatsoever he thought fit for the Preservation of himself*, and the rest of Mankind, *he gives up* to be regulated by Laws made by the Society."[25] But what does it mean to be "regulated by laws made by the society"?

At the very least, it means being subject to the ruler's power to punish violations of these laws. Hobbes suggests that a subject grants the ruler punishment power when he does three things:[26]

1. The subject must be disposed to obey the punishment orders of the person or group chosen as ruler.
2. The subject must surrender his right to come to the aid of another who is being punished by the ruler (although not, some might think, his right to defend himself).
3. The subject must oblige himself to assist the ruler in punishing others (but not, some might say, himself).

Regarding the first action: if we assume that the situation underlying the creation of a ruler is a battle-of-the-sexes dilemma, then once the subjects have agreed (implicitly or explicitly) that a certain person or group will be their ruler, obeying that person's punishment commands is identified as the way to achieve coordination in this situation; hence to the extent that obeying the punishment commands of any other person or group would disrupt this coordination, they have good reason not to do so.[27] Regarding the second action, it would seem that, in general, people are able to refrain from interfering with their government's punishment of people other than friends and relatives. Hobbes would point out that such punishment does not threaten their own well-being and insofar as allowing it to happen is a way of instituting a remedy to the warfare in that natural state, it is desirable to let it occur. Locke would point out that people are generally supportive, for moral as well as self-regarding reasons, of punishment of those who do not live by the law of reason and hence deserve the infliction of pain (indeed they support such punishment in the state of nature). Thus, any problems generated by those who do attempt to intervene on behalf of criminals for whom they care are small enough to be easily handled by a ruler who has sufficient police force to help him carry out the punishments.

But this brings us to the third action. In a community of any significant size the government will need help enforcing its edicts: police, judges, and jailers will all be required to make effective enforcement of the laws possible. Therefore, some percentage of persons in the community must be wiling to carry out these jobs in order that the government have power. If (as Locke contends) people have the capacity to act in other-interested ways even at some cost to themselves, the ruler could appeal to them to volunteer their services. If (as Hobbes contends) they have no such capacity, a natural way for the government to receive their services would be to make individual contracts with each of them to become part of that cadre, giving them goods in exchange for service. Moreover, such a contract would not require either the ruler(s) or the members of the cadre to be fine, upstanding promise-keepers: it would only require that they be self-interested and smart enough to see the repetitive prisoner's dilemma nature of the agreement.[28] That is, because the government will stay in power only for as long as this cadre functions, it is in its interest to pay cadre members in order to ensure their future service. And because members of the cadre will only get that pay if they do what the government wants, it is in their interest to follow its orders. So we can expect these cadres to develop, and it is in the other subjects' interest not to interfere with their formation. The upshot of this discussion is that *no general social contract* is necessary for a government's empowerment.

But is this all that is necessary for a state to exist? Some legal theorists have argued it is not; on their view the state not only has the power to punish but also the authority to rule.[29] What is state authority? Philosophers such as Raz or Anscombe understand it to be that which a state has, such that members of it believe they are obligated to obey its directives.[30] So on this view, if I am a subject of a political system, then I obey a command of the state not only because I am fearful of the sanction if I do not and I am caught, but also (and more importantly) because the command is authoritative for me. "I have to do this because it is the law!" I think to myself. The exact definition of state authority is the subject of controversy, but one recent philosopher argues for the following definition: "α has authority over β if and only if the fact that α required β to ϕ (i) gives β a content-independent reason to ϕ, and (ii) excludes some of β's reasons for not-ϕ-ing."[31]

Students of positivist legal theory know that it is important not to mistake a claim of authority for a claim of justification. As Hart was at pains to stress, to say that states have authority over their citizens is to make a purely descriptive statement, not a normative one. Whether or not a subject is right to obey the state, and whether or not a state deserves to have the obedience of its subjects, Hart claims that a coercive regime is only a state (as opposed to a group of gunmen coercing a population through the use of physical power) if the people accept a rule granting the regime the right to issue commands they will regard as binding upon them (i.e., that they will believe give them a content-independent reason for following them simply because they are issued by this regime).[32]

Now there are some who deny that states possess authority, even when this is understood in a purely positivist sense. But for those who believe it exists, the traditional, explicitly contractarian interpretation of the social contract argument might seem to promise an analysis of it. In the same way that my doctor has authority to take out my appendix if we have contractually agreed that she should do so, so too does it seem that my state has authority to dictate how I should behave in certain areas if we have contractually agreed for it to do so. Locke's appeal to promissorial consent is therefore explanatorily useful if one reads it as part of an explanation of how the state comes to have authority to command me. Someone who believes this may therefore want to supplement or replace any convention-based model of the state with an explicit appeal to an authority-giving contract between the ruler and the people.

But is this explanation of authority any good? Over and over again, from David Hume to Ronald Dworkin, the contract tradition has been ridiculed for failing to provide anything like a plausible explanation of the state's authority using the idea of a promissorial contract. Just when, asks Hume, have most of the world's population undertaken this contractual obligation? People, he notes, generally obey the state because they think they are "born to it," not because they have promised to do so. What about the notion of tacit consent? If tacit consent is understood simply as the acceptance of benefits, then it is hard to know why it obliges us (it certainly would not do so normally in a court of law—acceptance of benefits rarely, if ever, counts as making a promise), or why it obliges us members any more than it obliges any foreign traveller who enjoys the benefits of the state while she is here. And if we interpret this kind of consent such that it is more explicitly made and more explicitly promissorial, then it becomes increasingly difficult to argue that all or even most citizens of regimes around the world have ever given it.

Well then, might political authority be explained contractually if the contract explaining it is hypothetical rather than actual in nature? But here Dworkin has the appropriate rejoinder: "A hypothetical contract is not simply a pale form of contract; it is no contract at all."[33] We are not obliged by make-believe contracts, but by real ones. Hence, whatever excellent use a hypothetical contract has in defining justice or legitimating the state, a contract that never really took place cannot explain real authority.

I still think that there is something about a contractarian approach to state authority that is right, but I want to argue that this "something" can be best captured only by using the convention explanation of the state. The reason why explicitly contract-based explanations of the state's authority invariably fail is that they rest on a false history of the state.[34] But one can use the more plausible convention analysis to explain the state's authority by arguing that the process of generating a leadership convention involves not only the creation of rulers who have a virtual monopoly on force, but also (and perhaps more importantly) rulers who have authority to command. As Anscombe suggests, to create the state is to create *an authoritative office*.[35] An umpire in baseball has his authority by virtue of holding that authoritative office (required if the game is to be played), and not by virtue of any contract between him and the players that explicitly gives him the right to command them. Similarly, it is the nature of their office, and not any real or make-believe contract, which explains why our rulers have authoritative power. But that office is nonetheless one that, on the convention model, the people create and maintain through their participation in a certain kind of convention.

Now perhaps that participation is unwitting. A people who decide to regard a certain person as their queen because they believe that God has authorized her to rule and thus obey her are in fact giving her both power and authority through their obedience as a result of their interdependent acceptance of her as leader — so that God does not authorize her, they do. The fact that their consent to her rule is unwitting, i.e., that they do not know that it is they who are responsible for her holding that particular kind of office which exists because of their need for it, might be greatly to her advantage. In particular, it might give her more security of reign because her subjects would not see that they in fact have the ability and indeed good reason to strip her of her authority to command them if her performance as ruler were poor. Nonetheless, she gets both her power and her authority by virtue of their unwitting convention-generating activity.

If one adds to one's analysis of the state the idea that the state is an institution whose rule is ultimately authoritative in the community ("the final court of appeal" as Rawls puts it),[36] one is accepting a Hartian approach to the nature of a legal system rather than an Austinian approach.[37] Insisting that Austin was wrong to suppose that a legal rule could be binding simply because the rule-giver has the physical power to coerce people to obey it, Hart maintained that a binding rule can only be created by one who has the authority to give the people such a rule. And this authority, he argues, can only come from another rule accepted by the people which he calls the "Rule of Recognition."[38]

I want to argue that if the contractarian chooses to do so, she can give an account of the state that dovetails nicely with the Hartian legal theory.[39] On the convention analysis, the leadership convention created by the people generates rules which together constitute the Hartian Rule of Recognition. First, the convention defines governmental offices and establishes limits on the powers and duties of these offices. These powers and duties constitute what I will call the "operational" rules of government. Second, the convention bestows on some of these offices the authority to command, which involves giving the office-holder the power to make a command that the people will believe they have a *prima facie* reason to obey simply because these office-holders have made it. Call these "authority-bestowing" rules; they entitle the office-holder to make directives that are binding on the people, and making them is actually part of the process of defining the offices of government. (What kind of authoritative directives a particular-office holder can make is determined by the leadership convention.) And finally, there are rules which specify the process of filling these offices, such that the person selected by the process is entitled to the office.

Creating the leadership convention involves generating these sorts of rules. Together they constitute an *impersonal* authority in the legal system, and I would argue that it is part of the conceptual analysis of the state that this impersonal authority exists. These rules are obligating not because they are themselves dictated by an authoritative office-holder (this puts the cart before the horse — these rules define what counts as an authoritative office-holder), but because they are accepted, via convention, by the people. Indeed, as Hart points out, these rules can exist and operate effectively even when there are many who are not terribly clear about the details of the authority of different offices of the government which the convention establishes. As long as there are some people who know the details, and these few are trusted by the rest to monitor the performance of any office-holder on the basis of these details, the convention can be said to be accepted by everyone.[40]

Let me stress again that on this approach to understanding the state's authority, the issue of whether the state is morally justifiable is irrelevant. This model offers an explanation of what the institution is, not a normative defense of it. If a moral theorist desires to pursue the justification of this institution, she will morally evaluate at the very least its use of negative sanctions to enforce its dictates, and perhaps also the moral legitimacy of the authority the state has over its subjects. If she believes the institution is morally justifiable, how would she defend it? She would do so using her favorite moral theory. Utilitarians, Kantians, and divine rights theorists will have different ways of defending (or attacking, if they choose) the state's legitimacy. And, of course, there are also contractarian ways of doing so. Contemporary philosophy has seen the rise of what I call contractarian moral theory, in which the notion of "what we could agree to" is understood to be central to evaluating actions, policies, and social institutions. There are a variety of contractarian moral theories that have been developed, and all of them are controversial. Embracing the convention analysis of the state commits one to *none* of these views, because it is a non-normative analysis. So, of course, if one wants to legitimate the state one must supplement that analysis. Which theory one should choose, however, is a matter of independent philosophical assessment; there is no more reason to choose a contractarian defense of the state than to choose a contractarian defense of any institution or policy. One would only do so if one thought, on independent grounds, that this was the right moral theory to choose.

IV. SUMMARY

The contractarian explanation of the state can therefore be summarized as follows:

> The state is an institution whose primary role is to deter, prevent, and forestall conflict among people through the use of legislators, adjudicators, and coercive enforcers, and it is maintained by convention in which people are "in agreement" about what their government will be and who will rule within it; specifically, it establishes the offices of government and procedures for filling those offices, and it grants punishment power to some of these office-holders. Participating in that convention means, at the very least, not interfering with, and perhaps actively assisting in, the state's punishment activities — especially its formation and maintenance of punishment cadres. Hartian positivists will also argue that this convention is itself a complex set of rules entitling those selected by the procedures to hold office, obligating them to respect the terms of the office, and entitling them to make rules that are binding upon the people, so that it is an impersonal authority in the society by virtue of being accepted by the people.

The convention, once instituted, only exists for as long as the people maintain it, which involves their participation in the three punishment activities, and their continued acceptance and enforcement of the rules constituting it.

Note that the convention model presents the state as an institution whose primary role is to encourage cooperation and discourage conflict. For many this will be too limited a conception of the role of this institution, ignoring the way it may properly be engaged in the redistribution of assets in the name of justice, or in the education of its citizens, or in the promotion of cultural opportunities and endeavors. Contractarians can always argue for the addition of these duties to the state's agenda, but they would also argue that such additions do not change the fact that the state's power and authority to wield sanctions and issue binding commands are fundamental to understanding what it is, and how it is created and maintained.

What kind of relationship exists between the rulers and the ruled when the rulers' power is generated and maintained by convention? This is actually a complicated question, whose answer requires that we recognize that there is a hierarchy of what I will call (following Wittgenstein) "games" in a political society. First, there is the "political" game, in which the people are subordinated to government office-holders, who have the power to obligate them and to inflict sanctions upon them. So the relationship between people and ruler in this game is the relationship of a subordinate to a commander.

But second, there is the meta-game that creates and maintains this object-game, in which the people define and control the power of these offices and office-holders through their participation in the leadership convention. To understand the people's relationship with the rulers of this meta-game, let me use some of Locke's metaphors for a moment. Locke argued that creating the state involves the people becoming, after making contracts with one another, one unified entity – what he called a "political community." He then argued that the people, so understood, enter into contractual relations with the ruler. Of course literally there is rarely if ever such an explicit promissorial agreement between ruler and ruled, but if this language is metaphorical, it can be successfully cashed out using the convention model. That model places these parties in what I call an "agency" relationship, which is not contractual either in nature or origin, but which is similar enough to actual agency relationships, which are initiated by contract, to make any metaphorical talk of a social contract between ruler and ruled forgivable. Just as a principal gives (usually via contract) a person known as her 'agent' power to act by allowing her to wield a right belonging to the principal, so too do the subjects give a ruler political power through their generation of a leadership convention. And just as a principal can supervise the performance of her agent, and control the agent, by threatening to fire her if she does not use the principal's rights as the principal wished, so too can the people supervise the performance of the ruler-agent by threatening to depose him if he does not perform as the people wish. In figure 3 I give the game-theoretic structure of the ruler-subject relationship:

Figure 3:

Their preferences for the outcome created after
the people's second move (1 = highest, 4 = lowest)

RULER	PEOPLE	RULER	PEOPLE
	Keep in power	2	1
govern according to terms of empowerment			
	depose	4	3
	depose	3	2
ignore terms of empowerment			
	keep in power	1	4

Because the subjects in this game are able to make their move contingent upon how the ruler has moved, their possible moves, which are represented in the second column, are understood to be temporally posterior to the ruler's move. The two columns of numbers correspond to the players' preferences for outcomes created by the combination of their possible moves.

This game is not a prisoner's dilemma, and hence does not require promises to bind ruler and people effectively. The ruler knows that if she rules against the people's wishes, they will fire her: their keeping her in power when she rules badly ranks lowest for them while their firing her when she rules badly ranks second highest for them. She also knows that if she rules well they will keep her "employed": their keeping her employed when she rules well ranks highest for them; their firing her when she rules well ranks second lowest for them. So she has a choice between ruling well and staying in power (ranked second) or ruling poorly and being deposed (ranked last). So her best move is to rule well. But this is exactly the move by her that the people most want her to make. Their preferences and power in this situation force her to make a first move which allows them to achieve their favorite outcome, but the game is also such that she is able to retain power (a highly desirable outcome for her as long as she pleases them). However, note that she is not completely powerless in this situation. Because the people need her to rule, she can be assured that her least favorite outcome (i.e., her doing the job and their deposing her) is also one of their least preferred outcomes. So she has enough power over them (at least for the time-being) *because they need her* to secure a desirable outcome for herself (although not her most desirable outcome). Indeed, how well the agent needs to work is a matter of degrees: to stay employed she must work just well enough to make it more advantageous to the principal to keep her rather than incur the costs of firing her. (So, in the end, the people who are the principal in this relationship will be unlikely to be able to demand and get exactly the performance from their ruler/agent that they would like.)

As I shall discuss in the next section, this analysis of the relationship between ruler and ruled is too simplistic, and I shall be discussing how to make it more sophisticated. However, one correction is easy to make, and making it allows us to cash out another Lockean metaphor. Insofar as the ruler's power is created through the generation of a convention, her power is the result of many individuals determining that obeying the commands of only this ruler (in particular, her punishment commands) is rational. Hence a single entity called "the people" do not literally bestow or withdraw power; instead, whether or not a person rules depends upon many individuals determining whether or not obedience or rebellion is in their best interest (where that interest is defined either by a moral or religious law or by their desires). Nonetheless, there is this much truth to the idea that "the people" institute and depose rulers: In order for individuals to institute a ruler, *each must coordinate (either explicitly or implicitly) with one another* on who the ruler shall be and what the scope of her legitimate areas of command are; and in order for individuals to depose a ruler, they must, once again, coordinate (either explicitly or implicitly) with one another on the idea that an alternative state of affairs would be better than the present state. So although Locke is saying something literally false when he says that the people contract with one another to form a unified political community which contracts with the ruler, nonetheless a state only exists when the individuals composing it are "in agreement" with one another, coordinating such that a leadership convention is established and maintained, and thereby becoming, collectively, the principal in an agency relationship with the office-holders.

One of the difficulties of coming to understand the state is that it is an enterprise constituted by two distinct games, in one of which the people are the controllers of the rulers, and in the other of which, the people are controlled by them. We are indebted to the social contract theorists for trying, albeit with metaphors, to make that double relationship clear.

V. CRITICIZING THE CONVENTION MODEL

How successful is this model? In this section I want to evaluate two criticisms someone could make of my claim that the social contract tradition generates a historically plausible, convention-based model of the state's creation and maintenance. First, one might object that the model, regardless of its success as an explanatory theory, is simply not generated by the social contract tradition; second, one might argue that it cannot be successful as an explanation because it is not historically plausible. I will discuss each of these criticisms in turn.

A. The Convention Model and the Social Contract Tradition

To build the convention model out of Hobbes's and Locke's political writings using the resources of contemporary game theory strikes many as anachronistic at best, deeply distorting at worst. Are the language and tools that I use to state the model too dissimilar to the language and tools of the traditional contractarians to allow me to claim that it is nonetheless their model?

I do not believe so. We must resist the temptation to treat philosophical figures as museum pieces. Instead we should dissect, analyze, explicate, and respond to their arguments in order to see how far those arguments are right. Of course, it is anachronistic to read game theory back into traditional contractarian writings — that is not the point. The issue to be decided is whether or not we learn anything of value about Locke's and Hobbes's understanding of the state if we do so, and I think we do. These philosophers were groping for ways of understanding the state, not as the creation of God, not as ordained by nature, but as a human creation. The convention model explains how this is possible, and in the process, preserves two central ideas in the tradition: first, that there is a kind of agreement among the people that explains why the state exists; and second (although this point was contested by Hobbes), that there is an agreement between the people and the ruler setting out the terms of his rule. The first agreement is, on this model, a convention rather than an explicit promissorial agreement, whose generation could take many forms. The second agreement, on this model, is really an agency relationship between the people (who create and maintain the ruler's power for certain purposes) and the ruler (who must use that power to satisfy them or be deposed).

Still, I have made substantial revisions in the traditional contract argument by replacing talk of contracts with talk of conventions and agency relationships. I have argued that these revisions are consistent with and even required by the presuppositions of the traditional contractarians' arguments. By making these revisions have I vindicated the contractarian argument as an explication of the state, or have I refuted it?

Perhaps it really does not matter how one answers this question; what is important is the model itself and not its philosophical pedigree. Nonetheless, I tend to regard my analysis as a vindication of the contractarian argument. If one shows that the premises of a political argument require a different conceptual representation of the state than the representation given by the original users of that argument, then it is appropriate to say that the revisionist conceptual representation has been implicit in the argument all along (albeit unacknowledged by its previous users). It is because the preferences of the people in the traditional contractarians' state of nature establish battle-of-the-sexes dilemmas rather than prisoner's dilemmas that it becomes right to say that, on contractarian's view, the creation of government requires the generation of a convention.

Hume saw himself as an opponent of the social contract argument because he endorsed ideas which this analysis incorporates. But I would argue that he should be seen only as an opponent of the traditional contractarian's persistent use of the idea of contract, an idea which my analysis shows is not implicit in the argument itself and which, if inserted into it, damages the argument's operation as an explanation of a ruler's political power. Indeed, I would argue that both Hume and I are "revisionists" only in the sense that we are revising, and improving upon, the standard interpretation of the social contract argument.

B. Is the Model Right?

Critics may worry about the extent to which the model can be empirically veri-
fied. I think such worries have merit, but before I explain why, I want to show
that it does have some real explanatory power.

First, do the preferences of real people match the coordination-game preferences of Locke's or Hobbes's people on the question of whether or not to enter
civil society? This is an empirical question to be answered by empirical study,
but given that these philosophers show why moral, religious, and self-interested
motivations give rise either to pure or conflict-ridden coordination game preferences on the question of instituting the state, this suggests that a wide range of
real people, with any of these motivations, would nonetheless have preferences
that fit the convention model.

This model can also be used to illuminate the actual reasoning processes of
people who are considering whether or not to rebel against their government.
Consider Gregory Kavka's intriguing discussion of what he calls the paradox of
revolution. In Kavka's words, the paradox goes as follows:

> Exploited citizenry are apparently in a multiparty prisoner's dilemma sit-
> uation with respect to participating in a mass revolt. Collectively they
> have the power to overthrow their oppressors, and would probably be
> better off if they did so. But an individual's participation in a revolt is
> dangerous and will have only a minute effect on the prospect of the revolt
> succeeding, while the individual can expect to reap most of the benefits
> of a successful revolt (should one occur) without participating. Hence,
> rational individuals will not participate, and mass revolts of rational citi-
> zens will never occur even against tyrannical, repressive, or exploitive
> regimes. This odd conclusion—that the rationality of the members of a
> society prevents them from overthrowing a despised government—is
> called *the paradox of revolution*.[41]

Kavka contends that the paradox shows that people are in a multi-party prisoner's dilemma with respect to the question of revolution, and as all students of
this dilemma know, rational actions by rational people will lead to a suboptimal
outcome in a prisoner's dilemma—in this case, the outcome of continued submission. But in stating the paradox in argument form, Kavka does not explicitly
mention any game-theoretic situation. He presents it as follows:

1. Rational individuals act so as to maximize expected payoffs.
2. In a potentially revolutionary situation, the expected costs of participation are higher than the expected costs of nonparticipation, and there
   are no sufficiently compensating expected benefits of participation.
3. Therefore, rational individuals in a potentially revolutionary situation
   will not participate in a revolution.[42]

Of course, the argument cannot establish that revolution will never occur,
because, as Kavka notes, people sometimes act irrationally, and thus irrational

motives might explain revolutionary activity throughout history. Moreover, "the possibility of others irrationally joining a revolt may influence the cost-benefit analysis of *rational* potential revolutionaries."[43] With this in mind, Kavka proposes what he calls the "dynamic-maximizing" solution:

> Rational agents' expected utility calculations about participation in revolution will *change* as they observe others joining the revolutionary struggle. In particular, as a first approximation we would expect agents' estimates of the probability of the revolution succeeding to go up, and their estimates of the probability of being punished for taking part in the revolt to go down, as the number of people they observe taking part in the revolt increases. These changes in probability will in turn raise the expected benefits associated with participation (since the receipt of many such benefits is contingent upon the revolt succeeding) and decrease the expected costs (e.g., the risk of being punished for participating). It is also possible that the intrinsic payoffs of participation, such as the pleasure of taking part in a mass enterprise, and the intrinsic costs of nonparticipation, such as the guilt one may feel over being a free-rider, will increase as the number of others participating increases.[44]

So the idea is that as confederacies enlarge, more and more people will find it rational to participate. In particular, any individual will join the revolution when his or her "revolution-participation threshold" is reached. "Whether a revolution will occur will depend upon the distribution of revolution-participating thresholds among the members of a population."[45] It is possible that a population will have thresholds distributed such that revolution is essentially impossible, but it may also have thresholds distributed such that it is inevitable.

  I like Kavka's solution to this paradox, but I want to argue that it is only a solution because, in fact, the citizenry are *not* in a multi-party prisoner's dilemma with respect to the question of revolution. This should be evident because, in a real prisoner's dilemma, it does not matter how many of my fellow players are disposed to choose the cooperative action — *I* am still rational to refrain from cooperation. The fact that Kavka's solution has it that people will find cooperation in the revolution rational with increasing numbers of rebels shows that they are in a different kind of game.

  As I have argued at length elsewhere, problems can seem "prisoner's dilemma-like" even though they have a different game theoretic structure,[46] and that is what is going on here. In fact, parties are in a coordination game with respect to the question of revolution. Just as creating a state involves solving a host of potentially conflict-ridden coordination problems, so, too, does changing it. Imagine that I am a disgruntled citizen who would like a new ruler. What reasons do I have for maintaining what I take to be a bad convention? Consider the reasons I have for maintaining any convention, e.g., the convention to drive on the right. If there is no law requiring me to respect this convention I will respect it anyway if I believe: (a) that I am in a coordination dilemma; (b) that in fact driving on the right is the conventional solution to that dilemma; (c) that it is a convention that enables the community to achieve a desirable coordination equilibrium, so that it furthers the interest of those in the coordination dilemma; and most importantly (d) there is no other convention on a different coordination equilibrium which it is rational for me to pursue (given the costs and benefits of doing so) by (in part) not obeying the convention. Note (d) presupposes that by acting so as to respect a convention, I also help in a very small way to maintain it through my respect for it.

These four considerations are also central to explaining why and when a citizen has reason to obey her ruler. I have reason to respect a leadership convention about who should rule, and thus obey the ruler, when: (a') I am in a (conflict-ridden) coordination dilemma about who should rule; (b') in fact this ruler is the conventional solution to that problem; (c') it is a convention that enables us to realize a coordination equilibrium, so that it furthers the interests of those in the coordination dilemma; and (d') there is no other leadership convention that would realize a different coordination equilibrium whose adoption I believe it rational for me to pursue (given the costs and benefits of doing so) by (in part) not respecting this convention. Again, this last point presupposes that when I act so as to respect the leadership convention and obey the ruler's commands, particularly his punishment orders, I help in a small way to maintain this convention and keep him in power.

Now what happens when a subject believes (a') and (b'), but denies (c') — judging the convention to be bad either because it fails to realize a coordination equilibrium at all (so that, barring exorbitant costs, changing should be pareto efficient for everyone), or because there is a better coordination equilibrium available to the group (although perhaps not better for everyone). In either case he concludes that people have made a mistake, and would be better off, on the whole, deposing the present leader and replacing her with another ruler. He therefore wishes to take from her the authority to rule which this bad convention grants her. If they come to agree that they have a better alternative (so that for each of them [d'] is no longer true), then (as we discussed above) neither he nor they will believe they should obey her, and will rebel. But if they do not agree with him, then his unilateral action in support of another candidate will be useless. *In fact,* in this situation, a convention, albeit a bad one, does exist. And it is this fact which he is forced to take into account in his calculations. He might still draw the conclusion that he should obey the ruler if, for moral or self-interested reasons, the consequences of acting to change the convention will be worse than the consequences of acquiescing in the bad convention. He may make this judgment when he finds the present government bad but believes (given what he knows) that so few others agree with him that an attempt to change the convention by refusing to obey the ruler would be futile, or when he believes that they do agree with him that the present ruler is bad but disagree among themselves about what convention should replace it.[47]

However, there is one other reason why someone might obey a convention even when he judges it to be bad, and that is when there is no common knowledge of how the government is evaluated by the citizenry generally. Kavka gives a model for how this kind of situation inhibits revolution in his paradox of perfect tyranny. As Kavka explains, a tyrant who is universally disliked can, paradoxically, remain in power, when the situation is such that the people obey the tyrant out of fear of one another. That is, each citizen is obedient

> out of fear that some of his fellow citizens would answer the ruler's call to punish him if he were not. So citizen A obeys out of fear of citizens B, C, et al., B obeys out of fear of A, C, et al., and so on. In this situation, the beliefs of rational citizens that their fellows will punish them for not following the ruler's orders constitute a network of interlocking mutual expectations, a "net of fear," that provides each citizen with a sufficient motive of obedience.[48]

Kavka's remarks here fit with my analysis, given earlier, of sovereign empowerment through the citizenry's decision to obey and/or respect his punishment commands. This is, in effect, the decision by which people generate the leadership convention. Once in place, that convention yields considerable power for the ruler. But it is always power that, in the last analysis, can be traceable to the decisions of the individuals who are participating in the punishment process. Thus, if the frail and universally disliked ruler can inhibit the passing of information among the disgruntled citizenry, their knowledge of the convention's existence and their uncertainty about receiving support from others will likely make it irrational for them to risk opposing the ruler.

In this situation the people are "mastered" by their ruler, despite the fact that they empower him by their obedience to him. To be *mastered* is *to be subject to the use of coercion in a way that disables one from participating in the process of creating or changing a leadership convention.* Because there are degrees of disablement, there are degrees of mastery. The use of coercion against blacks in South Africa, against left-wing Chileans by Pinochet, and against Tibetans in China is substantial enough to inhibit such activity severely, rendering these people mastered to an extreme degree. But techniques of mastery are present in all Western democracies, as anyone whose name is on file at the FBI knows. A ruler has, and must have, significant coercive power over her citizens. That power makes her disproportionately more powerful than any of her subjects (or even fairly large groups of those subjects), and she may be able to use this power to disable, partially or totally, one or more of them from participating in or changing the leadership convention. And it is so tempting for rulers to do so that there probably never has been (nor ever will be) a regime in which such disabling does not go on to some degree or other.

Even worse, a portion of the population may approve of the mastery of the rest of the population and actively support their ruler's use of power to disable that portion from participation in the leadership convention. Those who are disabled may even be in the majority if the ruler and his supporters are clever enough to keep important technology from them, rendering them badly unequal (e.g., in South Africa).

So there are really two forms of political domination which our discussion has revealed: the domination of a master, and the domination of a "hired" protection agency. The contractarian story, which presupposes that every person involved in the creation of the state is the equal of every other, results only in the creation of the second form of domination. But if, as seems true in the real world, equality cannot be presupposed because of technological (if not natural) superiority, then mastery can and does exist. Indeed, insofar as the very empowerment of a ruler destroys equality by making her more powerful than those who are ruled by her, the seeds of political mastery are planted in the very act of generating a leadership convention.

A pure form of mastery in a human community is very unlikely. Given human frailty and technological limitations (Superman and James Bond movies to the contrary) no ruler can hope to master people all by himself: he needs supporters to do so, and this means there must be at least an agency relationship between him and his supporters. In this sense Pinochet, Stalin, and Idi Amin, despite their mastery of subject populations, have all been agents; the power relationship within the ruling clique supporting them fits the contractarian's agency analysis of a political regime.

On the other hand, a pure form of agency seems just as unlikely. Aside from the fact that a portion of the population may approve of the mastery of others and actively support their ruler's use of power to disable the rest from participating in the leadership convention, a ruler is always able to take advantage of the fact that the punishment power granted to him makes him disproportionately more powerful than any of his subjects (or even fairly large groups of those subjects) in order partially or totally to disable one or more of them from participating in or changing the leadership convention. For better or worse, when people create a state, they create a monster, over which it may not be easy to maintain control.[49]

Given both the reality and the limitations of technological dominance, the explanatory truth about political regimes would seem to be that they are mixtures, to various degrees, of the agency and mastery forms of domination. So what the contractarian "explains" with his convention model is only one aspect of our political reality: i.e., the extent to which rulers have power, and perhaps also authority, through some or all of the subjects' participation in a leadership convention. The convention model fails to accommodate the reality of the non-agency aspects of subjects' relationships with the regimes that rule them.

But even if contractarians have overemphasized the agency aspect of our political life, this may be because they have intuitively sensed that probably only the agency aspect can be morally justified. The convention model gives us the form of domination we would create if we were and always remained equal, and even as that state of equality is more ideal than fact, so too is the kind of political regime it generates.

NOTES

1. The project of developing a contractarian explanation of the state may, however, help one to understand how social contract talk can have justificatory force. It is hard to

understand how an appeal to a non-existent promissorial agreement to create the state can provide a foundation for the legitimacy of that institution. On the other hand, if we can develop a theory that explains in what sense citizens really do "consent" to the states that rule them, it may be easier to understand how that consent could justify the institution.

2. See *Leviathan,* chapter 15, paragraph 21 (pp. 76–77 in the 1651 pagination).

3. See Luce and Raiffa, *Games and Decisions* (New York, 1957), 90–94, and chap. 6.

4. From David Lewis, *Convention* (Cambridge, Mass., 1969), 24.

5. Kavka agrees, noting that people may also agree at this stage on a constitution, explicit legislation, procedural safeguards to be followed in the regime, and so forth. See his *Hobbesian Moral and Political Theory* (Princeton, N.J. 1986), 188.

6. Gregory Kavka cites *passages from Leviathan,* chap. 18, in support of a similar analysis of the game-theoretic structure underlying the state's creation but he does not go on to stress the way in which that structure underlies a convention-based rather than a contract-based explanation of the state. See *Hobbesian Moral and Political Theory,* 180ff; and see below, note 18.

7. See my *Hobbes and the Social Contract Tradition* (Cambridge, 1986), chap. 6.

8. See Locke's *Two Treatises of Government,* edited by P. Laslett (Cambridge, 1960, section 6 of the Second Treatise, p. 311).

9. Ibid., sec. 8, p. 312.

10. Locke writes, "it is unreasonable for Men to be Judges in their own Cases. . .Self-love will make Men partial to themselves and to their Friends. . . . Ill Nature, Passion and Revenge will carry them too far in punishing others." Ibid., sec. 13, p. 316.

11. Ibid.

12. Ibid.

13. Ibid., sec. 127, p.397.

14. Ibid., sec. 8, pp. 312–12; my emphasis, and see chapter 9 of the Second Treatise.

15. Only if considerable numbers of people believe that there is *no* candidate (outside of their favorite) to whom it is better to be subjugated than to remain in a total or partial state of war is the conflict so great that the battle-of-the-sexes character of the game is destroyed. But given the way in which Locke believes government secures peace, such radical preferences are not defensible on his view on either moral or self-interested grounds, and he does not take seriously in his political writings the possibility that people could come to have them.

16. From the Institute's *American Restatement of Contracts,* discussed by P. S. Atiyah, in *An Introduction to the Law of Contract,* 3d ed. (Oxford, 1981), 28.

17. From Atiyah, ibid., 32. There is also a species of contract which involves unilateral and not bilateral promising, but that species is not relevant to our concerns here.

18. In his book *Hobbesian Moral and Political Theory,* Gregory Kavka sends conflicting messages about how this question ought to be answered. He agrees that the battle-of-the-sexes game characterizes the problem people face when they want to create a commonwealth, but he characterizes Hobbes's theory of the social contract as follows:

> commonwealths are formed by institution, when a number of independent individuals create a common power over themselves by mutual agreement. This state-creating pact, or social contract, is pictured by Hobbes as having a complex structure. It is not really a single agreement, but a set of bilateral agreements linking each contractor with every other. Hence, a single party can rightly demand fulfillment of the agreement by each of the others. Each of these bilateral agreements surrenders the individual's right of self-rule to, and authorizes all the actions of, a sovereign person or assembly to be elected later by the parties by majority vote. In this two-stage process, the actual sovereign is selected only after the parties are joined into a social union by overlapping mutual agreements. The parties bind one another to confer on whoever is elected their combined power and authority, in hopes thereby of achieving protection against foreigners and one another. The sovereign is not, qua sovereign, a party to the social contract and is therefore not constrained by it. (p. 181)

Kavka's language here clearly signals that he sees this contract as not just an agreement but a promissorial agreement—one which binds and constrains.

19. Lewis, *Convention*, 83.

20. Lewis does not answer this question. My general answer to it in this essay is given in more precise form in my *Hobbes and the Social Contract Tradition*, chap. 6, 142–45.

21. See Lewis, *Convention*, 35.

22. Explicit mention of voting and democratic choice procedures occurs in *Elements of Law*, edited by F. Tönnies (Cambridge, 1928), 198–99. Kavka thinks it is also suggested in *Leviathan*, chaps. 18 and 20, but I do not see the idea explicitly present there.

23. See Robert Nozick, *Anarchy, State and Utopia* (New York, 1974), 16ff. Nozick actually constructs three scenarios, but the second and third are not sufficiently different from the first to merit discussion here.

24. In Nozick's words:

Invisible-hand explanations minimize the use of notions constituting the phenomena to be explained; in contrast to the straightforward explanations, they don't explain complicated patterns by including the full-blown pattern-notions as objects of people's desires or beliefs. Invisible-hand explanations of phenomena thus yield greater understanding than do explanations of them as brought about by design as the object of people's intentions. It is therefore no surprise that they are more satisfying. (Ibid., 18–29)

25. Second Treatise, sec. 129, pp. 397–98.

26. See *Leviathan*, chap. 28.

27. Of course the state is continually threatened by those who claim to be a higher authority than the ruler, e.g., religious figures. Hobbes was particularly contemptuous and hostile towards the Christians of his day who maintained their right to disregard the commands of their ruler because a higher authority (e.g., the Pope, a Protestant leader, even their own consciences informed by God through prayer and biblical revelation) permitted them to do so.

28. The literature on iterated prisoner's dilemma arguments is voluminous, but for a well-known discussion, see Robert Axelrod, *The Evolution of Cooperation* (New York, 1984).

29. In *Hobbes and the Social Contract Tradition* I failed to emphasize sufficiently the extent to which states have authority, and not merely coercive power, over the ruled. This discussion aims to correct that oversight.

30. See E. Anscombe, "On the Source of the Authority of the State," *Collected Papers, Volume III: Ethics, Religion and Politics* (Minneapolis, 1981), 130–55; Joseph Raz, *The Authority of Law* (Oxford, 1979); and Leslie Green, *The Authority of the State* (Oxford, 1988).

31. Green, *Authority of the State*, 41–42.

32. Indeed, one might believe that a state can only be properly said to have punishment power (as opposed to the mere physical power to coerce) if it is the authoritative command-giver in the society. I will not take up here to what purpose a state ought to punish; this would be part of a moral theory of the state's legitimate role.

Notice how much Hobbes suggests the idea that states have (and ought to have) not merely power but authority of this kind in the following passage:

And when men that think themselves wiser than all others, clamor and demand right Reason for judge; yet seek no more, but that things should be determined, by no other men's reason but their own, it is as intolerable in the society of men, as it is in play after trump is turned, to use for trump on every occasion, that suite whereof they have most in their hand. (*Leviathan*, chap. 5, paragraph 3 [pp. 18–19 in 1651 pagination])

33. Ronald Dworkin, "The Original Position," in *Reading Rawls*, edited by N. Daniels (New York, 1974), 17–18.

34. For this way of seeing the issue I am indebted to Alan Nelson, "Explanation and Justification in Political Philosophy," *Ethics* (1974).

35. "Authority arises from the necessity of a task whose performance requires a certain sort and extent of obedience on the part of those for whom the task is supposed to be done." Anscombe, "On the Source of the Authority of the State," 134.

36. Rawls uses this phrase to describe the authority of the principles of justice upon which he believes rulers should act. See *A Theory of Justice* (Cambridge, Mass., 1971), 135.

37. Hart's legal theory is set forward in his *The Concept of Law* (Oxford, 1961).

38. For a discussion of Hart's approach to authority, see Ronald Dworkin, "Model of Rules I," in his *Taking Rights Seriously* (Cambridge, Mass. 1977).

39. The relationship between political analyses of the state and positivist and natural law theories of jurisprudence is badly underanalyzed. The discussion here is merely a start at such an analysis.

40. See Hart's discussion in *The Concept of Law*, 111.

41. See Kavka, *Hobbesian Moral and Political Theory*, 267, who cites the work of Olson, Tullock, and Buchanan in his development of the paradox.

42. Ibid., 268.

43. Ibid.

44. See ibid., 273–74. Kavka proposes three possible solutions to the paradox. The first two are in Kavka's eyes problematic, and he is most pleased with the third. Hence this is the one I concentrate on here.

45. Ibid., 274.

46. See my "Free Rider Problems in the Production of Collective Goods," *Economics and Philosophy* 3 (1987): 245–73.

47. Hobbes argued that it was against reason for a subject to rebel against her government, but I have argued (in *Hobbes and the Social Contract Tradition,* chaps. 8 and 9) that the premises of his argument commit him to the rationality of rebellion in certain circumstances. That discussion runs along roughly the same lines as the discussion here.

48. Kavka, *Hobbesian Moral and Political Theory,* 257.

49. Thus many polities (e.g., the United States) rely on separation of powers to prevent any one individual or office from achieving significant degrees of mastery.

The Deductive
Method

DANIEL M. HAUSMAN

From the 1830s, when Nassau Senior (1836) and John Stuart Mill (1836) first wrote on economic methodology, until the 1930s, when positivist views become ascendent, there was a strong consensus among economists that economic methodology was in fact and ought to be deductive (see also, for example, Cairnes 1875 and Keynes 1917). The basic premises of economics—claims such as that people prefer more goods and services to fewer or the law of diminishing marginal utility—are established by introspection, casual experience, or direct test, and the rest of economics is then deduced from these established "laws" and descriptions of the particular material, institutional, and informational circumstances.

In the 1930s Lionel Robbins provided the following vivid statement of this view:

> The propositions of economic theory, like all scientific theory, are obviously deductions from a series of postulates. . . . The main postulate of the theory of value is the fact that individuals can arrange their preferences in an order, and in fact do so. . . . These are not postulates the existence of whose counterpart in reality admits of extensive dispute once their nature is fully realized. We do not need controlled experiments to establish their validity: they are so much the stuff of our everyday experience that they have only to be stated to be recognized as obvious. (1935, 78–79)

J. J. Klant (1984, 56f) aptly labels this view "empirical a priorism" (as opposed to the straight a priorism of von Mises [1981] and his followers). The basic "laws" are empirical, but they are so firmly established that the task of economics is merely to investigate their consequences.

1. THE INEXACT DEDUCTIVE METHOD

Let us look more carefully at this method of theory development and appraisal. John Stuart Mill provides the following general characterization and defense of the deductive method in science:

> When an effect depends on a concurrence of causes, these causes must be studied one at a time, and their laws separately investigated, if we wish, through the causes, to obtain the power of either predicting or controlling the effect; since the law of the effect is compounded of the laws of all the causes which determine it. (1843, 6.9.3)

Note that "compounding of the laws of all the causes" is *deducing* the consequences of the concurrence of a plurality of causes.

By a deductive method Mill does *not* mean the hypothetico-deductive method, which he calls "hypothetical method" and which he criticizes, when it fails to prove its conclusions inductively (1843, 3.14.4–5). In insisting on the need for a deductive method, Mill is also not primarily concerned with how laws are *discovered*. Mill makes clear that his methods of induction are most important for the justification of scientific claims, although they may also serve the purposes of discovery (1843, 3.9.6). What distinguishes the deductive method is not that one creates hypotheses rather than derives them from evidence. Quite the contrary, the deductive method is in part an account of how one can *derive* economic laws from inductive evidence of a different kind.

Mill's deductive method consists of three stages (1843, 3.11). In the first, one establishes laws by *induction*. For example, scientists interested in tides induce the laws of mechanics and of gravitation, or borrow the results of the inductions of others. Good evidence for these laws comes from diverse sources, but little comes from complex phenomena such as tides. Second, scientists deduce the laws of tides from these fundamental laws and specifications of the relevant circumstances. Third, scientists must verify the deductive results. But notice that they are not testing the basic laws, just their (inexact) lawlike consequences concerning the tides. Mill argues that the verification of derived laws provides additional confirmation to the inductively established laws upon which they are based, but the possibility of disconfirmation is not even considered, and the evidential weight of such results is slight (1843, 3.11.3). The more complex the phenomena, the less one can study it directly and the more one needs to develop one's science deductively on the basis of laws that are independently established.

To make clearer the basic idea, let me give two further simple illustrations. Suppose *W* is sick, and would like to know whether penicillin will help cure *W* (compare Mill 1843, 3.10.6). The empirical *a posteriori* method, or, as Mill calls it, the method of direct experience, would have us inquire whether others with symptoms resembling *W*'s recovered more often or more rapidly when given penicillin than when given nothing or a placebo. The deductive method or method *a priori* in contrast would have us draw upon our knowledge of the causes of *W*'s symptoms and on our knowledge of the operation of penicillin to decide whether penicillin will help cure *W.* Both methods are "empirical" and involve testing. The difference is that the former attempts to use experiment or observation to learn about the complex phenomenon directly, while the latter employs observation or experiment to study the relevant component causal factors. Similarly, one could determine empirically the range of an artillery piece directed at different angles with different wind conditions and atmospheric pressure. Or one could make use of the law of inertia, Galileo's law of falling bodies, and experimentally determined laws of air resistance to calculate the range. The latter deductive method is in Mill's view, the method of all advanced sciences, although, for practical applications, the method of direct experience is needed as a check on the deductive results.

Presented in conjunction with examples like those in the previous paragraph, the deductive method seems unobjectionable. One can get better evidence concerning the correctness of Galileo's law or the law of inertia from controlled experiments, in which the influence of other causal factors is almost absent, than from observations of the range of artillery pieces. So applications of these laws via the deductive method to complex phenomenon test these laws only slightly. Notice that the laws clearly do not say what will inevitably happen, but only what *would* happen in the absence of other causal factors or what will happen *ceteris paribus*.

The application of the deductive method to economics is problematic, because, especially in contrast to the example of determining the range of the artillery piece, causal factors that are known to be significant are left out of the story. The inexactness is not negligible. Indeed Mill criticizes members of the "school of Bentham" (especially, by implication, his father, James Mill) for analogous "geometrical" theorizing about government. James Mill argued for representative government on the ground that individuals pursue their own interests and rulers in non-representative governments will not have the same interests as those of the governed (1820). This account is, in the view of the younger Mill, not only empirically inadequate, but methodologically flawed, for it focuses on only one admittedly important causal factor and ignores many others. J. S. Mill writes:

They would have applied, and did apply, their principles with innumerable allowances. But it is not allowances that are wanted. . . . It is unphilosophical to construct a science out of a few of the agencies by which the phenomena are determined, and leave the rest to the routine of practice or the sagacity of conjecture. We either ought not to pretend to scientific forms, or we ought to study all the determining agencies equally, and endeavour, so far as it can be done, to include all of them within the pale of the science; else we shall infallibly bestow a disproportionate attention upon those which our theory takes into account, while we misestimate the rest, and probably underrate their importance. That the deductions should be from the whole and not from a part only of the laws of nature that are concerned, would be desirable even if those omitted were so insignificant in comparison with the others, that they might, for most purposes and on most occasions, be left out of the account. (1843, 6.8.3)

But when it comes to economics, John Stuart Mill apparently recommends just the methodological practice that he condemns in these remarks. For the correct method of including all of the "determining agencies" "within the pale of the science" is not feasible. Economists must set their sights lower and aim only at a *hypothetical* science of *tendencies* which is, in Mill's view, generally "insufficient for prediction" yet "most valuable for guidance" (1843, 6.9.3). Since in political economy "the immediate determining causes are principally those which act through the desire of wealth,. . ." (1843, 6.9.3), one can separate the subject matter of political economy from other social phenomena and theorize about political economy as if the desire for wealth were virtually the only relevant causal factor (see note 6 below).

Mill defends as follows this sort of partial deductive method, which so closely resembles the geometrical method of his father:

The motive which suggests the separation of this portion of the social phenomena from the rest, and the creation of a distinct branch of science relating to them, is, that they do *mainly* depend, at least in the first resort, on one class of circumstances only; and that even when other circumstances interfere, the ascertainment of the effect due to the one class of circumstances alone is a sufficiently intricate and difficult business to make it expedient to perform it once for all, and then allow for the effect of the modifying circumstances; especially as certain fixed combinations of the former are apt to recur often, in conjunction with every-varying circumstances in the latter class. (1843, 6.9.3)

The defenses Mill offers for employing this partial or inexact deductive method thus seem to be (1) practical, that there is no alternative, (2) metaphysical, that, although the results are only hypothetical the same causal influences persist even when there are other disturbing causes, and (3) pragmatic, that this is an efficient way of theorizing and that more order can be found this way than in any other.[1]

In the case of economics, theorists first borrow basic "laws" from the natural sciences or psychology (which Mill regards as an introspective experimental science). One tests the fundamental laws upon which economics is constructed on *other* phenomena where there are fewer disturbances or interferences. Then theorists develop economics deductively. Verification is essential, but not in order to test the basic laws; they are already established and could hardly be cast in doubt by the empirical vicissitudes of a deduction from a partial set of causes.

It should be stressed that the deductive development of economics is not a matter of proving theorems with nothing but established laws and true descriptions of the relevant circumstances as premises. The premises of the deductions include as well a number of other stipulations or auxiliary hypotheses, such as assertions that agents have perfect knowledge or that there are only two commodities in the economy. These often are poorly established, even known to be false.

The messiness of the "deduction" in the inexact deductive method as it is applied in economics makes such a method of discovering and justifying scientific theories both problematic and interesting. One task of a weak logic of discovery is to lay bare the reasoning which makes plausible first attempts at scientific theories, and deduction from somewhat plausible premises does make what is deduced plausible (Nooteboom 1986). If an economic claim can be shown to follow from more fundamental generalizations and auxiliary hypotheses, which are reasonable approximations or simplifications, one has reason to take that claim seriously. Principles such as Say's Law have been embraced by economists on such grounds.

It might be argued that the partial deductive method can do no more than help make economic hypotheses initially plausible. For, as Mill stresses (because of the *ceteris paribus* clauses in the basic laws and the other simplifications), the deduced implications must themselves be confirmed, and it might be contended that whether or not they are confirmed, the fact that they were deduced from inductively established laws (and various simplifications) seems irrelevant. Either way our confidence in the implications would depend on the extent to which they were confirmed.[2]

But this dismissal of the inexact or partial deductive method would be unjustified. There are degrees of confirmation and degrees of belief. Our confidence in generalizations such as those concerning market demand and supply may be rationally increased by showing that they can be derived from the inexact fundamental laws of the theory of consumer choice and various specifications of relevant circumstances. The general strategy of developing models that incorporate independently credible laws provides the implications of those models with a certain credibility in advance of and apart from any testing of them.

To sharpen the discussion, let us then formulate a schema, figure 1, expressing the broad outlines of the deductive, or *a priori* method, as it may have been conceived by Mill to apply to economics. Qualifications will be needed later, but at this point a bold formulation will provide a useful focus.

I have added the parenthetical "Inexact" in order to stress the fact that the deductive method need not leave out significant causal factors, as it inevitably will in economics. Indeed Mill regards this method as something of a cheat. The true deductive method will rely only on facts and causes, not on simplifications. I have left out the "proving" of the laws concerning relevant causal factors, which Mill takes to be the first step of the deductive method, because I want to focus on the tasks of economists, who are concerned with applying psychological and technical laws, not with establishing them. Formulating the deductive method in this way also helps to make clear how this method differs from the hypothetico-deductive method. The differences are in step 1, where one begins with proven (but inexact) laws rather than mere hypotheses to be tested, and in step 4. Since the laws are already established, they are not open to question in this judgment step. Apart from discovering logical errors in the deduction, all that is open to assessment are the sufficiency and accuracy of the other premises and the extent of the "coverage" provided by the borrowed laws.

Figure 1. The (Inexact) Deductive Method

1. *Borrow* proven *(ceteris paribus)* laws concerning the operation of relevant causal factors.
2. *Deduce* from these laws and statements of initial conditions, simplifications, etc., predictions concerning relevant phenomena.
3. *Test* the predictions.
4. *Judge* (a) whether there is any mistake in the non-law premises in the deduction, (b) what sort of interferences occurred, (c) how central the borrowed laws are (how major the causal factors they identify are) and whether the set of borrowed laws should be expanded or contracted.

Knowing that individuals seek wealth and that they tend to have many children, economists in Mill's day investigated deductively what follows from these tendencies in various circumstances. The deductive method is needed for all sciences, whether exact or inexact, in which the complexity of causal factors renders inductive methods such as Mill's inapplicable. In inexact sciences the implications of theory will, moreover, only agree with the results of experiment approximately for the most part.

2. QUALMS

During the past half century, most of those concerned with economic methodology have found something fishy or fraudulent in Mill's and Robbins's tolerant attitude toward inexact fundamental laws and their frequently disconfirmed consequences. For it seems that, on Mill's and Robbins's view, evidence can only confirm theory or show that there is some interference. There seems to be no real possibility of empirical criticism and, thus, no real empirical justification for the theory. In the judgment step, no judgment of the laws themselves is permitted.

Mill's inexact deductive method has been subject to logical, methodological and practical criticisms. The logical criticism maintains that statements that are vaguely qualified with *ceteris paribus* clauses are scientifically illegitimate because they cannot be conclusively refuted by empirical testing (Hutchison 1938, chap. 2). As I have argued at length elsewhere (forthcoming, chaps. 5 and 6), this criticism is misconceived. Not only is the methodological demand that scientific claims be conclusively verifiable or falsifiable untenable, but one can give truth conditions for inexact claims qualified with *ceteris paribus* clauses, and one can defend conditions for distinguishing when one is justified in accepting such generalizations (Hausman 1981a, 120–33 and forthcoming, chap. 4; Kincaid 1989).

The methodological criticism maintains that the rules implicit in the deductive method are unacceptably dogmatic (de Marchi 1970; 1986). In particular it may plausibly be argued that one ought not to regard the basic laws as proven or to refuse ever to regard unfavorable test results as disconfirming them. Adhering to the deductive method thus, it is alleged, impedes the progress of economics and leads to the sort of *ad hoc* response to apparent disconfirmation characteristic of a degenerating research program.

Furthermore, methodological vice is alleged to lead to practical impotence. The practical criticism maintains that by regarding apparent disconfirmations as inevitably the result of some disturbing cause, the inexact deductive method winds up justifying theories that cannot be of any practical use (Friedman 1953). For policy purposes we need to know what *will* happen, not what *would* happen in the absence of disturbing causes.

These are serious criticisms, and indeed, since the early 1940s, the only extended defenses of the traditional view of justification in economics have been I. M. W. Stewart's (1979), mine, and (usually on the basis of an anti-empiricist epistemology) that of the Austrian school (Dolan 1976). There has been a dramatic revolution in theorizing about economic methodology, which has led to a repudiation of the inexact deductive method in precept, although, interestingly, not in practice.[3] Perhaps methodological practice in economics is overdue for a major overhaul, but first let us look again at that practice to see whether it is as mistaken as has been asserted.

Can the methodological and practical objections be answered? Can something like the inexact deductive method and the existing methodological practice in microeconomics be defended? Can the apparent dogmatism be tempered or justified? Do economists disregard apparent disconfirmations? Must they fail to learn from experience? Can the method of discovery and appraisal employed by economists make it rational to rely on economic theories for policy purposes?

3. APPARENT DOGMATISM
AND THE THEORY OF CONSUMER CHOICE

Although I shall argue that the methodological rules of the inexact deductive method as presented in figure 1 cannot be defended, I shall nevertheless defend the existing practices of theory assessment among economists. These practices appear to be consistent with the inexact deductive method, but they are, I shall contend, also consistent with the recommendations of standard methods of theory appraisal given the particular circumstances with which economists have to cope. Although apparent Millians in practice, economists can be good Bayesians or hypothetico-deductivists in principle.[4] Given the tasks economists face, Bayesian and hypothetico-deductivist confirmation theories recommend confirmational practice that is almost indistinguishable from what Mill's inexact deductive method recommends. The methodological practice of economists may be defensible, even though the inexact deductive method is indefensible, and economists appear to conform to it.

To make this discussion concrete, let us focus on the standard theory of consumer choice, for its basic generalizations or behavioral postulates are both simple and revealing. Consumer choice theory is made up of the following five "laws":

1. (Completeness or comparability) Given any agent A and options x and y, either A prefers x to y or A prefers y to x or A is indifferent between x and y.
2. (Transitivity) Given any agent A and options x, y, and z, if A prefers x to y and y to z, then A prefers x to z.
3. (Utility maximization) Among the feasible or attainable options, an agent A chooses x if and only if A does not prefer any other option y to x.
4. (Nonsatiation) For all agents A and all commodity bundles b and c, A prefers b to c if and only if b is larger than c.
5. (Diminishing marginal utility) For all agents A, the amount by which an additional unit of a commodity or service t increases A's utility is a decreasing function of the amount of t that A possesses.

This characterization is rough and oversimplified in many ways. The notion of "larger" with respect to bundles or vectors of commodities or services needs spelling out. Contemporary economics is committed to diminishing marginal rates of substitution rather than diminishing marginal utility. Standard economic presentations do not distinguish sharply, as I have, between preference and choice. Weaker claims (such as acyclicity in place of transitivity) are sufficient in certain contexts. These claims must be supplemented by a continuity or closure axiom in order to entail the existence of a continuous utility function for individuals (where utility is simply an ordinal index of preference ranking (Debreu 1959, 54–59; Harsanyi 1977, chap. 3). But these and many other questions are not for this occasion. This rough characterization should provide a sufficient grasp of what the generalizations of consumer choice theory assert.

The most important feature of the "laws" of consumer choice theory for our purposes is that there is, obviously, a good deal of truth to each of them, but, equally obviously, they are not all true exceptionless universal generalizations. It is unquestionably sensible to regard them, at least in some qualified or hedged form, as possessing considerable initial credibility. Although the generalizations of consumer choice theory are hardly as well established as Newton's laws of motion (not that economists ever believed otherwise), it may still be reasonable to maintain that one has captured in these inexact generalizations significant causes of human behavior.

The credibility attributed to the generalizations of consumer choice theory thus falls short of the sort of proven or obvious truth that Mill and Robbins believe economists can begin with. Only some fancy philosophical footwork permits one to regard these generalizations as true at all, and it is questionable whether these axioms can be regarded as exactly well established.

One can thus defend one part of the inexact deductive method, although in a highly attenuated form: it may be intellectually legitimate to regard one's basic laws as possessing a high credibility apart from the successes or failures of the particular theory. In the particular case of economics, this initial credibility is only moderate, for the generalizations of consumer choice theory are problematic. They are plausible approximations, and they also have important pragmatic vindications.

The other main methodological recommendation of the inexact deductive method, that one *never* attribute apparent disconfirmations to shortcomings in one's laws, is defensible only as a rule of thumb that is appropriate for particular circumstances. It is unacceptable as a general methodological rule. To follow it would truly prevent one from ever discovering inadequacies in those laws. Except in the happy circumstances in which those laws possessed no inadequacies, it would hinder theoretical and empirical progress. Such a rule is unacceptably dogmatic.

Yet it is not unacceptably dogmatic not to find appreciable disconfirmation of economic "laws" in the welter of empirical failures to which economic theories are subject. Whether the correct response to empirical anomaly is to question the generalizations of consumer choice theory or to cite interferences depends on the particular circumstances. When the anomalies are those cast up by largely uncontrolled observation of complicated market phenomena, then it may be most rational to pin the blame on some of the many disturbing causes, which are always present. Since one's confidence in the simplifications and *ceteris paribus* assumptions necessary to apply economic theory to actual market phenomena will generally be much lower than one's confidence in the basic laws, the more likely explanation for the apparent disconfirmation will always be a failure of the simplifications rather than the laws. In consequence little can be learned about the purported laws from observation, but the failure will issue from the difficulties of the task not from methodological mistake. The possibility of discovering errors in the "laws" of equilibrium theory will be foreclosed by inadequate data and limited knowledge, not by unjustifiable methodological fiat.

Let me document this claim with respect to a simple Bayesian account of confirmation (see for example Eells 1983; Hesse 1974; Horwich 1982; Jeffrey 1983; or Rosenkranz 1977). Let H be either a "law" of consumer choice theory or a conjunction of such laws and A be the conjunction of all the other statements needed to derive a prediction, e from H. The prior probability of H, prob(H) is much larger than the prior probability of A, prob(A). (The probability of the conjunction, A, will, of course, be much smaller than that of the separate conjuncts, which are themselves improbable.) To keep things simple, although at the cost of unreality, let us suppose that H and A are probabilistically independent of each other, so that prob($H \cdot A$) = prob(H) $\cdot$ prob(A). Personalist Bayesians typically suppose that relevant probabilities are known, and I shall partially join them, although the assumption is fantastic (see Kaplan 1983; 1989).

Suppose now that $H\&A$ entail e, so that $\text{prob}(e/H{\cdot}A) = 1$. Given this fact, the independence of H and A, and Bayes' Theorem, we know that

(1) $\text{prob}(H{\cdot}A/e) = \text{prob}(H){\cdot}\text{prob}(A)/\text{prob}(e)$;

and, of course,

(2) $\text{prob}(H{\cdot}A/{\sim}e) = 0$, where $\sim e$ is the negation of e.

If e is borne out by observation, the (1) tells us that the ratio of the prior probability of $H\&A$ to the posterior probability of $H\&A$ is $\text{prob}(e)$. Since

(3) $\text{prob}(H/e) = \text{prob}(H{\cdot}A/e) + \text{prob}(H{\cdot}{\sim}A/e)$,

we know by Bayes theorem that

(4) $\text{prob}(H/\mathrm{e}) = \text{prob}(H){\cdot}\text{prob}(A)/\text{prob}(e) +$
$\qquad \text{prob}(H){\cdot}\text{prob}({\sim}A){\cdot}\text{prob}(e/H{\cdot}{\sim}A)/\text{prob}(e)$ or

(5) $\text{prob}(H/e) = [\text{prob}(H)/\text{prob}(e)]{\cdot}[\text{prob}(A) + \text{prob}({\sim}A){\cdot}\text{prob}(e/H{\cdot}{\sim}A)]$.

Since $\text{prob}(A)$ is small, and there is no reason in general to expect that $\text{prob}(e/H{\cdot}{\sim}A)$ will be close to one, H will be appreciably less well confirmed by e than is the conjunction $H\&A$. Since

(6) $\text{prob}(H/{\sim}e) = \text{prob}(H{\cdot}A/{\sim}e) + \text{prob}(H{\cdot}{\sim}A/{\sim}e)$,

and the first term on the right hand side of (6) is zero, we can see that the posterior probability of H given unfavorable evidence $\sim e$ will be larger as prob (A) is smaller. Expanding the second term by means of Bayes' theorem we find,

(7) $\text{prob}(H/{\sim}e) = \text{prob}(H){\cdot}\text{prob}({\sim}A){\cdot}\text{prob}({\sim}e/H{\cdot}{\sim}A)/\text{prob}({\sim}e)$.

Since there is no reason to expect that $\text{prob}({\sim}e/H{\cdot}{\sim}A)$ will be smaller than $\text{prob}({\sim}e)$ and $\text{prob}({\sim}A)$ is also large, the observation of $\sim e$ only weakly disconfirms H. Given how weakly evidence will bear on H (and the indeterminacies in our probability judgments, which are assumed away in this discussion), pragmatic factors may justifiably come into their own in influencing one's reactions to apparent disconfirmations.[5] So in non-experimental circumstances the credible "laws" with which economists begin will be *de facto* non-falsifiable.

If one never had any better data than casual experience and market statistics, then there would be no way to tell whether economists employed the unjustifiably dogmatic inexact deductive method presented in figure 1 or whether they were good Bayesians or hypothetico-deductivists hampered by lack of knowledge and evidence. But experiments are only difficult in economics, not impossible; and there is by now a good deal of experimental evidence bearing on consumer choice theory. Economists and decision theorists are thus in the interesting situation of possessing considerable experimental evidence that apparently disconfirms consumer choice theory.[6] In experimental circumstances, it is possible to become justifiably confident that the predictive failure is not due to errors in the other statements needed to derive predictions from the generalizations of consumer choice theory. Consequently, in such a setting, one must take seriously the possibility of disconfirming the generalizations of consumer choice theory. Only the unjustifiable Millian method *a priori* would permit one to discount this possibility altogether. Since a willingness to take the possibility of disconfirmation seriously in experimental circumstances is consistent with a general inclination to treat apparent disconfirmations as due to interferences, that general inclination is no proof of unjustifiable dogmatism.

4. PRAGMATIC CONSIDERATIONS

One important effect of taking seriously experiments that mitigate the empirical difficulties that stand in the way of testing inexact claims is to make the conceptual difficulties clearer. To explain away an apparent disconfirmation by changing an auxiliary hypothesis or citing a disturbing cause is to change one's applied theory in response to apparent disconfirmation. The new applied theory has, of necessity, different empirical consequences than the old. Hence it is wrong to say that those who always cite some interference to explain away unfavorable evidence *ignore* disconfirmations. Perhaps they do not react correctly, but they do react.

Disturbing causes, like all causes, have their (inexact) laws, and to explain away a disconfirmation by citing an interference thus may not be purely *ad hoc*. For the disturbing cause cited is to be expected in similar circumstances, and the modification has some non-vacuous empirical content — although the complexity of the phenomena may make testing impossible. The more general the disturbing cause, the more contentful and less *ad hoc* is the hypothesis that cites it.

The right question in a well-controlled experimental context is not "Is the theory disconfirmed or is there an interference?" but "What should one do about this disconfirmation? Should one add a qualification to the theory (which might in many contexts harmlessly be ignored), or should one revise the theory in a more fundamental way?" One cannot draw any sharp line between qualifications and modifications, but one does not need to do so. In both cases empirical evidence exerts real control over theory change. *The difference is pragmatic: qualifications can often be ignored, while modifications leave a permanent mark.* The significant question is whether one can fruitfully and frequently employ the unqualified theory; and the answer to this question depends both on the evidence and on one's purposes (see Mill's remarks quoted above, p. 000).

Another way of grasping the issue here would be to ask how one is supposed to know, in Mill's terminology, that economic theory has captured the *"greater"* causes of economic phenomena.[7] Introspection and thoughts about rationality can provide evidence that transitivity is a significant causal factor affecting choice behavior, but neither could give one solid reason to believe that transitivity is more important than, for example, attitudes toward risk.

How then can one decide whether a disturbing cause is major or minor and whether one may justifiably regard consumer choice theory as capturing the "greater causes" of consumer behavior? Do experimental anomalies demand fundamental revisions or merely qualifications that for many purposes need not even be noted? The decision depends on both pragmatic and empirical factors. In its pragmatic aspect this question demands that one be clear about both practical and theoretical *employments* and *aspirations* for the theory. What does one want the theory for and what sort of theoretical grasp of the subject matter does one think possible?[8] But the decision also hinges on the empirical scope, frequency, and distribution of the disconfirmations experimenters have uncovered. If, for example, the disconfirmations are slight in the range of phenomena that are of the greatest theoretical and practical importance, and one does not believe that a much better theory is likely to be found (which, obviously will depend on what alternatives have been suggested), then it would be reasonable to account for the disconfirmations in terms of "interferences." If, on the other hand, the qualifications need to be invoked often, and one believes that considerably more exactness is possible, then it would be more reasonable to seek to modify the theory decisively.

Notice how significantly the reasoning here differs from the deductive method. What drives economists to regard interferences as minor disturbing causes is not the manifest truth of the basic axioms nor any methodological rule prohibiting revisions of them, but the nature of the disconfirmations coupled with the pragmatic attractions of consumer choice theory.

The presence and promise of alternatives would and should also strongly influence one's decisions here. Indeed, it is fair to say (following to some extent Lakatos's view [1970], that what converts experimental results from anomalies or difficulties for consumer choice theory into disconfirming evidence demanding fundamental theory modification is the formulation of alternatives to consumer choice theory, which accommodate these anomalies within a theory that can do at least some of the work done by consumer choice theory. For some of these alternatives see Levi (1986), Machina (1987), and McClennnen (1990).

5. THE ECONOMISTS' DEDUCTIVE METHOD

We are now in a position to formulate a schema (figure 2) sketching a deductive method that is justifiable and consistent with existing theoretical practice. This schema is as much a repudiation of the inexact deductive method as it is a revision of it, for it is consistent with standard views of confirmation such as the hypothetico-deductive method or those espoused by Bayesians.

What justifies continuing to call it a deductive method, despite its concessions that the inexact laws with which one begins are not proven and that they can be refuted by economic evidence? First (in contrast especially to Popperian methodological views), independent confirmation of the basic inexact laws plays a crucial role. Second, refutation is still largely proscribed, albeit by the circumstances, not by methodological rule. Since economists are typically dealing with complex phenomena in which many simplifications are required and in which interferences are to be expected, the evidential weight of a predictive failure will be very small. It will rarely be rational to surrender a credible hypothesis because of a predictive failure in circumstances such as these.

The economists' deductive method suggests two grounds for judging how much disconfirmation results from unsuccessful prediction. The first derives from Lakatos and directs one to consider what sort of theory modifications or qualifications will most increase the confirmed empirical content of the theory. Given the acute *practical* Quine-Duhem problem here, which is a consequence of how dubious are the various auxiliary hypotheses necessary in order to perform any tests, it will be extremely difficult to judge theory modifications on empirical grounds. The second, pragmatic ground, may consequently play a justifiably large role. For if one cannot tell which theory modification is empirically better, it is sensible to choose the one that has greater pragmatic virtues — that is, the one that it is easier to use, gives sharper advice, lends itself to cleaner mathematical expression and development, and so forth.

Figure 2: Economists' Deductive Method

1. *Formulate* highly credible (*ceteris paribus*) and pragmatically convenient laws concerning the operation of causal factors that are relevant to the complex phenomena of concern.
2. *Deduce* from these laws and statements of initial conditions, simplifications, etc., predictions P concerning relevant phenomena.
3. *Test* the predictions.
4. If the predictions are correct, then regard the whole amalgam as confirmed. If the predictions are not correct, then *compare* alternative accounts of the failure on the basis of empirical progress and pragmatic usefulness.

The inexact deductive method, as formulated in figure 1, is indefensibly dogmatic, for evidence, even the weak evidence of uncontrolled observation, can occasionally force one to rethink basic laws, and, in any case, the basic "laws" of economics are a motley crew. One cannot rule out employing unfavorable evidence to argue against the "laws" themselves rather than the simplifications or the *ceteris paribus* assumption that interferences were not present. But the complexity and messiness of economic observations will largely nullify this possibility.

It is still thus perfectly rational to behave in very much the manner in which Mill recommended. (Hence one can see why Mill's views seemed so plausible, were so easily refuted, yet methodological practice continues apparently to conform to them.) The "laws" of consumer choice theory can be regarded as reasonable approximations that have a good deal of truth to them and great pragmatic convenience. One can, in this way, behave in an empirically responsive and rationally justifiable way and yet largely conform to the deductive method. Indeed, with respect to phenomena such as those of economies, one has no other good choice. Powerful tests require either experimentation with its possibilities of intervention and control, a great deal of knowledge, or fabulous good fortune, and without such tests (or superior alternatives) it would be irrational to surrender credible hypotheses with great pragmatic attractions in the face of apparent disconfirmation.

As formulated in figure 2 above, the economists' deductive method does not forbid fundamental theory revision. But given the circumstances in which economists find themselves, it is unlikely that market data will ever be taken to disconfirm the basic laws or behavioral postulates of consumer choice theory. The relevant features of those circumstances are: (1) the initial credibility of relevant, but highly inexact laws; (2) the difficulty of performing experiments; (3) the complexity of the phenomena (the significant influence of many different causes of many different kinds); and (4) the limitations of knowledge of economic phenomena. If economists can do experiments, they can control for various disturbances and avoid the complexity of the phenomena with which they are presented non-experimentally. If they knew enough, they could exert much the same control even if experiments were not possible. If, on the other hand, they were blessed with a comparatively simple set of phenomena such as those of celestial motion, then neither the inability to experiment nor the paucity of our knowledge would be crippling. But the combination of (2)–(4) makes knowledge of economic phenomena hard to garner.

When experiments are possible and when alternatives are available that have some of the initial credibility of the accepted theory and offer similar pragmatic advantages, then theory change is possible, according to the economist's deductive method. And if one studies how economists respond to experimental anomalies, one can, I think, see that they are not necessarily committed to a dogmatic view, such as the inexact deductive method. Although one finds, not surprisingly, some dogmatism in these responses, it is not the shared methodological rule and it is more the consequence of a commitment to a particular image of economics than to a dogmatic theory of confirmation.[9] Many modifications are in fact proposed, discussed, and tested.

6. THE DEDUCTIVE METHOD
AND THE DEMANDS OF POLICY

Although I have discussed at length the methodological criticisms of the inexact deductive method and have, depending on how one conceives of matters, either answered them or have shown them not necessarily to apply to the methodological practice of economists, I have not yet directly addressed the practical criticism that in following a deductive method, economists condemn their work to practical futility.

But having clarified the varieties of the deductive method, one can easily see that this criticism is specious. The economists' deductive method does not rule out theory changes when doing so will increase the empirical content of the theory — on the contrary it mandates them. Nor does it — or any other variety of the deductive method—condemn empirical generalization. Mill is explicit in endorsing obvious common sense on this point: if something works, use it (though with due caution). Moreover, the development of empirical generalizations for which no deductive derivation is currently possible is also of great *theoretical* importance for such generalizations constitute the most important *data* for which theories need to account.

The point of the deductive method is not to condemn useful empirical generalizations or to abandon accurate predictive devices. It is instead to condemn naive reliance on unreliable empirical generalizations and to provide an *additional* means of getting a predictive grasp on the phenomena. Whether the best way to aim an artillery piece is by firing it in various circumstances and fitting a curve to the data points or by calculating from fundamental laws is an empirical question. Rather than forbidding the first procedure, the deductive method offers a way of improving and correcting the results one gets by it.

If the standard neoclassical theory of the firm had all the empirical virtues claimed for it by economists such as Milton Friedman (1953), then one should make use of it for relevant practical purposes. The economist's deductive method does not recommend the sort of theoretical purism that spurns useful tools that are not in perfect condition and perfectly understood. But by considering the realism of the theory's assumptions—the constituent causal processes and their laws—one may be able to get some guidance concerning when the predictions of the theory are likely to break down and concerning how to modify the theory in the face of apparent disconfirmation.

NOTES

This paper is drawn from chapters 4 and 7 of my forthcoming book, *The Inexact and Separate Science of Economics*. Many people have helped clarify my thinking on these issues. Neil de Marchi deserves special thanks. After writing this essay, I discovered two relevant discussions, Howson and Urbach 1989, 96–103, and Dorling 1979, to which I should have referred when I discussed the Bayesian argument in section 3 below. My apologies to the readers and to those authors.

1. Surely much the same argument could have been given by Mill's father in his own defense. There is an irony here in the fact that recent extensions of neoclassical economic models to political phenomena recapitulate (although more subtly) the account of political behavior presented by James Mill. See, for example, Buchanan (1975; 1979).

2. I suggested this in a confused discussion of these points (1981b, 383). Among other failings in my discussion, I did not too clearly state that one employs the deductive method to justify the implications of the inductively derived fundamental laws, not to justify those laws themselves.

3. I have no systematic argument in support of this assertion, and I am not claiming that all branches of economics display the same methodology. In a decade of presenting this view to a large, but scarcely random sample of economists, I have found little disagreement with the contention that the practice of microeconomics still *appears to* conform closely to Mill's deductive method.

4. Mill might agree with my critique of what I have formulated as the inexact deductive method. It is, in my view, more consistent with the text to attribute to Mill the view that the invulnerability of the laws is due to the difficulties of disentangling the effects of different causes, not to any methodological rule.

5. Since (from a Bayesian perspective) theory choice, like all choice, depends on both probabilities and utilities, one might go on to attempt a systematic account of the importance of the pragmatic virtues of the standard theory.

6. I have in mind, for example, the experimental results concerning "preference reversal." For a useful overview, see Roth (1988). See also Lichtenstein and Slovic (1971), Grether and Plott (1979), Slovic and Lichtenstein (1983), Berg et al. (1985), Karni and Safra (1987), and Cox and Epstein (1989).

7. I am indebted for this way of thinking about this question to Joseph Stiglitz.

8. "[T]he critics of the simplified psychology used by economic theorists have made little headway in bringing forth substitute principles. I do not believe they ever will. Their strictures are valid as *limitations* on the familiar reasoning, not as negations. The principles of the established economics are partial statements, but sound as far as they go, and they go about as far as general principles can be carried" (Knight 1921, 145). This response supposes that the limitations are unsystematic errors.

9. This image of economics also goes back to Mill. It sees economists as focusing on only a small number of causal factors and developing a single systematic theory that, apart from various interferences or disturbing causes, is sufficient to account for all important economic phenomena. See chapters 4 and 7 of my forthcoming book.

REFERENCES

Berg, J., J. Dickhaut, and J. O'Brien 1985. "Preference Reversal and Arbitrage." In *Research in Experimental Economics* edited by V. Smith, 31–72. Greenwich.

Blaug, M. 1980. *The Methodology of Economics: Or How Economists Explain.* Cambridge.

Buchanan, J. 1975. *The Limits of Liberty: Between Anarchy and the Leviathan.* Chicago.

Buchanan, J. 1979. *What Should Economists Do?* Indianapolis.

Cairnes, J. 1875. *The Character and Logical Method of Political Economy.* 2d ed. Reprint New York, 1965.

Cox, J., and S. Epstein. 1989. "Preference Reversals Without the Independence Axiom." *American Economic Review* 79: 408–26.

Debreu, G. 1959. *Theory of Value.* New York.

de Marchi, N. 1970. "The Empirical Content and Longevity of Ricardian Economics." *Economica* 37: 257–76.

de Marchi, N. 1986. "Discussion: Mill's Unrevised Philosophy of Economics: A Comment on Hausman." *Philosophy of Science* 53: 89–100.

Dolan, E., ed. 1976. *The Foundations of Modern Austrian Economics.* Kansas City.

Dorling, J. 1979. "Bayesian Personalism, the Methodology of Research Programmes, and Duhem's Problem." *Studies in the History and Philosophy of Science* 10: 177–87.

Eells, E. 1983. *Rational Decision and Causality.* Cambridge.

Friedman, Milton. 1953. "The Methodology of Positive Economics." In *Essays in Positive Economics,* 3–43. Chicago.

Grether, D., and C. Plott. 1979. "Economic Theory of Choice and the Preference Reversal Phenomenon." *American Economic Review* 69: 623–38.

Harsanyi, J. 1977. *Rational Behavior and Bargaining Equilibrium in Games and Social Situations.* Cambridge.

Hausman, D. 1981a. *Capital, Profits and Prices: An Essay in the Philosophy of Economics.* New York.

Hausman, D. 1981b. "John Stuart Mill's Philosophy of Economics." *Philosophy of Science* 48: 363–85.

Hausman, D. Forthcoming. *The Inexact and Separate Science of Economics.*

Hesse, M. 1974. *The Structure of Scientific Inference.* Cambridge.

Horwich, P. 1982. *Probability and Evidence.* Cambridge.

Howson, C., and P. Urbach. 1989. *Scientific Reasoning: The Bayesian Approach.* La Salle, Ill.

Hutchison, T. 1938. *The Significance and Basic Postulates of Economic Theory.* Reprint with a new Preface, New York, 1960.

Jeffrey, R. 1983. "Bayesianism with a Human Fact." In *Testing Scientific Theories,* edited by T. Earman, 133–56. Minneapolis.

Kaplan, M. 1983. "Decision Theory as Philosophy." *Philosophy of Science* 50: 549–77.

Kaplan, M. 1989. "Bayesianism without the Black Box." *Philosophy of Science* 56: 48–69.

Karni, E., and Z. Safra. 1987. "'Preference Reversal' and the Observability of Preferences by Experimental Methods." *Econometrica* 55: 675–85.

Keynes, J. N. 1917. *The Scope and Method of Political Economy.* 4th ed. Reprint, New York, 1955.

Kincaid, H. 1989. "Confirmation, Complexity and Social Laws." In *PSA 1988*, vol. 2, edited by A. Fine, 299–307. East Lansing, Mich.

Klant, J. 1984. *The Rules of the Game.* Cambridge.

Knight, F. 1921. "Traditional Economic Theory – Discussion." *American Economic Review Papers and Proceedings* 22: 143–46.

Lakatos, I. 1970. "Falsification and the Methodology of Scientific Research Programmes." In *Criticism and the Growth of Knowledge,* edited by I. Lakatos and A. Musgrave, 91–196. Cambridge. Reprinted in Lakatos, *Philosophical Papers,* vol. 1, 8–101. Cambridge, 1978. (Page references are to the latter.)

Levi, I. 1986. "The Paradoxes of Allais and Ellsberg." *Economics and Philosophy* 2: 23–53.

Lichtenstein, S., and P. Slovic. 1971. "Reversals of Preference Between Bids and Choices in Gambling Decisions." *Journal of Experimental Psychology* 89: 46–55.

McClennen, E. 1990. *Rationality and Dynamic Choice: Foundational Explorations.* Cambridge.

Machina, M. 1987. "Choice under Uncertainty: Problems Solved and Unsolved." *Journal of Economic Perspectives* 1: 121–54.

Mill, James. 1820. *An Essay on Government.* Edited by Currin V. Shields. Reprint, Indianapolis, 1955.

Mill, J. S. 1836. "On the Definition of Political Economy and the Method of Investigation Proper to It." Reprint in *Collected Works of John Stuart Mill,* vol. 4. Toronto, 1967.

Mill, J. S. 1843. *A System of Logic.* London, 1949.

Nooteboom, B. 1986. "Plausibility in Economics." *Economics and Philosophy* 2: 197–224.

Robbins, L. 1935. *An Essay on the Nature and Significance of Economic Science.* 2d ed. London.

Rosenkranz, R. 1977. *Inference, Method and Decision.* Dordrecht.

Roth, A. 1988. "Laboratory Experimentation in Economics: A Methodological Overview." *Economic Journal* 98: 974–1031.

Senior, N. 1836. *Outline of the Science of Political Economy.* Reprint, New York, 1965.

Slovic, P., and S. Lichtenstein. 1983. "Preference Reversals: A Broader Perspective." *American Economic Review* 73: 596–605.

Stewart, I. 1979. *Reasoning and Method in Economics: An Introduction to Economic Methodology.* London.

von Mises, L. 1981. *Epistemological Problems of Economics.* Translated by G. Reisman. New York.

Vigotsky and Artificial Intelligence: What Could Cognitive Psychology Possibly Be About?

ROM HARRÉ

I am far from wanting to mount an attack on the general project of using the computer and its programs as a resource in the furtherance of psychological research. My concern in this essay is not at all Luddite. Instead, my aim is to develop an analysis of a problem field for a possible psychology so that a certain version of the artificial intelligence/cognitive science program (hereafter AI/CS) can actually be productive. So far as I can see, the promise of AI/CS has far exceeded any of its deliverances. I believe that the trouble lies in the use by AI/CS practitioners of a distorted version of what psychology could be and what language is. This has encouraged unfortunate trends in AI/CS that have led the field to the kind of impasse chronicled by Winograd and Flores (1986). Some authors, notably Fodor (1981) and Dennett (1978) perhaps more than others, represent the point of view that is responsible for the current crisis. By reworking our conceptions of what a discipline of psychology might be, free of assumptions about what it would take for it to be a science, I hope to revive the AI/CS approach in a more promising way.

I take the techniques of the AI/CS to be essentially modes of modeling. In this respect they are very similar to the modes of modeling in use in general engineering, so I shall be drawing on the kinds of analyses of iconic and homeomorphic modeling that are familiar in the philosophy of science. Models have served two main roles in physical science and engineering. Homeomorphic models like the pictures of blood vascular systems to be found in textbooks have been fruitful as devices for the schematic representation and so for the analysis of complex phenomenon. Paramorphic models like lines of force have been fruitful as devices for controlling the formulation of plausible theories in a realistic style. These are theories which purport to describe plausible but so far unobserved causal mechanisms productive of the phenomena in question. I hope to show which of these aims AI/CS as a modeling technique might fulfill and to which phenomena it has a proper application.

Preliminary philosophical work is needed to define the proper field of psychology because, despite the short history of AI/CS, there are already tendencies for this very important development to go off the rails – largely, I believe, because it has been hooked to the wrong ontological locomotive. Like much academic psychology of recent provenance, it assumes the unexamined thesis of individualism in psychology, whether this thesis is taken mentalistically or physicalistically. The divide between the defenders of alleged folk psychology and those who would like to replace it with a descriptive and explanatory rhetoric derived wholly from neurophysiology has already been rendered empty by Wittgenstein's insights into the role of words like belief, want, and so on and their place in the universe of interpersonal action and intrapersonal reflection. Beliefs, etc., are not hypothetical entities in an alleged folk psychology of a hypothetically deductive kind. The Hertzian model of explanation is proper only to the physical sciences as Wittgenstein realized. There is no false or inadequate folk psychology on the Hertzian model to be supplanted by something better of the same sort. Such an idea is at least partly a consequence of the 'individualism' assumption. I believe that the most fundamental error reproduced in such cognitive psychology has been an assumption about the very nature of psychological reality itself, and it is to a repair of this fundamental error that I shall be devoting most of this essay.

I shall set out five theses, all, to some extent, controversial. Using these theses as a touchstone, I propose "to check out" how far a cognitive science could be developed by being made compatible with them.

By AI/CS, I understand the following double-sided project: (1) to develop an analysis of all forms of human activity, including perception, judgment, action, and so on, relative to some conceptual system, the content of which is yet to be settled; (2) to invent programs, in the technical sense, which could be run on some conceivable but not necessarily actual computer. In running these programs the output of the machine would simulate, to any preassigned degree, the human activity as originally analyzed. In AI/CS there is a thorough-going interaction between, or involvement of, the mode of analysis of human activity and the form and status of the output of the programmed computer.

The metaphysical or ontological element, which has been present in cognitive science since the very beginning and which has proved attractive to scientific realists, is the assumption that structures of successful programs will, in some way, serve as models of the structure of the mind. Furthermore it is hoped that the structure of the computer, when so programmed, can serve as a model of the structure of the brain. At least these two modeling assumptions are built into the project. These assumptions are not in question in this essay. At issue will be: What is the psychological reality for the representation and understanding of which the modeling enterprise is to be undertaken? In particular, what is the nature of the mind?

The Five Theses

1. Hacking's Thesis: That Mind Is Not a Trans-historical Category

According to Hacking, there is no such thing as *the mind,* of which cognitive science could be true or false. The word "mind" does not refer to some genus of entities, innumerable examples of which have appeared and whose nature is open to investigation. It is not a word like "virus." "The mind" might figure in a theory of what it is for people to think. Such a theory might be modeled on the kind of theory exemplified by the idea of the molecule, which figures in a theory of gases expanding. An entity of this sort provides an ontological basis for an account of the genesis of a certain kind of process. According to Hacking, there are only 'local' concepts of "the mind" arising out of whatever psychological "science" is currently in favor. Thus, apropos of AI/CS, he says, epigrammatically, "'The mental life' is not modelled by the programme, it becomes the programme." So, in assessing the standing of AI/CS, we must compare the mental life as it emerges in cognitive science studies with the mental life as it emerges in other kinds of study, for example, socio-linguistic studies. The mental life is what we are trying to give an account of, but which aspects of our mental lives are in focus is determined by the *form* of the kinds of study that we are currently favoring. For instance, is it the kind of study whose form involves hypothetical entities? To make comparisons of mental life pictures properly we need to clear up certain muddles about the role of ordinary language in the production of minds. In particular we must clear up the folk psychology muddle that has been at the heart of much of the debate about the apparently bizarre proposals by the Churchlands (cf. P. Churchland 1986) for a neuropsychology which is to exclude all mentalistic concepts by relexicalizing all psychological terms as physiological technical expressions. It is worth remarking at this point, to forestall misunderstandings, that only a Luddite would think that the comparison between the mental life as it emerges in AI/CS and the mental life as it emerges in social linguistics leads to some kind of competition. It is not that one of these is going to stand in place of the other.

According to Hacking, AI/CS picks out certain aspects of the mental life, particularly those involving tasks and achievements, by virtue of the kinds of studies undertaken. It is not that something else could be studied by current AI/CS. This restriction is built into the very language in which the AI/CS project is presented. So AI/CS contributes to an understanding of an important part of human life as it is currently lived, namely that kind of life that is particularly associated with entrepreneurial capitalism. But that is by no means the whole of life, even life as lived by modern people. AI/CS as it is currently presented, that is, through a rhetoric by which its projects and results are told as narratives of a certain kind (celebrating success rather than salvation), runs the danger of reintroducing Lockean ideas with the use of the tendentious concept of mental representation and of reinventing Cartesian mind-stuff with the use of the tendentious concept of mental states. I shall return to the issue of mental states later. Since it is an essential part of what I shall call the Level One AI/CS rhetorical apparatus, its reevaluation will play an important part in defining Level Two AI/CS.

My problem is this: Can we innoculate AI/CS in its proper role as a way of contributing to the understanding of a certain part of contemporary life in such a way that it will not continually lead its practitioners to slip back into the reconstitution of the ontology of a seventeenth-century psychology that we ought long since to have abandoned? Hacking's thesis is an important contribution to this innoculation. If mind is not a transhistorical category, identifying a transhistorical ontological species that has been continuously reproduced as individual "minds," then the seventeenth-century thesis that minds are sets of ideas or immaterial substances is not something that needs to engage us at all in our construction of the psychology for current modes of everyday living.

2. Vigotsky's Thesis: "Mind" Is a Collective Production Largely Mediated by Language

According to this point of view, "minds" are continually being produced, partly publicly and partly privately, in the discursive practices of communities of speakers. Mentality consists, in part, of the products of these practices, like rememberings, emotings, etc. But an adequate psychology must also include in its field the powers and skills needed to produce them. In this way of thinking of the mind there is no substance. The mind products are activities or actions or processes. Nouns like "memories" are to be taken as substantive metaphors, convenient shorthand, hypostatizations for complex social acts or the conditions for their possibility, and not as the names of mysterious entities which it is the job of the psychologist to track down and study. Beliefs, memories, wants, and so on should not be taken as entities on the model of HIV viruses which it is the job of the virologist to track down and study. Emotions are abstractions from the everyday activity of emoting, of angry, penitent, cheerful *displays,* which are part of the ordinary conversational interaction of groups of human beings. Emotions are abstractions. At best, words like "anger," "sorrow," "happiness," and so on are stylistic devices for a rhetoric and not the names of mysterious entities. This is not the place to argue the Vigotsky thesis. I shall assume it as part of my resources for the project of revamping AI/CS.

In all of the cases of mind production that will be referred to in this essay, the human ground is primarily collective. Minds are produced in the joint activities of psychologically symbiotic diads, triads, and so forth of people engaging in conversation and other conversation-like symbolic activities. The grounding of individual skills is only secondarily personal, as individual and private versions of fragments and genres of the public and collective conversation.

I want to illustrate this point with the example of remembering as a human practice. I shall argue that characteristically remembering is a cognitive process that is accomplished in conversation distributed through the relevant collection. I shall also argue that, far from being an individual achievement, remembering is socially structured. One must distinguish between the personal and private phenomenon of recollection (the current presentation of some record of past events to oneself as such, the study of which was inaugurated by Ebbinghaus) and the full-blown human activity of remembering in which private recollections are certified as verisimilitudinous representations or presentations of some past occasion, state, or event. Clearly the psychology of remembering, in the full sense, cannot possibly be reduced to some feature of recollection, since there is nothing, and could be nothing, in recollections themselves that could enable anyone to determine whether his or her "memorial experiences" are verisimilitudinous or not, accurate or inaccurate, and so on. Something other than subjective conviction must enter into the process by which recollections are certified as memories.

One suggestion might be that certification takes place through some kind of testing procedure, a kind of archaeology of everyday life. Recollections are checked out against the traces that have been left by the events in question. For instance, a recollection might be checked out against an old photograph or it might be checked against a diary entry. One hardly needs reminding that checkings-out of this kind are really very rare. In most cases, recollection is not transformed into memory in that fashion.

If one thinks about how a committee organizes its memorial activities, it becomes clear that the transformation of a recollection into a memory is achieved very largely through a public and conversational process. It is often a matter of negotiation between the various parties with an interest in what is to count as the past of the institution or group of people in question. Recollections are set against one another, not against archaeological remains of everyday life. The minutes of a committee are constructed by the chairman and the secretary from the rough notes that have been taken during the meeting. With the certification of those minutes at the next meeting, a verisimilitudinous record is created there and then. There is no further question as to the true and accurate "record of the past." In this formal procedure, we have a kind of model of much of the memory work that goes on in everyday life (Haug 1987). The conversations that are common in families, in which members propose recollections and in which these are discussed and worked over to determine the family past, are very much the same sort of activity as the taking and certification of the minutes of the meeting. In each case recollections are juxtaposed to recollections and social power plays an important role in the outcome of negotiations of conflicting claims. However, in the case of those discussions in which the memories of families are created, the overt exercise of memorial power is much clearer than in the behind-the-scenes work of chairman and secretary in the preparation of the minutes of the meeting of an ordinary institution. Marga Kreckel, in her study of the conversations of the British Broadcasting Corporation's series "The Family," noticed on several occasions that discussions about the past were finally settled by the exercising of memorial rights by the mother, who simply declared what the past had been. Other research has shown a similar sort of power structure and the formation of memories in accordance with it.

There are plenty of other cases where we must free ourselves from the idea that something private and individual is behind a psychological process that occurs publicly and collectively. For example, if we consider emotions like indignation and regret, we have no need to say that a hidden moral assessment is behind the display of these emotions. Emotions, as displayed, are the form that the moral assessment sometimes takes. To display one's indignation is to make a moral assessment of some event that has occurred. Similarly to display one's regret is retrospectively to assess one of one's own actions unfavorably. Indeed, in some cases, one person's display may be defined as indignation, not by any intentional states of that person but by what the other people who will take part in the conversation do and say.

It was Vigotsky (1962) who first drew our attention to the fact that conversation is typical of the means of the collective production of mentality and also, one might add, the best model for other such production processes.

At this point we can begin to unravel the tangle of confusions about folk psychology. The main error, compounding their individualism, into which both the critics and defenders of folk psychology have fallen is to assume that the English words for all sorts of aspects of mentality work for the folk that use the language, as if they played a similar role to the theoretical concepts that are used in the terminology of physics to denote real or imaginary hypothetical entities. It was exactly this position that Wittgenstein pilloried in the psychological sections of Wittgenstein's *Philosophical Investigations* (1953). Both defenders and critics of "folk psychology" suppose that, for example, the folk treat beliefs as the mental states which purportedly lie behind declarations. Wittgenstein enabled us to see what is in front of our very eyes. Beliefs are the content of actual or possible declarations. A statement like "I believed so and so all along" is not to be interpreted as "somewhere in me was an entity, 'the belief in so and so' that, though, at that time unobserved, persisted in existence during the period in question." Rather it means something like "I would have been prepared to say or to declare all along that so and so." What is the temporally continuous grounding of this disposition? There need be nothing *behind* a declaration but physiology. But a declaration is not a disguised physiological phenomenon. That is the mistake which the Churchlands make. A declaration exists only in a collectivity. It is incorporated, and only exists as such, in a moral order in which people as speakers stand in certain relations of mutual trust and commitment.

Belief is a conversational phenomenon. So the idea that folk psychology is a kind of diaphanous physics of the mind with beliefs and desires as its theoretical entities is an error common to both sides of the debate. It is not that folk psychology can be defended against critics such as the Churchlands by advocates such as Dennent. The whole idea is radically misconceived. There is no folk psychology that could be displaced by neurophysiology. The collective production of mentality by symbolic means does not stand over against neurophysiology. On the 'Vigotskian' view a reformed psychology would be dominated by the study of the "grammars," that is, the norms of order of those conversations in which mental products, like rememberings, emotings, declarations of belief, etc., are produced. This is not exhaustive of psychology, only of mentation. There is the whole field of manual skill to be investigated, the conditions of acquisition and use, the physiological groundings and so on.

The remaining three principles could be thought of as special cases of the two general principles with which I have begun this discussion.

3. Winograd's Thesis:
Linguistic Productions Are More or Less Indeterminate,
Their Meanings Are Essentially Contestable, and Retrospectively Revisable

The ground for this principle or thesis is that we must acknowledge three particularizing aspects of acts of speaking: (1) their historicity, the way in which the meaning of an utterance depends on the actual history of past uses and which is specific to the present moment of its production; (2) contextuality, the way in which the meaning of an utterance is made relatively determinate in the immediate social and conversational context of its utterance; (3) indexicality, the way the meaning of an utterance is dependent on the identity of the engaged speakers as embodied beings and persons of a certain moral standing. The meaning of all linguistic items is subject to historicity, contextuality, and indexicality and, thus, so are the meanings of all linguistic acts. This is an important thesis, indeed, perhaps the most important thesis for the critical reconstruction of cognitive science. One of the striking consequences of accepting it is that now the existence of norms of order become a problem. Given the historicity, contextuality, and indexicality of all utterances, how then can we say that there are right and wrong things to say, correct and incorrect, proper and improper contributions to a conversation?

Since there are no such things as constant transhistorical, transituational, and transpersonal units of language as produced, all linguistic structures are indeterminate to some degree. Yet we are able to construct continuous conversations. This is achieved, I believe, by virtue of the general acceptance of some sort of principle of charity. For example, we overlook the minute contextual and indexical variance in the terms of a traditional syllogism. The difference in the context provided by the major and minor premises, together with the conclusion, are not sufficiently great to invoke serious equivocation. There will be equivocation but it may be of such little moment that the argument can be allowed to run through. However, it would be wise to assume that formal argument forms, if realized as conversation, are equivocal unless shown not to be, and so any kind of model using a formal calculus is to some extent suspect.

4. Davies's Thesis: Insofar as Mentality Is Produced Conversationally, Contradiction Is Sometimes To Be Tolerated

This thesis has been mostly developed in feminist linguistics to deal with the problems that are created, particularly for women, by the existence of a variety of discursive practices in which they must engage in order to complete, so to say, a day of ordinary life. In this context, a discursive practice is to be understood as

a locally recognized way of producing a proper conversation and thus of producing some aspect of one's mentality, in particular oneself as a 'singularity' —
a 'self'.

Many people organize their reflexive reasoning, their sense of themselves,
around apparently formally contradictory declarations. So for instance, we
might have the declaration "I am a mother of small children" framed within one
discursive practice and "I am an academic sociologist" framed within another,
both declarations made by the same publicly identified person (Smith 1987).
Considered relative to each distinctive discursive practice, there is microconsis-
tency. But since to live one's daily life requires the use of both discursive practices, there is no macroconsistency. There would be no matter of interest here
unless there was some way in which the discursive practices interacted with one
another and, indeed, that is exactly what happens.

Complications arise when there is a leakage between the constituent conversations. An interesting example (Davies and Harré 1990) is the Alwyn Peter
case. Alwyn Peter was an aboriginal Australian who was acquitted of murdering
his wife on the grounds that his culture had been destroyed. In a brief autobiog-
raphy, Alwyn Peter claims both that he did kill his wife, and that he did not. The
former declaration is made sense of within the discursive practices of the European system of legality and psychology in which intentional acts are ascribed to
the person who performed the action. Alwyn Peter does not deny that it was by
his hand that the fatal knife-thrust was made. However, the latter declaration
makes sense within the discursive practices of aboriginal Australians, in which
Peter's failure to conform to tribal law by marrying the woman he murdered was
a punishable offense. But since the traditional penalty of spearing is no longer
possible, Alwyn Peter believed that a collective tribal punishment was meted out
to him through a magical impulsion to kill his wife when he was drunk. The
suffering he has subsequently endured is the punishment for his violation of
tribal custom. The leakage between the two discursive practices occurs in his
account of the events that followed his second marriage. The second wife asked
him to leave on grounds defined within European discursive practice, namely
that he was dangerous (that is, not in control of his actions) when drunk. He
himself understands this action as rational in its own terms, but *also* as embedded within the aboriginal discourse. The second onset of misery, subsequent on
his expulsion by the second wife, is the indication that he is still being punished
for his original violation.

Even if we restrict the application of Davies's thesis to only some discursive productions of self, the necessity to tolerate contradiction is fatal to the idea
of a cognitive science program in which the whole of a person's language in use
is formally mapped onto some logical calculus. The contradiction condition
would be fatal to any such enterprise.

Theses three and four therefore impose constraints on the language models
which would be necessary to represent linguistically mediated mental processes.
They certainly run counter to naive cognitive science, but as I shall argue, they
do provide opportunities for a more sophisticated version of that project. Theses

three and four show, if they are correct, that standard formal logics cannot be adequate tools for representing mental processes or structures if the mentation is conceived according to the Vigotskian model, that is, conversationally. Thus we reach a disturbing intermediate conclusion: naive cognitive science is not an empirical descriptive project, but it is normative and prescriptive. It presumes individualism and logicism as essential conditions or perhaps even premises in its theoretical constructions. Sociologists and historians will recognize these for the political assumptions that they are.

5. Coulter's Thesis: Mentation Involves Whole Person Skills and Performances

Coulter has argued in several places (Coulter 1989) that it is a mistake to assign, either to the brain or to an information-processing module, aspects of human mentation that can only be ascribed to a whole embodied social being, a person. His argument is essentially based upon usage and borrowed consciously from Wittgenstein. For instance, everyday uses of 'remember', 'forget', and so on determine what, for this culture, at this moment, remembering and forgetting are, and these are always attributed to whole persons. We do not say, for instance, that part of ourselves forgets or part of our brains remembers. This is not just an accident of our ignorance. This is a feature of the logic of the concept itself, and it reflects the fact that remembering and forgetting are morally accountable and socially constructed phenomena, in the conversational production of which whole persons are engaged.

But there is a second argument, a moral argument. Declarations (for example, memories as claims to recollect a past event), displays of anger which involve moral commitments and moral stances, or displays of indignation and of regret are interjections into conversations which can only be made on behalf of moral beings. It is the whole person that is a moral agent, not some part of the person, and in particular it is not the brain that stands in moral relations to others.

Thesis five, if correct, would restrict the use of modularity treatments and support the project of AI/CS as a modeling of whole conversations rather than of mysterious goings-on in individual speakers.

THE TWO LEVELS OF COGNITIVE SCIENCE

Level One

I have tried to represent in figure 1 the overall structure of the naive form of AI/CS that I believe must be abandoned for research into most psychological topics. I shall call that AI/CS of Level One. In this scheme the tendentious concept of "mental state" is defined in terms of structural isomorphisms that can be set up between the structure of an abstract program, the structure of a brain, and the structure of a computer whose microswitches have been organized by the taking up of the program. The one thing such a "mental state" is for sure is not mental!

In terms of the scheme (figure 1), the upshot of the argument involving the five theses is that only p'' could be a mental state. S'' is a brain state under a mentalistic description.

There is a sharp clash between the technical expression "mental state" as it is defined in Level One AI/CS and the concept of "mental state" as it emerges from the application of the five theses about language and the production of mind that I have been developing in this essay. I believe that the clash is so severe that the project of a Level One AI/CS is actually impossible. What p'' is as a mental state (for instance, as an act of recollection made *relatively and for the moment* determinate as a memory through the developing structures of conversation and other social actions within which it has a place) exists only in a collective of persons. There is no finite determinate entity that is *the* mental state p''. As a memory claim, it is essentially contestable, and this is the case for all such mental products of conversational activity.

However, there could be a Level Two AI/CS in which the very same modeling techniques could be put to proper use, but it would be focused on something very different. It would involve the modeling of the very processes in which mental states of the kind I have argued for in this essay, would have their place. The pair $<S',S''>$, that is, the pair which is formed by the mapping of the structure of a program onto the structure of a brain, would be an incomplete but necessary part of the explanation of the ability of the group of people so trained as to produce a conversation, which would in its turn engender such and such a 'real' mental state, say, a certified act of remembering. But, of course, the pair $<S',S''>$ would be a formal model in neurophysiology. It would not, it could not, be a stand-in for a mental state. There is a project for cognitive science and an important one, but it is not at all the project that has been undertaken under the influence of the mistaken idea that in the total model expressed in figure 1, the computer is to the program as the brain is to the mind.

Figure 1

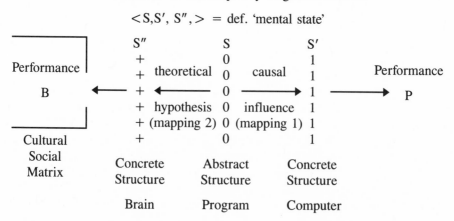

The Structure of Contemporary Cognitive Science

$<S,S', S'',> = $ def. 'mental state'

CONCLUSION

I would like to see AI/CS developed as a cluster of formal theories of conversation and, in this respect, it could become very deep. If this program were followed, it could become a theory of the mind in the only sense I can take seriously, that is, a theory of the discursive production of mentation. Just as quantum mechanics and relativity cannot be combined consistently into one overall physics of the universe, it may be that no consistent overall theory could be developed which incorporates all the individual theories of the clusters of formal representations of the procedures and conventions that we find necessary to develop our indexical, historical, and contextually specific conversations.

REFERENCES

Churchland, P. 1986. *Neurophilosophy.* Cambridge, Mass.

Coulter, J. 1989. *Mind: Action.* Cambridge.

Davies, B., and R. Harré. 1990. "Positioning." *Journal for the Theory of Social Behaviour* 20.

Dennett, D. C. 1978. *Brainstorms: Philosophical Essays on Mind and Psychology.* Brighton.

Fodor, J. A. 1981. *Representations: Philosophical Essays on the Foundations of Cognitive Science.* Brighton.

Hacking, I. 1988. "Making Up the Mind." *London Review of Books,* 1 September, 15–16.

Haug, F. (Ed.) 1987. *Female Sexualisation,* translated by E. Carter. London.

Smith, D. E. 1987. "Women's Perspective as a Radical Critique of Sociology." In *Feminism and Methodology,* edited by S. Harding. Indianapolis.

Vigotsky, L. 1962. *Thought and Language.* Cambridge, Mass.

Winograd, P., and F. Flores. 1988. *Understanding Computers and Cognition.* Reading, Mass.

The Disappearance
of Tradition in Weber

STEPHEN P. TURNER AND REGIS A. FACTOR

Traces of the evidence of Weber's academic origins in the study of the law are evident throughout his writings, and especially in his methodological writings. In the case of his employment of legal concepts of probabilistic causality and of the interest relativity of description, the sources are precisely attributed and the implications of the borrowings are readily understood.[1] But perhaps the most interesting case of Weber's reliance on, and modification of, the legacy of jurisprudential theory and legal modes of reasoning is in the passages in *Wirtschaft und Gesellschaft* in which Weber formulates his famous definitions of action, legitimacy, and forms of social order. Some of these definitions, notably the definition of the state as a territorial monopoly of legitimate violence, have become, in the later literature, links with Weber's name, and thought of as his own distinctive product; in fact, in this particular case, the formulation is found in the major work of the most famous jurisprudential thinker at the time of Weber's training in the law, Rudolph von Jhering.[2]

In this essay we will consider another basic topic: the problem of the nature of the distinctions between *Sitte, Brauch, Wert, Mode,* and *Recht,* on which Weber's discussion relies. These discussions typically involved the untranslatable concept of *Sitte,* which marks a contrast between practices or customs with normative force and "mere practice." There is a close parallel to this distinction in American social thought in W. G. Sumner's latinate distinction between the *mores* and folkways of a society. In what follows we shall simply use the German term as a reminder of its long history in German philosophy. Weber was obviously aware of this history, as was Jhering. Our aim will be to examine Weber's modifications of the received version of these distinctions and to consider the implications of these modifications. As we shall see, what Weber presents as an innocuous classificatory problem contains a much more significant conceptual transformation, which bears on the general image of modernity as rationalization constructed by Weber. One need not speculate on Weber's sources in these passages; the sources are identified by Weber himself. Weber not only cites Jhering, describing his major work, *Der Zweck im Recht,* then thirty-five years in print, as "still a significant contribution"[3] on the subject, he also cites Tönnies's *Die Sitte,*[4] which is itself in significant part a commentary on Jhering, as well as on such figures as the theorist of matriarchy Bachofen, who was influenced by Savigny. Tönnies's work concludes with a discussion of some passages from Nietzsche's *Morgenröthe* of 1881. For Weber's contemporaries, these writings were among the statements on the nature of morality and the moral basis of law that defined the problem-domain, and Weber treated them accordingly.

THE PROBLEM-SITUATION

The larger historical background to the problems, and the intellectual traditions that constituted them, gave them pivotal significance both in philosophy proper and in the political tradition of Germany, which was largely constituted by, and refracted in, the teaching of law. The main fact to which these distinctions were addressed was the problem of the relation between morals, which is to say the universal, and the particular or local practices to which moral significance is attributed, for example, such things as marriage customs. Many philosophical strategies were employed to resolve this conflict. In ethics, the typical solution was formalism—some version of an argument to the effect that the good in a practice was separable from the specific *content* of the practice, so that superficially conflicting practices could be treated as equally ethical in *form.* The point of these elaborate arguments was to avoid a certain kind of reduction, exemplified by Nietzsche. Nietzsche's early formulations served to reduce the universal claims of morality to the status of local custom, and custom to tradition, on genealogical grounds:

> Morality *(Sittlichkeit)* is nothing other (therefore nothing more!) than obedience to customs *(Sitten)*, of whatever kind they may be; customs, however, are the traditional *(herkommliche)* way of behaving *(handeln)* and evaluating. In things in which no tradition commands there is no morality; and the less human life is determined by tradition *(Herkommen)*, the smaller the circle of morality.[5]

This reductive reasoning employs, though with the aim of parodying and breaking down, distinctions and a strategy of analysis with a complex prior history, of which the history of law forms a conspicuous part. Savigny dealt with the diversity of law between societies through an assertion of the basis of law in custom, and he took this historical origin to establish the continuing primacy of custom or customary morals over law, at least with respect to the questions of the moral authority or force of the law, the common feeling of inner necessity which gave mere statutes their moral force.[6] This doctrine, which Weber, a Romanist in his legal philosophy, rejected, was based on a conception of the *Volksgeist* that was of course discredited by its subsequent uses: Weber faced *völkisch* thought as a living tradition.

To respond to the issues raised by this reduction of morality to the local (and by the universalistic dialectical responses to this reasoning evoked), Weber had to find a set of categories that reduced the conflict to less threatening dimensions. In this respect, his rhetorical strategy parallels Nietzsche's demotion of morality to convention. But his task is more delicate: for Weber it was essential to avoid reducing rationality to convention, or to a local tradition. Thus for Weber it is not the reductive strategy of genealogy, but the strategy of analytical separation that is demanded. Accordingly, where Nietzsche's and Jhering's vocabulary points to the filiations between ideas, notably between *Sitte* and *Sittlichkeit,* Weber's differentiates. He selects *Wert* in place of terms associated with *Sitte,* and the more neutral "Tradition" for *Herkommen.* Yet to make such substitutions persuasive, Weber also had to provide his own countergenealogy. In doing so, he relied on many of the conceptual markers established in the earlier discussion, transforming them to suit his own strategy. Nietzsche's strategy may be said to strengthen the philosophical conflicts by understanding them as historically real conflicts; Weber's strategy was to defuse the philosophical conflicts by turning the alternatives into historical types. Jhering and Tönnies had pursued this same strategy, so to understand Weber one must understand how he undermined and transformed the problematic that informed them. In each case, this issue was the binding character or the moral force of custom or laws: Nietzsche saw custom and conventional morality as historical and therefore not binding; Jhering and Tönnies wished to save the binding element in the face of historical change and diversity. In this particular aim Weber was conspicuously successful: today it is conventional, at least among social scientists, to think of the problem of the moral force of law as a problem of "legitimacy" and the problem of legitimacy in terms of the legitimating beliefs of the ruled.

Weber's approach was to create categorizations that were not class-concepts, but abstract paradigm cases or ideal-types. The approach itself derived not from the tradition of natural scientific definition or categorization, which would have aimed at objective criteria for membership in classes, but from the conceptual practices of Roman law, in which classifications express fundamental conceptual contrasts. These are to be applied to empirical material, but with the expectation that one could find many cases in which classification is difficult or impossible because the material falls between the ideal cases. Jhering's own philosophy of law utilized the same practices on much the same material, and the parallels in results are quite striking.[7]

There is, however, a fundamental difference in premises. Like many of his philosophical contemporaries, such as Durkheim's teacher Boutroux, and his sociological contemporaries, such as Spencer, to whose *The Data of Ethics Der Zweck im Recht* was favorably compared, Jhering was centrally concerned with the relation of purpose to causality. Just as the ethical formalists sought to resolve the problems raised by the diversity of morals by finding a universal formal element that held despite their diversity, Jhering sought a universal purpose, or more precisely a diversity of purposes with universal roots. To account for the diversity of societal purposes he relied on cause, particularly the diversity of local conditions, history, and conditions of social life, and, in a utilitarian fashion, on the causal effect of individual desires. The legitimacy and explanatory power of the teleological consideration of societal purposes was assured for him by the possibility of accounting for social purposes on individualistic premises. Jhering thus did not wish to argue that there was a distinctive kind of causally efficacious end or will beyond individual ends and individual will. But he denied that the notion of egoism contained in the narrow concept of self-preservation of early utilitarianism was sufficient to account for the law and social life.

ZWECK IM RECHT

For Jhering, the history of law is a history of the evolution of societal purposes. The problem of *Sitte* arises parallel to and in connection with his account of legal evolution. The "evolutionary" argument is that the law is a product of struggles between interests which represents the temporary resolution of the fundamental conflicts of interest within a given society. The role of revolutions and coups d'état is to create new legal orders by force. These new orders embody new compromises between interests, and then allow for the development of other interests; Jhering believed, and sought to demonstrate, that successive orders also serve successively larger societal interests. The difficulties in this reasoning are obvious, and were obvious to Jhering himself. It is paradoxical to speak of the imposition of law by force, when the specific instances of force in question, such as revolutionary violence, are extralegal. How does this kind of extralegal force *become* law? For Jhering, this was a central philosophical problem, but not a historical mystery. In history, legal orders arose in violence and came to be normative for the societies they governed. The problem, as Jhering put it, was of binding norm to force. Characteristically, Jhering thought of this problem in terms of sequential transitions: the binding of norm and force could arise, he thought, either by beginning with an agreement, and using force to compel adherence, or by force coming to be accepted as normatively valid law.

Jhering employed two bridge-concepts to connect the binding of norm to force to purposes. Both concepts were legal in character: "indispensability" and "necessity." Agreements, such as may be understood to underlie republican forms of government, may have as an "indispensable" part reliance on coercion in the sense that, without coercion or the threat of coercion, the agreement would be a nullity, as would be the case of a state in which individual citizens could repudiate their obligations to it without suffering serious consequences. This thought is fundamental for Jhering; the justification of law, or legal coercion, itself lies in its indispensability for the achievement of societal purposes. But force may be bound to law in another, and historically more important fashion: through "necessity," particularly the common recognition of the necessity of force for the attainment of common ends.[8] In earlier times, Jhering suggests,

> [the] relation between force and law corresponded to the conceptions of people at that stage. They did not look upon force with our eyes; they saw nothing improper or damnable in such a condition but only what was natural and self-evident. . . . They had an instinctive understanding that there is a need for an iron fist in a wild time to force resisting wills to common action, that there needs a lion to tame wolves, and took no offense at it devouring lambs.[9]

The purpose served by force in these cases was "self-evident": the purpose was peace. But if today "force constitutes the accessory element of law" rather than its most conspicuous feature, it is no less essential, and this becomes evident in moments of crisis.

The role of agreement in modern politics is highly visible; statutory law is the immediate product of procedures of agreement. The purposes which law serves, however, are perhaps more obscure—and certainly more obscure than the end he believed to be visibly served by force in times past—because they are more distant from the experience of the individuals in the society, more complex, and more difficult to understand. Yet they are, he believed, accessible to systematic rational analysis, and also open to rational improvement. Jhering's work was, in part, an account of these purposes.

While various social ends might easily be recognized retrospectively to be concealed in the practices of a society, from its manners to its statutory laws, it is not characteristically the case that people have a self-conscious understanding of the connection between the practices and their social purposes, much less a recognition that amounts to a warrant for the egoistic acceptance of the compulsory character of the practices. Nor did Jhering assume that the societal purposes served by various human aims are self-evident. In his discussion of "ideal interests," for example, he argued that such acts as dying for one's country or for particular principles in fact served societal purposes. So part of his own analysis is a kind of *Ideologiekritik* which shows the societal purposes behind such apparently non-egoistic, non-societal, human aims.[10]

> Behind the so-called ideal interests, which we pursue, behind the idea, for which we set our strength and life, stand real personalities, whose well-being, be it what it will, ought to be fostered, we ourselves, our supporters, our comrades in belief, our fellow citizens, the poor, scientists, etc., at a higher power, a whole *Volk,* at the highest humanity—every idea of a practical motive of our action ends finally in living essence.[11]

THE GENEALOGY OF *SITTEN*

Throughout the text of volume 1 of Jhering's work he refers to the coming discussion of this general topic in chapter nine, the first chapter of volume 2.

The chapter itself Jhering[12] clearly regarded as a significant achievement. The basic argument parallels the case of law: the claim that legal coercion was warranted by its indispensability also led to a recognition of the indispensability of the *Sittlich* realm to the societal purposes served by law, and to law itself, for while coercion is indispensable to the law, it is also insufficient. In short, from the point of view of the teleological side of his analysis, law and *Sitten* were analogous, in that both served societal purposes. The difficulty lay in extending the causal or genetic side of the analysis: the bridge-concepts that served in the case of law did not serve as readily in the case of *Sitten*.

The "lever" that is essential to state power is force. The levers that enforce conformity to *Sitten* differ. Jhering's analysis is a response to intuitionist accounts of moral feelings. *Sittlich* feeling, he argues, is the result, not the cause, of practice.[13] Normative custom or *Sitte* comes from custom in the sense of mere practice through the continuous repetition of an action until it becomes second nature or habitual, and therefore less dependent on will. The term *Gewohnheit*, which designates such habits, refers to their external properties; the term *Sitte* adds to this the inner element of bindingness or normativeness.[14] The source of this normativeness of the *Sitte* is the life of the *Volk,* the conditions of common life, to which the observance of the *Sitten* contributes. Thus the *Sitte* are relative to the historical situation of the *Volk,* and force of the *Sitte* rests on their being historically tested as obligations.

The latter steps in this argument may appear to be sleight of hand. It is unclear how "mere" practices come to be, or at what point and in what way they come to be, transformed into obligations, and how obligations to conform externally come to be transformed into a subjective sense of morals, into a matter of conscience as distinct from mere obedience or conformity. This last step, internalization of what Jhering calls the *sittliche Gesinnung* or moral intention is particularly puzzling. The command to obey the *Sitte* refers only to external conformity; morality refers to the internal, to the subjective realm of conscience and character.[15] Moralists had supposed that this means that the moral intention must then have a different source than *Sitten* do, perhaps an innate source. The difficulty with this theory is that *sittlich* feeling, however strong, varies historically and between societies.

Jhering deals with this problem in an interesting but roundabout manner. He considers various past philosophical discussions of the topic and settles on Locke's criticisms of the doctrine of innate moral ideas as the closest to the truth. Locke's error, he suggests, was one of emphasis. He should have stressed not only the negative side of the argument, but its positive suggestion that moral ideas are learned. The way in which this occurs is unfortunately mysterious in Jhering's own account. "Man has to learn that he may not rob, steal, kill; [or else] that common living cannot exist. Man must learn much through injury."[16] As he goes on to explain, "one rises to the *Sittlich* when one gains the insight that one's individual survival is conditioned via one's societal survival."[17] Thus, "[h]istory produces the *Sittlich Gesinnung*,"[18] which builds on the innate egoistic drive for well-being by showing what practices conduce to the societal good.

These practices are, of course, not presented to the individual as external imperatives which he or she might reject or accept, as *Sitten* themselves are, but as "descriptions of a *Geistig* world."[19] They are conceptual structures that are constitutive of the individual's moral life: its imperatives are experienced as conceptual necessities, and as an "emanation of his own *Sittlich* essence."[20]

This line of reasoning enabled Jhering to come to terms with the problem of the phenomenology of moral life, particularly the existence of an inner sense of correctness and conscience. Jhering distinguished four "social imperatives": style, *Sitte,* morals, and law.[21] The first, he argued, is distinguished by its transience, though he notes that modes of dress which serve the purpose of proclaiming the *volk*-community are long-term "fashions." The second, he said, borders on one side on custom, which is the non-obligatory "simple facticity of continued universal action" and on the other side, on morals. Customs would be *Sitte* and command, if they served not only the individual's interest but that of others or of the public at large by being linked through a chain of mutual interests.[22] Thus customs may be transformed in history into *Sitte.* "When individual action is imitated it becomes custom, and if the element of social obligation is attached to it, it is now *Sitte.*"[23] The practice of tipping is illustrative of this process.[24] *Sitte* differs from morality in that while morality forbids the harmful, *Sitte* forbids the merely dangerous.[25] Each of these imperatives, through practice, creates its own "sense" or feeling. Moral intuitions, involving the harmful, are only the most conspicuous kind of inner sense. The commands of *Sitte* are generally prophylactic in character and need to be obeyed only in an external fashion. But the practice of *Sitte* also brings forth its own kind of inner sense, the sense of propriety, decorum, and tact; analogously in the case of the law, practical familiarity brings forth the judicial sense possessed by a good judge.

THE PROBLEM OF WILL

While social ends may be made to explain individual behavior retrospectively, by translating these ends into individual advantages or goods, the same explanations do not hold prospectively. Thus while it may be evident that the adoption of some convention, such as the elimination of violent means to settle disputes, would be to the advantage of virtually all if virtually all adopted it, there would be no advantage to the first individual to lay down arms in the face of a violent world. The problem of accounting for obligation in terms of advantage is, of course, a fundamental problem for the individualists and rationalists of the present, whether utilitarians or game theorists. For thinkers like Tönnies, the most prominent Hobbes scholar of his day, these issues were also at the forefront of their thought. Their solutions to this problem were, like Hobbes's own, philosophical reconstructions of history as it must have been. They relied on ideas about the law-givers who established orders and a variety of psychologies in which the phenomenological feeling of the authority of tradition could be explained. Jhering's genealogy of *Sitten*, which he exemplified by the case of tipping, was just one of the available reconstructions. Others were more compelling, at least with respect to the weak spot in all rationalistic accounts, the phenomenological sense that a practice is an obligation.

Nietzsche, the author of the most compelling genealogy of morals, insisted on the inherent conflict between tradition and utility when he wrote that tradition is "a higher authority which one obeys, not because it commands what is *useful* to us, but because it *commands.*"[26] Indeed, as he insists,

> if an action is performed *not* because tradition commands it but for other motives (because of its usefulness to the individual, for example), even indeed for precisely the motives which once founded the tradition, it is called immoral and is felt to be so by him who performed it: for it was not performed in obedience to tradition.[27]

Jhering was compelled to assume that this separation between moral feeling and utility was something that had not existed originally, and he characterized the mentality of primitives accordingly, as when he discussed their acceptance of the necessity of force. But the argument rests on an asymmetry: the utilitarian person, the rational individual, is taken for granted as the starting point of explanation. Nietzsche challenged this historical picture by challenging the asymmetry.

> Originally. . .everything was custom, and whoever wanted to elevate himself above it had to become lawgiver and medicine man and a kind of demi-god: that is to say, he had to *make customs*—a frightful, mortally dangerous thing![28]

In short, the individual of Hobbism and utilitarianism did not exist in the primal community. In one sense, Nietzsche merely shifted the burden of proof, or inverted the asymmetry, so that the rational individual became the historical product to be explained rather than the object on which explanation rested. But he was also able to elaborate his account of tradition historically. Even in recorded history, he pointed out, we can see that individualism in our present sense was not intelligible.

> [T]o a virtuous Roman of the old stamp every *Christian* who "considered first of all his *own* salvation" appeared—evil.—Everywhere that a community, and consequently a morality of custom exists, the idea also predominates that punishment for breaches of custom will fall before all on the community: that supernatural punishment whose forms of expression and limitations are so hard to comprehend and are explored with so much superstitious fear.[29]

This was truer to the phenomenology of morals than Jhering's account had been, for although Jhering regarded *Sitte* as forbidding the dangerous, he could not easily account for the element of awe in attitudes toward customary practices. For Nietzsche,

> fear in the presence of a higher intellect which here commands, of an incomprehensible, indefinite power, of something more than personal—there is *superstition* in this fear.[30]

The possibility of transmitting and maintaining these feelings depends on the fact that the transmission of the feelings underlying tradition occurs subrationally:

> It is clear that moral feelings are transmitted in this way: children observe in adults inclinations for and aversions to certain actions and, as born apes, *imitate* these inclinations and aversions; in later life they find themselves full of these acquired and well-exercised affects and consider it only decent to try to account for and justify them. This "accounting," however, has nothing to do with either the origin or the degree of intensity of the feeling: all one is doing is complying with the rule that, as a rational being, one has to have reasons for one's For and Against, and that they have to be adducible and acceptable reasons. To this extent the history of moral feelings is quite different from the history of moral concepts. The former are powerful *before* the action, the latter especially after the action in face of the need to pronounce upon it.[31]

This analysis conflicts with Jhering's at its weakest point: the contrast between the phenomenology of moral feeling and its causal force, on the one hand and the purposive character, particularly the social purpose, which Jhering attributes to *Sitte* and whose conscious recognition in some sense is presumed to be a condition of their normative force. Yet while Nietzsche shifts the burden of proof, he does not provide an account of the diversity of morals, nor an analysis of the basic concepts—such as Community—on which his analysis relies. It is thus not surprising that Tönnies, the author of a famous book on community in addition to his Hobbes studies, took up these same issues when he published his own book on *Sitte* in 1909.[32]

TÖNNIES'S ORIGIN STORY

Tönnies's strategy was to find a more fundamental concept from which to derive a conception of *Sitte*. He posed the problem as one of properly relating "three ideas related to custom which must be differentiated conceptually. These are the ideas of actual usage, of norm, and of social will."[33] The novelty of his analysis was in his use of the concept of social will, which he had introduced in *Gemeinschaft und Gesellschaft*. When he asks "Can the essential substance of custom as a configuration of the general will be developed from its manifestations?"[34] he is asking whether some notion of social will can serve as this fundamental concept.

The concept of will had a long and curious history in this discussion prior to Tönnies's intervention, quite apart from Nietzsche's famous use of it. Jhering had criticized Kant in a famous passage in which he remarked that "You might as well hope to move a loaded wagon from its place by means of a lecture on the theory of motion as the human will by means of the categorical imperative."[35] The argument could be extended to criticize other formalist conceptions of ethics. He argued that the source of will was interest, meaning individual purposes, and that action had such purposes, of which social purposes were a particular, enlightened, variety. Tönnies sought to identify sources of social will which could not be reduced to utilitarian or quasi-utilitarian individual goods (such as Jhering's "well-being"). He could do so by extending the implicit personification of society found in the writings of Rousseau and many contemporary social theorists, and evident in remarks like Jhering's own comment[36] on the way in which society must "break the intractable will of the individual." He attributed to society, indeed both to *Gemeinschaft* and to *Gesellschaft,* "will." Like Jhering, this represents a rejection of formalism in ethics. But the derivation of will proceeds differently.

Tönnies's analysis of will begins with the concept of habit, which itself involves will — not in the sense of inherent or natural inclination, but as "second nature." Habit, he argues, becomes a power, as recognized in the expression "force of habit,"[37] and "established habits imperceptibly change into the instinctive" or "involuntary."[38] The relation between habit and instinct is that habit strengthens wishes and instincts,[39] which are themselves rooted in the "instinct of self preservation and emotions which stem from it."[40] Language does not adequately recognize this element of will in habit, but that is because

> [t]he real and essential will is not what lies on the surface of consciousness. These are only the busy servants and messengers who pave his way while the sovereign sits unseen in his coach. The real and essential will is habit — that is will which has become lord and master through practice.[41]

Jhering, Tönnies noted, had argued that custom and habit differ with respect to the normative or "command" element. He had based this argument on his analysis of language: "language. . .discerned the command of custom but not of habit."[42] But Tönnies wished to argue that the analysis of language is inadequate on its own terms. Contra Jhering, some *Sitten* command and others do not. This raises a prior question: whether there is a sense in which the "commanding" and "permitting" which language attributes to some *Sitten*, as in the expression "custom permits that the sexes bathe together" points to an "authority" or "powerful will" that must be a social will, and one which must be perceived and "analysed in analogy to individual will."[43]

Tönnies was, of course, already committed to this thesis, and his analysis of *Sitte* merely extends it. He characterizes this "social will" in a fashion reminiscent of Durkheim. It serves "to order and regulate every individual will. Every common will can be understood as expressing a 'thou shalt'."[44] This expression in itself, Tönnies held, implies the existence of a will, for the act of command implies the existence of autonomy and freedom whether it is the command of an individual to itself or the command of an association of individuals. But to "impute a will to custom, thus personifying it" is problematic on metaphysical grounds. "Custom cannot be imagined without people who want what custom wants." His solution to this problem of the seat of the social will is to locate it in the people. These "people" are the *Volk,* which connotes not only the living but the dead and the unborn.[45] It is thus the essential will, the "necessary and logical" will of the *Volk,* what Tönnies termed its *Wesenwille,* that is the source of *Sitten*. Custom is the self-regulation of this will and emerges "through habit and out of practice."[46] Tönnies is able to build on this a genealogical account of moral feeling that subsumes Nietzsche's. Habit inherently "points toward the past,"[47] and this is the source of the distinctive fact of reverence and honor which attach to *Sitten*. *Sitten* fall in the category of things learned by the "obedience and imitation through which the young and disciples follow their parents and masters and learn from them."[48]

Reverence "results from the actual state of affairs as an inference and a claim."[49] It is an inference from the fact of parental power and superiority that gets generalized. The reverence accorded past practice is a special case of the reverence of the living for the dead, which is itself a special case of the reverence of children for parents and the young for the old.[50] This reverence, in the last analysis, is based not on custom, but "actually on nature, on 'natural law' — that is, on a tacit understanding about what has to be"[51] that inheres in the fact of dependence on parents. The characteristic features of this "natural" reverence, fear, and honor attach to the *Sitte* that are transmitted. The belief which results from this "inference" is a generalized reverential belief in past things and practices. Tönnies called this belief a "custom of customs. . .as a custom which rises above custom, links itself with it, and sanctions it."[52]

Tönnies might have used this origin story to attempt to account for practices in terms of the facts of transmission and the historical contingencies in transmission that account for their diversity. He makes a number of suggestions along these lines, particularly with respect to the special role of women in the transmission of *Sitten*. But his main concern was to reanalyze Jhering's distinctions in terms of his own analysis of will. The distinction between *Sitten* which are mere practices or *Brauch* and those *Sitten* which genuinely "command" is explained by Tönnies by the contrast between *Sitten* which do and do not spring from the social will. The remaining categories may be generated by the use of two devices: the consideration of the extent of actual empirical performance of the practice and the concept of imitation. Morals, in distinction to *Sitten*, are ideals which are not necessarily followed or achieved; *Sitten* must be facts of practice to exist at all. Ideals of decorum, however, are ideal standards, which are thought to be valid, or hold as demands, whether they are followed or not. *Sitten* form the predominant basis of such ideals, but they are separate and may even conflict with the *Sitten*.[53] They are often imitated because they are thought to be a mark of social superiority. Imitation or behavior based on inferences from the external conduct of others is thus a means of transmission distinct from those that inspire awe. Duty, in contrast to moral ideals, is a matter of imitation of actual practice, based on the inference that what others do one must also do.[54]

Because Tönnies is concerned to make the case for a non-individual will, he is concerned throughout to stress conflicts between the demands of *Sitte* and other sources of conduct, such as fashion, ideals of decorum, and the like. The enlightenment notion of the conflict between reason and tradition might be supposed to fit this. But Tönnies wishes to sociologize this contrast by identifying the utilitarian social order, the order that arises from the impulses of rational individualism, with the *gesellschaftliche* elements of modern life. He constructs a genealogy to fit this. The original form of the contrast between reason and *Sitte*, according to Tönnies, arose from the variant interpretations of the idea of natural law. The "common idea of the Aryans before their separation," which appears in the *Veda,* treats the "regulation of nature" and "the regulation of human life" as one. In ancient Rome, however, a contrast developed between customary arrangements and those which are reasonable because they are purposeful or expedient. Modern rationalism, science, and critical philosophy have developed this contrast in a misleading manner. In large part because of the kinship of *Sitte* with superstition, rationalists have dismissed *Sitte* as subrational. Tönnies rejects this as an inadequate judgment. "The thinking person must recognize the unconscious creativity in the human, social and individual spirit, and must find rationality not only in what is rational in its *form.*"[55] He preferred to state the problem in terms of the relation among the two kinds of will and *Wissenschaft.* The *Kurwille,* the will which chooses and exhibits expediency, *may* be united with *Wissenschaft,* but *Wissenschaft* may be united with the *Wesenwille* as well.

This is the basis for Tönnies's positive message. In the closing paragraphs of *Die Sitte* where Tönnies referred to aphorism 9 of *Morgenröthe,* he assents to the characteristic modernist claim, which Jhering himself made, that the morality of *Sitte* has become inadequate and that it needs to be replaced. But Tönnies, like Nietzsche, cannot accept that the rationality of the *Kurwille,* the rationality of utilitarianism, is sufficient as a replacement. What is needed is a "conscious ethic — that is, the recognition of that which makes man human and the self-affirmation of reason" which partakes of a new kind of reason: "reason, precisely through this, must cease being merely a scientific analytic power. Rather it must develop into the joyous creation of *Gemeinschaft.*"[56]

THE PROBLEM RESTATED

Weber's alternative was not presented, as Tönnies's was, as a solution to the problem of *Sitte.* It appears in the series of definitions and methodological comments that formed the preface to *Wirtschaft und Gesellschaft.* The section may be read as Weber presents it, as a series of idiosyncratic but potentially useful distinctions, which occasionally appropriate ideas from the previous literature, of which the writings of Jhering and Tönnies form a part.[57] But one may also read the section as a radical remapping of the domain of human conduct in which the problem Jhering and Tönnies sought to solve does not arise. Thus the subtext may be read by noticing, at each step of Weber's discussion, how one portion after another of the domain of *Sitte* that is explained by the theories of Jhering and Tönnies is explained differently or described in a way that makes further social explanation unnecessary or irrelevant.

The structure of Weber's classification of action, and to some extent the structure of the text of *Wirtschaft und Gesellschaft* as a whole, parallels Jhering's *Der Zweck im Recht.* Jhering and Weber both begin with the distinction between purpose and cause. Weber makes a broad distinction between natural processes and processes with meanings, or intended purposes,[58] that parallels Jhering's distinction between mechanical "causes" and psychological "purposes." In both cases, the concepts are exclusive: in Weber the distinction is between processes which are natural or meaningless[59] and those that are meaningful; in Jhering, it is between influences on conduct that have or have not been converted into psychological motives.[60] Both accept, of course, that there are natural processes involved in various ways in action. For Weber, the category of natural processes includes memory, habituation, and such phenomena as can be attributed to racial or biological sources. Moreover, as we shall see, he is prepared to grant to these processes an extremely large portion of human conduct. The category of action proper, meaning action with an intended purpose, Weber draws more narrowly than Jhering. Where Jhering says "Purpose forms the only psychological reason of the will,"[61] hence "no volition, or, which is the same thing, no action, without purpose" (meaning that where there is volition there is "action"), Weber phrases the problem of "what is action" in terms of the "subjective meaning" an individual attaches to his action, and collapses the concept of subjective meaning into the concept of "intended purpose."

This stress on intentionality is a difference of some significance. It is evident that many of the cases in which the concept of purpose is employed in ordinary usage do not fully share the properties of the paradigm cases of purposive action, that is, those cases where the agent is fully conscious of the purposes toward which the action is directed, where these purposes are genuinely motivating, and where these purposes are articulable and comprehensible to others as purposes. Jhering and Weber handle deviations from this paradigm in quite different ways. Their divergent views of animal behavior are revealing in this respect. In the first edition of his book, Jhering had insisted that one fundamental difference between animals and humans was that animals used other animals only as means, and that animals do not learn and transmit their learnings. In later editions he recanted both claims, recognizing many cases of mutual aid and accepting that "even the idea of society, i.e., of regulated living together for the purpose of pursuing common ends, already appears in the animal world."[62] In this case, as elsewhere, Jhering is satisfied to infer purpose and declines to deny the animals' "purposing power the name of will because of a defective self-consciousness which is less complete than man's own."[63] Even "the idea of a future event," which is readily attributed to animals, "means an idea subsumed under the category of possibility," and this implies the "use of the categories of purpose and of means" and therefore the control of these by "understanding."

Weber begins with the epistemological problems of mental attributions and comes to drastically more stringent conclusions. Like Jhering, he accepts that "many animals 'understand' commands, anger, love, hostility, and react to them in ways which are evidently often by no means purely instinctive and mechanical and in some sense both consciously meaningful and affected by experience."[64] Jhering used this result to collapse animal behavior into the category of purposive action. Weber's strategy was the reverse. Although he was eager to deny that there is reason to believe that biology can contribute much to the understanding of human action, he makes an exception for certain areas of human action. He argues that "biological analogies" may prove suggestive in connection with "the question of the relative role in the early stages of human social differentiation of mechanical and instinctive factors, as compared with that of the factors which are accessible to subjective interpretation generally." Not only are these factors "completely predominant" in the earlier stages of human development, they are "often of decisive importance" in later stages, particularly in connection with "traditional action" and "many aspects of charisma" in which "lie the seeds of certain types of psychic 'contagion.'" These types of action, says Weber,[65] "are very closely related to phenomena which are understandable only in biological terms or are subject to interpretation in terms of subjective motives only in fragments and with an almost imperceptible transition to the biological." This is quite a drastic extension of the domain of the biological or, more precisely, a sharp restriction of the relevance of "interpretation in terms of subjective motives." Weber was quite explicit about this. At one point he remarks that "there is no a priori reason to suppose that our ability to share the feelings of primitive men is very much greater"[66] than our ability to share those of animals.

One might put this down to excessive *epistemic* scrupulousness. But Weber sees it as a *conceptual* issue, that is, a problem of the boundaries between categories. The case of imitation is illustrative of Weber's approach to these problems. Nietzsche located the transmission of tradition in the subrational realm of ape-like limitation. For Weber, imitation is not even in the category of action: in discussing the influences of crowds, Weber said that for his own purposes, "mere 'imitation' of the actions of others. . .will not be considered a case of specifically social action if it is purely reactive so that there is no meaningful orientation to the actor imitated."[67] But Weber also stresses that "the borderline is. . .so indefinite that it is often hardly possible to discriminate."[68] The reason for this indefiniteness, which he said holds for both traditionalism and charisma, is "that both the orientation to the behavior of others and the meaning which can be imputed to the agent himself, are by no means capable of clear determination and are often altogether unconscious and seldom fully conscious."[69] This last clause is crucial, for it goes beyond the epistemic.

Jhering handled the problem of self-consciousness differently. Since he recognized that there can be actions that have "become habitual to such a degree that we no longer think of anything in the doing of it,"[70] he insisted that "even habitual action, in which we no longer do conscious thinking at all, is still purposeful action." His point in doing so is of considerable importance for his view of the character of practice:

Habitual action represents in the life of the individual the same phenomenon as morality and customary law do in the life of a people. In both, the individual as well as the people, a more or less clearly conscious or felt purpose originally called for the action, but the frequent repetition of the same action from the same motives and with the same purpose has bound together purpose and action to such a degree that the purpose has ceased to be a consciously perceptible element of the voluntary process.[71]

In contrast, Weber places "purely traditional behavior" in the category of this "merely reactive" type.[72] He does not deny that the category is significant. Indeed, he remarks that the sociological importance of "merely 'reactive' imitative" may be "at least equal to that of the type which may be called social action in the strict sense."[73]

One may observe that this distinction between the category "natural processes" and action is not merely a classification. It is in part, the "natural" part, an aetiological or explanatory classification. To accept it is to accept the possibility that there may be a "racial" or other "natural" explanations of portions of human conduct. This step is an easy one to take if it is presented entirely as a category which may be empty. But this presentation is not entirely innocent. The arguments of Jhering and Tönnies, it should be recalled, are arguments that posit a problematic explanatory factor (in Tönnies it is the *Wesenwille*, in Jhering it is a particular account of human nature and the human past). We are not inclined to accept these problematic explanations unless we are compelled to: the arguments are arguments from explanatory necessity. To concede part of the domain, for example to concede Weber's reclassification of some of the phenomena into the domain of the "natural" is to concede part of the basis for the argument from explanatory necessity.

Weber does not, in fact, restrict himself to creating a conceptual category that might be empty. By suggesting that the conduct of primitive peoples is predominantly "natural," he removes a great deal from the category Tönnies and Jhering wish to explain and to explain with. This same strategy is repeated, in more or less subtle ways, throughout the discussion of the category of action and its subcategorizations. But in these discussions the problem of distribution is obscured by the character of the categories, which are explicitly ideal-typical.

TYPES AND CATEGORIES

Our inability to draw the line between intentional and "reactive" behavior results from a generic methodological problem: the relevant imputations employ ideal-types, and in the cases of human action in question, these types characteristically diverge significantly from the material to which they are applied *precisely with respect* to intentionality. Weber explained:

The theoretical concepts of sociology are ideal types not only from the objective point of view, but also in their application to subjective phenomena. In the great majority of cases actual action goes on in a state of inarticulate half-consciousness or actual unconsciousness of its subjective meaning. The actor is more likely to be "aware" of it in a vague sense than he is to "know" what he is doing or to be explicitly self-conscious about it. In most cases his action is governed by impulse or habit. Only occasionally and, in the uniform action of a large number of individuals, often only in the case of a few individuals, is the subjective meaning of the action, whether rational or irrational, brought clearly into consciousness. The ideal type of meaningful action where the meaning is fully conscious and explicit is a marginal case. . . . But. . .the sociologist may reason as if action actually proceeded on the basis of clearly self-conscious meaning. . . .[74]

Weber adds that the sociologist must often work with ideal-types because of their clarity, but he should keep in mind that he is in fact imputing motives and meanings on the basis of an ideal-type.[75] This means, in effect, that Weber claims that those actions in which the agent clearly is not consciously aware of the purpose of his action are nevertheless *to be understood on analogy* with ordinary intentional action, in which the agent is aware of his purposes, and that in the case of uniformities of action it is the conscious intentions of the *few cases in which conscious intentions figure* that are to be taken to be indicative of the unconscious intentions behind the rest, and that this kind of interpretation is sufficient (because, implicitly, it is the only kind possible).

In one sense, this alone settles the issue with Tönnies and Jhering, albeit on the most arbitrary of grounds. There is no point to the quest for underlying hidden intentions, because there are none of the appropriate kind that can be imputed in this fashion. What can be imputed will be the kinds of intentions Tönnies described as lying on the "surface of consciousness." Both Tönnies and Jhering inverted this analysis. They supposed that the underlying purposes were to be discerned in something lying beneath the surface; both of them regarded the reasons people gave for their conduct to be rationalizations of habit.[76] And they supposed that habit and its variations could not be accounted for without appeal to social purpose or will.

THE CLASSIFICATION OF "ACTION"

Weber responds to this argument indirectly by his classification of the kinds of actions that fall under the general heading of "habitual" by the next step in his classification, which is to divide actions (which he has predefined as intentional, in the odd extended sense discussed above) into a set of four categories what are, in effect, categories of intentions: *zweckrational, wertrational,* affectual, and traditional. The last category is something of an oddity in the classification itself, for it is properly not a subcategory of the intentional but an extension of the notion of habit. But Weber says that despite the fact that "the great bulk of everyday action to which people have become habitually accustomed" are almost all automatic reactions, "its place in a systematic classification is not merely that of a limiting case because, as will be shown later, attachment to habitual forms can be upheld with varying degrees of self-consciousness."[77] "Strictly Traditional" action thus appears in this scheme in accordance with the idea that there is a continuum between the habitual and the intentional cases of a type of action that is usually not performed with conscious intentions (and is therefore often on, or beyond, the borderline of "action" proper). This is an intriguing idea, for it serves to take back part of the ground ceded to the "natural," but only that part for which habitual action has a self-consciously intentional analogue.

"Affectual" behavior, in its pure form, "also stands on the borderline of what can be considered 'meaningfully' oriented, and often it too goes over the line" as, for example, when it is an "uncontrolled reaction to some exceptional stimulus."[78] So the categories of action that are action properly and unequivocally are *zweckrational* and *wertrational* action. Yet *zweckrational* action, strangely, is also a "limiting case," not because it is not "action" but because the orientation of action wholly to the rational achievement of ends requires ends, or as Weber puts it, a "relation to fundamental values," which cannot be chosen rationally.[79] Thus no action can be wholly *zweckrational*. The paradigm cases of *wertrational* action include "clearly self-conscious formulation of the ultimate values governing the action," which are thus the only cases which in their pure form properly speaking fall within rather than at the limits of the category of intentional action, and a *zweckrational* (or purposively rational, means-end) orientation to the achievement of these ends. The examples Weber gives are sacrifices for a cause, duty, honor, and the like.[80] These always involve, Weber says, "'commands' or 'demands' to the fulfillment of which the actor feels obligated."[81] Weber argues that this kind of conduct is rare. Jhering, it will be recalled, subjected these kinds of aims to an *Ideologiekritik* which interpreted them as serving social purposes.

One point of this strange categorization of what are, with one exception, limiting or borderline cases is to say that virtually all actions fall someplace in between the limits or borders. The categorization is thus a conceptual one, a mapping of a space in which actual cases may be located by placing them along continua. At the next level of classification the method of categorization changes: Weber divides action into class-like categories, uniform and nonuniform. The category of "uniformities" is then divided into subcategories and sub-subcategories which match, more or less closely, those familiar from Tönnies and Jhering. This is done by employing more than one level of subclassification. The level of uniformities includes four basic types: usages, actions involving legitimate orders, those that are *zweckrational*, and self-interestedly rational responses which are uniform because they are similarly rational responses to similar situations. The first two are in turn subdivided, but in the first subcategorization the same kinds of remarks as those initially made in connection with habit are made again. Thus we are told that the "transition from [mere practice] to validly enforced convention and to law is flowing."[82]

At the next lower level, however, the classifications are made on class-like, criteriological or empirical grounds rather than "conceptually" in terms of continua between pure types. The subcategorization of *Brauch* or usage reflects Tönnies's argument against Jhering's analysis of the relation between *Sitte* and *Sittlichkeit*. For Weber, a usage is an actually existent probability, the presence of which is "determined entirely by its actual practice." A usage is a *Sitte* if "the actual performance rests on long familiarity."[83] This is meant to distinguish *Sitte* from cases in which a "uniformity exists in so far as the probability of its empirical performance is determined by the *zweckrational* orientation of the actors to similar ulterior expectation."[84] The category of usage also includes *Mode*, or fashion, which is distinguished from other usages by the fact that in the case of *Mode*, "the mere fact of the novelty of the corresponding behavior is the basis of action." The motivation for adherence to *Sitten* distinguishes *Sitten* from the kinds of uniformities that fall under the heading of legitimacy-related.

> The actor conforms to them of his own free will, whether his motivation lies in the fact that he merely fails to think about it, that it is more comfortable to conform, or whatever else the reason may be. But always it is a justified expectation on the part of members of the group that a customary rule will be adhered to.[85]

One of the peculiarities of this particular categorization is that, although it is not presented as such, it is explicated in Weber's commentary as an aetiological classification, that is, it is a category that Weber defines by its causes, in this case the motives of the adherents.

The way in which the impression that the classification is merely a descriptive scheme is produced is by using the phrase "rests on long familiarity"[86] in the primary definition. But the phrase is blandly misleading. It is either an empty solecism for "done for a long time," so that *Sitte* would be merely old *Brauch,* or it is an explanation which points to a basis on which the practice rests. Weber says that the reasons for a person's adherence to the practice may vary, but he cites only such examples as "that he merely fails to think about it, that it is more comfortable to conform."[87] When Weber turns to the question of the "stability of customary action," he is more explicit: it "rests essentially on the fact that the person who does not adapt himself to it is subjected to both petty and minor inconveniences and annoyances as long as the majority of the people he comes into contact with continue to uphold the custom and conform with it."[88]

One may observe that this is an alternative to the account given by Jhering and Tönnies, but one with no basis in anything other than assertion. Uniformities based on comfortable habit and the avoidance of petty annoyance are hardly the place in which great hidden purposes are to be found. But we have no reason to accept this characterization of the motives for adherence to *Sitten,* to stop our analysis with these motives, or to conclude that there is nothing in the category of *Sitten* other than these kinds of uniformities. If one considers Jhering's examples, such as the practice of tipping, it is evident that in some sense the petty annoyances of which Weber speaks are a "lever" and are part of the process of learning and developing the practices which serve reciprocal relations in society.

Weber's next category is of uniformities of orders (which involve legitimacy) and includes law and convention. The procedure of subclassification Weber follows for these cases enables him to avoid giving any essentialist analysis to the distinctions among law, *Sitten,* and convention. Once he has defined *Sitten* as actual usages which do not involve external sanctions, he is free to distinguish law and convention similarly, as obligations *with* sanctions, but sanctions with distinct sources: in the case of law, sanctions by a special group, namely the juridical; in the case of convention by individuals acting on their own to compel conformity, by the "psychic sanction" of "disapproval."[89] These classifications, which resemble Jhering's discussions of the "lever" of coercion, are close to criteriological in character, easy to apply, and involve only the superficial aspects of the law. They do not answer any of the essentialist questions that Jhering or Tönnies wished to ask about the law, such as "What makes law obligatory and mere *Sitte* not?"

The answer to these questions is foreshadowed in Weber's discussion of *Wertrationalität*, rational ordering of values. At the beginning of the section on uniformities, Weber said that the classification would be based on "typically appropriate subjective meaning attributable to"[90] persons acting in accordance with the uniformities. In fact, the discussion proceeds at the first level of subcategorization by distinguishing the sources of the sanctions employed on behalf of the regularity. But in discussing the cases of law and convention, Weber adds to the scheme the consideration that these orders are distinguished by the existence of belief in their legitimacy. When he turns to the question of what upholds or guarantees[91] the legitimacy of an order, he argues that there are two principal ways: from disinterested motives, which may be affectual (such as loyalty), *wertrational* or religious in origin, or by self-interested motives. These are, so to speak, practical guarantees of obedience. They do not, he argues, interrelate in a systematic way with considerations of morality that have distant social purposes, as Jhering supposed: ethical ideas, Weber says, may have profound influence on action without any sort of sanction, and, indeed, "This is often the case when the interests of others would be little influenced by their violation."[92] Yet "every system of ethics which has in a sociological sense become validly established is likely to be upheld to a large extent by the probability that disapproval will result from its violation, that is, by convention."[93] So it is the sanction of disapproval that makes the ethic effective; in contrast, legal rules often are simply expedient, and thus do not rest on "ethical" grounds.

This absence of systematic relations suggests that what he calls the "bases" of legitimate orders are to be found not in some sort of consistent social purposes or in the *Volkswille,* but in the beliefs on the basis of which legitimacy is ascribed to orders by their subjects. This is the subject of the next subcategorization, the famous categorization (into traditional, charismatic, and rational-legal) of kinds of beliefs about the validity of orders. "Tradition" appears here under the following definition: "belief in the sanctity of tradition" which is described as "the most universal and primitive case."[94] "The fear of magical penalties confirms the general psychological inhibitions against any sort of change in customary modes of action."[95] This is, of course, Tönnies's "custom of custom."[96]

These categories of belief are ideal-typical constructions which must be applied where they do not fit precisely. There is, moreover, a by-now familiar difficulty: "In a very large proportion of cases, the actors subject to the order are of course not even aware how far it is a matter of custom, of convention, of law.

In such cases the sociologists must attempt to formulate the typical basis of validity."[97] This means, as in the case of traditional action, that the classification must be applied by attribution to persons who do not consciously hold the beliefs.

THE PROBLEM OF *SITTE*

The set of problems that concerned Jhering and Tönnies—the diversity of customs, the phenomenological sense of the "commanding" character of at least some of them, and the problem of explaining their evolution—disappears in this scheme. The category of *Sitte* or tradition is divided up into small portions. The problem of the identification of the *Sitten* of a given society, which Tönnies was careful to stress were hidden below the surface of consciousness, is resolved by the expedient of considering the case where *Sitten* are not consciously upheld as merely a variation of the few cases in which they *are* consciously upheld. This means, in effect, that there can be no mysterious category of compelling *Sitten* that are *in general* below the surface of consciousness. All that belongs to the category will have a conscious analogue, at least for some people in the group. The problem of compulsion is reduced to several distinct problems, each of which is solved differently: in the case of usage, it is a matter of petty annoyance or discomfort; in the case of conventions, it is the overt "sanction" of disapproval; in the case of law, it is the coercive sanctions of the specialized "legal" authorities. Each of these cases is in practice mixed, so that the load any given factor must bear is minimized by the fact that other factors, such as self-interest or mere habit, may bear the bulk of the load. So the problem of what makes *Sitten* compelling disappears.

Yet many of Weber's contemporaries, of whom Durkheim was the most notable, shared Jhering's and Tönnies's fascination for the problem of *Sitten*, and believed it to be fundamental. Durkheim treated the overt, conscious, forms of traditions as indications and incidental products of the existence of a causally powerful collective mental realm, the *conscience collectif.* This conception shared with Tönnies's the idea that consciously upheld ideals cannot be the model for *Sitte*, and, like Tönnies, Durkheim saw the problem as one of distinguishing habits which were mere habits from those which have normative force or reflect the force of society. Their "mapping" strategies are mirror images: where Weber divides the category into a long series of distinct problems, each of which is accounted for differently, Durkheim collects together a variety of apparently disparate phenomena under the heading of "constraint" and, like Tönnies and Jhering, proposes a univocal account of this unique category. Weber, in contrast, creates a vast four-sided gray area into which actions fall. But each of the sides is oddly defined. In the case of affectual and traditional action, the sides are vaguely defined borderlines between intentional action and mere behavior. In the case of *wertrational* action, the instances of the type are held by Weber himself to be historically unusual. In the case of *zweckrational* action, the pure form is a logical impossibility.

How compelling are these alternatives? How compelling is Weber's redrawing of the categories in terms of which the problem arises? An assessment of Weber's position that was true to its contextual origins – to Weber's own problem in revising his sources – might be organized around the following question: (1) How much of the realm of *Sitten* may be modeled on explicitly intended valued? (2) Is there much left over? (3) Where does the model of explicitly intended values leave the problem of the diversity of morals? (4) Where does it leave the problem of the phenomenological sense of command, externality, incorporation, and the like attributed to *Sitten*? (5) Where does it leave the problem of the transmission or learning of *Sitten*? The answer to the first of these questions depends on the question of the existence of habits which are social practices (or shared mental structures, in the "Structuralist" forms of this thesis), which are in some sense "transmitted" non-verbally or in a way that cannot be reduced to the verbal or conscious content of the practices. Weber must deny that there are any such practices: the negative implication of his insistence on attributing motives of action involving traditions as approximations to ideal-types which involve conscious adherence to traditions is that there is nothing in the category, nothing "left over." Weber gives no argument for this, but he could do so by successfully answering the remaining questions. Jhering and Tönnies both have accounts which at least point toward answers to the problem of the diversity of morals: Jhering's process of social learning, for example, makes circumstances and the evolution of reciprocal action and practice account for the divergent forms of *Sitten* that may be observed historically and in the present. This account, it may be noted, allows for that which is transmitted to change in ways which are intrinsic to the process of learning itself.

Weber's answer to this set of problems must be in the form of an account in which the concept of value-choice figures heavily, for this is his only alternative to the transmission of unchanging habit through "imitation." Indeed, his reliance on imitation forces him to look elsewhere for an account of change, and this places the burden of explanation, with respect to both change and diversity, on conscious departures from tradition, meaning such historical processes as charismatic moral prophecy, submission to a dominant group, or rationalization understood as or identified with self-conscious revision. As he puts it, an important aspect of the "process of the 'rationalization' of action is the substitution for the unthinking acceptance of ancient custom, of deliberate adaptation to situations in terms of self interest."[98] The other aspects, including "conscious rationalization of ultimate values" or moral skepticism are equally "conscious" in character.[99]

The source of compulsion must also be found in the rationally compelling character of the ultimate values in question, in the force of charisma, or in some combination of these, or of these and the habits acquired through their practice. To be sure, the role of the element of pure normative compulsion may be minimized, as Weber himself does when he suggests that considerations of convenience, notably the avoidance of petty annoyances, account for the stability of

Sitte, and that a system of ethics is "likely to be upheld to a large extent" by the probability of disapproval of violations of it.[100] But the phenomenological experiences of rational acceptance of a conclusion, or logical compulsion, or convenience, of habit, and of social disapproval are distinct experiences from that of a sense of the demands of morality, and these are, in turn, distinct from the sense of demands which arise from a conscious value-choice. These differences are obscured by the fact that his account of value-choice is dependent on an analogy between largely unconscious actual conduct and ideal-types of conscious moral choice of the same kind as one finds in his discussion of tradition.

The plausibility of Weber's categorization thus rests on the plausibility of this manner of eliminating the problem of the phenomenological sense of externality and command by taking the cases that Jhering and Tönnies took to be paradigmatic and relocating them in the mixed category between these ideal-types, each of which Tönnies and Jhering, and many others such as Durkheim, took to be qualitatively different from *Sitten*. So the persuasiveness of the notion of value-choice and *wertrational* action as a surrogate for the commanding power of *Sitten* is decisive both directly and indirectly, in connection with the problem of the change of *Sitten* and their diversity. Weber's overt rhetorical strategy conceals its centrality. Because he explicitly insists that empirical cases of action resemble the model of "pure rational orientation to absolute values"[101]. . ."for the most part only to a relatively slight extent,"[102] he does not invite empirical scrutiny of the question of the extent to which rationalization occurs.

Weber's highly persuasive picture of human history as emancipation from the enchanted world of unthinking, unchanging tradition into a world of subordination to an iron cage of rational self-consciousness depends on this unscrutinizable question. But if traditions—in the sense of practices not reducible to their conscious articulated expressions—are present and are constitutive parts of social life in the modern world as well as the world of our ancestors, Weber's methodological devices would conceal them from us. They will have disappeared in the categorization scheme, not in the world.

NOTES

1. Stephen Turner and Regis Factor,"Objective Possibility and Adequate Causation in Weber's Methodological Writings," *Sociological Review* 29 (1981): 5–28.

2. Stephen Turner and Regis Factor, "Decisionism and Politics: Weber as Constitutional Theorist," in *Max Weber, Rationality and Modernity,* edited by Scott Whimster and Jon Lash (London, 1987), 334–54.

3. Max Weber, *The Theory of Social and Economic Organization,* translated by A. M. Henderson and Talcott Parsons, edited and with Introduction by Talcott Parsons (New York, 1947), 122. (*Wirtschaft und Gesellschaft. Grundriss der verstehenden Soziologie,* Winckelmann [Tübingen, 1976], 15.)

4. *Social and Economic Organization,* 127 (*Wirtschaft und Gesellschaft,* 17.)

5. Friedrich Nietzsche, *Daybreak: Thoughts on the Prejudices of Morality,* translated by R. J. Hollingdale (Cambridge, 1982), aph. 9. (*Morgenröthe. Nachgelassene Fragmente* [Berlin, 1971], aph. 9.)

6. Julius Stone, *Social Dimensions of Law and Justice* (Stanford, Calif., 1966), 94.

7. See Turner and Factor, "Decisionism and Politics." One might construct a complete table of conceptual correspondences, which would be quite impressive, though that is not attempted here.

8. Rudolph von Jhering, *Der Zweck im Recht*, vol. 1, 2d ed. (Leipzig, 1884), 254-55. The legal use of "necessity" ordinarily relates to legally definable conditions under which the law does not hold. As Jhering observed, the Imperial Criminal Code itself held that an act which would ordinarily be a criminal act would not be under conditions of "necessity" for which the agent was not responsible; moreover, the state can declare a state of exception. See Turner and Factor, "Decisionism and Politics."

9. *Der Zweck im Recht*, vol. 1, 254-55.

10. Jhering might have dodged these difficulties, as Kelsen later did, by restricting himself to a pure theory of the law that treated the law as a separate object, a system, to be studied as such.

11. Rudolph von Jhering, *Der Zweck im Recht*, vol. 2, 2d ed. (Leipzig, 1886), 89.

12. *Der Zweck im Recht*, vol. 1, xii.

13. *Der Zweck im Recht*, vol. 2, x-xi.

14. Ibid., 21-22.

15. Ibid., 38.

16. Ibid., 112

17. Ibid., 198.

18. Ibid., 116.

19. Ibid., 99.

20. Ibid., 100. In this and other respects, such as his stress on the constitutive character of moral ideas, Jhering is reminiscent of Durkheim. If Jhering's is not a wholly successful solution to the problem of subjective feeling, it is striking in its consistent insistence on the social determination of morals and on the dependence of phenomenologically "private" experience on social facts. In one especially striking passage, Jhering discusses the role of fests. He (vol. 2, 203) argues that "every great societal act finds its expression in a fest" which are means by which "individual joy is raised to the height of the societal" and by which "one of the most beautiful bonds of the societal union" are built.

21. Vol. 2, 230-31.

22. Ibid., 247.

23. Ibid., 242.

24. Ibid., 249.

25. Ibid., 260-61.

26. *Daybreak*, aph. 9. (*Morgenröthe*, aph. 9.)

27. Ibid.

28. Ibid.

29. Ibid.

30. Ibid.

31. Ibid., aph. 34. (*Morgenröthe*, aph. 34.)

32. Ferdinand Tönnies, *Custom: An Essay on Social Codes*, translated by A. Farrell Borenstein (Chicago, 1961). (*Die Sitte* [Frankfurt am Main, 1909]. Page numbers of German editions will appear in parentheses in following notes.

33. Ibid., 114 (70).

34. Ibid., 41 (16).

35. *Der Zweck im Recht*, vol. 1, 51.

36. *Der Zweck im Recht*, vol. 2, 256.

37. *Custom*, 32 (9).

38. Ibid., 31 (9).

39. Ibid., 33 (10).

40. Ibid., 31 (9).

41. Ibid., 34 (11).

42. Ibid., 36 (12).

43. Ibid., 37 (13).
44. Ibid., 38 (14).
45. Ibid., 39 (15).
46. Ibid., 42 (17).
47. Ibid., 42–43 (17).
48. Ibid., 43 (18).
49. Ibid., 45 (19).
50. Ibid., 44 (19).
51. Ibid., 45 (19).
52. Ibid., 48 (21–22). In the case of religion, like the case of learning from parents, "reverence" derives from the manner of learning. In the case of the learning of ritual practices, "the natural sentiments, feelings of servility, of humility and diffidence, all of them expressions of reverence, are expressed strongly and distinctly through the performance" (*Custom,* 49 [22]).
53. *Custom,* 113 (69).
54. Ibid., 93 (42–43).
55. Ibid., 143 (92).
56. Ibid., 146 (94–95).
57. Weber's explicit intent in formulating the categories is not terribly clear. At one point, Weber (*Social and Economic Organization,* 115 [13]) denies that he has "intention here of attempting to formulate in any sense an exhaustive classification of types of action," and he goes on to suggest that "the usefulness of the classification for the purposes of this [sociological] investigation can be only judged in terms of its results" (*Social and Economic Organization,* 115 [13]) without saying what sorts of results it is supposed to achieve, except perhaps "clarity."
58. *Social and Economic Organization,* 91 (3).
59. Ibid.
60. *Der Zweck im Recht,* vol. 1, 12.
61. Ibid., 4.
62. Ibid., 5.
63. Ibid., 6.
64. *Social and Economic Organization,* 104 (7).
65. *Wirtschaft und Gesellschaft,* 8.
66. *Social and Economic Organization,* 104.
67. Ibid., 114 (11).
68. Ibid., (7).
69. Ibid., (12).
70. *Der Zweck im Recht,* vol. 1, 15.
71. Ibid., 21.
72. *Social and Economic Organization,* 90 (2).
73. Ibid., 114 (12).
74. Ibid., 111–12 (10–11).
75. Ibid., 112 (11).
76. See Tönnies's discussion of the drunkard (*Custom,* 32–33 [10–11]).
77. *Wirtschaft und Gesellschaft,* 12.
78. *Custom,* 36 (12).
79. Some of the subsequent history of these ideas of reason, in relation to "value" is discussed in Stephen Turner and Regis Factor, *Max Weber and the Dispute Over Reason and Value: A Study in Philosophy, Ethics, and Politics* (London, 1984). The sociological side of the reception history is discussed in Alan Sica, *Weber, Irrationality, and Social Order* (Berkeley, Calif., 1988).
80. *Social and Economic Organization,* 116 (12).
81. Ibid.
82. Ibid., 122 (15).

83. Ibid., 121 (15).
84. Ibid.
85. Ibid., 121–22 (15).
86. Ibid., 121 (15).
87. Ibid.
88. Ibid., 123 (16).
89. Ibid., 127 (17).
90. Ibid., 120 (14).
91. Ibid., 126–27 (17).
92. Ibid., 130 (19).
93. Ibid.
94. Ibid., 131 (19).
95. Ibid.
96. Like Tönnies, and in this respect like Nietzsche, this implies that "Conscious departures from tradition in the establishment of a new order" require special kinds of assertions of authority, either prophetic or assertions of return to supposedly earlier and more valid traditions (*Social and Economic Organization*, 131 [19]).
97. *Social and Economic Organization*, 132 (20).
98. Ibid., 123 (15).
99. Ibid.
100. Ibid., 130 (19).
101. Ibid., 116 (12).
102. Ibid., 117 (13).

Social Norms and Narrow Content

MEREDITH WILLIAMS

There are at least two forms of individualism about mental content: individualism as a principle of the individuation of the mental states and processes; and individualism as an ontological thesis. Individualism as a principle of individuation, or radical internalism, is typically characterized negatively: "An individual's being in any given intentional state (or being the subject of such an event) can be explicated by reference to states and events of the individual that are specifiable without using intentional vocabulary and without presupposing anything about the individual's social or physical environment."[1] The ontological thesis is a weaker form of individualism, according to which "an individual's intentional states and events (type and token) could not be different from what they are, given the individual's physical, chemical, neural, and functional histories."[2] This second form of individualism is a strictly individualistic thesis. For the argument of this essay, I want to keep these two forms of individualism distinct. Mental content is *internal* if it is in the head; and it is *individualistic* if social structures and institutions are irrelevant to, or unnecessary for, the specification and existence of the mental content. Internalism is the stronger position, for an internalist about mental content thereby holds an individualistic conception of content. However, the converse does not hold. One could be an individualist about content without being an internalist.[3] Tyler Burge, for one, has argued strenuously against an individualistic conception of mental states under either interpretation. In this essay, I shall support Burge's conclusions. The distinctive approach he uses, however, is limited in showing why internalism and individualism are mistaken. So, though I shall use the thought-experiment approach as a way into the problem of individuating mental content, the target is to show how individualism of either form goes wrong.

Burge's basic methodological tool is that of the thought-experiment. In each essay, he invites his reader to consider a real world case and a counterfactual world case in which the individual protagonists of each story can be described identically in terms of what goes on from the surface of the skin inwardly. Yet the content of their psychological lives differs and that difference, Burge maintains, can only be accounted for in terms of environmental differences, sometimes a difference in the physical environment and sometimes a difference in the social context.

Though Burge's conclusions have been met with criticism, I will argue that Burge is correct in his attacks on individualism. The mistake he makes is in assigning too much weight to our intuitive readings of his thought-experiments. His thought-experiments are readily susceptible to more than one reading; and so they invite the introduction of a more sophisticated version of individualism, one that rests on distinguishing narrow mental content from wide content. What is most important about Burge's work are the *theoretical* explanations he suggests (without full development) for *why* individualism fails. If Burge is right, what sets the standards for the correct use of concepts that figure in the individuation of beliefs or other intentional states are "archetypical applications" and "norms of understanding" which are operative within a social context. As I shall show in this essay, the ways in which theories of narrow mental content fail tie in with the social explanations of the formation and use of standards that Burge suggests. Mental content does involve the natural and social environments of the individual, as both are necessary to the ways in which standards and norms inform content.

In section 1, I characterize Burge's three most interesting thought-experiments, showing the distinctive contribution of each. The limitations of this approach are examined in section 2, where I develop the two arguments that figure most prominently in the idea that there must be individualistic narrow mental content. These arguments support two distinct theories of narrow content, one of which focuses on individualism as a principle of individuation (narrow content as conceptual role) and the other of which focuses on individualism as the ontological thesis of supervenience (narrow content as anchored). I argue in section 3 that both theories of narrow content fail, which calls for a new look at the way in which social practices in particular figure in the individuation and reality of intentional states (section 4).

1. INDIVIDUALISM AND THE THOUGHT-EXPERIMENT

The Thought-Experiments

Burge's cases split into two kinds: those that are held to show that the physical environment is involved in mental content (by way of reference) and those that are held to show that the social environment is involved (by way of social norms of understanding). Burge appeals to Putnam's original twin earth thought-experiment about water on earth and its counterpart on twin earth to show the role played by nature in fixing mental content.[4] Briefly, Oscar lives on earth where he drinks water, bathes in it, cooks with it and so on. Oscar$_2$, on the other hand, lives on twin earth where everything, including his own internal states, is exactly as it is on earth except for the liquid called 'water'. On twin earth, this liquid has a chemical composition XYZ that differs from that of our water, namely, H_2O. Though Oscar and $Oscar_2$ drink, bathe, and cook simultaneously in identical ways, they do so with different liquids. Burge endorses Putnam's conclusion that the contents of thoughts about water and $water_2$ cannot be the same because the referents differ in the two cases, and the referent of each concept is part of the content of that concept. Having thoughts about water requires being related to water (that very stuff) in the right sort of way. If Putnam and Burge are correct about this, then the contents of natural kind terms cannot be individuated by appeal solely to features internal to the individual. The subject's total ignorance of the true constitution of water is irrelevant to whether or not he is referring to water, thus revealing the slack between how the term 'water' applies to the world and what the subject knows or need know.

The second two thought-experiments concern the role of society, rather than nature, in fixing mental content. The first of these concerns the role that expertise plays in fixing the content of our specialized vocabularies.[5] Burge identifies it as a case of incomplete understanding. The subject Oscar on earth believes that he has arthritis in his thigh. This belief derives from a misunderstanding of what arthritis is. As the medical experts will tell Oscar, arthritis is an inflammation of the joints and so cannot occur in a muscle. What 'arthritis' picks out is determined by the medical experts of our society whereas what 'water' or 'tiger' pick out is determined by water and tigers. But this is not yet a case that supports radical anti-individualism. This is because it looks as though the experts stand in the same relation to arthritis as the layman does to water. The experts use 'arthritis' to pick out a particular type of disease. If arthritis were discovered to be caused by a particular virus or bacillus, then arthritis (if 'arthritis' is treated as a rigid designator by the experts) could be discovered to occur in muscles as well as joints provided the right kind of virus were discovered to be the cause of the thigh-pain. But Burge does not want to talk about the case in this way; he wants a case in which the role of experts is salient in fixing the content of a term, and I shall follow him in this emphasis as far as possible. To complete the thought experiment we must introduce $Oscar_2$ who lives on twin earth where the medical experts agree that $arthritis_2$ is an inflammation of both joint and muscle. Thus, though Oscar and $Oscar_2$ engage in the very same lines of thought and inference in their use of the expression 'arthritis', the contents of their thoughts are quite distinct: What Oscar believes is false whereas what $Oscar_2$ believes is true.

The last thought-experiment attempts to establish the more radical claim that a social element is constitutive of content itself. Accordingly, it does not involve dependence on experts. In this case, Burge hopes to show that a perfectly ordinary concept can be shown to implicate what he calls, the "norms of understanding" of the society.[6] The concept he chooses is that of sofa. In this case, Oscar entertains rather odd and certainly deviant beliefs about sofas. Sofas are, he believes, really religious artifacts, not pieces of furniture. Burge's contention is that Oscar can believe this of sofas only if indeed these objects are sofas. And whether they are sofas or not is not up to him but up to the community of which he is a part. He attempts to show that by contrasting Oscar with Oscar$_2$ who holds the very same beliefs (it would seem) about elongated chair-like objects existing on twin earth. The only difference between the world of Oscar and the world of Oscar$_2$ is that on twin earth these objects really are religious artifacts; only Oscar$_2$ does not know that everybody in his linguistic community knows this. He, like Oscar, believes that the members of his community think that the objects designated by 'sofa' are pieces of furniture. This single difference in social convention between earth and twin earth is enough to show, Burge holds, that the contents of 'sofa'-thoughts on earth and the contents of 'sofa$_2$'-thoughts on twin earth are distinct. After all, earth 'sofas' are indeed sofas whereas twin earth 'sofas$_2$' are sacred safos. One must not mistake a sacred relic for a trinket. Just so, one must not mistake a safo for a sofa.

This third case differs from the first two in a significant way. Oscar does not suffer from a failure of knowing what any competent speaker within the linguistic community knows; it is not that he is ignorant or has only a partial understanding of what sofas are.[7] It was this lack in Oscar in the first two cases that led Burge to conclude that nature and society took up the slack. But in this third case, Oscar has full understanding of what anyone in his community would take to be true of sofas; he just thinks that they are all wrong. He has formed an alternative and deviant hypothesis about sofas. The concept of sofa has a different "cognitive value" for Oscar than it has for the rest of his community. This slack between the way 'sofa' applies to the world (by way of conventional meaning) and what Oscar believes to be true about sofas is not due to his "beliefs" falling short of the world, but due to his forming a different conception of these objects. Burge's point here, though he does not put it this way, must be that the idiosyncratic cognitive value sofas have for Oscar presupposes the smooth functioning of our ordinary linguistic practices in the use of 'sofa'.

These thought-experiments certainly seem to be powerful devices for disclosing elements external to and independent of the subject in the identification of the contents of the subject's intentional states. But even if it is true that the individuation of particular mental states requires adverting to environmental factors, does this show that contentful mental states are not in the subject's head? Critics read these cases as showing that we must distinguish between narrow mental content and wide content, thus replacing a crude Cartesianism, which draws upon such rough and ready distinctions as that between my beliefs about water and the stuff that is really out there, my (limited) understanding of diseases and the experts' (full) understanding, my perspective and valuation of commonplace objects and the community perspective, for a more sophisticated version. Let us examine this more sophisticated view.

Narrow Content vs. Wide Content

Just what is the distinction between the narrow and wide content of mental states? As one advocate of individualism has put it, narrow content is what is left over after we "chop off" the referring and socially bounded arms that reach out to the world.[8] Narrow content is what is left over when all objects, persons, and institutions external to the individual are taken away. What we want to know in this essay is, what is this left-over part? Two strategies are available to those defending a place for narrow content: narrow content is to be identified with functional role within a complex internal causal system (conceptual role semantics); or narrow content is to be identified with the internal effect of certain environmental causes (causal theory of representation). I shall show that both strategies fail.[9] For both, narrow content becomes attenuated to the point of spontaneous elimination, the former through uncontrollable expansion and the latter through a shrinking to the point of invisibility. But before witnessing the demise of narrow content, we need to consider more carefully the case for the distinction.

Putnam's original twin earth case brings out some of the complexity.[10] The meanings of the expressions that enter into the specification of intentional states are irreducibly multifaceted. Factors external to the individual enter into the determination of the content itself. For natural kind terms like 'water', the determinant of its extension is the similarity of stuff in the world to *this* very stuff called 'water' right here. Nothing in the individual's head can play the normative role that this stuff in the world plays in fixing the extension of the term. This multifaceted view of content threatens the integrity of the Cartesian subject. The traditional Cartesian subject is autonomous (the contents of intentional states are in the head) and self-aware (the contents of her intentional states are latently if not actually available to the subject). If part of the content of the subject's mind is external to the subject and is such that the subject could be wholly ignorant of its nature, then the Cartesian subject has been lost, and with it the claim of internalism.

The twin earth argument thus creates a serious problem for the crude Cartesian picture, but at the same time it appears to provide the resources for solving the problem. The solution lies, of course, in distinguishing narrow content from wide content. Wide content is the full multifaceted content, which includes both internal and external determinants of meaning. Narrow content is what is left over after severing the subject's connection to the external determinants of meaning. That portion of content, it is maintained, is in the head of the subject and known by the subject. Following Putnam, we can say that the stereotype (itself a norm in that it sets criteria for correct use) — the assemblage of properties commonly used to pick out paradigm examples — and the indexical component of meaning are in the head, but the sample picked out by the indexical and which sets *the* standard for membership in the extension of the term clearly is not in the individual's head. This certainly seems a neat solution.

What could Burge object to here? How can Burge use the very same thought-experiment and yet draw such a different, and incompatible, conclusion? According to Burge,

> Putnam interprets the difference between Earth and Twin-Earth uses of 'water' purely as a difference in extension. And he states that the relevant Earthian and Twin-Earthian are 'exact duplicates in. . .feelings, thoughts,

interior monologue etc.'. On our version of the argument the two are in no sense exact duplicates in their thoughts. This shows up in oblique occurrences in true attributions of propositional attitudes.[11]

It is crucial for Burge's attack on internalism that the semantic role played by the environmental contributors to mental content not be lost when their referring terms occur in oblique contexts. In other words, Burge needs to block the move that some find natural from the occurrence of a term in an oblique context to the term's being literally in the head.[12] Far from this being an entailment of the claim that a term occurs obliquely, it can only be an explanation for its occurrence in the oblique context. The argument must go something like this: Consider the propositional attitude sentence, 'Oscar believes that water is refreshing'. The content of the that-clause identifies the particular belief that Oscar has. In so identifying this particular belief, each term embedded in the oblique context must occur opaquely, that is, co-referring expressions are not permissible substitutions. None of this carries with it the idea that the content-sentence of the belief-sentence must be in the head of the individual. That move comes with an explanation of the opacity of the terms. The reason, it might be held, that one cannot substitute co-referring expressions for obliquely occurring expressions is that opacity results from these expressions being the very ones that the individual uses, in her head as it were, in forming her particular belief. But this strong psychological explanation for opacity is not required; all that is required is that belief-content is sensitive to how something is described. And Burge holds that the description by which the content of a belief is expressed retains its semantic relations to the world. The oblique context does not sever semantic relations to the world. So whatever the argument is for narrow content, it cannot be that what occurs in oblique contexts must be "in the head" contents. Opacity is not internality.

But does opacity rule out internality? Of course not. After all, Putnam, like Burge, maintains that opaque terms do not lose their semantic relations to the world just in virtue of being opaque. Indeed the point of the thought experiment, for Putnam, is the opposite. So what is the difference in the way that Burge and Putnam interpret this twin earth thought-experiment?

The difference comes, according to Burge, in the way that they each explain the semantic bond itself between the referring term and its referent.[13] Putnam holds that the referring link itself is created and sustained because natural kind concepts like 'water' have an indexical component, and it is this indexical component that relates thought to the world. So Oscar and his twin, in virtue of being indexically related to different liquids, have beliefs with different extensions even though, in virtue of a shared stereotype, they have beliefs with the same intension. In this way the indexicality of natural kind terms explains both the difference and sameness of the twins' respective beliefs about water and water$_2$.

Burge objects to this way of explaining the semantic relation that obtains between 'water' and its extension. If extensions are fixed in virtue of natural kind terms having an indexical component, this would make their extensions subject to contextual constraints, depending upon where the individual happens to be. But this cannot be correct. The correct explanation, according to Burge, is that natural kind terms are rigid designators. They are originally fixed by the use of genuinely indexical expressions, but they are not indexicals themselves nor do they have an indexical component. If we accept this, then we can see that the opaque occurrence of the term 'water' in specifying the content of Oscar's (or his twin's) belief does not abnegate Oscar's semantic relation to the originating sample of H_2O. as Burge puts it, 'water' is a context-free term.[14] I agree with this but with one very important qualification: 'Water' is context-free *so far as any individual is concerned.* This is quite unlike genuine indexicals which are always used contextually and individualistically. That 'water' is a rigid designator means that the actual liquid out there in the world is implicated (1) in the opaque occurrence of 'water' in oblique belief-contexts, but (2) independently of the particular location of the individual. It is important for Burge's account that the individual need not be nor have been in any physical proximity to the liquid H_2O in order to have beliefs about water. Being a rigid designator (rather than an indexical term) allows for the environment playing an indispensable semantic role and for Oscar and his twin being identical "molecule-for-molecule."[15] This is just what Burge needs. There is a gap clearly between the individual, and everything that goes on in the individual, and the extension of the term; and yet the term guarantees that there is a semantic relation between the individual and the extension of the term. The semantic properties of the term accrue to the term independently of anything the individual does or fails to do.

What is crucial for Burge's interpretation of the thought-experiment is that natural kind terms are treated as rigid designators. If the meanings of natural kind terms were fixed by stereotypes, then, it might be held, meanings could be in the head. If they were fixed, in part, by an indexical component, then content could be narrow and wide. If meanings were fixed by what the individual happened to know or where the individual happened to be, then meaning would be context-bound. But Burge argues for a "context-free interpretation" of natural kind terms. For a term to be a rigid designator is for it to be context-free. This is where Burge goes wrong. As I shall argue later, rigid designators are not context-free in an absolute sense; rather they are *individual-context-free.* There is an indispensable role played by the community in fixing and sustaining the extension of rigid designators that cannot be performed by the individual alone. What is correct in Burge's explanation is that any given individual need not herself have or have had contact with the liquid H_2O. The individual is detachable from that part of the environment that contributes to determining meaning, but the content of her thought is not.

There is also a second and distinct sense in which natural kind terms are context free. It is possible for everyone on earth to have attitudes towards water without any of them knowing what water is, without, that is, realizing what its true microstructure is. Though the stereotype must be known to the subject, the real essence of water need not be known to the subject (or anyone else). Still what 'water' picks out in virtue of its referring relation must be water and nothing else. It is the great weight given to the referring relation that secures 'water' to water and not another thing, no matter what anyone knows or believes to be the case. Once the referring relation is in place, it is unbreakable. So the argument goes. This, of course, is a purely metaphysical point. So long as we hold this view of reference, then referring expressions are necessarily tied to the objects they pick out. But this is an overly inflated view of what reference can do. Our beliefs about water can be (and have been, before around 1700) *theory-context-free*. That is, we need not have any theoretical beliefs, or any accurate theoretical beliefs, about the microstructure of water in order to refer to it successfully. So the moral of the thought-experiment holds: Any time a referring expression forms part of the content of a mental state as expressed by the embedded that-clause of attitude statements, the individual subject is semantically tied to the referent no matter what the subject, *or anyone else,* may or may not know about the true constitution of the referent provided we, that is, our linguistic community, use the referring expression rigidly. Then rigid designators occurring in oblique contexts preserve the semantic relation to their referents.

Does the same explanation work for Burge's other two cases, the 'arthritis' case and the 'sofa' case? Structurally, the 'arthritis' case seems to mirror the 'water' case. Just as the full or wide meaning of 'water' depended upon the existence of an actual liquid in the world, so the full meaning of 'arthritis' depends upon the judgment of a group of experts. Just as the baptismal sample of water determines the extension of 'water', so the judgment of experts determines the extension of 'arthritis'. There is an important difference, however, between the two cases: For each, some initial referring act determines extension, but with 'water', a sample of the extension itself fixes membership in the kind (whatever is like *this* stuff) whereas with 'arthritis', the judgment of the experts fixes the stereotype for the rest of society. It must be this way; otherwise, we could simply forego appeal to the experts and treat 'arthritis' in exactly the same way as we treat 'water'. But Burge wants to show that in this case there is a social dimension to meaning that cannot be treated equivalently to the simple referring relation.

With terms of art or expertise, like 'arthritis', someone must know the stereotype, for the expression is tied to the stereotype as authorized by experts. This is quite unlike the 'water' case where no one's specialized knowledge or expertise is required for successful use of the term. This is part of the value of rigid designators. Thus, insofar as Burge's argument against internalism turns on the rigidity of referring expressions, it has limited scope. Our question becomes: Does this kind of rigidity belong to 'arthritis' as well? It would seem not. Though the subject in his use of 'arthritis' is thereby constrained by the experts, it certainly is not because 'arthritis' refers to the experts. Rather it is because a certain authority is accorded the experts. Unlike 'water', were the experts to revise their judgment, the meaning of 'arthritis' would thereby be altered. This cannot happen with 'water' unless we are changing concepts altogether, and merely using homophonic expressions for the two concepts. Oscar's belief that he has arthritis in his thigh involves an oblique occurrence of 'arthritis'. What is the character of the semantic relation of 'arthritis' to the group of experts? One might think that they are accorded authority because they know what 'arthritis' refers to. But then what would matter is the referring relation, and the authorities would only come into it in a secondary way, not a primary way. The thought experiment sheds no light on this, but merely draws attention to the fact that the only difference between earth and twin earth is a social difference, and so the explanation of meaning of 'arthritis' must implicate this social difference. But how?

What is needed here is not a Kripkean account but something more akin to a Gricean account. Oscar supports his use of 'arthritis' by certain second-order intentions, the most important of which are his intention to use the term in accord with the judgment of the experts and his willingness to allow his use to be overruled by their judgment. These "deference" intentions concern the status of his use of the term itself, and are indispensable to Oscar's using the expression at all.[16] This just is what the linguistic division of labor is about. Any attempt to eliminate the role of the expert in Oscar's use of 'arthritis' by eliminating these second-order epistemic beliefs renders his use of 'arthritis' so highly idiosyncratic that any similarity to our concept of arthritis is accidental. If Oscar protests that he does mean the same by 'arthritis' as we do, then *perforce* he acknowledges as his own the second-order epistemic intentions that link his use of 'arthritis' to the experts.

In these two cases, it is a contingent fact that Oscar lives in the world that he does, but once living in the world he does, the contents of his mental life are fixed in part by items in that world whether or not he knows what they are and whether or not he comes into contact with those items. In both cases the key term has an essential semantic link to an item in Oscar's environment. The item is essential because of the *normative role* it plays. The item actually sets the standard for correct application of the term in question. For 'water', that link is guaranteed by the term's being a rigid designator. For 'arthritis', that link is guaranteed by the term's being a medical term of art. But what of Burge's third case, the one concerning a completely ordinary concept, namely, that of a sofa?

Here there is no hidden but natural essence, nor is expertise required. Here a gap is created between the individual and the world he lives in by attributing a deviant belief to our Oscar. He believes that sofas are not pieces of furniture, but religious artifacts irreverently misused. It is important to Oscar's belief that he is talking about *sofas* and that he believes sofas are religious artifacts. What counts as a sofa is what any competent speaker of the language would pick out as a sofa. As a competent speaker himself, Oscar can pick out sofas as well as any one else in the community. In order to create the dissonance required by those thought experiments, the concept of sofa is held to have a different "cognitive value" for Oscar, where cognitive value is explicitly individualistic. The cognitive value of the concept of sofa is set over and against, though presumably dependent upon, the conventional meaning of 'sofa' which is fixed by community practice.

Unless we have an account of the dependence of cognitive value upon conventional meaning, the distinction invites the response that content can be both wide and narrow. Cognitive value is narrow content, it might be argued.

Since 'sofa' is not a rigid designator nor a term of art, just why does the oblique occurrence of 'sofa' carry with it a semantic tie to those pieces of furniture? Burge's claim must be that, whatever this tie is, the thought-experiment shows that it must exist, for our intuitions are that there is a difference in the contents of Oscar's thoughts and Oscar$_2$'s thoughts, and the only difference between the worlds are social differences. So the thought-experiment, as Burge wants to use it, must carry the full weight of the argument for anti-internalism in a way that it does not for 'water' or even 'arthritis'. But it simply cannot carry that philosophical weight. We need an explanation of why cognitive value is dependent upon conventional meaning.

2. DEFENSE OF INTERNALISM

So, do we have to look at the thought-experiments from Burge's recommended perspective? If we cease to take that God's eye point of view and look at the matter from the perspectives of our individual subjects, then it seems equally intuitive to say that there is something the same in what the twins believe about water, arthritis, and sofas.[17] Call that "cognitive value" or "narrow content," but the intuition is the same: It is what the individual thinks is going on, or how she conceives it, that matters both in individuating the contents of her beliefs and in explaining her behavior.

Advocates of internalism have looked for some way of making the classical semantic relations between terms and the world irrelevant to specifying narrow content, without, however, eliminating *all* normative properties of narrow content, and thus forfeiting the claim that narrow content is indeed content. The point of attack has not been, as one might have expected, Burge's argument that the semantic ties of terms occurring in oblique contexts are not broken within such contexts. Rather critics grant that Burge's thought-experiments do show that the natural and social environments are part of the oblique content that individuates particular beliefs, but object to his identifying this content with mental or psychological content.[18]

That-clause Content vs. Psychological Content

Individuating beliefs by appeal to the embedded that-clause is not as straightforward as Burge makes it seem. Looking at the thought-experiment from a different perspective or looking at more complicated cases can leave one certain that there must be something like narrow content. For example, if Oscar and his arthritic$_2$ twin could be instantaneously switched at the moment of their entering the doctors' waiting rooms, each would pursue his alternate's path, although the descriptions used to characterize their beliefs and desires would become extremely baroque if we were strict in maintaining Burgean principles of individuation. In fact, we would begin to lose a grip on just what Oscar really does believe. After all, Oscar's belief that he has an arthritic thigh pain is confirmed by the doctor$_2$; at the dinner table, he and his family$_2$ discuss his arthritic thigh pain; his friends$_2$ commiserate. We know that the doctor$_2$ was wrong in thinking that Oscar has an arthritic thigh-pain, though he was quite correct in diagnosing an arthritic$_2$ thigh pain. What does Oscar believe? After much discussion with family$_2$ and friends$_2$ on the nature of his complaint, does Oscar continue to believe that he has arthritis or does he come to form new beliefs (undetectable by himself) that he suffers from arthritis$_2$? When he remembers the first time he felt his arthritic pain, what is he remembering? The "false" memory that he had an arthritic pain; or the true "memory" that he had an arthritic$_2$ pain? Could both be involved? Just such confusion about how to individuate and count beliefs is exploited by critics of Burge, who want to make room for a notion of narrow content.

When confusion arises over how to individuate beliefs by appealing to the external component of their content (H_2O or XYZ; our doctors or their doctors), it is tempting to look for a different criterion for counting. The candidate cannot be the *de facto* semantic links to environmental items, for that is precisely what has been brought into question by switching Oscar and Oscar$_2$. Historic community and contemporary community push in opposite directions and so render Oscar's beliefs confused and obscure to us, although Oscar himself suffers no disability from his confusion. But perhaps that shows that the criteria that matter in individuating Oscar's beliefs are not the semantic links to the world, but something else. The most plausible candidate is the cognitive role the belief state plays in the utterances and behavior of our Oscar. Individuation by cognitive role and individuation by referent need not be the same. And so it looks as though we need to distinguish what Brian Loar calls the "social content" or "that-clause" content from the "psychological content" of a belief state.[19]

The case Loar uses is that of puzzling Pierre.[20] Pierre, while still in France, is told "Londres est jolie" and believes what he is told. Later he moves to London, not realizing that London is his "jolie Londres," and settles in Kensington. He comes to believe that London is a beautiful city. Let us agree that 'London' and "Londres' are both rigid designators, picking out the same city. This is Burge's strongest case for explaining the semantic tie between term and world. Does Pierre have one belief or two? On Burgean principles of individuation, Pierre has one belief, and the place occupied by 'Londres' and 'London' in his network of beliefs and other attitudes is quite irrelevant. And yet Pierre has a strong desire to visit Londres which is only checked by his pleasure of living in London. When away from his home in London, he experiences a deep melancholy whenever he thinks of London; to distract himself, he sometimes tries thinking about Londres instead. In such a situation, the only reasonably response is that Pierre has distinct beliefs about London and Londres. And in accepting this reading, we must conclude that social content and psychological content are distinct. This way of making space for psychological, or narrow, content is compatible with Burge's claim that 'London' and 'Londres' each occur obliquely in the beliefs we ascribe to Pierre as well as being the very terms Pierre uses himself when expressing his beliefs. Pierre picks out the city London in both cases, and so everything he believes about Londres is believed to be about the city itself, just as all his beliefs about water are beliefs about H_2O, even though he is ignorant of the chemical composition of water.

So the defender of internalism is ready with a reply to Burge. Burge goes wrong, according to his critics, in identifying that-clause content with psychological content. This may be due to a failure to distinguish between the first-person perspective and the third-person perspective;[21] or it may be dramatically shown in various thought-experiments in which the complexity of the subject's beliefs outstrip the relative simplicity of the that-clause description.[22] The gap that emerges, it could be argued, is not between "the relevant environmental facts and relations to the environment, on the one hand, and what the individual knows and can discriminate, on the other," as Burge says,[23] but a gap between the simplicity of ordinary belief ascriptions and the complexity of properly refined descriptions of the subject's mental state. The crudity, as it were, of ordinary attributions must be replaced by the refinement of in-depth attributions. This allows the defender of narrow content to grant Burge his point that social content retains semantic connections to the world. But these semantic ties are not essential to the identity of the underlying psychologically real mental content. Thus, whether or not it is correct to hold that when 'water' occurs in oblique context, it retains its semantic tie to water itself, we can readily "chop off" the individual's relation to the real stuff without affecting how he thinks about that stuff. Indeed, it could be argued, this was part of the thought-experiment. The defender of narrow content is merely exploiting the subject's ignorance. With respect to the 'sofa' case also, the defender of internalism can exploit features of the thought-experiment itself, namely, the introduction of cognitive value. Individual cognitive values may or may not conform to the conventional meanings of the community, but it is the former that are required to individuate the deviant beliefs of our subject. So the defender of individualism seems able to "chop off" the referent at one end of the continuum of cases (the 'water' case) and endorse the individualistic component at the other end (the 'sofa' case).

What about Burge's case of 'arthritis'? The defender of internalism cannot straightforwardly "cut off" the expert, for the focus is on the special role that the expert plays *for* the subject. Nor can the defender endorse the cognitive value in a straightforward way because the subject places authority for his beliefs outside himself. This is what is important about linguistic division of labor. In his own use of 'arthritis', the subject tacitly appeals to the authority of the expert. So here it might be said that because the subject is "borrowing" a concept, as it were, the oblique occurrence of the expression 'arthritis' is semantically tied to the group of experts. But here, too, this argument for the oblique occurrence of 'arthritis' opens the way for the defender's simply "chopping off" the experts as he "chopped off" the referent. There still seems to be left over what is known or is available to the subject even if it is not much. In this way the "chopping off" of the semantic links to the external world disparages, in a way, the importance of the referring and deferring relations of terms to items or persons in the world.

What is emphasized is the place of expressions within the subject's individual ecology of beliefs, desires, and behaviors. Assessing cognitive value locates the role played by the expression within this complex structure. Defenders of individualism who take this tack support a conceptual role semantics, and hold that conceptual role can be specified internalistically and individualistically. The weakness of the thought-experiment, thus, is that it only shows that (some) concepts *are* public and social, not that they must be.

What advocates of narrow content want to preserve is, as I would like to put it, the normativity of mental content. The classical semantic properties of reference and truth conditions require the relation of terms to the world, but the normativity of mental life, that concepts are rule-governed, can be individualistic and internalist. They are guided by logical principles, epistemic principles, rationality constraints, and other normative principles. Because they are normatively characterized, we can misrepresent items, draw fallacious conclusions, ignore relevant evidence, defy rationality. The important question is whether the individual is able to provide what is necessary to make these kinds of mistakes as well as being guided in the proper fashion. If narrow content fails to display these normative features, whatever happens to be picked out can hardly be described as "content." So sophisticated advocates of narrow content find themselves defending the following three claims:

(1) That-clause content has semantic ties to the natural and/or social world (the semantic condition).
(2) Psychological content is literally in the head of the individual (the internal reality condition).
(3) For anything to count as "content," it must be subject to standards for correctness (the normativity condition).

The first two conditions are apparently reconciled by distinguishing between *that-clause content,* namely, the proposition that is specified by the that-clause, and *psychological content,* namely, the inferential place of the item within the network of beliefs and desires of the subject. Psychological content differs from that-clause content in that relational semantic ties to the actual world are irrelevant to its identity. However, in order to count as content, psychological content must have some normative property, such that correct usage can be distinguished from incorrect usage. Moreover, though it is arguable that social content and psychological content are distinct, still there must be some interesting and nonaccidental relation between them. So this first reply to Burge's arguments leaves us with two new problems that need answering: First, if narrow content is this psychological content, how does psychological content set its own internal standards for correct vs incorrect usage? Second, how is this psychological content related to social content?

But why should we believe that these are distinct? Clearly there is a tension between two criteria for identifying content, namely, the appeal to the referent and the appeal to a system of beliefs within which the content is embedded. But does this show that we have two kinds of content? Why doesn't it show only that under abnormal circumstances, the two criteria do not dovetail as they normally do? This, it is arguable, is a mark of the strangeness of the circumstances, but not a sign of the existence of two kinds of content. What is needed for defending the stronger ontological thesis is the rationale for mental content. This, it seems to me, is provided by the argument from causation. This argument can be seen as a defense of a fourth condition on psychological content:

(4) States with psychological content have causal properties (the causal condition).

Narrow content is required if there is to be *mental* causation. But, *prima facie,* this conflicts with condition (3) that psychological content must be normative if it is to count as content at all. So the fundamental rationale for the internal reality of mental states makes their being contentful suspect, as both semantic and normative properties seem to be incompatible with mental states' being causes.

The Argument from Causation

The argument from causation is simple and direct, and for that reason quite powerful. It can be characterized as consisting of two stages, each reflecting a prior metaphysical commitment. First, a commitment to psychological realism, that is, to the idea that mental states, like belief and the other propositional attitudes, are discrete and causally efficacious; and second, a commitment to physicalism, which is the thesis that everything is explicable ultimately in terms of physical matter.[24] The first stage of the argument goes like this. There is no action at a distance, and so the mental causal states of behavior must *perforce* be local. If mental states have causal powers, then they must be states internal to the individual. And if these causal states are mental, then they must have content. If they cause in virtue of the content they have, then that content must likewise be internal to the individual. It clearly follows from this that if content is not internal to the individual, then mental states do not have the causal powers they do (if any) in virtue of their content. So it seems we must choose between the following: Either content is not in the head, in which case we must reject the idea that mental states are causally efficacious; or the causal efficacy of mental states is obviously correct, in which case content must be in the head.

The second stage is a defense of supervenience. At the very least, a commitment to physicalism requires that intentional states supervene upon physical states. As J. A. Fodor sums it up, "if mind/brain supervenience goes, the intelligibility of mental causation goes with it."[25] Thus, for Fodor and other advocates of psychological realism, Burge's arguments purporting to show that mental content involves social norms must be wrong. Fodor's central argument against Burge's anti-individualism is a "diagnosis" of how Burge goes wrong.

Burge's error, according to Fodor, is to conflate methodological individualism and methodological solipsism.[26] Methodological individualism, Fodor maintains, is a fully general methodological constraint on any science. That constraint is that any scientific taxonomy must be a taxonomy by causal powers. It is the causal power of objects that is relevant to scientific inquiry, including psychology. Just insofar as the referents and social norms that help individuate oblique content do not affect the causal power of the mental state itself, they are irrelevant to the formation of laws of psychological causation. But this, Fodor insists, is not tantamount to eliminating all relational properties from the individuation of appropriate taxonomic groups, for some relational properties can be relevant to the causal powers of members of the taxonomic group. Burge confuses this methodological principle, according to Fodor, with a substantive empirical thesis, viz., methodological solipsism. Methodological solipsism is the empirical hypothesis that mental states "are computational, hence syntactic."[27] Burge, thus, is alleged to take a methodological constraint on taxonomy formation for a substantive empirical hypothesis about psychological entities, namely, that they are (non-relationally individuated) formal entities. The difference between the two is as follows: If semantic (or other relational) properties can be shown to effect or bear upon the causal powers of the mental state, then they would be respectable candidates for constructing a scientific taxonomy. Methodological individualism allows for relational individuation. Methodological solipsism, on the other hand, explicitly rejects the relevance of any relational property to the individuation of psychological states. So the fact that relational properties may be useful or even required to construct a scientific taxonomy does not support the conclusion that an internalist and individualistic psychology is mistaken. And arguments against the empirical hypothesis that mental states are formal entities does not thereby entail that internalism or individualism has been discredited.

Is this what Burge has done? Has he (mis)construed arguments against methodological solipsism as arguments against methodological individualism? What are the relational properties that Burge argues individuate mental content? As we have seen, they are of two types, the referents of natural kind terms ('water') and social conventions as fixed by the community as a whole ('sofa') or by an expert subcommunity ('arthritis'). Fodor's position can accommodate these, for he himself develops a causal theory of meaning which calls for items in the environment to trigger appropriate mental representations, so that these representations can get on with their causal work in the production of other mental states and behavior. What Fodor finds unacceptable is Burge's idea that items of the environment figure in the individuation of mental states *whether or not* the individual has causally interacted with these items. This is the real source of disagreement, and it has nothing to do with conflating methodological solipsism and methodological individualism.[28]

Indeed, the confusion Fodor attributes to Burge is the same confusion Burge attributes, by another name, to critics making use of the argument from causation, the very argument Fodor constructs. Burge is attacking methodological individualism on the ground that it "conflat[es] causation with individuation."[29] How we individuate the content of our mental states need not be restricted to what has causal impact on our bodies. This presumably is the lesson of the thought-experiments. This lesson is supplemented with examples from other sciences in which individuation and attribution of causal powers diverge.

Continent shift is explained by appeal to peripheral impacts and chemically constituted events and objects, while we individuate continents themselves in part by their relations to other land masses. Similarly, intentional states and processes are identified by their propositional content, a content which adverts to social conventions and natural kinds. So there is a profound disagreement about the nature of mental content that can only be resolved by looking at the theories of content developed by each. It certainly cannot be resolved in favor of Fodor's position by the "diagnosis" offered, as that diagnosis misfires.[30]

Fodor's second objection to Burge's anti-individualism is that insofar as Burge's view is correct, it is not very interesting.[31] The thought-experiments only draw our attention to "a difference between the way psychology individuates behaviors and mental states and the way common sense does," and this kind of cross-cutting of taxonomies, Fodor reminds us, is a commonplace in science. So "mind/brain supervenience" need not extend to all ways of individuating mental content, only to the causally efficacious elements. But there is a hidden danger here for Fodor. More is at work than merely citing a truism of scientific practice. If the cross-cutting of taxonomies goes too far, few mental states will survive the cuts, leaving little for psychology to theorize about. As Fodor acknowledges, what might turn this banal observation about scientific taxonomies into an ominous-looking cloud hanging over intentionalist psychology is that psychology might cross-cut commonsense notions of mental content in a way that eliminates a place for intentionalist psychology.[32] The underside to the charge of banality against Burge is the charge of impoverishment of domain against Fodor. This strategy for undermining Burge's attack on individualism can be seen to cloak very serious concessions concerning what survives the cut, hence what counts as psychologically real.

3. TWO THEORIES OF NARROW MENTAL CONTENT

In sum, the two objections to Burge's anti-internalist conclusions were: first, social content and psychological content need not be identical, and so the semantic ties to the environment that characterize that-clause content need not belong to psychological content. Second, mental causation requires internal mental content. Separating that-clause content and psychological content results in an uneasy relation between the semantic condition and the internal reality condition by eliminating the relevance of that-clause content to psychological explanation. But this carries in its wake the problems of characterizing the relation between these two contents and of offering an account of *internal* normative standards. The argument from causation generates a conflict between the normativity condition and the causal condition. How can causal principles provide the normative standards by which to judge a causal occurrence as correct or incorrect? Both conflicts make providing an account of internal individualist norms crucial. Focusing on one or another of these conflicts has given rise to two prominent theories of narrow content: Giving preeminence to the first conflict, that between the semantic condition and the internal reality condition, gives us conceptual role semantics;[33] and giving preeminence to the second conflict between the normativity condition and the causal condition gives us causal theories of mental representation.[34]

"Anchored" Content: The Problem of Misrepresentation

Fodor's response to the arguments based on the original twin earth case (the 'water' case) is to grant that this case does show that intension by itself cannot determine extension while denying that this shows that the connection between intension and extension has been broken. On the contrary, Fodor argues that the twin earth thought-experiment does not show that there are two factors of meaning but that content determines extension *only relative to a context.* Narrow content must be "anchored." Meaning is univocal, it is the denotation of the representation. Thus, to "chop off" the referent is to eliminate content. There is no such thing as substantive narrow content to which extension can be added, thereby giving us full wide content. Narrow content can only be captured indirectly as "a function from contexts and thoughts onto truth conditions."[35] It is itself inexpressible.

So Fodor rejects the idea that that-clause content and psychological content differ. The cost of honoring the semantic condition, however, is the *nominal* satisfaction only of the internal reality condition. Fodor calls the internal function "narrow content." It is the advocate of a conceptual role semantics who wants a substantial notion of internal content and who, thus, insists upon the importance of this contrast. For Fodor, such a contrast is the beginning of the end for an intentionalist psychology (and he may well be correct once we acknowledge what is involved in specifying the full functional role of a belief). What remains for him is the conflict between the causal condition and the normativity condition. This, he attempts to resolve by arguing that normativity can be captured in purely causal terms.

To reconstruct his argument, we need to understand the two determinants of narrow content, viz., what it is to be "anchored" in a context and what thought it. Thoughts presumably can only be the sentence-like entities that are individuated syntactically. The context is the world of H_2O and other such physical stuffs. Mental content is the function that maps syntactic structures (thoughts) and local physical contexts onto truth conditions.[36] But how do we know which mapping is the correct one, i.e., is the one which maps syntactic structures onto the correct set of truth conditions? Fodor attempts to find the solution in certain causal relations between mental representations and the local environment of the subject: "a symbol expresses a property if it's nomologically necessary that all and only instances of the property cause tokenings of the symbol" (p. 100). In brief, 'horse' means horse in virtue of the fact that horses and only horses always cause tokenings of 'horse' in mentalese.

Clearly, this will not do as it stands: first, because not all horses have caused tokenings of 'horse' in anyone's mind; and second, because sometimes other creatures, such as cows, can cause tokenings of 'horse'. However, when something other than a horse causes a tokening of 'horse', this tokening is a mistake. But how can a causal theory of meaning account for error and misrepresentation? This is the problem of normativity. Fodor calls it the 'disjunction' problem in order to highlight the fact that tokens of an effect can result from more than one kind of cause. So if cows can on occasion cause the tokening of 'horse', why, on the causal theory of meaning, doesn't 'horse' mean horse or cow? Fodor interprets this as a challenge to provide a criterion for distinguishing the *relevant cause* of tokenings of 'horse' from irrelevant causes.[37] This distinction, however, must be drawn in wholly naturalistic terms. To use semantic or intentional terms would be begging the question, as Fodor is seeking to ground such properties in causal relations. So, it cannot be that cow-causes are ruled out because only horses are relevant to the meaning of 'horse'. The causal relations that obtain between tokenings of 'horse' and objects in the world must show that only horse-causes are relevant to the tokening of 'horse'.

Fodor quickly rejects one possible solution that has its origin in Dennis Stampe's important essay defending the causal theory of representation. The solution involves what I call a "natural teleological" account of normativity. This solution focuses on the background circumstances within which the object causes its representation. It involves the notion of a system's functioning as it is supposed to do so, where "well-functioning" and "function" are identified in terms of natural selection. The fallacy embodied in this approach to the problem, according to Fodor, is that this naturalism is only skin-deep. Smuggled into the notion of "well-functioning" or "fidelity conditions" or "optimal circumstances" is a normative standard; yet the point of going to a causal theory of representation was to ground the normative in the non-intentional and non-normative, namely, in the physical. Appeal to fidelity conditions assumes that there must be a fit between truth and well-functioning. Break that connection between truth and optimality, and the allure of the appeal to optimal conditions vanishes. "For the sake of" arguments, even of this biological sort, cannot explain mental representation without tacitly bringing in semantic notions. Fodor wants a strictly non-intentionalist criterion for distinguishing "relevant cause." He seeks to ground normativity in straight causal talk.

Fodor hopes to distinguish the relevantly (i.e., correctly) caused tokenings of 'horse' by providing a criterion for identifying mistaken, or wild, tokenings of the symbol. His claim is that wild tokenings of 'horse' presuppose veridical tokenings of 'horse' whereas veridical tokenings do not depend upon the wild tokenings (if any). This asymmetrical dependence can be expressed, without appeal to "wildness" and veridicality, in terms of the counterfactual properties of the symbol: "If B-caused 'A' tokenings are wild – if they falsely represent B's as A's – then there would be a causal route from A's to 'A' even if there were no causal route from B's to 'A's; but there would be no causal route from B's to 'A's if there were no causal route from A's to 'A's."[38] In other words, in nearby possible worlds where there are horses but no cows, there will be tokenings of 'horse'. But in other nearby possible worlds where there are cows but no horses, there will be no tokenings of 'horse'. In worlds, such as our own, where there are both cows and horses, there will be tokenings of 'horse' as effects of both horses and cows. Thus, an asymmetry is revealed in the counterfactual properties of symbols that is strong enough to support the normative distinction between correct representation and misrepresentation.

Whether these counterfactual properties are sufficient to make this distinction is the first question to ask. In the nearby world where there are no horses but there are cows, if 'horse' in our world is tokened by cows under certain conditions, namely, those abnormal conditions in which cows look like horses, then why wouldn't 'horse' be tokened on that cow-world provided the cow is in the right circumstances? After all, there are tokenings of 'horse' in the presence of cows in certain circumstances. As this is a purely causal connection, why wouldn't it obtain on cow-world? Fodor might say that in order to mistake a cow for a horse, one must have the concept of both cows and horses. No one would disagree with this; it is a truism that in order to take something for an *F*, one must have the concept of an *F*. What we want to know is why the cows on cow-world do not cause tokenings of 'horse' when the cows are in the right circumstances, namely, *those abnormal ones* in which cows look like horses? To take care of this, Fodor has only two options: (1) He can simply *stipulate* that these counterfactuals obtain in near-by possible worlds. Such stipulation in no way connects with the causal explanation that Fodor gives. There is no causal explanation for why cows in nearby possible worlds fail to cause tokenings of 'horse' when they are in the "right" abnormal circumstances. Perhaps in these nearby possible worlds, cows could cause tokenings of 'horse' just as, in our actual world, sea cows prompted mariners to token 'mermaid'. Either this stipulation is ad hoc and arbitrary, which is unacceptable; or it is introduced in virtue of some independent consideration. That independent characterization can only be that the asymmetric dependence must respect semantic distinctions. But then the asymmetric dependence presupposes the semantic distinctions it is intended to ground.

(2) The second option available to Fodor is to hold that the only way one can get the concept of 'horse' is by experiencing horses. In other words, the concept 'horse' must come from actual horses and no where else. This makes the asymmetric dependence a causal dependence. But, why should we believe this? Why can't the citizens of cow-world make up horses just as we have made up griffins and centaurs? Also if the meaning relation between horse and 'horse' is in fact causal, then presumably it is the horsey look of the horse that causes tokenings of 'horse'. And if it is the horsey look that matters causally to the tokening of 'horse', then cows, in those abnormal circumstances in which they look horsey, cannot but cause tokenings of 'horse'.

So either the asymmetrical dependence presupposes the semantic distinction it was intended to explain (option 1); or it in effect self-destructs, as there is no (causally) principled reason why the horsey looks of cows cannot cause tokenings of 'horse' even in worlds where there are no horses. In sum, the semantic properties of 'horse' cannot be explained solely by appeal to its causal relations to horses.

Fodor virtually admits this.[39] This simple causal theory cannot work for any complex concepts, not even of the sort like 'horse'.[40] If it can work anywhere, it is with concepts of phenomenal experiences, like the experience of red. This is because, according to Fodor, the circumstances in which red instantiations cause 'red' tokenings are "*nonsemantically, nonteleologically, and nonintentionally specifiable*. In fact, they're *psychophysically* specifiable."[41] Complex concepts can then be seen as constructions out of this base of experiential tokenings. From the tokenings or representations like 'red' to the fixing of beliefs like 'red there', horsey looks can be constructed that warrant the tokening of 'horse'. All this, of course, sounds remarkably familiar. It is the reintroduction of phenomenalism; and it carries with it all the difficulties traditional phenomenalism faced. Most importantly, there are principled difficulties with the idea of phenomenalistic constructions and there are principled difficulties with the phenomenal base as well. With Fodor we have a strong case for psychology recapitulating epistemology. And psychology is in no better shape than epistemology in sustaining such a picture of concepts and thought.

"Indexed" Content: The Problem of Interpretation

If the attempt to find a place for narrow content within a denotational semantics fails, perhaps it can be found in a conceptual role semantics, a fully internalist semantics. Advocates of this position explicitly adopt a two-factor theory of meaning, according to which the meaning or content of a symbol can be split into (at least) two components: the internal conceptual role played by the symbol and the external referential connection the symbol has to some state of affairs in the world. Fodor's denotational theory of meaning made the external referential connection basic and in doing so ran afoul of the problem of misrepresentation as there is no way that a purely causal theory of denotation can account for the normative dimension of representation. Not only does Fodor's denotational theory fail to accommodate the normativity condition, it also results in the atrophy of narrow content, reducing it to an inexpressible function from thought to the world. This only nominally satisfies the internal reality condition. Conceptual role semantics (CRS), on the other hand, promises to satisfy all four conditions and to provide a fully adequate account of narrow content: narrow content is something like Fodor's thought without regard to its referring relation to the world.

Thought is construed broadly to include thinking, believing, intending, wanting, and all the other propositional attitudes. What CRS exploits is the idea that meaning is given in the uses to which an expression is put, and not given by object(s) in the world (if any) to which it refers. What matters is the conceptual role played by the expression, and that can be specified fully in terms of the expression's characteristic roles in a system of expressions related by rules of logic, evidence, and rationality. With this emphasis on the complex logical network rather than the referents of particular representations, the fundamental unit of psychological reality cannot be the isolated mental representation but the thoughts in which the representation plays a role. As Ned Block, an advocate of CRS, puts it:

> the exact nature of the external factor does not matter. . . . The internal factor, the conceptual role, is a matter of the causal role of the expression in reasoning and deliberation and, in general, in the way the expression combines and interacts with other expressions so as to mediate between sensory inputs and behavioral outputs. A crucial component of a sentence's conceptual role is a matter of how it participates in inductive and deductive inferences. A word's conceptual role is a matter of its contribution to the role of sentences.[42]

It is also important to this view that the rules that govern the expressions need not be explicit; on the contrary, their operation is shown through the ways in which the expressions are, or can be, manipulated. I shall, for convenience's sake, call this system "the logical system."

As the quote from Block shows, internalist[43] CRS is tied to a functionalist theory of mind. Mental state types are individuated by their causal role in a larger system, a system consisting of perceptual inputs (really, proximal stimuli), behavioral outputs (motor commands), and other mental states and processes. The key to CRS is the idea that the logical system is *isomorphic* to this causal system. Thus, there is held to be, for any given expression, an isomorphism between the conceptual and logical roles played by that expression (its role within a rule-governed, or normative, system) and its causal role in mediating sensory inputs, behavioral outputs, and other internal processes.

CRS seems to be in a very strong position for accommodating all four conditions discussed above while resolving the apparent conflicts between the semantic condition and the internal reality condition and between the normativity condition and the causal condition. The semantic properties of that-clause content can be excised, leaving that which is wholly internal to the individual, namely, "the causal role of the expression in reasoning and deliberation." In this way, the advocate of CRS wholly endorses the distinction between that-clause content and psychological content, holding that psychological content is given by the conceptual roles expressions play (the narrow content) whereas that-clause content is to be identified in terms of the referent and/or truth conditions of the expression (the wide content). CRS also seems to resolve the conflict between the normativity condition and the causal condition. In severing connections to referents, truth conditions, and social conventions, the logical system is understood to be a closed system within which the expressions or symbols of the system are fully governed by the (implicitly) determinate rules of the system. The functionalist theory of mind also posits a system whose elements can only be individuated within the system itself. Although the logical system is a normative system (though not a semantic system, strictly) and the functional system is a causal system, the idea of narrow content is nonetheless preserved because the causal connections of the functional system mirror the logical and inferential connections of the normative system. It is in virtue of this mirroring relation, and only in virtue of it, that the causal system – a neural system after all – can be said to be contentful, subject, that is, to the normative constraints of rules. For the advocate of narrow content, this isomorphism *must* obtain. If it does not, there is no hope for an internalist psychology. This isomorphism, then, between the logical system and the causal system requires close examination.

We need to look both at the relata and at the relationship itself. One suggestion is that there is a *de facto* correlation between words or sentences of natural language and expressions of mentalese and between the logical relations among the former and the causal relations among the latter. This is a curious idea. The alleged correlation is not empirically grounded. As a matter of fact, actual *tokens* of natural language sentences are simply not produced for the most part, and so are not available for correlating empirically natural language tokens with tokens of sentences in mentalese. The point here is not that we have no independent way of individuating tokens of mentalese – though that is true also – but that no such actual contingent correlations exist. When I pick up my umbrella upon noticing the dark clouds in the sky, I do not typically (if ever) utter the sentences 'There are dark clouds in the sky' and 'Dark clouds mean rain'. So the isomorphism is not one that obtains between the actual tokenings of natural language sentences and tokenings of corresponding sentences in mentalese.

The natural language sentences can only be part of something like rational reconstructions of inferences, such that behavior can be interpreted as something like the conclusion of an Aristotelian practical syllogism. So the correlations must obtain between appropriate interpretive redescriptions of the aetiology of behavior, descriptions expressed in natural language sentences, and tokenings of sentences in mentalese. But because these natural language sentences are themselves part of a theory of behavior that looks very much like the theory in which sentences in mentalese are postulated, it is difficult to see how we have discovered *contingent* correlations. For this approach to work, it is necessary to assume that the natural language reconstruction is the same as the mentalese pattern of inference and deduction. The correlations that matter most for CRS must be found to hold between explicitly displayed inferential systems and neural systems. This is typically the way in which examples are constructed in order to persuade the reader of the intuitive plausibility of CRS.[44] A simple form of deductive reasoning, such as modus ponens, could be mirrored, it is suggested, by neural activity in the brain. So for the reconstructed inference that is alleged to explain my picking up my umbrella, there is a corresponding causal path instantiated in my brain. That inferential pattern looks something like this:

> There are dark clouds in the sky.
> If (or nearly always when) there are dark clouds in the sky, there is rain.
> Therefore, there [will be] rain.
> Rain gets unprotected bodies wet.
> Therefore, if my body is an unprotected body, my body [will get] wet.
> My body will not get wet.
> Therefore, it is not the case that my body is unprotected.

The final conclusion of this enthymeme is held to be a behavior (such as my picking up an umbrella) or a motor command (issued to the relevant set of muscles). The fully articulated inference, even in a simple case like this, is extremely lengthy, of course, but the point of such illustrations is clear: The inference consists of repeated applications of simple logical argument-forms like modus ponens and modus tolens. Provided we can associate each sentence type, and/or each element type of the sentences, with a neural type, we can mirror the inferential connections that obtain among the sentences and their elements with causal connections that obtain among the neural states. The inferential patterns go through whether or not the sentences are interpreted or have any semantic properties at all. In this way, we seem justified in saying, with Block, that "conceptual role is *total causal role,* abstractly described."

Despite the apparent plausibility of this picture, closer examination shows serious strains within CRS. Theoretical problems arise for both relata of the isomorphism. Neither the logical system nor the causal system can provide what is necessary to make CRS plausible. The logical system itself must be such that each of the lengthy enthymemes implicated in a decision or an action or a perception or a whim is fully explicit and fully determinate with respect to both its elements and its inferences. It must be fully explicit in that each step of the pattern of reasoning must be statable; and it must be fully determinate in that each premise and each element within each premise must be formed precisely correctly. The simple enthymeme above clearly fails to honor both of these requirements. The premises themselves are conclusions from other inferences. *Ceteris paribus* clauses are understood to hold, but have not been made explicit. The shapes of the elements in each line of the enthymeme must be fixed precisely. So although (in the rough and ready way in which this was presented as an illustration) it did not matter whether a proposition type was inscripted as 'there is rain' or 'there will be rain', for the purposes of CRS there can be no such laxity.

Each of these problems is familiar. The first gives rise to the frame problem that so plagues artificial intelligence research. The second gives rise to the problem of specifying the class of formal or syntactic items that can be substituted for each other without disrupting the inferential pattern. Though in this illustration, the first premise was given as the sentence 'There are dark clouds in the sky', intuitively it ought not to make any difference to the explanation of behavior if we substitute 'Dark clouds are in the sky' or 'Dark clouds are overhead' or 'The sky is full of clouds that are dark' and so on and so on. They belong together because they mean the same thing and so these slight variations in sentence structure should not matter. Yet on this view of mental activity, such differences can make all the difference. From the point of view of the resources available to CRS, there is no reason why they should belong together. Such groupings can only be seen as ad hoc and coincidental. Moreover, if we were to substitute of the members of this group, such as 'The sky is full of clouds that are dark', the enthymeme would fail to go through, and I would leave the house without my umbrella. For 'The sky is full of clouds that are dark' and 'If there are dark clouds in the sky, there is rain' do not match properly to derive the sentence 'Therefore, there will be rain'.

The second problem area concerns the causal system. Semantic properties and constraints, provided by reference or truth conditions, are, by design, irrelevant to CRS. This means that other kinds of normative constraints are crucial to the intelligibility of this position. We may not be able to assign truth values to any of the sentences of mentalese nor appeal to the referents of any of its terms, but nonetheless the terms and sentences of mentalese are normatively guided and evaluable. There can be correct or incorrect use of terms; valid or invalid patterns of reasoning; efficient or inefficient use of data; and so on. Yet no causal system can deliver normative principles. The normativity of the causal system can only be derivative, depending upon its instantiating valid or correct or efficient patterns of reasoning. Suppose that upon seeing the dark clouds, I take off my coat as I leave the house. Have I made a mistake? Or have I engaged in a different pattern of reasoning? Or is there no connection at all between my perception and my action? The causal system cannot distinguish among fallacious reasoning and novel interpretation of premises and different rules. Only in the context of the logical system do we get a handle on these normative notions, so "conceptual role" cannot be identified with "total causal role" simpliciter, for what is relevant is not the *de facto* total causal role, but only that aspect of the causal role that is isomorphic to the logical system. And this means that the criterion of causal relevance is given by the normative rules. So CRS, construed as requiring a correlation between two independently characterizable systems, fails.

The difficulties with this direct approach to the isomorphism, namely, that there must be a correlation between the elements and patterns of inference within the logical system expressed in natural language sentences and neural states and patterns of neural activity within the causal system, suggest that CRS might be better defended by an indirect approach. This is the strategy developed by Brian Loar.[45] The relata are persons and propositions; and the relation is not one of the subject's "having" a proposition but one of the proposition's indexing the underlying functional state.

Propositions, Loar tells us, are"sets of possible worlds" individuated in a fine-grained way.[46] The function of belief ascriptions is to "index underlying states with propositions which. . .encode counterfactuals about that state."[47] The counterfactual relations that obtain among the underlying states mirror the logical relations among propositions. So "by virtue of its unique place in the logical network a proposition can index a belief's unique functional role."[48] Can this isomorphic relation between underlying mental states and abstract logical systems save the notion of narrow content?

I need to preface the discussion of indexing by pointing out two important features of propositions. First, though beliefs are relations to propositions, this does not require that propositions be something that actually exist. They are not to be construed as abstract entities existing in some platonic realm.[49] Propositions are to be construed as sets of possible worlds.[50] The only way to do this, it seems to me, is, in effect, to treat beliefs as expressing sets of dispositions to behave in certain ways under certain conditions.

The second important feature of propositions is their relative flexibility compared with sentences. They can be tailored to fit exactly the psychological or mental content of the subject's belief. This is what Loar means in holding that fine-grained propositions are to be associated with fine-grained functional roles for beliefs.[51] Even though mental content can be more fine-grained than the typically crude specification of oblique content, there is no one particular sentence that must be identified as specifying *the* content of the particular belief. In this way, it avoids one of the difficulties that arises in searching for a correlation between sentences and functional roles. Thus, Pierre's beliefs about London and Londres can be distinguished without having to specify the particular sentences that capture the exact contents of the two beliefs.

By identifying propositions as the objects of belief, Loar can accommodate the distinction between that-clause and psychological contents while avoiding the impossible task of trying to identify the very sentence that captures the precise psychological contents of Pierre's beliefs. Psychological content is given by the propositional index, which encodes the full functional role of the underlying state. That-clause content is given by our commonsense psychological specifications and explanations that "are so generally shot through with social and causal presuppositions that narrow content cannot in general be captured thus."[52] This alleged distinction, however, is harder to draw than it appears. Loar argues that there are two kinds of content. In distinguishing these two kinds of content, two criteria operate, neither of which draw the distinction in the way that Loar wants. The first identifies that-clause content with wide content, namely, content identified by its semantic properties, especially its socio- and referential-causal relations to the world. This distinction can apply both to our that-clause content and our psychological content. The second criterion also blurs the alleged distinction between two kinds of content, for it seems to turn on a consideration of the *degree of crudeness* or refinement in the specification of the propositional content. 'London is beautiful' and 'Londres is beautiful' are crude propositional indices of Pierre's beliefs, retaining their semantic properties, whereas something more fine-grained like 'London, the city to which I moved in 1988, is beautiful' and 'Londres, the city I have never visited, is beautiful' captures more fully the actual psychological content of Pierre's beliefs and shows the way in which they diverge. It is very difficult to say whether our commonsense belief ascriptions posit a wholly different kind of content or are simply crude. What is wanted, of course, are appropriately refined propositional specifications of content, stripped of referring or truth conditional relations to the natural and/or social world. What is most important in substituting propositions for sentences as the objects of belief is that Loar has thereby substituted sets of possible worlds for referents in the actual world as semantically more important, and has thus freed the individual mind from more than accidental constraint by this actual world. The success of this strategy turns on the work being done by "indexing."

What is this indexing relation that associates propositions to underlying states? As the name indicates, they are a special kind of "label" for identifying psychological states. They individuate the psychological state they index without describing that state. The psychological state itself, e.g., the belief, is a functional state, meaning that the particular belief's "possible states are counterfactually related to each other, input and output thus and so."[53] Thus, indexing is another way of characterizing the "standard association" between the causal structures that are literally in the head, and their counterfactual properties, and the abstract logical and inferential structures that characterize the propositional system. In brief, the proposition indexes a distinct functional role.

There are two ways of interpreting this relation, neither of which is very satisfactory for the advocate of narrow content. It could be treated as a name which labels a set of states.[54] This is a very unhappy solution, as the logical interconnections that obtain among propositions in virtue of their logical form is lost. So, from 'Sam believes that Sally plays the piano very well', we cannot directly infer the truth of 'Sam believes that Sally plays the piano'. The latter is a distinct name or label that must be discovered to apply to another set of Sam's underlying states. This is clearly an unsatisfactory tack to take. But if indexing is not a naming relation, what is it?

Loar's view is that propositional indices are a special kind of label for psychological states. "Labels" of this sort, it seems to me, can be characterized in terms of the following three features:

(1) These "labels" are introduced for the benefit of the theorist about mental states. They are introduced as part of a theory about the underlying states that cause behavior, especially verbal behavior. As such, they are *convenient fictions*, abbreviations for the full specification of the underlying state.[55]

(2) But they are not ordinary labels, as the indexing proposition, in all its internal logical complexity, is indispensable for the individuation of the underlying state and all its counterfactual properties. It is this internal logical complexity that enables the proposition to encode all the counterfactual properties of the underlying state. The proposition provides the *individuation conditions* on psychological states.

(3) Finally, a proposition P is the correct label for an underlying state M if and only if the causal properties of M track the logico-inferential properties of P. Contingent counterfactual relations among the underlying states *mirror* necessary logical relations among propositions.

It seems to me that propositions are being asked to function both as names for states (convenient fictions), such that their logical structure is irrelevant, and as interpretations of the underlying states, such that what they mean and what logical structure they have is indispensably important. Loar's naturalism demands that propositions be eliminable and his desire to explain mental content requires that they be essential. So the tension that exists in satisfying the causal condition and the normativity condition is masked in part by describing propositions as indices. At the very least, to describe them as convenient fictions is misleading, and for two reasons. First, as "fictions" it is suggested that the full specification of all that is abbreviated by their use is both possible and, if done, explanatory. Both claims are dubious. Second, as "fictions" it is suggested that they were never necessary to the theory of mental states, but only used for pragmatic reasons. Yet this is false on Loar's own account of how such a theory appealing to propositional indices could have developed.

The first objection. If these fictions are eliminable, with what are they to be replaced? According to Loar, they are to be replaced with grotesquely complicated constructions which consist of hugely long conjunctions of all the instantiations of all the conditions of all nominalized belief-desire sentences. As Loar says himself, "To each sentence 'x believes that p', there corresponds a preposterously unmanageable sentence that does not quantify over propositions and is equivalent to 'x believes that p' apart from the latter's reference to a proposition."[56] The equivalence between the individuation of the belief by appeal to its propositional index and this grotesquely large sentence lies in the alleged fact that "they agree exactly on x's functional state."[57] This alleged agreement is a fiction. This entire approach assumes that all possible conditions in which x believes that p can be specified in advance; that the notoriously troublesome *ceteris paribus* clauses that are always associated with specifying conditions and behaviors can be unpacked in a full and perspicuous manner. No such analyses have ever succeeded; and there is no reason to believe that they will succeed in this case.[58] Moreover, one of the seeming advantages of taking propositions rather than sentences as the objects of belief is lost. Difficulties with specifying the very sentence that captures the exact content of belief that arose for a sentential CRS now arise for Loar's propositional CRS.

In addition, no such sentential replacement is at all explanatory. Loar is right in his observation that "the unwieldy theory, with indices eliminated, seems to have no claim to express intentionality apart from its relation to the theory with indices."[59] This is not just a pragmatic matter. The propositions we use in individuating the underlying states determine what is relevant. In eliminating the proposition we would eliminate our criterion for sorting out the relevant causal connections from the irrelevant ones. So the appeal to indices does provide a way of determining which causal connections are relevant to being a particular belief. This leads directly to the second objection.

Loar's own story of how we could have come to develop the belief-desire theory makes propositions theoretically indispensable. The idea is that our early theorists of the mind hypothesized underlying functional states as the normal cause of utterances of s. This supports a classical dispositionalist account of beliefs as dispositions to assert s under appropriate conditions. "But that causal relation," Loar tells us, "may itself be then *reconstructed within the theory*; we come to say that x uttered s because x had certain communicative purposes and beliefs, where these are referred to via the more abstract indexing system."[60] However, the very idea of such a reconstruction requires the use of propositions as theoretically essential, as providing the "defining properties" of belief. This hypothesized reconstruction is only possible given appeal to propositions; it would not be possible using the long sentences as replacements for the propositions.

My final objection concerns the "mirroring" conditions: Causal properties of the functional state must track the logical properties of the proposition. This ideal is the real motor behind all versions of CRS. Equally all versions of CRS face the same difficulty. The causal interrelations of the functional state are contingent. That these interactions track logical relations is contingent. Logical relationships, however, are necessary. Suppose some functional state of a living organism has successfully tracked the logical relations of some proposition. Suppose further that at some time in the life of the organism the causal relationships diverge from the logical relations of the proposition. Has the organism made a mistake? Have the causal relationships been tracking a different proposition than the one used to describe and explain the organism's behavior? Or has that causal pathway nothing to do with tracking at all? Nothing within CRS provides a way of distinguishing among these different possibilities. *How* the functional state is interpreted or indexed is crucial to determining what went wrong. But nothing in the causal nexus of the functional state can resolve this normative problem.

Loar acknowledges this anti-internalist argument that no internal properties of an individual can determine how a thought represents something.[61] But he argues that the anti-internalist conclusion that takes the representational properties of thoughts to be essential to psychological explanation is mistaken. It is mistaken, he maintains, because "representational properties that are essential to psychological explanation need be representational or intentional only from a subject/projective perspective."[62] What he means by this is that our "primitive notion of aboutness is subjective, and this is the foundation of the semantic"[63] where "subjective intentionality is the disposition of thoughts to reveal themselves 'as intentional' upon reflection."[64] Reflection reveals that "my thoughts appear *self-interpreting*."[65] Intentionality thus is an artifact of reflection, for which there may be explanation, but it is not essential theoretically to the explanation of behavior. That is given by the causal/functional roles of neural states within the neurophysiological system of the organism. The conflict between the normativity condition and the causal condition is thus resolved by arguing that the normativity, or intentionality, of psychological states is irrelevant to psychological explanation. Intentional states, namely, self-interpreting states, are nomological danglers.

But even if we hold that intentionality is epiphenomenal, there are still two difficulties for Loar: What makes the study of these functional systems an inquiry into *psychological* processes? This position looks like a form of eliminativism in favor of the neural sciences. The second problem is that this account of intentionality does not really answer to the normativity condition. That condition required that psychological representations and states be rule-governed, where specification of the rules reveals what is a correct or incorrect representation. A purely causal account cannot mark this normative distinction.

So it would seem that the subjective intentionality revealed by reflection provides the criterion for distinguishing relevant from irrelevant features of the total causal system. The selectivity, then, of psychological states is revealed through primitive subjective reflection. This makes the *sui generis* self-evidence of psychological states indispensable. It also shows why Loar picks self-interpretation as the product of primitive reflection (rather than say incorrigibility of primitive mental states), for he is looking for a way to ground rule-governed content. Loar, thus, comes to identify narrow content with the self-interpreting inner state. The naturalism that first motivated hypothesizing CRS has collapsed.

In conclusion, both Fodor and Loar come to agree that no naturalistic account can be given for intentionality, representationality, or normativity. Because both are committed to internalism and individualism, both revive previously discredited accounts of the mental, Fodor in terms of incorrigible phenomenal experiences and Loar in terms of self-interpreting private inner states. It is my view that none of these three features of mental life can be understood from the perspective of this strong internalism. Content must be rooted in the public and social domain.

7. NORMS AND SOCIAL PRACTICE

What Burge draws our attention to is the importance of social practices and the linguistic division of labor in understanding individual mental life. No purely internalist and/or individualist account of mental content can explain or ground the normativity of our practices or the intentionality of our mental states. Both Fodor's denotational theory and Loar's conceptual role theory fail to solve the problem of normativity. As shown above, for Fodor, this becomes the problem of specifying the relevant cause of the tokening of a neural state that endows that state with representational content; for Loar, the problem of normativity becomes the problem of how to characterize the "standard association" between a logical network of propositions and a functionally described physical system. Neither anchoring nor indexing can solve the problem of normativity without presupposing the very standards of correctness anchoring or indexing was to explain. As I suggest above, recognition of this failure is shown, it seems to me, by the return of both Fodor and Loar to phenomenal experience and subjective intentionality respectively as the *sui generis* source of intentionality. This is the only recourse open so long as internalism and individualism are held to be unrevisable givens.

Social Theory of Normativity

But if these individualist positions cannot account for the intentionality of mental content, how can a social theory? The key to understanding the social theory of mental content turns on seeing that normativity is basic to *human* intentionality. Human intentionality (unlike animal intentionality) is marked by its sensitivity to norms and standards. Thus, the problem of normativity is the problem of understanding how standards are set that fix meaning and provide the guide and/ or justification for subsequent use. The normativity of intentional states, that is, their being accurate or inaccurate, correct or incorrect, is dependent upon their relation to socially fixed standards, what Burge calls "norms of understanding." Neither anchoring nor indexing can perform this role. Both presuppose the very normative standards they are supposed to ground. The setting of standards is thus simply not within the provenance of the radically isolated individual.

As already indicated in the discussion above, each of Burge's three thought-experiments highlights different roles played by the community in fixing the standards for use of a term. With natural kind terms like 'water', being a rigid designator explains why even in oblique contexts the expression 'water' retains its semantic connection to H_2O. Yet rigid designation obtains only within a social structure. This is so for two reasons: first, the original baptism that fixes the relation between term and object or person requires a setting that is rich enough to make room for naming. This is the Wittgensteinian point that a certain stage-setting is required in order to name, as naming is not the mere association of a word with a place, person, or object. What is to be named has to be made salient against a background of the myriad simultaneously occurring properties and aspects that could be named. At this point, I shall simply make the claim that a social practice is necessary for setting the stage. I shall return to this point shortly. Second, once an object or person has been named, the causal chain that preserves the connection between name and referent is a socially sustained chain, one in which the members have an interest (even if unarticulated) in maintaining the relation between name and referent, an interest which is expressed in the continuation of the appropriate causal chain. The appropriate causal chain is, of course, the one that originates in the baptismal object. In normative terms, the baptismal object sets the standard for correct and incorrect future use of the naming expression. That future usage and the baptismal object are related by a *social* chain is obvious. What may seem less obvious is that the originating baptismal act itself requires a social practice.

With the concept of arthritis, however, its relation to the experts is not explained by the term 'arthritis' being a rigid designator; likewise with 'sofa'. So what is the relation of the individual's use of 'arthritis' to the experts? There must be a more Gricean explanation: When I use terms of art or expertise, I use them intending to use them as the experts do and intending my audience to so understand my usage.[66] Satisfying this "deference condition" is part of the layman's successful use of terms of expertise. The experts are accorded a special epistemic status because of their specialized knowledge; and it is for this reason that their judgment provides the standard for correct usage of the term by the layman. An important part of what this means is that I am aware of my limitations, and so knowingly open myself to correction by the experts. In sum, the layman's use of terms of expertise must satisfy a deference condition. This condition consists of two parts: first, expert judgment provides the standard of correct usage for the layman; and second, the layman acknowledges his own limitation in this matter. The very way in which the layman's use of terms of art is related to the experts shows that these cases do not reveal anything basic about the social dimension of normativity. They concern a limited range of cases, all dependent upon our ordinary linguistic competence.

It is to be hoped that Burge's 'sofa' case, on the other hand, will shed light on this basic competence, and for this reason it requires close examination. For 'sofa' there is a third explanation for how environmental factors, this time the linguistic community, are involved in fixing and sustaining norms. The explanation is not that 'sofa' is a rigid designator, so come what may, when Oscar uses 'sofa' he thereby refers to sofas. Nor is this a matter of his use being parasitic upon community use in the way that his use of 'arthritis' is parasitic upon the judgment of the doctors. Oscar does not intend to use 'sofa' as those in the know do. This is because Oscar is just as much "in the know" as anyone else. So neither does he take himself to be open to criticism and correction by other competent speakers. He *is* a competent speaker. Neither feature of the deference condition characterizes his use of 'sofa'. So if 'sofa' does not rigidly designate what a particular linguistic community says (any more than 'arthritis' designates what a group of experts say) and if the subject is not self-consciously dependent upon those in the know, what is the relation of the individual in his use of ordinary terms to the community?

The relation is twofold: first, in the process of learning language, the child is clearly dependent upon the adult in a way that is similar to the relation of the layman to the expert. It is similar but not the same. The deference condition that marks adult use of terms of expertise does not govern the child's early uses of language. The child is not a small adult using words with the intention of using them in accord with expert judgment. This intention of the adult is too sophisticated for a child to have. This intention presupposes a general mastery and competence against which the importation of the exotic, the unknown, and the theoretical is intelligible, and so it cannot ground such competence.[67] The young child, in using ordinary words of ordinary discourse, is not using them against such a background of knowledge and linguistic competence. Her dependence upon the adult world is much more thorough-going than that of the layman or the expert. Her use is sustained, not by her own background competence, but by the competence of the adult world. In first acquiring language, she does not intend to use words as adults do; she just uses them, increasingly in the right contexts. The child is not open to correction because she knowingly places herself in that position; the child just is corrected. In these ways, the young child's relation to language is external. It is, then, a misdescription of the child's relation to the adult to characterize it as one of deference.

The second relation that the individual's use of such ordinary notions of 'sofa' has to the linguistic community is more important for the purposes of this essay. It concerns the normativity of linguistic usage more directly. In representing a part of the world we thereby open ourselves to misrepresenting it. We can use our words correctly or incorrectly. The account of this normative dimension of language use involves the community but not in the obvious and direct way in which a rigid designator is related to its referent nor in the way in which lay use of terms of art are parasitic upon expert judgment. The subject does not open herself to correction from the community; if she does make an error, she is as much able, from a linguistic stance, to correct it as anyone else. So if a person mistakenly takes a cow for a horse, given the surrounding circumstances, her linguistic competence is not impugned, but the difficult circumstances are. The problem here is to account for the fact that words are normative, that they can be used correctly or incorrectly. We know why the experts are given the authority they are. Because they know about the obscure or exotic phenomenon, experts are accorded a special epistemic status. But the community is not accorded a special epistemic status; and so the way in which the community grounds the normativity of ordinary linguistic practices cannot be in the way in which the experts do. The community does not have a special authority, which is why individual community practices can be challenged even by a competent individual. The point is that the activity of members of the community, as expressed in the *de facto* harmony and agreement of their judgments, grounds the fundamental contrast between correct and incorrect.

It is no accident that Burge's third case involving an ordinary concept is a case of deviant belief, not an error as with 'arthritis'. In this case, it is important that Oscar is not making a mistake similar to that of wrongly believing that arthritic pain can occur in muscles or similar to mistaking a cow for horse. He has not mistaken a sofa for a religious artifact in the way that one might, for instance, mistake a bead necklace for a rosary. Nor does he intend to use 'sofa' as the furniture experts do, willingly reforming his own usage if it conflicts with that of the experts. He is not in poor or abnormal conditions for recognizing these perfectly familiar objects. He, like any other competent speaker, can identify sofas without help. But it is only in virtue of his membership within the linguistic community that enables him to form deviant individualistic conceptions of ordinary objects. Community judgment as expressed in the actual uses of ordinary terms in context just *is* the norm or standard of correct usage. The authority of the community derives from the fact that it is only within a community that the primitive distinction between correct and incorrect can get a hold. The most primitive form that a norm takes is expressed in the conformity of the individual's behavior to the community of which she is a part.[68] There are three features of this conformity that are of especial interest. In order of importance, the first is that this basic or primitive conformity is necessary for human intentionality and genuine individualism; the second is the non-theoretical and non-reflective character of our engagement in various language-games; and the third is the importance of exemplars as norms or standards. In order of explication, however, I shall begin with the role of exemplars.

The point at which language most obviously connects with items in the world is with the use of ostensive definitions, archetypical applications, indexicals, and rigid designators. As we have already seen, the two most promising alternatives to the social theory of content, namely, the causal theory of reference and conceptual role semantics, fail, in distinct but complementary ways, to account for ostensive definitions (and their kin). The causal theory cannot account for the stage-setting needed to isolate the baptismal object and appropriate causal chain; and conceptual role semantics cannot get from functional roles to referents without independent interpretation of the functional roles. Both failures have to do with the background network necessary for the activities of naming, referring, and ostending. Neither a logical system nor a complex causal nexus can provide the right kind of background. But social practice can, for the community provides the stage-setting within which any of these world-referring activities occur.

No object in itself can stand as paradigm for a class or kind of object nor can the usage of an expression in itself count as an archetypical application, as Burge expresses it. For a pool of water to count as a standard-setting sample, that pool must be accorded a special status. That status is manifested by its place within the behavioral and verbal activity of a socially structured group. The arguments for meaning holism and attitude holism, that a concept or belief is only what is within a network, support such a view. But rather than looking for an explicit list of propositions and their logical and evidential relations, one looks for the way in which a community uses language in their practices, the usage thereby displaying (rather than describing) the normative role assigned certain objects.

This assigning of normative roles need not be understood as an actual ritual occurring at some definite time (though it may be this); rather the assignment is shown in the actions of the community. The point to be emphasized here is that the background network is not something that occurs in the head. Social practice provides the needed context, and that just consists in the patterned and harmonious ways of acting and judging that exist among the members of the community. The beliefs, desires, and other attitudes of the individual are embedded within this natural and social environment. They are best understood as dispositions, the analysis of which would appeal both to kinds of behavior and kinds of contexts. This is not a recommendation to revive a strongly reductionist account of these dispositions. But it is a recommendation to see beliefs and other such states as dispositions, the exercise of which involves both patterns of behavior and structured circumstances. This enables us to account both for the way in which society can contribute to the content of a belief or thought without directly causally effecting the individual and for the sense in which it is true that beliefs are psychologically real states.

Since the individual's personal experiences do not themselves fix the meaning of terms,[69] though the socially constrained actions of the members of the community do, it is possible for an individual to use a word meaningfully without ever having come in contact with a member of the class of objects referred to. This is clearly the case with both natural kind terms and terms of expertise. The use of such terms is individual-context-free; that is, a substance like water need never have been in the local environment of the individual who successfully uses the term 'water' and forms appropriate beliefs about the liquid. These beliefs are psychologically real, not in the sense that there are literally contentful states internal to the individual, but that there are real patterns of action within the social and natural world that are the exercise of the water-beliefs. In emphasizing patterns of action, I intend to press against the idea that where there are dispositions, there must be the categorical bases of the dispositions, bases *whose properties explain the disposition* itself. In the case of psychological states, there is no reason to expect to find such underlying bases. Indeed much suggests the contrary. Even advocates of an intentionalist psychology acknowledge that ordinary psychological concepts may cross-classify scientific psychological concepts; and, of course, the cross-classification diverges even more and more strikingly between neurological-level descriptions and ordinary descriptions. There may well be no interesting and systematic correlations between neural patterning and ordinary dispositional patterning. This gap does not warrant, however, the conclusion that ordinary descriptions are to be eliminated on the ground that they constitute a bad theory of human behavior. This is because they are not part of a theory in rivalry with neurophysiology.

This takes us to the final feature of ordinary linguistic competence. Not only does ordinary competence involve the use of objects as normal samples by our community practices, ordinary competence also is non-theoretical and non-reflective. Part of what this means is that the attempt to model such basic competence upon the basis of theory construction and use is going to distort the character of this competence. Theory construction is a more sophisticated cognitive enterprise, one that presupposes basic competence, and so cannot be used to explain that competence.[70] This basic competence, which embodies both understanding of the world one lives in and understanding of language, is not a way of interpreting the world but a way of acting and judging non-reflectively in accord with others. This marks another great difference between the use of ordinary expressions like 'sofa' and expressions of expertise like 'arthritis'. Expert terms are embedded within theories whereas ordinary terms are not. As I expressed it earlier in this essay, ordinary terms whether of natural kinds or not, are theory-context–free unlike terms of expertise. They do require a context of use, but that context is not a theory. We can now understand why it is important that Oscar's deviant belief is a *hypothesis* about the value and proper use of these objects. Like any hypothesis or theory, it presupposes a stable background of linguistic practice against which the hypothesis may be formed and evaluated.[71] But, as I have been emphasizing, this background itself is not a system of hypotheses.

CONCLUSION

What I have tried to show in this essay is that the notion of narrow mental content is in serious trouble, and that trouble derives from stresses and tensions within the two most promising theories of narrow content. The causal theory of representation and conceptual role semantics, though bedeviled by different problems, end up in curiously similar positions. Both theories treat the referential function of narrow content as an inexpressible function from what goes on within to something external; both theories are forced to broadly dispositionalist accounts of psychological attitudes by way of possible worlds; and both save internalist intentionality by appeal to a given subjective experience.

The most plausible alternative to these internalist and individualist theories is a social theory of normativity. This requires giving up homogeneous conceptions of belief and learning. In particular and most importantly, the models of belief as hypothesis, of learning as hypothesis formation, and of norms as algorithmic rules cannot serve as *general* models for all cases of belief, belief fixation, and normative practice. This is because these practices of hypothesis formation and testing *presuppose* a mastery of rule-governed competence. This basic cognitive competence is possible only against a background of dynamic social practices in which primitive normativity is grounded in social conformity, belief in complex dispositions to behave verbally and otherwise, and explicit norms in objects accorded the status of exemplars.

NOTES

1. Tyler Burge, "Individualism and Psychology," *Philosophical Review* (1986): 4.
2. Ibid.
3. Cf. Colin McGinn, *Mental Content* (Oxford, 1989).
4. Tyler Burge, "Other Bodies," in *Thought and Object,* edited by Andrew Woodfield (Oxford, 1982).
5. Tyler Burge, "Individualism and the Mental," *Midwest Studies in Philosophy* IV (1979).
6. Tyler Burge, "Intellectual Norms and Foundations of Mind," *Journal of Philosophy* (1986).
7. This is not so for $Oscar_2$, however. He has at best a partial understanding of what the term 'sofa$_2$' means.
8. See Ned Block, "Advertisement for a Semantics for Psychology," *Midwest Studies in Philosophy* X (1986).
9. See sections 4 and 5.
10. Hilary Putnam, "The Meaning of 'Meaning'," in his *Mind, Language, and Reality* (Cambridge, 1975).
11. Burge, "Other Bodies," 102–103.
12. J. A. Fodor commits just this fallacy in his "Methodological Solipsism Considered as a Research Strategy in Cognitive Psychology," *Behavioral and Brain Sciences* (1981). See my "Language Learning and the Representational Theory of Mind," *Synthése* 58 (1984).
13. Burge, "Other Bodies." Burge acknowledges that Putnam's position is more complicated than the position ascribed to him, but that nonetheless he is justified in his interpretation of Putnam. I am going to follow Burge in this.
14. Ibid., 107.
15. Like most everyone else, I will also ignore the fact that Oscar and $Oscar_2$ could hardly be "molecule-for-molecule" identical given the different chemical composition of water and water$_2$.
16. Please note that although these second-order intentions concern the use of the word 'arthritis', this account of the semantic link of terms of expertise to the experts is not a variant on the objection that Oscar's error is really a metalinguistic error. Burge is quite correct in rejecting this reinterpretation of Oscar's predicament. I am not saying that Oscar's belief that he had arthritis in his thigh is to be reinterpreted as a belief that 'arthritis' applies to some ache in his thigh. See "Individualism and the Mental," 93. Rather Oscar intends that his use of 'arthritis' conforms to expert use, such that he is correct in believing that it is arthritis that he is suffering from and not another disease.

17. See Graeme Forbes, "A Dichotomy Sustained," *Philosophical Studies* (1987). Forbes emphasizes the need to distinguish between a third-person perspective and a first-person perspective.

18. See Brian Loar, "Social Content and Psychological Content," in *Content of Thought*, edited by D. Merrill and R. Grimm (forthcoming); and Kent Bach, "Burge's New Thought Experiment," *Journal of Philosophy* (1986).

19. Loar, "Social Content and Psychological Content." Also see Brian Loar, "Subjective Intentionality," *Philosophical Topics* (1987). I shall use the expression "that-clause content" to mark this distinction.

20. Loar uses the case of puzzling Pierre (see Saul Kripke, "A Puzzle about Belief," in *Meaning and Use,* edited by A. Margalit (Dordrecht, 1979) to make his point. I am not developing the case exactly as Loar does though I do retain the point Loar wanted to make using this case.

21. See Forbes, "A Dichotomy Sustained"; and Loar, "Subjective Intentionality."

22. See Loar, "Social Content and Psychological Content"; and Bach, "Burge's New Thought Experiment."

23. Burge, "Intellectual Norms and Foundations of Mind," 709.

24. Let me make two points about this characterization of physicalism. First, I do not equate physicalism with naturalism. Naturalism is best construed negatively as the denial of the existence of anything supernatural or metaphysical. Second, physicalism does not have to be reductionist. To be explicable ultimately in terms of physical matter does not require that the explanations and vocabulary of one level are replaceable by explanations and vocabulary of another level, though it does require that we can understand how processes and states of the higher level are instantiated at the level of physical description.

25. J. A. Fodor, *Psychosemantics* (Cambridge, Mass., 1988), 42.

26. Andrew Woodfield raises a related objection when he argues that Burge has conflated a theory of content with a theory of content specification. Once these are kept distinct, Woodfield argues, there is space both to acknowledge Burgean points about the social character of content specification and to develop a strongly internalist account of mental content itself. See his "Thought and the Social Community," *Inquiry* 25 (1982).

27. Fodor, *Psychosemantics*, 43.

28. Moreover, there is no reason to believe that Burge has fallaciously drawn conclusions about the necessity for using relational properties to individuate mental states from arguments against the computational theory of mind.

29. Burge, "Individualism and Psychology," 16.

30. I think that Fodor's use of this "diagnosis" reflects his own commitment to the computational theory of mental processes. In other words, something very close to methodological solipsism tells us what counts as affecting causal powers when it comes to constructing a scientific taxonomy of mental causes.

31. Fodor, *Psychosemantics*, 44.

32. This is, of course, precisely the position of those who argue that there is no real subject matter for scientific psychology to study. See P. S. Churchland, *Scientific Realism and the Plasticity of Mind* (Cambridge, 1979) and P. M. Churchland, *Neurophilosophy* (Cambridge, Mass, 1986).

33. See Brian Loar, *Mind and Meaning* (Cambridge, 1981) and Block, "Advertisement for a Theory of Semantics for Psychology."

34. See Dennis Stampe, "Towards a Causal Theory of Mental Representation," *Midwest Studies in Philosophy* II (1977); and Fodor, *Psychosemantics*.

35. Fodor, *Psychosemantics*, 47.

36. Ibid., 48.

37. See Stampe, "Towards a Causal Theory of Mental Representation." Stampe interprets the problem as requiring that we specify the fidelity conditions under which a cause has the requisite effect. Thus, Stampe considers the problem from the point of view of the cause's being sufficient for producing 'horse' whereas Fodor treats the problem from the point of

view of the cause's being necessary for producing 'horse'. Also see Fred Dretske, "Misrepresentation," in *Belief: Form, Content, and Function,* edited by Radu J. Bogdan (Oxford, 1986).

38. Fodor, *Psychosemantics*, 108.

39. Ibid., 111–112.

40. Ibid., 116.

41. Ibid., 112.

42. Block, "Advertisement for a Theory of Semantics for Psychology," 628.

43. I preface "conceptual role semantics" with "internalist" to underscore the fact that CRS is distinct from a Wittgensteinian view of meaning as use. There are two important differences between CRS and the Wittgensteinian view. First, for CRS, conceptual systems are private and individualist whereas on a Wittgensteinian view, use is public and social. Second, CRS, in excising all relations to the world in specifying conceptual roles, has no place for objects to function as paradigms or exemplars. Though the Wittgensteinian view rejects a denotational theory of meaning, nonetheless exemplary objects play an indispensable role in language use.

44. See, for example, Block, "Advertisement for a Theory of Semantics for Psychology," 628; and, for an interesting early defense of this view, Paul E. Meehl, "Psychological Determinism and Human Rationality," *Minnesota Studies in the Philosophy of Science* IV, edited by Michael Kadner and Stephen Winokur (Minneapolis, 1970).

45. My discussion of Brian Loar derives from his *Mind and Meaning*.

46. Ibid., 58.

47. Ibid., 62.

48. Ibid.

49. Ibid., 142.

50. Loar appeals to Robert Stalnaker's way of doing this in *Inquiry* (Cambridge, Mass., 1984).

51. Cf. Loar, *Mind and Meaning,* 58.

52. Loar, "Social Content and Psychological Content," 14.

53. Loar, *Mind and Meaning,* 44.

54. Cf. Ibid., 59–60.

55. Ibid., 144.

56. Ibid.

57. Ibid.

58. Loar is aware of this kind of problem. See his remarks on phenomenalism, ibid., 128, but he identifies these problems as having to do with epistemological concerns, not concerns of explication. But that is not so. Phenomenalist reductions were introduced explicitly as the analyses of certain statements.

59. Ibid., 126–27.

60. Ibid., 124.

61. Loar, "Subjectivity Intentionality."

62. Ibid., 114.

63. Ibid., 116.

64. Ibid., 102.

65. Ibid., 99.

66. This Gricean account has the virtue of indirectly drawing our attention to the fact that paradigmatic cases of kinds of terms does not rule out marginal or vague or ambiguous uses of the same terms. What I mean is that a word like 'arthritis' can be used more like an ordinary word like 'sofa', in which case it is not used as a term calling for expert knowledge. Folk wisdom can have it that arthritis is any kind of joint or muscle ache and can be alleviated by wearing a copper bracelet. It is quite clear that terms of art can also become assimilated into general usage and become interchangeable with some non-technical word or descriptive phase. 'H_2O' is a clear example of this; and in philosophical circles 'the firing of C-fibers' became a virtual substitution for 'being in pain', and *not* because the identity theory was found

to be true. Such devaluing of the technical term is not what is intended in the discussion of the linguistic division of labor.

67. See my "Language Learning and the Representational Theory" (*Synthése* [1984]) for a more complete discussion of this issue.

68. For a more detailed account and defense of this social view of normativity, see my "Rules, Community, and the Individual," in *Meaning-Scepticism,* edited by K. Puhl (Berlin/ New York, forthcoming).

69. And I would argue, but not here, they cannot fix the meaning of terms. See my "Representation, Privileged Objects, and Private Languages," *Canadian Journal of Philosophy* (1981).

70. See my "Language Learning and Representational Theory of Mind," for the full argument.

71. As a hypothesis, this deviant belief is much more difficult to state and sustain than Burge allows for in his description of earth and twin-earth. Indeed, if it is really true on twin earth that sofas$_2$ are religious objects, then it is simply not possible that they could have been used, bought and sold in just the same ways as sofas are on earth.

Contributors

Cristina Bicchieri, Department of Philosophy, Carnegie Mellon University
David Braybrooke, Department of Philosophy, Dalhousie University
Regis A. Factor, Department of Philosophy, University of South Florida
Arthur Fine, Department of Philosophy, Northwestern University
Richard Foley, Department of Philosophy, University of Notre Dame
Richard Fumerton, Department of Philosophy, University of Iowa
Margaret Gilbert, Department of Philosophy, University of Connecticut
Gary Gutting, Department of Philosophy, University of Notre Dame
Jean Hampton, Department of Philosophy, University of California, Davis
Rom Harré, Sub-Faculty of Philosophy, Oxford University
Daniel M. Hausman, Department of Philosophy, University of Wisconsin
Terence Horgan, Department of Philosophy, Memphis State University
Gregory S. Kavka, Department of Philosophy, University of California, Irvine
Joseph Margolis, Department of Philosophy, Temple University
Alan J. Nelson, Department of Philosophy, University of California, Irvine
Frederick A. Olafson, Department of Philosophy, University of California, San Diego
Hilary Putnam, Department of Philosophy, Harvard University
Alexander Rosenberg, Department of Philosophy, University of California, Riverside
David-Hillel Ruben, Department of Philosophy, Logic, and Scientific Method, London School of Economics and Political Science
Theodore R. Schatzki, Department of Philosophy, University of Kentucky
Lawrence H. Simon, Department of Philosophy, Bowdoin College
Brian Skyrms, Department of Philosophy, University of California, Irvine
Jordon Howard Sobel, Scarborough College, University of Toronto
John Tienson, Department of Philosophy, Memphis State University

464

Stephen P. Turner, Department of Philosophy, University of South Florida
Meredith Williams, Department of Philosophy, Northwestern University
Robert Paul Wolff, Department of Philosophy, University of Massachusetts

Peter A. French is Lennox Distinguished Professor of Philosophy at Trinity University in San Antonio, Texas. He has taught at the University of Minnesota, Morris, and has served as Distinguished Research Professor in the Center for the Study of Values at the University of Delaware. His books include *The Scope of Morality* (1980), *Ethics in Government* (1982), and *Collective and Corporate Responsibility* (1980). He has published numerous articles in the philosophical journals. **Theodore E. Uehling, Jr.,** is professor of philosophy at the University of Minnesota, Morris. He is the author of *The Notion of Form in Kant's Critique of Aesthetic Judgment* and articles on the philosophy of Kant. **Howard K. Wettstein** is professor of philosophy at the University of California, Riverside. He has taught at the University of Notre Dame and the University of Minnesota, Morris, and has served as a visiting associate professor of philosophy at the University of Iowa and Stanford University. He is the author of *Has Semantics Rested on a Mistake? and Other Essays* (Stanford University Press, forthcoming).